Brussels

timeout.com/brussels

Time Out Guides Ltd
Universal House
251 Tottenham Court Road
London W1T 7AB
United Kingdom
Tel: +44 (0)20 7813 3000
Fax: +44 (0)20 7813 6001
Email: guides@timeout.com
www.timeout.com

Published by Time Out Guides Ltd, a wholly owned subsidiary of Time Out Group Ltd.
Time Out and the Time Out logo are trademarks of Time Out Group Ltd.

10 9 8 7 6 5 4 3 2

This edition first published in Great Britain in 2010 by Ebury Publishing.
A Random House Group Company
20 Vauxhall Bridge Road, London SW1V 2SA

Random House Australia Pty Ltd 20 Alfred Street, Milsons Point, Sydney, New South Wales 2061, Australia

Random House New Zealand Ltd 18 Poland Road, Glenfield, Auckland 10, New Zealand

Random House South Africa (Pty) Ltd Isle of Houghton, Corner Boundary Road & Carse O'Gowrie, Houghton 2198, South Africa

Random House UK Limited Reg. No. 954009

Distributed in the US and Latin America by Publishers Group West (1-510-809-3700)
Distributed in Canada by Publishers Group Canada (1-800-747-8147)

For further distribution details, see www.timeout.com.

ISBN: 978-1-84670-193-1

A CIP catalogue record for this book is available from the British Library.

Printed and bound in Great Britain by Butler Tanner & Dennis, Frome, Somerset.

The Random House Group Limited supports the Forest Stewardship Council® (FSC®), the leading international forest-certification organisation. Our books carrying the FSC label are printed on FSC®-certified paper. FSC is the only forest-certification scheme supported by the leading environmental organisations, including Greenpeace. Our paper procurement policy can be found at www.randomhouse.co.uk/environment.

While every effort has been made by the author(s) and the publisher to ensure that the information contained in this guide is accurate and up to date as at the date of publication, they accept no responsibility or liability in contract, tort, negligence, breach of statutory duty or otherwise for any inconvenience, loss, damage, costs or expenses of any nature whatsoever incurred or suffered by anyone as a result of any advice or information contained in this guide (except to the extent that such liability may not be excluded or limited as a matter of law). Before travelling, it is advisable to check all information locally, including without limitation, information on transport, accommodation, shopping and eating out. Anyone using this guide is entirely responsible for their own health, well-being and belongings and care should always be exercised while travelling.

MIX
Paper from
responsible sources
FSC® C023561

Contents

Introduction

It's fair to say that when the word Brussels is mentioned it comes loaded with pre-conceived attitude. This is largely to do with the fact that the media uses it as a catch-all term for everything that it perceives as wrong with the European Union. Brussels is doing this, Brussels will dictate that, Brussels has decided that pounds and ounces are the devil's work. Of course, Brussels as a city has done no such thing.

As the undeniable capital of the EU, it's a problem the city elders have had to deal with for years, a PR sword of Damocles forever nagging away at everything else Brussels is. But deal with it they have. Over the last decade, since being one of the European Cities of Culture in 2000, Brussels has totally transformed itself in terms of its living standards, its visitor offerings and how it feels about itself. What it has managed to do is to identify itself, accept its quirky foibles and give itself distinctive brands for each of its identities.

Of course, the EU and its attendant organisations are vitally important to the city's global importance, economic viability and cultural mix, but the EU Quarter remains a city within a city; sit in a Lower Town café and you are blissfully unaware of all the goings-on just 15 minutes away. Prime ministers come, foreign affairs ministers go, but it's likely you'll know nothing about it. And this is where Brussels comes into its own – it's a city for living in, even in the historical centre, a place where you can still buy a flat on the Grand'Place. And it's most certainly a city for visiting. The tourist authorities are handing over the Brussels brand on a plate with spot-on information, joined-up services and scrubbed-up attractions and set pieces. For the visitor this is a win-win situation, where a mix of impressive sightseeing, going with the flow and breezing along like a local gives the best opportunity to understand this endearing muddle of a city.

Gary Hills, Editor

Brussels in Brief

IN CONTEXT

The history of the Low Countries is complex and is detailed here in a chronological description. There is a feature on the architectural gem that is Brussels art nouveau and another on the brilliant comic book art that is famed the world over. Brussels Today looks at the current challenges facing the city and the country, in particular the ongoing politics of language and regionality.

▶ For more, see pp13-45.

SIGHTS

The Grand'Place is the first port of call for most visitors and from here the main sights are within walking distance. A hill connects the older Lower Town and more opulent Upper Town with its major galleries and seats of state. A short métro or bus ride gets you to the EU Quarter, elegant, quirky Ixelles and St-Gilles or to one of Brussels' fine parks.

▶ For more, see pp47-95.

CONSUME

Brussels is renowned for its restaurant and café culture. The quality of food and Belgian beer is second to none. Bar life is ingrained in everyday life and the best are listed to help you on your way. Also in this section you'll find a comprehensive guide to the city's shopping scene, including antiques and vintage, and the lowdown on Brussels' best hotels.

▶ For more, see pp97-174.

ARTS & ENTERTAINMENT

Brussels is packed with international culture all year round. In the summer festivals take the lead, headlined by music, theatre and proud Belgian cultural events. Brussels also has a world-class nightlife scene, often buzzing till dawn, and we show you the city's finest clubs. And if you've got kids in tow, there's a guide to the best children's activities on offer.

▶ For more, see pp175-229.

ESCAPES & EXCURSIONS

Nowhere in Belgium is too far from Brussels, and the country's efficient, cheap train services can transport you around with ease. In this section you can find details of where to escape the capital for a day or two. From the great city states of Antwerp, Bruges, Ghent, Liège and Leuven to the handsome sweep of the Belgian coast, there's plenty to choose from.

▶ For more, see pp231-294.

Brussels in 48 Hours

Day 1 Up the Hill and Down Again

10AM Stand in the Grand'Place and spend some time looking at the varied architecture of the **Hôtel de Ville** (*see p51*) and **Guildhouses** (*see p48*). The **Musée de la Ville de Bruxelles** (*see p52*) is great for a potted history of the city. This is also a good time for coffee in any of the square's cafés.

11AM Leave the square and walk up rue de la Madeleine then continue up the Mont des Arts. This takes you to the Royal Quarter and the city's major cultural institutions. Here you have a choice of the **Musée des Instruments de Musique** (*see p64*), the **Magritte Museum** (*see p64*), the **Musées Royaux des Beaux-Arts** (*see p64*), the **Musée BELvue** (*see p64*) or the **Palais Coudenberg** (*see p65*).

1PM Head along rue de la Régence to the lovely Gothic church of **Notre-Dame du Sablon** (*see p68*). Afterwards, nearby place du Grand Sablon makes the perfect place for lunch.

2.30PM Walk down to the bottom end of the square and into rue Stevens. Here you can visit **Notre-Dame de la Chapelle** (*see p59*) before taking a stroll around the antiques shops of the **Marolles** (*see p58*). Start in rue Haute and cut down any of the small streets.

3.30PM Walk back past Notre-Dame de la Chapelle, cross the dual carriageway and head down rue de l'Escalier to place de la Vieille Halle aux Blés, home to the **Fondation Internationale Jacques Brel** (*see p54*). Continue down rue du Chêne for a glimpse of the **Mannekin-Pis** (*see p54*).

4.30PM Walk along rue de l'Etuve until you cut across the top end of the Grand'Place. Continue into rue de la Colline and into the **Galeries Royales St-Hubert** (*see p155*). Time for window shopping followed by a well-deserved drink at **Mokafé** (*see p117*). For dinner, head to nearby rue du Fossé aux Loups for a seafood platter at drop-dead gorgeous **Belga Queen** (*see p114*).

NAVIGATING THE CITY

Most of the sights in the Lower Town and Upper Town are manageable on foot. If you don't want to walk up the Mont des Arts, bus 95 from the Bourse gets you up the hill quickly to either the Sablon or the Royal Quarter. It also continues on to place du Luxembourg, a good jumping off point for the EU Quarter where the European Parliament is located. Another way of getting around is **Villo!** (*see p298*), an urban cycling scheme that allows you to pick up a bike from any one of 180 stations around the city.

The once-simple métro system has recently become a little more complex. This is nothing to do with adding more lines, it's a case of reorganising the existing ones into a bowl of spaghetti. The important thing is to find the name of the line's end point and use that for navigation (*see p336*). Public transport is very efficient in Brussels. Remember, once you validate your ticket it is valid for

Day 2 Further Afield

9AM Take the métro to Merode. Take the avenue des Gaulois exit and pop into the **Maison de Cauchie** (*see p74*). From here, head into the Parc du Cinquantenaire through Léopold's grandiose arch. The park is home to the **Musées Royaux d'Art et d'Histoire**, the **Musée Royal de l'Armée et d'Histoire Militaire** and **Autoworld** (for all, *see p74*).

11AM Walk through the park, looking out for the **Pavillon Horta** (*see p74*). Emerging at the Schuman roundabout, you are in the heart of the EU district – check out the political goings-on at the **Berlaymont** and **Justus Lipsius** buildings (*see p70*). Follow rue Froissart to place Jourdan, a good place to stop for coffee or an early lunch.

1PM Walk through Parc Léopold to métro Maelbeek. Take métro line 1 or 5 to Beekkant and change on to line 6, direction Roi Baudoin. Alight at Heysel. From here you can visit the renovated **Atomium** (*see p88*), designed by André Waterkeyn for the 1958 World Fair, and the **Pavillon Chinois** (*see p88*). During May, you can also visit the **Serres Royales** (Royal Greenhouses, *see p88*).

4PM Take métro line 5, direction Herrmann-Debroux, and alight at De Brouckère. After a spot of afternoon tea at the grand fin-de-siècle **Café Métropole** (*see p139*), cross place de Brouckère and walk to Ste-Catherine. Here you can check out the exhibition spaces of **De Markten** (*see p123*) or **La Centrale Electrique** (*see p192*). Alternatively, discover the designer boutiques along chic **rue Antoine Dansaert** (*see p160*), a Flemish heartland of fashion, style and culture.

6PM Spend some time sizing up the many fine fish restaurants along Quai aux Briques for later – **Bij den Boer** (*see p121*) does one of the best *moules-frites* in town. If the weather's warm, join the locals under the trees on the place du Vieux Marché aux Grains. If not, pop into **Monk** (*see p142*) for an artisan beer.

one hour on all forms of transport. For full details of transport, *see pp296-298*.

SEEING THE SIGHTS

Museums are closed on Mondays. Some of the smaller museums also close for lunch or have variable opening times. Always check before setting off.

PACKAGE DEALS

If you're planning on visiting a number of museums and using public transport, the

Brussels Card is an essential purchase. It is available for one-, two- or three-day periods. The card offers free entry to around 30 museums, along with free transport on the entire STIB public transport network and discounts and special offers from certain bars and shops. The card costs €24 for 24hrs, €34 for 48hrs and €40 for 72hrs. It can be bought at the city's tourist offices (*see p304*) or online. See www.brussels international.be for details.

Brussels in Profile

THE LOWER TOWN

This is the heart of the city, radiating out from the Grand'Place. The maze of streets, still muddled along medieval lines, gives way to broader boulevards, especially Anspach where the old River Senne once ran. This leads to the drinking quarter of St-Géry (the site of the first settlement) and the boutiques and fish restaurants of Ste-Catherine. Finally, the earthy Marolles provides an intriguing link through to the posher Upper Town.

▶ *For more, see pp48-59.*

THE UPPER TOWN

Once the preserve of kings and still the home of government, the lofty Royal Quarter looks down on its lower neighbour. Here lies not just royalty but politics, justice and high art. The main thoroughfare says it all: rue Royale leading into rue de la Régence. The Sablon is Brussels' poshest village, a collection of high end shops, restaurants and cafés all around what could be a village green but is a decidedly 21st-century car park.

▶ *For more, see pp60-68.*

THE EU QUARTER & ETTERBEEK

The steel and glass edifices of the main EU complex are gathered around the Schuman roundabout, with iconic buidlings such as Berlaymont, Justus Lipsius and the European Parliament dominating proceedings. The area is also home to Brussels' largest, most impressive and best-known park, the Parc du Cinquantenaire. Further west, the terraced townhouses of Etterbeek stretch out into the distance.

▶ *For more, see pp69-74.*

IXELLES & ST-GILLES

There are significant contrasts from one street to the next here. The upmarket swathe of avenue Louise gives way to the African Matongé quarter, while to the west place du Châtelain is where the smart set play. Parvis St-Gilles attracts the locals to its bars and quirky restaurants. The area is also home to some magnificent houses, including many of the city's most remarkable art nouveau designs.

▶ *For more, see pp75-82.*

ANDERLECHT & THE WEST

Starting at the Gare du Midi, Anderlecht is one of Brussels' largest communes. Post-industrial and now largely residential, Anderlecht seems to be in search of its modern identity. Smaller neighbour Molenbeek St-Jean nestles in to the north and is bordered by the old Brussels canal. The canal area has been earmarked as up-and-coming for years. But apart from the impressive Tour & Taxis cultural centre, it still waits.

▶ *For more, see pp83-86.*

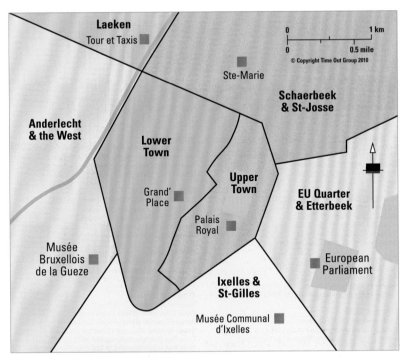

Laeken
Tour et Taxis

Ste-Marie

Schaerbeek
& St-Josse

Anderlecht
& the West

Lower
Town

Upper
Town

EU Quarter
& Etterbeek

Grand'
Place

Palais
Royal

Musée
Bruxellois
de la Gueze

European
Parliament

Ixelles &
St-Gilles

Musée Communal
d'Ixelles

0   1 km
0   0.5 mile
© Copyright Time Out Group 2010

SCHAERBEEK & ST-JOSSE

At its southern end, Schaerbeek speaks of
grand avenues and gentlemen's houses.
Its town hall is like a Gothic wedding cake,
its cultural centre a lofty old market hall.
But Schaerbeek is also home to a sizeable
immigrant population with its attendant poor
housing, something that crosses over the
border into neighbouring St-Josse, a vibrant
area that is almost entirely North African and
Turkish in character. If it's ethnic shopping
you're after, these are the areas to head for.
▶ *For more, see pp89-92.*

LAEKEN

This wealthy and green area some distance
to the north-west of the city centre is home
to the Belgian royal family, Belgian football,
the iconic Atomium and the immense art
deco Parc des Expositions – or Brussels
Expo, as it is now called. It's a rarefied
atmosphere up here and you may even get
to see King Albert taking his daily drive
from Laeken Palace into the city centre.
▶ *For more, see pp87-88.*

TimeOut Brussels

Editorial

Editor Gary Hills
Copy Editors Dominic Earle, Elizabeth Winding
Listings Editor Philip Sheppard
Proofreader Tamsin Shelton
Indexer Neelanjona Debnath

Managing Director Peter Fiennes
Editorial Director Ruth Jarvis
Series Editor Will Fulford-Jones
Business Manager Dan Allen
Editorial Manager Holly Pick
Assistant Management Accountant Ija Krasnikova

Design

Art Director Scott Moore
Art Editor Pinelope Kourmouzoglou
Senior Designer Kei Ishimaru
Group Commercial Designer Jodi Sher

Picture Desk

Picture Editor Jael Marschner
Acting Deputy Picture Editor Liz Leahy
Picture Desk Assistant/Researcher Ben Rowe

Advertising

New Business & Commercial Director Mark Phillips
International Advertising Manager Kasimir Berger
International Sales Executive Charlie Sokol
Advertising Sales (Brussels) Pascale Zoetaert

Marketing

**Sales & Marketing Director, North America
& Latin America** Lisa Levinson
Senior Publishing Brand Manager Luthfa Begum
Group Commercial Art Director Anthony Huggins
Marketing Co-ordinator Alana Benton

Production

Group Production Director Mark Lamond
Production Manager Brendan McKeown
Production Controller Katie Mulhern

Time Out Group

Director & Founder Tony Elliott
Chief Executive Officer David King
Group Financial Director Paul Rakkar
Group General Manager/Director Nichola Coulthard
Time Out Communications Ltd MD David Pepper
Time Out International Ltd MD Cathy Runciman
Time Out Magazine Ltd Publisher/MD Mark Elliott
Group Commercial Director Graeme Tottle
Group IT Director Simon Chappell

Contributors

Introduction Gary Hills. **History** Gary Hills. **Brussels Today** Gary Hills. **Art Nouveau** Derek Blyth, Gary Hills. **Cartoon Brussels** Peterjon Cresswell, Lucy Mallows. **Sights** Gary Hills, Lucy Mallows. **Hotels** Sue Heady, Gary Hills. **Restaurants & Cafés** Gary Hills, Lucy Mallows. **Pubs & Bars** Gary Hills, Peterjon Cresswell. **Shops & Services** Sue Heady, Anouk Vandeneijnde, Lucy Mallows. **Calendar** Gary Hills. **Children** Derek Blyth. **Film** Jonathan Murphy, Gary Hills. **Galleries** Sarah McFadden, Gilbert West. **Gay & Lesbian** Gary Hills. **Music** Julius Stenzel, Gary Hills, Cyrus Shahrad. **Nightlife** Gary Hills. **Sport & Fitness** Alita Byrd, Peterjon Cresswell. **Theatre & Dance** Gary Hills, Lucy Mallows. **Escapes & Excursions** Gary Hills, Derek Blyth, Lucy Mallows. **Directory** Gary Hills, Alita Byrd.

The Editor would like to thank: Sophie Bouallegue (Belgian Tourist Office/Brussels & Wallonia), Jon Gilmartin, Rym Neffoussi (Belgian Tourist Office/Brussels & Wallonia) and Peter Soetens.

Maps JS Graphics (john@jsgraphics.co.uk). Maps are based on material supplied by Mapworld.

Photography by Oliver Knight except pages 3, 6, 8 (top right, bottom left & right), 9, 36, 37, 49 (bottom right), 51, 53, 55 (right), 65, 66, 73, 76, 81, 84, 87, 89, 90, 99, 110, 112, 113, 117, 129, 131, 146, 153, 156, 158, 159, 162, 163, 166, 168, 169, 173, 184, 186, 196, 198, 202, 205, 208, 210, 215, 216, 219, 224, 231, 232, 234, 237, 240, 242, 243, 246, 249, 251, 253, 254, 257, 259, 262, 263, 264, 269, 270, 275, 276, 277, 279, 280, 281, 282, 287, 288 Matthew Lea; pages 4, 5 (bottom left), 8 (second top right), 13, 31, 64, 97, 122, 123, 125, 127, 137, 145, 150, 160, 170, 175, 190, 191, 192, 193, 194, 195, 199, 223, 228 Jonathan Perugia; page 14 Popperfoto/Getty Images; page 19 Bridgeman Art Library/Getty Images; page 43 Nicolas Borel, Atelier de Portzamparc 2009; page 62 Saskia Vanderstichele; page 93 Hadley Kinkade; page 109 Serge Anton; page 147 Jael Marschner; page 176 Bruno Vessié; page 177 Alexandre Miodezky; page 178 Fred Pauwels; page 180 Daan Roose; page 181 Gaston Batistini, Labo River; page 197 Melanie; page 209 Greg Van Oz; page 229 Sammi Landweer.

The following images were provided by the featured establishments/artists: pages 5 (bottom right), 23, 31, 98, 102, 103, 108, 229 (top left), 235, 239, 256, 258, 260, 272, 274, 283, 284, 334.

About the Guide

GETTING AROUND

The back of the book contains street maps of Brussels as well as a map of the Laeken complex. The maps start on page 313; on them are marked the locations of hotels (**❶**), restaurants and cafés (**❶**), and pubs and bars (**❶**). The majority of businesses listed in this guide are located in the areas we've mapped; the grid-square references in the listings refer to these maps. City centre maps for Antwerp, Bruges and Ghent can be found at the start of their chapters.

THE ESSENTIALS

For practical information, including visas, disabled access, emergency numbers, lost property, useful websites and local transport, please see the Directory. It begins on page 295.

THE LISTINGS

Addresses, phone numbers, websites, transport information, hours and prices are all included in our listings, as are selected other facilities. All were checked and correct at time of going to press. However, business owners can alter their arrangements at any time, and fluctuating economic conditions can cause prices to change rapidly.

The very best venues in the city, the must-sees and must-dos in every category, have been marked with a red star (★). In the sights chapters, we've also marked venues with free admission with a **FREE** symbol.

PHONE NUMBERS

The area code for Brussels is 02. You need to include this code even when dialling from within the city. From outside Belgium, dial your country's international access code (00 from the UK, 011 from the USA) or a plus symbol, followed by the Belgian country code (32), 2 for Brussels (dropping the initial '0') and the seven-digit number as listed in this guide. So, to reach the Brussels Info Point, dial +32 2 563 63 99. For more on phones, including mobile phone access, *see p303*.

FEEDBACK

We welcome feedback on this guide, both on the venues we've included and on any other locations that you'd like to see featured in this guide. Please email us at guides@timeout.com.

Time Out Guides

Founded in 1968, Time Out has grown from humble beginnings into the leading resource for anyone wanting to know what's happening in the world's greatest cities. Alongside our influential weeklies in London, New York and Chicago, we publish more than 20 magazines in cities as varied as Beijing and Beirut; a range of travel books, with the City Guides now joined by the newer Shortlist series; and an information-packed website. The company remains proudly independent, still owned by Tony Elliott four decades after he launched *Time Out London*.

Written by local experts and illustrated with original photography, our books also retain their independence. No business has been featured in the guides because it has advertised, and all restaurants and bars are visited and reviewed anonymously.

ABOUT THE EDITOR

Gary Hills lives in Brussels and has been writing for Time Out since 2001. As Consultant Editor and Editor, he has now worked on four Brussels City Guides as well as other Time Out publications, in-flight magazines, hospitality industry publications and online.

A full list of the book's contributors can be found opposite.

In Context

History

From feral Belgae to federal Belgians.

TEXT: GARY HILLS

When Julius Caesar first arrived in what is now known as Belgium in 59 BC, the area was inhabited by Celtic and Germanic tribes who had been drifting into the region since 2000 BC. The Belgae, as the Romans then called them, were notoriously tough and resistant, but they were simply no match for the formidable Roman army, which settled comfortably into control of what it then called Gallia Belgica, a useful cushion between the Rhine and the provinces of Gaul. The Roman settlements, therefore, were largely in the south-east, though we know that they also used the coast for salt production, the south-west for quarrying and the region near Ghent for ironworks.

Brussels as we know it today simply did not exist at this time. The site was an inhospitable one, with marshy flood plains from the multi-directional River Senne making settlement extremely difficult. Surrounding the marsh was a vast forest, the Silva Carbonaria (Charcoal Forest), which had been providing fuel and iron ore for weapons long before the Romans first arrived. The Forêt de Soignes to the south-east of modern Brussels is now the last remaining remnant of what once covered huge swathes of Gaul. The importance of the forest as a source of fuel can still be seen reflected in Brussels street names such as rue du Marché au Charbon and quai au Bois à Brûler.

THE FRANKS

The Roman empire in Gallia Belgica first began to founder in the third century AD, when the Franks, a coalition of Germanic tribes, began attacking its northern borders. This was also compounded by constant flooding, an ongoing problem throughout the history of the Low Countries, and by the fifth century the last of the Romans were gone. From 350 onwards, the Franks were beginning to settle into the more economically viable parts of the region, but Gallia Belgica remained volatile as waves of invaders passed through to continue attacking Roman armies in Gaul. These invasions are now seen as the first stage in the process that would lead to the deep linguistic division that cuts across present-day Belgium, since they caused the northern areas to become German-speaking, while to the south, Latin-based languages remained dominant.

The presence of the Franks in the Brussels region is largely unrecorded, although burial sites provide pretty solid evidence that they were around from the fifth century, and were almost certainly using the tributaries of the River Senne as a trading post. The rest is largely conjecture, although it seems an early church was erected in the hamlet of Brosella, the first mention of the place known today as Brussels. The first more reliably documented reference to Bruocsella (dwelling in the marsh) dates from 695, when it was a stopover on the trade route from Cologne to Bruges and Ghent.

King Charlemagne ruled from 768 to 814 and built an empire from Denmark to southern Italy, all the way from the Atlantic to the Danube. When he died in 814, his sons and grandsons went to war with each other over the fine print of their respective royal inheritances. As a result, in 843 the kingdom was split between his three grandsons by the Treaty of Verdun: Louis the German received East Francia, which roughly corresponds to modern-day Germany; Charles the Bald was given control of West Francia, which equates more or less to France plus Flanders; and Lothair received Middle Francia, or the Middle Kingdom. This was a thin strip of land between the River Scheldt and Germany in the north, and stretching down to the Mediterranean.

During the ninth and tenth centuries, the old Frankish kingdoms found themselves subjected to regular invasions by marauding Vikings, who took advantage of the power vacuum. There was a gradual disintegration of central power and a rise of feudal domains. Flanders became one of the most powerful of all of these, and although it was theoretically ruled by the kings of France, the Flemish counts were virtually autonomous. Other fiefdoms were Liège, Hainaut, Namur, Luxembourg and Brabant.

Around 1000 a church dedicated to St Géry was erected on an island formed by the River Senne. This Ile St-Géry or Grand Ile was later to become the heart of the city; it still exists today in the shape of place St-Géry, although the early fortifications have given way to an agricultural hall and numerous trendy bars. Walk along the narrow street called Borgwal and you retrace the line of the original wooden palisades. Borgwal, therefore, can lay claim to being the oldest street in Brussels. From 1020, Brosella started to be mentioned as a port and in 1047 its ruler, Lambert II, Count of Louvain (Leuven), built a fort on Coudenberg Hill, overlooking the flood plains (*see p22* **A View from Above**). The growing strategic and military importance of the Brussels settlement saw the erection of the original city walls over an 80-year period. Referred to as the *première enceinte*, or first enclosure, they constituted an impressive run of towers and gateways that kept the inhabitants in and the attackers out. All that is left of them now is a pair of isolated towers, including the Tour Noire, sandwiched between blandish modern buildings by place Ste-Catherine.

THE DUKES OF BRABANT

From 1106, the Counts of Louvain began to be known as the Dukes of Brabant, even though they continued to rule Brussels from the city of Louvain. They started to use the surrounding forests as hunting grounds and the city soon started to spread out from the marshy valley of the River Senne into the hills and plateaux around it. The new city walls gave confidence to build grand stone houses, which can still be seen reflected in central street names such as Plattesteen. Also at this time, Brussels became an important commercial centre, mainly for wool and cloth production, and by the 12th century Flemish cloth was being sold in France, Italy and England, and the basis of an Anglo-Belgian trading partnership had been firmly established. In 1282, there is the first recorded mention of the Drapers' Guild, something that indicated the importance of the cloth trade, and the future of Brussels itself.

The economic health of Flanders depended not only on the state of its trade relations with England, but also on Anglo-French relations, with Flanders often suffering from English reprisals against the French. Despite the fact that the Flemish counts were in the pockets of the French royals, the Flemish remained often hostile to the French. On 11 July 1302, at the Battle of the Golden Spurs, the French knights suffered a shock defeat, the victorious Flemish collecting 700 pairs of spurs from the fleeing French. It was a milestone in Flemish resistance and the victory became ingrained in the Flemish and Belgian consciousness (11 July is still a public holiday across Flanders). The balance of the England–France–Flanders triangle became even more fragile in 1337, when the Hundred Years War began. At the outset of the war, a Flemish landowner called Jacob van Artevelde led a rebellion in Ghent against the pro-French counts of Flanders, who fled to France. Flanders had been officially neutral, but Van Artevelde actively allied it with the English.

During this time, Brussels continued to grow dramatically. While Louvain officially remained the capital of Brabant, the rulers were already receiving dignitaries in Brussels, and the city's jurisdiction widened to take in places such as Schaerbeek and Ixelles. But in 1356 there was a power struggle between the daughters of Duke John III, resulting in a deadly battle won by Count Louis de Malle of Flanders. For the first time in its history, Brussels was ruled for a short while by the Flemish.

This brutal shock forced the city's elders to recognise the need for stronger defences, and in 1357 construction began on a new set of walls, the *seconde enceinte*, or second enclosure. It was these walls that gave the centre of Brussels its pentagonal shape and now provide the city with its inner ring road: le Petit Ring. The names of the gates are still with us: Porte de Namur, Porte d'Anderlecht and so on, but only the Porte de Hal remains, a lonely Cinderella castle on a traffic island.

THE DUKES OF BURGUNDY

A process of great cultural change began in the 1360s when Margaret of Malle, daughter of Count Louis de Malle, married Philip the Bold, Duke of Burgundy. When Louis died in 1384, Flanders and other provinces came together in a loose union under the authority of the Dukes of Burgundy. The key figure was Philip the Good (Philippe le Bon), grandson of Margaret and Philip the Bold. Having inherited Flanders, Burgundy, Artois and other provinces, he then acquired Brabant, Holland, Hainaut, Namur and Luxembourg through a combination of politics, purchase and military action.

Although the Dukes of Burgundy ruled for less than a century, the cultural changes during this period were significant. In addition to their ducal palace in Dijon, they had important residences in Lille, Bruges and Brussels. The court moved regularly between them, although from 1459 it became based mainly in Brussels. The Dukes of Burgundy initiated their own court culture in the Low Countries, and were active patrons of the arts. Parades, tournaments, jousting and pageants were a major part of city and court life under the Dukes, as a means of displaying their power and wealth. This was also apparent in the great building works that now took place. The first university in the Low Countries was founded in Leuven in 1425; work on Brussels' formidable Town Hall, still the dominant feature of the Grand'Place, started in 1402; the awesome tower of Mechelen Cathedral was begun in 1452. In the arts, the best-known evidence of the Dukes' patronage was in 15th-century painting: the Brabant-born painter Jan van Eyck worked in Ghent and Bruges; Rogier van der Weyden worked in Brussels as the city's official painter; and German artist Hans Memling settled in Bruges in 1465.

'The Edict of Blood in 1550 demanded the death penalty for all those convicted of heresy.'

Although the textile industries were swiftly declining in the 14th and 15th centuries, mainly as a result of cheaper competition from England, other industries were replacing them. Brussels was now producing tapestries, was becoming a centre for goldsmiths, and its first printing works opened in 1475. Brussels soon became the centre of Philip the Good's court and the Coudenberg Palace undoubtedly ranked as one of Europe's finest.

With the death of Philip the Good in 1467, the end of the rule of the Dukes of Burgundy was in sight. Philip was succeeded by his son Charles the Rash (Charles le Téméraire), who disliked Brussels and so moved his court to Mechelen. There was no great grief when he was killed at the Battle of Nancy in 1477. He was succeeded by his daughter Mary, whose death five years later left the Netherlands in disarray. Mary had married Maximilian von Habsburg of Austria, and their son Philip was only four when she died. The Low Countries were then ruled by Maximilian for the next ten years, making them part of the Habsburg empire.

THE SPANISH NETHERLANDS

Maximilian's son Philip married Juana, the daughter of King Ferdinand and Queen Isabella of Spain. Their son Charles was born in Ghent in 1500 and, after an extraordinary series of premature deaths and childless marriages among the ruling families of Europe, he had inherited most of Europe by the time he was 20. He became Lord of the Netherlands in 1506 and King of Spain in 1516, and he was made Emperor Charles V of Germany when his grandfather Maximilian died in 1519. In this way, a native of Ghent found himself ruling the Netherlands, Austria, the Tyrol, Spain, Mexico, Peru, the Caribbean, Sicily, Naples and the German empire. Charles spent much of his earlier reign in Brussels and spoke both Dutch and French. While the connections with Spain were to prove quite disastrous in the future, Charles understood the Belgians well and he became a popular ruler. He returned great wealth and prosperity to Brussels, just as its fading medieval glories needed a kick-start.

Brussels had its new statement-piece Town Hall in place with its 90-metre (300-foot) tower (*see p26* **Power to the People**) and the palaces on the hill beamed prestigiously over the city. The first regular international mail service was set up in Brussels in 1520 by Jean-Baptiste de Tour et Taxis. Antwerp was even more prosperous than Brussels, as it was the crossroads of the trading routes between Spain, Portugal, Russia and the Baltic. Each day, some 5,000 merchants would gather in the exchange, and anything up to 500 ships came and went from the port.

Charles's reign saw the beginning of the Reformation, which would have devastating consequences for Europe. Lutherans from Germany extended their influence westwards into the Netherlands, while Calvinism spread northwards from Geneva. Although Charles was prepared to negotiate with Luther and his followers, he would also deal harshly with Protestants, whom many considered heretics. The first Lutheran martyrs were burned in Brussels in 1523, and in 1550 Charles passed the Edict of Blood, which demanded the death penalty for all those convicted of heresy.

Charles abdicated in 1555, in an emotional ceremony at Brussels' Coudenberg Palace, and handed over the reins of the Netherlands to his son Philip, who became Philip II of Spain. Like his father, Philip inherited a collection of provinces in the Low Countries, rather than a nation. There was no common ancestry or language among the 17 provinces, and the French and Dutch language split was already patently evident to all.

IN CONTEXT

The problems afflicting the Netherlands during Philip's rule were very similar to those suffered under Charles: heavy taxation and the gradual spread of Protestantism. But whereas Charles had remained popular, Philip was never liked. He was Spanish by birth and sentiment, he didn't speak French or Dutch and he had very little affection for his subjects in the Low Countries. He was also rather more hard-line in his defence of Catholicism than his father. In this he was aided by the Inquisition. Although the Spanish achieved the greatest infamy, their Belgian counterparts were hardly moderate. A poor citizen in Bruges who happened to trample on a consecrated wafer had his hand and foot wrenched off by red-hot irons and his tongue ripped out, before being slowly roasted over an open fire. Brussels' Grand'Place became a grisly home to executioners.

THE DUTCH REVOLT

Philip's troubles in the Netherlands started fairly quickly. He appointed his half-sister Margaret of Parma as regent, but power was mainly in the hands of two hated pro-Spanish councillors, Cardinal Granvelle and Count Berlaymont. Philip's most prominent opponents were Prince William of Orange, Count Egmont and Count Hoorn. In 1565, a group of nobles opposed to Philip formed the League of Nobles. Berlaymont referred to them disparagingly as 'ces gueux', beggars, and 'Vivent les gueux!' became their rallying cry. They objected to Philip's refusal to tolerate Protestantism, his attempt to centralise power, the heavy taxes imposed on the provinces, and the presence of Spanish troops in the Netherlands.

The spread of Protestantism was not merely confined to the League of Nobles. It burgeoned equally among the poor in the towns of Flanders, Brabant, Holland and Zeeland. In the 1560s, Calvinist preachers attracted huge crowds, and part of their attraction to the poor was that they railed against the wealth of the Catholic Church. The preachers also criticised the imagery and art in the Catholic churches. In the Iconoclastic Riots of 1566, raging Calvinist mobs destroyed Catholic churches all across the Netherlands. In Antwerp, crowds attacked the cathedral with axes: they hacked up the Madonna, pulled down the statue of Christ at the altar, destroyed the chapels, drank the communion wine, burned manuscripts and rubbed the sacred oil on their shoes. They then did the same to 30 other churches in the city.

Philip duly appointed the Duke of Alva as the new governor in the 17 provinces, and he soon arrived with an army of 10,000. One of his very first acts was to set up the 'Council of Blood' (officially the Council of Troubles or Tumults). On 4 January 1568 alone he had 84 people executed on the scaffold. In March, there were 1,500 arrests, 800 of them in one day, and in June Counts Egmont and Hoorn were beheaded in the Grand'Place. Their deaths marked the start of a full-scale revolt in the Netherlands that would last for 80 years.

Although Calvinism had first taken hold in the south, the southern provinces were now also coming under the influence of the Counter-Reformation, and in 1579 the ten southern provinces formed the Union of Arras, accepting the authority of Philip, and of Catholicism. The north's response was the 1581 Union of Utrecht, which was essentially a declaration that the seven northern provinces no longer recognised Philip's authority. By the end of the century the northern provinces had formed the Republic of the United Netherlands, also known as the United Provinces, while the southern provinces were known as the Spanish Netherlands, a split that became irreversible.

In 1598, Philip handed over his remaining territories in the Netherlands to his son-in-law, Archduke Albrecht of Austria. Philip hoped this might make reconciliation between the north and south possible. However, when Albrecht died without an heir in 1621 the provinces reverted to Spanish rule, although Philip's daughter Isabella remained governor until her death in 1633. Isabella and Albrecht maintained a lavish court, with court painter Peter Paul Rubens as its focal point.

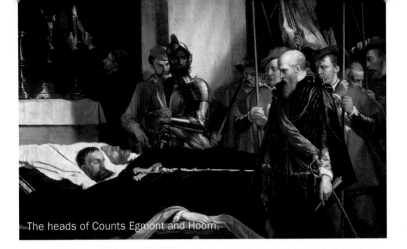
The heads of Counts Egmont and Hoorn.

They negotiated an uneasy truce with the Dutch in 1609, but this lasted just 12 years, with the war subsequently continuing until 1648. During its last phase, the religious gap widened between the two sides, with the United Provinces becoming more firmly Calvinist and with the Spanish Netherlands in the grip of the Catholic Counter-Reformation. The war ended in 1648 with the Treaty of Munster, in which Spain recognised the independence of the north's United Provinces, with the agreed borders corresponding to the present-day Belgian-Dutch border.

In the second half of the 17th century, King Louis XIV of France had grand ambitions to dominate Europe at the expense of the Dutch, the English and the Habsburgs. Spain's former power had dwindled so far that it was no longer able to defend its own territory. The late 17th century brought a succession of gruelling wars: the War of Devolution, the Dutch War and the War of the Grand Alliance, in all of which the Spanish Netherlands were either attacked or occupied. The ensuing peace treaties led to the territory of the Spanish Netherlands being slowly whittled away, with France finally taking hold of both Artois and Ypres.

All this time, Brussels was still producing a range of luxury goods, including ornamental lace, tapestries and porcelain, some bound for export and some earmarked for the nobles and merchants still making their homes in the Spanish Netherlands. It was at this time, in 1695, that Louis XIV, unable to enter Brussels to claim the Spanish Netherlands, ordered the pointless and barbaric bombardment of the city, destroying most of its medieval fabric. *See p26* **Power to the People**.

THE AUSTRIAN NETHERLANDS

When Philip IV of Spain died in 1665 the Spanish throne passed directly to his sickly four-year-old son Charles. Despite two separate marriages, Charles II remained childless and for most of the 1690s he seemed to be teetering on the verge of death. Eager to fill a vacuum, the French, English, Dutch and Austrians began plotting over who would succeed him. By the time Charles II died in 1700, there were two candidates: Archduke Charles of Austria and Philip of Anjou, grandson of Louis XIV of France. Charles favoured the Frenchman as his heir and in 1701 the French Duke of Anjou entered Madrid as King of Spain. The French occupied Dutch-held barrier fortresses in the Spanish Netherlands, and the English and the Dutch declared war on France. The War of Spanish Succession lasted from 1701 to 1713 and was fought in Germany, the Netherlands, Italy and Spain, as well as at sea. During the war, the Spanish Netherlands were governed by the French and the English. Peace was made at the 1713 Treaty of Utrecht and the 1714 Treaty of Rastatt. Philip of Anjou kept the Spanish throne, but the Austrians came away with the Spanish Netherlands, henceforth known as the Austrian Netherlands.

The main effect of the Austrian Netherlands during the first years of the 18th century was peace, for the country was no longer the prey of French armies. Only once during Austrian rule were the Netherlands invaded by the French, in 1744. Emperor Charles VI of Austria wanted his daughter Maria Theresa to inherit his empire, but the rest of Europe refused to accept this. France invaded and occupied the Austrian Netherlands until the Treaty of Aix-La-Chapelle restored Austrian rule in 1748 and gave the throne to Maria Theresa's husband, Francis I.

The real power, however, lay solely with Maria Theresa. Her rule, lasting until 1780, brought considerable economic renewal in the Austrian Netherlands. This was partly a result of peace, and partly because of efforts by her governor, Charles of Lorraine, to build roads and waterways. There were also improvements in agricultural technology – so much so that the late 18th century was the only time in Belgium's history when it was self-sufficient in grain. There were also new glass, coal and cotton industries, which, unlike the trades that came before, did not revolve around the power of the guilds. Smaller industries – paper mills, sugar refineries and silk factories – also grew.

Cultural life developed, censorship relaxed, French books circulated freely and bookshops were opened in the outlying towns. There was a growing printing industry too. However, the Austrian Netherlands were scarcely at the fore of the Enlightenment, and rural culture still followed traditional values, with companies travelling around the countryside performing medieval mystery plays.

In 1731, the Coudenberg Palace burnt down after a vat of boiling sugar started a fire in the royal kitchens. In 1740, work began on a new palace, the Palais du Roi, which is currently the town residence of the Belgian royal family. The neo-classical place Royale and the Palais de la Nation, the seat of the Belgian parliament, were built in the 1770s and 1780s. In 1782, work started on the official residence of the Belgian royal family at Laeken.

Maria Theresa was succeeded by her son Joseph II in 1780. His rule was far more radical than his mother's. He immediately attempted to modernise the country, closing monasteries and seminaries, taxing the Church and reforming both the judicial system and governmental administration. In 1781, he passed the Edict of Toleration, recognising religious freedoms. Joseph was loathed by the more conservative Belgians, who saw their traditional privileges and vested interests threatened by his wayward spate of reforms. The result was the Brabançon Revolution of 1789-90, which involved all the provinces except Luxembourg. The rebels, led by a Brussels lawyer, wrote a new constitution inspired by the US Articles of Confederation, and formed the Confederation of the United Belgian States. But the revolution collapsed into chaos as a result of the widening split between conservative and progressive rebels. Around 100,000 peasants, led by priests, marched en masse through the centre of Brussels to register their protest against the progressives, many of whom were subsequently forced to flee to France. Austrian authority was finally restored in 1791, and when Joseph II eventually died, he was succeeded by the liberal Leopold II, who had less enthusiasm for reform, preoccupied as he was with events in other parts of his increasingly less stable empire.

FRENCH REVOLUTIONARY RULE

In 1792, the French declared war on Austria and Prussia, occupying the Austrian Netherlands and independent Liège. The French armies were initially greeted as liberators, but the welcome quickly faded, and when the loathed French temporarily withdrew from Brussels after a defeat in 1793, the people of Brussels ransacked the houses of pro-French families. When France reoccupied the Austrian Netherlands in 1794, tens of thousands of Belgians emigrated. The French exacted strict war levies and military requisitions and set up an *agence de commerce* to take anything from cattle to art back to France. Among their booty was Jan van Eyck's religious painting *The Adoration of the Mystic Lamb*, now hanging in Ghent's cathedral, and they also

IN CONTEXT

confiscated the palace at Laeken. In 1795, the French absorbed the former Austrian Netherlands and set up a new administration. They abolished the former provinces and created nine new *départements*. Brussels itself became a departmental capital answering to Paris. Liège and the Netherlands were united for the first time, and the region was referred to by the French as *Belgique*.

The French passed new laws suppressing feudalism and the guilds and from 1796 applied French law to Belgium. The Belgians accepted the occupation and annexation passively but unenthusiastically; French leaders complained of their apathy. The leading opposition to French rule came in 1798, after the French introduced conscription. There were riots in east and west Flanders and about 10,000 peasants formed an army in Brabant. The uprising was soon crushed, brutally and bloodily, and hundreds were executed. The last five years of the century saw industry in decline, the depopulation of towns, new taxes, economic hardship, and organised gangs of robbers roaming the highways. Slowly, the French encouraged the growth of industries such as coal and cotton, which benefited from the new markets in France. The new industries were capitalist, funded by entrepreneurial nobles and traders who had bought former monastery lands cheaply. One of the most notable beneficiaries of the French occupation was Antwerp, where Napoleon constructed a new harbour and port, which he described as 'a pistol aimed at the heart of England'.

He also made his mark on Brussels, ordering the city's old walls to be demolished and then replaced with open boulevards. He bought the palace at Laeken as his official residence, but only used it occasionally before trading it for the Elysée Palace in Paris in a legal settlement with the Empress Josephine. French rule of the Netherlands came to a sharp end in 1814, when Napoleon was forced to abdicate as Emperor of France, following his defeat at the Battle of Leipzig. His opponents (Britain, Prussia, Russia, Austria) recaptured Brussels in February 1814 and appointed a council of conservatives to govern the city. The council was very keen for Belgium to return to Austrian rule. In 1814, the Congress of Vienna began its work to break up and redistribute Napoleon's empire.

On his return from exile, Napoleon rounded up an army. The Congress of Vienna quickly condemned the landing and Europe prepared for war. The armies of the British, Spanish, Prussians, Austrians and Dutch numbered over one million men between them. Napoleon had gathered about 375,000 soldiers. The Duke of Wellington, commander-in-chief of the British, Hanoverians and Belgians, established his headquarters in Brussels. One of the legends of Waterloo is that Wellington was attending a ball hosted by the Duke and Duchess of Richmond in the rue de la Blanchisserie when he heard of Napoleon's approach on 18 June. The battle lasted for ten hours and 50,000 soldiers were killed. Napoleon escaped to Paris, where he abdicated and surrendered to the British. He was banished to the island of St Helena, where he died in 1821.

UNITY AND REVOLUTION

The Congress of Vienna redrew the map of Europe after Napoleon. One main dilemma was the Netherlands. The north had existed as an independent state since 1648, but the former Spanish and Austrian Netherlands had no tradition of independence and Congress was reluctant to create one. Austria had no desire to recover these provinces, and there was no question of their going to France. So what was to become of them? The Congress of Vienna decided to unite the Netherlands with the Austrian Netherlands and form the United Kingdom of the Netherlands, thereby creating a strong buffer between France and Prussia. It was a solution that few inhabitants had asked for, other than some Belgian entrepreneurs who realised that union with the Dutch might compensate for the loss of markets in France.

The United Kingdom of the Netherlands was created as a constitutional monarchy ruled by William of Orange. He was installed as its sovereign prince on 31 July 1814,

A View from Above

Cold Hill made the perfect perch for the powers-that-be.

Since 1047, when Lambert II first built a fort on Cold Hill, the powers that be have chosen to survey the local hoi polloi from on high. Historically, this enabled them to escape the murk of the marshes below and to defend their seat of power both psychologically and physically. During the Middle Ages, Brussels had to defend itself aggressively against powerful Leuven as the seat of power of the Dukedom of Brabant; the hilltop palace and defences of the Coudenberg became an important part of that struggle.

Philip the Good (1396-1467) decided that the palace on the hill should become his main residence, and it was during this same period that the palace became an important part of placing Brussels firmly on the path to diplomatic ascendancy. Philip had a great hall built – the Magna Aula – with an open-beam, unsupported roof and wooden ceiling. It was 40 metres (131 feet) long and 16 metres (53 feet) wide, and became a magnificent place for receptions, assemblies and celebrations. One such gathering was described by Antonio de Beatis in 1518: 'We also saw the Catholic King's palace where his father King Philip was born. It contains a large and very lofty hall where they joust without saddles when the weather is too bad for jousting outside.'

It was Charles V who commissioned the massive chapel (it took 32 years to build), which was justifiably renowned throughout Europe for its Gothic splendour. In fact, the palace at Coudenberg was regarded as one of Europe's greatest royal residences. Imagine, then, the horror when, during the night of 3 February 1731, a large vat of boiling sugar overheated and set fire to the palace kitchen. Attempts to put it out failed and the whole building was engulfed in flames. Everything apart from a portion of the library and a few works of art was destroyed, and the palace remained in ruins until 1774, when building once again started on the site.

This new incarnation became what we now know as the Royal Quarter in the Upper Town, constructed during the reign of Empress Maria Theresa and designed by noted French architect Barnabé Guimard. To accommodate it, parts of the old palace were blown up or simply built over. The ruins remained under place Royale for centuries and were largely forgotten until the 1990s, when they were finally excavated and underwent extensive archaeological research before being fully restored and opened to the public.

It's now possible to recreate the footsteps of the illustrious residents and visitors of the past and visit the palace in its underground setting, just beneath street level. Walking around this ancient site is evocative and eerie – it's quite possible to be completely alone down there. When you buy your ticket at the desk of the **Musée BELvue** (*see p64*), you're given a code to open the door to this dark kingdom. You descend to a lower level where there's a looped film showing – take the time to watch it before you enter. Once inside, you find yourself in a hugely atmospheric pink-brick space, gently lit and strangely silent, save for the muffled moan of traffic above.

One thing you'll notice is the contour of the hill and how the construct of this vast palace was cleverly designed to follow the steep drop while keeping everything on the level. Don't expect anything overly grand or spectacular; these are ruins at their most basic and you'll need to use your imagination to rebuild the structures above their base levels. But you'll also see the footprint of the Magna Aula, remains of the chapel, parts of kitchens, store cupboards and courtyards. Piecing it all together with the help of the excellent free guide brochure (and the film) is a fascinating exercise in and of itself, as is trying to place your bearings in relation to the modern world still rolling on above you.

Of special note are the crumbling remains of rue Isabelle. Guimard had the street vaulted over for use as cellars, so you really need to use your imagination to visualise it as an exterior street running along the natural contours of the Coudenberg. It had existed since the Middle Ages, but the Archduchess Isabelle wanted it widened and lengthened so she could slip out of the palace and make her way down the hill to the cathedral without fuss or ceremony. It was here that Charlotte Brontë lived at No.32 – the site of that house is now under the entrance hall of the Palais des Beaux-Arts in rue Ravenstein.

It's a truly enchanting experience; apart from patches of the old city walls and the remaining gates, the palace ruins are the best of what is left of medieval Brussels.

Fire engulfs the Coudenberg Palace in 1731.

'Belgium's history as a nation state began with the French speakers in the ascendant.'

and declared king in 1815. As well as its 17 provinces, the new kingdom also had two capitals, The Hague and Brussels. William I was eager to promote prosperity and unity, and although he largely succeeded in the former, he failed in the latter. The southerners found many reasons to resent the new state. The south of the kingdom was already industrialised and had become wealthy as a result. Although Brussels was joint capital, the new country was governed by a Dutch king, Dutch ministers and Dutch civil servants. While being more numerous and prosperous, Belgians had very little political power at the outset and gained little more over time.

Many Belgians took refuge in memories of the earlier grandeur of Antwerp and Brussels, regarding the Dutch as upstarts. There was also fury at the government's attempts to introduce Dutch as the standard national language. This resentment was not confined to just French speakers – those who spoke Flemish dialects also protested against the blanket use of Dutch. Belgium's Catholics were opposed to the new government because it had declared religious freedom and removed the Catholic bias in the education system. Belgian liberals also opposed the new state, seeking freedom of the press and a less autocratic style of government. In 1828, the Catholics and liberals formed an unlikely alliance, demanding that the Belgians, not the Dutch, become the dominant force in the Netherlands. The government did make some concessions, repealing the language decrees in the south and guaranteeing freedom of education, but it would neither accept Belgian supremacy nor grant freedom of the press.

The winter of 1829-30 was very severe and farmers suffered accordingly. On top of that, overproduction in the industries of the south had caused wage cuts, bankruptcies and a rash of unemployment. Workers in both sectors were quickly turning mutinous, and there were regular protests and demonstrations in Brussels as a result. On 25 August 1830, an opera called La Muette de Portici, by Daniel Auber, was performed in Brussels' Théâtre de la Monnaie. Its subject was the Naples rebellion of 1647 and the opera had been banned since being written in 1828. During an aria called 'L'Amour Sacré de la Patrie' (Sacred Love of the Fatherland), liberals and students in the theatre started rioting, then joined the workers protesting in the square outside.

This was the start of the Belgian Revolution. The Dutch government negotiated with the leaders of the revolution and there seemed a possibility of administrative separation. But William I prevaricated and the impatient and disillusioned rebels decided to go for secession. William sent 10,000 troops into Brussels at the end of September, and while the numbers were insufficient to crush the revolution, they were enough to inflame the southern provinces into joining the uprising. Belgian soldiers deserted their regiments, and William's troops were soon driven out of Brussels. A new government was rapidly assembled. On 4 October 1830, the rebels declared an independent state and provisional government; on 3 November they held elections for a National Congress. It met on 10 November and comprised 200 people, mostly intellectuals, lawyers and journalists. There were very few representatives from industry or finance.

On 22 November the new Congress set out a constitution. Belgium would be a parliamentary monarchy and unitary state of nine provinces, with freedom of religion, education, assembly, press and language, and a separate church and state. On 3 March 1831, the Congress passed an electoral law defining the electorate, which consisted of about 46,000 men of the bourgeoisie. This meant that one out of every 95 inhabitants had the vote, a relatively high proportion – in France, it was one in 160.

The rest of the world soon recognised the new nation, and in January 1831 the Great Powers met in London to discuss the issue. Britain advocated creating a Belgian state, France and Germany agreed, and Belgium was recognised as an independent and neutral state. Deciding on a new king was less easy, but eventually Léopold of Saxe-Coburg-Gotha was selected. He was related to the major European royal households, most famously as uncle to both Victoria and Albert. He took an oath to the constitution on 21 July, now Belgium's National Day. Shortly afterwards, the Dutch invaded Belgium, and this helped prolong a sense of unity among the Catholics and liberals. The Dutch beat the Belgian rebels at Leuven and Hasselt but then retreated on hearing reports of an approaching French army of 50,000. They did not recognise the new country until 1839.

INDEPENDENT BELGIUM

It was more or less inevitable that the coalition between liberals and Catholics in the new state of Belgium would be neither harmonious nor long-lived. The political history of Belgium in the 19th century was of a tug of war between the two, the main bones of contention being the education system and the language split. Belgium's history as a nation state began with the Catholics and the French speakers in the ascendant. The new constitution allowed people to use whichever language they desired, but French was the language spoken in the courts, the education system (apart from some primary schools) and the administration. In the country as a whole, Flemish was more widely spoken, with 2.4 million Flemish speakers to 1.8 million French ones. The majority of Belgians were being governed in an alien language.

Intellectuals in both Antwerp and Ghent soon began to resent the predominance of French. In 1840, they organised a petition demanding the use of Flemish in the administration and law courts of Flemish-speaking provinces. To begin with, the Catholics were dominant at most levels. Membership of monasteries and convents more than doubled during the 1830s and 1840s, and in 1834 a new Catholic university was founded at Mechelen, moving to Leuven in 1835. The Catholic Church also controlled most secondary education. In 1846, the liberals held a congress in Brussels to clarify the points of their political programme and plan an election strategy. The Catholics did not start to organise themselves in anything like the same way until the 1860s. Charles Rogier first formed a liberal government in 1848, and the liberals governed, albeit with a few gaps, until 1884.

Although Belgium lost the Dutch East Indies markets when it split from the Netherlands, there was industrial expansion from the 1830s, at a time when much of Europe had plummeting industrial prices. With its programme of railway construction and industrial investment, Belgium was the first country in Europe to undergo the Industrial Revolution. In Brussels the canal system was extended with the new Canal de Charleroi, and with it a whole new industrial complex was built on the western side of the city in Anderlecht, Forest and Molenbeek. It became known as Little Manchester. The king wished to maintain his capital as a prestigious centre of commerce, banking and luxury goods rather than a hub of manufacturing. There were also political reasons: with economic problems all across the country, an industrialised urban workforce was seen as dangerous. The Belgian Workers' Party was founded in 1885 and the Socialists would soon exert political influence.

Universal male suffrage was introduced in 1893 and in 1894 the Socialists gained their first parliamentary seats – but with the bulk of their support in Flanders, the Catholics retook power until 1917. There had already been concessions to Flemish speakers, and the Catholics sped up the process. Language remained a big problem. Legislation had introduced bilingualism in Flanders and strengthed the Flemish position in law and education, but the Flemings were still governed and tried in French. In 1898, Flemish was given official equality with French, though the electorate (only taxpayers could vote) was almost entirely French-speaking.

IN CONTEXT

Power to the People

The rise and fall of the guilds of the Grand'Place.

What is now the **Grand'Place** was a marshy area before the first market began life around the present St Nicholas church in the 11th century. The current square was paved over in the 12th century and the first of its buildings appeared to the south and west of the square. Over time, the tangle of medieval streets around the Grand'Place became home to a mix of markets, traders and craftspeople, something that's still identifiable in today's street names. It's no wonder, then, that the powerful medieval guilds began to establish themselves on this square, the economic and spiritual focus of the city.

But the guilds were not simply bodies of skilled craftsmen – they were a politically powerful mix of union, local magistrate and charity. What started out as an occupational organisation soon developed into something that stipulated work hours and conditions, lengths of apprenticeship and rules governing mastership. In Ghent the guilds also built almshouses and charity was given to those in their professions who had fallen on harder times. But the guilds also had a political role: run by the wealthiest families, they were able to exert influence on the authorities of the time to further their own economic interests. This same lobbying function allowed them to provide a counter-balance to aristocratic taxes, levies and trade restrictions, and to fund small rebel armies to ferment popular unrest in the face of impositions. Guild militias even took part in the Battle of the Golden Spurs in 1302.

The powerful textile guilds were the most troublesome to the authorities, followed by the smiths, brewers, butchers and then the carpenters. As the textile industry declined and new non-guild industries developed, the guilds lost much of their influence and towards the end of the 16th century their great era was on the wane.

Despite this loss of power, what we now see on the Grand'Place is a result of the guilds' irrepressible wealth that was still in place following the French bombardment of Brussels in 1695. Over three days and three nights the French reduced medieval Brussels to rubble – on the Grand'Place only the tower of the Hôtel de Ville survived. It took the guilds only five years to rebuild their lost houses in the stunning Baroque style that to this day makes the Grand'Place one of Europe's finest squares. As well as numbers, the houses were given names, something that provided them with the prestige they demanded.

Yet it was only in 1852 that a law was finally passed to protect the buildings, while the city agreed to pay for the upkeep of the façades in 1883. These days only one guild still occupies the same house it built for itself – the Brewers' House at No.10 (officially L'Arbre d'Or, or the Golden Tree). The rest are occupied by bars, shops and restaurants, and filled with tourists, although nothing can take away from their magnificence.

EXPANSION AND EXPLORATION

Despite constant dispute over particular issues, the Belgians did demonstrate a sense of unity in some areas of public life. Independence led to a building spree in Brussels. Among the earliest additions were the Galeries St-Hubert in the 1840s. These were then followed by a spate of official buildings and commemorative projects as Belgium began celebrating its own existence, culminating in the construction of the Parc du Cinquantenaire for the 50th anniversary exhibition. The Palais de Justice was completed in 1883 on the Galgenberg Hill, the site of the gallows in past times. The first railway station in Brussels opened in 1835 where Yser métro station now stands, with a line to Mechelen.

The major town-planning feat of the 19th century was the covering over of the River Senne. The river had become a repository for industrial and agricultural waste, including effluent from breweries and textile industries that had deliberately set up shop on its banks. Periodic cholera outbreaks led to an epidemic in 1866, when 3,500 people died. Rather than develop civil engineering schemes to clean up the river, the authorities decided on the more radical approach of a *voûtement*, or covering up. The idea was not just for sanitary reasons. Central Brussels was short of grand property in the 19th century, and its tangle of streets resembled Bruges more than a major European capital like London or Paris. The *voûtement* gave the opportunity for grand boulevards, big hotels and Parisian-style apartment blocks for the wealthy. Property developers jumped for joy at the idea. Above the *voûtement* appeared the new boulevards Anspach, Lemonnier and Adolphe Max, achieving the required design, but never the social cachet. The city elders hadn't thought that wealthy residents would much rather buy grand houses in Ixelles and St-Gilles than live in close quarters to others.

The grand plans of Léopold II, who succeeded his father in 1865, weren't limited to Belgium. As crown prince, he had been looking around for potential new territories, considering British-run Borneo, the Philippines, South Africa and Mozambique. Finally, he decided to grab a piece of the 'magnificent African cake'. Much of Central Africa was still unexplored and in 1876 Léopold set up the Association Internationale Africaine with the help of the explorer Henry Stanley. Although other European governments and the United States expressed qualms about Léopold's activities in Africa, he dismissed them sufficiently for the Berlin Declaration of 1885 to recognise the independent state of the Congo, with Léopold as its head of state. He referred to himself as its proprietor and ruled his new territory with absolute power and pure terror. Léopold's colonial adventures were to cast a dark shadow on Belgium's reputation. From 1895, when he started exporting wild rubber, it generated huge revenue, much of which was passed back to Belgium and used for massive public works such as the Musée Royal de l'Afrique Centrale at Tervuren. Local entrepreneurs, industrialists and engineers who grew rich on the Congo Free State built great houses in the extravagant art nouveau style, with little regard for the expense.

By the early 20th century, Léopold's policy of extracting maximum profit from the Congo, regardless of ecological and human cost, was exposing Belgium to international criticism, particularly from Britain. In 1908, the Belgian government forced Léopold to hand it over to the nation, and it remained a Belgian colony until independence in 1960.

WORLD WAR I

On its creation in 1830, Belgium declared itself to be perpetually neutral. But on 2 August 1914, Kaiser Wilhelm of Germany demanded that Belgium give its troops free passage on their way to invade France. Belgium had half a day to respond to the ultimatum, which it rejected. On 4 August German troops entered the country and the government took refuge in Antwerp. Seven hours later Britain declared war on Germany. By midnight, five different empires were involved in the war. German forces

IN CONTEXT

entered Brussels on 20 August; it was a strategic city for them, being a useful staging post between Aachen and the Western Front. English nurse Edith Cavell, who had stayed on in the city and was later executed by the invaders, said that conversations with the Germans revealed they were surprised to find themselves there, having believed they were marching on Paris. Once in place, the Germans demanded a massive war indemnity and huge amounts of food for the troops, meaning a real possibility of starvation for the locals. The situation in Brussels was largely saved by the intervention of the Americans, who organised the Commission for Relief in Belgium and set up charitable aid. The US ambassador, Brand Whitlock, became something of a Belgian national hero as a direct result.

Yet Belgium suffered horribly in World War I. At the village of Hervé, the Germans set an example: within a few days, only 19 of the 500 houses remained standing, the church smoking in ruins, and the shattered village littered with corpses. Other massacres occurred elsewhere: the Germans shot 110 people at Andenne, 384 people at Tamines, and 612 people, including a three-week-old baby, at Dinant.

By the end of September Antwerp was under siege and fell on 10 October, despite the arrival of British troops, including the poet Rupert Brooke, in a fleet of London buses. Over half a million refugees left Antwerp, among them thousands who had fled there from all over Belgium. Some 1.5 million had already left the country, although many would later return. The government went to Le Havre, while King Albert I, successor to his uncle Léopold II, took up position with the small Belgian army in the north-west of the country. Widely known as 'le Chevalier' (the Soldier King), he won acclaim from his people by fighting with his troops in the trenches alongside the French and British.

The four-year-long German occupation had terrible consequences. A total of 44,000 war dead might be dwarfed by the losses of Russia and France, but 700,000 Belgians were deported to Germany to work on farms and in factories, including the burgomaster Adolphe Max. The economy was devastated. Belgium had once depended on other countries to power its raw materials and its export markets, and it lost both. Much of its rail system was destroyed in an attempt to prevent the German invasion, agricultural production slumped, and there was widespread poverty and hunger. Belgium was liberated in 1918, and until 1921 the prevailing consideration of the post-war governments was how to rebuild the country. It is estimated that its losses represented about one-fifth of its total national assets in 1914, and not all of them were recovered in war reparations.

The Germans had been pro-Flemish, and a small group of Flemish politicians had been enthusiastic collaborators. In 1916, the Germans had declared the University of Ghent Flemish-speaking. It reverted to French and did not adopt Flemish again until 1930. Having just recovered what they had lost after World War I, the Flemings made a series of language gains during the 1930s. In 1932, French and Flemish ceased to have equality in Flanders, where the official language now became Flemish.

The period following World War I had been marked by brief political unity, as Catholics, liberals and Socialists worked together to rebuild the country. This unity soon dissipated, however, particularly after the introduction of proportional representation. The first universal male suffrage elections without multiple votes for the bourgeoisie were held in 1919 (women had to wait until 1949), and resulted in a series of coalition governments: between 1918 and 1940 Belgium had 18 different administrations. After a slight respite, the country slumped into depression in the 1930s, with unemployment, social unrest and a move to the right. In the 1936 elections Flemish nationalist and right-wing parties in Wallonia and Brussels made big gains, blaming the economic depression on the weak parliament, lack of strong leadership and the unions. Also, the Soldier King, Albert I, had died under suspicious circumstances in a rock-climbing accident in 1934, and his son, Léopold III, lacked the same charisma.

WORLD WAR II

After allying with France, Belgium reasserted its neutrality following the German invasion of Poland in 1939. It did little good. Hitler attacked on 10 May 1940. Showing opposite traits to his father, Léopold III surrendered after just 18 days. Much of the population was in support of Léopold's action, but the government itself was not. Believing that Belgium should commit itself to the Allies, it became a government-in-exile in Le Havre and then London. Despite having initially espoused a policy of normalisation, the Germans gradually became more authoritarian during the course of the war, creating greater resistance. Belgium suffered the same problems as it had in World War I: deportations, forced labour, poverty and food shortages. In Brussels there was a Gestapo HQ in avenue Louise and the Résidence Palace in rue de la Loi was the Nazi administrative centre for Belgium. From 1 June 1942, Belgian Jews were required to wear the yellow Star of David.

The Germans created a deportation centre in Mechelen and, between 1942 and 1944, sent 25,257 people to Auschwitz. Two-thirds of those died on arrival. Against all the odds, a network of Belgian resistance and opposition managed to save thousands of others from a similar fate. Concentrating on the children, Belgians from all classes and backgrounds risked their own lives by taking Jewish children into their families and homes, creating new identities for them. In that respect, Belgium saved more Jews per capita than any other occupied country.

Belgium was finally liberated in September 1944 and one of the first tasks was to tackle the thorny issue of collaboration. The war tribunals considered 405,000 cases, reaching 58,000 guilty verdicts, of which 33,000 were within Flanders. Then there was the behaviour of Léopold III. In a non-binding referendum, only 57 per cent voted in favour of his return (72 per cent of those in Flanders and 42 per cent in Wallonia), and when he did come back there were serious disturbances. In 1951, Léopold stepped aside in favour of his son Baudouin.

Even today, the issue of collaboration is an extremely sensitive one: up to 15,000 Belgians convicted of collaboration receive reduced pension and property rights as a direct result. In February 1996, a military court in Brussels reconsidered the case of one Irma Laplasse, a Flemish farmer's wife who had betrayed resistance fighters to the Nazis in 1944; she was executed by a firing squad for her crime in 1948. The court upheld her conviction, but ruled that the death sentence should have been commuted to life in prison. The judgement was met by protests from both sides. Concentration camp survivors and former members of the resistance and the Belgian secret army were outraged at any moves to rehabilitate Nazi collaborators; for its own part, the far-right Flemish Vlaams Blok party controversially campaigned for an amnesty for all those accused of collaborating, insisting that the tribunals were an attempt to victimise and repress the Flemish people as a whole.

POST-WAR BELGIUM

World War II had made it clear that Belgium's traditional neutrality was untenable, and even before the war was over the government-in-exile set about rejecting the policy in favour of international alliances. It signed the Benelux Customs Union with Luxembourg and the Netherlands, thus abolishing customs tariffs and setting a common external tariff. Belgium became an enthusiastic participant in post-war international relations; as an export-driven economy it needed to belong to the growing international relations superstructure. Belgium was one of the first signatories of the UN Charter in June 1945, joining the Organisation for European Economic Co-operation in 1948. It also became a member of the Council of Europe and the European Coal and Steel Community, as well as the HQ of the European Economic Community (EEC) when it was set up in 1957.

Brussels' new integrated role in a European context saw major upheavals in the capital. First proposed in 1837, a rail link through the city – the so-called Jonction Nord-Midi, directly connecting the main stations – was not adopted until 1901, and begun in

IN CONTEXT

earnest until 1911. The more pressing need for post-war reconstruction in 1919, and then again in 1945, stalled the project. In the meantime, a third station, Gare Centrale, was created, according to plans left by Victor Horta, one of the key architects of the city's art nouveau and art deco style. The line now had to run through three stations, and caused city planners to tear down thousands of buildings to make way for it. Building the entire 3.5-kilometre rail link involved removing one million cubic metres of earth, placing 85 kilometres (53 miles) of reinforced concrete pillars, and using 42,000 tonnes of iron. Some 1,200 homes were destroyed. Brussels had lost its soul and gained a global reputation as an architectural nightmare. Commerce and convenience – Eurostar travellers now benefit most from this cross-city access, decades after a young King Baudouin opened it in 1952 – won the day. It set a dangerous precedent for how the city would shape up in the second half of the 20th century.

Brussels' hosting of the World Fair of 1958 allowed for further rapid modernisation, the ring boulevards becoming a network of highways and tunnels. Brussels became the HQ of NATO in 1967, the same year that the EEC main offices of the Berlaymont building were opened. Its enormous structure typified the grandiose, impersonal quarter of steel and glass growing up around it, as the EEC took on yet more members. Officials and diplomats swamped the old Léopold quarter and created, in effect, two Brussels in one: an international zone around Schuman and the rest of the city.

During the EEC era King Baudouin became a highly respected monarch, concerning himself as he did with the well-being of his subjects and important social issues. A quiet, unassuming man, he is credited with preventing Belgium from splitting into two. He was childless until his death in 1993, after which the crown passed to his brother, the present King Albert II.

The language barrier separating French-speaking Wallonia from Flemish-speaking Flanders was formally created in 1962, leaving Brussels with an officially bilingual status. In 1965, the political parties also split into Flemish and Walloon wings, exacerbated by economic developments. Successive Belgian governments then made a series of reforms, granting greater autonomy to each community and changing Belgium from a centralised to a federal state; the 1993 fourth state reform also split Brabant into Flemish Brabant and Walloon Brabant. In 2001, Guy Verhofstadt's government introduced a fifth state reform and transferred yet more powers to the communities and the regions, including agriculture, fisheries, foreign trade and the responsibility for running local elections – the first of which took place in 2006.

In between, the public scandal surrounding Mark Dutroux galvanised the country in the late 1990s. Huge public protests from all sides broke out over police handling of the Dutroux affair, in which the multiple child murderer escaped detection and then captivity. This unity was further bolstered by the marriage of the royal heir, Prince Philippe, to an ordinary Belgian citizen in 1999. In 2003, Prince Laurent married Belgo-British Claire Combs. Laurent has not been without controversy, though. The youngest son of Albert II, once third in line to the throne, is now 11th. A party-goer as a bachelor, Laurent made the headlines in 2007 for being the first senior royal to testify in open court concerning alleged embezzlement of funds – in this case from the Belgian navy.

Belgium's history has always been allied to the history of other European countries and the new millennium continued the pattern. Brussels was officially named as the capital of Europe under the Treaty of Nice, and in 2001 the euro was adopted. With the swift expansion of the European Union, Brussels saw a large influx of diplomats, officials and staff from new member countries. In 2003, Belgium joined its European neighbours in opposing the Iraq War, supporting diplomacy through the UN – although, as part of its NATO commitment, it supports forces in Afghanistan with 560 personnel and six F-16 fighter planes. It has recently agreed to remain until the end of 2011.

For Belgium, though, the most critical battle is on home ground as successive, fragile coalition governments attempt to tackle the country's deep-rooted political and linguistic divisions.

Brussels Today

*Politics to the fore as talk of
independence rumbles on.*

TEXT: GARY HILLS

Because of its strategic importance at the heart of a small
country, Brussels is intrinsically linked to and involved
with all that happens around it. The politics of Brussels
are the politics of Belgium and vice versa. As one of the
three regions of the country, Brussels-Capital (Flanders
and Wallonia are the other two) needs to steer its own
independent way through the choppy waters of nationalism
and old rivalries. Regionality and language are the big issues
in Belgian politics today. The country is split horizontally and
almost neatly in two, with Dutch-speaking Flanders to the
north and French-speaking Wallonia to the south. In the
middle, but surrounded by Flanders, is the officially bilingual
Brussels-Capital Region.

The language history of Brussels is a complex one, but in
short French was made its official language after the Belgian
Revolution, despite a Dutch-speaking majority, and today
it is estimated that 85 per cent of Brussels residents are
French speakers. This is all well and good in the city's 19
communes, but the trouble starts when French hits Dutch
in the surrounding Flanders region. Nowhere is this more
strongly felt than in the Brussels-Halle-Vilvoorde (BHV)
electoral and judicial district (*see p33* **Lost in Translation**)
where the ongoing political wrangles encapsulate everything
that is immoveable in Belgian politics.

LONG-HAUL FIGHT

After the general election of June 2007, six parties – three Flemish, three French-speaking – began negotiations to form a coalition government. One of the sticking points between them was the issue of constitutional reform, and in particular reform of the BHV electoral district. Never had there been a more prolonged and bitter negotiation period with little give from either side; on 6 November the talks became the longest in Belgian history. All in all, it took 196 days to form an interim government under Prime Minister Guy Verhofstadt that would last until March 2008. Some commentators noted that this crisis could be the beginning of the end for Belgium as a federal state.

In August 2007, the Flemish commercial television station VTM conducted a survey of 1,300 Flems to ask about Flemish independence; the results were almost as inconclusive as the concurrent political negotiations, with 45.8 per cent wanting an independent Flemish state and 54.2 per cent against the idea. Interestingly, 78 per cent of respondents could not understand why the French-speaking opposition was being so intransigent over BHV and wider state reform.

The mess continued into 2010 under a new government, and again BHV was at its heart. This time the Open Flemish Liberal and Democrat party decided to leave the coalition after failing to reach an agreement on the future of BHV. When Prime Minister Yves Leterme offered his resignation to the king in April, it was accepted and an election was called for June 2010. Even before the election began there was a suggestion from Marc Bossuyt, Flemish president of the Constitutional Court, that the election could be ruled unconstitutional unless the BHV district was split in advance. This didn't happen and Belgium went with some trepidation to the polling booths.

2010 ELECTION

The 2010 general election was held on 13 June; Belgium goes to the polls on a Sunday as there is a legal obligation to vote. Bearing in mind that there are no national parties, the country braced itself yet again for a drawn-out process to form a new coalition. Two major outcomes of the election again typified the complexity of current Belgian politics. The party that won most MP seats was the Flemish separatist New Flemish Alliance (N-VA) headed up by 39-year-old Bart de Wever. The pledge was that Flanders would eventually break from the south and become a member of the European Union in its own right. Winning 27 of the 150 seats was a major achievement for the N-VA considering the fractured nature of the party system.

Herman van Rompuy.

Commission europe
Europese Commiss

Lost in Translation

BHV encapsulates Belgium's deep-rooted language divide.

The electoral district, or constituency, of Brussels-Halle-Vilvoorde (BHV) has been a major sticking point in Belgian politics since the Belgian Revolution. The district comprises the 19 communes of Brussels-Capital and the Dutch-speaking area around it in the province of Flemish Brabant. This makes it the only constituency that overlaps the regions and language areas, something decidedly sensitive in a country like Belgium.

What it means in reality is that residents of BHV can vote for either Dutch-speaking or French-speaking parties in Federal and European elections. It also means that French speakers from the district (ie, Brussels) can stand for election even in the Dutch-speaking area. Confused? It's the nitty gritty of this historic anomaly that has been taxing politicians and decision makers for years. It's spoken about in bars and discussed constantly in the newspapers and on television, but no one can seem to move the issue on. What complicates the matter even further is that the considerable number of French-speaking residents of the area have 'language facilities' that offer them rights such as requesting official forms or a court hearing in French, something unheard of in the rest of monolingual Flanders.

The Flemish parties, and in particular the separatists, would like to see the constituency split along language lines. The French-speaking politicians are completely opposed to this, fearing they could lose the Halle-Vilvoorde vote and their connection with voters with language facilities. They also see a split in the constituency as the final nail in the coffin for Belgian unity. One of the main current criticisms by the Belgian electorate is the seeming unwillingness of politicians to find a way through the mire of the issue. Successive parties have walked out of negotiations, others have gone it alone and voted in an unconstitutional ballot just because it made them feel better. Parliament has tried to introduce bills for sensible debate, but the French-speaking parties have used delaying tactics to put a halt to proceedings. If nothing else, BHV has become a symbol of the disquiet in the country as a whole and Bart de Wever (*see left*) has it in his mind to split the constituency with no concessions to the French community.

'There is speculation about what Brussels could look like in a devolved country, where each region could become a state in its own right.'

Just one seat behind with 26 seats was the Brussels-based Socialist Party (PS) led by Italian immigrant and French-speaking Elio di Rupo, one of the more flamboyant of Belgium's political figures. As the largest francophone party and with support from Flemish Socialists this could yet prove to be the biggest group in parliament. At the time of writing, negotiations are still ongoing with a caretaker government in place. De Wever has made it clear he has no objection to di Rupo becoming prime minister, as long as a new government would devolve more power to the regions. The Socialists remain opposed to any move that would threaten a unified Belgium, but there is also a shadow over di Rupo as his limited knowledge of Dutch could be a barrier.

The N-VA's success is based on a more moderate rationality than that expressed by the right-wing Vlaams Belang, a party that wants immediate secession and sanctions against immigrants. De Wever's approach is more measured. He sees independence as a slow, negotiated settlement rather than a revolution. With Belgium's reputation for political negotiations, though, this could be even slower than he expected.

EU COMPLICATIONS

Brussels is obviously at the heart of the European Union, and recent EU developments strike a louder resonance here simply because it happens in the city's backyard. In November 2009, Brussels-born Herman van Rompuy was surprisingly elected as the first full-time president of the European Council, something that up to then had been shared by EU states on a rotational basis. EU politicking and reasoning aside, Van Rompuy was seen as a safe bet in an arena where there could be national rumblings with an appointment such as Tony Blair. For Belgium, this was an historic moment – Van Rompuy had been prime minister as part of the 2007-2008 election fallout and resigned at the end of 2009 to take up his EU position.

Now his influence is needed as Belgium takes on the six-month presidency of the Council of the European Union from 1 July 2010. At first it was thought that the lack of a permanent government could harm the efficacy of the presidency. But commentators now believe that the interim government has prepared sufficiently, and a new incoming coalition at this time could be harmful to the process. In true Belgian style, van Rompuy is selling the presidency as low-key, particularly as he is now at the head of the Council.

BRUSSELS TOMORROW

With all this talk of Flemish separatism there is ongoing speculation about what Brussels could look like in a devolved country, where each region could become a state in its own right. As things stand Brussels-Capital, made up of 19 communes, is a region. It's only Brussels City (Ville de Bruxelles/Stad Brussel) that is the capital of Belgium. If, and it's still an if, the country were to split, Brussels-Capital would be left in an extraordinary position. If Charles Picqué, minister-president of Brussels-Capital, had his way, Brussels would become a city state like Vatican City, raising taxes from the EU to pay for it. This city state scenario would also mean that Brussels could join the EU independently. Another suggestion is that Brussels could become a capital district along the lines of Washington DC and even be administered by the EU, despite there being no precedent for anything like this. Understandably, the EU remains silent on the matter, but you can't help feeling that Mr van Rompuy is keeping a quiet but steady eye on the city he views from his presidential office window in the EU Quarter.

Flemish flag.

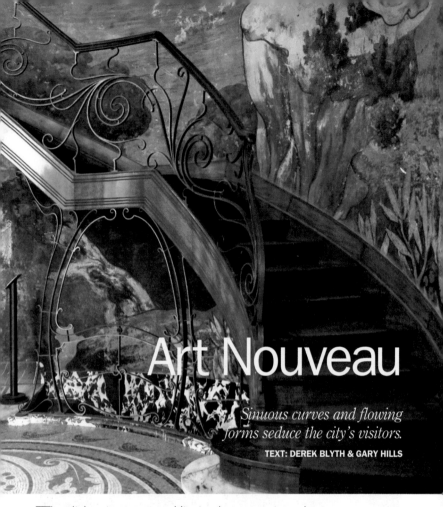

Art Nouveau

Sinuous curves and flowing forms seduce the city's visitors.

TEXT: DEREK BLYTH & GARY HILLS

The city's art nouveau architectural movement was born in 1893, in the suburbs of Brussels. Two houses built almost simultaneously just a few blocks apart provided the inspiration for a style that then spread to Paris, Barcelona and Glasgow, and between 1893 and the 1910s the city was the scene of an extraordinary revolution in architecture.

Dozens of architects embraced the bold new style, which used materials such as iron, stone and mosaic tiles in combination with motifs adopted from the natural world, and undulating, flowing lines. Increasingly daring buildings were designed by the likes of Henri van de Velde, Ernest Blérot, Gustave Strauven and Octave van Rysselberghe – and although numerous masterpieces were demolished in the 1960s in shamefully cavalier fashion, the capital of art nouveau still has an abundance of architectural gems.

'Art nouveau was condemned by Catholics as a godless extravagance and embraced by a middle class eager to break with old traditions.'

OUT WITH THE OLD, IN WITH THE NEW

Most critics agree that art nouveau originated in England around 1890, with the Arts and Crafts movement. Spreading across Europe and beyond, it became known as Jugendstil in Germany, Modernista or Modernismo in Spain, Stile Floreale or Stile Liberty in Italy and Sezessionstil in Austria.

Art nouveau combined the linear patterns of the Arts and Crafts movement with curving motifs modelled on plants and flowers. It also borrowed heavily from Japanese wood prints, which melded angular shapes with the movement of free-flowing kimonos and trees. By blending traditional craftsmanship with contemporary style, art nouveau architects created a totally new form, concentrating on every detail down to doorknobs and window panes. The style is marked by sinuous lines, ornate cast ironwork, rounded windows, tiled floors, stained glass and winding staircases; many houses also incorporate elaborate sgraffito murals, in which the top layer of glaze or plaster is etched away to reveal the layer below.

The preferred medium of free-thinkers and socialists, art nouveau was condemned by Catholics as a godless extravagance and embraced by an emerging middle class eager to break with old traditions. Clients included industrialists and engineers who had amassed enormous wealth in the Congo Free State, and could commission at will; although not everyone could afford the likes of Victor Horta, who lavished attention on every detail, his followers adapted the style for less wealthy clients, who saved money by preserving a traditional Belgian interior.

IN CONTEXT

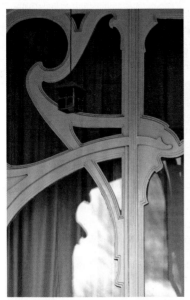

Maison de St-Cyr. *See p38.*

TOWARDS A NEW AESTHETIC

Many important art nouveau houses were built on the streets around avenue Louise, including Horta's debut **Hôtel Tassel** at 6 rue Paul Emile-Janson – an elegant townhouse, among the buildings that UNESCO would later describe as 'works of human creative genius'. At the same time, Paul Hankar was working on the **Maison Hankar** at 71 rue Defacqz, whose exquisite façade incorporates sgraffito tiles by Adolphe Crespin. He also built the art nouveau house at 48 rue Defacqz for the symbolist painter Albert Ciamberlani, easily recognisable from its two large north-facing windows and faded sgraffito decoration. The house next door was also designed by Hankar, as were several shopfronts in the city centre – an example of which survives at 13 rue Royale.

The streets and squares of St-Gilles are also liberally dotted with houses built by Horta and his followers. The most important is the Hôtel Horta at 25-26 rue Américaine, the architect's home and office. Now the **Musée Horta** (*see p82*), its stunning interior boasts mosaic floors, Asian tapestries and elaborate staircases.

The style gained a hold in Schaerbeek after Mayor Louis Bertrand decreed it to be in favour. One of Horta's earliest works here was for wealthy lawyer Eugène Autrique at **266 chaussée de Haecht**. Horta refused any payment, on condition that the money saved was devoted to the construction of the building's stylish white stone façade.

In 1889, Horta won a commission to design a temple in the **Parc du Cinquantenaire** (*see p73*), to contain Jef Lambeaux's *Passions Humaines*; alas, the nude figures of Lambeaux's monumental marble bas-relief unleashed a storm of controversy, and the building was closed after just three days. Art nouveau houses also line the streets around the park. The **Maison de St-Cyr** (*see p71* **Take a Break**) in square Ambiorix was designed by 22-year-old Gustave Strauven in 1905. With its narrow façade, ironwork and round loggia at the top, it is one of the most striking buildings in the city. Unlike Horta's houses, however, this building is all about surface decoration, with the interior divided up into conventional rooms.

DECLINE AND FALL

Gradually, the style faded in favour of the more geometrical architecture of early 20th-century Vienna and Glasgow – a shift already in evidence in Paul Cauchie's **Maison de Cauchie** (*see p74*) on rue des Francs, built in 1905; inside, it is richly decorated with gilded murals of beautiful women in long gowns, echoing the style of Gustav Klimt. Klimt himself designed a magnificent frieze for the dining room of the **Palais Stoclet** (avenue de Tervuren), built by the Austrian architect Josef Hoffman between 1905 and

Walk Art Nouveau

The remarkable architecture of St-Gilles and Ixelles.

Our tour starts at the No.94 Bailly tram stop by rue du Bailly. At 224 avenue Louise is **Hôtel Solvay**, built by Victor Horta in 1898. He was largely unknown when he designed this fine house of wrought iron and curvaceous stone.

Back down avenue Louise, a left turn takes you down rue Paul-Emile Janson and Horta's **Hôtel Tassel** at No.6. At the end of the street and right to the end of rue Faider is **48 rue Defacqz**, built by Paul Hankar in 1897. Right along Defacqz is Hankar's studio at **No.71**.

At the end of Defacqz, turn left down the chaussée de Charleroi; the next street on the left is rue Américaine, where Victor Horta built a home and studio at Nos.25-26. It is now the **Musée Horta** (*see p82*). Heading back

down chaussée de Charleroi/Brugmann, a left turn takes you to No.55, and a house called **Les Hiboux** (The Owls), built by Edouard Pelseneer in a curious art nouveau style. Next door, the impressive **Hôtel Hannon** was designed by Jules Brunfaut in 1903. It is now the **Contretype** photo gallery (*see p82*).

Behind it, in rue Félix Delhasse, are two houses in the Glasgow style of Mackintosh, at **Nos.13-15**. Right along rue de la Glacière and left on to the chaussée de Waterloo brings you to **Horta métro station**, its artwork made from Horta's demolished works. A 15-minute walk leads to rue Vanderschrick and a row of art nouveau houses by Ernest Blérot. Here, too, is **La Porteuse d'Eau** café, done out in Horta style.

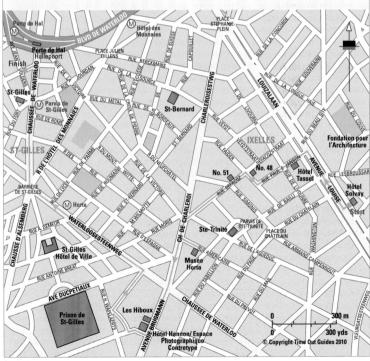

Behind Closed Doors

A look at the city's gems, with the group that helped to save them.

The demolition of Horta's famous Maison du Peuple helped spark the creation of the Atelier de Recherche et d'Action Urbaines, or ARAU, in 1969. Formed by a group of concerned citizens, the organisation set out to confront a city government callously neglecting its architectural heritage. The immediate aim was to save and renovate historic buildings, and fight against a policy that was turning large areas into barren office districts.

As well as campaigning, ARAU runs insightful guided tours. The most popular ones, covering the city's art nouveau and art deco architecture, are organised on Saturday mornings (walking tours €12, bus tours €17) from May to December, and take visitors around many remarkable art nouveau interiors that are usually closed to the public. Other walking tours (€10) focus on particular districts or themes. Tours are usually in French, although regular English ones are scheduled from May to September. Book through the TIB tourist office (*see p304*) or directly with ARAU (02 219 33 45, www.arau.org).

1911. It is considered the prime example of the Wiener Werkstätte style, the Arts and Crafts workshop Hoffman co-founded as part of the Vienna Secession movement. The marble-clad exterior has art nouveau influences, but is stripped of ostentation and gives a determined nod to modernism. Hoffman, like Horta, designed everything down to the last doorknob; sadly, the exterior is all you will see of the building.

Even Horta himself abandoned art nouveau, adopting a modern, more linear style when he came to design the **Palais des Beaux-Arts** (*see p65*) and the **Gare Centrale**. Nonetheless, there are still hints of art nouveau in his final buildings, suggesting that he never wholly abandoned his love of organic curves.

In the 1960s, hundreds of exceptional art nouveau buildings were torn down by city planners, often replaced by uninspired office blocks. With alarming speed, the city lost most of its wonderful art nouveau shopfronts, almost all of Victor Horta's department stores and a beautiful private home once owned by Blérot. The most scandalous demolition of all came in 1964, when Horta's **Maison du Peuple** was torn down to make way for a banal office building, despite vociferous protest. Considered Horta's finest work, the Maison was a stunning glass and cast-iron palace with an auditorium, café and shops; although its remains were numbered and stored, much of the ironwork was lost. Some balustrades are now displayed in Horta métro station, and part of the building has been incorporated into a café in Antwerp.

REMAINS OF THE DAY

After decades of indifference, the city has finally recognised its architectural heritage, and art nouveau survivors are now properly protected. Some have been put to imaginative new uses, such as the Old England department store – now reincarnated as the **Musée des Instruments de Musique** (*see p64*). Meanwhile, Horta's last art nouveau commission before wartime exile in the US, the Waucquez fabric warehouse, has been lovingly restored as a home for the **Centre Belge de la Bande Dessinée** (*see p56*).

In all there are around 2,000 surviving art nouveau buildings in Brussels, mainly concentrated in the 19th-century communes of Ixelles, St-Gilles and Schaerbeek. The winding streets of Ixelles are especially rewarding for explorers (*see p39* **Walk**), and the TIB tourist office (*see p304*) has maps showing the most important buildings. To get behind the façades, take one of the excellent guided tours organised by **ARAU** (*see above* **Behind Closed Doors**), which visit private homes usually closed to visitors.

Cartoon Brussels

Comics are serious stuff in this part of the world.

TEXT: PETERJON CRESSWELL & LUCY MALLOWS

Belgium's cultural identity is forever linked to a young man with a blonde quiff who saves the day. Belgium is the home of the comic strip (*bande dessinée,* or BD for short), and Tintin is the country's most easily identifiable popular icon. The cub reporter and his various friends and associates – his faithful white fox terrier Snowy, gruff companion Captain Haddock (known for his extravagant curses and 'blistering barnacles!' catchphrase), the bespectacled genius Professor Calculus and others – shift more postcards, T-shirts and books than anything else Belgian. To date, some 200 million Tintin comic books have been sold around the world, more than half of them in French, the rest in Basque, Afrikaans, Faroese and 50 other languages.

'Georges Rémi – or Hergé as he signed himself – is the father of what Belgians call the 'Ninth Art'. Before he emerged, comic strips were little more than a light chortle.'

A HERO IS BORN

Born in 1907, Georges Rémi – or Hergé as he signed himself – is the father of what Belgians call the 'Ninth Art'. Before Hergé emerged, comic strips were little more than a light chortle. The father of the contemporary European comic book and creator of the clear graphic that would inspire the pop art of Warhol and Lichtenstein, Hergé transformed the genre, heading a local cottage industry that has now gone global. Major Brussels-based studios accommodate design talent from Belgium, Holland and the francophone world, publishing houses churn out 40 million comic albums a year, while tales of Tintin and other Belgian BD stars are animated for TV series or the cinema screen. In Brussels, as well as a museum dedicated to the genre and 40 or more BD stores, downtown façades have been colourfully transformed into murals of cartoon characters. These comprise the Comic Strip Walk, a tour of painted street corners (*see p44* **Strip Search**).

The centenary year of Hergé's birth, 2007, was celebrated with events and exhibitions taking place on a global scale. In Brussels, at Gare du Midi, a giant fresco was unveiled on 10 January, 78 years to the day after Tintin's first appearance in *Le Petit Vingtième* in 1929. It can be seen inside the station on the left as you enter via the Eurostar entrance. The Pompidou Centre in Paris staged an exhibition entitled 'Hergé', placing the cartoonist under the same roof as Picasso and Matisse. In May, the month of Hergé's birth, the first stone was laid at the Musée Hergé (*see right* **Profile**) in Louvain-la-Neuve. This temple to Tintin – a short train ride from Brussels – opened in 2009, and has become the world's most important Hergé archive. Tintin and his friends seem more alive than ever.

FROM TOTOR TO TINTIN

When Georges Rémi was born to middle-class parents in Etterbeek, the comic strip was in its infancy. A Swiss illustrator, Rodolphe Töpffer, had produced early narrated drawings in the 1830s, followed by a few French artists, whose work ran in occasional periodicals. By the late 19th century, American broadsheets were publishing a cartoon of vignette adventures; the French press ran the best ones, as well as work by native artists. In England, children's comics started to catch on.

Boy scout Rémi began to contribute drawings to the monthly *Le Boy Scout Belge*, and got a job at Catholic daily *Le Vingtième Siècle*. He created a character, Totor, who later became Tintin. His first published adventure, *In the Land of the Soviets*, appeared in its children's section, *Le Petit Vingtième*. Four months later, the paper staged Tintin's triumphal return from Russia in a stunt at Brussels' Gare du Nord; Tintin, played by an actor, and his white dog Milou (later known to English-speaking readers as Snowy), were swamped by fans. After more adventures in the Congo in 1931, the Gare du Nord was packed. In 1934, the stories were compiled into their first comic album books by Tournai publisher Casterman.

Until then, Tintin's adventures were simple, puerile even. The Soviets were firmly castigated for their communist ways, the native Congolese subjected to paternalistic colonialism. Then, for *The Blue Lotus*, Hergé met Chang Chong-Yen, an émigré Chinese studying in Brussels, whose tales of the Japanese occupation of his homeland

Profile Musée Hergé

Step inside Tintin's world at this stunning new museum.

In June 2009, the Musée Hergé opened its doors to an eager public. The museum was a long time coming, with the idea first being mooted in 1979, and the Studios Hergé (originally the Fondation Hergé) has been amassing artefacts relating to Georges Rémi's life and work with a view to finding it a permanent home since 1986. The museum is largely privately financed – Hergé's widow, Fanny, contributed $20 million to ensure that her husband's work could be brought out of bank vaults and into the light.

The choice of Louvain-la-Neuve, a new university town south-east of Brussels, was an inspired one, enabling award-winning French architect Christian de Portzamparc to experiment with an urban structure in a woodland setting. The result is a playful series of colours, angles and cubes, reflecting the boxed nature of Tintin's life and adventures. Nothing is quite as it seems, and even the central lift shaft is chequered black and white, resonant of the famous rocket. Walking through the museum is akin to embarking on one of Tintin's journeys, as odd steps and walkways lead you into the unknown – you could almost be a character in one of the books. As you explore, you'll discover an impressive archive of photographs, drawings and research materials used by Hergé

in building his meticulously accurate stories and pictures.

One gallery is devoted to the science of Tintin and shows how Hergé, a man who rarely travelled, was able to bring realism to his stories with a complete understanding of the way things work. There are also examples of Hergé's other work: the extravagantly quiffed boy reporter wasn't his only invention.

With a ground-floor shop, restaurant and library as well, the museum is definitely worth the 30-minute train ride out of Brussels.
Musée Hergé, Louvain-la-Neuve (02 62 62 421, www.museeherge.com). Open 10am-6pm Tue-Sun. Admission €9.50; €5 reductions. No credit cards.

CARTOON CLASSICS Another must-see for comic aficionados is the **Centre Belge de la Bande Dessinée** (*see p56*).

IN CONTEXT

Centre Belge de la Bande Dessinée.

Strip Search

Seeking out the city's vibrant comic murals.

In 1991, local comic book illustrators hit upon the idea of brightening up their city with a series of comic murals. Using original drawings by each artist, the group Art Mural created a series of 20 works, a number slowly being added to. There are also underground stations gaily decorated with cartoon heroes, plus a walking tour that allows visitors to glimpse grey streets they wouldn't otherwise venture down.

For a detailed outline of the six-kilometre route, follow the tour with a map from the TIB tourist office (*see p304*). Walkers are welcomed by a statue of Franquin's error-prone Gaston Lagaffe, before being pointed in the direction of the nearby **Centre Belge de la Bande Dessinée** (*see p56*). This art nouveau former department store explores the history of cartoons over three floors of exhibits. Tintin is the highlight; families should note that

the erotic works on the top floor are perhaps not suitable for kids.

The route then runs by Willy Vandersteen's Bob and Bobette; Suske and Wiske, as they are known in their original Flemish, became the biggest post-war smash after Tintin. Next, it goes through the heavily muralled Ste-Catherine and St-Géry quarters, passing Lucky Luke, before heading, via Edgar P Jacobs' Yellow M on rue du Petit Rampart, to myriad murals on and around the lively rue du Marché au Charbon. Notice Frank Pé's Broussaille at the top of the street. The trail winds through the Marolles (Hergé's wily Quick et Flupke on rue Haute are suitably in character with the area) right down to the Gare du Midi.

You are ushered on to the Eurostar by Philippe Geluck's Le Chat and, fittingly, the figures of Tintin and Snowy atop the Lombard Publications building.

IN CONTEXT

'The Tintin comic folded in 1988. He and Snowy now sit atop the vast office block of Lombard Publications outside Midi station.'

persuaded Hergé of the need for documentary research. Thereafter, whether it was Australia or the moon, Hergé would painstakingly refine each detail. A new clarity – of plot, dialogue and draughtsmanship – came to light, the influential *ligne claire* that makes every box stand out and contribute to the overall narrative. Characters emerged, starting with Captain Haddock in *The Crab with the Golden Claws*, then Professor Calculus and the Thom(p)son Twins. With his own weekly comic in 1946, the foundation of the Hergé Studios in 1950 and a film adaptation in 1960, Tintin became a legend.

GOING GLOBAL
While their American, French and British counterparts used superheroism and sci-fi, Belgian cartoonists stuck to funny, character-driven everyday situations, in particular detective stories. Strong plot and dialogue kept the pages turning. Once Hergé had set the rules for content and continuity, Belgian artists could delve deep into their irreverent and surrealistic heritage, showcased by the seminal Marcinelle School. Based in Hainaut, a new group of cartoonists sprang up with *Spirou* magazine, launched by publisher Jean Dupuis in 1938.

It was Dupuis who turned a hobby into an industry. An apprentice printer, he kept a foot-operated pedal press at home, printing leaflets and newsletters. His workshop extended to the parish press before he launched weeklies for adults and, in 1938, children. Spirou featured key artists such as (André) Franquin, creator of Gaston Lagaffe, and Peyo (Pierre Culliford), father of the Smurfs (les Schtroumpfs). Along with Jijé (Joseph Gillain) and Morris (Maurice de Bevere, creator of Lucky Luke), and EP Jacobs of the Tintin School, the quintet brought Belgian comic strips on to the world stage. Some would collaborate with the staff of *Mad* and *Superman* magazines in America, others helped with artistic development when Astérix creator René Goscinny set up *Pilote*, France's pioneering BD publication. Major cartoonists had their own studios, backed by a skilled labour pool of letterists and colouring artists. Dupuis, along with Casterman, became one of Belgium's leading publishers.

The 1960s and 1970s saw great changes in the industry. While Tintin and the Smurfs became global TV stars, comic sales decreased as animated versions became more popular. Artistic integrity was sacrificed to the demands of commercial logic. Belvision became one of Europe's biggest manufacturers of televised animation. After boardroom disputes, Dupuis was swallowed into a publishing conglomerate. The Tintin comic folded in 1988. He and Snowy now sit atop the vast office block of Lombard Publications outside Midi station, greeting travellers on their arrival to Brussels.

Comics began to appeal to baby boomers who had grown up with Tintin and *Spirou*, and now wanted something more adult, erotic even. Albums took the place of magazines. Casterman launched a new generation of cartoonists with the series *A Suivre* in 1978, with contemporary themes for a more demanding readership. Its key auteur was François Schuiten, whose collaboration with Benoît Peeters gave rise to the *Obscure Cities* series, exploring themes of urbanisation gone mad and social isolation. Taking the peeling grandeur of Schaerbeek as their inspiration, Schuiten and Peeters redefined their native city, much as Hergé defined foreign climes for his readership. Their success illustrates that the Ninth Art can appeal to an adult readership and the television screen too. Schuiten's computer-generated TV series *Quarxs* found fans across the generational divide in the late 1990s.

IN CONTEXT

Discover the city from your back pocket

Essential for your weekend break, over 30 top cities available.

TIME OUT GUIDES WRITTEN BY LOCAL EXPERTS
visit timeout.com/shop

Sights

Maison de Cauchie. *See p74.*

The Lower Town

Landmark sights and market bargains.

The Lower Town is the spiritual heart of Brussels. It falls into three main areas: firstly, the Grand'Place & around, a showcase of medieval and 19th-century streets with a commercial area to the north and an urban tangle of quirky stores (and a gay quarter) to the south. Then there's St-Géry and Ste-Catherine, adjoining quarters on the other side of arterial boulevard Anspach, dotted with restaurants, chic bars and designer stores.

Finally, the shabby but loveable Marolles is an authentic working-class area, stretching from Upper Town Sablon to the concrete wastes of the Midi railway estuary, home every Sunday morning to one of Europe's biggest and best markets.

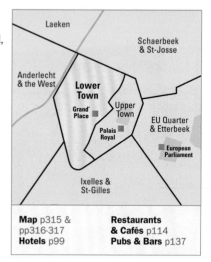

Map p315 &	Restaurants
pp316-317	& Cafés p114
Hotels p99	Pubs & Bars p137

SIGHTS

GRAND'PLACE & AROUND

Métro Gare Centrale, pré-métro De Brouckère or Bourse, tram 3, 4, 31, 32, 33 or bus 48, 95.

The Grand'Place is Brussels' most obvious and always outstanding set piece. It's hard to dispute Victor Hugo's description of it as 'the most beautiful square in the world', and it is now a UNESCO-designated World Heritage Site. The Place has always been a focus for the social and cultural life of the city, whether as a medieval market, a parade ground, a place of execution, a concert venue or, until the 1980s, a shortcut for traffic and a car park for coaches. Now a pedestrian zone, it changes colour and character according to the season: flower-strewn in summer, fairy-lit for Yule. It is the starting point for any tour of the Lower Town, with the tower of the **Hôtel de Ville** (Town Hall) as its distinctive landmark.

The houses on the square were made of wood until the French bombardment of 1695 (*see p26* **Power to the People**), which destroyed over 4,000 buildings and flattened everything except the tower of the Hôtel de Ville, which was used by the gunners to take aim. Under the command of the mercantile guilds, the square was rebuilt

in under five years, in stone, with fine bronze and gold detail. As each guild jostled for influence, it branded each house with individual markings and a name (although some pre-date the guilds). The following are among the most spectacular: Nos.1-2 **Le Roi d'Espagne**, also the bakers' guild, now a pub (*see p141*). The Spanish king is Charles II, whose bust is on the front façade. No.3 **La Brouette** (the wheelbarrow). The tallow dealers' guild, with a statue of patron St Gilles above the door.
No.4 **Le Sac** (the sack). The joiners' and coopers' guild, with a carving of a man diving into a sack above the door.
No.5 **La Louve** (the she-wolf). The archers' guild, with a phoenix at the top to symbolise the building's two burnings and rebuilds.
No.6 **Le Cornet** (the horn). The boatmen's guild, with a façade designed to resemble the stern of a galleon.
No.7 **Le Renard** (the fox). The haberdashers' guild, with a female statue representing each of the world's continents.
No.9 **Le Cygne** (the swan). The butchers' guild. Marx and Engels (who wrote the *Communist Manifesto* in Brussels) drank in a bar here, and the house witnessed the birth of the Belgian Workers' Party.

Grand'Place.

Whatever your carbon footprint, we can reduce it

For over a decade we've been leading the way in carbon offsetting and carbon management.

In that time we've purchased carbon credits from over 200 projects spread across 6 continents. We work with over 300 major commercial clients and thousands of small and medium sized businesses, which rely upon our market-leading quality assurance programme, our experience and absolute commitment to deliver the right solution for each client.

Why not give us a call?

T: London (020) 7833 6000

No.10 **L'Arbre d'Or** (the golden tree). The brewers' guild, and the only building still under guild ownership. Note the hop plant detail. It houses the **Musée des Brasseurs Belges**. Nos.24-25 **La Chaloupe d'Or** (the golden galleon, now a brasserie) and **La Maison des Tailleurs** (the tailors' house). The tailors' guild is topped by St Boniface, holding a symbolic pair of scissors.

No.26 **Le Pigeon** (the pigeon). The artists' guild. Victor Hugo stayed here in exile in 1852.

No.8, L'Etoile (the star), was knocked down in 1850 to accommodate tourists. Burgomaster Charles Buls was so incensed he had it rebuilt over an arcade, which serves as shelter for the much-caressed recumbent figure of Everard 't Serclaes, the guild leader who fought off a Flemish attack on Brussels in 1356. Soldiers from Gaasbeek tore his tongue out, prompting locals to destroy Gaasbeek castle. Stroking the statue's worn limbs is supposedly meant to bring good luck.

On the east side of the Place is a terrace of six houses with a single façade, designed by Willem de Bruyn in 1698. The grouping is known as the House of the Dukes of Brabant because of their sculptures on the front. The Brussels commune has bought two of them and is currently converting them into apartments and a new exhibition centre.

Facing the Hôtel de Ville is the Maison du Roi, which houses the **Musée de la Ville de Bruxelles**; the highlight here is the costume collection of the Manneken-Pis.

The patron saint of merchants is **St Nicolas**, whose church – the oldest in Brussels – stands off the Place by the Roi d'Espagne on rue au

INSIDE TRACK
GOING UNDERGROUND

Stand in front of the Bourse and look along boulevard Anspach. This was where the unhygienic, disease-carrying River Senne once ran, until it was covered over and later re-channelled. Now, water is replaced by metal as the city centre trams run along its course.

Beurre. Diagonally opposite is the **Bourse**, the old Stock Exchange. This grand, neo-classical building boasts a decorative frieze by Carrier-Belleuse, with statues by Rodin adorning the top. Underneath, in Bourse métro station, is the hands-on **Scientastic Museum**, bringing science alive for children. Flanking the Bourse are two classic cafés, the **Falstaff** (*see p117*) and **Le Cirio** (*see p115*).

★ **Hôtel de Ville**
Grand'Place (02 279 43 65, tourist information 02 513 89 40). Pré-métro Bourse or métro Gare Centrale. **Open** *Guided tours* (in English) 3.15pm Tue, Wed. Apr-Sept also 10.45am & 12.15pm Sun. **Admission** €3. **No credit cards.** **Map** p315 C5.
Construction work on this superb edifice, adorned with elaborate sculptures, took no less than 50 years. The left wing (1406) was built by Jacob van Thienen and, for balance, a right wing was later introduced by an unknown architect. The old belfry was too small for the new structure, so Jan van Ruysbroeck added the splendid 113m (376ft) tower, an octagon

SIGHTS

Manneken-Pis souvenirs.

sitting firmly on a square plinth. In 1455, a dramatic gilt statue of St Michael slaying the dragon was erected at its pinnacle. The tower seems to unbalance the rest of the building and legend has it that, in despair, the architect climbed to the top of his masterpiece and threw himself from it. This is unlikely; the simple reason for the imbalance is that the left wing is smaller than the right in order to preserve the street pattern. You can't climb the tower, but a series of elegant official rooms can be visited on the guided tour. The most flamboyant of them is the 18th-century Council Chamber, awash with gilt, tapestries, mirrors and ornate ceiling paintings. Brussels' only secular Gothic building, the town hall remains in practical use as the seat of the Mayor of Brussels and is also the official marriage venue for Brussels commune residents. *Photo p54.*

Musée des Brasseurs Belges
10 Grand'Place (02 511 49 87, www.beer paradise.be). Pré-métro Bourse or métro Gare Centrale. **Open** 10am-5pm daily. **Admission** €6. **No credit cards. Map** p315 C5.

Run by the brewers' confederation, this permanent exhibition displays traditional techniques, and has a new high-tech brewing centre.

Musée du Cacao et du Chocolat
9-11 rue de la Tête d'Or (02 514 20 48, www. mucc.be). Pré-métro Bourse or métro Gare Centrale. **Open** 10am-4.30pm Tue-Sun. **Admission** €5.50; free under-12s. **No credit cards. Map** p315 C4.
Founded by Jo Draps, a third generation Belgian chocolatier, the museum traces the history of chocolate from its discovery by the Aztecs, through its arrival in Europe, and on to the development of the praline and other Belgian specialities.
▶ *For advice on where to invest in the city's finest chocolate, see p165.*

Musée de la Ville de Bruxelles
Grand'Place (02 279 43 50, www.brussels.be/ artdet.cfm/4202). Pré-métro Bourse or métro Gare Centrale. **Open** 10am-5pm Tue-Sun. **Admission** €3. **No credit cards. Map** p315 D4.

Meet the Locals The Manneken Dresser

The city's most famous statue is never knowingly underdressed.

Jean-Marc Ahime had to fight off five other applicants for the most prestigious job in Brussels: the dresser to the city's most famous little statue. Ahime covers up the nudity of the **Manneken-Pis** (*see p54*) on a regular basis, and also supplies the beer,

wine and sometimes even champagne for the little boy to spout forth on special occasions when plain water won't suffice.

The costume tradition started in the 1700s. One of Louis XV's soldiers had stolen the little statue and left him outside a brothel. Louis apologised by offering the boy his first outfit: a stylish gold brocade suit. From then on, *ketje*, as he's fondly known in Bruxelloise, received sumptuous outfits four times a year.

Today his wardrobe contains a total of 784 costumes, the most recent displayed at the top of the grand staircase at the **Musée de la Ville de Bruxelles** (*see above*). Ahime still works here as a security guard, doubling up as a dresser when the occasion requires.

Now in his thirties, jovial Bruxellois Ahime was trained by the previous *habilleur*, who held the post until retiring. The position requires a real interest in costumes and an in-depth knowledge of fabrics, as many – a Soviet cosmonaut's outfit, say, or spangly Elvis jumpsuit – are quite fragile. Ahime receives a new outfit about once a month. Anyone can offer to clothe the Manneken and each proposal goes before a committee. Once it's accepted, Ahime then dresses the statue at a formal ceremony, famously turning wee into wine.

Constructed in the 13th century and thrice rebuilt, the Musée de la Ville is known in Dutch as the Broodhuis (bread house) – a more accurate title since it was owned by the bakers' guild. Shored up after 1695, it was left to crumble until Mayor Jules Anspach decided to rebuild it in fashionable neo-Gothic style in 1860. A museum since 1887, it now houses a somewhat dowdy collection of paintings, photographs, documents, tapestries and models that chronicle the history of Brussels. You'll find enlightening sections on the bombardment of 1695 and Léopold II's ambitious building programme, but the dizzying impression is one of constant invasion. The museum also contains the vast wardrobe of the Manneken-Pis (amounting to almost 800 costumes, of which around 200 are on permanent display) plus some impressive paintings, including Pieter Bruegel the Elder's *Wedding Procession*.

FREE St-Nicolas

1 rue au Beurre (02 267 51 64). Pré-métro Bourse. **Open** phone for details. **Map** p315 C4.
Founded in the 11th century, this model of medieval sanctity survived the 1695 bombardment. Its curved shape follows the old line of the River Senne and has tidy little houses (now shops) built into its walls. Over the centuries the church became gloomy and stained, but in recent years it has been lovingly and painstakingly renovated. It now sits again in warm, honeyed splendour.

Ilot Sacré

Just north of the Grand'Place is the **Ilot Sacré** (Holy Isle), saved by locals and now one of the Lower Town's liveliest areas. At the time of the World Expo of 1958 city authorities were looking to redevelop the streets here to ease the traffic flow. Shopkeepers in the neighbourhood were outraged and the plans were axed. After the Expo, the authorities decided to create seven protected 'isles' with stringent planning rules to protect their identity, and in 1960 the Ilot Sacré was created.

It is an evocative medieval tangle of small streets, devoted almost entirely to restaurants, many of which entice tourists with stupendous displays of fresh fish and seafood reclining on mountains of ice. Rue des Bouchers is the main thoroughfare with the street names around it appetisingly evoking the Middle Ages, with the likes of rue des Harengs (Herring Lane) and rue du Marché aux Herbes (Grassmarket). Rue des Bouchers is today still full of original houses with stepped gables and wooden doors mostly dating from the 17th century. At the end of the street, near No.58, a narrow passage leads to the **Résidence Centrale**, a modern development in a traditional style with a tranquil courtyard and an elegantly modish bronze fountain. Not quite so elegant is **Jeanneke-Pis**, the female

SIGHTS

counterpart to the Manneken, installed in 1985 to raise money for charity, and still squatting in nearby impasse de la Fidélité.

Petite rue des Bouchers has more of the same brash restaurants, but it was here, at No.30, that La Rose Noire jazz club gave Jacques Brel his first success in 1953. The renowned Théâtre du Toone, a puppet theatre and café, is in an alley off here in a building put up a year after the bombardment.

In contrast to the bustle of medieval markets evoked nearby, **Galeries St-Hubert** suggests the seeds of the modern mall (*see p155* **All Under One Roof**). Europe's oldest glass arcade was designed by JP Cluysenaar and opened by Léopold I in 1847, at the time, as Karl Marx cynically observed, of a potato famine. It still sparkles, equalling the glitter of the jewellery shops that it harbours. Set out in three sections (galeries de la Reine, du Roi and des Princes), it also houses keynote cultural venues such as the **Arenberg Galeries** (*see p188*), a fabulous independent arthouse cinema, the **Théâtre Royal des Galeries** (*see p226)*, with a noted Magritte fresco on the ceiling, and the **Théâtre du Vaudeville**, which now boasts a fine pedigree as a restaurant and events venue. Restaurants such as **Ogenblik** (*see p117*) and cafés such as **Mokafé** (*see p117*) echo the splendour of their surroundings.

By the arcade's southern entrance stands busy place d'Agora, an oasis of waiting taxi cabs with a small craft market on most days. It's marked on most maps as place d'Espagne,

which is, strictly speaking, the desolate area behind with the giant statue of Don Quixote looking over the old town.

South of the Grand'Place

The south side of the Grand'Place is quieter, characterised by idiosyncratic shops and odd vendors of strange plastic figurines. Follow the crowds from the square, past the lace and tapestry shops into rue de l'Etuve, and you come across the **Manneken-Pis**, famous as a national symbol but eternally disappointing as a tourist spectacle, though you wouldn't believe it when you see the crowds. Like the *Mona Lisa* it's so much smaller than you expect, but the boy is fortunately elevated on a Baroque pedestal to give him some grandeur. Around him are gated railings, only opened by the person whose sole job it is to dress him in his various costumes: Euro-jogger, Santa Claus, a condom on World AIDS Day, and so on (*see p52* **Meet the Locals**). A framed sign gives a calendar of upcoming costume days. The current statue was made in the 17th century by Jérôme Duquesnoy. Stolen by the British in 1745, then again by the French in 1777, it was smashed by a French ex-con in 1817, who was given life for doing so. Its origins are unknown, though it is naturally endowed with local myth as well as a never-ending pee.

A short walk east, up the hill and on the Vieille Halle aux Blés, is the **Fondation Internationale Jacques Brel**, dedicated to

Hôtel de Ville. *See p51.*

the famed chanteur; a short walk west, rue du Marché au Charbon is the main gay quarter of town with a bar in almost every building. Perhaps the loveliest of the Lower Town's half-dozen churches also stands here: **Notre-Dame de Bon Secours**.

FREE **Notre-Dame de Bon Secours**
Rue du Marché au Charbon (02 514 31 13). Pré-métro Anneessens. **Open** 9am-5.30pm daily. **Services** 11am Sun. **Map** p315 C5.
Built in the late 1600s, this Baroque masterpiece, designed as a collaboration between Jan Cortvrindt and Willem de Bruyn, remains a superb example of Flemish Renaissance style.

North of the Grand'Place

Much of the historical heart of Brussels was tragically lost when the River Senne was covered over and straight avenues and formal squares were constructed between the Gares du Nord and Midi. Distinguished architectural ensembles included place De Brouckère, whose grandeur – and fountain – gave way to build the métro station. Although home to the classy **Hotel** and **Café Métropole** (*see p99* and *p139*), these days it is merely a traffic intersection, dominated by the awful Centre Monnaie mall. It overshadows the neo-classical opera house **Théâtre de la Monnaie** (*see p201*), built here in 1819. As well as being historically significant (in 1830 it staged the opera that led to the uprising for Belgian independence), the venue is worth visiting for its ornate interior. Sadly, the exterior has been ruined by what seems like a shed attached to its roof to house the mechanicals.

Arrowing north from the plaza in front of the theatre is gaudy rue Neuve. It could be any high street in any town, a crowded, pedestrianised stretch of brand names culminating in the ugly shopping centre **City 2** (*see p153*). It's hard to believe that this was the site of the Duchess of Richmond's famous musical ball on the eve of the Battle of Waterloo – although the airy **Notre-Dame du Finistère** does provide some architectural relief. Near it is the place des Martyrs, home to a large monument to the 445 revolutionaries who gave their lives for Belgium in 1830. It was a cobbled ruin until the Flemish authorities took the initiative to restore some buildings as government offices. Their French counterpart then responded in turn by renovating another part of the square.

SIGHTS

It is lined with fine neo-classical buildings, including the impressive **Théâtre des Martyrs** (*see p225*).

Around the corner is one of Brussels' most popular museums, the **Centre Belge de la Bande Dessinée**. Located in a beautifully restored Victor Horta department store (whose ground-floor café can be partaken of without a ticket), it features a revamped Tintin section, as well as displays on lesser-known Belgian comic characters – many of whom feature on a comic strip walk of the city (*see p44* **Strip Search**).

Running parallel to rue Neuve is the grand boulevard Adolphe Max, with some stunning buildings if you look up beyond the ground-level shops. To the north, the boulevard peters out into sex shops and hostess clubs.

★ Centre Belge de la Bande Dessinée

20 rue des Sables (02 219 19 80, www.comics center.net). Métro/pré-métro De Brouckère or Rogier. **Open** 10am-6pm Tue-Sun. **Admission** €7.50; €3-€6 reductions. **No credit cards.** **Map** p317 E3.

Set on three floors of a beautiful Horta-designed department store, the Comic Strip Museum greets you with a statue of Tintin, Snowy and the iconic red and white rocket they took to the moon. The Tintin collection, revamped for the 75th anniversary celebrations in 2004, is the highlight of the exhibition, which covers the history of comics and cartoons from Winsor McCay's early Gertie the Dinosaur (1914) to the heroes of today. If you've got kids in tow, beware of the erotic works lurking on the third floor.

▶ *See also pp41-45.*

FREE Notre-Dame du Finistère

Rue Neuve (02 217 52 52). Métro/pré-métro De Brouckère or Rogier. **Open** 8am-6pm Mon-Sat; 8am-noon, 3-6pm Sun. **Services** 9.15am, 12.10pm, 5pm Mon-Fri; 4.30pm, 6pm Sat; 9am, 11am, 4pm, 5.30pm Sun. **Map** p317 D3.

Largely built in the early 18th century on the site of a 15th-century chapel, the church's Baroque interior is most notable for its almost stupendously over-the-top pulpit.

ST-GERY & STE-CATHERINE

Métro Ste-Catherine, pré-métro Bourse or bus 86.

Restaurants, bars and churches are the key features of sassy St-Géry and former quayside Ste-Catherine, two small and self-contained quarters across boulevard Anspach from the Bourse. Both neighbourhoods have undergone major renovations, turning once-shabby districts into likeable but somewhat sterile and sanitised versions of their former selves.

St-Géry is centred on the square of the same name, composed mostly of a great number of swanky designer bars converging around the grand **Halles St-Géry**, an erstwhile covered market that's now a large bar and exhibition space, with a nightclub situated down in the basement. St-Géry was originally revived by entertainment mogul Fred Nicolay, who set up a string of trendy cafés and bars and spread word of a cool scene. On summer nights the busy terraces of the bars, which include Mappa Mundo and Zebra, create a Mediterranean atmosphere around the square.

The former desolate inner-city quarter was ripe for modernisation. Chic **rue Antoine Dansaert** (*see p160* **Style Street**) is the city's fashion centre and heart of the Flemish revitalisation of the area, including the right-on **Beursschouwburg** theatre (*see p224*) and the upmarket rue des Chartreux shopping scene (*see p170* **Chain-free Chic**). This has led to an influx of young professionals, and made it popular with the gay community.

By contrast, set around the quays of the old harbour, where a thriving traffic of fishing boats was grounded with the filling in of the Senne in 1870, Ste-Catherine still feels like a port. Fountains and paved walkways now cover what locals (but not maps) refer to as the **Marché aux Poissons**, the Fish Market, either side of the métro stop. Hosting, indeed, a large fish market once a week, lined with fish restaurants lit up with vast red neon lobsters – and turned into a market and giant outdoor skating rink over Christmas (*see p179* **Festive Frolics**) – Ste-Catherine is dominated by its namesake church. The belfry of an earlier, 13th-century Ste-Catherine is nearby, as is the **Tour Noire** (Black Tower), a rare remaining remnant of the first city wall, rescued from demolition by Mayor Charles Buls.

Beside the church, **place Ste-Catherine** has been completely rebuilt, losing some of its old character, but no one bemoans that it is no longer a car park. On the contrary, since the restorations a small vegetable market has returned, as has the oyster man (*see p130* **Profile**). A little further away but still in the locality are the churches of **Notre-Dame aux Riches Claires** and **St-Jean-Baptiste au Béguinage**. The latter was once the centre of Brussels' largest *béguinage*, a charitable community for single women founded in the 13th century.

In tandem with picturesque slices of history, the knock-on effect of St-Géry has crossed over into Ste-Catherine; everyday Belgian bars, cafés and shops are now becoming interspersed with nods to minimalist chic. A classic example is **De Markten** (*see p123*) on rue Vieux Marché aux Grains, an old refurbished building with a

SIGHTS

Profile Midi Market

Get down to Gare du Midi for a Sunday morning bargain-hunting bonanza.

The new development around and under the Gare du Midi is an urban travesty, bleak by day and barren at night. Yet come here on a Sunday morning and you'll find one of Europe's biggest and brightest markets in full swing – the brilliant **Midi Market**.

One of the greatest frustrations of visiting markets when you're abroad is that you can't buy much of the stuff you want: the cheese will be too smelly, and that cheap crate of avocados won't last the journey. Of the 450 stalls at Midi, though, around half are non-comestibles. The clothing section alone is vast; you'll need to develop a strong sense of what is tat and what is not, though the €3 price tags on the bras give a good indication. Better value and quality are the kids' clothes, and basics like T-shirts and socks.

Do take in the food, even if you can't take it home. Most of the stallholders are North African, and peddle their wares with all the catcalling vim and vigour of downtown Marrakech. Fruit and veg comes in a wave of towering primary colours and is sold either individually, in boxes or by the bag (you'll be given a plastic carrier to fill yourself). Bunches of fragrant herbs are stacked high, but it's the olive stalls that truly impress, with every colour, size, marinade or sauce imaginable – if you're not sure, one will be thrust at you to taste. These stalls are also excellent for buying nuts, dried fruit, dates and figs.

Another highlight is the flower and plant section. Imagine a whole street of flora, brimming with cut roses, tulips and bargain mixed bunches. You'll also be almost blinded by the fluorescent sweep of bedding plants; Belgians have a weakness for bright red geraniums and begonias.

So what else can you get your hands on? Well, what do you want? Coffeepots, pans, kids' toys, mobile phone covers, tablecloths, foam rubber offcuts, shoes, purses, handbags, tools, mops and bin bags; it's all there. Above and through it all is the thumping of the latest Arabic disco music – available to buy on CD, of course.

SIGHTS

EATING UP YOUR BRUSSELS
For a round-up of the capital's other popular food markets, *see p168*.

Walk Strolling the Marolles

Flea market finds and no-frills cafés in working-class Brussels.

Until the urban developers had their way, the Marolles had the reputation of being the working-class, radical underbelly of Brussels. In its narrow streets and tenement blocks the gritty locals slogged away and gave authority the finger. Walking through the Marolles today it's unlikely you'll feel that same infamous grit, though with a bit of imagination and a look behind the façades you still get a sense of real life rippling around you.

Start out along the two main streets, rues Haute and Blaes, which form a squashed ellipsis through its heart. From place de la Chapelle, head into rue Haute, the higher of the two. Here you're in **Breugel** land, though apart from his house at No.132, there's not much left of what he would have seen. Rue Haute is more or less dedicated to interior design shops: kitchens, bathrooms, sofas and an impressive selection of colonial stores selling teak furniture or bits and bobs from India. Also look out for art deco gems.

Take your time to look left and right, up and down the hill. These narrow little streets give the best idea of how the Marolles must once have looked, with its diminutive houses and unsanitary conditions. The steepness of the rat runs made daily life a sheer slog; now, though, they are cauterised at the top end by the developed Upper Town (in particular the **Palais de Justice**; *see p68*) and at the bottom by the main railway line.

If you continue along the whole length of rue Haute, you'll come to the busy ring road and see the imposing old city gate, **Porte de Hal** (*see p80*); or take a right-hand turn into any of the hilly streets leading down to the other thoroughfare, rue Blaes. Rue des Renards leads you, via quirky second-hand shops, to the corner of place du Jeu de Balle with its daily morning flea market and a selection of cafés and bars. You'll find nothing frilly or frothy here. These are honest-to-goodness drinking holes that see nothing wrong with a coffee and cognac at eight in the morning; you'll also be able to get a decent omelette or *steak frites* at lunchtime.

Rue Blaes is a little more higgledy-piggledy than its haughtier cousin Haute. The shops along here are full of random jumble and ethnic curiosities, as well as antique reclamation and clothing. All the shops are independent, and browsing is expected. Feel free to pop in and out and have a nose. Zig-zagging away from the main street will give you another taste of the area and show that there is still life in the old streets; look out for the dance venue **Chapelle des Brigittines** (*see p228*) and the radical culture space **Recyclart** (*see p205*) under Chapelle station.

Finally, stand at the bottom end of rue de Notre Seigneur. Get the restaurants **Les Petits Oignons** (*see p125*) and **La Grande Porte** (*see p125*) in your sights and block out everything else, and you'll have a rare glimpse of a little corner that is forever the Marolles.

Antiques market, **Rue Blaes**.

SIGHTS

café on the ground floor and a popular Flemish arts centre behind. The square out front is packed with drinkers and diners and live sound stages in the summer. But turn in to rue de Flandre and once again you are presented with a vivid image of how the area used to look: traditional restaurants, quaint old shops selling caged birds, bridal gowns, bakeries and delis.

West of central Ste-Catherine, on the edge of town, is all that remains of the river: the **Canal de Charleroi**, a thin stretch of water running north–south. Along the bankside boulevard Barthélémy, an art gallery complex housing **Kanal 20** has tried to boost an urban revival in this forgotten quarter; activities at the old customs building **Tour et Taxis** *(see p208)*, further north, show more promise.

FREE Notre-Dame aux Riches Claires

23 rue des Riches Claires (02 511 09 37). Pré-métro Bourse. **Open** 4-6pm Sat; 9.30am-2pm Sun. **Services** 9.30am, 11.30am Sun. **Map** p315 B4.
This charming asymmetrical structure, built in 1665, is probably the work of Luc Fayd'herbe, a pupil of Rubens.

FREE Ste-Catherine

Place Ste-Catherine (02 513 34 81). Métro Ste-Catherine. **Open** 8.30am-5pm (summer until 6pm) Mon-Sat; 9am-noon Sun. **Services** *Chapel* 8am. *Church* 10am. **Map** p315 C3.
Almost as unkempt as its surroundings (and with an ancient *pissoir* built between the buttresses), Ste-Catherine was designed in 1854 in neo-Gothic style by Joseph Poelaert, and almost became the stock exchange before opening as a church in 1867. One treasure is a 15th-century statue of a Black Madonna, supposedly rescued from the Senne after being thrown in by angry Protestants.

FREE St-Jean-Baptiste au Béguinage

Place du Béguinage (02 217 87 42). Métro Ste-Catherine. **Open** 10am-5pm Tue-Sun. **Services** 5pm Sat; 10am, 8pm Sun. **Map** p316 C3.
One of the best examples of Flemish Baroque architecture in the city, this large church, attributed to Luc Fayd'herbe, has a fluid, honey-coloured façade. Its light-filled interior houses a beautiful pulpit and 17th-century paintings by Theodoor van Loon.

THE MAROLLES

Pré-métro Porte de Hal or bus 27, 48.

The Marolles is Brussels' traditional working-class district: all too rapidly gentrifying, but for now a tatty but durable resistance to the urban expansion and standardisation of the 19th and 20th centuries. These days the area is an incongruous mix of shabby shops, restored antique boutiques and interior design palaces.

The population is largely immigrant, with some nouveau-riche interlopers and a few deep-rooted locals who still speak odd words of Marollien, the fantastically rude dialect. At night, legions of trendy drinkers congregate in the Sablon before making their way down the hill to eat, or move on to Brussels' top techno spot **Fuse** *(see p211)*. As they tip out at daybreak, and the market sets up, so the cyclical life of the Marolles starts all over again. *See left* **Walk**.

The name derives from an order of nuns, the Mariam Colentes (devotees of Mary), who lived in a convent on the corner of rue Montserrat and rue des Prêtres; now all that remains as a reminder of them is a statue of the Virgin in rue Prévoyance. The area stretches haphazardly from the slopes of the imposing **Palais de Justice** down to the Gare du Midi. To the east it runs up against adjoining Sablon, up the hill and suitably upmarket. A public lift – and slow improvement in antique shopping down below – now link the Upper and Lower Towns.

At the north end of the district is place de la Chapelle where **Notre-Dame de la Chapelle** stands. The church is widely known as the burial place of Pieter Bruegel the Elder, though he is, in fact, buried elsewhere. This infamous confusion arises from a memorial plaque laid by his son in the fourth chapel. The house where Bruegel once lived is nearby at 132 rue Haute, the 16th-century **Maison de Bruegel**. Although it doesn't contain any of the artist's works or artefacts, it's open to groups by written request. Short, narrow streets proclaim their roots: rue des Orfèvres (Goldsmiths' Lane); rue des Tonneliers (Barrelmakers' Lane); and rue des Ramoneurs (Chimney Sweeps' Lane).

Midway along rue Blaes is **place du Jeu de Balle**, Marolles' epicentre, where a daily flea market is surrounded by earthy bars and cafés. Although you'll still see a few locals jigging to the accordion playing on a Sunday, these days tipplers are more likely to be shoppers back from a browse in the local bric-a-brac shops.

The burial of the Senne saw much industry move out of the centre, and the Marolles was left to rot. Thousands of homes were destroyed to make way for the railway and Palais de Justice. The railway arches now provide space for the energetic **Recyclart** *(see p205)*.

FREE Notre-Dame de la Chapelle

Place de la Chapelle (02 512 07 37). Pré-métro Anneessens or bus 20, 48. **Open** 9.30am-4.30pm Mon-Fri; 12.30-5pm Sat; 8am-7pm Sun. **Services** 4pm Sat; 8am, 10.30am, 4.30pm, 6.30pm Sun. **Map** p315 C6.
Part of the chapel dates from the 12th century, while the transepts are Romanesque and the nave 15th-century Gothic. Most of the paintings within date from the 19th century.

SIGHTS

The Upper Town

Lofty by name, lofty by nature.

The Coudenberg (Cold Hill) has, from the 11th century, provided the ruling classes with a psychological advantage over their subjects as they looked loftily down on them from their castles and palaces. There were practical reasons, too: it provided a defence against enemies, and was a good distance from the infested River Senne on the marshland below.

Even today there remains an air of superiority, reflected in the neo-classical architecture. Here are the seats of royalty and government, the stately squares and public spaces, as well as the city's most illustrious museums, all linked by the grand, stern rue Royale. From the Lower Town it's a right royal climb, though the ascent is gentler if you start from the classy Sablon.

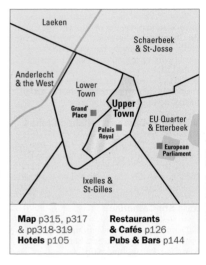

Map p315, p317 & pp318-319 Hotels p105	Restaurants & Cafés p126 Pubs & Bars p144

Mont des Arts. *See p63.*

ROYAL QUARTER

Métro Parc or Trône, tram 92, 94 or bus 27, 38, 95.

Ten minutes' walk uphill from the Grand'Place stands the **Cathédrale des Sts Michel et Gudule**. Although it is isolated from the city by a crowd of modern buildings, it's easy to imagine the Cathédrale dominating the medieval skyline, a constant reminder to the hapless Bruxellois of the power of the Church. To the left and rear is rue du Bois Sauvage where, between Nos.14 and 15, stands a solitary scrap of the old city wall.

Walk up the steep hill and you come to the determinedly straight **rue Royale**, the main artery of the Upper Town, punctuated at one end by the Palais de Justice and at the other by the church of Ste-Marie. This is the 'royal route', linking the Royal Palace in Laeken (*see p88*), home to the royal family, with the Royal Palace off place Royale, used for state ceremonies. The king is driven along it most days. Tourists can jump on the No.92 or 94 tram and let it take them along the road with as many stop-offs as they like for the hour validity of a normal ticket.

Palais de la Nation.

Running alongside rue Royale is the 18th-century **Parc de Bruxelles**. First laid out in classic French style, the design of its avenues is largely based on a Masonic pair of dividers. It's dotted with strange classical statues – armless, but with toes peeking out at the bottom. You'll notice that some also have their noses missing; Lord Byron was believed responsible for this vandalism, but eventually the Austrian Count Metternich owned up to the not so statesman-like behaviour. The park was once a chic strolling ground, although in the revolution of 1830 its avenues ran with blood. These days it's packed full of joggers and office workers on their lunch breaks. It also makes the perfect setting for the chocolate-box **Théâtre Royal du Parc** (*see p226*).

At the park's northern end stands the Belgian parliament building, the **Palais de la Nation**, graced by a lovely 18th-century façade by Guimard, the architect responsible for the homogeneous nature of the area. At the southern end is the king's starkly imposing official residence, the **Palais Royal**. It has never been much in favour with the royals, who prefer the airiness of Laeken, and the flag only flies on the rare occasions when the

monarch is home and on official duties. It is open to the public in the summer.

At the western end of the palace is the Hôtel Belle Vue, built as a swanky hotel in 1777. It was Wellington's headquarters at the time of Waterloo but now houses the **Musée BELvue**, where memorabilia, documents and photographs chronicle the short history of the Belgian monarchy since 1831. Directly behind the palace is the narrow rue Brederode, where Joseph Conrad first visited the Congo Trading Company in 1889; it's as creepy today as when it was first described in his *Heart of Darkness*.

West of the Palais Royal stands the **place Royale**, built on the site of the 15th-century Coudenberg Palace, a name remembered in the church of **St-Jacques-sur-Coudenberg** at the top of the same square. The statue here is of Godfroide de Bouillon, who led the successful first Crusade in the 11th century; he remains blissfully unaware of the trams that now circle beneath him. From here you get one of the best views in Brussels, looking directly down to the Grand'Place. Underneath these streets are the remains of the original **Palais Coudenberg** (*see p22* **A View from Above**), which burned down in 1731 when a fire started in the kitchens. When the square was rebuilt under the orders of Empress Maria Theresa, the ruins were buried for cost reasons and then forgotten about until the 1930s. They were re-exposed in 2000 during major renovations and – in typical Brussels style – were subsequently earmarked for an underground car park. Mercifully intact, they are now open to the public.

At the western corner of place Royale are Brussels' two major art galleries, the Musée d'Art Ancien and the Musée d'Art Moderne. Linked by an underground passage, they make up the **Musées Royaux des Beaux-Arts** (*see p66* **A Brush with Genius**). Attached and alongside the galleries is the splendid new **Magritte Museum**, which opened in 2009. At Nos.2-4 is the main Brussels Info Point (BIP) centre (*see p304*).

Downhill from place Royale on rue Montagne de la Cour are two architectural landmarks. The first is one of the great triumphs of art nouveau in the city: the spiky Old England department store, long ago shuttered up but reopened in 2000 as the **Musée des Instruments de**

Meet the Locals Paul Dujardin

The man who is shaking up cultural complacency.

As the youngest in a family of nine, Paul Dujardin knows something about battling to get his own way. In 2002, he took over as chief executive officer and artistic director of **Bozar** (*see p65*) – a disparate group of artistic institutions lurking together in the gorgeous Horta building over on rue Ravenstein – and immediately gave the cultural centre the shake-up it needed to launch it into the 21st century.

A youthful 47, Dujardin is slightly built and bursting with energy – four children await his arrival at the family home every night. Dujardin embodies the image of the European, having graduated in archaeology from Brussels Free University and completed yet further studies in Spanish, music and literature at universities in Oviedo and Berlin. He speaks six languages, and his carefully selected team

at Bozar is effortlessly trilingual. Dujardin may describe managing such a prestigious institute as problematic, but it's clear he has the vision and drive to blend a wide variety of programmes that appeal to both undemanding provincials and culture nerds, all gathered together under one roof. A colleague describes him as 'demanding and impossible' and 'a rebel', but it's clear there's a great deal of mutual respect. 'He wants to launch 300 projects all at the same time and he loves to rock the boat.'

In its first four years, the rebranded Bozar doubled its annual visitors from half a million, and its popularity shows no sign of abating; in 2008, there were almost a million visitors in total, and over 700,000 tickets issued at the box offices. Dujardin, it seems, is doing the business and making Horta's place a palace of the people.

Musique. It's one of the most distinctive and best-known buildings in Brussels. Further down the street, as it sweeps right into rue Ravenstein, is the red-brick, gabled **Hôtel Ravenstein**. This 15th-century building, the only significant survivor from the original Coudenberg quarter, was the birthplace of Anne of Cleves, fourth wife of Henry VIII.

Descending Ravenstein, to the left is the classic shopping arcade Galerie Ravenstein, now sadly faded and echoingly empty. To the right is the main entrance to the city's rebranded and revived cultural centre, the **Palais des Beaux-Arts** or 'Bozar' (*see left* **Meet the Locals**), and, alongside on rue Baron Horta, the **Musée du Cinema**, both a film museum and working picture house.

From here, you can climb the steps back up to rue Royale, or take the steep descent down Ravenstein to the Mont des Arts (*photo p60*), a 1950s piazza that joins the Upper and Lower Towns. It's flanked on one side by the **Palais du Congrès** and on the other by the **Bibliothèque Royale de Belgique** and adjacent **Palais de Charles de Lorraine**, and on both by skateboarding teenagers. An all-in museum pass and kids' events on Sundays have seen the staircased piazza become a major part of family weekends.

FREE Cathédrale des Sts Michel et Gudule

Place Ste-Gudule (02 217 83 45, www.cathedrale stmichel.be). Métro Gare Centrale or Parc or tram 92, 93, 94. **Open** 7am-6pm Mon-Fri; 8.30am-3.30pm Sat; 2-6pm Sun. **Admission** free. *Crypt by appt €2.50.* **No credit cards.** **Map** p317 E4.

This wonderful cathedral was dedicated to the male and female patron saints of Brussels – and while St Michel is the better known, Ste Gudule is by far the more popular of the two in local lore. Her symbol is a lamp, blown out by the devil but miraculously relit when she prayed. The cathedral stands on the site of a Carolingian-era chapel on the Treurenberg (Hill of Sorrows), which gained importance when Lambert II decided to move the saint's relics there from St-Géry. The current Gothic building (replacing a second church that had been built in 1072) was begun in 1226 and completed in 1499, with later chapel additions in the 16th and 17th centuries.

The Cathédrale's darkest moments came with the mass defacement in 1579, perpetrated by Protestant iconoclasts, and in the late 18th century, when French revolutionary armies largely destroyed the interior along with priceless works of art. The renewed interior is splendidly proportioned and happily retains a host of its original treasures. Most impressive are Bernard van Orley's stunning 16th-century pictorial stained-glass windows in the transepts, and the 13th-century choir. Both the

Musée des Instruments de Musique. *See p64.*

SIGHTS

SIGHTS

interior and exterior were heavily renovated during the 1990s, when remnants of the 11th-century Romanesque church were unearthed in the crypt.

★ Magritte Museum

1 place Royale (02 508 32 11, www.musee-magritte-museum.be). Métro Gare Centrale or tram 92, 94. **Open** 10am-5pm Tue, Thur-Sun; 10am-8pm Wed. **Admission** €8; €2-€5 reductions; free under-18s. Combined ticket with Musées Royaux des Beaux-Arts €13; €9 reductions. **No credit cards. Map** p319 E6.
Until June 2009, the only place of homage to René Magritte was the museum in his little house. That all changed when the Musées Royaux des Beaux-Arts opened this new museum in a stunning building on the place Royale. The museum is ordered chronologically; on entering you are elevated up to the third floor then work your way back down, with each floor representing a period in the artist's life. It's all very theatrical, and of course you get to see some of Magritte's most famous works. The museum has been an astounding success, with half a million visitors in its first year. Book online to avoid the queues.
▶ *For a more intimate look at Magritte, visit his modest former home in Anderlecht where he lived and painted for 24 years; see p85.*

Musée BELvue

7 place des Palais (070 22 04 92, www.musbelle vue.be). Métro Trône or tram 92, 94. **Open** 10am-5pm Tue-Fri; 10am-6pm Sat, Sun. **Admission** €5; €3 reductions. Combined ticket with Palais Coudenberg €8; €5 reductions; free under-18s. **No credit cards. Map** p319 E6.
Along with chronicling the Belgian royals, this museum – formerly the Musée de la Dynastie – has become of wider interest since the Fondation Baudouin installed an exhibition on the life of the popular last king, including his office and relics of his childhood. It's all rather voyeuristic, which makes it bizarrely irresistible.

Musée du Cinéma

Palais des Beaux-Arts, 9 rue Baron Horta (02 511 19 19, www.cinematheque.be). Métro Gare Centrale or Parc or tram 92, 94. **Open** from 4.30pm Mon, Tue, Fri; 2.30pm Wed, Sat, Sun; 12.30pm Thur. **Admission** €3. **No credit cards. Map** p317 E5.
This modest but fascinating little museum traces the early days of cinema, and the inventions that led to the development of cinematography by the Lumière brothers.
▶ *This place is still used as a working cinema, with piano accompaniment to silent films in the two projection rooms; see also p189.*

★ Musée des Instruments de Musique

2 rue Montagne de la Cour (02 545 01 30, www.mim.be). Métro Gare Centrale or tram 92, 94. **Open** 9.30am-4.45pm Tue-Fri; 10am-4.45pm Sat, Sun. *Restaurant* until 11pm Thur-Sat. **Admission** €5; €1.50-€4 reductions; free under-12s. **Credit** MC. V. **Map** p319 E6.
Designed by Paul Saintenoy in 1899, with curving black wrought ironwork framing large windows, the former Old England department store emerged a century later – and after a decade of restoration – as a museum housing a 6,000-strong collection of instruments (the world's largest), of which 1,500 are on display at any one time. Look out for the bizarre saxophone types dreamed up by the instrument's inventor Adolphe Sax. The top-floor restaurant offers panoramic views of the city. *Photo p63.*
▶ *Free music events take place regularly, from funk orchestras to school choirs; see p200.*

★ Musées Royaux des Beaux-Arts

3 rue de la Régence (02 508 32 11, www.fine-arts-museum.be). Métro Gare Centrale or tram 92, 94. **Open** *Museum* 10am-5pm Tue-Sun. *Café* 10am-5pm Tue-Sun. **Admission** €8; free-€5 reductions; free under-18s. Combined ticket with Magritte Museum €13; €9 reductions. **Credit** AmEx, MC, V. **Map** p315 D6.
The collection at the city's Fine Arts Museum covers the art of the Low Countries over the past six centuries, from masterworks by Rogier van der

Weyden, Hans Memling and Pieter Bruegel the Elder to a great spread of Belgian surrealist work.

A new wing carved out of two landmark buildings (one art nouveau, the other neo-classical) adjacent to the museum contains a bookstore, a sleek café and an upscale restaurant, all accessible from the street. This expansion made more room for the museum's marvellous collection of 17th- and 18th-century Flemish paintings, now cleaned, restored, and exhibited in superior numbers. A colossal gallery, the Patio, has been created for the display of a rare suite of eight vast Renaissance tapestries made in Brussels, and the museum is now looking like the world-class institute that it always promised to be. *See p66* **A Brush with Genius**.

Palais des Beaux-Arts ('Bozar')

23 rue Ravenstein (02 507 84 44/02 507 82 00, www.bozar.be). Métro Gare Centrale or Parc or tram 92, 94. **Open** 10am-6pm Tue, Wed, Fri-Sun; 10am-9pm Thur. **Admission** varies. **Credit** AmEx, MC, V. **Map** p317 E5.

The Bozar is the most dynamic element in the cluster of cultural attractions around the Mont des Arts. Once a moribund site of disparate arts disciplines, the Beaux-Arts has been transformed by director Paul Dujardin (*see p62* **Meet the Locals**) into the Bozar, a modern, multi-purpose cultural institute not unlike the Barbican in London. Designed by Victor Horta in 1928, the fabulous art deco building has also been revamped, with its false ceilings ripped out and original features restored.

Palais Coudenberg

Entrance through Musée BELvue, place des Palais (070 22 04 92, www.coudenberg.com). Métro Trône or tram 92, 94. **Open** 10am-5pm Tue-Fri; 10am-6pm Sat, Sun. **Admission** €5; €3 reductions. Combined ticket with Musée BELvue €8; €5 reductions; free under-18s. **No credit cards. Map** p319 E6.

Begun in the 11th century and enlarged by Philip the Good in the 15th century to become one of Europe's finest palaces, the Coudenberg was razed

SIGHTS

Palais des Beaux-Arts.

A Brush with Genius

Spend an hour exploring the galleries of the Musées Royaux des Beaux-Arts.

Together, Brussels' two major art galleries, the Musée d'Art Ancien and the Musée d'Art Moderne, comprise the **Musées Royaux des Beaux-Arts** (*see p64*), covering everything from 15th-century Gothic to 20th-century surrealism. It can be a daunting prospect if you're short of time, so we've suggested an itinerary to follow if you've only got one hour – though note that certain galleries close for lunch between noon and 2pm.

Start by picking up a map at the information desk and head straight across the grand main hall and up the stairs to the blue section (rooms 10-45), featuring 15th- and 16th-century art. Countless religious paintings depict the life of the Virgin Mary; if that's not your bag, follow the circuit directions to find Roger van der Weyden's sensitive *Portrait of Anthony of Burgundy* and, in a room on its own, a 1475 masterpiece by Dieric Bouts the Elder, *The Justice of Emperor Otto and Beheading of the Innocent Man*, a violently detailed triptych. Hieronymus Bosch's *The Temptation of St Antoine* is further along. You'll then pass through rooms lined with portraits of sad, pasty-faced young men to the burgundy walled gallery (30-31) displaying works by the Bruegel family: Pieter the Elder and Younger. There are two versions of *The Massacre of the Innocents* – busy, bloody scenes in the snowy white landscape – and a wonderful pile of drunken bodies in the elder Bruegel's *St Martin's Wine*.

Next, swoop up the grey marble staircase to the vast 17th- and 18th-century section, home to works by Rubens, Rembrandt and masters from the Low Countries. Rubens' *The Fall of Icarus* (room 51) is full of elemental energy, with delicate yet brisk brushstrokes. In the next room, his vast canvases with rippling torsos and fleshy nudes are just what we expect. Flemish landscapes, portraits and still life paintings are shown in an elegant green room (54-55); Dutch master Melchior d'Hondecoeter's *Le Paon* is a fabulously baroque composition of peacocks, ducks, swallows and a spaniel. Room 58 features a superb donated collection, including works by Bruegel the Elder's son, Jan.

Then it's back along the gallery looming over the main hall and straight towards the entrance, checking out the strange blue and beige forests by Belgian Constant Montald (1862-1944). Head down the linking escalator to the Musée d'Art Moderne, through the red section, with its temporary exhibitions, to the green area (19th and 20th centuries).

Four spacious floors hold a huge collection spanning a range of styles and movements, including Jacques-Louis David's ground-breaking masterpiece *The Death of Marat*. There are also lots of pastoral scenes by Hippolyte Boulenger, and some rustic Courbets. Léon Frederic's 1883 *Le Marchands de Craie* is a powerful triptych showing a peasant family in a muted Low Countries colour scheme. The museum has a large collection of works by Belgian Impressionist James Ensor and by his compatriot, the symbolist Fernand Khnopff, who painted some evocative, ethereal portraits of women and children – though the lady in his best-known work, *The Caress*, has a leopard's sinuous body. Finish your grand tour with a peep at Georges Seurat's *La Seine de la Grande Jatte* – a sunlit, soothing expanse of blue.

SIGHTS

Place du Petit Sablon.

by fire in 1731. Built over to create place Royale, the Coudenberg was excavated in recent times to allow visitors a glimpse of its past glory. The cellars of the Aula Magna, a huge reception chamber with a capacity of 1,400, used by Charles V in 1555 for his farewell address, are among the relics. For more on the Palace's history, *see p22* **A View from Above**.

FREE Palais Royal

Place des Palais (02 551 20 20, www.monarchie. be). Métro Trône or tram 92, 94. **Open** *Late July-early Sept* 10.30am-5.30pm Tue-Sun.
Admission free. **No credit cards.**
Map p319 E6.

The current, charmless building is an amalgam of styles created originally by Dutch king William I, remodelled in 1825 and again in 1904. As this is a residential palace, there's nothing much of historic interest here, so don't expect to see a fur wrap thrown casually over a Louis XV chair.

FREE St-Jacques-sur-Coudenberg

1 impasse Borgendael, place Royale (02 511 78 36). Métro Trône or tram 92, 93, 94. **Open** 1-6pm Tue-Sat; 8.45am-5pm Sun. *Services* 5.15pm Tue-Thur; 9am, 9.45am (English), 11am Sun.
Admission free. **Map** p319 E6.

This church was built in 1775 to resemble a Roman temple, although an incongruous belltower was added in the 19th century, giving it a strange Pilgrim Fathers-New England sort of look. The interior is as peculiarly imposing as the exterior, and you can

imagine that it served perfectly as a temple of reason and then as a temple of law when Brussels was under the sway of revolutionary France, before being returned to Catholicism in 1802.

SABLON

Tram 92, 94 or bus 27, 48, 95.

Stroll on south past the Musées Royaux des Beaux-Arts and you come to upmarket and sophisticated Sablon. The local landmark is **Notre-Dame au Sablon**, most likely the loveliest Gothic church in Brussels. Across busy rue de la Régence from the church is **place du Petit Sablon**. Its centre is taken up by a small park, whose railings, by art nouveau architect Paul Hankar, are carefully divided by 48 columns, each with a statuette representing one of the ancient guilds of Brussels. Its chief dedicatees are the 16th-century counts Egmont and Hoorn (*see p18*), both of them executed on the Grand'Place in 1568.

At the top end of the square stands the **Palais d'Egmont**. Begun in the 16th century, it was enlarged in the 18th century and had to be rebuilt at the start of the 20th after a fire. It is now used for receptions by the Ministry for Foreign Affairs and it was here that Britain, Ireland and Denmark signed their entry to the then EEC in 1972. The rooms are superb, but only the gardens are open to the public. Look

Notre-Dame au Sablon

out for the statue of Peter Pan, a copy of the one in London's Kensington Gardens.

Behind Notre-Dame is the **place du Grand Sablon**, a major square lined with glitzy restaurants and high-price antiques shops. Small independent art galleries and some of Brussels' finest chocolate shops (*see p165* **Confection Perfection**) complete the picture. At weekends, an antiques market adds colour to the foot of the church. Grand Sablon is full of life and verve, although it is always bisected by a stream of cars and buses, and there remains an unfortunate and inappropriate car park at its centre. This doesn't stop the magic of white lights at Christmas or numerous festivals.

At the lower end of rue de la Régence stands the unloved (by critics and criminals) **Palais de Justice**, completed in 1883 by Joseph Poelaert, Léopold II's favoured architect. It was the death of him, brought about, it was said, by a witch from the Marolles in revenge for the site's 3,000 demolished houses. The steps are a perfect stage for demonstrations, and the terrace affords panoramic views. You can take the lift or descend the steps down to the more endearing streets of the Marolles. The public are allowed into the main hall – a free municipal lift drops you next to the Palais entrance.

★ FREE Notre-Dame au Sablon

38 rue de la Régence (02 511 57 41). Métro Porte de Namur or tram 92, 94. **Open** 9am-7pm Mon-Sat. **Admission** free; guided tours available on request. **Map** p315 D6.

Built in the 15th and 16th centuries, Notre-Dame au Sablon was once home to a statue of Mary shipped in from Antwerp on account of its reputed healing powers. A carving of the boat can be seen in the nave, but the statue was demolished by Protestants during the Iconoclastic Riots. The current impressive structure boasts some stunning 14m (46ft) high stained-glass windows.

▶ *The statue's arrival is still celebrated in July, with the Ommegang parade; see p178.*

FREE Palais de Justice

Place Poelaert (02 508 64 10). Métro Louise or tram 92, 94, 97 or bus 20, 48. **Open** 8am-5pm Mon-Fri. **Admission** free. **Map** p318 C7.

The largest of Léopold II's grandiose projects, this intimidating colossus caused the demolition of 3,000 houses and demise of its architect Poelaert, driven mad by his need for symmetry. Few critics agree on its style even today. The strange exterior is supposedly Assyro-Babylonian, though it is really a mishmash of styles that has suffered some ridicule over the centuries. The interior is equally imposing – and flawlessly symmetrical – with grand magisterial statues of Demosthenes and Cicero, and an echoing waiting room, the Salle des Pas Perdus (Hall of Lost Steps). Kafka would have loved it.

SIGHTS

The EU Quarter & Etterbeek

The beating heart of Europe.

In the 1960s, an attractive 19th-century quarter around the Schuman roundabout was torn down to allow the construction of office buildings for the burgeoning European institutions. In the 1980s, the once-lively Quartier Léopold suffered a similar fate when the European Parliament complex was built, partly on the site of an old brewery.

Most Bruxellois are appalled at the damage that has been done to the fragile urban fabric of their city, with soaring glass and steel office blocks nudging out lovely townhouses, and local communities gone forever. Now, there's a move to make the EU Quarter more appealing to workers and residents alike in an attempt to improve quality of life and the perception of the institutions themselves. Already, a former car park has been turned into attractive place Jean Ray, the abandoned Van Maerlant chapel has been converted into an EU library and a new park has been set next to the Charlemagne building.

Laeken

Schaerbeek & St-Josse

Anderlecht & the West

Lower Town

Grand' Place

Upper Town

EU Quarter & Etterbeek

Palais Royal

European Parliament

Ixelles & St-Gilles

| **Map** p320 & pp322-323 | **Restaurants & Cafés** p128 |
| **Hotels** p106 | **Pubs & Bars** p146 |

AROUND THE AREA

It will be many years before the scars of EU expansion have healed. While the needs of locals are set against those of the Eurocrats, the sweep of Etterbeek from the east of the Petit Ring to the Fôret de Soignes remains a mix: elegant squares are overlooked by tower blocks, art nouveau treasures sit alongside glass edifices, rows of terraced streets are girdled by stately parks. This is Brussels at its most fractured. Do look out, though, for local gems such as the city's finest chips at **Maison Antoine** on place Jourdan (*see p122* **On the Hoof**) and the colourful weekend market on the same square. An enjoyable afternoon can be spent exploring in and around **square**

Marie Louise (*see p72* **Calm Waters**) or, for Europhiles, an hour amid the edifices, greenery and quality restaurants (*see p71* **Take a Break**).

EU QUARTER

Métro Schuman.

The EU Quarter is a series of office and policy-makers' buildings linked by streets that echo an older Brussels. The area has long been the focus of attentions of urban heritage action groups, who refer nostalgically to pre-EU days when it was the lively Quartier Léopold with its characteristic local bars and beautiful houses. Patches of these still exist, but as the heritage

Time Out Brussels **69**

Arc de Triomphe.
See p73.

SIGHTS

activists lament, the heart has been torn out. Recent times have at least seen a more decisive architectural style, and many of the heavy grey office blocks are being replaced by more daring sculptured buildings that may one day be seen as standard bearers of their time.

A good starting point is to take the métro to Schuman. Exiting on the Schuman roundabout, your attention is snagged by the (in)famous **Berlaymont building**, a star-shaped symbol not just of the EU, but of the bureaucratic nightmares associated with it. This was the original home for the European Commission until 1991, when it was deemed too dangerous because of its outrageous asbestos content. It would have been cheaper to pull it down, but local disquiet – yes, the locals learned to love it – and its tricky foundations meant renovation was the only option.

After years under white plastic, it is now a gleaming, state-of-the-art smart building, which more or less breathes for its computerised self. It reopened in 2004, late and millions over budget, and now houses the whole Commission and 3,000 officials.

Opposite the Berlaymont is the **Justus Lipsius building**, first opened in 1995 for the Council of Ministers. Its frontage of pink granite and fluttering flags will be familiar as the backdrop to countless newscasts as it's the place where the world's media gather on high days. Since the decision was taken to hold all

EU summits in Brussels, this little corner can be security-cordoned for days, which is not something that endears the EU to locals. By 2012, these summits will be switched to the **Résidence Palace** nearby.

Away to the south, shining like a crystal palace in the far distance, is the **European Parliament** (*photo p73*). It is known locally as the *Caprice des Dieux* (Folly of the Gods), which strangely enough is also the name of an identically shaped supermarket cheese. The best view of this undeniably impressive set of buildings is from the attractive but unexceptional **Parc Léopold**. Briefly the site of a zoo, this was one of the world's first science parks in the late 19th century and it remains dotted with impressive research institutes. One of the park's public attractions is the **Institut Royal des Sciences Naturelles**, famous for its dinosaur skeletons and the robotic wonders of 'dinamation', a hit with kids. On the other side of the same street is the **Musée Wiertz**, home and studio of the oddball 19th-century artist, and now a showcase for his works.

Turn right out of the park and you'll come to **place Jourdan**, a slice of Brussels life, lined with bars and restaurants in the old style. The queue here is for the most famous *friterie* in town, **Maison Antoine**. Turn left out of the park and you'll see the back of the **Résidence Palace**, a superb honey-brick art deco block originally built as an apartment complex in the 1920s, complete with a pool, theatre and roof garden. It was later the Nazi administrative headquarters. It now houses the International Press Centre and thus one of the world's largest press packs.

Circling south of Parc Léopold then following the train tracks north brings you to busy **place du Luxembourg** and the original Luxembourg railway station booking hall. This same station became a key chapter in the saga of resistance to development when squatters moved in to protest against its demolition. To no avail: the bulldozers prevailed, wiping away the old billiard room and waiting room, and with them a cherished piece of urban history. The remaining booking hall looks like an afterthought to appease the critics, a strange, lonely little piece of old Brussels. The square itself has kept much of its charm, although the cafés and restaurants lining it are rather bland.

North of place du Luxembourg are two major roads, rue Belliard and rue de la Loi. Scoot over them and through the area beside Maelbeek métro station, known as the Maelbeek valley (the Maelbeek is a tributary of the River Senne). For decades this was a wasteland, but there are finally signs of regeneration as dereliction is replaced by new housing stock. Running parallel to rue de la Loi is the more pleasant rue

Take a Break

There's plenty to see beyond the suits around planet EU.

You're on an hour's lunch break, it isn't raining and you fancy a mooch around and beyond planet EU. Where's best to go?

The main EU complex is clustered around the Schuman roundabout, by far the finest starting point. Around you will be the iconic Commission building **Berlaymont** and the **Justus Lipsius building** for the Council of Ministers. Just along the rue de la Loi is the stately **Résidence Palace** (for all three, *see left*), home to the international press corps. Walking along the length of rue Archimède takes you to the tranquil square Ambiorix, a pretty little park surrounded by a mix of architectural styles. Look out for No.11, the **Maison St-Cyr**, an outrageously fluffy art nouveau house like no other. Follow the lie of the land as it drops down to avenue Palmerston, named after the great statesman who lived here. The **Van Eetveldehuis** at No.4 was designed by Victor Horta himself. This then brings you into the top of square Marie Louise and

its famous pond (*see p72* **Calm Waters**). Cutting through rue du Taciturne leads you straight back to Schuman.

The other option is to head up rue Stevin to the corner of the **Parc du Cinquantenaire** (*see p73*). Beyond the mosque, you'll see the classically inspired **Pavillon Horta** (*see p74*), which puts you in a good position to look up the park towards that undeniably impressive yet flamboyant folly of Léopold II, the **Arc de Triomphe** (*see p73*). The arch is surrounded by museums such as **Autoworld** and the **Musées Royaux d'Art et d'Histoire** (for both, *see p74*). Entry prices are modest – check the web to see what exhibitions they have on. A stroll back through the park or a one-stop hop on the métro from Mérode takes you straight back to Schuman.

There is, of course, one more option. Pick up the phone and make a lunch reservation at **Le Midi Cinquante** (*see p128*). All in all, an hour very well spent.

SIGHTS

Berlaymont.

Calm Waters

Green living in the midst of bureaucratic Brussels.

Before the extension of the suburbs at the end of the 19th century, there were 48 ponds across the city. Now only six remain: Parc Léopold (*see p70*), Abbaye de la Cambre (*see p79*), Josaphat Park and the two *etangs d'Ixelles* (*see p78* **Water World**) make five, and the sixth forms a beating heart for elegant square Marie Louise.

The Marie Louise site was designed and developed by Gédéon Bordian, who took advantage of the hilly lie of the land to create a cascade of gardens with water features running over the rocks. These also provide shelter and a shower for the wildfowl that make the pond home. Dotted among them are sculptures by Consantin Meunier and Victor Rousseau. In the middle of the pond, a powerful fountain adds grace and spectacle, though it's nigh on impossible to know when it will be switched on – high days and holidays are a safe bet.

Surrounding the square is a very eclectic assortment of houses, providing one of the most intriguing architectural skylines in the city. To the north and west, mid 20th-century purpose-built blocks have an attraction of their own. Stylish, compact and with neat gardens, there is an air of affluent Manhattan about them. On the opposite side, stately terraces of 19th-century townhouses make their mark – each individually designed and quite independent of the others, they make for a curious hotch-potch. Some have been converted into apartments, others keep their original purpose as family homes. Take time to look at the intricate skyline; towers, turrets, oriole windows, spikes and spires create classic contrasts. In 1938, the poet WH Auden lived at No.70.

At ground (and water) level, sandy footpaths allow breathing space for both city dwellers and EU functionaries. Toddlers waddle with the ducks, old men sit and stare, young lovers canoodle and business deals are done down the phone. This is green urban living at its most attractive and individual.

Square Marie Louise.

Joseph II with rows of terraced townhouses punctuated by the odd ugly office building. Near its Petit Ring end is the **Musée Charlier**, an unusual collection of art and furniture.

Back east along **rue du Marteau** – a charming street full of eclectic architectural styles – is **square Marie-Louise**. It has a fanciful pond frequented by waterfowl and is flanked on two sides by rows of charming fin-de-siècle houses, each one tall and narrow but otherwise unique (*see left* **Calm Waters**). East again, along avenue Palmerston (named after the British PM, who early in his political career had been a staunch supporter of independence for Belgium; a blue plaque at No.26 marks where he lived), is **square Ambiorix**, its grassy expanse surrounded by lovely art nouveau houses. To the south, **rue Archimède** is alive with restaurants; north-east, sloping **rue des Confédérés** is where the English poet WH Auden spent five months in 1938 'bathing and café-crawling'.

Institut Royal des Sciences Naturelles

29 rue Vautier (02 627 42 38, www.natural sciences.be). Métro Trône or bus 34, 80. **Open** 9.30am-5pm Tue-Fri; 10am-6pm Sat, Sun & school hols. **Admission** €7; €6 reductions; free under-5s. **Credit** MC, V. **Map** p322 H7.
The Royal Natural History Museum contains one of the world's finest collections of iguanodons, as well as a deep-sea diving vessel that plunges down to see a scrap between a sperm whale and a giant squid. These now vie for visitors' attentions with the sumptuous Arctic and Antarctica Room.

Musée Charlier

16 avenue des Arts (02 220 26 91, www.charlier museum.be). Métro Arts-Loi or Madou or bus 29, 63, 65, 66. **Open** noon-5pm Mon-Thur; 10am-1pm Fri. **Admission** €5. **No credit cards. Map** p320 F4.
Guillaume Charlier was an active figure in Brussels in the early 1900s, when he was taken under the wing of Henri Van Cutsem, a patron of the arts. Charlier moved into van Cutsem's house, the site of the museum, where he hosted concerts and salon discussions. The house, whose interior was redesigned by Horta, is filled with tapestries, furniture and works by Ensor, Meunier and Charlier himself.

FREE Musée Wiertz

62 rue Vautier (02 648 17 18, www.fine-arts-museum.be). Métro Trône or bus 34, 38, 54, 59, 80, 95. **Open** 10am-noon, 1-5pm Tue-Fri; Weekends by appt for groups. **Admission** free. **No credit cards. Map** p322 G7.
Antoine Wiertz (1806-65) painted vast canvases of the most gruesome subjects: biblical and mythical scenes with gratuitous violence thrown in. Well regarded in his time (not least by himself – he put

European Parliament. *See p70.*

his own work on a par with that of Michelangelo and Rubens), Wiertz persuaded the state to buy him this house and studio in return for inheriting his works when he died. The museum contains 160 pieces and makes for an unusual, if slightly bizarre, diversion.

PARC DU CINQUANTENAIRE

Métro Schuman or Mérode.

If it's overblown and neo-classical in Brussels, it's probably the work of Léopold II. The king had 300 labourers working day and night to complete the massive **Arc de Triomphe** (*photo p70*) that stands at the centre of the single largest, most impressive and best-known Brussels park. The overdrive was an attempt to meet the deadline of Belgium's 50th anniversary, celebrated in 1880. In the event, construction was not completed in time and the Arc had to be substituted with a wooden stand-in for official ceremonies. It wasn't completed until 1910, a year after Léopold's death. Hugely impressive in scale, it is a monument that singularly fails to stir the emotions – a reflection perhaps of Léopold's own failed ambitions of glory.

On either side of the Arc, colonnades front wings that house three museums. The northern wing is also the site of the **Musée Royal de l'Armée et d'Histoire Militaire**, which provides an enjoyably retro journey for military buffs of all ages; the southern wing is shared by

SIGHTS

INSIDE TRACK SUMMIT DAY

Beware – if you travel to the EU Quarter on a summit day (when the prime ministers meet at the Council) the streets will be cordoned off with blue and white police tape. Only residents and workers with ID are allowed through. The métro train is also unlikely to stop at Schuman station, delivering you at the next stop, Mérode. Mind, it's a pleasant enough walk back through Léopold's arch and the park.

motor vehicle museum **Autoworld** and the **Musée du Cinquantenaire**.

Over in the north-west corner of the park, the rather unexpectedly neo-classical and austere **Pavillon Horta** (www.kmkg-mrah.be) is an early piece (1889) by the architect who was later to become synonymous with art nouveau in Brussels (*see pp36-40* **Art Nouveau**). The real interest, however, is inside with Jef Lambeaux's luxuriant reliefs *Les Passions Humaines*. After years of being locked away – they were considered too lewd – they are now being renovated. Ironically, the pavilion stands within the grounds of Brussels' largest mosque. On the south side of the park, on avenue des Nerviens, is the **Centre d'Art Contemporain**

Maison de Cauchie.

(*see p192*), devoted to modern Wallonian art; nearby, on rue des Francs, is the **Maison de Cauchie**, home of painter Paul Cauchie.

Also on the east side of the park, built by Léopold II to link it with his **Musée Royal de l'Afrique Centrale** (*see p95*) at the other end, is the avenue de Tervuren, flanked on both sides by highly impressive fin-de-siècle housing. Ahead, a statue of Field Marshal Montgomery calmly observes the square that bears his name.

Autoworld
11 parc du Cinquantenaire (02 736 41 65, www.autoworld.be). Métro Mérode. **Open** *Apr-Sept* 10am-6pm daily. *Oct-Mar* 10am-5pm daily. **Admission** €6; €3-€4.70 reductions. **No credit cards. Map** p323 K6.
The venue for Belgium's motor show since 1902 and one of the biggest automobile museums in Europe.

★ Maison de Cauchie
5 rue des Francs (02 733 86 84, www.cauchie.be). Métro Mérode. **Open** 10am-1pm, 2-5.30pm 1st weekend of mth & by appt. **Admission** €5; free under-12s. **No credit cards. Map** p323 L7.
Entirely refurbished in 2001, the former home of painter and architect Paul Cauchie was built in 1905 in the twilight of Brussels' art nouveau period. It shows the influence of the Vienna Secession with its geometric shapes – the gilded mural of the lovely maidens in long gowns is slightly reminiscent of Gustav Klimt and was actually designed to be an advertisement of Cauchie's art.

FREE Musée Royal de l'Armée et d'Histoire Militaire
3 parc du Cinquantenaire (02 737 78 11, www.klm-mra.be). Métro Mérode. **Open** 9am-noon, 1-4.45pm Tue-Sun. **Admission** free. **No credit cards. Map** p323 K6.
A revamp has added a new department covering international conflict from 1918 to the present day – the European Forum on Contemporary Conflicts. The display dealing with the 1830 Belgian uprising and the hangar filled with aircraft from the two world wars are also particularly striking.

Musées Royaux d'Art et d'Histoire
10 parc du Cinquantenaire (02 741 72 11, www.kmkg-mrah.be). Métro Mérode. **Open** 9.30am-5pm Tue-Fri; 10am-5pm Sat, Sun. **Admission** €5; €1.50-€4 reductions; free 1st Wed of mth from 1pm. **Credit** V. **Map** p323 K7.
The antiquity department has a huge collection of artefacts from the ancient worlds of Egypt, Greece, the Near and Far East, and pre-Columbian America. Other collections include European art from the Middle Ages, art deco glass and metalwork, lace and 18th-century carriages. You can also buy tickets for the Pavillon Horta here.

Ixelles & St-Gilles

A mix of African spirit and belle époque grandeur.

The adjoining communes of Ixelles
and St-Gilles, covering a swathe of
southern Brussels before it becomes
forest, represent what living in this city
is all about. Here, stylish cosmopolitan
life meets an earthier ethnic mix, and
simply turning a corner can take you
from one world to another.

If you want to get to know Brussels,
explore these areas. From fine belle
époque and art nouveau townhouses
to the vibrancy and bustle of the
African quarter of Matongé, which
takes its name from an area of Kinshasa
in the Congo, and from the fashionable
restaurants of the Châtelain and Ma
Campagne areas to the homely tagine
spots of St-Gilles, this is Brussels at
its most diverse.

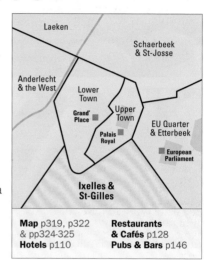

Map p319, p322	Restaurants
& pp324-325	& Cafés p128
Hotels p110	Pubs & Bars p146

IXELLES

Métro Porte de Namur, tram 94 or bus 38, 71.
The Bois de la Cambre is Brussels' answer to
Central Park. It's a vast wooded parkland
located on the edge of the city centre that
was originally part of the wild and greater
Fôret de Soignes.

In 1859, construction began on a grand,
broad avenue – avenue de la Cambre – giving
citizens in the city centre easy access to the
wide, open, green spaces beyond. In 1864,
Léopold II decreed that the new avenue should
be named after his eldest daughter, Louise,
and it was around this same avenue that
Ixelles slowly took shape.

Beginning at **place Louise** on the Petit
Ring (keeping the Palais de Justice behind you),
the top end of the imperial avenue has human
proportions. Sophisticated shops and galleries
line each side, although the portentously named
Galeries de la Toison d'Or (Golden Fleece
Galleries) are more of a mixed bag, with
everyday shops nestling in among the jewellery
and fake fur. Two small pedestrianised streets,
rue Jordan and **rue Jean Stas**, are full of
small restaurants, and in summer the terrace
tables are packed with chattering shoppers.

As soon as you reach **place Stéphanie**
(the younger sister of Louise), the reality of the
avenue hits home: double-lane highways on
each side of a central tree-lined reservation
lined with tram tracks. Scale and traffic render
pedestrians insignificant – don't even think
about trying to cross the road.

By far the best way to experience avenue
Louise is by taking the No.94 tram which runs
from place Stéphanie and turns left just before
the Bois. Along the way keep a look out for
the Horta-designed **Hôtel Solvay** at No.224,
built for the son of a noted industrialist. The
33-year-old Horta was given free rein to produce

INSIDE TRACK
CHI-CHI CHATELAIN

It's not just a weekly market that happens
around place Châtelain every Wednesday
afternoon and continues into the early
evening. It's also a gathering point for
the area's cocktail crowd, turning day
into night as they spill on to the terraces
of the bars and restaurants – and there's
no better place to see and be seen.

Châtelain food market.

a work of fluid, intricate, symmetrical lines, with gigantic windows and imaginative use of stone. At **No.453**, what is now a high-rent apartment block was a Nazi HQ in the war. This became the scene of one of the most audacious fightbacks of the occupation (*see p82* **All Guns Blazing**).

It's worth hopping out of the tram halfway down Louise, where down a sidestreet off to the east is the **Fondation pour l'Architecture**, a centre for architecture, urban planning and landscape gardening, whose bookshop features models of local buildings. Opposite you'll find the **Musée d'Archives d'Architecture Moderne** (86 rue de l'Ermitage, 02 649 86 65), an old Masonic lodge boasting exhibitions of neglected local architects.

At almost the same point on Louise but west of the avenue, just a short stride down rue du Châtelain, is **place du Châtelain**. Ringed with hip but affordable restaurants, it manages to maintain a neighbourhood feel despite throngs of bright young things drawn by its buzzy nightlife. There's an excellent **food market** on the square every Wednesday afternoon. **Rue du Page**, which runs south-west off Châtelain, is home to some of Brussels' most enduring restaurants, while the small square of **parvis de la Trinité**, north-west of Châtelain, is an assemblage of graceful houses around a lovely church, which looks as if it might well belong somewhere in Latin America.

Further south, after avenue Louise makes a slight swing to the right to home in on the Bois de la Cambre, one block westward on rue de l'Abbaye is the **Musée Meunier**, which showcases just over a quarter of the artist's prolific output. A small garden to the east, meanwhile, is home to the **Abbaye de la Cambre**, which dates back to the 12th century. The Bois de la Cambre itself is described in the Green Brussels chapter: *see pp93-95.*

Chaussée d'Ixelles

For a grittier take on Ixelles, head east from avenue Louise to Porte de Namur (one stop on the métro) where the twin chaussées of Wavre and Ixelles fan out. Between the two spreads the Matongé area – predominantly Congolese, but also with Indian and North African communities. The quarter's colourful shops and cafés are a welcome change from the more staid retail blandness of avenue Louise.

At the centre of the area are **rue Longue Vie** and **rue de la Paix**, the former a gaudy, paved strip lined with bars and restaurants that gradually become more and more upmarket the closer you get to **place St-Boniface**. A centre for classy nightlife, the square is signposted by the sinister, turreted church of St-Boniface.

Profile The Matongé

The Congo meets Belgium in the Matongé district.

Hidden in suburban Ixelles, beyond the bland glitz of avenue Louise, Brussels is home to a small corner of Africa. Taking its name from an area of Kinshasa in the Congo, the Matongé is located between chaussée d'Ixelles and rue de Trône, bringing vibrant music and bursting colour to what is otherwise still a gently decaying district. In the early 1960s, a wave of students came to Brussels after the independence of the former Belgian Congo. Congolese intellectuals gathered in clubs such as Les Anges Noirs and bars around Porte de Namur métro, and this became the main jumping off point for the Matongé.

At the heart of the Matongé is the **Galerie d'Ixelles**, the arcade linking chaussées de Wavre and d'Ixelles. The gallery's two sides take their names from Kinshasa's two main streets of Inzia and Kanda-Kanda.

Inzia is filled with snack bars, while Kanda-Kanda's many hairdressers – Chez Maman Henriette, Maman Jolie and Maman Alphonsine – double up as packed social centres, where customers debate local goings-on and the latest hair extensions. Also here is **Musicanova** (24 Galerie d'Ixelles), one of Europe's best African music shops, offering a great stock of pulsing sounds.

Elsewhere, **chaussée de Wavre** is lined with grocer's shopfronts, piled high with imported plantains, manioc leaves, yams, sugar cane and guava; inside, the shelves are stacked with giant sacks of rice, huge drums of palm oil and heaps of fragrant dried fish. Traders thrust forward cheap shoes 'direct from Abidjan', cotton *kangas* (shawls) and colourful *bazin* (wraps).

Bustling by day, Matongé also springs to life at night. The main drag is **rue Longue Vie**, a pedestrianised section of street between chaussée de Wavre and rue de la Paix jam-packed with upbeat bars and restaurants, all of them blazing forth the sounds of African artists like Salif Keita and Manu Dibango. Most open late and offer spicy stews, fiery chicken piri-piri, *foufou* and *chikwangue*, a starchy cassava root mash, washed down with Congolese Tembo beer or palm wine. Around the corner on rue Francart they serve grilled gazelle or *n'dole* (a powerful meat and dried fish stew).

EXTRA HELPINGS More mainstream dishes and Caribbean rums can be found at nearby **L'Horloge du Sud** (*see p148*), a less hectic introduction to African cuisine.

Water World

Grand living by the Ixelles Ponds.

The two *étangs d'Ixelles* (Ixelles Ponds) are actually the remains of four natural ponds that partially dried up around 1860. They lie along the course of the Maelbeek stream, stretching in a chain from the Abbaye de la Cambre over ground covered by place Eugéne Flagey to parc Josephat in Schaerbeek.

The two lakes lie north to south. The eastern side of the ponds is flanked by upmarket *maisons de maître*: swanky townhouses built for families at the turn of the 19th century. These ultra-desirable addresses are now divided up into apartments, mostly occupied by wealthy expatriates and embassy workers. Many have fabulous art nouveau façades and crazy doors, often designed by Ernest Blérot (1870-1957), a lesser-known art nouveau architect who created homes for those who couldn't afford a Horta pad. One façade worth noting stands at 29 avenue des Klauwaerts – a hulking behemoth of a building, whose aesthetic lies somewhere between a stone tomb and a Wurlitzer organ.

The western side contains a rag-bag mix of 1930s art deco apartment blocks and some tasteful art nouveau terraced houses. At the northernmost tip of the top lake, between the water and avenue Général de Gaulle, the Saturday market's stalls sell giant vats of fresh olives, Italian deli produce, home-made quiches, smouldering waffles and the occasional bargain Chinese tracksuit.

Ixelles' cultural life was given a shot in the arm by the opening of the **Flagey** centre (*see right*), in a landmark art deco building that had been boarded up for a decade after large chunks of asbestos were discovered. The *paquebot* (steam ship) and *l'usine à son* (sound factory), as it was variously nicknamed, revitalised place Flagey, dominating the square and luring back trendy young Flems with a lively programme of movies, concerts and the culturally hip **Café Belga** (*see p129*).

A sign warns visitors not to feed the ducks, white geese, doves and pigeons that populate the lake as there is a risk of botulism, and you're not supposed to climb over the low railings on to the grassy slope leading down to the water – though many do, especially in summer. It's packed with sunbathers, lunching office-workers and grannies defying the bird-feeding ban.

To the south of the ponds, the **Abbaye de la Cambre** (*see right*) is a beautiful group of buildings, with custard-yellow walls surrounding a white church, the National Geographic Institute and an art school. The formal French garden provides a peaceful place for a stroll, dotted with conical yew bushes and gravelled terraces to swish one's crinoline along.

GRANCHE.R —LAMBIO
—MAHIEU.L —MARCEL
ELS P —MINISCLOUX.
CI —PETYT.A —PHILIP
ROOTEN.P —SCALLIE
NS.A —STUYCK.L —SU
NTELS.H — VAN AERD
N.F —VANDERMEYLEN
—VEECKMAN.G —VER

SIGHTS

Further south, down chaussée d'Ixelles, the
uneven square of **place Fernand Cocq** is an
attractive evening option, with half-a-dozen
lively bars. In summer, when customers sip
their drinks outside, the square mutates into
a Mediterranean terrace, looked over by the
Riviera-styled **Maison Communale** at the
far end. Surrounded by gardens, this large,
pleasant residence belonged to the violinist
Bériot and his Spanish wife, the famous singer
La Malibrán, who bought the house as a
monument to their newly-wed love.

As it slowly meanders southwards, chaussée
d'Ixelles becomes both sparser and significantly
darker, dotted with little more than the
occasional bar or low-range retail name. There
is one notable bright spot, just off the chaussée
up steep rue Van Volsem, and that's the **Musée
Communal d'Ixelles**, an art museum housed
in a former abattoir that is renowned for the
quality of its exhibitions.

The chaussée ends at the **Etangs d'Ixelles**
(Ixelles Ponds; *see left* **Water World**), pretty
in spring and summer and filled with ducks
and fishermen. It's not the tranquil locale that
it once was, though, thanks to the rebirth of
Flagey (*photo p81*). When it was completed in
1938, the ocean-liner-profiled building was the
world's most advanced communications centre.
Its moment passed, however, and the place fell
into disrepair; it was quite literally left to rot
throughout most of the 1990s. A recent revival
as a studio, concert venue (*see p203*) and
cinema (*see p188*), and a stylish bar (**Café
Belga**; *see p129*), has brought thousands down
to this once-forgotten corner of Ixelles. Finally,
after many years of major roadworks and
deep digging, the whole square has become
sparkling and sophisticated.

Close to the southern end of the ponds is
the splendid **Musée des Enfants**. Hands-on
activities are at its core: there are art and
puppet workshops, and the programme is
completely revamped every three years.
Labelling is in French and Dutch only. East of
here is the bilingual university, the French side
being the ULB and the Flemish the VUB. They
are both enclosed by boulevard du Triomphe,
within a pleasant campus. This is a lively area,
with a sweep of bars and restaurants along the
chaussée de Boondael, between the university
and the Abbaye de la Cambre.

Further south extend the leafy expanses of
Watermael-Boitsfort and the Forêt de Soignes:
see pp93-95 **Green Brussels**.

FREE Abbaye de la Cambre

*11 avenue Emile Duray (02 648 11 21). Tram
23, 94 or bus 71.* **Open** 9am-noon, 3-6pm
Mon-Fri, Sun; 3-6pm Sat. **Admission** free.
No credit cards. Map p325 G13.

SIGHTS

Founded in the 12th century by the noble Gisèle for the Cîteaux Order, the Abbaye de la Cambre was badly damaged during the Wars of Religion and later rebuilt in both the 16th and 18th centuries, although the 14th-century church attached to the abbey survives. It's all set in elegant French gardens, alongside the National Geographical Institute and an exhibition centre.

Fondation pour l'Architecture

55 rue de l'Ermitage (02 642 24 80, www.fondationpourlarchitecture.be). Tram 81, 82, 94 or bus 38, 54, 60. **Open** noon-6pm Tue-Fri; 10.30am-6pm Sat, Sun. **Admission** €6; €5 reductions. **No credit cards. Map** p319 F9.
This converted pumping house should be the first port of call for anyone interested in Brussels' architectural heritage. Exhibitions are varied and well put together, with models, photos, videos and furniture, and there is a first-class bookshop too.

Musée Communal d'Ixelles

71 rue Van Volsem (02 515 64 21, www.musee-ixelles.be). Bus 38, 54, 60, 71, 95. **Open** 11.30am-5pm Tue-Sun. **Admission** €7; €5 reductions. **Credit** AmEx, DC, MC, V. **Map** p322 G9.
This excellent little museum, founded in 1892, is justifiably well known for its exhibitions of mainly modern art. Its permanent collection features works by local artists such as Magritte, Delvaux, Spilliaert and Van Rysselberghe, along with original posters by Toulouse-Lautrec. Two wings blend perfectly for a well-lit and interesting space.

FREE Musée Meunier

59 rue de l'Abbaye (02 648 44 49, www.fine-arts-museum.be). Tram 94 or bus 38. **Open** 10am-noon, 1-5pm Tue-Fri. **Admission** free. **No credit cards. Map** p324 F12.
The house and studio of the renowned 19th-century Belgian sculptor and painter is home to more than 170 of his sculptures and 120 of his paintings (of an output of 800), the best known being his bronze figures of workers. Meunier began painting religious scenes, but turned to sculpture inspired by social realism: farmers, miners and workers heroically labour in grim surroundings.

ST-GILLES

Pré-métro Horta; or tram 81, 92
St-Gilles is easily one of Brussels' most beautiful residential areas. It's built on a hill that climbs roughly north to south, and as the altitude increases, the changes are subtle but significant. Terraces of rooming houses and tacky shops slowly give way to row upon row of well-groomed, middle-class townhouses, culminating in the magnificent belle époque and art nouveau mansions located around avenue Brugmann.

A good starting point for any exploration of the area is the atmospheric 14th-century **Porte de Hal**, located down on the Petit Ring and the sole surviving medieval gate of the many that once studded the old city walls. Over the centuries the gate has been used as a prison, a toll booth and a grain store; it is now a museum, showing mainly temporary exhibitions. A tunnel redirects local traffic underground, so the gate sits in relatively peaceful gardens.

Running south from the Porte is chaussée de Waterloo. Its lower end is generally uninspiring, although the local Spanish community has peppered it with cheap (but not necessarily cheerful) restaurants. For the real St-Gilles, you need to head uphill toward the main square, the **parvis de St-Gilles** which, like the wider neighbourhood, has a quiet, contemplative air – except for the bustling market on Sunday mornings. This is very much a residential part of town: if you move away from the main thoroughfares, you'll find yourself in small, quiet streets, most with their own bars and local shops.

Further up the hill, beyond the **Barrière de St-Gilles**, where several large avenues converge on the charming little square, the richer St-Gilles appears; the houses are truly monumental, although the traffic and trams cutting through their midst do detract from the grandeur somewhat.

Clearly visible to the south of the Barrière, occupying a commanding position at the head of avenue Dejaer, is St-Gilles' **Hôtel de Ville**, an impressive 19th-century building in French Renaissance style. Originally designed by Albert Dumont in 1900-04, the building's most visually arresting features are the frescoes on the ceiling above the main staircase and in the Marriage Room. Behind this bit of civic monumentalism, on rue de Savoie, is the old **Chez Moeder Lambic** (*p151*) bar, worth a visit or even a peek through the window.

St-Gilles' golden age came at the end of the 19th century, when a few wealthy men commissioned fabulous art nouveau residences (*see pp36-40* **Art Nouveau**). With their swirling, daring lines and elaborate friezes, the houses appear both flamboyant and insouciant beside their more stalwart neighbours. The majority can be found in the area south of the Barrière de St-Gilles and to the east of the immense Prison de St-Gilles. Most, sadly, are closed to the public, but one striking exception is architect Victor Horta's own house, the **Musée Horta**, at the heart of the art nouveau area in rue Américaine.

The prison itself is remarkably in keeping with its genteel surrounds, with fairly low walls and bisected by pleasant avenue de la Jonction. At the head of the avenue is the art nouveau

SIGHTS

Flagey. *See p79.*

SIGHTS

, built in 1902 by Jules Brunfaut.
es the **Espace Photographique**
…etype photo gallery.

To the west of the prison extends the easily accessible greenery of the Parc de Forest and Parc Duden: *see pp93-95* **Green Brussels**.

Espace Photographique Contretype

1 avenue de la Jonction (02 538 42 20, www.contretype.org). Tram 81, 91, 92, 97 or bus 54. **Open** 11am-6pm Wed-Fri; 1-6pm Sat, Sun. **Admission** €2.50. **No credit cards**.
Jules Brunfaut built this house in art nouveau style for the industrialist Edouard Hannon, who was also a keen amateur photographer. His photographs are on display, along with works by various photographers in residence. The interior features light, lofty salons and a staircase with a vast fresco by PA Baudouin. Stripped of its original furniture, the house has the echoing impersonality of a grand showpiece studio.

▶ *For more on the city's art galleries, see pp190-193.*

★ Musée Horta

25 rue Américaine (02 543 04 90, www.horta museum.be). Tram 81, 91, 92, 97 or bus 54. **Open** 2-5.30pm daily. **Admission** €7; €3.70 reductions. **No credit cards. Map** p324 D11.
Horta built this house in 1899-1901 as his home and studio. The exterior is plain enough, and is nothing compared to the Hankar-designed house round the corner in rue Defacqz. This external reticence is fairly typical of an architect who was Belgian enough to want to keep his delights hidden away indoors. The interior is astonishingly light, graceful and harmonious. It was clearly designed as a place to live in; there's no attempt to dazzle or disturb. The attention to detail is astonishing, with every functional element, even down to the door handles, designed in the fluid, sensuous architectural style Horta helped to create. The staircase and stairwell are particularly breathtaking: an extravaganza of wrought iron, mirrors and floral designs, topped by a stained-glass canopy. A word of warning: the museum is often crowded and even Horta's wonderful staircase loses its appeal when you have to queue to climb it.

All Guns Blazing

The pilot who took on the Gestapo.

The innocuous-looking apartment building at 453 avenue Louise has a surprisingly dark past. It was here that the occupying Nazi forces of World War II installed the dreaded Gestapo, converting the building into a base for surveillance and a detention centre. The locals knew what it was and what went on in there, but there was little they could do in the face of brutal security. One heroic Belgian changed all that, and brought some much-needed patriotic cheer to the dark days of war.

Jean-Michel de Selys Longchamp fled Belgium after the German troops arrived

in May 1940. He made it safely to England, where he joined up with a Belgian air force squadron attached to the RAF. In January 1943, he took off with another pilot from the Manston airfield in Kent on a mission to strafe German railway movements in north Belgium. With their mission duly accomplished, the planes returned to England – but not Selys Longchamp, who decided to turn and head for Brussels. He had already approached RAF bosses about an idea he had to destroy the Gestapo HQ, but had been given no answer. This, he decided, was his chance to try his luck.

Flying in low over Brussels, he sped towards the building in his Typhoon and set off his guns, destroying great lumps of the façade in a cloud of concrete and glass. As he zoomed up above the building he let the flags of Belgium and Britain fall on to the wreckage before flying back to Manston. His audacious attack killed a top Gestapo officer, while at the same time boosting morale within the Resistance. Selys Longchamp was both demoted and awarded the Distinguished Flying Cross, in recognition of his insubordination and his bravery. Seven months later he was killed in a mission over Ostend, but Longchamp had already entered Brussels lore as the man who took on the Gestapo and won.

Anderlecht
& the West

Head to the suburbs for some quirky surprises.

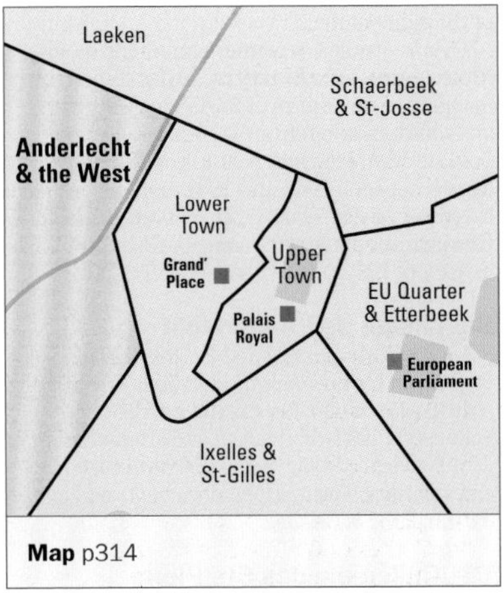

Despite being situated just across the main canal from central Brussels, Anderlecht, Koekelberg, Molenbeek and Jette are unlikely to feature on most visitors' lists of must-see sightseeing spots.

Ex-industrial, largely grey and uninspired for the most part, they are nevertheless home to a couple of appealingly offbeat attractions, including the bizarre Basilica in Koekelberg and the Musée Magritte, set in the artist's former home in Jette.

Another cultural draw, beside the railway yards and factories of the Willebroek Canal in run-down, residential Molenbeek, is **Tour et Taxis** (*see p208*). This stately, turn-of-the-century warehouse and railway sheds complex now houses offices, restaurants and a handful of design shops, and has become one of the city's major events and exhibition spaces.

Laeken

Schaerbeek & St-Josse

Anderlecht & the West

Lower Town

Grand' Place ■   Upper Town

Palais Royal ■   EU Quarter & Etterbeek

■ European Parliament

Ixelles & St-Gilles

Map p314

ANDERLECHT

Métro St-Guidon or Clemenceau, tram 81 or bus 49.

Type the word 'Anderlecht' into an internet search engine and the first entries refer you to RSC Anderlecht, Belgium's biggest football club (*see p216*). The commune appears to have a modest self-image all the same, allowing the **Vanden Stock stadium** in Parc Astrid to be its biggest asset. Match nights bring the football bars that stretch all the way along avenue Théo Verbeek to life.

Most days, though, Anderlecht is sombre. At its Midi end, station developments encroach on what were once grand boulevards of upper middle-class living. Muddled streets of mostly run-down neighbourhoods finally give way to green spaces, punctuated by café-lined squares

such as place de la Vaillance. But then, this is Brussels: even in Anderlecht, surprises abound.

Anderlecht is a rough translation of 'love of Erasmus', after the great humanist who lived here for only five months but whose influence on the Low Countries can still be felt to this day (*see p86* **The Human Touch**). The **Maison d'Erasmus**, where he stayed, is now a quiet sanctuary amid city life, where the atmosphere seems little changed over the centuries.

The majority of sights in Anderlecht are near St-Guidon métro station. Leaving the station, you'll see the beautiful Gothic **Collégiale des Sts Pierre et Guidon**, gracefully aloof from the shopping arcade. Behind it is the 17th-century **Béguinage de l'Anderlecht**, now a museum. The *béguinages* were groups of lay sisterhoods whose members lived in religious communities, unbound by vows. Their charity work was prevalent across the Low Countries.

Back east, the area towards the train station is mostly seedy but still dotted with strange attractions. The local abattoir houses a crazy, tacky **market** (24 rue Ropsy Chaudron, open from 7am Fri, Sat), with anything from plastic mosque alarm clocks to cheap electronics, and mountains of melons and tomatoes. The modern abattoir still manages to shift an abundance of meat. Opposite, the **Brasserie La Paix** (49 rue Ropsy Chaudron, 02 523 09 58) has been serving spectacular Belgian fare since 1888. Nearby, on rue Gheude, is the **Musée Bruxellois de la Gueuze** at the brewery of the same name.

Off rue Emile Carpentier stands the moving **Monument aux Martyrs Juifs**; etched into its side are the names of 23,838 men, women and children taken from the Nazi collection point in Mechelen and sent to concentration camps between 1942 and 1944; not one of those listed survived. Nearby, the **Musée de la Résistance** illustrates some of the secret history of Belgium's World War II experience.

Béguinage de l'Anderlecht

8 rue du Chapelain (02 521 13 83). Métro St-Guidon. **Open** 10am-noon, 2-5pm Tue-Sun. **Admission** €1.50. **No credit cards.**
Founded in 1252, this ancient and atmospheric convent consists of four modest 16th-century houses and a garden. The museum documents and evokes the life of the *béguinage*.

FREE Collégiale des Sts Pierre et Guidon

Place de la Vaillance (02 523 02 20). Métro St-Guidon. **Open** 9am-noon, 2-5pm daily. **Services** 8.45am Mon-Fri; 6pm Fri; 4.30pm, 6pm Sat; 9.30am, 11am, 5pm Sun. **Admission** free.

Founded before the tenth century, the current Collegiate Church is late 15th-century Gothic. Inside, a long altar is illuminated by light filtered through the stained-glass windows; below is one of the oldest Romanesque crypts in Belgium.

Maison d'Erasmus

31 rue de Chapitre (02 521 13 83, www. erasmushouse.museum). Métro St-Guidon. **Open** 10am-6pm Tue-Sun. **Admission** €1.50. **No credit cards.**
The house where Erasmus stayed is a small, well-preserved, red-brick seat of learning set in a shady garden. A museum, it contains first editions of his *In Praise of Folly* and *Adages*, and letters from Charles V and Francis I. There are also portraits of the great man by Dürer and Holbein, and a medal by Cellini. For more on Erasmus's stay here, *see p86* **The Human Touch**.

Musée Bruxellois de la Gueuze

56 rue Gheude (02 521 49 28, www.cantillon.be). Métro Clemenceau or pré-métro Lemonnier. **Open** 8.30am-5pm Mon-Fri; 10am-5pm Sat. Last entry 4pm. **Admission** €5. **No credit cards. Map** p318 A6.
At the Musée Bruxellois de la Gueuze you can enjoy a tasting tour around Brussels' last working brewer of Gueuze, the unusual beer fermented naturally in Anderlecht's gloomy climate. The entrance price includes a glass of beer.

FREE Musée de la Résistance

14 rue van Lint (02 522 40 41). Métro Clemenceau. **Open** 9am-noon, 1-4pm Mon, Tue, Thur, Fri. **Admission** free.
Members of Belgium's resistance put together this striking collection of original documents relating to their struggle in the war years.

Tour et Taxis. *See p83.*

Profile Musée Magritte

Step inside the artist's former home.

Brussels initially appears conventional and conservative. Scratch beneath the surface, however, and you'll find it to be one of the most subversive cities in Europe. One artist embodies this like no other. René Magritte lived and painted for 24 years in the grey, suburban residence at 135 rue Esseghem in Jette. This modest terraced house, today the **Musée Magritte** (*see p86*), became the spiritual home of Belgian surrealism, a more radical branch of the Paris-born movement.

The surprisingly large house was divided into three separate apartments, with René and his wife Georgette renting the ground and attic floors. Visitors can see many elements of the building in his paintings: the blue walls and fireplace from *La Durée Poignardé* – although there's no steam locomotive puffing forth – and the sash windows, glass doors, staircase and other bourgeois elements that Magritte manipulated so effortlessly.

The Magrittes came to a compromise over the colour scheme: Georgette preferred brown for the doors, stairs and panelling, while René insisted on the clashing salmon pink dining room, electric blue lounge and lime green bedroom. René and Georgette led quiet lives; the artist painted some of his masterpieces from his Renoir and Vache periods in a suit and bow tie. Visitors can see original works, documents, letters and photos on the first and second floors, and 17 of the 19 rooms are open to the public.

The Magrittes moved out in 1954, and the building was bought by two Belgians. It was restored between 1993 and 1999 as a permanent homage to a surreally typical *belge*. Make of it what you will: as Magritte said of *Man in the Bowler Hat*, in which a face is obscured by a bird: 'Everything we see hides another thing, we always want to see what is hidden by what we see, but it is impossible. Humans hide secrets too well.'

MORE MAGRITTE Another must-see for admirers of the artist is the glorious new **Magritte Museum** (*see p64*) in the Upper Town, which showcases over 200 of his works.

JETTE & KOEKELBERG

Métro Simonis, tram 19 or bus 49, 89.

The large, anonymous commune of Jette is set
in between the western canal districts and
Laeken (*see p87*). Its very anonymity made
it the perfect home for that most respectable
and bourgeois of surrealists, René Magritte.
The equally anonymous house where he lived
with his wife and muse Georgette between 1930
and 1954 opened as the **Musée Magritte** in
1999, and is an essential stop for anyone with
more than a passing interest in the artist
(*see p85* **Profile**). The Magrittes lived on
the ground floor (although they also used the
garret; the first and second floors were occupied
by others), and it has since been restored to as
authentic a condition as possible.

The tiny border commune of Koekelberg is
home to Brussels' most bizarre and overblown
church: the **Basilique du Sacré Coeur**.

Basilique du Sacré Coeur

*1 parvis de la Basilique (02 425 88 22). Métro
Simonis.* **Open** *Church* winter 10am-5pm daily;
summer 8am-6pm daily. *Dome* winter 10am-4pm
daily; summer 9am-5pm daily. **Admission**
Church free. *Dome* €3. **No credit cards.**
Commissioned by Léopold II in 1905, this vast structure, an extraordinary mix of Gothic and art deco
with a lit-up cherry-coloured crucifix on top, took
seven decades to finish.

★ Musée Magritte

*135 rue Esseghem (02 428 26 26, www.magritte
museum.be). Métro Belgica or tram 51, 94.*
Open 10am-6pm Wed-Sun. **Admission** €7;
€6 reductions. **No credit cards.**
Magritte's house is a fittingly bizarre monument
to the artist. The window and fireplace in the front
room appear in numerous Magritte paintings, but
perhaps the most surprising discovery is the tiny
back room where he executed hundreds of his works.
See also p85 **Profile**.

The Human Touch

The Maison d'Erasmus is a fine tribute to the legendary theologian.

Maison d'Erasmus.

The legendary writer, thinker, theologian
and philosopher Erasmus spent much
of his short life on the move. Born in
Rotterdam in 1469, he worked his way
around Europe, leaving his mark on history
and the minds of men as he went. His
most famous treatise, *In Praise of Folly*,
was written as he headed for England from
Italy, a gift to his friend Thomas More.

At that time, Anderlecht was a small
village of a few hundred people, but was
important as a stopping point for pilgrims
en route to Compostela. Significant
religious buildings included the **Béguinage**
(*see p84*) and the **Collégiale des Sts Pierre
et Guidon** (*see p84*). Around the latter a
number of houses sprang up, and for five
months in 1521 Erasmus occupied one
with his friend Pieter Wychman.

Such was his celebrity status that people
flocked to see where the great Erasmus
lived. After his departure and death in
Basel in 1536, the house became a site of
pilgrimage and homage to a man who stood
for a more human approach to religion.

Considering the history of the region
and the piecemeal wrecking of historical
buildings over the centuries, it's a miracle
that this place of learning has survived.
The house remains in all its simplicity and
is now used as a museum, the **Maison
d'Erasmus** (*see p84*), as well as a study
centre housing rare books and manuscripts.
The house also boasts period furniture,
sculptures and paintings by the Flemish
Primitives. Outside is a herb garden
containing plants Erasmus mentions using
when he was ill, and a 'philosophical
garden' based on his text *The Religious
Banquet*, with sculptures by different artists.
Between them, they offer a restful balance
between the body and the mind. Erasmus
would have approved.

Laeken

A stately royal retreat and a wealth of iconic landmarks.

Laeken stretches over a huge green area some distance north of the centre, divided into a royal estate and residence, and the public leisure complex of Heysel. It seems an unreal, artificial city hovering outside Brussels proper, pieced together by jigsaw designers. Each of its main sights are in themselves worthy of a visit; they just make unlikely neighbours. Here you will find the national stadium, the renovated Atomium, theme parks, a multiplex cinema, the Royal Palace and two Léopoldine follies.

It's easy to reach by métro (get off at Heysel) or, for a more interesting ride, by taking the Nos.18, 23 or 81 trams. The sights are all situated within walking distance of one another.

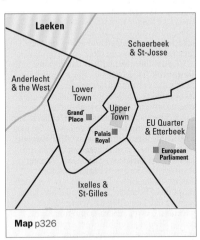

Map p326

EXPLORING THE AREA

Métro Heysel or tram 3, 19.

The **Stade Roi Baudouin** (*see p216*) was previously the Heysel Stadium, where 39 people died in 1985 before the Liverpool vs Juventus European Cup Final, when terrace violence brought about the sudden collapse of a wall. Its cool Bob van Reeth redesign kept the original neo-classical entrance by Joseph van Neck from 1929. Next door is the immense **Parc des Expositions**. Eleven palaces were built here, the first in 1935, to mark a century of Belgian independence. The largest, the Grand Palais built by van Neck, is a classic art deco triangular composition with ever-decreasing pavilions flanking the imposing, four-columned centre building. The halls now house a constant stream of major trade fairs, detailed at www.bruexpo.be.

Directly down the boulevard du Centenaire is the iconic **Atomium**. At 102 metres (335 feet) tall, it never fails to impress by its sheer size and scale; a crystal molecule of metal magnified 165 billion times. Built for the 1958 World Fair – and certainly not meant to last over half a century – it has been

Tour Japonaise.

completely overhauled and buffed up, and gleams with renewed vigour.

Close to the silver balls is the entrance to the **Bruparck** (*see p182*), an offbeat conurbation of family amusements. The complex includes **Kinepolis** (*see p188*), the original multiplex cinema with nearly 30 screens and a capacity of 7,500. There's also **Océade**, a water park with a tropical theme, but by far and away the most irresistibly kitsch attraction is **Mini-Europe**. Here, exact copies of famous landmarks are laid out in a park to a scale of 1:25. Among them are the Houses of Parliament, the Acropolis, the Eiffel Tower and a rather good mock-up of Brussels' own Grand'Place. Kids seem to like launching an Ariane rocket, watching TGV trains rush into tunnels or seeing Vesuvius bubble over. Around it all is the Village, an uninspiring name for an uninspiring set of kit-built gable houses with the usual fast food restaurants and shops.

For something more subtle, more peaceful and more entrenched in real history, walk south to glorious **Parc du Laeken**. Its main centrepiece is the **Château Royal**, the residence of the Belgian royal family. Built in 1782-84 for the Austrian governor-general, it was originally called Schoonberg, but after the arrival of the French in 1794 it lost both its name and family. It lay abandoned until Napoleon decided he'd like it; it was here that he planned the catastrophic invasion of Russia. Eventually, he did a deal with Josephine and swapped Laeken for the Elysée Palace in Paris. Now it is very much a private residence, and unlike the **Palais Royal** in town (*see p67*), is sadly not open to the public. However, the magnificent **Serres Royales** – the Royal Greenhouses – do open at certain times each year. Try to visit at night when they are lit up by spotlights. The tourist information office has details.

Also in the park are a couple of royal follies, whims of King Léopold II after he visited the 1900 Paris Exhibition and saw two oriental buildings he wanted in his own back garden. The **Tour Japonaise** is a five-level red tower that now holds temporary exhibitions, but is interesting enough at any time. Across avenue Jules van Praet, the **Pavillon Chinois** is yet another curiosity offering oriental ceramics.

Ten minutes' walk from the Château Royal is **Notre-Dame de Laeken**, the burial place of Belgium's royals. Viewing is restricted.

★ Atomium
Boulevard du Centenaire (02 475 47 75, www. atomium.be). Métro Heysel or tram 23, 81. **Open** 10am-6pm daily. **Admission** €11; €4-€8 reductions. Combined ticket to Bruparck, see website. **Credit** AmEx, DC, MC, V. **Map** p326 B2.
Designed by André Waterkeyn for the 1958 World Fair, this iconic structure has a classic *Flash Gordon* look about it, giving it a retro appeal for modern times. After years of neglect, dynamic curator Diane Hennebert negotiated a €24 million renovation between the state, Brussels City and the owners to renovate the iconic molecule, which reopened in 2005. Now it has interactive exhibitions, a new visitors' centre and a restaurant at the top.

FREE Notre-Dame de Laeken
Parvis Notre-Dame (02 479 23 62, www. ndlaeken-olvlaken.be). Métro Bockstael or tram 81, 94 or bus 53. **Open** 2-5pm Tue-Sun. **Admission** free. **Map** p326 E3.
Although opening times are restricted, the huge, neo-Gothic exterior, designed by Poelaert in 1851, is worth a wander. Look out for the 13th-century Madonna on the altar. In the cemetery are tombs of important Belgians – including Poelaert himself.

Pavillon Chinois
44 avenue Jules van Praet (02 268 16 08, www.kmkg-mrah.be). Tram 23, 52. **Open** 9.30am-5pm Tue-Fri; 10am-5pm Sat, Sun. **Admission** €4 combined tour with Tour Japonaise. **No credit cards. Map** p326 D1.
Built as a restaurant for Léopold II, then left to its own devices for years, the pavilion is now home to a collection of fine Chinese porcelain.

★ Serres Royales
61 avenue du Parc Royal (02 513 89 40). Métro Heysel. **Open** May. **Admission** €2; free under-18s. **No credit cards. Map** p326 D1.
This sequence of 11 linked greenhouses was built on the orders of Léopold II by Balat and the young Victor Horta in the 1870s. They are soaring edifices, forming an iron and glass cathedral to botany. Léopold moved into one on his deathbed, and other royals have in the past set up writing desks and seating areas in others.

Tour Japonaise
44 avenue Jules van Praet (02 268 16 08, www.kmkg-mrah.be). Tram 23, 52. **Open** 9.30am-5pm Tue-Fri; 10am-5pm Sat, Sun. **Admission** €4 combined tour with Pavillon Chinois. **No credit cards. Map** p326 D1.
This mock pagoda, set around Japanese gardens, houses temporary Japanese exhibitions.

Schaerbeek & St-Josse

Faded grandeur meets urban reinvention.

Once a wooded hunting ground, and later famed for its blossom-laden cherry orchards, Schaerbeek covers a vast swathe of northern Brussels. Before the construction of the Gare du Nord in 1841, the area was a mellow backwater of family-run bakeries and breweries. These days, though, it is a rather gloomy mix of industry and grand avenues, and is home to significant immigrant populations.

It touches on the smaller and poorer commune of St-Josse, which hugs the north-east portion of the Petit Ring and is almost completely North African and Turkish in character. Although neither district has many tourist set pieces, both offer up a distinctly different slice of Brussels life.

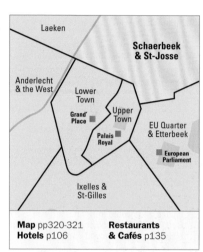

Laeken

Schaerbeek & St-Josse

Anderlecht & the West

Lower Town

Grand' Place

Upper Town

Palais Royal

EU Quarter & Etterbeek

European Parliament

Ixelles & St-Gilles

Map pp320-321   **Restaurants**
Hotels p106   **& Cafés** p135

SCHAERBEEK

Métro Botanique or Gare du Nord, or tram 92, 94.

Schaerbeek was once a bucolic idyll of cherry orchards, but the commune expanded during the latter part of the 19th century and developed with the new Belgian state. At independence in 1830 there were 1,600 people living here; by 1900 there were 65,000, travelling to work in trams rattling down busy boulevards and past grand houses –

GENERAL

St-Josse.

INSIDE TRACK FAMOUS SONS

Celebrated former residents of Schaerbeek include singer Jacques Brel, the late *Spirou* cartoonist Roger Camille, surrealist artist René Magritte and pianist Claude Coppens.

many built in art nouveau style for and by the country's new bourgeoisie.

Such grandeur had faded by the time the prodigal son of Schaerbeek, *chanteur* Jacques Brel, grew up here. A plaque at 138 avenue du Diamant marks the house where he was born. Schaerbeek shaped his eye for everyday detail in his songwriting, but Brel first made it big in town, at the long defunct Rose Noir cabaret in the petite rue des Bouchers. He then found global fame in Paris. His parents moved to Anderlecht, which today has the honour of having a métro station named after him. There is little else in Schaerbeek to commemorate him.

Modern times left Schaerbeek behind. In the area to the west of rue Royale, around the Gare du Nord, drab sex shops are being replaced by Moroccan stores selling halal meat, miniature indoor waterfalls and suitcases. Chaussée de Haecht is the place to find Turkish bakeries, Muslim butchers and cafés filled with Turkish football flags. Without its own métro station, Schaerbeek is a visibly poor neighbourhood – bad street lighting, erratic refuse collection and no glamorous shops – but don't let that deter you from a visit.

Renowned cartoonist François Schuiten, who has lived in Schaerbeek all his life and used its peeling grandeur as inspiration for epic urban comic tales such as his seminal *Brüsel*, has been occupied with renovating the commune's most treasured art nouveau legacy, the **Maison Autrique** (266 chaussée de Haecht,

Relics Reborn

The cultural reclamation of two historic venues.

Schaerbeek and St-Josse may be poorer cousins to other Brussels communes, but they contain a pair of arts complexes vital to the cultural lifeblood of the city.

The most enigmatic is the stately **Halles de Schaerbeek** (*see p92*). Built as a covered market in 1865, the Halles are a monument to the industrial age, a temple of glass and riveted iron. After a fire in 1898, World War I and changes in shopping habits, the building stood empty by the

1920s. The Halles were used as a warehouse, workshops and even a car park until they were finally sold on to a development agency that planned to convert them into housing.

A group of locals led by Jo Dekmine (*see p225* **Meet the Locals**), director of the influential **Théâtre 140** (*see p226*), petitioned for the building to be saved and reconfigured as a cultural centre for the commune and city. It was saved when the

Halles de Schaerbeek.

www.autrique.be), which was Victor Horta's first design commission. It is a typical three-storey Brussels townhouse, known here as an *enfilade*: tall, narrow and four rooms deep. Behind a white stone façade, its sober domesticity is enlivened by characteristic details such as the carved wooden staircase and the swirling mosaics on the ground floor. Persuading the local authorities to buy this 1893 gem, and collaborating with his co-author Benoît Peeters, Schuiten has transformed it into an imaginative exploration of the city's past. The Schuiten and Peeters revamp is half-museum and half-theatrical *mise-en-scène*; visitors can walk through the rooms, from the laundry to the attic, experiencing local life the way it was lived a century ago.

Parallel to rue Royale, chaussée de Haecht is the spine of Schaerbeek, built on a rather grandiose scale with long avenues sweeping down to monumental buildings and churches overlooking the city. Branching off from rue Royale, the royal route leading past the palaces of the Upper Town down to the jaws of the Palais de Justice, chaussée de Haecht links the local landmarks of the churches of Ste-Marie and St-Servais, the Halles de Schaerbeek and the Hôtel Communal on place Colignon.

Place Colignon was constructed around the Hôtel, its houses equally grand with gables, turrets and flagpoles. The Hôtel itself was inaugurated in 1887 by Léopold II. Damaged by fire at the beginning of the 20th century, the Flemish Renaissance-style building is made

ministry of the French community took it on and raised the money to start renovations, completed in 1997. Now the Grande Halle can seat 2,000 people, while the Petite Halle – once the fish market – is a space for smaller concerts and theatre. The original cellars accommodate the bar and small performance spaces. Of course, the Halles are big enough to hold major rock concerts and touring operas, but not to the detriment of its use as a place for kids, circus workshops, local Arabic-speaking groups or the international dance and theatre companies who represent the commune's neighbourhoods.

The French community also opened another cultural door in nearby St-Josse, where the greenhouses of Brussels' original botanical gardens were in need of nurture. Laid out in 1829, the gardens were bought by the state in 1870 for furthering conservation and an understanding of plant life. In the 1930s, the trans-Brussels rail link uprooted the gardens and they were moved out of the city. The grounds and grand buildings were left derelict until the ministry of the French community acquired them in 1978, with the intention of establishing a cultural centre.

In 1984, the Rotonde and the Orangerie, relics of a botanical past, were transformed into **Le Botanique** (*see p92*), a venue for concerts, film festivals, theatre and literary evenings. The stage and seating in the Rotonde maintains its circular aspect, making it one of the city's most unusual and vibrant performance spaces.

Le Botanique.

from red brick, with numerous towers and windows. Down rue Royale Ste-Marie from the square is the large, beautiful and decaying church of **St-Servais**. It holds services in Spanish and Italian, and has a commanding view over avenue Louis Bertrand. This formerly grand boulevard leads east to pretty **Parc Josaphat**. Here you'll find ponds, an animal reserve, a sculpture museum, sporting facilities and free concerts on summer Sundays.

Close to St-Servais stand the **Halles de Schaerbeek**. A rare example of 19th-century industrial architecture, the Halles are another example of a Brussels renovation success story. *See p204, p228* and *p90* **Relics Reborn**. Beside the Halles, and dominating the northern end of the rue Royale, the church of **Ste-Marie** is a neo-Byzantine mosque-like building, arched and curvaceous, with an octagonal dome.

It marks the border with the commune of St-Josse, as does the **Gare du Nord**, once the centre of the red-light district.

ST-JOSSE

Métro Madou or Botanique; or bus 29, 63.

Almost completely North African and Turkish in character, vibrant St-Josse is full of bustling fruit shops and intimate little ethnic eateries. Situated near the Petit Ring, its most popular attractions are a quick and easy hop from the city centre, in particular the arty **Le Botanique** (*see p204, p177* and *p90* **Relics Reborn**) – an inspired mixture of neo-classicism, glass and iron, built in 1826. Formerly the city's greenhouse, it is now the cultural centre for the francophone community.

Meet the Locals The Pioneering Priest

How one man brought mass to the métro.

Softly spoken and dressed in a chunky grey jumper, Father Christian Haudegard doesn't look like your average priest. Nor is his chapel your typical place of worship.

Commuters rushing through the Madou métro subway might not even notice the tiny chapel occupying a dingy shopfront next to a discount clothing store.

Father Christian.

Lunchtime passers-by, though, might be lured by sacral singing emerging from La Dame de l'Unité. Father Christian has never ridden the Brussels métro, but in 1967, while walking through the station, he saw that the outlet was up for rent. He paid up and opened it as a chapel, without support from the Church, offering a traditional apostolic service funded solely from donations. It turned out to be an astute move. Recently, in Istanbul, he saw that someone had opened a mini-mosque in a station there and proudly displayed a poster of him inside, the pioneering *Père* of métro religion. He even runs another chapel, Ste-Rita, at nearby Rogier métro.

Father Christian has worked in a factory all his life and only comes in to lead the daily 12.30pm mass; retired Ursuline nun Sister Christine volunteers when he's not around. Often both chapels are deserted, but the doors are left open for the faithful to pop in and light a candle. Father Christian is dismayed that he recently had to install iron bars and close early. 'For my first 20 years here nothing disappeared. Now they take flowers, paintings, everything.'

The location may be highly unusual, but the chapels retain a solemn atmosphere. At one Friday mass at Ste-Rita only five middle-aged women turned up, all Belgian African, but Father Christian says it's always packed on Thursdays. 'That's the day of our patron Saint Rita, the patron of lost causes, illness and domestic abuse.'

Green Brussels

Head south for leafy surrounds and bucolic villages.

Beyond Ixelles and St-Gilles spreads a vast swathe of greenery. Not too long ago it was all the Forêt de Soignes, the hunting ground of the Dukes of Brabant. In the 18th and 19th centuries its bounds decreased considerably, and over 20,000 oaks were felled on the orders of Napoleon to build the Boulogne flotilla.

Nearer to town, the forest is divided between the leafy southern and eastern communes. In Forest and Uccle, green patches such as the Parc de Forest and Parc Duden were set aside for urban use in the 19th century. At the same time, immediately south of Ixelles, the forest's northern tip was landscaped as a leisure park and christened Bois de la Cambre. Closed to cars on Sundays, it's also the haunt of joggers, cyclists and in-line skaters. To the south-east are various villages that make for fine afternoons out, either by virtue of their bucolic setting (such as Watermael-Boitsfort or Genval) or because of a notable cultural attraction such as the Musée Royal de l'Afrique Centrale in Tervuren.

SIGHTS

FOREST & UCCLE

The once-elegant but now rather ramshackle Parc de Forest and Parc Duden lead you from the southern edge of St-Gilles into Forest, where the houses are notably less elegant and the shops notably cheaper. Further south stretch the sedate, suburban streets of Brussels' largest commune, Uccle, a quaint area that is filling up fast with nouveaux riches eager for green surrounds close to town. Cutting right through Uccle, the lengthy chaussée d'Alsemberg is dotted with terrace bars such as Ici le Bô-Bar (02 343 43 03, www.icile bobar.be), which attract the in-crowd.

The house at 41 avenue Léo Errera was built in 1928 for David van Buuren, a Dutch banker enamoured of the art deco style. Opened as the **Musée David et Alice van Buuren**, it combines art, architecture and landscaping to stunning effect. Beyond the museum extends plenty of verdant greenery – perhaps the most charming example being the expansive Parc de Wolvendael, owned by successive royals through the centuries.

Musée David et Alice van Buuren
41 avenue Léo Errera (02 343 48 51, www.museumvanbuuren.com). Tram 3, 23, 24 or bus 38, 60. **Open** *Museum & garden* 2-5.30pm Mon, Wed-Sun. **Admission** *Museum* €10; €5-€8 reductions. *Garden* €5. **No credit cards**.
Every object here – even the custom-made piano – conforms to the highly polished lines of the art deco movement favoured by its pre-war owner, David van Buuren. His large art collection, spanning five centuries, is remarkable; there is a version of Bruegel's *Landscape with the Fall of Icarus*, as well as works by Ensor, Wouters and Van de Woestyne (a friend of the Van Buurens), plus a Braque, and a Van Gogh charcoal and watercolour sketch of *The Potato Eaters*. A framed letter from David Ben Gurion shows the Van Buurens' dedication to the Zionist cause. Outside, the garden is laid out in a maze that was designed by Belgian landscape architect René Pechère.

WATERMAEL-BOITSFORT

South-east of Ixelles, Boitsfort – or Watermael-Boitsfort (www.watermael-boitsfort.be), to give

Ticket to Tervuren

Hop on a tram to the countryside.

The city's best tram ride, the No.44, emerges from the dark of Montgomery métro terminus to hit the daylight and wind its way towards the picturesque village of Tervuren, ten kilometres east of town. If you're riding it to the end of the line, specify this when you buy your ticket.

It's best to sit on the right-hand side for the finest views as the tram emerges into wide, tree-lined avenue de Tervuren and passes the impressive Palais Stoclet at No.281. Just past it, you'll see the lovely hills and lakes of Parc de Woluwe, a mercifully natural and wild green space. Directly opposite the park is the **Musée du Transport Urbain Bruxellois** (*see below right*), packed with restored trams and memorabilia; en route you'll also be able to glimpse grand embassy houses and consulate buildings through the trees.

The tram then starts to pass through the Forêt de Soignes. There's a distinct change of atmosphere and mood as the city begins to drop away – quite extraordinary, considering you're so close to a major

SIGHTS

it its official title – makes a fine half-day detour. With 24,000 inhabitants, W-B hits the spot between city and country, a bustling suburb of Brussels half-covered by the Forêt de Soignes. Expats love the village feel, large houses and the huge International School here. Watermael and Boitsfort were entirely separate entities until Napoleon combined them by imperial decree in 1811. They still have separate railway stations, Watermael's a pretty little design from 1844.

Watermael-Boitsfort's three main squares are Bischofsheim, Gilson and Wiener, a good place to get off the No.94 tram from town. Wiener's Sunday morning market provides the focus for village life, with spice stalls, authentic Spanish food, Thai goodies and a farm dairy selling lumps of cheese and fresh milk and cream.

Boitsfort is known for its ponds and sculpture gardens. In 1922, two residential areas were selected to become showcases of floral urban living. Le Logis, centred around the Trois Tilleuls area with streets named after birds, is laid out in the English style. Cottages have green doors and shutters, with hedges and cherry trees in their gardens. Le Floréal is on the other side of the forest, and a short taxi ride away, but is another charming

example of model city living. The streets here are named after flowers, and the similarly styled houses have a dominant yellow theme. Other buildings of architectural note are the Maison Haute and the Maison Communale, both on place Gilson, the administrative offices for the commune. The striking church of St-Hubert (Jagersveld 6, 02 672 23 95) has a tall, cathedral-like spire and nave, which rather dominate the landscape.

Up in Watermael, the attractive little church of St-Clément (50 rue du Loutrier, 02 672 52 29) has a tower dating from the tenth century. From here it's only a short walk to café-lined place Keym, the renovated central square.

AVENUE DE TERVUREN

Tervuren is an old Flemish municipality bordering Boitsfort deep in the Forêt de Soignes, whose link with Brussels was established by Léopold II. Having found a suitable venue to show off his ill-gotten gains from the Congo – on the site of Charles of Lorraine's old palace in Tervuren – Léopold II ordered the construction of a ten-kilometre avenue, running from his grand monuments in the Parc du Cinquantenaire to what is now the **Musée Royal de l'Afrique Centrale**. It's capital. The beech forest once served as the hunting grounds of the Dukes of Brabant and has been reduced by two-thirds since its heyday, but it remains an impressive sight.

When you arrive at the Quatre Bras stop, you'll see the outer Brussels ring road. This is technically the end of the Brussels region and you're about to enter into Flanders (remember to buy a full single ticket for this journey, as métro tickets are valid for Brussels only). It was at Quatre Bras that the Hussar regiment met Napoleon's troops in 1815 and fled right back into town.

The carriages trundle on through ever more dense forest, where the little tram stops are like country halts. As the tram finally circles into the Tervuren terminus, whole families of rabbits sit staring defiantly before darting away for safety. All of a sudden you find yourself in the countryside, and everything is in Flemish. From here it's only a short walk to the **Musée Royal de l'Afrique Centrale** (*see below*), diagonally opposite.

Palais Stoclet.

diagonally opposite the terminus of the No.44 tram (*see above* **Ticket to Tervuren**) from the Montgomery transport hub back in town; the quaint **Musée du Transport Urbain Bruxellois** also stands along the route.

Brussels' most controversial museum houses the world's largest collection of African ethnography. The building itself – built between 1904 and 1910 – was inspired by Versailles and the Petit Palais in Paris. Surrounding it are the grounds of a previous royal palace, which still contain the remains of 18th-century stables and the Renaissance Chapelle St-Hubert. Beyond is the rambling Parc de Tervuren, full of canals, woodlands and a lake, ideal for picnics and much less formal than the inner-city parks.

Musée Royal de l'Afrique Centrale

13 chaussée de Louvain, Tervuren (02 769 52 11, www.africamuseum.be). Tram 44. **Open** 10am-5pm Tue-Fri; 10am-6pm Sat, Sun. **Admission** €4; €1.50-€3 reductions. Free after 1pm 1st Wed of mth. **No credit cards**.
As well as major ethnological and zoological collections, the museum is home to the archives of Henry Morton Stanley, the explorer commissioned by Léopold II to help found his despotic empire in the Congo. Sadly, some 95 per cent of the collection remains stored away from the eyes of the public. This sorry state of affairs is loaded with historical baggage, and successive governments and funding cuts means the museum has hardly changed since the current permanent exhibition was established in the 1960s, a time when the European 'look what we got' view of the colonies was rather different from today's. It's a state of affairs that museum director Guido Gryseels is committed to putting right, and bringing the museum's message and image up to date is the aim of a major overhaul, originally scheduled for completion in time for the museum's centenary celebration in 2010. However, the design only received approval by all parties in spring 2010. After four years of delicate negotiation the work can begin; the museum says it will stay open throughout.

Musée du Transport Urbain Bruxellois

364 avenue de Tervuren, Woluwe-St-Pierre (02 515 31 08, www.trammuseumbrussels.be). Tram 39, 44. **Open** 1-7pm Sat, Sun, public holidays. **Admission** €5. **No credit cards**.
The Brussels Transport Museum houses a collection of beautifully restored old trams and trolleybuses dating as far back as 1869. A vintage tram makes a regular journey from Parc du Cinquantenaire to Tervuren; tickets cost €8, which includes entrance to the museum itself.

/orld Class

ect places to stay, eat and explore.

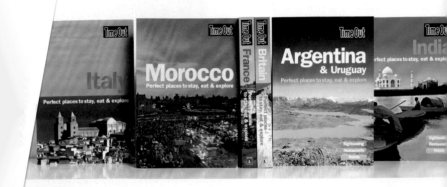

TIME OUT GUIDES
WRITTEN BY
LOCAL EXPERTS
visit timeout.com/shop

Chez Moeder Lambic. *See p151*.

tels

...weekend bargain in a city awash with business beds.

...has many more hotels than most other
...ts size. This is largely because of the
...all the institutions that service it, along
...e fact that multinationals set up base here
...ose to the action.

...s means that significant numbers of visitors
...pense accounts come to the three- to five-star
...ory hotels and rates are usually geared to
... So you'll find the usual international chains,
... as Novotel, Hilton, Marriott and Sheraton,
... a scattering of charming independents, like
Plaza and **Métropole**, all trying to attract the
spenders. This is ironically advantageous for the leisure traveller as hotels
...p their rates considerably at weekends and in the summer months to avoid
...ng empty. It's worth doing some research – availability and prices change
... a daily basis – and experimenting with some of the quirkier independents;
...e **Noga**, **Hotel Orts** and **Welcome**, for example.

PRICES & CLASSIFICATION

In Belgium, hotel stars are awarded according
to the quantity and type of services a hotel
offers, rather than the innate quality of the
property. As a result, a nondescript hotel with
a slew of services will have more stars than one
with character that doesn't see the need for
trouser presses and 24-hour room service.

We have classified hotels according to their
location, then by their rack rate price for a
standard double room: **Deluxe** (€250 or
over), **Expensive** (€150-€249), **Moderate**
(€90-€149) and **Budget** (under €90). In
addition, we have listed the best B&Bs and
hostels. Most establishments can easily cope
with your enquiries in English.

Rooms tend to be of a decent size, but can
vary dramatically, not only between hotels but
also within the properties themselves. For the
many hotels created out of townhouses, the
rooms found inside are usually more compact,
although their high ceilings give an impression
of space and period details often make up for
the lack of elbow room.

All prices quoted for the hotels below apply
to rooms with a toilet and a shower or bath and
include breakfast, unless otherwise stated.
Some of the cheaper hotels listed often offer
communal washing facilities, rather than en
suite bathrooms, so be sure to check when
booking your stay.

BOOKING

Resotel (02 779 39 39, www.belgium
hospitality.com, call centre open 8.30am-6pm
Mon-Fri) is a free booking service for hotels in
Belgium. The service negotiates rates with the
hotels and can offer up to 50 per cent off the
rack rates. For UK travellers, a full list of hotels
in Brussels is available from the **Belgian
Tourism brochure line** (0800 954 5245).

THE BEST HOTEL BARS

Le Dixseptième
Order a cognac, settle back and believe
you're in another age. *See p101.*

Manos Premier
The Kolya Lounge's sweeping terrace
is the perfect spot for summer drinking.
See p111.

Métropole
The grande dame of Brussels cafés.
See right.

GRAND'PLACE & AROUND
Deluxe

★ Hotel Amigo

1-3 rue de l'Amigo, 1000 Brussels (02 547 47 47, www.hotelamigo.com). Métro Gare Centrale or pré-métro Bourse. **Rates** €660. Breakfast €30. **Credit** AmEx, DC, MC, V. **Map** p315 C5 **①**

The height of luxury, steeped in history and decked out *à la mode*, the Amigo accommodates pop stars and politicians alike. Strange, then, that it started life as a prison – according to the city records from 1522. Although it has been razed to the ground twice since, the hotel's polished flagstones date from the middle of the last millennium. Equally impressive are the beautiful 18th-century Aubusson tapestries and paintings of the Flemish and Italian schools. The rest, however, is wonderfully contemporary, thanks to a €15-million refurbishment when the Rocco Forte group took over in 2000. Sir Rocco's sister, designer Olga Polizzi, created 155 elegant rooms and 19 suites, using the finest linens and leathers, embellishing with little touches of Belgium – an image of Tintin here, a Magritte print there. Nothing, however, reaches the heights of the Blaton Suite, named after the Belgian family who owned the hotel from 1957 to 2000. Larger than most one-bedroom flats in central London, it boasts its own kitchen, dining room, living room and a huge terrace with views over the rooftops from the Amigo's vantage point right by the Town Hall.

Bar. Business centre. Concierge. Disabled-adapted rooms. Gym. Internet (wireless). No-smoking rooms. Parking. Restaurant. Room service. TV.

Métropole

31 place de Brouckère, 1000 Brussels (02 217 23 00, www.metropolehotel.com). Métro/pré-métro De Brouckère. **Rates** €250. **Credit** AmEx, DC, MC, V. **Map** p315 D3 **②**

The Métropole deserves a mention simply because it is the grande dame of the Brussels hotel scene (it opened in 1895) and displays the most stunning architecture in its public areas, including its renowned café (*see p139*). The French Renaissance main entrance leads into an Empire-style reception hall, with gilt flourishes, columns and stained-glass windows. An original cage lift conveys guests up to rooms in the main building, which are disappointing by comparison and lack the luxury touches of other top hotels. The 1925 extension at the back of the building has some nice art deco fittings. *Photo p100.*

Bar. Business centre. Concierge. Internet (wireless). No-smoking rooms. Restaurant. Room service. TV.

Le Plaza

118 boulevard Adolphe Max, 1000 Brussels (02 278 01 00, www.leplaza-brussels.be). Métro/pré-métro Rogier or De Brouckère.

Hotel Amigo.

CONSUME

Métropole. *See p99.*

Rates €250. Breakfast €20. **Credit** AmEx, DC, MC, V. **Map** p317 D2 ➌
Le Plaza, like the Métropole, is an independent hotel owned by a well-known Belgian family. Dating from 1930, the building was the headquarters of the Nazis and later the Allied Forces in the war, so the (now listed) structure was largely spared the bombing. The winter garden, which did suffer, was rebuilt and now houses the restaurant. The rest of the building, with original fittings (amethyst crystal chandeliers, Gobelins tapestry, marble bas-reliefs), has been restored to its former glory. The sumptuous rooms are decorated in shades of cream, beige and ochre, and an ornate Moorish-style theatre is used as a function room. The only drawback is the surroundings – the boulevard has more than its fair share of sex shops.
Bar. Business centre. Concierge. Gym. Internet (wireless). No-smoking rooms. Parking. Restaurant. Room service. TV.

Radisson SAS Royal Hotel
47 rue du Fossé aux Loups, 1000 Brussels (02 219 28 28, www.royal.brussels.radisson sas.com). Métro/pré-métro De Brouckère. **Rates** €250. **Credit** AmEx, DC, MC, V. **Map** p315 D4 ➍
Behind the elaborate art deco façade of the Radisson SAS lies a truly top-class business hotel with good leisure facilities and a well-deserved reputation for serving great food. Choose from four different styles of room (Maritime, Oriental, At Home and Business Class); all come with luxury fittings, wireless internet access and tea/coffee-making facilities, but lovely little flourishes set each style apart – opt for a Maritime room if you prefer wooden rather than carpeted floors, for instance. You can indulge yourself at the fitness centre or at the Bar Dessiné, with Belgian cartoons on the walls and a superb selection of malt whiskies behind the bar. The hotel's executive chef is Yves Mattagne, who has earned two Michelin stars for the in-house Sea Grill (*see p119*), so expect to eat well, even if you have to pay handsomely for the pleasure.
Bar. Business centre. Concierge. Disabled-adapted rooms. Gym. Internet (wireless). No-smoking rooms. Parking. Restaurant. Room service. TV.

Expensive

Atlanta
7 boulevard Adolphe Max, 1000 Brussels (02 217 01 20, www.nh-hotels.com). Métro/ pré-métro De Brouckère. **Rates** €199. Breakfast €22. **Credit** AmEx, DC, MC, V. **Map** p315 D3 ➎
The Spanish NH Hoteles chain has been making huge inroads into Brussels and, at the last count, had five properties in the city. The Atlanta is its flagship. Housed in an elegant early 20th-century building, the

hotel boasts modern, bright and cheerful decor, thanks to the Mediterranean influence. A terrace attached to the breakfast room offers great rooftop views, a real bonus in summer. The highlight, though, of any stay at an NH hotel is the excellent attention to detail: for example, you can choose the type of pillow you want.
Bar. Business centre. Concierge. Disabled-adapted rooms. Gym. Internet (wireless). No-smoking rooms. Parking. Restaurant. Room service. TV.

★ Le Dixseptième
25 rue de la Madeleine, 1000 Brussels (02 517 17 17, www.ledixseptieme.be). Métro Gare Centrale. **Rates** €200. **Credit** AmEx, DC, MC, V. **Map** p315 D5 ➏
Le Dixseptième is a real gem: a boutique hotel with just 24 individual rooms in a great location not far from the Grand'Place. Popular with business people looking for a hotel with a more personal touch, the 17th is also an ideal destination for a romantic weekend in Brussels. Twelve of the rooms are housed in the 17th-century building that was the home of the Spanish ambassador, while the other 12, equally spacious but more prosaic, are in a new block to the back. There's a bar and a lovely period salon overlooking an inner courtyard where breakfast is served. Service is impeccable.
Bar. Business centre. Concierge. Internet (wireless). Room service. TV.

Dominican
9 rue Léopold, 1000 Brussels (02 203 08 08, www.thedominican.be). Métro Gare Centrale. **Rates** €150. Breakfast €27. **Credit** AmEx, DC, MC, V. **Map** p315 D4 ➐
Opened back in 2007 on the site of a 15th-century Dominican abbey, the Dominican's decor mixes high ceilings, original stone floors and tranquil cloisters. A private courtyard, which most rooms face, enhances the calm atmosphere. The bright, airy lobby and lounge contrast with the bedrooms, decorated in more muted tones. All rooms incorporate a small seating area, espresso machine and pillow menu. The buffet breakfast can be taken in the courtyard or in cosy velvet chairs in the Grand Lounge restaurant. *Photo p102.*
Bar. Business centre. Concierge. Disabled-adapted rooms. Gym. Internet (wireless). No-smoking rooms. Restaurant. Room service. TV.

Floris Arlequin Grand'Place
17-19 rue de la Fourche, 1000 Brussels (02 514 16 15, www.florishotels.com). Métro/pré-métro De Brouckère. **Rates** €195. **Credit** AmEx, DC, MC, V. **Map** p315 D4 ➑
The contrast between this modern, 92-room hotel and the little cobbled street on which it stands could not be more stark. The rooms vary in size (but are uniformly comfortable, bright and clean), and three of them, as well as the top-floor breakfast room, offer

panoramic views over the rooftops. Internet rooms are only available on weekdays.
Bar. Business centre. Concierge. Internet (wireless). Room service. TV.

Saint-Michel

15 Grand'Place, 1000 Brussels (02 511 09 56, http://atgp.be). Métro Gare Centrale or pré-métro Bourse. **Rates** €150. **Credit** AmEx, DC, MC, V. **Map** p315 C5/D5 ❾
If you want to wake up and look out over one of Europe's most beautiful squares, then stay at the Saint-Michel. However, be warned that there's no double glazing, so if there's an event on in the Grand'Place you might not get the earliest of nights. Situated behind a picturesque façade on the south-eastern side of the square, the building (dating to 1698) belonged to the Tanners' Guild before becoming a private residence after the French Revolution, and then a hotel.
Bar. Internet (wireless). Restaurant. Room service. TV.

Budget

A la Grande Cloche

10-12 place Rouppe, 1000 Brussels (02 512 61 40, www.hotelgrandecloche.com). Pré-métro Anneessens. **Rates** €79. **Credit** AmEx, MC, V. **Map** p315 B5 ❿

This family-run hotel is located in a quiet square equidistant from Midi station and the Grand'Place. The rooms are clean and fairly comfy. Each one has a queen bed: roomy for one, but a bit of a squeeze for two (the twin rooms avoid the problem and are usually spacious). The cheaper rooms tend to have a small shower box.
Internet. TV.

STE-CATHERINE & ST-GERY

Deluxe

Atlas

30 rue du Vieux Marché aux Grains, 1000 Brussels (02 502 60 06, www.atlas-hotel.be). Pré-métro Bourse or métro Ste-Catherine. **Rates** €250. **Credit** AmEx, DC, MC, V. **Map** p315 B4 ⓫
Behind the 18th-century façade of the Atlas lie acceptable rooms that teeter on the edge of sterility. Location scores highly here over style. It's near the trendy shops of upmarket rue Antoine Dansaert and the throbbing nightlife hub of St-Géry – reserve one of the five four-person split-level duplex rooms if you're making a party of it. For an early night, book a back room overlooking the courtyard. A complimentary drink is served on weekday evenings.
Business centre. Concierge. Disabled-adapted rooms. Internet (wireless). Parking. Room service. TV.

Dominican. *See p101.*

Marriott

1-7 rue Auguste Orts, 1000 Brussels (02 516 90 90, www.marriott.com/brudt). Pré-métro Bourse. **Rates** €275. Breakfast €25. **Credit** AmEx, DC, MC, V. **Map** p315 C4 ⓬

While the façade of the Marriott is a beautifully restored remnant of the 19th century, most of the interior is completely new, creating a nice blend of original and modern. As you'd expect from an American chain, the rooms come fitted to a high standard, and include large beds and wireless internet access. The room decor is bright, but the bathrooms – in muted shades of beige – are a tad more relaxing. A nice touch is the free tea and coffee served in the ground-floor bar before 9.30am. *Bar. Business centre. Concierge. Disabled-adapted rooms. Gym. Internet (wireless). No-smoking rooms. Parking. Restaurant. Room service. TV.*

Expensive

George V

23 rue 't Kint, 1000 Brussels (02 513 50 93, www.hotelgeorge5.be). Pré-métro Bourse. **Rates** €160. **Credit** AmEx, DC, MC, V. **Map** p316 B4 ⓭

The George was completely renovated when new owners moved in during 2009. The rooms have been decorated to a much higher standard than before, though some do remain on the small side. That said,

the hotel is in a quiet location, close to the area's fashionable shops and bars, and the option of triples makes it an attractive deal for weekend parties. *Bar. Internet (wireless). TV.*

Moderate

Hotel Orts

38-40 rue Auguste Orts, 1000 Brussels (02 517 07 07, www.hotelorts.com). Pré-métro Bourse. **Rates** €130. **Credit** AmEx, DC, MC, V. **Map** p315 C4 ⓮

The Orts opened its doors in 2006, injecting some style into this previously lacklustre area. The architecture is grand fin-de-siècle Brussels and looks particularly stunning at night with its theatrical lighting. The individually colour-themed rooms are spacious and finished to a high standard. The corner rooms are more modest in size but benefit from a double vista. It's a perfect location for sightseeing and nightlife – its street-level café (*see p121*) has made a mark already. Weekend deals can be up to 50% less than standard rates. *Photo p104.* *Bar. Internet (wireless). TV.*

Noga

38 rue du Béguinage, 1000 Brussels (02 218 67 63, www.nogahotel.com). Métro Ste-Catherine. **Rates** €135. **Credit** AmEx, DC, MC, V. **Map** p316 C3 ⓯

Hotel Orts. *See p103.*

Noga means star in Hebrew and this hotel, located on a charming and tranquil street in Ste-Catherine, lives up to its name. The atmosphere is friendly and delightfully kitsch, with nautical-themed knick-knacks in the airy public areas jostling for space with pictures of royals and assorted bric-a-brac. The rooms, which have showers but no baths, are a tad more restrained, but each is individual in its design fittings. That said, you can pretty much guarantee they'll be bright, spacious and comfy. *Photo p107. Bar. Internet (wireless). TV.*

Welcome

23 quai au Bois à Brûler, 1000 Brussels (02 219 95 46, www.hotelwelcome.com). Métro Ste-Catherine. **Rates** €135. **Credit** AmEx, DC, MC, V. **Map** p315 C3 ⑯

The typical 19th-century façade of the Welcome belies the guest rooms inside: each one is unique and has been decorated with genuine antiques and arte-facts to represent a different destination, among them Bali, India, Japan and Morocco. Other options include the Tibet room, which has a small terrace and is decorated in dramatic shades of red and black, or the Jules Verne room, which follows a round-the-world theme and boasts a large balcony. The exotic interior, paired with the friendliness of the owners, the Smeesters, make this a great spot.
Bar. Internet (wireless). No-smoking rooms. Parking. Room service. TV.

THE MAROLLES & GARE DU MIDI
Moderate

Agenda Midi

11 boulevard Jamar, 1060 Brussels (02 520 00 10, www.hotel-agenda.com). Métro/pré-metro Gare du Midi. **Rates** €140. **Credit** AmEx, DC, MC, V. **Map** p318 A7 ⑰

Most people wouldn't stay in the insalubrious area around the Gare du Midi out of choice, but if you find yourself forced to seek a bed for the night because you've missed the last Eurostar to London, you could do a lot worse than the Agenda Midi. With a welcoming bright yellow façade, it's not hard to find, and its rooms, though neither huge nor spectacular, are decorated with warm Mediterranean colours and have mosaic-tiled bathrooms. The town centre is easily reached by pré-métro – or even on foot, if you're feeling energetic.
Internet (wireless). No-smoking rooms. TV.

Budget

Galia

15-16 place du Jeu de Balle, 1000 Brussels (02 502 42 43, www.hotelgalia.com). Métro/pré-métro Porte de Hal or Gare du Midi. **Rates** €80. **Credit** AmEx, DC, MC, V. **Map** p318 B7 ⑬

The Galia is a simple, family-run hotel offering good-value accommodation overlooking the square where the flea market is held, making it the ideal place for bargain hunters to stay. The hotel is decorated with images of Belgian comic strips and the cheerful rooms are basic but clean and pleasant, with fairly large triples and quads available. The brighter front rooms are triple-glazed to block out the sound of the market and surrounding bars. An extension pro-gramme brought the total number of rooms to 40 and also includes a new brasserie.
Bar. Internet (wireless). No-smoking rooms. Restaurant. TV.

UPPER TOWN
Deluxe

Eurostars Sablon

2-8 rue de la Paille, 1000 Brussels (02 513 60 40, www.eurostarssablon.com). Tram 92, 93, 94 or bus 95. **Rates** €250. **Credit** AmEx, DC, MC, V. **Map** p315 D6 ⑲

In the heart of the Sablon antiques area and only five minutes' walk from the Grand'Place, this intimate hotel of just 28 rooms and four suites is tucked away on a quiet cobbled street. Don't be put off by the modern façade – once inside you'll find a beautiful boutique hotel with elegant rooms. There's also a sauna in the basement.
Bar. Business centre. Concierge. Internet (wireless). No-smoking rooms. Room service. TV.

Stanhope Hotel

9 rue du Commerce, 1000 Brussels (02 506 91 11, www.thonhotels.be/stanhope). Métro Trône. **Rates** €350. Breakfast €25. **Credit** AmEx, DC, MC, V. **Map** p319 F6 ⑳

The Stanhope has almost doubled in size in recent years, but that has not changed the calm and inti-mate atmosphere of the hotel. Book one of the origi-nal rooms, carved out of a row of elegant townhouses, if you want a stay that evokes an idealised 19th-century English country home. But check into a new room if you prefer antique-style furnishings, but also want modern wooden floors and high-tech bathroom facilities. Check the excellent internet rates.

INSIDE TRACK SLEEP WELL

If it's peace and quiet you're after, do a little research before booking a central hotel, particularly in the Lower Town. That fantastic view of the Grand'Place or the buzz of the lively streets of Ixelles won't necessarily quieten down once you do. It's not just voices, Belgian drivers are notoriously honky. Reserve a room at the back or at least check for double glazing.

CONSUME

Bar. Business centre. Concierge. Disabled-adapted rooms. Gym. Internet (wireless). No-smoking rooms. Parking. Restaurant. Room service. TV.

Moderate

Du Congrès

42-44 rue du Congrès, 1000 Brussels (02 217 18 90, www.hotelducongres.be). Métro Madou. **Rates** €130. **Credit** AmEx, DC, MC, V. **Map** p317 F4 ㉑

The four elegant townhouses that constitute the Du Congrès have been beautifully renovated to create a sleek, modern hotel with original fin-de-siècle features. Some rooms have high ceilings, a stunning fireplace and original cornicing, with a simple modern bathroom en suite. Others may not include as many authentic features, but what they lack in detail they make up for in space and/or tranquillity. This is particularly true of those overlooking or opening on to the back garden and split-level terraces, where residents can breakfast in summer. Guests at the one-star sister hostel Madou (45 rue du Congrès, 02 217 18 90) opposite can use the facilities here. Nearby, the two-star Sabina (78 rue du Nord, 02 218 26 37, www.hotelsabina.be) is also in the same family.

Bar. Business centre. Internet (wireless). TV.

NH Hotel du Grand Sablon

2 rue Bodenbroek, 1000 Brussels (02 518 11 00, www.nh-hotels.com). Tram 92, 93, 94 or bus 95. **Rates** €120. **Credit** AmEx, DC, MC, V. **Map** p315 D6 ㉒

Antiques hunters will enjoy a stay at the NH, on pretty place du Grand Sablon, site of the weekly antiques market. A great location in a handsome building at great rates.

Bar. Business centre. Concierge. Disabled-adapted rooms. Internet (wireless). No-smoking rooms. Parking. Restaurant. Room service. TV.

PLACE ROGIER & ST-JOSSE

Deluxe

★ Crowne Plaza Brussels City Centre – Le Palace

3 rue Gineste, 1210 Brussels (02 203 62 00, www.crowneplaza.com). Métro/pré-métro Rogier. **Rates** €350. Breakfast €25. **Credit** AmEx, DC, MC, V. **Map** p317 E2 ㉓

The Crowne Plaza dates back to 1908 and is one of Brussels' hotel landmarks. Major refurbishment has seen the faded 1930s updates replaced with an art nouveau look, all lines and curves, in keeping with the building's age. There's no stinting on modernity, though, with all the comforts you'd expect from a contemporary hotel. If you want to splash out, book the hotel's pride and joy: Grace Kelly's wedding tour suite.

Bar. Business centre. Concierge. Disabled-adapted rooms. Gym. Internet (wireless). No-smoking rooms. Restaurant. Room service. TV.

Sheraton Brussels Hotel & Towers

Manhattan Center, 3 place Rogier, 1210 Brussels (02 224 31 11, www.sheraton.be). Métro/pré-métro Rogier. **Rates** €375. **Credit** AmEx, DC, MC, V. **Map** p317 D2 ㉔

With 508 rooms, this is the biggest of all Brussels' hotels, boasting no fewer than 30 floors of spacious, elegant rooms with large beds and all the usual comforts and services you'd expect from an American chain. Constant modernisation has resulted in a newly renovated lounge bar and 'smart rooms', an added perk for high-powered business types, on the exclusive top five floors. Further draws include the panoramic views of the city from the upper storey rooms and the top-floor heated indoor pool.

Bar. Business centre. Concierge. Disabled-adapted rooms. Gym. Internet (wireless). No-smoking rooms. Pool (indoor). Restaurant. Room service. TV.
▶ *The in-house Crescendo is a seafood restaurant of some note.*

Expensive

Hilton Brussels City

20 place Rogier, 1210 Brussels (02 203 31 25, www.brussels-city.hilton.com). Métro/pré-métro Rogier. **Rates** €209. **Credit** AmEx, DC, MC, V. **Map** p317 E2 ㉕

If you want the standard five-star Hilton, go to the Hilton Brussels on boulevard de Waterloo. If you prefer smaller boutique hotels (and lower prices), then head for the four-star Hilton Brussels City. This stylish modern property, which is housed in three buildings dating from the 1930s and still retains some of the original features (such as the art deco lights in the restaurant), offers a more personalised service with the help of some of the best hotel staff in town. The rooms in the different buildings offer various configurations, but the decor remains the same and features pale wooden floors. A modest fitness centre, sauna and steam room, plus a decent buffet breakfast, make this a great place to stay.

Bar. Business centre. Concierge. Disabled-adapted rooms. Gym. Internet (wireless). No-smoking rooms. Restaurant. Room service. TV.

EU QUARTER & MONTGOMERY

Deluxe

★ Silken Berlaymont

11-19 boulevard Charlemagne, 1000 Brussels (02 231 09 09, www.hoteles-silken.com). Métro Schuman. **Rates** €295. **Credit** AmEx, DC, MC, V. **Map** p321 J5 ㉖

CONSUME

Noga. *See p103.*

Boutique Chic

Paint your palette blue, grey or whatever colour you fancy in Brussels' designer hotels.

Pantone Hotel.

Boutique hotels have been creeping into Brussels slowly over the last decade. Some are beautifully designed in the classical style, notably **Le Dixseptième** (*p101*) and the **Manos Premier** (*p111*). Both of these places make visitors feel like house guests at a private home, and it can be easy to forget that there's a bill to pay at the end of it all. The Poulgouras family has developed the Manos brand into something even more boutique by opening **Be Manos** on a quiet square near the Gare du Midi (02 520 65 65, www.bemanos.com). Unlike the grandeur of its big sister, this is a palette of greys, blacks and whites with metal edging and splashes of orange.

The trend for designer boutique hotels originally kicked off when the **Monty Small Design Hotel** (*see p110*) transformed a 1930s townhouse into a new, modern interior done out in reds, whites and greys with striking individual bibelots and artistic statements. It showed that the classic Brussels townhouse was perfect for small hotel development; the rooms are sizeable and lofty, and the stairs and original features add character and style.

The next logical step was to look at other, more modern spaces to see what could be achieved. Brussels has its fair share of boxy apartment and office blocks, and some enterprising designers have found a way to use this in terms of space and light. The **White Hotel** (212 avenue Louise, Ixelles, 02 644 29 29, www.the whitehotel.be) looked at both architecture and design at the same time, working the whole together in blocks of white. For some the rooms will be too austere, and the breakfast room too much like a school canteen; for others it is pearly heaven.

The latest place to use cool, open spaces is the **Pantone Hotel** (1 place Loix, St-Gilles, 02 541 48 98, www.pantone hotel.com). The theme here is colour and is part of the colour matching group's design-driven arm, Pantone Universe. Feeling daring, fiery or tranquil? Simply choose a room depending on your mood, or even hire a bike in your colour of choice.

There's no knowing where the trend will lead next – there are hundreds of buildings waiting for a new life. With Brussels' insatiable need for hotel rooms and its love of quirky design, anything could happen.

White Hotel.

Eurostars Montgomery.

The Silken B's location in the heart of the EU district, its rooms (each with a desk and internet connection) and the slick staff mark it out as a business hotel, while the modern architecture, spa and arty streak give it a certain funkiness. What sets the hotel apart, though, is the photography collection that adorns the walls of the rooms and the basement Zoom Gallery, with some 450 images from photographers across the EU. The hotel strikes the right balance between business and pleasure, although leisure visitors may find it a little out of the way. That said, the in-house L'Objectif restaurant with its artful modern cuisine and garden views means that some might need an excuse to leave in the first place. The Silken also runs 12 apartments nearby.
Bar. Business centre. Concierge. Disabled-adapted rooms. Gym. Internet (wireless). No-smoking rooms. Parking. Restaurant. Room service. TV.

Expensive

Eurostars Montgomery

134 avenue de Tervuren, 1150 Brussels (02 741 85 11, www.eurostarshotels.com). Métro Montgomery. **Rates** €189. **Credit** AmEx, DC, MC, V.

The Montgomery is a lovely, small hotel in an upmarket residential area, beside a métro station six stops from the city centre. The rooms are all beautifully decorated in English country style, but come equipped with all the latest gadgets, including wireless internet access and DVD players (DVDs can be borrowed from reception). As most guests are here on business, the restaurant only opens on weekdays. So although it's a peaceful place to stay, if you like to be at the heart of the action look elsewhere.

Bar. Business centre. Concierge. Gym. Internet (wireless). No-smoking rooms. Restaurant. Room service. TV.

Moderate

Monty Small Design Hotel

101 boulevard Brand Whitlock, 1200 Brussels (02 734 56 36, www.monty-hotel.be). Métro Montgomery. **Rates** €149. **Credit** AmEx, DC, MC, V.

Located in a 1930s townhouse, the Monty was utterly transformed by Thierry Hens' mix of modern and traditional. The interior sparkles with contemporary items of classic design by Philippe Starck and Charles Eames, and grey and red decoration throughout sets an understated but eminently stylish tone. The 18 rooms are simple but sexy, with en suite shower rooms, and guests seem happy to mingle around the breakfast table in the reception area. There's a front terrace and courtyard garden, as well as a fashionable lounge that adds a welcome touch of home – especially when juxtaposed with the sterility of the EU façades nearby.

Bar. Business centre. Internet (wireless). No-smoking rooms. TV.

IXELLES

Deluxe

Conrad Brussels

71 avenue Louise, 1050 Brussels (02 542 42 42, www.conradhotels.com). Métro Louise. **Rates** €550. **Credit** AmEx, DC, MC, V. **Map** p319 D8 ㉗

Some would say there are only two true five-star hotels in Brussels: the Conrad and the Amigo (*see p99*). It's certainly hard to fault the quality of the Conrad's decor, even if it's not to everyone's liking. The service is perfect, perhaps too perfect, with rooms tidied almost too frequently. Room service, though, is tailor-made: you can choose exactly which ingredients go into your sandwich, salad or main course. To work off that in-bed brunch, head downstairs to the in-house Aspria fitness centre (*see also p220*). Given all the swank – flunkies in top hats, chandeliered reception area the size of a small airport – it's no surprise that the Conrad is set on the smartest shopping street in town. The only real criticism: it can feel a little soulless in its pursuit of excellence.
Bar. Business centre. Concierge. Disabled-adapted rooms. Gym. Internet (wireless). No-smoking rooms. Parking. Pool. Restaurant. Room service. TV.

★ Manos Premier

100-106 chaussée de Charleroi, 1060 Brussels (02 537 96 82, www.manoshotel.com). Métro Louise. **Rates** €345. **Credit** AmEx, DC, MC, V. **Map** p319 D8 ㉘

With its ivy-clad front, dotted with fairy lights, there's something undeniably romantic about the Manos Premier. It's a converted townhouse with just 50 rooms, so when you step inside it feels like you're entering someone's home (which is not surprising, since it's been run by the same Greek family for more than three decades). While the rooms are comfortable and elegantly fitted, with antiques and Louis XVI-style decor, the hotel's real attractions lie elsewhere. The Kolya restaurant, open for lunch and dinner, has a lovely conservatory; there's a great African-themed bar with striped carpets, curvy velvet armchairs and leopard skin; and the spacious, terraced garden is a real oasis of peace. There's even a fully equipped gym. The icing on the cake, however, is the magnificent, Moorish-styled hammam, with a jacuzzi and sauna. The hotel's plainer, four-star sister, the Manos Stéphanie, is located along the street. *Photo p112.*
Bar. Business centre. Concierge. Gym. Internet (wireless). No-smoking rooms. Parking. Restaurant. Room service. Spa. TV.
► *For more about the Manos boutique hotel brand, see p108.*

Thon Hotel Bristol Stéphanie

91-93 avenue Louise, 1050 Brussels (02 543 33 11, www.thonhotels.be/bristolstephanie). Métro Louise. **Rates** €350. **Credit** AmEx, DC, MC, V. **Map** p319 E9 ㉙

The lobby of this hotel is strangely old-fashioned and slightly kitsch, with its swagged curtains and over-the-top sofas. Once you get beyond that, though, things rapidly improve. Thon claims to have the biggest hotel rooms in Brussels; they certainly are spacious, all with room for a desk. The Superior rooms have a sofa, while the Club rooms can sleep up to four people. There are even rooms for people with allergies.
Bar. Business centre. Concierge. Disabled-adapted rooms. Gym. Internet (wireless). No-smoking rooms. Parking. Pool. Restaurant. Room service. TV.

★ Warwick Barsey

381 avenue Louise, 1050 Brussels (02 649 98 00, www.warwickbarsey.com). Métro Louise then tram 94. **Rates** €350. **Breakfast** €25. **Credit** AmEx, DC, MC, V. **Map** p324 F12 ㉚

As soon as you walk through the door of this luxurious boutique hotel, you know that you're somewhere really special. The interior was designed by none other than Jacques Garcia, who created an opulent reception area in his signature rich red with Napoleon III-style furnishings and neo-classical relief work. The restaurant (with occasional DJs) and rooms are similar in style, exuding a warmth and intimacy that make the Barsey a perfect winter hotel. And there's also a courtyard terrace, making it the perfect summer residence as well. The only real downside is the location: set at the leafier end of avenue Louise, it's quite a hike from the centre of town, though not too far from Brussels' luxury shops.
Bar. Business centre. Concierge. Internet (wireless). No-smoking rooms. Parking. Restaurant. Room service. TV.

Expensive

Agenda Louise

6-8 rue de Florence, 1000 Brussels (02 539 00 31, www.hotel-agenda.com). Métro Louise then tram 94. **Rates** €160. **Credit** AmEx, DC, MC, V. **Map** p319 E9 ㉛

The Agenda Louise is an unassuming, friendly and comfortable hotel. With its quiet location just off avenue Louise and clean, spacious rooms, the hotel is popular with families. A nice touch in each room are the framed photos of Brussels and the accompanying book giving details of the subjects in the pictures. The Agenda is also keen to attract more business guests during the week and has installed desks and free Wi-Fi in its rooms.
Internet (wireless). No-smoking rooms. Parking. TV.

CONSUME

Manos Premier. *See p111.*

Budget

Les Bluets
124 rue Berckmans, 1060 Brussels (02 534 39 83, www.bluets.be). Métro Hôtel des Monnaies. **Rates** €75. **Credit** MC, V. **Map** p318 C9 ❷

This place is as colourful as the couple who run it: an eccentric Belgian-English lady and her Colombian husband. Set in a building dating from 1864, Les Bluets has been a hotel for more than 30 years and has acquired a fair amount of decorative features in that time. Every room is crammed with antiques, kitsch holiday souvenirs and what look like jumble sale buys, while plants and flowers spill out from balconies and bathrooms. Nothing is standard – the decor, the room sizes or the amenities. Smokers and noisy young people are not welcome as guests. Check-in is from 11am to 10pm, and cash payments are preferred.
Internet (wireless). No-smoking throughout. TV.

Rembrandt
42 rue de la Concorde, 1050 Brussels (02 512 71 39, http://rembrandt.dommel.be). Métro Louise then tram 94 or bus 71. **Rates** €75. **Credit** MC, V. **Map** p319 E8 ❸

There's something rather quaint about this one-star hotel, with its reception that closes at 10pm and a breakfast room filled with twee china ornaments and gilt-framed still lifes. The rooms are similarly homely, with high ceilings, flowery wallpaper, old

dark wood furniture and framed prints on the wall. It's clean, quirky and great value.
Internet (wireless). No-smoking throughout.

BED & BREAKFAST

B&Bs in Brussels (also known as *maisons* or *chambres d'hôtes*) are traditional in that they involve staying in someone's house – it's not a euphemism for a cheap hotel. Be prepared to respect the owner's foibles and accept that hotel-style services are not on offer. A B&B stay here is more suited to the less frantic traveller, rather than the boozy weekender. The appeal lies in the chance to stay with Belgians, often eager to regale you with insider tips.

Bed & Brussels
02 646 07 37, www.bnb-brussels.be. **Rates** vary. **Credit** MC, V.

B&Bs throughout Brussels can be booked through this friendly agency that visits homes regularly. The website has plenty of good quality pictures and also allows you to see a 360-degree panorama of the place you're booking. Weekly rates and longer rentals are also available.

Chambres en ville
19 rue de Londres, 1050 Brussels (02 512 92 90, www.chambresenville.be). Métro Trône. **Rates** €90; €10 supplement for one-night stay. **No credit cards. Map** p319 F7 ❸

There's no better endorsement for a place than word of mouth, and most of Philippe Guilmin's custom comes via recommendations. You could easily walk past the ordinary front door, behind which lies a very attractive, good-value place to rest your head. The sympathetic, erudite and competently English-speaking Guilmin is hospitality itself, his handful of rooms all individually decorated and boasting spacious en suite bathrooms. The rooms feature stone or stripped wooden floors, high ceilings and windows (so they're naturally light), wall hangings and homely touches such as fresh flowers. The large breakfast table is often shared with Guilmin's cosmopolitan and friendly clientele – such as middle-aged academics, art historians, Brussophiles – pleased with the proximity to the restaurants of Ixelles, the palaces of the Royal Quarter, a métro station, and peace and quiet.

YOUTH HOSTELS

There are three hostels in Brussels belonging to Youth Hostelling International and one self-styled 'youth hotel'. All tend to enforce a maximum stay of one week, although this is sometimes negotiable.

YHI hostels require a membership card purchased in your country of residence. (If you don't have one, you will be charged an extra

€4-€5 per night.) It's also advisable to book through www.hihostels.com, as this guarantees that your bed will be kept longer than usual (so you can arrive later in the day). The use of bed sheets is compulsory – rental is usually included in the price, but at the **Centre Vincent Van Gogh** you can bring your own or use your sleeping bag.

Prices quoted below include breakfast and are per person.

Bruegel (YHI)

2 rue du St-Esprit, Lower Town, 1000 Brussels (02 511 04 36, www.youthhostels.be). Métro Gare Centrale. **Rates** (incl sheet rental) €18.90-€35.50. **Credit** MC, V. **Map** p315 C6 ③⑤
This hostel is set on a pleasant church square near the Sablon, a short walk from the Gare Centrale and the Grand'Place. Another plus is the recent renovation programme, removing the 12-person rooms and introducing a chill-out area for every floor (the first floor also has a TV). On the downside, it's the only hostel to impose a curfew (1am), but the basement bar stays open until the last person goes to bed, so there's always time for a nightcap.
Bar. Disabled-adapted rooms. Internet. No-smoking throughout. TV.

Centre Vincent Van Gogh (CHAB)

8 rue Traversière, St-Josse, 1210 Brussels (02 217 01 58, www.chab.be). Métro Botanique. **Rates** €33.50 single; €26.50 double (incl sheet rental). **Credit** AmEx, DC, MC, V. **Map** p320 F2 ③⑥

This may be the largest hostel in town, but it's still advisable to book your bed at least a month in advance (especially in holiday season), because it's used by school groups visiting the European Parliament. Housed in two buildings, the hostel has bright, modern rooms, some with en suite facilities. Public areas include a bar (which is open from 6.30pm) and a farmhouse-style kitchen for self-catering. Nearby is the cheery Jacques Brel (30 rue de la Sablonnière, Upper Town, 1000 Brussels, 02 218 01 87, www.laj.be).
Bar. Internet. No-smoking throughout. TV.

Sleep Well Youth Hotel

23 rue du Damier, Lower Town, 1000 Brussels (02 218 50 50, www.sleepwell.be). Métro/pré-métro Rogier or De Brouckère. **Rates** €35 single; €26 double (incl sheet rental). **Credit** MC, V. **Map** p317 D3 ③⑦
This 'youth hotel' feels less institutionalised than youth hostels. Although the basic formula is still bunk beds in bare rooms (adapted for disabled use), an on-site tourism adviser, comfy armchairs in the communal areas and a comic strip mural in the lobby are bonuses. The location also scores highly: just behind the main shopping street of rue Neuve and a five-minute walk to the Grand'Place. Guests must be 35 years or under, although this doesn't apply to the Sleep Well's newest wing. The more cheerful rooms have en suite showers, with en suite baths a luxury in the triple rooms.
Bar. Concierge. Disabled-adapted rooms. Internet. No-smoking throughout. Restaurant. TV.

CONSUME

Centre Vincent Van Gogh.

Restaurants & Cafés

Discerning diners, ambitious chefs and legendary double-fried frites.

In 2010, Belgian restaurants were awarded a total of 114 Michelin stars – more per capita than France. Impressive as this is, you don't need to fork out Michelin-rated money to eat well in this little country – or in Brussels, with its 2,000 restaurants. Most have been around for years: if a new establishment arrives and doesn't come up to scratch, it soon closes. Brussels diners know what they like, and are not prepared to compromise on their expectations.

Although Belgian-style kitchens still reign supreme, global influences are making their presence felt. The financial downturn, meanwhile, seems to have had little impact on the dining scene, as cafés and restaurants remain packed out at lunchtime and in the evening.

PRACTICALITIES

Brussels is not particularly cheap for eating out, nor do all its restaurants offer a set menu. The best bargains can be found at lunchtime (*midi*) when you can order the *plat du jour*, often with a free glass of wine or a coffee thrown in.

The website www.resto.be is the most wide-reaching resource, and also includes visitors' reviews. The search engine works in French, Dutch and English, though is hyper-sensitive and not smart enough to find a restaurant if you mis-type the name.

Bills come with service included, so there is no obligation to tip. Most diners leave a little extra to round off the evening; in top-quality restaurants, a healthier contribution is expected.

Throughout the chapter, we've listed the price of an average main course (or equivalent, such as the price of a sandwich in a café) to give a rough indication of price. Venues that represent good value for money are denoted by the € symbol.

INSIDE TRACK ON THE HOUSE

While eating out in Brussels isn't cheap, the price of spirits and wine is more reasonable than in other cities, and can help balance out the bill. House wines are usually of a high standard too.

LOWER TOWN

Grand'Place & around

The tiny streets around the Grand'Place are alive with restaurants and bars. Somewhat surprisingly, their location in tourist central doesn't mean they're either of poor quality or overpriced. Many have been here for decades, and used by generations of locals.

Aux Armes de Bruxelles

13 rue des Bouchers (02 511 50 50, www. armebrux.be). Métro Gare Centrale. **Open** noon-10.45pm Mon-Fri; noon-11.15pm Sat; noon-10.30pm Sun. **Main courses** €28. **Credit** AmEx, DC, MC, V. **Map** p315 D4 ❶ Belgian
Sitting like a grounded galleon in the gaudy sea of fish restaurants near the Grand'Place, Aux Armes is a classically mullioned institution, beloved by business folk and middle-aged, middle-class Belgians since 1921. The art deco interior is as classy as the waiters, who slide around with the utmost professionalism, delivering plates of mussels, turbot and the occasional steak. It's seafood that folk come for, including perfect *moules-frites* and creamy fish *waterzooi*.

Belga Queen

32 rue du Fossé aux Loups (02 217 21 87, www.belgaqueen.be). Métro/pré-métro De Brouckère. **Open** noon-2pm, 7-10pm daily. **Main courses** €28. **Credit** AmEx, DC, MC, V. **Map** p315 D3 ❷ Belgian

Everything about this glitzy place is unashamedly Belgian. The design, the menu, the produce; even the wine is sourced from Belgian producers abroad. The restaurant sits in a vast bank building with original pillars and a massive stained-glass skylight, giving it a lofty, spacious air. Yet once at your table, it can feel surprisingly intimate (though couples alone are rare – this seems to be a place to go with a crowd). The BQ is renowned for its oyster bar, where heaving seafood platters are composed. The hot food is inventive and thoroughly modern; the famous farm bird, Coucou de Malines, is sat on gingerbread with a hot pear sauce, though more traditional methods, such as braising in beer, are also used. The unisex toilet doors are transparent, and it's up to you to work them out. Don't expect us to give the game away.

Chez Léon
18 rue des Bouchers (02 511 14 15, www.chez leon.be). Métro Gare Centrale or pré-métro Bourse. **Open** 11.30am-11pm Mon-Thur, Sun; 11.30am-11.30pm Fri, Sat. **Main courses** €20. **Credit** AmEx, DC, MC, V. **Map** p315 D4 ❸ Belgian
Léon Vanlancker first opened a tavern in 1893, and ten years later unveiled a frites shop on the site of the current restaurant. How times have changed: Chez Léon now weaves through nine interconnecting houses and can seat 400 people. Its fast food feel and atmosphere keep the nose-in-air locals away – or maybe it's the paper napkins and menu featuring photographed dishes. On the culinary front, this

place is a temple to mussels and other Belgian classics, such as rabbit in sour cherry beer. You may not be treated like a king, but you'll surely eat like one. Léon is also good for families; under-12s get a free set menu as long as they're with two paying adults.

€ Le Cirio
18-20 rue de la Bourse (02 512 13 95). Pré-métro Bourse. **Open** 10am-1am daily. **Main courses** €10. **No credit cards.** **Map** p315 C4 ❹ Café
Le Cirio is named after the Italian grocer, remembered on a million sauce cans, who shipped wagons of goodies over the Alps from Turin to his ornate delicatessen, set by the stock exchange. Both the Bourse and deli have since folded, but the decor remains – beautiful fittings and Vermouth promotions, cash registers and century-old gastronomy awards – along with the eternally popular *half-en-half* wine (half sparkling, half still, wholly Italian). Grandes dames and their lookalike poodles sip away the afternoon, the former from a stemmed glass, the latter from a bowl of tap water. Pre-war toilets complete the experience.

★ Comme chez Soi
23 place Rouppe (02 512 29 21, www.comme chezsoi.be). Pré-métro Anneessens. **Open** noon-1.30pm, 7-10.30pm Tue, Thur-Sat; 7-10.30pm Wed. **Main courses** €65. **Credit** AmEx, DC, MC, V. **Map** p315 B6 ❺ French

Belga Queen.

CONSUME

Get the local experience

Over 50 of the world's top destinations available.

Restaurant Vincent. *See p119.*

Pierre Wynants, Belgian hero and one of Europe's top chefs, has now passed the baton over to his son-in-law, Lionel Rigolet, at this Michelin two-star establishment. Immaculate food is served in a mannered art nouveau dining room: typical dishes might include sole fillets with a mousseline of riesling and shrimps, or lobster salad with black truffles and potatoes. Old habits die hard: after a beautifully sculpted course arrives at your table, waiters return with an unassuming bowl of second helpings, proving that artistically small portions are never enough in Belgium.

€ Le Falstaff

19-25 rue Henri Maus (02 511 87 89, www.lefalstaff.be). Pré-métro Bourse. **Open** 10am-2am daily. **Main courses** €15. **Credit** AmEx, DC, MC, V. **Map** p315 C4 ➏ Café
Probably the most famous café-restaurant in Brussels, and certainly the most evergreen. An awning on one side of the Bourse barely prepares the first-time visitor for the eye candy of the art nouveau interior, which has been attracting Bruxellois of every stripe for the better part of a century. The reasonably priced mains are but a side dish to the range of beers, while extended opening hours are another major draw. A mere step from the main square, this is more than most European capitals can dream about.

€ Mokafé

9 galerie du Roi (02 511 78 70). Métro Gare Centrale. **Open** 7am-midnight Mon-Sat; 8am-midnight Sun. **Main courses** €9. **Credit** AmEx, DC, MC, V. **Map** p315 D4 ➐ Café
Located near the opera and opposite Brussels' best classical music shop, the Mokafé attracts a terrace full of arty types year round, protected from inclement weather by covered galleries. It's good for lunch, with reasonably priced Belgian café grub and pasta. On Sunday mornings, locals bring their newspapers and sit for hours with coffee and a croissant. Everyone pretends to be in their own little world, but just watch eyes dart and ears prick when a newcomer takes a table; knowing nods to regulars and faux acts of interest at strangers.

★ Ogenblik

1 galerie des Princes (02 511 61 51, www.ogenblik.be). Métro Gare Centrale.

THE BEST SET MENUS

Bosquet 58
So plentiful and so cheap, you wonder how the place makes a profit. *See p132.*

Divino
At lunch, choose any main menu dish, plus a drink and coffee, for €12. *See p121.*

Jaloa
It's classy, it's expensive, it's unforgettable. *See p123.*

Bags packed, milk cancelled, house raised on stilts.

You've packed the suntan lotion, the snorkel set, the stay-pressed shirts. Just one more thing left to do – your bit for climate change. In some of the world's poorest countries, changing weather patterns are destroying lives.

You can help people to deal with the extreme effects of climate change. Raising houses in flood-prone regions is just one life-saving solution.

**Climate change costs lives.
Give £5 and let's sort it *Here & Now***

www.oxfam.org.uk/climate-change

Oxfam is a registered charity in England and Wales (No.202918) and Scotland (SCO039042). Oxfam GB is a member of Oxfam International.

Be Humankind (Ω) Oxfam

Open noon-2.30pm, 7pm-midnight Mon-Sat.
Main courses €28. **Credit** AmEx, DC, MC, V.
Map p315 D4 **❽ French**
Set on the edge of the glamorous covered galleries, this place is a must for flash-the-cash professionals. The eclectic interior is sort of old-railway-station-meets-Conran, with a sprinkle of salt on the floor to give it that old soak feel. The menu is a polished affair: try the millefeuille of lobster and salmon with a coulis of langoustines. Watch the prices, though, as the bill tends to start mounting up in an *ogenblik* (blink of an eye). Also be sure to look out for Madame, who takes the bookings and prepares the bills; she sits at an ancient shop till with a little wooden footstall, dancing pumps, half-moon glasses and a mess-with-me-and-you're-dead look. Classic.

€ Plattesteen

41 rue du Marché au Charbon (02 512 82 03).
Pré-métro Anneessens. **Open** 11am-midnight daily. **Main courses** €18. **Credit** AmEx, DC, MC, V. **Map** p315 C5 **❾ Café**
This multifunctional bar-café acts as both a neighbourhood bar and an inexpensive restaurant. It's something of a melting pot, joining shopping Brussels to gay Brussels and the rue du Marché au Charbon, so the clientele might include ladies with poodles, ladies with men and men with men. As a result it makes for a great meeting place – especially in summer, when you can sit on the terrace and watch the world cruise by arm-in-arm. It's a true Brussels contradiction, with homely and unexceptional decor slap in the middle of the new trendsville.

Restaurant Vincent

8-10 rue des Dominicains (02 511 26 07,
www.restaurantvincent.com). Métro/pré-métro
De Brouckère. **Open** noon-2.45pm, 6.30-11.30pm Mon-Sat; noon-3pm, 6.30-10.30pm Sun. **Main courses** €25. **Credit** AmEx, DC, MC, V.
Map p315 D4 **❿ Seafood**
Up a little side street from the main glare of rue des Bouchers is the unassuming frontage of Vincent. Newcomers hesitate to enter because there seems to be only a kitchen entrance. Correct. Be brave and walk past the steaming chefs, and the dry maître d' will meet you at the other side. Vincent's fame comes from its tiled dining room, with a mural depicting old-time fishing and wild seas that dates from 1905. Some of the tables are shaped like fishing smacks, just in case you missed the theme. Ask for this when booking, or you could end up in the unexceptional dining room next door. Unsurprisingly, fish and seafood are the main draws, cooked to perfection. This is one of those places where the final touches are rustled up at table by epauletted waiters keen to show off their flambé skills. *Photo p117.*

★ La Roue d'Or

26 rue des Chapeliers (02 514 25 54, www2.
resto.be/rouedor). Pré-métro Bourse. **Open** noon-midnight daily. **Main courses** €25. **Credit** AmEx, DC, MC, V. **Map** p315 C5 **⓫ Belgian**
The Golden Wheel takes its name from the gold motif at the heart of a stained-glass window above the open kitchen. Through the window you can watch the team of chefs toiling away at what can be described as grandma's cooking. The fine spread of time-honoured Belgian classics includes mussels, oysters, lamb's tongue, pig's trotter, brawn, rabbit and slabs of beef; not surprisingly, vegetarians will feel rather left out. While the ingredients are no-nonsense, presentation and flavours are impeccable; as a result it remains a favourite with locals, who adore the wholesomeness of the place. So you know what you're letting yourself in for, the menu is also offered in English.

★ Sea Grill

Radisson SAS Royal, 47 rue du Fossé aux Loups
(02 227 91 25, www.seagrill.be). Métro/pré-métro
De Brouckère. **Open** noon-2pm, 7-10pm Mon-Fri.
Main courses €55. **Credit** AmEx, DC, MC, V.
Map p315 D4 **⓬ Seafood**
The Sea Grill – regarded by many as Belgium's top seafood restaurant – is buried inside the five-star Radisson SAS Royal Hotel, so while the entrance is rather corporate, the interior is seriously luxe. Chef Yves Mattagne seems to win every award going for his masterful pairing of traditional French techniques with modern international touches. Red

Bij den Boer. *See p121.*

CONSUME

Bonsoir Clara.

mullet with truffle risotto and roast tuna with
sautéed goose liver are among the specialities. Be
aware that a starter here could set you back more
than an entire meal elsewhere, however.

St-Géry & Ste-Catherine

Bij den Boer

*60 quai aux Briques (02 512 61 22, www.
bijdenboer.com). Métro Ste-Catherine.* **Open**
noon-2.30pm, 6-10.30pm Mon-Sat. **Main courses**
€20. **Credit** AmEx, DC, MC, V. **Map** p315 C3 ⑬
Belgian
The Farmer's looks a bit like a transport caff, and
can seem a little intimidating from the outside as it's
always packed with local customers – you get the
feeling you're gatecrashing a private do. Once inside,
the decor isn't awe-inspiring but is made up for by
a noisy, chattering atmosphere. The restaurant is
famous for its mussels and bouillabaisse, and prices
are good for the area – especially if you opt for the
four-course menu. On the other hand, the service is
infuriatingly slow. The staff are friendly enough,
and dash around at quite a rate, but never, it seems,
towards your table. Persevere, though, and you will
leave feeling mightily satisfied. *Photo p119.*

Bonsoir Clara

*22-26 rue Antoine Dansaert (02 502 09 90,
www.bonsoirclara.be). Pré-métro Bourse.* **Open**
noon-2.30pm, 7-11.30pm Mon-Thur; noon-2.30pm,
7pm-midnight Fri; 7pm-midnight Sat; 7-11.30pm
Sun. **Main courses** €25. **Credit** AmEx, MC, V.
Map p315 C4 ⑭ **Modern European**
Bonsoir Clara is the restaurant that started it all off
for rue Antoine Dansaert, a beacon of trend in an
area that was just waiting to happen. It still pulls in
the crowds with its understated sophistication and
brilliantly eclectic food. To say it's modern French
is too simplistic – the menu borrows from around
the world and incorporates Asian spices, Italian delicacies and Californian reductions. Seared tuna,
carpaccio of duck, and a pair of quails stuffed with
dried fruit and ginger give some idea of the range.
The look is clean and streamlined, with white tablecloths and white lilies, while a vast panel of back-lit
coloured glass adds a bit of flair.
▶ *Pause here for lunch after a leisurely morning
spent browsing the street's boutiques.*

Comocomo

*19 rue Antoine Dansaert (02 503 03 30,
www.comocomo.com). Pré-metro Bourse.*
Open noon-2.30pm, 7pm-late daily. **Main
courses** €10. **Credit** AmEx, DC, MC, V.
Map p315 C4 ⑮ **Tapas**
Set amid designer shops and other chic eateries,
Comocomo has proved a roaring success. It owes
its popularity to both the food and the concept:
it's a Basque *pintxo* (tapas) bar, with a sushi-style
conveyor belt. Clean and modern, with splashes of

coloured light, the restaurant feels inv
to-the-minute, with a Wi-Fi connection i
can't bear to be offline. The *pintxos* we
around the snaking belt in colour codes, depending
on theme: purple for pork, blue for fish, green for
veggie and so on, in seven categories. Try fried
quails' legs, boar carpaccio, octopus or black olives
and mushrooms. You get charged for the amount of
empty plates at the end. *Photo p124.*

€ Divino

*56 rue des Chartreux (02 503 39 09, www.
restodivino.be). Pré-métro Bourse.* **Open** noon-
2.30pm, 6.30-11.30pm Mon-Fri; 6.30-11.30pm Sat.
Main courses €15. **Credit** AmEx, MC, V.
Map p315 B4 ⑯ **Italian**
The influence of the St-Géry area slowly spreads
along this charismatic street, with its abundance of
idiosyncratic shops and eateries. Divino is a splash
of inspiration in a row of old houses still waiting to
find its identity. Owner Moses Guez has created a
retro-minimalist dining space that buzzes as diners
attack gigantic pizzas topped with goats' cheese
and parma ham or carpaccio of beef. The pasta
dishes are brilliantly subtle and make liberal use
of seafood and fresh vegetables. A lovely brick-
walled terrace means the front of house is empty in
summer, but don't think for a moment that it's fallen
out of favour.

€ Hotel Orts Café

*38-40 rue Auguste Orts (02 517 07 00,
www.hotelorts.com). Pré-métro Bourse.* **Open**
9am-2am daily. **Main courses** €15. **Credit**
AmEx, DC, MC, V. **Map** p315 C4 ⑰ **Café**
Once upon a time, the White Horse, a tired and
moody men's teashop, sat on this busy corner. After
it closed the building slowly deteriorated, until renovation work began. Locals were thrilled to discover
that an original belle époque canopy had been lurking under the plywood, and ever-packed Orts
opened up for business. Tourists and locals use it
for different purposes throughout the day – breakfast, lunch, evening drinks or for a good late-night

---

THE BEST MOULES-FRITES

Bij den Boer
No nonsense, no messing, no leftovers.
See above.

Le Pré Salé
The window claims they're the best
Moules Golden, and they're pretty
moreish. *See p123.*

La Roue d'Or
Copper-panned, and overflowing with the
fattest frites in town. *See p119.*

On the Hoof

There's more to fast food than frites.

Chez Jef & Fils.

Under the bright blue awning of the **Mer du Nord** fish shop on the corner of place Ste-Catherine, well-dressed locals stand chatting, shopping bags in hand. Wafting through them is a fishy head of steam from an enamel cooking pot on a flame; as well as buying their turbot and mussels, they are tucking into bowls of *escargots* – not the snails we know from France, but rubbery North Sea whelks. On the square itself, a quieter group stands at the oyster stall (*see p130* **Profile**), taking a dozen *fines claires* with a glass of wine. This is fast food Brussels-style, where eating on the street doesn't always mean greasy napkins and mayonnaise moustaches.

Of course, this is the more genteel take on eating on the move, but it neatly sums up the democracy of enjoying food in Belgium. Across from the Bourse is the more working-class **Chez Jef & Fils** van, which has been serving *escargots* to regulars and passers-by for several generations. No chardonnay here, just a side serving of good old-fashioned gossip.

Street snacks cut across age and class, so long as unspoken – but well-understood – rules are observed. People will not blink at you eating a sandwich on the métro,

but try a burger and chips and you'll soon know about it. Fast food detritus is much less in evidence here than in other cities. Sure, there are kebab shops and snack bars around the downtown bars, not least along gaudy rue du Marché aux Fromages, but it's a localised scene. In burger chains, people prefer to sit in and eat. Belgian chain **Quick** dominates the market, and the golden arches of McDonald's are few and far between.

The best frites in town, though, come from the little stalls dotted around the city (the best being **Maison Antoine** on place Jourdan). They are double-fried in beef dripping and served up in a cone with a plastic fork, accompanied by an astonishing array of sauces.

Then there's the famous waffle, or *gaufre chaud*. The plain *gaufre de Liège*, sugary sweet but smaller, is popular, while the Brussels version is more full-on, with toppings such as cream and strawberries. For a sugar boost without the mattress, stop at any **Leonidas** (or even upmarket Wittamer) and ask for one praline of your choice. They are sold by weight, and staff are more than happy to pop a single one in a bag for you.

booze-up on Guinness or the excellent collection of Belgian brews. The terrace is open year-round, despite the traffic.

Jacques

44 quai aux Briques (02 513 27 62, www. restaurantjacques.be). Métro Ste-Catherine. **Open** noon-2pm, 6.30-10pm Mon-Sat. **Main courses** €28. **Credit** AmEx, DC, MC, V. **Map** p315 C3 ⑱ Seafood

A favourite with locals, Jacques oozes traditional Belgian charm, especially in summer when the huge windows are open and the restaurant meets the street. An old-fashioned, wood-panelled interior, tiled floors and globe lamps give the place its atmosphere, although the back room is lacklustre and merely acts as a sounding board for the kitchen. Service is efficient but abrupt. Jacques is famous for its sublimely light and buttery turbot with sauce mousseline, but the *moules-frites* make an excellent alternative. Booking is essential.

★ Jaloa

4 quai aux Barques (02 513 19 92, www. jaloa.com). Métro Ste-Catherine. **Open** noon-2.30pm, 7-10.30pm Tue-Fri; 7-10.30pm Mon, Sat. **Main courses** €40. **Credit** AmEx, MC, V. **Map** p316 B2 ⑲ French

French-born chef Gaëtan Colin has opened this new restaurant in a classy 17th-century townhouse at the bottom end of Ste-Catherine. Small and cosy, with a covered terrace at the back, it exudes understated style. The set menus come in four-, six- or nine-course versions, with the option of adding matched wines into the equation. Expect resolutely modern French cooking with Asian influences and an appealing lightness of touch: think carpaccio of scallops with asparagus sorbet and you'll get the idea. ► *On a budget? Prices are lower at its offshoot on place Ste-Catherine, Jaloa Brasserie (Nos.5-7, 02 512 18 31, www.brasseriejaloa.com).*

€ De Markten

5 rue Vieux Marché aux Grains (02 512 91 85, www.demarkten.be). Métro Ste-Catherine. **Open** 8.30am-midnight Mon-Sat; 10am-6pm Sun. **Main courses** €10. **No credit cards**. **Map** p315 B3 ⑳ Café

Before you enter this ground-floor café, take a step back and admire the magnificent building. The café is part of a cultural centre, and as such attracts young arty types from the Flemish school of thought. Inside, the style is postmodernist industrial chic. OK – it looks like a school canteen, but minimalism is just what these folk want. A terrace, filled with deckchairs in summer, looks on to the square.

Le Pré Salé

20 rue de Flandre (02 513 65 45). Métro Ste-Catherine. **Open** noon-2.30pm, 6.30-10.30pm Wed-Sun. **Main courses** €25. **Credit** AmEx, MC, V. **Map** p315 B3 ㉑ Belgian

De Markten

CONSUME

CONSUME

Comocomo. *See p121.*

What an institution this is. A white tiled dining room leads through to an open kitchen at the back, where you can see madame chef slaving away with her little helpers, cooking everything to order. When she's done, she comes out for a drink and a chat with friends. Friday night is cabaret night, a decades-old tradition with *Bruxellois* jokes, bawdy humour and a bit of a knees-up; it's near impossible to get a table for this, so book at least three weeks in advance. Food comprises hefty meat and fish dishes, with excellent cod, salmon and mussels and a huge beef rib for two people. There's absolutely no subtlety at the Pré Salé – it's all bright lights, big noise and vast plates of food, which is why we love it.

€ Thiên-Long

12 rue van Artevelde (02 511 34 80). Pré-metro Bourse. **Open** noon-3pm, 6-11pm Mon, Tue, Thur-Sun. **Main courses** €12. **No credit cards. Map** p315 C4 ㉒ Vietnamese
First impressions of this Vietnamese restaurant are of a wooden-tabled caff incongruously set in a jungle of kitsch artefacts from the Far East, including the obligatory fluoro waterfall and red-tasselled lanterns. Despite this outlandish decoration, this place is too self-effacing for its own good. It calls itself a *snack-resto*, but it's so much more than that. Steaming bowls of hot chilli soup, lacquered duck, beef with bamboo and crunchy stir-fried vegetables sum up one of the longest menus this side of Hanoi. The food is sublime, the portions are huge, and they're all concocted by one of the smallest chefs you've ever seen.

Le Vistro

16 quai aux Briques (02 512 41 81). Métro Ste-Catherine. **Open** noon-2.30pm, 7pm-midnight Mon-Fri; 6.30pm-midnight Sat. **Main courses** €25. **Credit** AmEx, DC, MC, V. **Map** p315 C3 ㉓ Seafood
Occupying the narrowest house of a terrace of fish restaurants, this is a compact and welcoming bistro. There are no fussy pink tablecloths and silk flower arrangements here; just brick and natural wood. The fish is on the traditional French side – think buttery sauces – but what makes Vistro special is its mighty platters of fresh seafood. They groan with oysters, mussels, clams, winkles and whelks, and are crowned with a choice of crab or lobster. No starter is needed, but as it's all opened fresh you should be prepared to wait. Across the way in the summer is a canopied terrace, where waiters have to dodge the traffic to get to your table.

The Marolles

A la Clef d'Or

1 place du Jeu de Balle (02 511 97 62). Métro/pré-métro Porte de Hal or bus 27, 48. **Open** 5am-5pm Tue-Sun. **No credit cards. Map** p318 B7 ㉔ Café

This large, loud caff is a favourite with locals, so it can be a bit of a squeeze for the casual visitor. Sunday mornings are the best and busiest, thanks to the earnest accordionist and party atmosphere. Unintentionally retro, the interior sports vinyl chairs and pink neon advertising signs. The food is of the *croque monsieur* and fried egg variety. Madame skates around in her mules and black leggings, while monsieur stands at the coffee machine, barking orders to the overworked staff; he's also in charge of the *soupe du jour* pot.

La Grande Porte

9 rue Notre-Seigneur (02 512 89 98). Bus 27, 48, 95, 96. **Open** noon-3pm, 6pm-2am Mon-Fri; 6pm-2am Sat. **Main courses** €18. **Credit** MC, V. **Map** p315 C6 ㉕ **Belgian**

Through the huge, studded wooden door that gives this establishment its name lies a cosy room, with an old bar running along one wall. Turn the corner, though, and you could be in a different world. It seems as if this restaurant has been stitched together from two different patterns, the modern addition quite soulless compared to the buzz of the main room. Wherever you sit, however, this place is great for late-night Belgian classics: mussels, steaks with sauce, *stoemp* and *waterzooi*, served with deep bowls of fresh frites. Expect to find an eclectic mix of artists, actors, musicians and groups of chums who just don't want to go home. *Photo p126.*

★ L'Idiot du Village

19 rue Notre-Seigneur (02 502 55 82). Bus 27, 48, 95, 96. **Open** noon-2pm, 7.15-11pm Mon-Fri. **Main courses** €25. **Credit** AmEx, DC, MC, V. **Map** p315 C6 ㉖ **Modern European**

This small bistro, beloved by celebs, is hidden away in a side street off the antiques hub of rue Blaes. The chairs and tables are of the type you'd hope to find in the nearby flea market, the walls midnight blue and deep carmine, the flowers dried, the chandeliers camp. It sounds clichéd but works perfectly, as does the eclectic food by chef Alain Gascoin, which is down to earth but well executed. Try the succulent rabbit and leek stew, full of wine and herbs. The feel is of being a guest in a private home, and booking is a must. *Photo p129.*

Les Petits Oignons

13 rue Notre-Seigneur (02 512 47 38, www. petits-oignons.be). Bus 27, 48, 95, 96. **Meals served** noon-2.30pm, 7-11pm Mon-Fri; 7-11pm Sat. **Main courses** €20. **Credit** AmEx, DC, MC, V. **Map** p315 C6 ㉗ **French**

From the outside, this fine old vine-covered house from the 1600s looks as if it could be straight out of a Breugel painting. Walking in you feel warm and welcomed, despite an odd 1970s air. In winter there's a log fire, in summer a green and lantern-lit terrace at the back. The unfussy French/Belgian food is cooked with finesse, arriving at the table in hefty

Le Perroquet. *See p126.*

CONSUME

La Grande Porte. *See p125.*

UPPER TOWN

€ ★ Le Cap Sablon

75 rue Lebeau (02 512 01 70, http://sites. resto.com/capsablon). Métro Gare Centrale or bus 95. **Open** noon-midnight daily. **Main courses** €15. **Credit** AmEx, MC, V. **Map** p315 D6 ㉙ Modern European

Among all the upmarket glitz of the Sablon, this understated little brasserie continues to shine, year after year. Its simple, understated art deco interior gives a homely, comforting feel, which is reflected in the menu. Basic but succulent roasts and grills, fish livened up by oriental spices and wicked desserts all make for a satisfying, reasonably priced meal. The chattering Sablon set knows all about this place, but the Cap has thus far resisted any social pressure to trendify. If you want to dine alfresco on the small terrace, specify when booking.

Lola

33 place du Grand Sablon (02 514 24 60, www.restolola.be). Bus 95. **Open** noon-3pm, 6.30-11.30pm Mon-Fri; noon-11.30pm Sat, Sun. **Main courses** €25. **Credit** AmEx, MC, V. **Map** p315 D6 ㉚ Modern European

Lola is one of those institutions loved by urban professionals and consistently recommended in guidebooks. It has the name, it has the location, it has the right clientele. The food is absolutely fine, in a modern brasserie way: rabbit with almonds and orange blossom or, for vegetarians, risotto and parmesan chips. This is not a place to whisper sweet nothings – it's loud and gregarious and has everything the young set needs. Go for the buzz, but, as with so many places of this genre, you may leave wondering if anyone ever noticed you were there.

€ Le Perroquet

31 rue Watteau (02 512 99 22, http://newsites. resto.com/leperroquet). Bus 95. **Open** 10am-1am daily. **Main courses** €9. **Credit** MC, V. **Map** p319 D6 ㉛ Café

An authentic art nouveau café, Le Perroquet features mirrors aplenty, plus stained glass, a striking black and white tiled floor and a summer terrace. A popular haunt of well-to-do young things in summer, before it's reclaimed by the autumnal flock of EU *stagiaires*, it's a stylish complement to the bland upmarket terrace bars of place du Grand Sablon, which is a two-minute walk away. It's quite dinky inside, so expect a scramble for a table after office hours on a Friday. Plentiful salads and imaginative stuffed pittas form the core of the menu. *Photo p125.*

Soul

20 rue de la Samaritaine (02 513 52 13, www. soulresto.com). Bus 48, 95. **Open** noon-2.30pm, 7-10pm Wed-Fri; 7-10pm Sat, Sun. **Main courses** €17. **Credit** MC, V. **Map** p315 C6 ㉜ Organic

See right Green Cuisine.

portions. A veal cutlet looks like the side of a horse, while the fillet of dorade is thick and fleshy. Depending on the menu, you may be asked to order desserts at the beginning of the meal – which can be annoying, but only goes to show that this is a restaurant that likes to get things right. This place suits any reason to eat out, from laziness to celebration.

Au Stekerlapatte

4 rue des Prêtres (02 512 86 81, www. stekerlapatte.be). Métro Hôtel des Monnaies. **Open** noon-2.30pm, 7-11pm Tue, Wed; noon-2.30pm, 7pm-midnight Thur-Sat. **Main courses** €20. **Credit** MC, V. **Map** p318 C8 ㉘ Belgian

A late-night restaurant for traditional food at no-nonsense prices. At first glance you may think it full and turn to leave, but there is a warren of rooms and corridors: there's bound to be a table somewhere in the maze. It's a friendly place, despite its darkness and offbeat location, becoming more desirable as the area improves. Prepared in the time-honoured way, there are steaks and sauces with great fat fries, grilled pig's trotter, spare ribs and black pudding (vegetarians beware).

Green Cuisine

Fresh thinking on the city's restaurant scene.

Healthy and ethical eating is making a slow but sure inroad into the food culture of Belgium, although there remains a deep-rooted suspicion in traditional quarters. Although Belgium still needs its old stalwarts – its super-calorific *sauce poivre-vert* to drape over steaks, or its egg yolk and cream enrichment for *waterzooi* – you'll find an ever-increasing emphasis on the ingredients and on simpler preparations in more forward-looking restaurants, while the organic Bio label is a fixture in local supermarkets nowadays.

At the acclaimed **Bon-Bon** (*see p134*), the quality of the produce is paramount. Chef Christophe Hardiquest will only use traceable sources, preferring even the olive oil to come with its own *appellation contrôlée*. The effect this picky approach has on the restaurant's menus is that they are a thrillingly moveable feast, changing according to market availability and in line with the seasons. In the EU Quarter, the little weekday lunch-only **Au Bain Marie** (*see p128*) prides itself on its meatless, *frite*less menu and serves up great wedges of freshly made quiches, home-made pastas and verdant salads. Such is its popularity, it is impossible to get in without a reservation.

The **Exki** (www.exki.be) chain has seen such a take-up of its wholesome, inventive sandwiches, pastas and salads that it now has shops all over town (and has expanded into France and Italy). This is fresh, ethical fast food at its best, with tapenades instead of butter and no sell-by dates; any leftovers are given to homeless charities at the end of each day.

A new organic restaurant that has made its mark is **Soul** (*see left*), in the Upper Town. Its menu eschews additives, refined sugar, butter and cream in favour of nutritious, often organic ingredients, with typical mains running from carrot and nut falafel with spiced lentils and raita to salmon fillet and quinoa risotto with green beans, seeds, feta and dill.

Soul.

CONSUME

CONSUME

EU QUARTER & ETTERBEEK

L'Atelier Européen

28 rue Franklin (02 734 91 40, www.atelier-euro.be). Métro Schuman. **Open** noon-2.30pm, 7-10pm Mon-Fri. **Main courses** €19. **Credit** AmEx, DC, MC, V. **Map** p321 J5 ❸
Modern European
The former wine warehouse, with a leafy courtyard out front, was converted into a studio and then a restaurant, though the studio feel remains – it's light and airy, with a beamed roof and whitewashed brick walls. The food is a mix of Belgian and French, with a focus on fish, though the buffet is a good alternative. Prices are reasonable for the area, which makes the place lively – especially in summer.

Au Bain Marie

46 rue Breydel (02 280 48 88). Métro Schuman. **Open** noon-2pm Mon-Fri. **Main courses** €13. **Credit** AmEx, DC, MC, V. **Map** p323 J6 ❸
Italian
See p127 **Green Cuisine**.

L'Esprit de Sel Brasserie

52-54 place Jourdan (02 230 60 40, www.esprit desel.be). Métro Schuman. **Open** noon-2.30pm, 7-10pm midnight daily. **Main courses** €18. **Credit** AmEx, DC, MC, V. **Map** p322 H7 ❸
Brasserie
What used to be two restaurants have now become one. The menu is the same, but the looks are different: one section is slightly more trad, with an amazing Murano glass chandelier, while the other is all wood, marble and copper. But it matters not a jot when you get round to tucking into the best of Belgian, from simple roast chicken and chips to rabbit in sour beer or beef tournedos with port. Popular with artistes, free thinkers and the odd celebrity.

Kafenio

134 rue Stevin (02 231 55 55, www.kafenio.be). Métro Schuman. **Open** noon-3pm, 6-11pm daily. **Main courses** €15. **Credit** MC, V. **Map** p320 H5 ❸ Greek
It's at lunchtimes that this Greek-inspired restaurant and bar really swings into action, with every table taken and a queue forming at the door. The reason is the buffet meze bar, where – accompanied by a waiter – you can make your selection from 50 hot and cold dishes, sit down with a drink and await delivery.

Le Midi Cinquante

Musées Royaux d'Art et d'Histoire, 10 Parc du Cinquantenaire (02 735 87 54). Métro Mérode. **Open** 10.30am-4.30pm Tue-Sun. **Main courses** €12. **Credit** AmEx, MC, V. **Map** p323 K6 ❸
Modern European
This classy, distinctive restaurant attracts not just visitors to the museum, but the movers and shakers of the EU Quarter. Renowned for its pasta dishes, Le Midi is all about generous portions, perfectly prepared and cleanly presented. Also on offer are innovative soups and lighter dishes, as well as Moroccan tagine and oriental-inspired salads. As befits so grand a building, the dining room is eloquent and elegant; the lovely terrace overlooking the park is packed solid in summer.

La Terrasse

1 avenue des Celtes (02 732 28 51, www. brasserielaterrasse.be). Métro Mérode. **Open** 8am-midnight Mon-Wed; 8am-1am Thur-Sat; 10am-midnight Sun. **Main courses** €14. **Credit** AmEx, DC, MC, V. **Map** p323 L7 ❸ Belgian
Set on the other side of the Parc de Cinquantenaire from the EU institutions, this bar makes an ideal meeting spot thanks to its proximity to Mérode métro, and the sun-dappled terrace from which it takes its name. Set back far enough from the traffic of avenue de Tervueren to give the illusion of rustic supping, La Terrasse is more than just a summer retreat; in autumn, while the kitchen is cooking up mussels in eight varieties, the respectable clientele moves inside to a chatty, old-style brasserie of wooden furnishings beneath globe light fittings.
▶ *Follow lunch with a walk around the green expanses of the Parc de Cinquantenaire.*

IXELLES & ST-GILLES
Ixelles

L'Ancienne Poissonnerie

65 rue du Trône (02 502 75 05, www.ancienne poissonnerie.be). Métro Trône. **Open** noon-3pm, 7-11pm Mon-Fri; 7-11pm Sat. **Main courses** €20. **Credit** AmEx, DC, M, V. **Map** p322 F7 ❸
Italian
The art nouveau Poissonnerie began life as a baker's, then became a fish and seafood emporium. It is now a listed monument so, mercifully, its exterior cannot be changed. In its third incarnation, owner Nicola Piscopo has created a rather beautiful Italian restaurant in a white and bleached wood setting, an imaginative mix of the old and new working in harmony. Classic meat, fish and own-made pasta dishes are served from an open-view, white

tiled kitchen; the food is Italian, but with a nod to French and other world influences. It attracts the suits at lunchtime and the well-heeled in the evening, but the AP remains a bastion of democratic eating.

Café Belga
18 place Flagey (02 640 35 08, www.cafebelga.be).
Bus 71. **Open** 9.30am-2am Mon-Thur, Sun; 9.30am-3am Fri, Sat. **Main courses** €12.
No credit cards. Map p322 G10 ⓴ **Café**
The shop window of the prestigious Flagey arts complex, Café Belga spreads itself over the ground floor of this former broadcasting house, its zinc and chrome 1950s look another attractive design by leisure guru Fred Nicolay and his team. It's sleek and spacious, certainly, but not without charm, and always, always busy. Unless you're eating here – options include soups, salads and sandwiches – it's counter service only, and not cheap, but that doesn't stop the flow of young arty types through its rather grandiose doors.

★ Chez Marie
40 rue Alphonse de Witte (02 644 30 31).
Tram 81, 82 or bus 71. **Open** noon-2.15pm, 7.30-10.30pm Tue-Fri; 7.30-10.30pm Sat.

L'Idiot du Village. *See p125.*

Main courses €26. **Credit** AmEx, MC, V.
Map p325 G10 ㊶ **French**
Marie's has become a little star in the restaurant scene, especially after super-chef Lilian Devaux won herself a Michelin sparkler for her efforts. Sitting by the ponds, the diminutive restaurant smacks of country living, with wood panelling, an old bar, an open kitchen, rustic checks and homely curtains. The contrast comes in the modern take on French cooking, which eschews heavy, cream-laden sauces in favour of fresh reductions and concentrated flavours. The fact that seafood is brought in from Brittany and pigeon and duck from the south west of France give some idea of the attention to detail and the quality of the food. Not surprisingly, booking is essential.

Cose Cosi
16 chaussée de Wavre (02 512 11 71, www2.resto.be/cosecosi). Métro Porte de Namur.
Open noon-3pm, 6-11.30pm daily. **Main courses** €18. **Credit** AmEx, MC, V. **Map** p319 E7 ㊷ **Italian**
From the outside, Cosi looks just a bit smarter than your average Italiano. Inside, the first surprise is the size of the place and how many diners it manages to pack in. Then you notice the antelope heads, animal skins, Zulu spears, faux shuttered windows, tropical plants; you could be in a safari lodge, except there's a baby grand piano where staff step up for a quick song. As bizarre as it may sound, it hangs together surprisingly well, with a lively atmosphere and generous plates of finely prepared Italian staples and grilled meats and fish. The staff are exceedingly friendly and efficient, the wine flows and the chatter is loud. All in all, a fine night out.

★ Le Deuxième Element
7 rue St-Boniface (02 502 00 28, www.2eme element.be). Métro Porte de Namur. **Open** noon-2.30pm, 7-11.30pm Mon-Fri; 7-11.30pm Sat, Sun.
Main courses €12. **Credit** AmEx, DC, MC, V.
Map p319 F7 ㊸ **Thai**
Instead of bamboo and Buddhas, this place favours chic minimalist, with wooden café tables and stylish modern art. The food is authentic Thai, though, with simple ingredients and menu choices ensuring there's no meddling with time-honoured flavours; plenty of ginger, lemongrass and fresh basil ensure a perfect red curry. Lunchtime shoppers and business people refuelling with a *plat du jour* make way for large groups of loud friends in the evening. Le Deuxième gets mobbed every mealtime, so it's always best to book.

L'Elément Terre
465 chaussée de Waterloo (02 649 37 27, www.resto.com/lelementterre). Tram 92. **Open** noon-2.30pm, 7-10.30pm Tue-Fri; 7-10.30pm Sat. **Main courses** €18. **Credit** DC, MC, V. **Map** p324 D12 ㊹ **Vegetarian**

CONSUME

Profile Jeannot

Muscadet and molluscs make the perfect lunch.

Jean Krol.

'*Le roi des moules!*' proclaims a portly man, dunking the king of mussels raw into a muddy vinaigrette on place Ste-Catherine's historic square.

'Don't listen to him, he's Italian,' laughs Jean Krol, known to locals as Jeannot. For the last two decades, Jeannot has been setting up his stall at 8.30am and selling fresh shellfish until 6pm. The mussels in question are all gobbled up – without ever seeing a pan of boiling water – by 2pm.

You can't miss his slightly tatty stall announcing six kinds of raw *huîtres* (oysters) and *moules* (mussels) straight from La Manche, to be washed down with muscadet wine, never beer.

'I'm always here,' he says, 'although during the Christmas market they shove me around the back of Ste-Catherine church as I'm not as aesthetic as the others.' Nonetheless, his humble stall attracts the great and the good; former prime minister Guy Verhofstadt, for one, who regularly showed up with a minister or two for a vitamin-packed shellfish lunch.

Shellfish arrive from Colchester, Zeeland and off the Brittany and Aquitaine coastlines. A middle man ships them over daily from the world's largest wholesale fresh produce market, Rungis, near Paris. Oysters come in six different sizes, and you can buy a plate of six or a dozen to eat on the spot or take away; new methods of oyster farming mean they're safe to eat all year round, not just in the 'r' months. The French eat mussels all year, but Belgian *moules*-munchers don't like the milky substance they produce during the reproductive season, May to July. Jeannot himself only eats mussels at the beginning of the season ('I get a bit fed up with them after that'), but consumes a dozen oysters every day, and giggles when declaring their legendary aphrodisiac qualities.
Jeannot Moules & Huîtres/ Mosselen & Oesters, place Ste-Catherine (02 410 09 44).

Le Pré Salé.

MUSSEL-BOUND
Prefer your mussels cooked and accompanied by chips? Try **Bij den Boer** (*see p121*) or **Le Pré Salé** (*see p123*), both of which are nearby.

CONSUME

The 'Elementary' is a small vegetarian place that also serves meat dishes. Confused? This is Brussels. The excellent food seems to arrive wearing slippers, and voices are rarely raised, maybe in reverence for the fine organic, chargrilled, caramelised vegetables, and the clever combinations of pulses and grains. The 'discovery plate' is a good way into the menu, offering a taste of this and that. Tasty, perhaps, but not the most riotous night out.

Le Fils de Jules

35 rue du Page (02 534 00 57, www.filsde jules.be). Tram 81, 92, 97. **Open** noon-2.30pm, 7-11pm Tue-Thur; noon-2.30pm, 7pm-midnight Fri; 7pm-midnight Sat, Sun. **Main courses** €20. **Credit** AmEx, DC, MC, V. **Map** p324 D11 ᐊ⑮
French

Jules is an integral part of Châtelain, pulling in classy urbanites hungry for its authentic French foodie experience. The difference here is that the menu is firmly based in the Landais and Basque region, with dripping duck products, chunks of fish, thick lentils and Salardais potatoes drenched in garlic. The wine list is a discovery, too, with its illegible local-language labels. The decor is a blend of New York art deco and 1970s copper, but the punters add the real colour; set Sunday menus ensure a full house.

La Porte des Indes

455 avenue Louise (02 647 86 51, www.laporte desindes.com). Tram 97. **Open** noon-2.30pm, 7-10.30pm Mon-Thur; noon-2.30pm, 7-11pm Fri, Sat; 7-10.30pm Sun. **Main courses** €22. **Credit** AmEx, DC, MC, V. **Map** p324 G13 ⑯ Indian

Not for the curry-and-pint-of-Kingfisher crowd, this. La Porte is refined and expensive, hushed and cushioned, decorated in Maharaja baroque with vast palms and over-the-top lighting and artefacts. It all hangs together in a rich and warming way, creating the perfect backdrop for the top-notch southern Indian food (with nods to the north). A dish from the royal court of Hyderabad – lamb cutlets soaked in garam masala, ginger and lemon – is an example of the finesse and careful balance achieved in the kitchen. Dress well and expect to spend liberally.

La Quincaillerie

45 rue du Page (02 533 98 33, www.quincaillerie. be). Tram 81, 92, 97. **Open** noon-2.30pm, 7pm-midnight Mon-Sat; 7pm-midnight Sun. **Main courses** €25. **Credit** AmEx, DC, MC, V. **Map** p324 D11 ⑰ Brasserie

The name means ironmonger, but don't think this is any old theme restaurant. The fine interior is largely untouched, its tables set with the original wooden drawers for holding nails, screws and widgets. A cast-iron gallery circles the ensemble, overlooked by a giant clock. The seafood bar, piled with crustaceans, is considered one of the best in the city, and the restaurant attracts a wealthy set. It's puzzling

that the service is often abrupt, even rude, although that doesn't seem to scare anyone off – book for any night of the week.

Rick's Bar

344 avenue Louise (02 647 75 30). Métro Louise then tram 97. **Open** 11am-midnight Mon-Sat; 10am-4pm Sun. **Main courses** €15. **Credit** AmEx, DC, MC, V. **Map** p324 F11 ᐊ⑱
American

Rick's is by far and away the best-known of all the American bars in Brussels, almost as well known in these parts as the *Casablanca* bar that spawned its concept. Housed in a magnificent three-storey townhouse on avenue Louise, it's swish and chic but serves what is arguably the best bar brunch in town. There are full meals, too – T-bone steaks, Rick's ribs and the like – but it's mainly used as a networking bar. Frequented by suits, it's a busy after-office haunt, and the rear terrace is glorious in summer.

Saint Boniface

9 rue St-Boniface (02 511 53 66). Métro Porte de Namur or bus 71. **Open** noon-2.30pm, 7-10pm Mon-Fri. **Main courses** €20. **Credit** AmEx, MC, V. **Map** p319 F7 ᐊ⑲ French

La Quincaillerie.

The Boniface looks as if it has stood on its little plot forever, beamed up from a distant Dordogne village. It cares not a jot for its trendier neighbours, its red and white checked cottage feel throwing out a warm, traditional light. Old posters and oil lamps stand guard over a menu of rich and hearty Périgordine classics: duck, puy lentils, foie gras, lamb studded with garlic and sliced potatoes soaked in goose fat. Notices pinned to the wall warn that mobile phones are not welcome. All well and good – you shouldn't be distracted from the authentic eating in this timewarp joint.

★ De la Vigne à l'Assiette

51 rue de la Longue Haie (02 647 68 03, http://sites.resto.com/delavignealassiette). Métro Louise. **Open** noon-2pm, 7-10pm Tue-Fri; 7-10pm Sat. **Main courses** €20. **Credit** AmEx, MC, V. **Map** p319 E9 ❺⓪ **Modern European**
Eddy Dandimont, joint owner of this tiny brasserie, is an award-winning sommelier. His stunning and reasonably priced wine list complements the menu perfectly, which serves up dishes that are French based but make quirky use of spices, herbs and subtle infusions. Much care is taken with the vegetables and salads, and nothing screams for lack of attention. The room is rustic in feel, with globe lamps and scrubbed walls, while the youngish Ixelles clientele adds to the atmosphere.

St-Gilles

€ Bosquet 58

58 rue Bosquet (02 544 13 15). Métro Hôtel des Monnaies. **Open** noon-3pm, 6-10pm Mon-Fri; 6-10pm Sat, Sun. **Main courses** €15. **Credit** MC, V. **Map** p319 D8 ❺① **French**
Hidden away in a quiet residential street and set in an old bar, Bosquet has a reputation based on word of mouth alone. Fed up of the stress of big kitchens, French chef Marc Louradour decided to set up this modest establishment, serving a two- or three-course *menu resto*. And what menus they are: duck breasts, leg of lamb, sole, all served with masses of veggies and sauce. It's only him cooking (even his own bread) and his wife serving out front, so it can be a bit slow at weekends when it's busier.

Café des Spores

103 chaussée d'Alsemberg (02 534 13 03, www.cafedesspores.be). Tram 55, 90. **Open** 7pm-midnight Mon, Sat; noon-2pm, 7pm-midnight Tue-Fri. **Main courses** €12. **Credit** AmEx, MC, V. **Modern European**
Anyone for mushrooms? If not, you're better off elsewhere. At the Café des Spores, earthy fungi feature in every dish on the menu. Cartoonist-cum-chef Pierre Lefèvre has fallen in love with the humble mushroom, forever experimenting with its possibilities and describing his culinary endeavours as 'cuisine ruled by nature'. People travel from afar to try

his imaginative menus, which change daily according to his mood and what's available. Even the decor is woodland inspired, with autumnal stripes.
▶ *Just opposite, La Buvette is Pierre's original venture – an old horse butcher's shop turned into a place for pre-dinner drinks.*

Ma Folle de Soeur

53 chaussée de Charleroi (02 538 22 39, www.mafolledesoeur.be). Métro Louise or tram 92. **Open** noon-2.30pm, 6-10.30pm Mon-Sat. **Main courses** €16. **Credit** MC, V. **Map** p319 D8 ❺② **Modern European**
Run by two sisters, this small restaurant has a huge picture window facing on to the street and an understated and mellow dining room, its wooden bar and tables softened by yellow walls and soft candlelight in the evening. The menu has flair and a touch of adventure – it's Belgian in nature, with French bistro influences. Meat (duck, steak and even horse) is to the fore, and dressed with imaginative sauces. The suits give way to young lovers and groups of friends in the evening. There's a back garden too.

€ Maison du Peuple

39 parvis de St-Gilles (02 850 09 08, www.maison-du-peuple.be). Pré-métro Parvis de St-Gilles. **Open** 8.30am-1am daily. **Main courses** €8. **Credit** MC, V. **Map** p318 B9 ❺③ **Café**
Situated on the ground floor of a wonderful turn of the century building, MdP is a vibrant blend of café culture, live music and art. Exhibitions and parties are attended by an ever-so-cool but friendly crowd, and there's an early-evening happy hour. Breakfast is available first thing, then the kitchen turns its attention to well-made antipasti, *croque monsieurs*, quiches and panini. It goes without saying that MdP offers free Wi-Fi to its customers.

Aux Mille et Une Nuits

7 rue de Moscou (02 537 41 27, www.milleetune nuits.be). Pré-métro Parvis de St-Gilles. **Open** noon-3pm, 6-11.30pm Mon-Sat. **Main courses** €15. **Credit** MC, V. **Map** p318 B9 ❺④ **Tunisian**
You might think twice before walking into this pink-painted Tunisian restaurant, but its full-on lighting and kitsch decor give it an edge in an area packed with North African restaurants. It resembles a modern Bedouin tent, with oriental rugs hanging from the walls and thousands of tiny lights sparkling brightly above like stars. And the food? Out of this world. For starters, try the harira chickpea soup or honey-soaked chicken in crisp pastry. Then there's the eternal dilemma of tagine or couscous, although you really can't go far wrong with either the caramelised lamb couscous or chicken tagine with grapes and honey. The service is impeccable.

Salons de l'Atalaïde

89 chaussée de Charleroi (02 538 29 29, http://lessalons.be). Tram 92. **Open** 11.30am-

CONSUME

11.30pm Mon-Fri; 7pm-midnight Sat. **Main courses** €21. **Credit** MC, V. **Map** p319 D9 🕔
Modern European
This former auction house is now an off-the-wall, over-the-top restaurant. Baroque mirrors, ornate chandeliers, oversized paintings, Gothic candles and ostentatious palms combine to give it a slightly unreal edge. The menu reflects a fresh take on Franco-Belgian cooking, so seasonal ingredients replace the old year-round staples.

FURTHER AFIELD

Les 2 Frères
2 avenue Vanderaey, Uccle (02 376 76 06, www. les2freres.be). Tram 52. **Open** noon-2.30pm, 7-11pm Mon-Fri; 7-11pm Sat. **Main courses** €20. **Credit** AmEx, DC, MC, V. French
Ex-maths teacher Patrick Roth has created an unusual equation between rustic and urban style in this classy French brasserie. Highlights of the menu

Belgian Bounty

Sturdy, satisfying classics are the mainstays of the local cuisine.

The Romans may have made mussels and oysters fashionable, but it was later invaders who gave Belgium its cuisine. Dutch, French, Spanish and Austrian rulers introduced a rich array of cooking styles – and as Breugel's vivid paintings and the banqueting scenes depicted in old Flemish tapestries testify, eating has always been a national pastime.

Belgium's fields are ideal for growing the potatoes, chicory and asparagus so central to its cuisine. They also support the famous Blanc-Bleu Belge cattle, for the ubiquitous *steak-frites*. The forests of the Ardennes are home to the venison, boar and wild hare that appear on menus in the *chasse* season, while the cold North Sea offers up tiny shrimps (*crevettes grises*), sole, crab and, of course, mussels and oysters (*see p130* **Profile**) from Zeeland.

Fussy presentation is generally frowned upon. Take *anguilles au vert*, a thick soupy affair in which chunks of eel lie suspended in a startling green sauce; although powerful and filling, it is less than pleasing to the eye. *Andouillette*, meanwhile, is a massive banger packed full of springy innards. Spiced and seasoned, the sausages are graded according to roughness. Their slightly softer cousin is the *boudin* from Liège, in a black (blood) or white form. *Filet américain* is raw, minced and spiced-up beef. Order this and you'll have a soft pink mound on your plate, looking a little like cat food, though surprisingly tasty. A much safer bet is *waterzooi*, found on every traditional Belgian menu. Made with chicken or fish, this stew from Ghent is rich with egg yolk and cream.

include cutlets of suckling pig caramelised with honey and lime, and tuna sashimi in a herb crust. As the kitchen closes the 2 Frères turns into a bar.

★ Bon-Bon
93 rue des Carmelites, Uccle (02 346 66 15, www.bon-bon.be). Tram 92. **Open** noon-2pm, 7-10pm Tue-Fri; 7-10.30pm Sat. **Main courses** €40. **Credit** AmEx, DC, MC, V. **French**
Bare brick and natural woods contrast nicely with crisp linen in this classy, Michelin-starred restaurant. Young chef Christophe Hardiquest honed his skills in some of Brussels' top establishments, including Sea Grill (*see p119*), La Villa Lorraine and the Conrad Brussels hotel. He and his team are artisans, crafting each day's menu from the best seasonal ingredients. It might be fish in a salt crust or tuna tartare with herb sorbet, but you'll never know until you get there. The simple, fresh flavours come with a strong Mediterranean influence.

Les Brasseries Georges
259 avenue Winston Churchill, Uccle (02 347 21 00, www.brasseriesgeorges.be). Tram 23, 90.

Deciphering the Menu

Know your andouillette from your anguille.

Virtually all menus in Brussels are written in French, though most restaurants in the centre also have versions in Dutch and English.

Meat (viande)
agneau lamb; **andouillette** chitterling sausage of offal; **biche** venison (doe); **boeuf** beef; **boudin noir/boudin blanc** black or white pudding; **caille** quail; **canard** duck; **confit de canard** preserved duck leg; **magret de canard** duck breast; **caneton** duckling; **cerf** venison (stag); **cervelle** brain; **cheval** horse; **chevreuil** venison; **dinde** turkey; **escargot** snail; **faisan** pheasant; **foie** liver; **gésier** gizzard; **gibier** game; **(cuisses de) grenouille** frog's legs; **jambon** ham; **jambonneau** ham (normally knuckle) on the bone; **langue** tongue; **lapin** rabbit; **lard** bacon; **lardon** small cube of bacon; **lièvre** hare; **oie** goose; **perdreau** young partridge; **perdrix** partridge; **pied** foot/trotter; **pintade/pintadeau** guinea fowl; **porc** pork; **poulet** chicken; **ris** sweetbreads; **rognon** kidney; **sanglier** boar; **saucisse** sausage; **tripes** tripe; **veau** veal; **volaille** poultry/chicken; **suprême de volaille** chicken breast. *Cooking terms* **bleu** all but raw; **saignant** rare; **rosé** pink (for lamb, duck, liver and kidneys); **à point** medium rare; **bien cuit** well done.

Fish & seafood (poisson & fruits de mer)
crustacé shellfish; **anguille** eel; **bar** similar to sea bass; **barbue** brill; **brochet** pike; **cabillaud** cod; **carrelet** plaice; **coquille St Jacques** scallop; **colin** hake; **crevette** shrimp; **crevettes grises** tiny sweet shrimps; **daurade** sea bream; **écrevisse** crayfish (freshwater); **eglefin** haddock; **espadon** swordfish; **flétan** halibut; **hareng** herring; **homard** lobster; **huître** oyster; **langoustine** Dublin Bay prawn/scampi; **limande** lemon sole; **lotte** monkfish; **loup de mer** similar to sea bass; **maquereau** mackerel; **merlin** whiting; **merlu** hake; **morue** dried salt cod; **moule** mussel; **palourde** clam; **plie** plaice; **poulpe** octopus; **raie** skate; **rouget** red mullet; **roussette** rock salmon/dogfish; **St-Pierre** John Dory; **sandre** pike-perch; **saumon** salmon; **scampi** prawn; **seiche** squid; **thon** tuna; **truite** trout.

Vegetables (légumes)
ail garlic; **artichaut** artichoke; **asperge** asparagus; **aubergine** aubergine/eggplant; **betterave** beetroot; **céleri** celery; **céleri**

Open 11.30am-12.30am Mon-Thur; 11.30am-1am Fri, Sat. **Main courses** €25. **Credit** AmEx, DC, MC, V. **Brasserie**

At Les Brasseries Georges, the feel of a fin-de-siècle Parisian brasserie is generated to perfection by the twisting copper and brass, the vast stained-glass windows, potted palms and statuettes of classical muses, all opened up by the obligatory red curtain as you walk through the doors. The specialities are the crustacea: oysters, whelks and the like, brought together either as a starter or a vast *plateau de fruits de mer.*

Senza Nome

22 rue Royale Ste-Marie, Schaerbeek (02 223 16 17, www.senzanome.be). Tram 92, 93, 94. **Open** noon-2pm, 7-9.30pm Mon-Fri; 7-9.30pm Sat. **Main courses** €25. **Credit** MC, V. **Italian**

Senza Nome steers clear of predictable Italian fare with a short, seasonal menu, offering the likes of stuffed sardines, *sèche* (whole baby squid, guts included) black-inked pastas or *branzino* (sea bass), bursting with citrus flavours and sun-ripe tomatoes.

▶ *Book ahead, as it's popular with audiences at the nearby Halles de Schaerbeek.*

---

rave celeriac; **cèpe** cep mushroom; **champignon** mushroom; **chicon** chicory/Belgian endive; **chou** cabbage; **choucroute** sauerkraut; **chou-fleur** cauliflower; **cresson** watercress; **échalote** shallot; **épinards** spinach; **fève** broad bean/fava bean; **frisée** curly endive; **girolle** pale wild mushroom; **haricot** bean; **haricot vert** French bean; **morille** morel mushroom; **navet** turnip; **oignon** onion; **pleurotte** oyster mushroom; **poireau** leek; **poivron vert/rouge** green/red pepper/bell pepper; **pomme de terre** potato; **truffe** truffle.

Fruit (fruits)

ananas pineapple; **banane** banana; **cassis** blackcurrant; **cerise** cherry; **citron** lemon; **citron vert** lime; **fraise** strawberry; **framboise** raspberry; **griotte** morello cherry; **groseille** redcurrant; **groseille à maquereau** gooseberry; **marron** chestnut; **mûre** blackberry; **myrtille** blueberry/bilberry; **pamplemousse** grapefruit; **pêche** peach; **poire** pear; **pomme** apple; **prune** plum; **pruneau** prune; **raisin** grape.

Desserts (desserts)

crème anglaise custard; **crème chantilly** whipped cream; **Dame Blanche** vanilla ice-cream with hot chocolate sauce; **feuilleté** layers of puff pastry; **gâteau** cake; **glace** ice-cream; **glacé** frozen or iced; **île flottante** soft meringue floating on custard sauce; **macédoine de fruits** fruit salad; **massepain** marzipan; **mignardises** small biscuits or cakes to accompany coffee; **soufflé glacé** iced soufflé.

Herbs & spices (herbes & épices)

aneth dill; **basilic** basil; **cannelle** cinnamon; **cerfeuil** chervil; **ciboulette** chive; **citronelle** lemongrass; **estragon** tarragon; **fenouil**

fennel; **muscade** nutmeg; **persil** parsley; **romarin** rosemary; **sauge** sage; **thym** thyme.

General

amande almond; **beignet** fritter or doughnut; **beurre** butter; **chaud** warm/hot; **chèvre** goat's cheese; **cru** raw; **farci** stuffed; **frites** chips; **froid** cold; **fromage** cheese; **fumé** smoked; **gaufre** waffle; **gelée** aspic; **haché** minced; **lentille** lentil; **miel** honey; **moutarde** mustard; **noisette** hazelnut; **noix** walnut; **nouilles** noodles; **oeuf** egg; **pain** bread; **pâtes** pasta; **poivre** pepper; **potage** soup; **riz** rice; **sel** salt; **sec/sèche** dry; **sucre** sugar; **thé** tea; **végétarien(ne)** vegetarian.

CONSUME

Pubs & Bars

A drink for every occasion.

Drinking is a part of Belgian culture, just as ingrained with time, honour and smoke as the Gothic stones of the Grand'Place itself. The range of bars and beers speak not only of the national history, but also of a drinking culture that is easily as significant as wine with Burgundy or tea with England.

At the centre of this culture is beer. Not just any old beer, but some 600 varieties in almost as many colours and flavours, and brewed by everyone from reclusive Trappist monks to major multinational concerns (*see p147* **A Beer for All Seasons**).

The sizeable expat population in Brussels has introduced the ubiquitous Irish pub into the cityscape; go to these to drink Guinness, speak English and watch sport on large screens.

DRINKING IN BRUSSELS

Ask for '*une bière*' and you'll get a standard glass of standard draught lager, invariably Maes, Stella or Jupiler, costing €1.50-€2. French speakers should note that asking for a '*demi*', as you would do for a standard small glass in France, will get you a half-litre and nods from fellow drinkers. '*Une blanche*' will get you a €2 glass of draught wheat beer. For a bottle of one of the more interesting brews, choose by name from a lengthy menu. As a starting point, it may be helpful to distinguish between *blonde* and *brune* types, light or dark. Most also have their alcohol content marked.

Bar opening hours are gloriously lax in Brussels. Drinking until midnight almost anywhere in town is easy; past 1am, you'll need to be in the centre, where dawn is not an uncommon closing time.

Downtown drinking begins, inevitably, with the Grand'Place, lined with imposing, terraced guildhouse pubs where aproned waiters serve hulking portions of food. Prices are higher here, but not budget-bustingly so. Around it fans a large network of bar-starred streets. South-westward snakes rue du Marché au Charbon, the spine of the gay quarter, Brussels' best bar-hop. Across boulevard Anspach, St-Géry is home to style cafés instigated by bar guru Fred Nicolay. Elsewhere, bars tend to reflect the area they serve. Sablon's are as glitzy as the neighbouring Marolles' are scuzzy. Ixelles' are a mixture of African (rue de Longue Vie), trendy (around place St-Boniface), student-oriented (near Ixelles cemetery) and snobbish (avenue Louise). More modern establishments on the Ixelles-St-Gilles corridor are sure to have been trendified. Those in the heart of St-Gilles will have a villagey feel, while the pubs of the EU Quarter provide expats with a drinking and networking facility.

LOWER TOWN
Grand'Place & around

A la Bécasse
11 rue de Tabora (02 511 00 06, www.ala becasse.com). Pré-métro Bourse. **Open** 11am-midnight Mon-Thur, Sun; 11am-1am Fri, Sat. **Credit** MC, V. **Map** p315 C4 ❶

INSIDE TRACK
TO SMOKE OR NOT TO SMOKE

Smoking in restaurants is banned, but bars are allowed to make up their own minds. Depending on layout, bars can be all-smoking, have a designated smoking area or ban their customers from lighting up at all. It's easy to work out which is which; if in doubt, check the door or window for the little red circle.

This bar comes as a surprise. From the street, all that marks its presence is a red neon light, hinting there's something tacky involved. Not at all. Look down at your feet, where a stone and brass welcome mat is fixed to the pavement. Follow the alley through the houses and you'll see the Dickensian-style bottle windows. Behind is an ancient tavern where customers sit at long tables and have their beer, including draught Lambic, poured from jugs by aproned waiters.

▶ *Nearby is another tucked-away beer-lover's paradise: L'Imaige de Nostre-Dame (8 rue du Marché aux Herbes, 02 219 42 49).*

Le Cercle des Voyageurs

18 rue des Grandes Carmes (02 514 39 49, www.lecercledesvoyageurs.com). Pré-métro Bourse. **Open** 11am-11pm Mon, Wed, Thur; 11am-midnight Fri; noon-midnight Sat; noon-10pm Sun. Closed Mon mid June-mid Aug. **Credit** MC, V. **Map** p315 C5 ❷

As the name suggests, the Cercle des Voyageurs is a place for travellers to meet. So as well as drinking in a laid-back, colonial-inspired setting in a grand old Brussels house, there are lots of events and talks about all aspects of travel. Check the website for upcoming turns. It's perfect for those on the road wanting some inside information – speak to the regulars or consult books and periodicals in the library. It even offers international dance classes in salsa and flamenco.

THE BEST BARS

For philosophising
Au Daringman is just right for putting the world to rights. Even if you're alone, you'll soon find someone to chew the fat with. *See p141.*

For beers on tap
Head to **Chez Moeder Lambic Fontainas** for beer nirvana (and possibly oblivion). The 40 draughts, plus guests, are glorious to behold. *See above.*

To preen and be seen
Anywhere in the Châtelain area will do the trick, but draping yourself around **OENO TK** will up your cred no end. *See p151.*

For genteel sipping
Polish your shoes, don your pearls and make for the **Métropole**. *See right.*

For hanging out in the Lower Town
Fontainas is *the* place to be in the Lower Town. Gay, straight – whatever you want to be is just fine here. *See right.*

★ Chez Moeder Lambic Fontainas

8 place Fontainas (02 503 60 68, www.moeder lambic.eu/sitebar/). Pré-métro Anneessens. **Open** 11am-1am Mon-Thur, Sun; 11am-2am Fri, Sat. **No credit cards**. **Map** p315 C5 ❸

The new and thoroughly modern daughter of the older St-Gilles Moeder Lambic (*see p151*) is a splendid addition to the city's bar scene. This bright young thing sits in an old townhouse on the unglamorous place Fontainas, right at the end of the Marché au Charbon crawl, providing a punctuation mark to a long evening of drinking. Its 40 lesser-known draught Belgian beers make this a place of discovery, along with a menu more befitting a wine bar. The crowd ranges from nouveau Goth to clipped professional, all there for a glass or two of something special.

▶ *For more on Moeder Lambic, see p150.*

Délirium Café

4a impasse de la Fidélité Carmes (02 514 44 34, www.deliriumcafe.be). Pré-métro Bourse. **Open** 10am-4am daily. **Credit** AmEx, DC, MC, V. **Map** p315 D4 ❹

In a tiny alley off rue des Bouchers lies the big and brash Délirium, named after the powerful (8.5%) Belgian pale ale brew Délirium Tremens. The pink elephant tells you all you need to know. But don't think you're hallucinating when you see the menu of 2,000 Belgian and international beers and 500 genevers. This alone makes the DC one of the world's favoured meeting places for beer-lovers. The knowledgeable staff will help you around the menu, but keep an eye on the alcohol strengths unless you want to become a victim of the troublesome pachyderm.

La Fleur en Papier Doré

55 rue des Alexiens (02 511 16 59, www.lafleur enpapierdore.be). Pré-métro Anneessens. **Open** 11am-midnight Tue-Sat; 11am-7pm Sat, Sun. **No credit cards**. **Map** p315 C6 ❺

As the haunt of the surrealists, this quirky venue would make a mint from the tourist trail were it not stuck on an obscure, steep, grey street whose only function is to connect the Lower and Upper Towns. It's not that La Fleur is far from the action: it's just that it's the wrong side of a pleasant stroll. It attracts the more unusual tourist, happy to gawp at the doodles and sketches and stagger around in Magritte's wonky footsteps. An artistically active bunch of regulars, albeit a modest one, alleviate their solitude.

★ Fontainas

91 rue du Marché au Charbon (02 503 31 12). Pré-métro Anneessens or Bourse. **Open** 10.30am-1am Mon-Thur, Sun; 10.30am-2am Fri, Sat. **No credit cards**. **Map** p315 C5 ❻

Possibly – no, probably – the best bar on Brussels' best stretch for bar crawling, the Fontainas is wonderfully understated. Set opposite the equally enjoyable Au Soleil (*see p141*), it is full of lovely little retro

La Lunette.

touches – old beaded curtains, Formica chairs with chrome legs, vintage advertising – that would do justice to a 1950s milk bar. Yet the place is as determinedly 21st century as the gay/straight mixed clientele: reliably excellent sounds from fiery resident DJs; strong cocktails; rare Orval and Maredsous brews. Throw in a few terrace tables when the sun's out and you have somewhere simply head and shoulders above anything going on in St-Géry.

Goupil le Fol
22 rue de la Violette (02 511 13 96). Métro Gare Centrale. **Open** 7.30pm-5am daily. **No credit cards. Map** p315 C5 **7**
Goupil – the stocky, grey-haired gent handing out sweets by the front door at the end of the night – can but cash in. He has his staff urge questionable house fruit wines upon many a tourist, while only providing standard Jupiler (at €2.50 a glass!) by means of any beer alternative. So, what is there to recommend? Well, Goupil is a kooky labyrinthine junkshop of a bar, where all trace of time can be lost thanks to a jukebox of 3,000 choice slices of vinyl. It's eccentric, velvety and nostalgic; check the beads and commie kitsch. On the right night – in a group, or better still, *à deux* – it is perfect.

La Lunette
3 place de la Monnaie (02 218 03 78). Métro/ pré-métro De Brouckère. **Open** 9am-1am Mon-Thur; 9am-2am Fri, Sat; 10am-1am Sun. **No credit cards. Map** p315 D3 **8**
This has become a bit of an institution, partly because of its location near the commercial zone and

partly because of its beer list, with eight welcome on-tap varieties. Measures here come in a standard glass or a Lunette, which is like a magnum champagne glass. That's a polite way of putting it; ask for a Lunette and you get a bucket. A sleek two-floor interior of curved green banquettes would be much admired somewhere like Amsterdam; in Brussels it's par for the course. The clientele includes shoppers, drifters and folk waiting for a film to start.

Métropole
31 place de Brouckère (02 217 23 00, www.metropolehotel.be). Métro/pré-métro De Brouckère. **Open** 9am-1am daily. **Credit** MC, V. **Map** p315 D3 **9**
For a little fin-de-siècle finesse, pop into the café of the grand Hotel Métropole. This place is of a different age: over-burdened chandeliers, mirrored walls, ornate ironwork and a hush that hasn't changed for a century. A pillar of guests' autographs features Emerson Fittipaldi and Vera Lynn; Sarah Bernhardt also stayed here, and is reincarnated in the ladies with elaborate hairdos who sit on the terrace in sunglasses and fur coats all year round. Aperitifs dominate the drinks menu, along with champagnes offered by the bottle, half-bottle and quarter-bottle, delivered by bow-tied waiters. It's not all glamour, though – note the Heinz ketchup on each table.

★ A la Mort Subite
7 rue des Montagnes aux Herbes Potagères (02 513 13 18, www.alamortsubite.be). Métro Gare Centrale. **Open** 11am-12.30am Mon-Sat; 1pm-12.30am Sun. **Credit** MC, V. **Map** p315 D4 **10**

CONSUME

A la Mort Subite. *See p139.*

Named after a card game and a variety of fruit beer whose hangovers easily assume the mantle of sudden death, the popularity of this classically dissolute café soon saw the name pass into legend. Earning such post-booze pain is a real pleasure in this narrow, wood-and-mirror haven of ensozzlement. You could write your life's work novel before any of the waiters deign to serve you – in fact, attempting to do so would fail to raise many eyebrows – but it's all part of the character. Be warned: this is one of few venues to serve the local Gueuze, which is to be handled with care.

O'Reilly's
1 place de la Bourse (02 552 04 81, http:// oreillys.nl/brussels). Pré-métro Bourse. **Open** 11am-2am Mon-Thur, Sun; 11am-4am Fri, Sat. **Credit** AmEx, MC, V. **Map** p315 C4 ⑪
It's not to everyone's taste in a city where the quirky and the individual take pride of place, but there's no denying O'Reilly's part in the grand scheme of serious drinking and partying. For a start it occupies the most in-your-face plot in the Lower Town, immediately opposite the Bourse and at the entry to the St-Géry watering hole. Its bright green exterior is hard to miss, with customers spilling out on to the terrace and prime-seating micro balcony. It is from here that the stags, hens and footie fans shout their allegiance to the bewildered crowd below. There's a mix of Belgian and Irish draughts, along with sustaining Irish breakfasts from 11am.

Le Roi d'Espagne
1 Grand'Place (02 513 08 07, www.roidespagne. be). Pré-métro Bourse. **Open** 10am-1am daily. **Credit** AmEx, DC, MC, V. **Map** p315 C4 ⑫
The king of the guildhouses on the gilded square (it was the HQ of the bakers' guild), Le Roi is a classic spot in a prime location, taking full advantage of the tourist trade by filling its warren of dark rooms and corners with dangling marionettes, old prints and pigs' bladders. By all means pity the poor pigs, but also save some sympathy for the waiters in monk outfits, as they struggle to keep tabs on busy tables while tourists scrap it out for a seat with that view over the Grand'Place. Many a diplomatic incident has been caused grabbing one.
▶ *For a quick rundown of the guilds and their emblems, see p48.*

Au Soleil
86 rue du Marché au Charbon (02 513 34 30). Pré-métro Anneessens or Bourse. **Open** 10am-1am Mon-Thur, Sun; 10am-2am Fri, Sat. **No credit cards. Map** p315 C5 ⑬
Set in an extravagant old tailor's premises, Au Soleil is filled with a constant buzz from early doors – so much so that passing by without popping in can be difficult. Everyone seems to be talking on top of one another, when they're not looking impossibly interesting amid the fug of fumes. It's all a pose, of course,

but it's quite fun for all that, and it lures punters to tumble down Charbon like lemmings. The somewhat stern interior features plenty of marble and weighty metal, backdropped by picture windows and passers-by out on the town. *Photo p142.*

Toone
21 petite rue des Bouchers (02 513 54 86, www.toone.be). Pré-métro Bourse. **Open** noon-midnight Tue-Sun. **No credit cards. Map** p315 D4 ⑭
This might be a well-known spot on the tourist trail, but to call it a trap would be doing the Toone family a great injustice. Eight generations have worked the puppet theatre here, cynical in six tongues. This cosy, two-room dark-wood establishment is the old theatre bar, a familiar stop for many Brussophiles as it's quirky enough to show to first-time visitors (dangling marionettes and the like), quiet enough to enjoy in whispered intimacy, and not too quaint to put you off coming again. It's signposted by the Musée de la Ville de Bruxelles on the Grand'Place.

Ste-Catherine & around

★ Au Daringman
37 rue de Flandre (02 512 43 23). Métro Ste-Catherine. **Open** noon-1am Tue-Thur; noon-2am Fri; 4pm-2am Sat. **No credit cards. Map** p315 B3 ⑮
Also known as Chez Haesendonck or Chez Martine, this entertainingly retro brown bar is hidden between the fashion quarter and the canal. It attracts an enjoyably varied clientele, with theatregoing older couples sharing tobacco smoke and squeezed-in tables with folk of a younger, more boho bent. Surrounding them, jumble-sale shots of Elvis, Ella and others contrast with the wood panelling and an iconic Stella sign from the 1950s. It's bookended by a modest bar counter and regularly topped up with flyers and listings leaflets covering every art form, over- and underground.

CONSUME

CONSUME

Au Soleil. *See p141.*

Kafka

21 rue des Poissonniers (02 513 54 89). Pré-métro Bourse. **Open** 4pm-2am daily. **Credit** MC, V. **Map** p315 C4

If it's late and you're lashing back the vodkas, chances are you're in the Kafka. Not that you'll remember the next day, but this place boasts a heady array of vodkas, genevers and other assorted white spirits, plus all the usual beers to chase the chasers down with. Regulars may remember the bar being at a different address; in 2009, new owner Patrice moved it along the road to a bigger spot, but lovingly re-created the interior of the original, Kafka prints and all.

Monk

42 rue Ste-Catherine (02 503 08 80). Métro Ste-Catherine. **Open** 11am-2am Mon-Thur; 11am-4am Fri, Sat; 4pm-2am Sun. **No credit cards.** **Map** p315 C4

Occupying a 17th-century gabled house close to the main square, Monk is set apart by its big picture window and contemporary logo, a lettered square used on its sign and stickers. The interior comprises a long, dark-wood bar, soft-lit by railway carriage wall lights above a row of mirrored panels. Jazz sounds go with the territory – that's Monk as in Thelonious Monk, just so you know.

▶ *The city has long been renowned for its vibrant jazz scene, and there's still plenty going on; see p205.*

La Tentation

28 rue de Laeken (02 223 22 75, www.la tentation.org). Métro/pré-métro De Brouckère. **Open** 9am-4am Mon-Fri; 5pm-4am Sat, Sun. **Credit** V. **Map** p315 C3

Oozing urban chic, this converted drapery warehouse has huge windows, brick walls and effective low lighting. Staff are relaxed and friendly, and there's a stylish and civilised vibe, making it a good spot to start the evening or head to for a quiet drink. It's run by Brussels' Galician community, hence the menu (Spanish liqueurs, tapas, cheese and cold meats) and the odd flamenco night.

De Walvis

209 rue Antoine Dansaert (02 219 95 32, www.cafewalvis.be). Métro Ste-Catherine. **Open** 11am-2am Mon-Thur, Sun; 11am-4am Fri, Sat. **No credit cards.** **Map** p316 B3

Deep at the dark, canal end of Antoine Dansaert, the Whale is beached between kebab joints and shabby phone centres – but this bar is no small fry. It's another venture from the Nicolay team, responsible for revamping St-Géry at the more fashionable end of this same street. This venue has been given more gaudy retro touches than most of the others in the empire. Traffic-light red is the *couleur du choix* in an otherwise bare interior, offset by a quite bizarre ceiling. You'll find Chinese Tsing-Tao beer among the usual Belgian faves, a modest menu of snacks and

CONSUME

sandwiches, and an up-for-it clientele. Occasional jazz and regular DJs on Saturday nights bring in crowds from across Brussels.

St-Géry

★ L'Archiduc
6 rue Antoine Dansaert (02 512 06 52, www.archiduc.be). Pré-métro Bourse. **Open** 4pm-5am daily. **Credit** AmEx, MC, V. **Map** p315 C4 ⑳

The duke of all dives, the baron of all bars, the art deco L'Archiduc was reopened by Jean-Louis and Nathalie Hernant in 1985 in time to be part of the cultural wave that swept down rue Antoine Dansaert and washed over the rest of Brussels. Its predecessor dated back to 1937 and boasted an impeccable jazz pedigree. Charlie Parker played here, as did Nat King Cole. Class will out, and L'Archiduc proved the perfect vehicle for fashionistas and their chic cohorts, with its curvaceous, two-floor interior resembling an ocean-liner's ballroom, drifting across the Atlantic. It's a fine line here between decadence and decorum, with doorbell entry, pre-dawn drinking and *demi-monde* regulars adding to the appeal.

Le Coq
14 rue Auguste Orts (02 514 24 14). Pré-métro Bourse. **Open** 10am-late. **No credit cards**. **Map** p315 C4 ㉑

It's hard to know why certain unassuming, plain-looking bars make the mark on the Brussels scene. You could walk past Le Coq without giving it a moment's thought, its wood panelled walls and flat lighting resembling any bar in any town. But there's magic inside, from the indifferent professionalism of the older-generation staff (who close up when people have gone) to the eclectic mix of daytime boozers and night owls, all there for an unpretentious drink and deep philosophical banter.

Gecko
16 place St-Géry (02 502 29 99, www.gecko cocktailbar.be). Pré-métro Bourse. **Open** 9am-2am Mon-Thur; 10am-3am Fri; 10am-3am Sat, Sun. **No credit cards**. **Map** p315 B4 ㉒

This once in-the-know splinter of St-Géry, narrow of interior and thin in customers, is now a full-blown bar attracting an across-the-board clientele with cut-price lunches, zingy cocktails and – after a welcome expansion – cosy alcoves and casual furnishings. Above a bar counter of colourful mosaic, a friendly face beckons. Come in. Pull up a wooden fold-up chair or commandeer one of the dinky cushions. It's characterful and jazzy on certain nights; check the website for the latest line-up. *Photo p146.*

Le Greenwich
7 rue des Chartreux (02 511 41 67). Pré-métro Bourse. **Open** 10.30am-1am Mon-Thur; 10.30am-2am Fri, Sat. **No credit cards**. **Map** p315 C4 ㉓

**INSIDE TRACK
THE ST-GERY EFFECT**

Place St-Géry is always buzzing with action. Pavement terraces are set up whatever the weather and season, but in the summer the place is packed. With bars on every corner, each is much of a muchness – it's the generic overload that everyone likes, and the melting pot vibe. Service at all of the bars here can be slow and a little abrasive; some only have bar service. Get your bearings before you sit and wait, or you could be there a long time.

The Greenwich is one of Brussels' institutions, a brown bar whose whole raison d'être is the studied patience of chess. Grab a chair, a beer, a board and a Tupperware box of chess pieces and become part of the furniture. Or order up a drink, open up a book and observe. It's got history, too: Magritte hustled pictures and Bobby Fischer hustled chess here. The Greenwich temporarily shut up shop in 2010 and the workmen moved in; seemingly the cellars have asbestos and there is to be a complete update of its component parts. Mercifully, though, the main bar and frontage remained intact at the time of writing. *Photo p148.*

Le Java
22 rue de la Grand Ile (02 512 37 16). Pré-métro Bourse. **Open** 5.30pm-4am Mon-Thur, Sun; 5.30pm-5am Fri, Sat. **No credit cards**. **Map** p315 C4 ②
An imposingly cool bar composing the bow of St-Géry as it meets rue de la Grande Ile, Le Java makes the best of its corner plot. The interior is dominated by a heavy round bar counter, foot-railed by Gaudiesque twisted metal and offset by half a tree and half a globe. Daily specials complement Bel pils and Steendonk beers on draught, all served with the same smile that welcomed you in. Cocktails are available too.

The Marolles

Chez Marcel
20 place du Jeu de Balle (02 511 13 75). Métro/pré-métro Porte de Hal or bus 27, 48. **Open** 6am-midnight daily. **No credit cards**. **Map** p318 B7 ㉕
Other bars may be more comfortable, but of all the venues in this downbeat flea market square, this one is the most true to local life. As tatty as the traders it serves, Marcel's stocks Cantillon Gueuze, a rarity from the Anderlecht brewery of the same name, cheaper more standard beers, toasted sandwiches and heavy lunches. A Manneken-Pis in local Union

football colours and prints of the market from a similar bygone era complete the authenticity. Plonk your market purchase on the modest terrace, call up a beer and listen out for banter.
▶ *The daily flea market and nearby shops offer plenty of scope for bric-a-brac browsing.*

UPPER TOWN

Le Bier Circus
89 rue de l'Enseignement (02 218 00 34, www.bier-circus.be). Tram 92, 94. **Open** noon-2.30pm, 6-11pm Tue-Fri; 6-11pm Sat. **Credit** AmEx, MC, V. **Map** p317 F4 ㉖
This somewhat bland brick bar wouldn't merit mention, save for its quite astonishing range of beers. There are around 200 to choose from, filling 17 pages of a menu directory handed to you by a well-informed barman. Vintage beers – Oude Krieke 35% at €25 a bottle, Gueuze aged in Cognac barrels at €20 – warrant four pages. It's then that you notice the mounted beermats and a blackboard of seasonal beers breaking the monotony of brick. Delve a little deeper and you'll find an intimate side room, and a back room decked out in cartoon characters.

The Flat
12 rue de la Pépinière (02 502 74 34, www.theflat.be). Métro Porte de Namur. **Open** 6pm-2am Wed-Sat. **Credit** AmEx, DC, MC, V. **Map** p319 E7 ㉗
This unusual bar may seem a bit theme park-ish at first glance, but it works well as a sophisticated place to drink with friends and colleagues. The rooms are laid out as if they are part of someone's home, so you can quaff a beer in the lounge, the dining room, the candlelit bedroom or even the bathroom. Meanwhile, television screens flash a stock market-type pricing index for drinks, which change according to how they're selling; get stuck into the margaritas, say, and the price comes down. Well worth a try.

Le Grain de Sable
15-16 place du Grand Sablon (02 513 18 44, www.legraindesable.be). Bus 95 or tram 92, 94. **Open** 8.30am-2.30am daily. **Credit** AmEx, MC, V. **Map** p315 D6 ㉘
Despite being set on one of Brussels' poshest squares, surrounded by big and blousy establishments, there is no fear of Le Grain suffering from an inferiority complex. Outside, the pavement terrace snakes its way around a corner, and in warm weather becomes a right-angle of bright buzz and cheerful rendezvous. Inside, funky Latin jazz plays in the tiny ground-floor bar, while the flickering candles seem to find their own bossa rhythm. The customers tend towards the vodka-Schweppes rather than the beer bottle. There are no startling effects here, just a modest room filled with beautiful people and the friendliest of muscular staff.

Place St-Géry.

CONSUME

Gecko. *See p143.*

CONSUME

EU QUARTER & ETTERBEEK

Chez Bernard

47 place Jourdan (02 230 22 38). Métro Schuman. **Open** 7am-2am daily. **No credit cards. Map** p322 H7

Sitting unfazed amid the mock-nouveau wine bars and brasseries on this busiest of squares, Bernard's Place remains rock-solid traditional to the last. A long mirrored room leads to an unlikely glass conservatory at the back, giving the impression that a tearoom has been stuck on the back of a beer hall. It greets in equal measure Eurocrats feeling good about mixing with locals, locals feeling indifferent about mixing with Eurocrats, Sunday morning shoppers and diners from Maison Antoine, the famous frites stall opposite (*see p122* **On the Hoof**). Yep, you can buy your chips, bring them here and staff will offer you a napkin and a beer list.

Fat Boy's

5 place du Luxembourg (02 511 32 66, www.fatboys-be.com). Métro Trône. **Open** 11am-late daily. **Credit** MC, V. **Map** p322 G7

Fat Boy's is Brussels' main expatriate sports bar, conveniently set in the considerable shadow of the European Parliament. Although it's categorically American in style, Brits flock here in droves to spend beery Sunday afternoons gawping at any of nine screens showing Premiership action and scoffing their way through the meaty menu of ribs and burgers. Fat Boy's improves when the post-work crowd descends to fill its long interior, spilling on to the terrace on summer evenings.

Schievelavabo

52 rue du College St-Michel (02 779 87 07, www.leschievelavabo.be). Métro Montgomery. **Open** 11am-2.30pm, 7pm-midnight Mon-Fri; 7pm-midnight Sat, Sun. **Credit** AmEx, DC, MC, V.

The Schievelavabo (literally translating as 'Wonky Washbasin', or – if you prefer – 'Skewiff Sink') brings a little much-needed bonhomie and retro conviviality to this otherwise grey and uninspired residential patch stuck between the EU Quarter and Woluwe Park. Although somewhat smaller than its sister branch, the formula here is exactly the same: solid wooden furniture; an enticing variety of well-sourced local beers; dependable staff; and a young, salaried clientele.
Other locations 344 Chaussée de Wavre, place Jourdan, EU Quarter (02 280 00 83).

IXELLES

L'Atelier

77 rue Elise (02 649 19 53). Tram 94 or bus 71. **Open** 4pm-3am Mon-Thur, Sun; 4pm-4am Fri; 4pm-5am Sat. **No credit cards. Map** p325 J13

A Beer for All Seasons

Tuck into the finest brews in the world.

Beer has been brewed in this part of Europe since the Middle Ages, and over the centuries has become Belgium's beloved national treasure. The range of 600 beers (1,000 if you count one-off specials) is unequalled for such a small country.

What beer-lovers appreciate is not just the quality but the variety of what is on offer. From pump lagers to sublime, finely honed ales brewed by monks – even medieval recipes. As with fine wines, the brewing process can take years, and there are strict controls governing how any company can describe its brew.

The more serious beers tend to be served in bottles, although every bar will stock at least one draught lager – generally Stella, Maes or Jupiler. White wheat beer ('*blanche*' or '*witte*') will also be on tap; the major brand is Hoegaarden, but Brugs and Limburgse are similarly ubiquitous. The beer is cloudy and refreshing and often served with lemon, so don't be alarmed when asked if you want it with *citron*. Different bars will also offer a selection of slightly more adventurous ales on draught (*au fût/van't vat*).

But it's to the beer temples that you must turn to find an encyclopaedic range on tap and from the bottle. **L'Atelier** (*see left*), **A la Bécasse** (*see p137*), **Le Bier Circus** (*see p144*) and **Chez Moeder Lambic** (*see p151*) offer a bewildering choice. In the Lower Town, the **Délirium Café** (*see p138*) guarantees to stock some 2,000 beers from around the world, including a stellar array of local brews.

Many Belgian brews hint at monastic origins, but only Chimay, Orval, Rochefort, Westmalle and Westvleterenand Achel carry the hexagonal Authentic Trappist Product logo, which means they have been brewed within the walls of a Trappist monastery. Aside from the dark, unclassifiable Orval, the tricky exception, all are deep brown and creamy; for deep brown and creamy with a kick, select the *dubbel* or *trippel* versions, which deliver the wallop of up to nine per cent ABV. The next ecclesiastical step down are the abbey beers – never to be confused with the Trappists. These include Leffe and Grimbergen, frequently found on tap thanks to national distribution deals.

The most unusual family of beers is the Lambics, particular to the Brussels area.

Lambics are naturally fermented with no added yeast, a process that takes at least a couple of years. A young Lambic is called a Faro, and is quite rare. Straight Lambic is very hard to find, but it provides the base for two of Belgium's most popular and idiosyncratic types of beer: Gueuze and fruit Lambics. Lambic's tart, wince-inducing taste makes it the perfect base in which to mix fruit such as cherries (*kriek*) and raspberries (*framboise* or *frambozen*).

Finally come the hundreds of ales of all colours and flavours. Look out for red beers from Rodenbach, strong golden ales such as the notorious Duvel and the amber De Koninck from Antwerp, and seasonal beers such as special Christmas and Easter brews.

Almost every variety of beer will be served to you in the correct glass, which has now become as important a part of the brand as the label. Look out for the round-bottomed glass from Kwak, which is held in a wooden stand and looks like something from a school science lab.

Don't let Belgian beers flummox you; there's no social stigma to any beer you choose from often extensive beer menus, and bartenders will be more than happy to talk you through them. Beer, remember, is a matter of national pride and drunk by all – male, female, young and old.

CONSUME

Tucked away amid drab streets 'twixt Ixelles lakes and cemetery, L'Atelier is a gem: a cosy, candlelit wood and brick scout hut of a bar, with a broad counter separating a conspiratorial back room from the front of house. Behind the dividing line is a vast fridge of bottled beers. Draught options – Kriek, Barbar, Chouffe, Pecheresse among them – are chalked up, as are local genevers and wines. Also displayed is a league table in honour of the diversity of Belgium's ales. Beer buffs mingle with the intellectual end of the student fraternity from the university.

Banco!

79 rue du Bailli (02 537 52 65, www.banco bar.be). Tram 92, 94. **Open** 9am-2am daily. **Credit** AmEx, MC, V. **Map** p324 E10 ⬤

Strange how an exclamation mark can change a brand. This old bank building used to house an Irish pub called the Bank. But give it a new look to better fit this now-happening street, change its name to something vaguely international, add a punctuation mark and voila! The old bank fittings remain, including the vaults and overnight safes, but everything is now brighter and blousier. The young Châtelain crowd loves this place for its informal drinking and big sports screen; cocktails are the early-evening preference, but there's no getting away from the past – Guinness, Kilkenny and Celtic Irish Cider remain at the core of the beer menu.

Couleur Pourpre

463 avenue de la Couronne (02 646 11 78). Bus 95, 96. **Open** 10am-2pm daily. **Credit** MC, V.

A stylish haunt in the busy student quarter in the far south of Ixelles, by the cemetery, the Colour Purple is a seductive bar whose vast interior is personalised by oriental furnishings and walls of purple. Communal ingestion of coffee, croissants and light lunches give the daytimes here an academic feel, but come dusk, the mortarboards are cast aside with gusto. Strong cocktails, as long a selection of whiskies as you'll find anywhere in town, and endless caipirinhas are devoured amid filtered disco lighting, while an acceptable DJ beat taps away.

★ L'Horloge du Sud

141 rue du Trône (02 512 18 64, www.horloge dusud.be). Métro Trône or bus 95, 96. **Open** 11am-3pm, 6pm-midnight Mon-Fri; 6pm-midnight Sat. **Credit** AmEx, MC, V.

Near the vibrant heart of Brussels' African quarter of the Matongé, L'Horloge du Sud is a far cry from the tacky, lurid and almost perpetually crowded bars of nearby rue de Longue Vie. Spacious and comfortable, L'Horloge comprises a loose collection of old tables and chairs, plants, warrior statues, musical instruments and a massive mirror, all of which merge woozily as the drum rhythms and plentiful selection of Caribbean rums and cocktails kick in. There's African and Belgian cuisine on offer, occasional live music, regular DJ sets at weekends, and the reliably constant vibe of a totally mixed clientele having barrels of fun. Praiseworthy and unique.

▶ *For more on the colourful Matongé quarter, see p77 Profile.*

Le Greenwich. *See p143.*

Ma Cabane Bambou

11 rue du Prince Royal (02 512 26 86, www. macabanebambou.be). Tram 92, 94. **Open** 7pm-late Tue-Sat. **No credit cards. Map** p319 E8 ㉝

For two decades this was Le Requin Chagrin, where Marlène Dépêche offered the exotic cuisine of Réunion, running a little rum as a side attraction. Marlène then transformed the Despondent Shark into a merry rum bar of broader provenance, with cane spirits from Réunion and other former French territories, including those in the Caribbean. They are put to excellent use in a vibrant cocktail selection, which includes an Aphrodisiaque with fresh ginger, and a variation of a strong Antillean punch known to Marlène as 'Le P'tit Pépé Loulou'.

Roxi

82 rue du Bailli (02 646 17 92, www.roxi.be). Métro Louise then tram 93, 94. **Open** 8am-1am Mon-Wed, Sun; 8am-2am Thur-Sat. **Credit** MC, V. **Map** p324 E10 ㉞

This trendy bar and gathering place attracts the chic urbanites of the Châtelain quarter with its three floors of stark decor, all-day cuisine and unfussy background sounds. Metal staircases link the floors, from the ground-floor bar with its wide windows to the dinky red stools of the tearoom, and on up to the modest balcony with its welcome panorama.

Winery

18 place Brugmann (02 345 47 17, www.winery online.be). Tram 92. **Open** 11am-8pm Mon-Sat. **Credit** MC, V. **Map** p324 D13 ㉟

The Winery is a clever little venture, attached to a wine shop in the shadows of the old church on the square. Wine bars are not that big in Brussels, so it's good to know that this place has attracted a goodly local crowd who appreciate its unpretentious decor and prices. In fact, it doesn't look like a wine bar at all, with its black and white tiled floor and tall, bleached wood stalls and tables. There's a short but intense wine list of new discoveries.

▶ *This place is perfect for a quick stop-off if you're on the art nouveau trail (see p39) and in need of a little light refreshment.*

A Tale of Two Bars

Moeder Lambic enters the 21st century.

The old **Chez Moeder Lambic** (*see right*) in the shadow of St-Gilles town hall has been part of the drinking scene for 25 years. Renowned as a place to get hold of some of the rarest brews with rare prices to match, it has long attracted an eclectic mix of thirsty locals, students and bearded beer pundits from around the world. Before Pierre Emmanuel Raymond took it over in the late 1990s there were no fridges, and its 1,000 bottles were stored precariously in an upstairs room; its loos, meanwhile, were outside.

A succession of modernisers have managed to maintain the unique atmosphere of the old Moeder while making it more appealing to modern drinkers. A mezzanine now relieves the pressure of the ground floor, meaning there's plenty of room for boxed games and large groups of pint-sharing beeristas. The cellars have been renovated, and beer tasting introduced (from €35; see website for details). At the

same time, thankfully, it feels as if nothing has really changed: the crowd is the same, the beers are as magnificent as ever, and the corner of St-Gilles that is Moeder Lambic remains perfectly intact.

In 2009, however, ripples ran through the Brussels bar and beer scene with the news that the Moeder was going trendy. Not in rue de Savoie, though, no indeed; we'll have none of that. Instead, Moeder was extending her reach, building her brood and moving into Lower Town trendsville.

A prime spot was found in a superbly renovated townhouse at the end of rue du Marché au Charbon, famed for its drinking scene. The new locale would be perfect for attracting the downtown arty crowd, gay boozers and anyone wanting something a little different to the usual Jupiler and Hoegaarden. And the new sprog couldn't be more different to its alter ego in St-Gilles, with minimalist, industrial styling, a sweeping bar that must have cost a

Chez Moeder Lambic.

pretty penny, and 40 beer pumps all in a gleaming row. In one fell swoop, Moeder cleverly rebranded itself without alienating its old faithfuls. **Chez Moeder Lambic Fontainas** (*see p138*) serves nothing but draught artisanal beers, largely unknown and, until now, largely untested by your average beer-buying punter. Here's a Jambe du Bois, mistily amber; there an Adelardus as deep and shiny as a fresh chestnut. Beers are classified by type to help you on your way, while the highly trained staff offer friendly advice. This is a beer hall for a new generation, the powerful brews aided and abetted by funky DJs at weekends.

Moeder Lambic is seemingly at the start of an extraordinary renaissance, with partnerships being forged with bars in the USA, Italy and Spain. Keep your eye on this beery lady; Moeder may be popping up in your part of the world before too long.

ST-GILLES

Brasserie de l'Union

55 parvis de St-Gilles (02 538 15 79). Pré-métro Parvis de St-Gilles. **Open** 7.30am-1am daily. **No credit cards**. **Map** p318 B9 ㊱

A tatty-round-the-edges bohemian bar, happy to serve the local community at large – some befriended solely by spaniels, and deep in one-way conversations – the Union comprises one large, busy room propping up a corner of the focal parvis de St-Gilles. Sunday morning market browsing here is accompanied by an accordionist squeezing out tunes – though nothing can quite drown out the din of children running amok. After they depart, along with the spaniels, the squeezeboxer and the senile, the night is claimed by characters from the covers of pulp fiction novels.

Brasserie Verschueren

11-13 parvis de St-Gilles (02 539 40 68). Pré-métro Parvis de St-Gilles. **Open** 8am-2am daily. **No credit cards**. **Map** p318 B9 ㊲

The classier of the corner bars serving the parvis, the Verschueren twinkles with art deco touches. Three rows of tables and banquettes are waited on by rather erratic staff, safe in the knowledge that few of the boho-intellectual regulars are paying much attention; the Verschueren is simply their natural habitat, drink or no drink. If they cared to look up, they'd find a more than adequate selection of beers – including bottled rarities such as Pecheresse. Rather incongruous alongside the classic station clock and delicate window panelling, a vast league ladder of football club names from the lower local divisions occupies the back wall, each team name delineated in bright Subbuteo colours.

★ Chez Moeder Lambic

68 rue de Savoie (02 539 14 19, www.moeder lambic.eu). Pré-métro Horta or Albert. **Open** 4pm-3am daily. **No credit cards**.

Happy to collect dust in its own little corner, the collectors' cavern of Chez Moeder Lambic hides from the soaring St-Gilles town hall behind beer-labelled windows. Inside it's a dark hive, with three long shelves of obscure bottles framing the bar counter and wooden tables. It would take a lifetime to sample every cobwebbed variety here – some of shabby ilk are still trying – but to pass the time, racks of comic books line one wall. Outsiders can only guestimate the number of brews, daring to stab at 300. Its sister establishment, Chez Moeder Lambic Fontainas, is very different; *see p138* and *left* **A Tale of Two Bars**.

OENO TK

29-31 rue Africaine (02 534 64 34, www.oeno tk.be). Tram 92, 94. **Open** 11am-8pm Mon, Tue; 11am-10.30pm Wed-Sat. **Credit** MC, V. **Map** p324 D11 ㊳

CONSUME

OENO is so cool, it should be kept in an ice bucket along with its vast selection of wines. Sleekly designed, with exposed brick and statement lighting, the bar is a place to discover and be discovered. A central table with bar seats provides a place for the glamorous people to mix and mingle. The blackboard above the bar area lists special wines, most of which are available by the glass or bottle. To accompany your vintage of choice, there's charcuterie, cheese plates and tasty little snacks such as grilled artichokes. This place is also a shop, so you can taste first then tuck a bottle in your bag for later.

UCCLE

Ici le Bô-Bar

22 parvis de St-Pierre (02 343 43 03, www.icile bobar.be). Tram 55, 92. **Open** noon-1am Mon-Fri; 2pm-2am Sat. **No credit cards**.

This clean-cut designer bar attracts the bright young things of Uccle with its showy interior, giant screen of pop videos and classy, if standard, cocktails. A bay window gives out on to a front terrace. There's nothing the Bô-Bar likes more than putting on an event, from a masked ball to a big-screen game.

Banquette Etiquette

The seat of power and influence.

It may be velvet, it may be striped, it may be shabby cloth or shiny vinyl; but whatever its state, the humble banquette continues to outlive fickle trends. The high-backed, bench-like seat lines the walls of many of Brussels' traditional bars, while the trendier set can't resist covering it in zebra skin. Calling it just a seat does the banquette a disservice: this is a time-honoured

institution that comes with its own socio-cultural impact and etiquette. For a start, all its inhabitants sit next to one another irrespective of age, class, gender or civil status. They are also all looking inwards, allowing for a communion between the drinker, the waiter and the rest of the bar.

The elderly shopper can sit alone; she needn't worry about taking a single chair at a table for four and so she feels part of the bar, part of the banquette community. She can choose to guard her space and look ahead, or she may strike up a conversation with a neighbour (even then there's no need for eye contact). The banquette is a social leveller. It is also a social marvel. There is nothing like a friendly banquette conversation, slightly turned in to each other and with no table dividing you.

It can be formal or informal (the sit-up-and-beg backs force you to be either alertly upright or lazily slouched); it can be a place to share business plans or family photographs; an intimate seat for all seasons. One thing you will notice is that banquette seats tend to be the ones taken first, drinkers staking their advantageous places before even considering filling the spaces in the middle. Banquette dwellers are also an active audience – they see all that passes them by, they know who's coming in and going out, who's off to the loo and who's seeing who.

Finally, consider the surrealist artists trying to hawk their radical new pieces around the bars in the 1920s. What chance would they have had if everyone had been huddled around tables looking at each other? The banquetteers may not have bought the avant-garde pieces being touted, but at least they would have had to have a look.

Shops & Services

Head to Brussels for boutiques, beer and boxes of chocs.

Shopping isn't high on the agenda for most visitors to Brussels, but trawling the city's quirkier boutiques can be fun. Brussels' little specialist shops offer everything from second-hand clothes and vinyl to homeware and ethnic imports. Antiques, bric-a-brac, chocolate (*see p165* **Confection Perfection**) and beer are on most people's shopping lists and for good reason.

Independent designers abound in the capital, but fashion shoppers should also consider a day trip to nearby Antwerp (*see p232*). The town that gave birth to the now world-renowned Antwerp Six group of designers, including Ann Demeulemeester and Dries Van Noten, is just 40 minutes away by train.

LOWER & UPPER TOWNS

Around the Grand'Place are tourist-dependent chocolate, lace and EU merchandise shops. You don't have to go very far to find better stuff. To the south-east, **rue des Eperonniers** has quirky old-fashioned gift shops; south-west, **rue du Midi** has stamp, camera and art shops. **Boulevards Anspach** and **Maurice Lemmonier** have comic shops, second-hand book and record stores and an assortment of dusty but quirky little businesses. In between, **rue des Pierres** and **rue du Marché au Charbon** are home to a mix of vintage clothes shops and streetwear boutiques.

North-east of the square are the Galeries St-Hubert, the most famous of the city's *galeries*, or shopping arcades, opened in 1847. Divided into the Galerie du Roi, de la Reine and du Prince, they accommodate expensive, old-fashioned boutiques selling gloves, hats, bags and accessories. *See p155* **All Under One Roof**.

Pedestrianised **rue Neuve**, Brussels' main shopping drag, is a nightmare. Think Croydon at its worst. It's home to high-street names alongside lesser-known but similar brands such as Vero Moda and Bershka. At its northern end are the landmark department store **Inno** and the horrendous **City 2** shopping centre, the highlight of which is the comprehensive bookstore **Fnac**. South of the place de la Monnaie are **rue des Fripiers** and **rue du Marché aux Herbes**, both offering high-street shops and independent boutiques.

Ste-Catherine, known for its seafood restaurants, is also home to good food shops. In adjoining **St-Géry**, **rue Antoine Dansaert** and **rue des Chartreux** contain trendy streetwear, cool gift shops, modern furniture stores and boutiques of established and up-and-coming Belgian designers. *See p160* **Style Street** *and p170* **Chain-free Chic**.

Sablon is the place to go if you're looking for antiques. Expensive boutiques are to be found along **rue Lebeau**, **rue des Minimes** and **place du Grand Sablon**, where an antiques market is held every weekend. More downmarket – and more exotic – antiques shops are found down below in the adjoining neighbourhood of the Marolles, on **rues Blaes**

**INSIDE TRACK
LATE NIGHT THURSDAYS**

In 2010, the powers-that-be in Brussels launched the idea of a late shopping night in the city centre. The coverage is not blanket like London's Oxford Street and it has more of a festival feel than a commercial drive. Shops are drip-dripping their way into the scheme, some dipping their toes, others going the whole mile. With strong unions and a strong desire for dinner, it's difficult to tell how this will develop, but check www.afterworkshopping.be for updates.

CONSUME

Antiques markets on **rue Blaes** and (*below*) **place du Jeu de Balle**.

and **Haute**. In the centre is **place du Jeu de Balle**, site of a daily flea market. *See p58* **Walk**.

AVENUE LOUISE & IXELLES

Avenue Louise and **boulevard de Waterloo** are where foreign money and Belgian inheritances are spent in the boutiques of MaxMara, Chanel, Gucci, Cacharel and Bulgari – just a sprinkling of the big names dotted along these two wide, tree-lined streets.

Avenue de la Toison d'Or (the name given to the southern side of boulevard de Waterloo) is more mid-range, with international clothing shops such as Women'Secret, Massimo Dutti and Petit Bateau. The three *galeries* leading off, de la Toison d'Or, Porte Louise and Espace Louise, are linked and play host to a mix of shops selling high-street and designer labels.

Halfway along avenue Louise, running west, is **rue du Bailli**. Here, and radiating out to the surrounding streets, is a selection of gift shops and clothing boutiques, interspersed with chic cafés and restaurants, which converge around place du Châtelain. Shoe shops abound.

Chaussées d'Ixelles and **de Wavre** contain chains and ethnic shops. In between, rue St-Boniface is lined with unusual boutiques.

TAX-FREE SHOPPING

Prices include a sales tax of up to 21 per cent. Rates vary depending on the item. In many shops, non-EU residents can request a Tax-Free Cheque on purchases of more than €145, which can be cashed at customs when leaving the EU to reclaim VAT. Savings Shops in the scheme have a 'Tax-Free Shopping' sticker on their door. Do ask if they don't.

SALES & OPENING TIMES

Historically, sales have been strictly regulated in Belgium. For the first few weeks in January and July stores slash prices across the board. Savvy shopkeepers also manage to offer a few specific discounts and promotional prices around special events, such as Valentine's Day.

Most shops are closed on Sundays and bank holidays. Smaller ones also close on Mondays.

General

DEPARTMENT STORES

Hema
117 rue Neuve, Lower Town (02 227 52 109, www.hema.be). Métro/pré-métro De Brouckère. **Open** 9am-6.30pm Mon-Thur; 9am-7pm Fri, Sat. **Credit** MC, V. **Map** p317 D2.

All Under One Roof

Wander through the Galeries Royales St-Hubert, Europe's first arcade.

From its opening day in 1847, its motto *Omnibus omnia* ('everything for everyone') announced that the Galeries Royales St-Hubert would be a microcosm of Brussels life. Everything that goes on in Brussels goes on in miniature within this elegant T-shaped cluster of three glass-roofed arcades. In 1836, a dynamic young Dutch architect, Jean-Pierre Cluysenaer, built a covered gallery linking two markets, and a decade later the first stone was laid by King Léopold I. Stretching for more than 200 metres (650 feet), and beautifully lit thanks to an elegant glass roof, the Galeries Royales were the first arcade in Europe.

Entering from place d'Espagne, Galerie de la Reine features the majority of little craftsmen's workshops and original store fronts. Those aspiring to dress like a 19th-century Belgian noble could find an entire wardrobe here, selecting some lambskin gloves at **Ganterie Italienne** (No.3, 02 512 75 38) or a rakish hat from **Monsel Parapluie** (No.4, 02 511 41 33). **Coutelier Tilquin** (No.5, 02 512 76 63) has a wonderful window display of knives, penknives and scissors.

At No.15, **Théâtre du Vaudeville** opened in 1884. First a casino, then a cabaret and a private club, it has been restored as a venue for all kinds of events, with a stylish café out the front. Opposite, **Philippe** makes superbly crafted shoes at No.18 (02 511 98 28). The **Thalassotherapy Centre** (No.21, 02 513 75 15) offers seaweed wraps, mud scrubs and tranquillity amid the chaos, while **Neuhaus** (No.25, 02 512 63 59) was established by a Swiss pharmacist in 1857 to dispense chocolate to take away the taste of medicine. The excellent arts cinema **Arenberg Galeries** at No.26 (*see p188*) dates back to the first film show in Belgium, 1 March 1896. A plaque at 7 Galerie du Roi, on the façade of the Nicholson clothes shop, is a homage from the Lumière brothers to their Belgian precursor Joseph Plateau. In 1836, he invented a stroboscopic device that led to the development of the cinema.

Back in Galerie de la Reine, the **Taverne du Passage** (No.30, 02 512 37 31) was once a meeting place for an artistic circle that included Dumas, Hugo, Apollinaire and Verlaine. Opposite, **Maison Delvaux** (No.31, 02 512 71 98), purveyors to the royal court, has provided travelling bags, purses and trunks since 1828. At the junction where the two arcades meet, **Kaat Tilley** (*see p161*) runs her designer clothes shop, a hot destination for well-dressed locals.

Turning left off the Galerie du Roi is the shorter, less attractive Galerie des Princes, whose best draw is the eccentric **Ogenblik** restaurant (*see p117*). In a custom reaching back 50 years, sand is sprinkled on the floor each morning to soak up customers' chewing tobacco and spittle. Dressmakers **Danaqué** are at No.2 (02 511 35 33), opposite the cavernous **Tropismes** bookstore (No.11, 02 512 88 51).

Back on the Galerie du Roi, stop for a well-deserved coffee break at **Mokafé** (*see p117*), before launching forth to see **Nicholas Witmeur's** antique jewellery creations (No.13, 02 513 72 53). The **Théâtre Royal des Galeries** (*see p226*) was first built here in 1847, but was pulled down and rebuilt in the 1950s. There's a Magritte ceiling fresco but the city fathers have obscured it with a huge chandelier. Emerging into the outside world, reward yourself with a Sudden Death beer at **A la Mort Subite** (*see p139*) pub over the road.

Galeries Royales St-Hubert.

CONSUME

Hema is like a Flemish Woolworths. Its two floors are filled with basics – candles, underwear, kitchenware and other random goods – of varying quality but at ludicrously cheap prices. Have a good rummage around and you may just leave triumphant. **Other locations** throughout the city.

Inno
111 rue Neuve, Lower Town (02 211 21 11, www.inno.be). Métro/pré-métro Rogier. **Open** 9.30am-7pm Mon-Thur, Sat; 9.30am-8pm Fri. **Credit** AmEx, DC, MC, V. **Map** p317 D2.

Inno is Brussels' main department store. Established in 1897, it has 15 shops in Belgium, four in Brussels. This is the largest of them, with five floors featuring all the usual departments: menswear, womenswear, childrenswear, shoes, home furnishings and so on. The handbag, jewellery and lingerie departments are notably good.

Other locations 12 avenue Louise, Ixelles (02 513 84 94); 699 chaussée de Waterloo, Uccle (02 345 38 90); 150 avenue Paul Hymans, Woluwe-St-Lambert (02 771 20 50).

Specialist

BOOKSHOPS & NEWSAGENTS

L'Ame des Rues – Librairie de Cinéma
49 boulevard Anspach, Lower Town (02 217 59 47). Métro/pré-métro De Brouckère. **Open**

Pêle-Mêle. *See p158.*

noon-6pm Mon-Sat. **Credit** AmEx, DC, MC, V. **Map** p315 C4.

A real mecca for film buffs, packed as it is with film stills, posters and postcards, plus television- and film-related books and memorabilia.

★ Filigranes
39-40 avenue des Arts, EU Quarter (02 511 90 15, www.filigranes.be). Métro Arts-Loi. **Open** 8am-8pm Mon-Fri; 10am-7.30pm Sat; 10am-7pm Sun. **Credit** AmEx, MC, V. **Map** p317 F5.

This labyrinthine bookstore has a decent English books section, as well as international magazines and newspapers. The art department is outstanding and the kids will love the children's area. You can also enjoy a drink in the central café, surrounded by books and browsers. Filigranes is totally un-Belgian in that it's open 365 days a year.

★ Fnac
City 2, rue Neuve, Lower Town (02 275 11 11, www.fnac.be). Métro/pré-métro Rogier. **Open** 10am-7pm Mon-Thur, Sat; 10am-8pm Fri. **Credit** AmEx, DC, MC, V. **Map** p317 D2.

Head to the top of the City 2 shopping centre to find this ever-dependable mammoth store that sells all kind of media. The book stock is excellent in all disciplines and languages (the French section is particularly strong), and the prices aren't bad. There are also CDs, videos, DVDs, computer games and assorted audio-visual and computer equipment. By the door is a ticket office for concerts around town.

Sterling
38 rue du Fossé aux Loups, Lower Town (02 223 62 23, www.sterlingbooks.be). Métro/pré-métro De Brouckère. **Open** 10am-7pm Mon-Sat; noon-6.30pm Sun. **Credit** AmEx, MC, V. **Map** p315 D3.

The ground floor of this bookshop has an excellent range of contemporary fiction, children's books, magazines and newspapers in English, while the first floor stocks classic fiction, plus non-fiction (such as computer and travel books). There's also a comprehensive section of books on Brussels.

Waterstone's
71-75 boulevard Adolphe Max, Lower Town (02 219 27 08, http://users.skynet.be/waterstones). Métro/pré-métro Rogier. **Open** 9am-7pm Mon-Sat; 10.30am-6pm Sun. **Credit** AmEx, MC, V. **Map** p317 D2.

The local Waterstone's has a good collection of English-language reading material (books, magazines and newspapers) on its two floors. The prices are on the steep side, though.

Comics

For a detailed history of the comic strip genre, see *pp41-45* **Cartoon Brussels**.

Stijl. *See p161*.

La Boutique Tintin

13 rue de la Colline, Lower Town (02 514 51 52, www.tintin.com). Métro Gare Centrale. **Open** 10am-6pm Mon-Sat; 11am-5pm Sun. **Credit** AmEx, DC, MC, V. **Map** p315 D4.

If you're a Tintin fan, then it's going to be hard to walk into this shop and not leave without buying something, even though prices are high. The range includes clothes, stationery and soft toys, as well as the comic strip books themselves. If you're a serious collector, there are also some limited edition miniatures (and not so miniatures).

★ Brüsel

100 boulevard Anspach, Lower Town (02 511 08 09, www.brusel.com). Pré-métro Bourse. **Open** 10.30am-6.30pm Mon-Sat; noon-6.30pm Sun. **Credit** AmEx, DC, MC, V. **Map** p315 C4.

One of the best comic shops in Brussels, with a huge choice of national favourites, as well as the most popular European and American comic strips in English, French and Dutch. The shop also stocks accompanying plastic and resin miniatures, posters and lithographs.

Le Dépôt

108 rue du Midi, Lower Town (02 513 04 84, www.depotbd.com). Pré-métro Anneessens. **Open** 10am-6.30pm Mon-Sat. **Credit** MC, V. **Map** p315 B5.

This store buys and sells all types of new and old comic strips, as well as figurines, cards, posters, limited edition lithographs and DVDs.

Other location 142 chaussée d'Ixelles, Ixelles (02 511 75 04).

Super Dragon Toys

6 rue Ste-Catherine, Lower Town (02 511 56 25, www.superdragontoys.com). Pré-métro Bourse. **Open** 10am-6pm Mon-Thur; 10am-6.30pm Fri, Sat. **No credit cards**. **Map** p315 B3.

Everything a manga fan could possibly want or need, from DVDs to figurines, video games and music. A huge range of manga comics is available in French, English and Flemish, and if a particular comic strip you've been looking for is not available, never fear: it can be ordered.

Utopia

39 rue du Midi, Lower Town (02 514 08 26, www.utopiacomics.be). Pré-métro Bourse. **Open** 10am-6pm Mon-Fri; 10am-7pm Sat. **Credit** MC, V. **Map** p315 C4.

Utopia specialises in American comic strips, plus TV and film merchandise, with a good collection of *Batman* and *The Simpsons* gear.

INSIDE TRACK BAG A BARGAIN

For flea market aficionados, there's nothing better than finding a gem lurking at the bottom of a rubbish heap. For the best finds and prices at the daily market at **Jeu de Balle** (*see p154*) get there early, at around 6am. This is when the vendors unload their vans and the pros are there waiting to see what comes out. For some reason, Tuesday is regarded as the best morning by those in the know.

Francis Ferent. *See p161.*

Second-hand

Nijinski
15-17 rue du Page, Ixelles (02 539 20 28). Tram 81, 82 or bus 54. **Open** 11am-7pm Mon-Sat. **No credit cards**. **Map** p324 D11.
A large second-hand store, Nijinksi sells books in many languages, including English. A play area has toys and children's books in English too. Staff are relaxed and friendly, and prices are reasonable.

Pêle-Mêle
55 boulevard Maurice Lemonnier, Lower Town (02 548 78 00, www.pele-mele.be). Pré-métro Anneessens. **Open** 10am-6.30pm Mon-Sat. **No credit cards**. **Map** p315 B5.
Pêle-Mêle is stuffed with books, comics, magazines, CDs, records, videos, DVDs and computer games, which it buys and sells. There is a decent English section too. Patient delving usually proves rewarding, and prices are more than fair. *Photo p156.*

CHILDREN
Fashion

Baby 2000
35F Weiveldlaan, Zaventem-Zuid (02 725 20 13, www.baby2000.be). Bus 351, 358. **Open** 10am-7pm Mon-Fri; 10am-6pm Sat. **Credit** MC, V.
A vast store near the airport, with a wide selection of clothes, toys, pushchairs, car seats, highchairs and bath paraphernalia from major manufacturers.

Kat en Muis
33 rue Antoine Dansaert, Lower Town (02 514 32 34). Pré-métro Bourse. **Open** 10.30am-6.30pm Mon-Sat. **Credit** AmEx, DC, MC, V. **Map** p315 C4.

This is the children's version of the cutting-edge fashion store Stijl that you'll find further along the street (*see p161*). In other words, expect designer clothes at high prices. Ideal for muddy weather as the wellies and hats are rather fetching.

Toys & magic

A&T Lewis Magic Circus Shop
45 rue Van Artevelde, Lower Town (02 511 24 07). Pré-métro Bourse. **Open** 10am-6.30pm Mon-Fri; 10.30am-6.30pm Sat. **Credit** MC, V. **Map** p315 B4.
A full-on magic store with a cordoned-off section that is out of bounds to non-magicians, as well as some costumes and masks.

★ The Grasshopper
39 rue du Marché aux Herbes, Lower Town (02 511 96 22, www.thegrasshopper.be). Métro/pré-métro De Brouckère or métro Gare Centrale. **Open** 10am-7pm daily. **Credit** AmEx, DC, MC, V. **Map** p315 C4.
This fantastic toy store, with eye-catching window displays, begins with a ground floor of trinkets and classics (yoyos, kaleidoscopes), novelty lamps and lots more. Upstairs are puzzles, educational and craft-based games, and larger items.

★ Serneels
69 avenue Louise, Ixelles (02 538 30 66, www.serneels.be). Métro Louise. **Open** 9.30am-6.30pm Mon-Sat. **Credit** AmEx, DC, MC, V. **Map** p319 D8.
Just about every toy a little heart could desire is stocked at this deluxe store – at high-flying prices. There are modern electronic favourites, as well as beautiful traditional toys and puzzles too.

CONSUME

ELECTRONICS & PHOTOGRAPHY

Ali Photo Video

*150 rue du Midi, Lower Town (02 512 34 55).
Pré-métro Anneessens.* **Open** 9am-6pm Mon-
Fri; 10am-6pm Sat. **Credit** AmEx, DC, MC, V.
Map p315 C5.
Ali Photo Video sells new still and video cameras of
all makes, as well as buying, selling and exchang-
ing second-hand ones. Staff develop photos, slides
and black-and-whites.

Media Markt

*111 rue Neuve, Lower Town (02 227 15 70,
www.mediamarkt.be). Métro/pré-métro Rogier.*
Open 9.30am-7pm Mon-Thur, Sat; 9.30am-8pm
Fri. **Credit** AmEx, DC, MC, V. **Map** p315 D3.
This giant German electronics emporium has taken
over the top floor of the Inno department store (*see
p156*). Great prices in a superstore environment.

Technoland

*22-24 rue Haute, Lower Town (02 511 51 04,
www.technoland.be). Bus 20, 48.* **Open** noon-7pm
Tue-Sat. **Credit** MC, V. **Map** p318 C7.
Come here for second-hand, high-end audio-visual
equipment and computers, usually at fair prices.

FASHION

Boutique

Autour du Monde (Bensimon Collection)

*70 rue de Namur, Upper Town (02 503 55 92,
www.bensimon.com). Métro Porte de Namur.*
Open 10am-6.30pm Mon-Sat. **Credit** AmEx,
MC, V. **Map** p319 E7.
This is the Brussels branch of a perennially popular
Parisian lifestyle boutique, which sells a nicely co-
ordinated mix of clothes, bags, toiletries, home furnishings, stationery and accessories in various
colours and prints, teamed with classic designs.
Highlights include leather jackets and coats, simple
tops and jumpers.

Ethnic Wear

*25 rue des Chartreux, Lower Town (02 514 78
08). Pré-métro Bourse.* **Open** 11am-7pm Mon-
Sat. **Credit** MC, V. **Map** p316 B4.
Ethnic Wear opened in autumn 2003 in a beautiful
building that once housed the quirky Album
Museum. It sells ecologically sound (and generally
brightly coloured) clothes, shoes and accessories
designed and made on site by Marie Cabanac, as
well as a few pieces made on a fair-trade basis. Men,
women and children are all catered for.

Icon

*5 place du Nouveau Marché aux Grains, Ste-
Catherine (02 502 71 51). Pré-métro Bourse.*
Open 10.30am-6.30pm Mon-Sat. **Credit** MC, V.
Map p315 B3.
At this stylish boutique you'll find a mix of casual
and elegant items aimed at young, urban women.
Pieces by Helmut Lang, Isabel Marant and Philip
Lim all feature.

Isabelle Baines

*4 rue de la Longue Haie, Ixelles (02 502 13 73,
www.isabellebaines.com). Métro Louise.* **Open**
2-6.30pm Mon; 10.30am-6.30pm Tue-Sat.
Credit MC, V. **Map** p319 E9.

Chine Collection. *See p162.*

CONSUME

Style Street

Rue Antoine Dansaert is one long catwalk.

It wasn't so long ago that rue Antoine Dansaert was just another scruffy Brussels thoroughfare, a quick route out of the centre towards the ring road. You may still get much the same impression as you dodge the hefty traffic, but look more carefully at its constituent parts and you begin to realise that this is a street with attitude.

Simply put, Dansaert is a Flemish heartland of fashion, style and culture, spawning myriad little hotspots in and around its main artery. The regeneration all started in 1984 when a small fashion shop opened, selling designs that had never been seen before. **Stijl**, the brainchild of Sonia Noël (*see right*), championed the work of young graduates from the fashion wing of the Antwerp Art Academy: the Antwerp Six. Brussels-based designers have also found a home on Antoine Dansaert. **Annemie Verbeke**'s (*see right*) sober silhouettes belie an enfant terrible of fashion who likes to push limits in line and form. French-born **Johanne Riss** (35 place du Nouveau Marché aux Grains, 02 513 09 00, www.johanneriss.com)

designs elegant wear for day and evening, along with bridal dresses, although her use of Lycra and other tight fits tends to suit more petite figures. Other highlights include **Kat en Muis** (*see p158*), a wacky clothes shop for children selling floral wellies and funky knits.

For accessories head to art deco store **Les Précieuses** (*see p164*), run by architect and fashion designer Pili Collado, or **Christa Reniers**' jewellery shop (*see p164*). There's designer eyewear at **Theo** (*see p172*), exotic footwear at **Hatshoe** (*see p166*) and fine hats at **Christophe Coppens** (*see p164*).

To learn more about Belgian designers take a look at **Modo Bruxellae** (www.modobruxellae.be), which is the *de facto* ambassador for the Belgian fashion industry. It organises Mode Design Brussels, during which various Belgian designers choose a special location – from cafés and galleries to shops and apartments – in which to display their clothes. If there's one thing Dansaert loves, it's a fashion show.

CONSUME

Local designer Baines opened her first boutique in Brussels in 1986, selling her machine-knitted but hand-finished jumpers, cardigans and gilets. The winter collection is made from wool and cashmere, while the summer clothes are cotton. Top-quality, long-lasting classic pieces with a modern twist.

Kaat Tilley

4 galerie du Roi, Lower Town (02 514 07 63, www.kaattilley.com). Métro Gare Centrale. **Open** 10am-6.30pm Mon-Sat. **Credit** AmEx, DC, MC, V. **Map** p315 D4.
Kaat Tilley opened her shop in the Galeries St-Hubert after studying fashion in Brussels and Antwerp. Her designs are ingeniously constructed out of delicate materials, sewn together in layers. The different lines are bridal and eveningwear, prêt-à-porter, knitwear, casualwear and womenswear.

Maison Degand

415 avenue Louise, Ixelles (02 649 00 73). Métro Louise. **Open** 10am-7pm Mon-Sat. **Credit** AmEx, DC, MC, V. **Map** p324 F13.
Maison Degand, housed in a grand fin-de-siècle mansion with most of the original interior preserved, sells luxury clothes for men and women, including made-to-measure suits and cashmere sweaters. It also stocks accessories, such as cufflinks, ties, cravats, cigar cutters and hip flasks. The annex sells more casual weekend wear.

Nina Meert

1 rue St-Boniface, Ixelles (02 514 22 63). Métro Porte de Namur. **Open** 2.30-6.30pm Mon; 10.30am-6.30pm Tue-Sat. **Credit** MC, V. **Map** p319 E7.
Nina Meert was born into a family of painters and worked at Pucci in Florence and Cacharel in Paris before opening her own shop in Brussels in 1979. Isabelle Adjani and Meryl Streep are just two of the famous names who have worn her creations, which are simple, comfortable and made from natural fibres such as wool and silk. Her top-notch knitwear collection has also been very successful.

Ramona

21 rue de la Grande Ile, Lower Town (02 503 47 44). Pré-métro Bourse. **Open** noon-6.30pm Tue-Sat. **Credit** AmEx, MC, V. **Map** p316 B4.
Enter this boudoir and you're likely to find Chilean Ramona Hernández Collao lying on a chaise longue, knitting her latest creation. She will turn her hand to any kind of clothing, including jumpers, trousers, coats, dresses and tops. Each piece is unique, being a different colour, texture and design.

★ Stijl

74 rue Antoine Dansaert, Lower Town (02 512 03 13). Pré-métro Bourse. **Open** 10.30am-6.30pm Mon-Sat. **Credit** AmEx, DC, MC, V. **Map** p316 B3.

The stark interior of Stijl contains some of the most cutting-edge design that Belgium has to offer – at a price. Owner Sonia Noël has a knack for spotting home-grown talent, having signed up first-time collections from Ann Demeulemeester, Dries van Noten and Martin Margiela, as well as Olivier Theyskens and Xavier Delcour. *Photo p157.*

Designer

★ Annemie Verbeke

64 rue Antoine Dansaert, Lower Town (02 511 21 71, www.annemieverbeke.be). Pré-métro Bourse. **Open** 11am-6pm Mon, Wed-Sat. **Credit** AmEx, DC, MC, V. **Map** p315 B3.
Fashionistas flock to Annemie Verbeke's shop, in a beautiful old building, for her classic clothes. The exquisite knitwear is simple but often features subtle detailing around the sleeves and neckline.

Francis Ferent

60 avenue Louise, Ixelles (02 545 78 30, www.ferent.be). Métro Louise. **Open** 10am-6.30pm Mon-Sat. **Credit** AmEx, DC, MC, V. **Map** p319 D8.
This is the flagship store of a small empire of boutiques stocking international labels for men, women and children. Brands include DKNY, Dolce & Gabbana, Sonia Rykiel, Miu Miu, Marc Jacobs, Helmut Lang and Prada. You might get an icy reception, though – the assistants seem to think they own the place. *Photo p158.*

Greta Marta

11 rue du Grand Cerf, Upper Town (02 648 62 24, www.gretamarta.be). Métro Louise. **Open** noon-6.30pm Mon; 10am-6.30pm Tue-Sat. **Credit** AmEx, DC, MC, V. **Map** p324 D10.
The shop may bear the owner's name, but 80% of the stock carries the label of Diane von Furstenberg, the Belgian designer who made her name in the 1970s with her classic wrap dress and is now experiencing a renaissance. The boutique aims to sell unique pieces within Belgium, stocking just one size of each design. Naturally, such exclusivity comes at a price.

★ Martin Margiela

114 rue de Flandre, Lower Town (02 223 75 20, www.martinmargiela.com). Métro Ste-Catherine. **Open** 11am-7pm Mon-Sat. **Credit** AmEx, DC, MC, V. **Map** p316 B3.
Keep an eye on the street numbers, as Martin Margiela's store, like his men's and women's clothes and accessories, is unlabelled. The Paris-based Flemish designer opened this shop (the first branch in Europe) in 2002. Run by Sonia Noël, owner of the Stijl designer emporium (*see p161*) and renowned fashion connoisseur, it's an all-white space housing black clothes and accessories, with just the odd splash of colour for good measure.

CONSUME

CONSUME

Nicolas Woit

80 rue Antoine Dansaert, Lower Town (02 503 48 32, www.nicolaswoit.com). Pré-métro Bourse. **Open** 10.30am-1pm, 2-6pm Mon-Fri; 10.30am-6.30pm Sat. **Credit** AmEx, MC, V. **Map** p315 B3.

Woit studied fashion in Paris before opening this store in 1998. Taking inspiration from period fabrics as well as Asian influences, he creates garments from luxuriant materials that have a bold, girlie and lightheartedly glamorous feel. Accessories such as hats, scarves, bags and jewellery adorned with semi-precious stones are integral to the outfit.

Olivier Strelli

72 avenue Louise, Ixelles (02 512 56 07, www.strelli.be). Métro Louis. **Open** 10am-6.30pm Mon-Sat. **Credit** AmEx, DC, MC, V. **Map** p319 D8.

Born of Italian parents in the former Belgian Congo, Olivier Strelli focuses on creating contemporary classics – simple designs that he brings to life with the vibrant colours of his birthplace, plus various hues of black and grey. He designs own labels for both sexes, plus a women's casualwear range.

Other location 44 rue Antoine Dansaert, Lower Town (02 512 09 42).

General

Chine Collection

82-84 avenue Louise, Ixelles (02 512 45 52, www.chinecollection.com). Métro Louise then tram 94. **Open** 10am-6.30pm Mon-Sat. **Credit** AmEx, DC, MC, V. **Map** p319 D8.

Designer Guillaume Thys launched this upmarket Belgian chain in 1991, with a prêt-à-porter range for women that aims to produce feminine clothes that are also functional, versatile, ultra-light and easy to wear. Printed and plain silks sourced from the Far East are a mainstay, although fur, leather, denim, wool and cashmere also feature. A range for girls, Mimi Chine, was recently introduced. *Photo p159.*

Massimo Dutti

47 avenue de la Toison d'Or, Ixelles (02 502 23 91, www.massimodutti.com). Métro Porte de Namur or Louise. **Open** 10am-6.30pm Mon-Sat. **Credit** AmEx, DC, MC, V. **Map** p319 D7.

Another successful Spanish clothing export, Massimo Dutti serves up smart, classically styled clothes for men, women and children. The elegant, practical attire is good-quality, although not usually breathtakingly exciting.

Other location Woluwe Shopping Centre, rue St-Lambert, Woluwe-St-Lambert (02 779 81 88).

Rue Blanche

39-41 rue Antoine Dansaert, Lower Town (02 512 03 14, www.rueblanche.com). Pré-métro Bourse. **Open** 11am-6.30pm Mon-Sat. **Credit** AmEx, DC, MC, V. **Map** p315 C4.

Two Belgian designers, Marie Chantal Regout and Patrick van Heurck, launched Rue Blanche in 1987, with seven different styles of cotton knitted jersey. From such lowly beginnings their business has expanded to include more than 100 timeless items in gorgeous fabrics, as well as beautiful evening bags, scarves and shoes. Household items, such as candles, vases and glossy books, complete the stock and ensure beautiful surroundings.

Streetwear

Privejoke

76-78 rue du Marché aux Charbon, Lower Town (02 502 63 67, www.privejoke.be). Pré-métro Bourse. **Open** 11am-7pm Mon-Sat; 2-7pm Sun. **Credit** AmEx, MC, V. **Map** p315 C5.

Privejoke, another of Brussels' original streetwear boutiques, is a funky choice. At least it is if you make your way to the back of the shop, where the men's clothes are to be found in a dark room. The women's section at the front, dotted with chandeliers, is far more bright and girlie. Brands stocked include Kangol, Pringle, Seven Jeans and Puma.

Twelvestar

12 rue des Riches Claires, Lower Town (no phone, www.myspace.com/magtwelvestar). Pré-métro Bourse. **Open** 12.30-6.30pm Tue, Thur; 2.30-6.30pm Wed; 12.30-7pm Fri, Sat. **Credit** MC, V. **Map** p315 B4.

Twelvestar's style is designer street-cred grunge, stocking male and female baggies, hyper-cool skate shoes, hoodies, tops and bags. Slightly offbeat brands such as ILI, Fenchurch and Vestal give this friendly and funky shop an exclusive feel. A nice touch is the sense of community; emerging

Rue Blanche.

Bernard Gavilan.

musicians and artists are encouraged to use the shop as a depot to showcase and sell their work.

Used & vintage

★ Bernard Gavilan
146 rue Blaes, Marolles (02 502 01 28, www.bernardgavilan.com). Métro Porte de Hal. **Open** 2-7pm Mon; noon-7pm Tue-Sat. **No credit cards. Map** p318 C7.
Local gay celebrity Bernard reopened his stylish shop in 2010, selling classy designer second-hand and customised vintage clothes, including trainers, sports bags and a huge selection of accessories.

Dod
16 chaussée de Louvain, St-Josse (02 218 04 54, www.dod.be). Métro Madou. **Open** 10am-6.30pm Mon-Sat. **Credit** AmEx, DC, MC, V. **Map** p320 G4.
Dod, which takes a warehouse approach to selling end-of-line designer fashion at discount prices, has now been in business for over 20 years. There are various shops, each specialising in either menswear, womenswear, childrenswear or, more recently, shoes. Along with this menswear branch, there's a womenswear outlet at No.44 (02 219 80 42) and a children's one at No.41 (02 217 52 08).
Other locations *Children* 8 rue du Bailli, Ixelles (02 640 64 83); 179 avenue Louise, Ixelles (02 640 60 40). *Men* 89 rue du Bailli, Ixelles (02 538 02 47). *Women* 64 rue du Bailli, Ixelles (02 640 38 98).

Les Enfants d'Edouard
175-177 avenue Louise, Ixelles (02 640 42 45, www.lesenfantsdedouard.net). Métro Louise then tram 94. **Open** 10am-6.30pm Mon-Sat. **Credit** AmEx, MC, V. **Map** p319 E9.
Edouard's Children sells second-hand designer labels and end-of-line stock. All of it is in excellent condition, and as a result prices can lean towards the expensive. Brands include Guess, Balmain, Charles Jourdan and Ferragamo.

★ Gabriele Vintage
27 rue des Chartreux, Lower Town (02 512 67 43). Pré-métro Bourse. **Open** noon-6pm Tue-Fri; 1-7pm Sat. **Credit** AmEx, DC, MC, V. **Map** p315 B4.
Gabriele Wolf, who owns this vintage clothing boutique, started collecting period hats when she worked in the theatre. In addition to hats, her rue des Chartreux shop sells clothes such as elegant evening dresses, coats and shoes, all dating from the 1920s onwards. Look out for the lopsided dummy standing on the street.

Idiz Bogam
76 rue Antoine Dansaert, Lower Town (02 512 10 32, www.myspace.com/idizbogam). Pré-métro Bourse. **Open** 11am-7pm Mon-Sat. **Credit** AmEx, DC, MC, V. **Map** p315 B3.
Idiz Bogam is a quirky little boutique selling second-hand and vintage clothing for both men and women from London, New York and Paris, much of it customised with sequins, ruffs and so on. There are also some wacky wedding dresses, as well as a fairly decent assortment of old and new shoes, hats and retro furniture.

Look 50
10 rue de la Paix, Ixelles (02 512 24 18). Métro Porte de Namur or bus 71. **Open** 10.30am-6.30pm Mon-Sat. **No credit cards. Map** p319 F8.
Look 50 is vintage at its rawest. No glam, no horrifying price tags, no pretence. Here, customers dig through the tightly packed mess of clothes to find the item that suits them best. The dominating era is the 1970s, with leather jackets, polyester dresses, funky vibrant shirts and fun hats.

Modes
164 rue Blaes, Marolles (02 512 49 07). Métro/pré-métro Porte de Hal or bus 27, 48. **Open** 10am-2.30pm Tue-Fri; 10am-3.30pm Sat, Sun. **Credit** AmEx, MC, V. **Map** p318 C7.
Modes specialises in vintage clothing made prior to 1950. Most pieces are for women, but there is a small children's section and a room at the back for men. The amazing collection includes furs, coats, dresses, shirts, skirts and hats, plus glasses, gloves, hat pins, purses and boas. There's also a limited range of linens, laces, ribbon and fabric.

CONSUME

Ramon & Valy

19 rue des Teinturiers, Lower Town (02 511 05 10). Pré-métro Bourse. **Open** 11am-7pm Mon-Sat. **Credit** AmEx, DC, MC, V. **Map** p315 C5.

An elegant corner shop that stocks only the best vintage clothes from French designers such as Yves Saint Laurent, Dior, Givenchy and Christian Lacroix, as well as Italian labels like Gucci and Roberto Cavalli. Vintage shoes and accessories are aimed at women but there are a few offerings for men and children.

FASHION ACCESSORIES & SERVICES

Cleaning & repairs

De Geest

41 rue de l'Hôpital, Lower Town (02 512 59 78). Métro Gare Centrale. **Open** 8am-7pm Mon-Fri; 8am-6.30pm Sat. **No credit cards.** **Map** p315 D5.

Spilled some wine? Dropped the jam? De Geest will launder virtually anything, including leather and suede items and upholstery.

Hats

★ Christophe Coppens

2 rue Léon Lepage, Lower Town (02 512 77 97). Métro Ste-Catherine. **Open** 11am-6pm Tue-Sat. **Credit** MC, V. **Map** p316 B3.

Flemish Christophe Coppens' hats are mainly for women, using all kinds of materials and ranging in price from around €150 to seriously pricey.

Gillis

17 rue du Lombard, Lower Town (02 512 09 26, www.gillismodistes.be). Pré-métro Bourse. **Open** 10am-6pm Mon-Sat. **Credit** AmEx, DC, MC, V. **Map** p315 C5.

Gillis is something of a Brussels institution, dating from 1910 and also known for supplying theatre costumes and hats. There's a small range of ready-made hats, which are mostly for women, but in winter a few men's hats are also available. However, the real speciality is made-to-measure hats, which are created on the premises using more than 300 wooden blocks.

Tarlatane

22 rue Ernest Solvay, Ixelles (02 502 79 29). Métro Porte de Namur or bus 54, 71. **Open** 11am-6.30pm Tue-Sat. **Credit** MC, V. **Map** p319 E7.

Valérie Janssens makes a range of accessories with a very girlie feel. Among the goodies are hats (particularly cloches and berets), bags (recycled wool day bags, silk evening bags), jewellery (made from sparkly cut-glass and buttons) and scarves.

Jewellery

Annick Tapernoux

28 rue du Vieux Marché aux Grains, Lower Town (02 512 43 79). Pré-métro Bourse. **Open** 1-6pm Fri; 11am-6pm Sat; also by appt. **Credit** MC, V. **Map** p315 B4.

Annick Tapernoux studied in Antwerp and then London's Royal College of Art, prior to setting up her eponymous shop, which displays both her silver jewellery (inspired by the elegance of the 1920s and '30s) and her silver homewares, such as bowls and vases. She also works to commission, either adapting existing designs or creating new pieces.

Arcane

54 rue du Midi, Lower Town (02 511 91 42). Pré-métro Bourse. **Open** 10.30am-6.30pm Sat. **Credit** AmEx, DC, MC, V. **Map** p315 C5.

Arcane has a wide range of affordable jewellery in all shapes and sizes, some incorporating leather, satin ribbons and beads. Many pieces are made from silver; some are classic, simple designs, while others come from India, Mexico, Thailand and Israel.

★ Christa Reniers

196 rue Antoine Dansaert, Lower Town (02 510 06 60, www.christareniers.com). Pré-métro Bourse. **Open** 11am-1pm, 2-6.30pm Mon-Sat. **Credit** AmEx, DC, MC, V. **Map** p315 C4.

Since she sold her first piece of jewellery in the early 1990s, Christa Reniers has become Belgium's most famous jewellery designer. Self-taught, she creates several new designs each season, adding to the already exquisite collection. Each piece is hand-cast and finished in the workshop located above this flagship store.

Other location 61 rue Lebeau, Sablon (02 514 91 54).

Marianne Timperman

50 rue Antoine Dansaert, Lower Town (02 675 53 82, www.mtimperman.com). Pré-métro Bourse. **Open** 11am-6.30pm Mon-Sat. **Credit** MC, V. **Map** p315 B4.

Marianne Timperman makes the majority of the jewellery on display herself, but there are a few pieces by Italian designer Tiziana Redavid. Marianne's speciality is silver; some items are oxidised so that they appear black, while others are made from granulated silver, resulting in a bobbly effect. She also incorporates semi-precious stones and pearls into various designs, and sells gold work too. Prices are reasonable.

Les Précieuses

83 rue Antoine Dansaert, Lower Town (02 503 28 98). Pré-métro Bourse. **Open** 11am-6.30pm Mon, Wed-Sat. **Credit** MC, V. **Map** p315 B3.

Pili Collado (Belgian of Portuguese descent) designs beautiful jewellery, using velvet ribbons, fine strands and polished chunky semi-precious stones and pearls. She also sells Jamin Puech's sequinned and embroidered bags and flamenco-inspired shawls, Diptyque candles and perfume, and scarves and tops by Japanese label Antipast.

Lingerie

★ Eva Luna
41 rue du Bailli, Ixelles (02 647 46 45, www. evaluna.be). Tram 92, 94. **Open** 1-6.30pm Mon; 11am-6.30pm Tue-Sat. **Credit** AmEx, MC, V. **Map** p319 E10.
Eva Luna describes itself as a love shop rather than a lingerie retailer and as such sells not only romantic, sexy and sassy underwear, but also the fragrant massage oils and cheeky sex toys to go with them. Designed primarily for women, the shop is soft and sensual.

Underwear
47 rue Antoine Dansaert, Lower Town (02 514 27 31, www.dunderwear.be). Pré-métro Bourse. **Open** 10.30am-6.30pm Mon-Sat. **Credit** AmEx, DC, MC, V. **Map** p315 B4.
Men's and women's undies, homewear, nightwear and beachwear by Hanro, Eres and Oxo.

Women'Secret
2 rue Neuve, Lower Town (02 217 10 28, www.womensecret.com). Métro/pré-métro De Brouckère. **Open** 10am-6.30pm Mon-Sat. **Credit** AmEx, DC, MC, V. **Map** p315 D3.
Women'Secret stocks an excellent selection of fun and reasonably priced lingerie, nightwear, beachwear, maternity wear and comfortable clothes for anyone lounging stylishly around the home. **Other location** Woluwe Shopping Centre, rue St-Lambert, Woluwe-St-Lambert (02 772 20 04).

Confection Perfection

A box of Belgium's finest.

Belgian chocolatiers base their luxury creations on three concepts: freshness, generosity and heritage. So it's almost impossible to go wrong in Brussels when choosing chocolate, except around the Grand'Place where the more obvious tourist-trap chocolate emporia can sometimes offer boxes of disappointment.

For everyday choccies at everyday prices, you really can't go wrong with **Leonidas** (www.leonidas.com). In 1913, a young Greek chocolatier, Leonidas Kestekides, fell in love with a local girl and settled here, opening a series of tearooms. These evolved into city-wide outlets for his value-for-money pralines, adorned with a profile of the eponymous king of Sparta, sold through the famous 'guillotine windows' straight on to the streets.

To take home the very best of Belgian chocolate-making, head for the place du Grand Sablon, home to two of the finest chocolate-makers on the planet. It may cost you an arm and a leg, and several inches on the waist, but the pralines are nothing short of sublime. **Wittamer** (*see p167*), easily spotted on the square with its lurid pink canopies, is the grand old dame of the

two. The founder, Henri Wittamer, opened his shop on the square in 1910 and it's still a family-run business, with siblings overseeing the three operations: grandchildren run the chocolate shop at No.6 and pâtisserie at No.12; next door, the upmarket tearoom at No.13 is run by great-granddaughter Leslie. Chocolates are still made at the back of the store, which features eye-catching designer-inspired window displays that change every three months. Across the square stands **Pierre Marcolini** (*see p167*), the eponymous shop and pretender to the Wittamer crown. Brussels-born with Italian lineage, Marcolini opened his first chocolate shop just 12 years ago and immediately won praise and awards for his cocoa creations: a ganache with earl grey tea, a Brittany caramel with salted butter and four spices. Pedestrians stop by his elegant window displays and gaze at the edible works of art. Marcolini is expanding fast, with branches in London, New York, Tokyo and Paris, and even the Belgian prime minister took a box of his chocs to Washington to sweeten the most pressing of deals.

Pierre Marcolini

CONSUME

CONSUME

Luggage

★ Delvaux

*27 boulevard de Waterloo, Upper Town (02 513
05 02, www.delvaux.com). Métro Louise or Porte
de Namur.* **Open** 10am-6.30pm Mon-Sat. **Credit**
AmEx, DC, MC, V. **Map** p319 D7.

Delvaux is something of an institution in Belgium,
creating top-quality leather products since 1829.
Expect to find handbags, wallets, belts, and a
small range of hand luggage, silk scarves and ties, and
desk accessories – all at luxury prices.
Other location 31 Galerie de la Reine, Lower Town
(02 512 71 98).

Shoes

Hatshoe

*89 rue Antoine Dansaert, Lower Town (02 512
41 52). Pré-métro Bourse.* **Open** 12.30-6.30pm
Mon; 10.30am-6.30pm Tue-Sat. **Credit** AmEx,
DC, MC, V. **Map** p315 B3.

Designer footwear for both men and women by
Patrick Cox, Costume National and Belgian designers Dries van Noten and Veronique Braquinho. Hats
and scarves are by Cécile Bertrand.

People Shoes Design

*14-18 rue du Lombard, Lower Town (02 502 18
01). Pré-métro Bourse.* **Open** 11am-7pm Mon-Fri;
10.30am-7pm Sat; 1.30-6.30pm Sun. **Credit** DC,
MC, V. **Map** p315 C5.

The focus of this shop (previously mad hatter Elvis
Pompilio's store) has changed, so that it now sells
as much street fashion for men and women as it does
designer-trendy urban footwear. Kids, however, still
only get shoes. Brands stocked include Diesel, Puma,
Dirk Bikkembergs and G-Star.

Sacha Shoe Design

*27 rue des Fripiers, Lower Town (02 218 79 65).
Métro/pré-métro De Brouckère or pré-métro
Bourse.* **Open** 10am-6.30pm Mon-Wed; 10am-
8pm Thur; 10am-7pm Fri, Sat; 1-6.30pm Sun.
No credit cards. **Map** p315 C4.

This funky, Dutch-owned shoe mecca sells everything from eccentric clubbing heels and boots to conventional office shoes for men and women. All the
latest trends and top brands are covered, including
Le Coq Sportif, Converse, Diesel and Dr Martens.
Other location 123 rue Neuve, Lower Town
(02 218 12 67).

Y-Enzo

*27 Galerie Espace Louise, Ixelles (02 514 65 68,
www.y-enzo.be). Métro Louise.* **Open** 10am-6.30pm
Mon-Sat. **Credit** AmEx, DC, MC, V. **Map** p319 D7.

Ultra-upmarket footwear by Yves Saint Laurent,
Gucci, Stephane Kélian and Dirk Bikkembergs,
among others, plus a limited number of designer
bags and clothes.

AM Sweet.

FOOD & DRINK

Bakeries

AM Sweet

*4 rue des Chartreux, Lower Town (02 513 51
31). Pré-métro Bourse.* **Open** 9am-6.30pm Tue-
Sat. **No credit cards**. **Map** p315 C4.

This lovely old-fashioned tea house and sweet shop
sells biscuits, chocolate by Laurent Gerbaud, cakes,
sweets, teas and coffees, most of which are made in-
house. The foodstuffs range from traditional recipes
(such as *pain d'épices*) to the latest innovative con-
coctions, such as French crystallised flowers, made
from real rose, lavender, violet and mint leaves.

★ Dandoy

*31 rue au Beurre, Lower Town (02 511 03 26,
www.biscuiteriedandoy.be). Pré-métro Bourse.*
Open 8.30am-7pm Mon-Sat; 10.30am-6.30pm
Sun. **Credit** MC, V. **Map** p315 C4.

The oldest cookie shop in town sells the best melt-
in-your-mouth *speculoos* (traditional Belgian ginger
biscuits), *pains d'amande* (wafer-thin biscuits), *pain
d'épices* and *pain à la grecque*.
Other location 14 rue Charles Buyls, Lower Town
(02 512 65 88).

Le Pain Quotidien

*16 rue Antoine Dansaert, Lower Town (02 502
23 61, www.painquotidien.com). Pré-métro
Bourse.* **Open** 7am-7pm daily. **Credit** MC, V.
Map p315 C4.

This successful chain of café-bakeries has branches around the world. This flagship Brussels branch is the most centrally located, but the one on avenue Louise is a favourite with its conservatory. Shoppers can pick up a loaf or croissant – or delicacies such as raspberry clafoutis, *tarte au citron*, and the legendary chocolate bombe cake. Brunch can be enjoyed with complete strangers around a warm, rustic setting of shared tables.
Other locations throughout the city.

Chocolate

See also p165 **Confection Perfection**.

Corné Port-Royal
9 rue de la Madeleine, Lower Town (02 512 43 14, www.corneportroyal.be). Métro Gare Centrale. **Open** 10am-8pm daily. **Credit** AmEx, DC, MC, V. **Map** p315 D5.
A good-quality chocolatier (similar to Neuhaus and Godiva), with franchises around town. Look out for the rather theatrical store at 5 Galerie de la Reine.
Other locations throughout the city.

★ Pierre Marcolini
1 rue des Minimes, Upper Town (02 514 12 06, www.marcolini.be). Bus 95, 96. **Open** 10am-7pm Mon-Thur; 10am-8pm Fri; 9am-8pm Sat; 9am-7pm Sun. **Credit** AmEx, DC, MC, V. **Map** p315 D6.
Pierre Marcolini is Brussels' biggest and brightest international name in chocolate. *See also p165* **Confection Perfection**.
Other locations 75 avenue Louise, Ixelles (02 538 42 24); 1302 chaussée de Waterloo, Uccle (02 372 15 11); 14 avenue de Hinnisdael, Woluwe-St-Pierre (02 771 27 20); Eurostar departure lounge (02 523 58 97).

Planète Chocolat
24 rue du Lombard, Lower Town (02 511 07 55, www.planetechocolat.be). Pré-métro Bourse or Anneessens. **Open** 11am-6.30pm Tue-Sun. **Credit** AmEx, MC, V. **Map** p315 C5.
As well as being a chocolate shop and a tea house, Planète Chocolat offers (bookable) group demonstrations of chocolate-making. The chocolate itself is among the funkiest in town: chocolate lips and bouquets of chocolate 'flowers' are specialities.

★ Wittamer
12 place du Grand Sablon (02 512 37 42, www.wittamer.com). Tram 92, 94 or bus 95. **Open** 9am-6pm Mon; 7am-7pm Tue-Sat; 7am-6.30pm Sun. **Credit** AmEx, DC, MC, V. **Map** p315 D6.
Wittamer is a renowned chocolate dynasty on the Sablon with a glitzy store and café along the street at 6 place du Grand Sablon. *See also p165* **Confection Perfection**.

Drink

See also p147 **A Beer for All Seasons**.

Beer Mania
174-178 chaussée de Wavre, Ixelles (02 512 17 88, www.beermania.be). Métro Porte de Namur. **Open** *Jan-Nov* 11am-9pm Mon-Sat. *Dec* 11am-9pm daily. **Credit** MC, V. **Map** p319 F7.
Beer Mania has been open for more than 20 years and now boasts a range of over 400 beers, along with matching glasses, gift packages, accessories and books. There's even a bar, so that you can sit down and sample the beers in comfort.

Délices et Caprices
68 rue des Bouchers, Lower Town (02 512 14 51). Pré-métro Bourse. **Open** *Winter* noon-8pm Mon, Thur-Sun. **Credit** AmEx, MC, V. **Map** p315 D4.
Délices et Caprices is run by a Swiss, Pierre Zuber, who's been in Belgium for 20 years and knows his beers. In addition to ale, beer glasses and other paraphernalia are sold, plus a few quality wines and genevers. Tastings are held on site.

Mig's World Wines
43 chaussée de Charleroi, St-Gilles (02 534 77 03, www.migsworldwines.be). Métro Louise then tram 92. **Open** 11am-7pm Mon-Sat. **Credit** AmEx, DC, MC, V. **Map** p319 D9.

Dandoy.

CONSUME

Maison d'Art G Arekens.

Best known for its Australian wines (owner Miguel Saelens stocks around 100 varieties), this store also sells wines from around 30 other regions and countries, including Belgium and Eastern Europe, plus fruit wines, grappa and whisky. Go on a Saturday for wine tasting.

Le Palais des Thés

45 place de la Vieille Halle aux Blés, Lower Town (02 502 45 59, www.palaisdesthes.com). Métro Gare Centrale. **Open** 11am-6.30pm daily. **Credit** AmEx, DC, MC, V. **Map** p315 C5.
A stylish shop, with around 250 varieties of tea from 30 countries, including Georgia and Turkey. Free tastings are offered, while gift ideas include beautiful teapots and scented teas.
Other location 25 chaussée de Charleroi St-Gilles (02 537 89 07).

International

Gallaecia

6 rue Charles Martel, EU Quarter (02 230 33 56). Métro Maelbeek. **Open** 11am-7pm Mon-Fri; 11am-3.30pm Sat. **No credit cards**. **Map** p320 H5.
If you can't live without Spanish produce, then this is the place to come. It sells *empañadas*, as well as olive oil, manchego cheese, serrano ham, tinned fish and preserves. Sweet treats such as *turrones* and *polvorones* are popular, as are the wines and cava.

Tagawa Superstore

119 chaussée de Vleurgat, Ixelles (02 648 59 11). Tram 81, 82, 93, 94 or bus 38, 60. **Open** 10am-7pm Mon-Sat. **No credit cards**. **Map** p324 F11.
Fresh and frozen Japanese specialities and dishes, plus wasabi – and newspapers.

Thai Supermarket

3-9 rue Ste-Catherine, Lower Town (02 502 40 32). Pré-métro Bourse or métro Ste-Catherine. **Open** 9.30am-6.30pm Mon-Sat; 10am-3pm Sun. **No credit cards**. **Map** p315 C4.
Next door to a vast Chinese supermarket is this more manageable Thai supermarket. Expect to find exotic fresh, dry and tinned produce as well as homewares. The staff are helpful and speak English.

Markets

Brussels has a number of food markets easily accessible from the city centre. The largest and most colourful is around the **Gare du Midi**, on Sundays from 8am, with a Mediterranean and North African flavour. Others are more akin to farmers' markets, with cured meats, fine cheeses and so on. The most popular is at **place du Châtelain** in Ixelles on Wednesdays from 2pm to 7.30pm. There's a lively one at **parvis de St-Gilles** on Sundays.

Treats & *traiteurs*

Claire Fontaine

3 rue Ernest Allard, Upper Town (02 512 24 10). Tram 92, 93, 94. **Open** 10am-6.30pm Tue-Sat. **No credit cards**. **Map** p319 D6.
It's pretty well impossible to walk past Claire Fontaine, just off the Sablon, without popping in just to have a taste of some delight. As well as sandwiches, quiches, soups and pastries to take away, there's a host of international gastronomic delights such as foie gras, lobster soup, olives, dry goods, teas and tisanes, absinthe and Belgian fruit wines.

★ Oliviers & Co

28 rue au Beurre, Lower Town (02 502 75 11, www.oliviersandco.net). Pré-métro Bourse. **Open** 10.30am-6.30pm Mon-Thur; 10am-8pm Fri, Sat; 11am-7pm Sun. **Credit** AmEx, DC, MC, V. **Map** p315 C4.
An atmospheric shop specialising in olive oil from around the world. You can buy in bottles or retro tins, and pick up the paraphernalia to go with it – pourers, jugs and table sets. There are exotic ranges such as truffle oils and pastas, bags of chillies and olive oil-based skin products.

Le Tartisan

27 rue de la Paix, Ixelles (02 503 36 00, www.tartisan.be). Métro Porte de Namur or bus 54, 71. **Open** 10am-7pm Mon, Tue; 10am-10pm Wed-Sat. **Credit** AmEx, DC, MC, V. **Map** p319 F8.
Le Tartisan deli was so popular that it moved around the corner from its old location and added a restaurant section. The speciality of the house is, not surprisingly, tarts – savoury and sweet, all made on site according to traditional recipes. They're

Plaizier.

astonishingly light, and come in both veggie and meat options, with lemon, walnut and chocolate or frangipane for sweet-toothed customers. **Other locations** throughout the city.

GIFTS & SOUVENIRS

Bali-Africa

154-156 rue Blaes, Marolles (02 514 47 92, www.baliafrica.com). Métro/pré-métro Porte de Hal or bus 27, 48. **Open** 10am-5pm Tue-Sun. **Credit** AmEx, DC, MC, V. **Map** p318 C7.

It's easy to get lost in this giant maze of a shop, though luckily the owners have signposted the rooms and provided a painted yellow line on the floor and stairs to help you find your way around. Wares include statuettes, masks, bongos and furniture from across the globe.

La Maison du Miel

121 rue du Midi, Lower Town (02 512 32 50, www.lamaisondumiel.be). Pré-métro Anneessens. **Open** 10.30am-6.30pm Mon-Fri, Sun; 10.30am-7pm Sat. **Credit** AmEx, MC, V. **Map** p315 C5.

Make a beeline for this shop, which was founded in 1887 and sells all things honey-themed, scented and flavoured, from edible goodies to toiletries. **Other location** 13 rue Marché aux Herbes, Lower Town (02 513 57 50).

INSIDE TRACK CHOCS AWAY

Brussels Airport sells more chocolate than any other sales point in the world. In 2007, more than 850 tonnes of the stuff made its way into travellers' bags.

Maison d'Art G Arekens

15 rue du Midi, Lower Town (02 511 48 08). Pré-métro Bourse. **Open** 10.30am-1pm, 2-6pm Mon-Sat. **Credit** MC, V. **Map** p315 C5.

You'd think this place was simply a picture-framing gallery, but pop inside and you'll find a variety of religious icons such as crucifixes and triptychs. There are also small plaster-cast reproductions of non-religious statues, but the real highlights are the 55,000 postcards and reproduction etchings.

Ma Maison de Papier

6 Galerie de la rue de Ruysbroeck, Upper Town (02 512 22 49, http://mamaisondepapier.be). Métro Gare Centrale or bus 34, 48, 95, 96. **Open** 1-7pm Wed-Fri; 3-7pm Sat. **No credit cards. Map** p315 D6.

A store of treasures, with its drawers of prints, plaques and posters of art exhibits and adverts from the late 1800s to the present.

★ Plaizier

50 rue des Eperonniers, Lower Town (02 513 47 30, www.plaizier.be). Métro Gare Centrale. **Open** 11am-6pm Mon-Sat. **Credit** AmEx, DC, MC, V. **Map** p315 D5.

Most people come here for the excellent postcards, generally original and artistic, but there's also a well-chosen selection of books, posters and diaries. Plaizier also specialises in retro photographs of Brussels from the 1940s and '50s – look out for the annual retro calendar.

Rosalie Pompon

1 rue de l'Hôpital, Lower Town (02 512 35 93). Métro Gare Centrale. **Open** noon-6.30pm Mon; 10.30am-6.30pm Tue-Sun. **Credit** AmEx, DC, MC, V. **Map** p315 D5.

CONSUME

CONSUME

Chain-free Chic

Rue des Chartreux is perfect for a spot of offbeat shopping.

Running at an angle from fashionable rue Antoine Dansaert (*see p160* **Style Street**), quainter, quieter rue des Chartreux stands strong against corporate or chain store development. It's never been a main thoroughfare because it leads to the place du Jardin aux Fleurs, part of a residential area. This creates a village effect and a sense of community among residents and retailers alike. This is a timeless street of shopping baskets, bicycles and dogs on leads, although the dawning of the new millennium didn't pass it by completely. Of constant interest to tourists is the life-size statue of a peeing dog that appeared as part of the City of Culture shenanigans in 2000. He stands in mid-spray on the corner with rue du Vieux Marché aux Grains.

To its left at No.27 is another half-cocked sight, **Gabriele**'s 1960s mannequin standing skew-whiff outside her impossibly packed vintage clothes shop (*see p163*). Sticking with the clothes theme, Chartreux has some slick little boutiques – don't be afraid to venture in. Designer **Louise Assomo** has her own outlet at No.64 (mobile 0485 91 20 57) and her eveningwear brings a touch of glamour – some might say respectability – to the street.

For foodies, **AM Sweet** (*see p166*) is a real treat, full of old-fashioned charm. This is the village tea room where you can get a real pot of leaf tea to go with that delicious slice of home-made cake. It also sells hot Brussels chocolatier Laurent Gerbaud's chocolate. At No.66, **Den Teepot** (02 511 94 02) also serves tea and cake but of the green variety. In its organic grocery you can find a vast selection of green goods, from kitchen roll to fresh veggies. The place hums with local bio warriors.

Interior design gets a look in with **Toit** (*see right*), and next door at No.44 is quirky new arrival **Brocéliande** (mobile 0477 353 607), a whacky upmarket flea market shop selling retro stuff from the 1950s to the 1980s. In a similar vein is the fabulous **Boutique Lucien Cravate** (No.24, 02 647 04 54), which dispenses cheerful, retro bric-a-brac from the 1950s and '60s. Along the street at No.14 is great gift shop **Whazup** (02 503 47 57), selling a range of toys for boys and household items. Add in a couple of watchmakers and clock repairers, the most grotesque (locked) art collection you could hope to see (at No.12), plus private men's club Le Gentleman at No.34, and you have one of the most offbeat streets in town.

A cross between a gift shop and toy shop, attracting both the young at heart and the young in age. Papier-mâché giraffes and elephants jostle for space with flower-adorned wellies, colourful fairy lights, wacky lamps and clocks and old-fashioned puppets.

Rose

56-58 rue de l'Aqueduc, Ixelles (02 534 9808). Tram 91, 92. **Open** 10.30am-6.20pm Tue-Sat. **Credit** MC, V. **Map** p324 D10.
Rose was established in December 2003 by Elodie Gleis, who gave up a job in advertising to open this temple to all things girlie. She sells a mix of decorative objects for the home, fashion accessories and small gifts, which she sources from different parts of Europe (including Cath Kidston).

Toit

46 rue des Chartreux, Lower Town (02 503 33 38, http://users.skynet.be/toit-bruxelles). Prémétro Bourse. **Open** 11am-7pm Wed-Sat. **Credit** MC, V. **Map** p315 B4.
This bright homeware boutique on this happening street sells glass, vases, framed pictures, CDs and bags. It also has a natty line in tinned and bottled food – jars of squid in its own ink, for example.

Yannart-Remacle

11 rue du Marché au Charbon, Lower Town (02 512 12 26, http://users.skynet.be/fa367721). Pré-métro Bourse or Anneessens. **Open** 8.30am-5.30pm Mon-Fri; 8.30am-12.30pm Sat. **No credit cards. Map** p315 C5.
This old-fashioned shop sells everything that a jeweller could need to perfect his or her art, including crystals and semi-precious stones.

Z'art

223 chaussée d'Ixelles, Ixelles (02 649 06 53, www.zart-shop.com). Bus 54, 71. **Open** 10.30am-6.30pm Tue-Sat. **Credit** AmEx, DC, MC, V. **Map** p322 F8.
Z'Art is the perfect place to browse for a gift, because it specialises in novelty items with a function: think octopus salt shakers, snail-shaped Sellotape dispensers and cow-adorned toilet roll holders. And if you don't want to carry it home, there is a new Z'art online shop.

Florists

★ Bo Flowers

49 place du Chatelain, Ixelles (02 646 66 96, www.boflowers.be). Tram 92, 94. **Open** 9am-8pm Mon-Thur, Sat; 9am-9pm Fri; 9am-6pm Sun. **Credit** MC, V. **Map** p324 E11.
Bo Flowers is open late and produces beautiful flower arrangements at reasonable prices.
Other locations 378 avenue Rogier, Schaerbeek (02 726 28 20); 107 avenue du Panthéon (02 428 78 68).

Fleurop-Interflora

0800 99669/02 242 29 64, www.interflora.com. **Open** 24hrs daily. **Credit** AmEx, DC, MC, V.
For those who want to say it with flowers, at any time of the day or night.

★ Het Witte Gras

7 rue Plétinckx, Lower Town (02 502 05 29, www.hetwittegras.be). Pré-métro Bourse. **Open** 9am-6pm Mon, Tue, Thur, Sat; 9am-7pm Fri. **Credit** AmEx, DC, MC, V. **Map** p316 B4.
Het Witte Gras is a pretty corner shop out of which house plants and flowers spill on to the pavement. Inside is an abundance of attractive vases and pots, plus plenty of expert advice.

HEALTH & BEAUTY
Cosmetics & perfume

Ici Paris XL

37 rue Neuve, Lower Town (02 219 22 07, www.iciparisxl.be). Métro/pré-métro De Brouckère or Rogier. **Open** 9.30am-6.30pm Mon-Sat. **Credit** AmEx, DC, MC, V. **Map** p315 D3.
Founded in Belgium in the late 1970s, this is the largest chain of perfumeries in the country. Each shop is stylish, while the range of luxury fragrances in most stores includes all the top brands.
Other locations throughout the city.

Planet Parfum

Centre Monnaie, place de la Monnaie, Lower Town (02 218 48 58, www.planetparfum.be). Métro/pré-métro De Brouckère. **Open** 9.30am-6.30pm Mon-Sat. **Credit** AmEx, DC, MC, V. **Map** p315 D4.
Ubiquitous fragrance store selling a wide selection of perfumes and some cosmetics.
Other locations throughout the city.

Hairdressers

Anthony-And

165 rue de Linthout, EU Quarter (02 736 45 35, www.anthony-and.com). Métro Mérode. **Open** 9am-7pm Mon-Sat. **No credit cards. Map** p321 L5.
Trendy yet unpretentious, this salon has quality hairdressers and great prices. Not only that, but you can boogie while you're blow-dried on Saturdays, when a resident DJ spins the vinyl.

Nicole Jocelyn

37 chaussée de Wavre, Ixelles (02 511 28 74). Métro Porte de Namur. **Open** 9.30am-7pm Mon-Sat. **No credit cards. Map** p319 E7.
One of the largest and most popular hairdressers in the area, specialising in Afro hair. Men, women and children are all catered for.

CONSUME

Kartell.

CONSUME

★ **Toni & Guy**
*28 rue de Namur, Upper Town (02 213 70 90,
www.toniandguy.be). Tram 92, 94 or bus 95.*
Open 10am-7pm Mon-Wed; 10am-8pm Thur,
Fri; 9am-7pm Sat. **Credit** AmEx, MC, V.
Map p319 E6.
Prices at Toni & Guy depend on who cuts your hair
– ranging upwards from a lowly stylist to the dizzy
heights of the creative director. The Brussels outlets
come with multilingual staff, with English, French,
Dutch, Spanish and Italian all spoken.
Other location 124 rue Stévin, EU Quarter
(02 737 52 80).

Opticians

Pearle
*22 rue Neuve, Lower Town (02 223 05 40,
www.pearle.be). Métro/pré-métro De Brouckère.*
Open 9.30am-6.30pm Mon-Sat. **Credit** AmEx,
DC, MC, V. **Map** p317 D2.
Pearle is one of Belgium's main optician chains,
offering walk-in eye tests and a wide range of
glasses and sunglasses. Prescriptions take around
five days to process.
Other locations throughout the city.

Theo (Depot)
*81 rue Antoine Dansaert, Lower Town (02 511
04 47, www.hoet.be). Pré-métro Bourse or métro
Ste-Catherine.* **Open** 10.30am-6.30pm Mon, Wed-
Sat. **Credit** AmEx, DC, MC, V. **Map** p315 B3.

Theo's trendy specs and sunglasses have a very distinctive look, with thick, brightly coloured frames.

HOUSE & HOME
Design & interiors

The best place for a browse is the Marolles, and
the two main streets of rues Blaes and Haute
leading to the daily flea market on place du
Jeu de Balle. *See p58* **Walk**.

Art & Influences
*221 avenue Louise, Ixelles (02 643 2843). Métro
Louise then tram 93, 94.* **Open** 10am-7pm Tue-
Sat. **Credit** MC, V. **Map** p319 E9.
A huge store stocking an amazing range of household items, from delicate little vases to large sofas,
in a wide range of colours and styles, including modern, African and Asian. There's also a café on site.

Cap Orient
*123 & 133 rue Haute, Marolles (No.123 02 513
13 02/No.133 02 513 13 05). Métro/pré-métro
Porte de Hal or bus 27, 48.* **Open** noon-6.30pm
Mon-Thur; 10am-6.30pm Fri-Sun. **Credit** AmEx,
DC, MC, V. **Map** p318 C7.
The shop at No.123 specialises in Chinese antiques
and reproduction furniture, while the sister shop
at No.133 focuses on Indian antiques, antique-style
furniture and artefacts.

Dille & Kamille
*16 rue Jean Stas, St-Gilles (02 538 81 25,
www.dille-kamille.be). Métro Louise or tram 91,
92, 94.* **Open** 9.30am-6.30pm Mon-Sat. **Credit**
MC, V. **Map** p319 D8.
Dille & Kamille is a chi-chi garden and home store.
Plants and decorative baskets are at the front, while
foodstuffs (olive oils, mustards, herbs, teas) are
towards the back. The middle section features lots
of household basics, kitchen gadgets, cookbooks and
traditional wooden toys. Great for browsing.

Espace Bizarre
*19 rue des Chartreux, Lower Town (02 514 52
56, www.espacebizarre.com). Pré-métro Bourse.*
Open 10am-7pm Mon-Sat. **Credit** AmEx, DC,
MC, V. **Map** p315 B4.
Big and blousy, Espace Bizarre sells an astonishing
range of high-end designer furniture and accessories, all influenced by the clean lines of Japanese
designs. Sliding screens, Futon bed bases and
original lighting form the core range. The shop also
stocks Fatboy hammocks.

Kartell
*2 rue Antoine Dansaert, Lower Town (02 514
79 45, www.kartell.it). Pré-métro Bourse.* **Open**
11am-6.30pm Mon-Sat. **Credit** AmEx, DC,
MC, V. **Map** p315 C4.

Fashionable plastic designs for furniture and lighting dominate this bright corner store. Philippe Starck is much in evidence.

Maisons du Monde
Boulevard Anspach, Lower Town (02 217 66 41, www.maisonsdumonde.com). Métro/pré-métro De Brouckère. **Open** 10am-7pm Mon-Thur, Sat; 10am-8pm Fri. **Credit** MC, V. **Map** p315 C3.
This international homewares chain, a newcomer to Brussels, serves up cushions, glassware, beds, cupboards and chairs with an Indian influence. Upstairs the sections are organised by colour, perfect for swatching things together.

Max
90-101 rue Antoine Dansaert, Lower Town (02 514 23 27). Pré-métro Bourse or métro Ste-Catherine. **Open** 11am-1pm, 2.30-6.30pm Tue-Fri; 11am-6pm Sat. **Credit** MC, V. **Map** p316 B3.
The designer furniture on show here tends be somewhat minimalist in look and predominantly dark in colour. However, the odd splash of brightness is provided by curvy armchairs, wacky cartoon-like sofas and papier-mâché sculptures.

Les Memoires de Jacqmotte
92-96 rue Blaes, Lower Town (02 502 50 83, www.lesmemoiresdejacqmotte.com). Métro/pré-métro Porte de Hal or bus 27, 48. **Open** 10am-6pm Mon, Tue, Thur-Sat; 10am-4pm Sun. **Credit** MC, V. **Map** p318 C7.

Arlequin. See p174.

About ten years ago the warehouse of the Jacqmotte coffee emporium was converted into this space, where dealers can rent a pitch and display their goods. Expect to find art deco antiques, including furniture, porcelain and jewellery, plus earlier pieces.

Philippe Lange
2a place de la Justice, Upper Town (02 503 46 18, www.philippelange.be). Métro Gare Centrale or bus 48, 95. **Open** 11am-1pm, 2-6pm Tue-Sat; Sun by appt only. **Credit** AmEx, DC, MC, V. **Map** p315 D5.
Art deco, art nouveau, 20th-century antiques and new design are specialities, along with Panton chairs and Knoll furniture from the 1950s and '60s.

Hobbies, arts & crafts

De Banier
85 rue du Marché au Charbon, Lower Town (02 511 44 31, www.debanier.be). Pré-métro Bourse or Anneessens. **Open** 10am-1pm, 2-6pm Mon-Fri; 10am-1pm, 2-5pm Sat. **No credit cards**. **Map** p315 C5.
This quiet little shop is packed with an extensive selection of arts and crafts supplies, including wood, paints, dyes, felt and beads. There are also 'how to' books and magazines, mainly in Dutch and French.

Schleiper
149 chaussée de Charleroi, St-Gilles (02 541 05 41, www.schleiper.com). Tram 92. **Open** 9.30am-6.30pm Mon-Sat. **Credit** AmEx, DC, MC, V. **Map** p319 D9.
An excellent choice of all types of art supplies, as well as an efficient framing service, framed art for sale and some office supplies.

Les Tissus du Chien Vert
2 rue du Chien Vert, Molenbeek (02 411 54 39, www.chienvert.com). Métro Comte de Flandre. **Open** 10am-6pm Mon-Sat. **Credit** AmEx, DC, MC, V. **Map** p316 A2.
There are three parts to this textile store: Les Tissus du Chien Vert is the specialised outlet with smart furnishing fabrics, silks and leathers, which also includes a second section, Les Puces du Chien, a bargain area of remnants. The third section, along the road, is Le Chien du Chien (50a quai des Charbonnages, 02 414 81 00), which is more of a general cloth store. The shops have been built out of canal-side buildings and are filled with boats (the owner is a keen sailor), a car, a rickshaw and a number of water features. Les Tissus, meanwhile, is home to a light aircraft. A quirky and refreshing shopping experience.

MUSIC & ENTERTAINMENT

Fnac (*see p156*) and **Media Markt** (*see p159*) also sell music and DVDs.

CONSUME

CONSUME

Arlequin

7 rue du Chêne, Lower Town (02 514 54 28,
www.arlequin.net). Pré-métro Anneessens or
Métro Gare Centrale. **Open** 11am-7pm Mon-
Sat; 2-7pm Sun. **Credit** MC, V. **Map** p315 C5.
Arlequin has all kinds of second-hand music, but
focuses on rock, punk, import and jazz; its sister stores
specialise in soul, funk, jazz, rap, reggae, classic and
world music. Quality is high, and staff are friendly.
This branch opens on Sundays. *Photo p173.*
Other location 90 rue d'Andenne, St-Gilles
(02 512 15 86).

BCM

6 Plattesteen, Lower Town (02 502 09 72).
Pré-métro Bourse. **Open** 11am-6.30pm Tue-Sat.
No credit cards. **Map** p315 C4.
The best place in Brussels to find dance music on
vinyl: techno, house, garage and drum 'n' bass. The
staff are very helpful, and this is a good source of
information for prospective clubbers.

Caroline Music

20 passage St-Honoré, Lower Town (02 217
07 31, www.carolinemusic.be). Métro/pré-métro
De Brouckère or pré-métro Bourse. **Open** 10am-
6pm Mon; 10am-6.30pm Tue-Sat. **Credit** MC, V.
Map p315 C4.
Caroline Music stocks an extensive range of
CDs, with huge sections devoted entirely to indie
and French music.

Free Record Shop

Centre de la Monnaie, place de la Monnaie, Lower
Town (02 218 62 26, www.freerecordshop.be).
Métro/pré-métro De Brouckère. **Open** 10am-7pm
Mon-Sat; 1-6pm Sun. **Credit** AmEx, DC, MC, V.
Map p315 D4.
As well as CDs, the Free Record Shop stocks videos,
DVDs and computer games. There's also a ticket
booth for gigs.
Other locations throughout the city.

Musical instruments

Azzato

42 rue de la Violette, Lower Town (02 512 37
52, www.azzato-music.com). Métro Gare Centrale.
Open 9.30am-6pm Mon-Sat. **Credit** AmEx,
DC, MC, V. **Map** p315 C5.
A wide range of guitars, string and wind instruments,
plus instruments from around the world.

Hill's Music

37-39 rue du Marché au Charbon, Lower Town
(02 512 77 71, www.hillsmusic.be). Pré-métro
Bourse or Anneessens. **Open** 9.30am-12.30pm,
1.30-5.45pm Tue-Sat. **Credit** AmEx, MC, V.
Map p315 C5.
Hill's specialises in quality acoustic string instruments, from guitars to harps.

Music Office

156 rue du Midi, Lower Town (02 502 38 70).
Pré-métro Anneessens. **Open** 10.30am-6.30pm
Mon-Sat. **Credit** AmEx, DC, MC, V. **Map** p315 C5.
The Music Office is the place to go for musical
instruments and recording equipment.

SPORT & FITNESS

Entre Terre et Ciel

20 place Stéphanie, Ixelles (02 502 42 41,
www.entreterreetciel.be). Métro Louise. **Open**
10.30am-6.30pm Mon-Sat. **Credit** MC, V.
Map p319 D8.
Between Earth and Sky is a luxury megastore for
fans of outdoor pursuits, including skiing, snow-
boarding, sailing, camping and mountaineering.

Montagne & Randonnée

27 rue des Vergnies, Ixelles (02 640 58 20).
Tram 81, 82 or bus 38, 60, 71. **Open** 10am-
1pm, 2-6.30pm Mon-Fri; 10am-6pm Sat.
Credit AmEx, MC, V. **Map** p322 G9.
A specialist store for climbing and camping, staffed
by experts in the field. Detailed local maps too.

Ride All Day

39 rue St-Jean, Lower Town (02 512 89 22,
www.rideallday.be). Métro Gare Centrale. **Open**
noon-6.30pm Tue-Sat. **No credit cards**.
Map p315 D5.
Ride All Day sells boards, shoes and clothing to the
skate rats who congregate around the skating
hotspot of the neighbouring Mont des Arts. The
staff, die-hard skaters, are happy to provide tips.

Sports World

City 2, rue Neuve, Lower Town (02 217 46 23,
www.sportsdirect.com). Métro/pré-métro Rogier.
Open 10am-7pm Mon-Thur, Sat; 10am-7.30pm
Fri. **Credit** AmEx, MC, V. **Map** p317 E2.
A massive depot of reduced price sportswear and
equipment including cycle, gym and hiking gear.

Velodroom

41 rue Van Artevelde, Lower Town (02 513
81 99, www.velodroom.net). Pré-métro Bourse.
Open noon-2pm, 4-7pm Tue-Fri; noon-5pm Sat.
Credit MC, V. **Map** p315 B4.
Velodroom is run by a non-profit organisation that
promotes cycling in Brussels as an environmentally
friendly alternative to cars. It also does repairs. If
you prefer not to be rushed, call for an appointment.

TRAVEL AGENTS

For cheap flights, try **Airstop** (28 rue du
Fossé aux Loups, Lower Town, 070 233 188,
www.airstop.be) or **Connections** (19-21 rue
du Midi, Lower Town, (070 233 313, 02 550 01
00, www.connections.be).

Arts & Entertainment

Calendar

Traditional treats, from floral carpets to full-on festivals.

Brussels has plenty of events all year round but truly comes into its own during the spring and summer months. The major exception to this is the magnificent Christmas market, when it's time to wrap up and drink hot wine.

Belgians delight in tradition and folklore, and it is not unusual to come across an unexplained procession of giant mannequins or a marching band as you walk around Brussels at the weekend. Old habits die hard, and rituals are played out as they have been for centuries.

For details on seasonal events and festivals around the city, the **Brussels Tourist Information Board** (02 513 89 40, www.brusselsinternational.be) is the best source. For events taking place further afield, try the **Belgian Tourist Information Office** (02 504 03 90, www.belgiumtheplacetobe.com).

SPRING

Brussels International Festival of Fantastic Film

86c avenue du Port, Molenbeek (02 201 17 13, www.bifff.org). Métro Yser. **Map** p316 B1. **Tickets** available by phone, from FNAC or the website. **Date** mid Mar.

This two-week horror/sci-fi festival continues to pack in the gore-loving punters. With more than 150 films from all over the world (40% of them Belgian), fans of the genre have plenty to feast on. In addition, there are body-painting competitions, wacky fashion shows and the Vampire's Ball – entrance in costume only.

Ars Musica

Various venues (02 219 26 60, www.arsmusica.be). **Tickets** available by phone or from the Bozar box office (23 rue Ravenstein, Lower Town, 02 507 82 00). **Date** Mar, Apr.

This festival of contemporary classical music sets the scene for the upcoming season and has become one of Brussels' best-loved music festivals. It's an event of discovery and education, where new composers are given a chance to show their pieces. Work by young people is given emphasis. *Photo p178.*

★ Kunsten Festival des Arts

Various venues (information 02 219 07 07, tickets 070 222 199, www.kfda.be). **Open**

Box office Mar, Apr 11am-6pm Mon-Wed, Fri; 11am-8pm Thur. *During festival* 11am-8pm daily. **Admission** €12-€20. **Credit** MC, V. **Date** May.

What makes this major three-week arts festival so different is that it appeals to all Belgians, refusing to identify itself solely with French or Flemish. Established in 1994 by Frie Leysen, Kunsten is an all-encompassing festival, attracting important and often controversial international names.

Zinneke

Various venues (02 214 20 07, www.zinneke.org). **Date** May.

See p180 **Zany Zinneke**.

Jazz Marathon

Various venues in Brussels & nearby towns (02 456 04 86, www.brusselsjazzmarathon.be). **Admission** free. **Date** May.

For three days, jazz-lovers can see live music in bars, clubs and restaurants all over Brussels. In 2010, the event attracted over 300,000 fans to 125 venues.

Dring Dring Bike Festival

Parc du Cinquantenaire, EU Quarter (02 502 73 55, www.provelo.org). Métro Mérode or Schuman or tram 27, 80, 81, 82. **Admission** free. **Map** p323 K6. **Date** May.

Belgium's die-hard army of cycling fanatics love this popular bike festival centred around the Parc du Cinquantenaire, with bikes for hire, guided tours around Brussels and its outskirts, and riding and maintenance classes. Pro-Vélo (*see p298*), which organises the event, rents out bikes during the event and throughout July and August.

Les Nuits Botanique

Le Botanique, 236 rue Royale, St-Josse (02 218 37 32, www.myspace.com/nuitsbotanique). Métro Botanique. **Tickets** phone for details. **Map** p317 F2. **Date** mid May.
For a fortnight bands play in the various rooms, marquees and gardens at the Botanique cultural centre. Groups are of the indie variety, many from the UK, appearing in the size of venue they would have played before they became famous. All the atmosphere of a festival without the mud. *See also p90* **Relics Reborn**.

Brussels 20km

Race begins & ends in Parc du Cinquantenaire (02 511 90 00, http://20km.chronorace.be). **Admission** €15 participants; free spectators. **Date** last Sun in May.
This event starts and finishes in the Parc du Cinquantenaire, passing through the Bois de la Cambre and avenue Louise along the way. First held 25 years ago, it is now an established part of the Brussels calendar, attracting 20,000 mainly amateur runners. Witness as this bustling city comes to a complete standstill.

★ Concours Musical International Reine Elisabeth de Belgique

Bozar, 23 rue Ravenstein, Upper Town (information 02 213 40 50, box office 02 507 82 00, www.concours-reine-elisabeth.be). Métro Gare

Centrale or Parc or tram 92, 93, 94. **Open Information** 9am-7pm Mon-Sat. *Box office (23 rue Ravenstein)* 11am-7pm Mon-Sat. **Tickets** prices vary. **Date** May-mid June.
Regarded as one of the world's foremost music competitions, the Concours was founded over 40 years ago by Belgium's former Queen Elisabeth, a keen violin player. Aimed at young professional musicians and singers, it alternates between three categories – singing, violin and piano – with the final featuring 12 competitors. The final concert is at the Bozar; others are held at the Conservatoire Royal de Bruxelles (*see p200*).

SUMMER

Brussels International Film Festival

Various venues (02 533 34 20, www.fffb.be). **Admission** varies. **Date** June.
This festival, now mainly based at Flagey (*see p203*), features various themes, with Belgian films

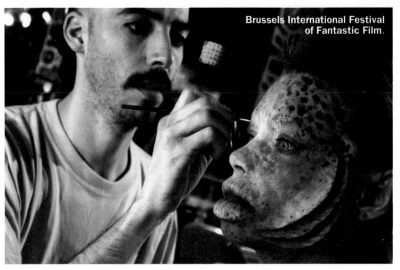

Brussels International Festival of Fantastic Film.

Ars Musica. *See p176.*

running alongside shorts and other European/US mainstream and arthouse pictures. There is also a European competition for features, and a Belgian one for shorts and documentaries.

Battle of Waterloo

Waterloo Visitors' Centre, 254 route du Lion, Braine l'Alleud (02 385 19 12, www.1815.be). **Open** *Nov-Mar* 10am-5pm daily. *Apr-Oct* 9.30am-6.30pm daily. **Date** every 5yrs in mid June.

A large-scale and visually stunning re-enactment of the legendary 1815 Battle of Waterloo takes place every five years in this Brussels suburb (the next one is set to take place in 2015). It's a spectacular event: about 2,000 men get dressed up in period uniforms, wield vintage guns and play war – some under Wellington and Blücher, others in the charge of Napoleon.

Festival of Wallonia

Various venues in Brussels & Wallonia (081 73 37 81, www.festivaldewallonie.be). **Admission** prices vary. **Date** June-Sept.

Belgian and international orchestras play in a vast musical programme all over francophone Belgium, with major events in Brussels. From churches to main concert halls, the festival's reach is impressive.

Festival of Flanders

Various venues in Flanders (tickets 070 77 00 00, www.festival.be). **Admission** prices vary. **Date** June-Oct.

One of the two major Belgian classical music festivals, this one is in fact eight separate festivals, with different themes playing in all the major Flemish cities. Look out for the KlaraFestival (www.klara festival.be), with everything on offer from classical to jazz and roots.

★ Ommegang

Grand'Place, Lower Town (02 512 19 61, www.ommegang.be). Pré-métro Bourse or métro Gare Centrale. **Admission** *Grand'Place performance* €35-€75. **Map** p315 C4. **Date** last Tue in June & 1st Thur in July.

This popular event is marked by a spectacular parade of enthusiastic Belgians dressed as nobles, guildsmen, jesters and peasants marching from the Sablon to the Grand'Place, some on horseback, others on foot, but all commemorating the glorious entry into Brussels of Charles V, the new emperor of the Spanish Netherlands, 500 years ago. It ends up with a horse parade, stilt-fighting and a jousting tournament in the Grand'Place. You can also buy seats for the grandstand in the Grand'Place (you'll need to book by May for a space), sit at a bar in the place du Grand Sablon and watch the start or simply catch the parade en route.

Drive-in movies
Esplanade du Cinquantenaire, EU Quarter (www.driveinmovies.be). **Tickets** €19 per car; €14 reductions. **Map** p323 K6. **Date** July-Sept.
At 10.30pm on Friday and Saturday evenings in July and 10pm in August, the Parc du Cinquantenaire turns into a drive-in cinema. Films are current and culturally relevant, and the sound system is truly first rate. An awesome audio-visual experience.

Brosella Jazz & Folk Festival
Théâtre de Verdure, Parc d'Osseghem, Laeken (02 270 98 56, www.brosella.be). **Métro** Heysel. **Admission** free. **Map** p326 B1. **Date** early July.
An annual outdoor festival of folk and jazz in the shadow of the Atomium. Brosella attracts a cross-section of music-lovers, including families who take a picnic along for the Sunday afternoon.

Foire du Midi
Boulevard du Midi, Lower Town (no phone, www.foiredumidi.be). **Métro/pré-métro** Gare du Midi. **Map** p318 B7. **Date** mid July-mid Aug.
Each year the largest travelling funfair in Europe arrives in Brussels and sets itself up along a 1km stretch of the inner ring road near the Gare du Midi.

There has been a fair on this site since the Middle Ages, but today's hyper-electric affair bears no resemblance whatsoever to the spit-roasted suckling pig event of yesteryear. Families turn up after midday and enjoy the rides and games until early evening, when a more adult crowd arrives.

National Day
*Parc de Bruxelles, rue Royale, place des Palais, Upper Town. **Métro** Gare Centrale, Parc or Trône.* **Map** p317/319 E5. **Date** 21 July.
National Day is taken seriously in Belgium, and the festivities naturally focus on Brussels. The royals are out in force and there's a large military parade – tanks, artillery, the lot. The rest of the day settles down into more lighthearted fairs, neighbourhood celebrations and fireworks late into the night.

Meyboom (Planting of the Maytree)
Rue des Sables & rue du Marais, Lower Town (www.meyboom.be). Métro/pré-métro De Brouckère. **Map** p317 E3. **Date** 9 Aug.
This ancient and unusual ceremony dates back to 1308, when the first tree planting took place. It's all to do with fighting off rebels from Louvain and the ensuing thanksgiving to the patron Saint Laurent, whose symbol is the fabled tree. It's also an excuse to dress up, parade around the city with the tree, plant it before 5pm by the Centre Belge de la Bande Dessinée and party into the night.

Festive Frolics
Sip mulled wine and skate beneath the stars in Brussels' winter wonderland.

Christmas in Brussels (*see p181*) seems to get bigger every year. Since the decision was made in 2001 to move the market out of the Grand'Place (it had become an overcrowded danger zone), it has extended along the streets to Ste-Catherine, covering almost two kilometres. In 2009, around 3.5 million people trod the festive path, passing 220 market stalls selling everything from garish candles to reindeer hats.

It still all starts on the Grand'Place, though, a stunning natural theatre set for Christmas. Electricity company Electrabel is currently sponsoring the deal, and as such the square is lit imaginatively with spots and lasers. In 2009, an electric-blue tree formed the centre point of a laser show picking out the Baroque relief of the square. A scaffolding gateway leads you from the square to the market proper, which begins at the back of the Bourse and follows a festively lit trail across boulevard Anspach and onward to Ste-Catherine. Each market stall is a little wooden-roofed hut

(some with illuminated sheep), selling mainly arts and crafts or food and drink, all of them having a pan-European flavour, tying Brussels in neatly with the Utopian single-market dream.

By the time you reach place Ste-Catherine and the quays beyond, not only are you decently warmed up, but you're at the heart of the festivities. The quaint stalls continue, punctuated every now and again by Heath Robinson-esque merry-go-rounds, a cycling course, the largest travelling big-wheel in Europe (with 18,000 lights) and, of course, a skating rink. Set up for the whole month, it's overlooked by a Liberace-style mirror ball, throwing pinpoints on the old gabled houses. It's here that the crowds gather and settle; in the beer tents, at the food stands, in the surrounding restaurants and bars as they watch their kids or mates glide. The festive atmosphere is thick and warm, as are the plastic cups of mulled wine, both doing a good job of helping keep out the bitterly cold air.

Zany Zinneke

A wild parade that makes you glad to be alive.

Brussels loves nothing better than a street knees-up with noise, colour and painted faces, gigantic figures, stilt-walkers, flags and fireworks. Deep inside that studied reserve is a carnival just waiting to burst out, a deep-rooted chaos that has been simmering since medieval times.

What a magical concept, then, is **Zinneke**, a biennial parade and festival (*see p176*). At its heart lies tradition and a uniquely Bruxellois way of celebrating, but it's a thoroughly modern, urban phenomenon aimed at galvanising the spirit of this multicultural city.

Zinneke was born in 2000 when Brussels was a European City of Culture, from which came a deluge of social and urban renewal projects. The idea was to develop creative workshops throughout the city, particularly in communes where life was tough. The aim? To bring together whole communities, regardless of their age, race, culture or gender, in a massive extravaganza of artistic endeavour. So professionals work with amateurs in the

fields of art, music, theatre and circus, in schools, youth centres, cultural spaces, folklore associations and all the groups and gangs that make up a living community. Language takes on new meaning – this is a movement that celebrates linguistic diversity and promotes a tongue of its own. Zinneke is for locals, or Zinnekes, who work in the Zinnôpoles (five regions) at the Zinnodes (local workshops). Together, they aim to make one big melting pot of the capital of Europe, the capital of Belgium, the city of Bruzzel. The parade, of course, is only the tip of it all: the workshops are ongoing throughout the year, where work and skills are developed and shared, and the Zinnodes perform in local and major events. But when Z-Day arrives, the Zinnekes leave their communes and retake the city in a spirit of sovereignty. The parade is awe-inspiring in its size and energy; it takes hours to pass by and fills the streets of downtown Bruzzel. Simply put, Zinneke is unlike anything you'll have ever zeen before.

★ Tapis des Fleurs

Grand'Place, Lower Town (no phone, www.flower carpet.be). Pré-métro Bourse or métro Gare Centrale. **Map** p315 C4. **Date** mid Aug.

For three days each year the Grand'Place is the scene of a floral carpet (*tapis*) made up of a million cut begonia heads. The flowers are supplied and designed by growers from Ghent, and laid painstakingly on the ground in a different design each year. The balcony of the Hôtel de Ville is open for an aerial view (admission €3).

★ Brussels Summer Festival

Various venues in Brussels (tickets 070 660 601, www.bsf.be). **Admission** €20 10-day pass. **Date** mid-end Aug.

A ten-day festival of rock, pop and world music in venues throughout Brussels, including outdoors in the Grand'Place. Organised by the city council, it is regarded as the most important music festival in the Brussels calendar.

AUTUMN

Journées du Patrimoine

Brussels (02 204 24 49, www.monument. irisnet.be). **Admission** free. **Date** early Sept.

A once-a-year chance to peek inside hundreds of historical buildings around Belgium usually closed to the general public. After Flanders (03 212 29 55, www.monument.vlaanderen.be) and Wallonia (081 332 384, www.skene.be), it is Brussels' turn to fling open the doors of homes and businesses for a glimpse of hidden history. The choice of buildings changes every year, as does the theme around which events revolve. The royals also open their greenhouses, the Serres Royales (*see p88*), to the public in May, and the Palais Royal (*see p67*) from late July through to September, after National Day.

Circuses

TIB 02 513 89 40. **Date** Oct, Nov.

A number of circuses visit Brussels every year – usually in October and November, and sometimes until Christmas and the New Year. Regular ones include the Bouglione circus in place Flagey and the Florilegio at the Hippodrome de Boitsfort. Some shows can be traditional and, for many, objectionable: there are performing tigers and elephants, as well as dogs and even, on occasion, ducks and geese. For dates, call the tourist information number above or look out for posters around town.

Independent Film Festival

Centre Culturel Jacques Franck, 94 chaussée de Waterloo, St-Gilles (02 649 33 40, www.centre multimedia.org). Métro/pré-métro Porte de Hal. **Tickets** vary. **Map** p318 B9. **Date** early Nov.

This festival began in 1974, when Super8 reigned supreme. Now incorporating a mix of media, the philosophy remains the same: to allow young directors

Tapis des Fleurs.

to find a springboard for their work. Expect some 100 films from 60 countries, many of them being shown for the first time.

WINTER

Ice skating

Place du Marché aux Poissons, Lower Town (02 513 89 40, www.plaisirsdhiver.be). Métro Ste-Catherine. **Admission** €6; €4 reductions. **Map** p315 C3. **Date** Dec-early Jan.

See p179 **Festive Frolics**.

★ Marché de Noël

Grand'Place to place Ste-Catherine (02 513 89 40, www.plaisirsdhiver.be). Pré-métro Bourse or métro Gare Centrale. **Admission** free. **Map** p315 C4. **Date** Dec-early Jan.

See p179 **Festive Frolics**.

New Year's Eve

Grand'Place & around. Pré-métro Bourse. **Map** p315 C4. **Date** 31 Dec.

Crowds pour into Grand'Place on 31 December. The atmosphere is good, the crowds friendly and high-spirited, but it's certainly not for the faint-hearted. The jollity extends to the streets around the square, as you're more likely to find a comfortable niche there. As the square thins out, music is played over the speakers and folk start dancing – it all becomes magical from that moment on. There's also a dramatic fireworks display from the Parc de Bruxelles.

Children

There's plenty of fun for youngsters in cartoon city.

Families tend to really enjoy Brussels. There are a couple of children's museums, a hands-on science museum, several grand parks complete with adventure playgrounds, natural woodlands, dedicated skateboard zones and bowling alleys. Films are shown in their original language, and there are plenty of children's theatre and puppet shows. On top of all that, theme parks, wildlife centres and a sandy coastline are within easy reach of the city too.

If your trip happens to coincide with Belgium's month-long carnival season (around Shrove Tuesday), then you're definitely in for a good time. In the run-up to Christmas, meanwhile, the circus comes to town and the ice rink and Christmas market burst forth with stalls, merry-go-rounds and a big wheel. On the downside, pushchair access is poor, pavements are cobbled and parking is tricky – so carrying tinies is the most sensible option.

BABYSITTING

A handful of Brussels' upmarket hotels also offer a babysitting service. *See pp98-113.*

La Ligue des Familles
109 avenue E de Béco, Ixelles (02 507 72 11, www.citoyenparent.be). **Phone** 9am-12.30pm, 1-4pm Mon-Fri. **Rates** vary.
The leading French-language resource for families in Belgium runs a babysitting service. You might be asked to take out an annual membership.

Office de la Naissance et de l'Enfance (ONE)
95 chaussée de Charleroi, St-Gilles (02 542 12 11, www.one.be). **Phone** 9am-5pm Mon-Fri.
For longer-term childcare arrangements, the ONE can send you a list of state and private nurseries, crèches and registered childminders around town.

Service des Etudiants de l'ULB
02 650 21 71. **Phone** 10am-noon Mon-Fri. **Rates** vary.
A reputable babysitting service run by students at the city university. Ring at least one day in advance.

ENTERTAINMENT

It may have a reputation for being among Europe's more sedate cities, but the Belgian capital provides plenty of opportunity for children and teenagers with excess energy to burn. Venues across the city offer all kinds of high-octane sports and activities, from bowling to skateboarding. For more information, *see pp216-222.*

Attractions

Several circuses put up tents in Brussels around Christmas time. The more traditional ones tend to be criticised by animal rights activists, but **Florilegio** (www.florilegio. com), which makes an annual visit to the Hippodrome de Boitsfort (51-53 chaussée de la Hulpe, Uccle, 02 533 10 80), is acclaimed for its showmanship and acrobatics.

Bruparck
1 avenue du Football, Laeken (02 474 83 83, www.bruparck.com). Métro Heysel. **Credit** AmEx, DC, MC, V. **Map** p326 A2/B2.
Mini-Europe *02 478 05 50, www.minieurope. com.* **Open** *mid Mar-June* 9.30am-6pm daily. *July, Aug* 9.30am-6pm. *Sept* 9.30am-7pm. *Oct-early Jan* 10am-5pm daily. Closed mid Jan-mid Mar. **Admission** €13.10; €9.80 reductions.
Océade *02 478 43 20, www.oceade.be.* **Open** *Apr-June* 10am-6pm Tue-Fri; 10am-9pm Sat, Sun. *July, Aug, school holidays* 10am-9pm daily. *Sept-Mar* 10am-6pm Wed-Fri; 10am-9pm Sat, Sun.

Admission €16.50; €13.50 reductions.
Atomium *02 475 47 77, www.atomium.be.*
The main draw at this attraction park at the foot of
the Atomium (*see p88*) is Mini-Europe, with its
miniature replicas of European landmarks such as
the Eiffel Tower and Big Ben (listen out for its
sonorous chimes). Bruparck also takes in the Océade
pool, with its child-friendly slides and chutes, along
with a fairground carousel and assorted fast
food joints and cafés. Ask about special deals and
family tickets.
▶ *The complex is also home to the multi-screen
Kinepolis cinema; see p188.*

Théâtre du Ratinet

*44 avenue de Fré, Uccle (02 375 15 63,
www.theatreduratinet.be). Bus 38, 41, 43 or
trams 18, 51, 91, 92.* **Shows** *Oct-June* Wed, Sat,
Sun afternoons. Closed July, Aug. **Tickets** €6.50.
No credit cards.
One of several small puppet theatres across the city
offering shows for children. The productions are
usually in French, but the atmosphere is infectious
even if your offspring don't really grasp the intricacies of the plot.
▶ *Théâtre du Toone puts on puppet versions of
classic plays with adult audiences in mind; see p227.*

Museums

Brussels has more than its fair share of decent
museums, several of which are likely to appeal
to kids. Almost every child is fascinated by the
huge iguanadon dinosaur skeletons displayed
in the awesome **Institut Royal des Sciences
Naturelles** (*see p72*), although it's also worth
noting that small kids are sometimes terrified
by the life-size automated models. Alternatively,
head out of town by a lovely old tram (*see p94*
Ticket to Tervuren) to the **Musée Royal
de l'Afrique Centrale** (*see p95*) for dioramas
of stuffed animals in African landscapes.

The **Musée des Instruments de
Musique** (*see p64*) is another attraction likely
to appeal to young ones, mainly because they
get to don cool headphones and listen to the
various musical instruments. For cartoon fans,
there's the **Centre Belge de la Bande
Dessinée** (*see p56*), where children can find
out how animated films work and step inside

full-size replicas of comic book scenes (though
it's not a place where they can run wild). Kids
can also spot the cartoon murals that sprinkle
the city streets (*see pp41-45*).

Many museums in Brussels run workshops
for children, usually on Wednesday afternoons,
weekends and during school holidays.

★ Musée des Enfants

*15 rue du Bourgmestre, Ixelles (02 640 01
07, www.museedesenfants.be). Tram 23, 90
or bus 71.* **Open** 2.30-5pm Wed, Sat, Sun,
school holidays. Closed Aug, weekends July.
Admission €7. **No credit cards. Map**
p325 H12.
A rambling townhouse in Ixelles has been turned
into a superb children's museum, with rooms for theatre, dressing up, giant interactive puzzles, educational games, painting and clay modelling. There's
a kitchen where kids are taught baking, a domestic
animal enclosure and an adventure playground. Not
surprisingly, it can get mobbed. *Photo p184.*

Musée du Jouet

*24 rue de l'Association, Upper Town (02 219
61 68, www.museedujouet.eu). Métro Botanique
or Madou.* **Open** 10am-noon, 2-6pm daily.
Admission €5.50; €4.50 reductions. **No credit
cards. Map** p317 F3.
This cluttered private museum is run by an enthusiastic toy collector. It displays a vast collection of
gaily painted train sets and tin cars, fantastic clock-
work toys (including a jumping zebra), puzzles, ted-
dies and dolls' houses; check the website for details
of special events such as the teddy bears' weekend.

★ Scientastic Museum

*Underground level 1, Bourse, boulevard Anspach,
Lower Town (02 732 13 36, www.scientastic.com).
Pré-métro Bourse.* **Open** 10am-5.30pm Mon, Tue,
Thur, Fri; 2-5.30pm Wed, Sat, Sun. **Admission**
€7.70; €5.20 under-26s; free under-2s. **Credit**
MC, V. **Map** p315 C4.
This private museum is set in a dingy underground
concourse at Bourse station, but inside it's a magi-
cal place, crammed with all sorts of interactive
experiments aimed at kids (though fun for grown-
ups too). There are factsheets in English and work-
shops in French and Dutch.
▶ *Small science buffs will also adore the mighty
Technopolis; see p185.*

PARKS

The cobbled streets of Brussels aren't exactly
made for pushchairs, so you may find yourself
spending a lot of time in the city parks. Most
are well suited to young children, boasting good
playgrounds with safe, modern equipment.

Close to the city centre, the **Parc de
Bruxelles** (*see p61*) has a good playground

ARTS & ENTERTAINMENT

Musée des Enfants. *See p183*.

and a café selling ice-cream. The **Bois de la Cambre** at the end of avenue Louise (entrances on chaussée de Waterloo and avenues Louise and Roosevelt) is a large landscaped park with a lake, lawns, horse-riding trails and woodland rambles. There are also two cafés, one with a playground and the other facing a rollerskating rink. Several main roads through the park are closed to traffic at weekends, creating a huge loop that is popular with cyclists, in-line skaters and kids learning to ride bikes. The small **Parc Tenbosch** (entrances on chaussée de Vleurgat and place Tenbosch) in Ixelles has a safe playground with well-maintained wooden equipment, a sandpit, football pitch and pond complete with lazy terrapins.

Some wilder retreats are found in Uccle, the city's leafy southern commune, including the **Sauvagère** nature reserve (entrance on avenue de la Chênaie), which has an outdoor playground ideal for young children, a picnic area, basketball court, duck pond and farm animals in enclosures. Also in Uccle, the lovely **Parc de Wolvendael** (entrances on avenues de Fré and Paul Stroobant) has an outdoor café, minigolf and a playground. It is located on a sloping hill that makes a perfect place to ski or sledge in winter. The **Parc de Woluwe** (entrance on avenue de Tervuren) is another popular spot for sledging.

The **Rouge Cloître** park on the edge of the Forêt de Soignes has two relatively new playgrounds with excellent climbing equipment. Further out, the **Park van Tervuren** (entrance on Leuvensesteenweg) has woodland rambles and cycle trails. Tram 44 runs from Montgomery through the forest (*see p94* **Ticket to Tervuren**).

OUT OF TOWN

It's fairly easy to get out of Brussels for a day at the beach or a canoe trip in the Ardennes. This small country has an expansive network of motorways, but there's also a good, cheap train service that runs to most places of interest. Belgian Railways (www.sncb.be) publishes a free brochure listing special excursions, many of them suited to kids.

On the domestic SNCB (02 528 28 28, www. b-rail.be) rail network, children under 12 travel free if travelling with an older ticketholder. Women in the last four months of pregnancy can travel in first class on a second class ticket – although you must be able to wave an official document showing the due date.

Day trips

★ Kayak Ansiaux
Kayak Ansiaux, 15 rue du Vélodrome, Anseremme (082 21 35 35, www.ansiaux.be). Train to Anseremme. **Open** Apr-Oct daily. **Price** €10-€19. **Credit** MC, V.
The biggest of the many kayak centres in the Ardennes, based at Anseremme on the River Lesse, near Dinant. From the station, a minibus takes you to the starting point a few kilometres upstream.

Pairi Daiza
Domaine de Cambron, Cambron-Casteau (068 45 46 53, www.pairidaiza.eu). Train to Cambron-Casteau. **Open** *Easter-June, Sept-early Nov* 10am-6pm daily. *July, Aug* 10am-7pm daily. **Admission** €22; €17 reductions. **Credit** MC, V.
The grounds of an old abbey near Ath have been turned into an exotic bird sanctuary boasting a river,

several lakes, water gardens and flowerbeds. The main attractions for kids are the giant walk-through aviary for birds of paradise, a giant tortoise and an Antarctic section. There's also an adventure playground, a petting farm and a restaurant.

Parc d'Aventures Scientifiques (Pass)

3 rue de Mons, Frameries (070 22 22 52, www.pass.be). Bus 1, 2 from Mons station. **Open** *early Sept, late Oct-June* 9am-4pm Mon, Tue, Thur, Fri; noon-6pm Sat, Sun. *July, Aug, school holidays* 10am-6pm daily. Closed early Sept-late Oct. **Admission** €12.50; €7.50-€10 reductions. **Credit** MC, V.

Belgium's interactive science centre is located in a former coal mine near Mons, restyled by French architect Jean Nouvel. The centre hosts hands-on exhibitions that are both innovative and educational.

Planckendael

582 Leuvensesteenweg, Muizen, near Mechelen (015 41 49 21, www.planckendael.be). Bus 284, 285 from Mechelen station or canal boat from station in summer. **Open** *Jan, Feb, Nov, Dec* 10am-4.45pm daily. *Mar, Apr, Oct* 10am-5.30pm daily. *May, June, Sept* 10am-6pm daily. *July, Aug* 10am-7pm daily. **Admission** €19.50; €14.50 reductions. **Credit** AmEx, MC, V.

The wide open spaces of Planckendael wildlife park provide an ideal habitat for rhinos, deer, antelope, wolves, birds and cranes. Founded by Antwerp Zoo as a breeding park, the estate has a restaurant, adventure playgrounds and rope bridges.

★ Technopolis

Technologielaan, Mechelen (015 34 20 00, www.technopolis.be). Train to Mechelen then bus 282, 283. **Open** 9.30am-5pm daily. Closed 1st wk Sept. **Admission** €11; €9 reductions. **Credit** AmEx, DC, MC, V.

Undoubtedly one of the best science museums in Europe. Kids can ride a bike along a high wire, try out a flight simulator, lie on a bed of nails or star in their own pop video. The staff are friendly and well informed, and only too pleased to explain Newton's Third Law in English to eager beavers.

Walibi Belgium & Aqualibi

9 rue Joseph Deschamps, Wavre (010 42 15 00, www.walibi.be). Walibi-Bierges station. **Walibi Open** *Apr-Oct* 10am-6/8/11pm daily. **Admission** €30; €26 reductions; free under-6s. **Credit** AmEx, MC, V.
Aqualibi Open *Jan-Mar, Nov, Dec* 2-10pm Wed, Fri; 10am-10pm Sat, Sun. *Apr, May-mid June* 1-10pm Wed-Sun. *Mid June-mid July* 2-10pm daily. *Mid July-Aug* 6-11pm daily. *Sept, Oct* 2-10pm Wed, Fri-Sun. **Admission** phone for details.

The biggest and oldest theme park in Belgium is back to its original name of Walibi. The park has several merciless water rides plus a few relics,

---

INSIDE TRACK NICE ICES

In summer, Brussels is teeming with ice-cream vans, generally parked up near playgrounds. But the best ice-cream comes from the salons dotted around the suburbs. It's hard to resist the authentically Italian **Il Gelato** at 168 rue Vanderkindere (02 344 34 95, www.ilgelato.be) or, almost directly opposite, **Zizi** (57 rue de la Mutualité, 02 344 70 81, www.glacierzizi.be). Another favourite is **Capoue**, whose seven city outposts include a branch at 36 avenue des Celtes in Etterbeek (02 733 38 33, www.capoue.com).

---

including a boat ride past a collection of somewhat dilapidated *Tintin* characters. Aqualibi, a big water park with chutes, wave machines and several pools, is closed for renovation until mid 2011. Check www.aqualibi.be for updates.

The Belgian coast

The 14 resorts along the 65-kilometre (40-mile) Belgian coastline (*see p283*) boast wide sandy beaches and a solid infrastructure of swimming pools, bowling alleys, minigolf courses, cinemas and ice-cream shops. They also lay on busy summer programmes featuring kite-flying festivals, Flemish *Pop Idol* contests and beach races. Kids will also insist that you rent one of the little go-karts that are found in every resort. They come in every imaginable design.

Ostend, the biggest resort, may be the most fun for adults but is the least suited to children. The busy resort of **Blankenberge** has more for kids to do, with its modern Sea Life Centre (116 Koning Albert I Laan, Blankenberge, 050 42 43 00, www.sealife europe.com, open 10am-6pm daily) allowing intimate contact with sharks. **Knokke-Heist** is more elegant, and has a butterfly park and bird sanctuary. Elsewhere, there are fishing boats to watch in **Nieuwpoort**, and a former Russian submarine moored at the Seafront centre (www.seafront.be) in **Zeebrugge**.

Young children might be equally as happy muddling around with Belgian families in quieter resorts. **Oostduinkerke**, for example, has shrimp fishermen on horseback and a fishing museum, while **De Haan** has, well, nothing much except for picturesque fin-de-siècle architecture. All of the resorts are linked by a coast tram that runs from De Panne to Knokke-Heist. Brussels' TIB tourist office (*see p304*) can provide further practical information to help you plan.

Film

A capital collection of mega multiplexes and arthouse alternatives.

With plenty of original language offerings, reasonably priced tickets, and film festivals and special events galore, Brussels is a brilliant destination for film buffs.

The choice of films on show here extends way beyond what you'll find in other cities of comparable size, with a healthy mix of big-budget blockbusters and less mainstream arthouse flicks. If you want to catch a major new release at the weekend, though, you'll have to book seats in advance – you're not the only cinephile in town.

WHERE TO GO

Local screens fall into two main categories: the UGC and Kinepolis circuit, which mainly shows blockbusters and takes the lion's share of the audience; and an arthouse circuit, showing repertory films as well as world and Belgian cinema (*see right* **Director's Cut**). When these latter cinemas started to feel the pinch, the various councils dug deep and came up with extra grants for almost all of the local screens, ensuring they could continue to offer their own particular brand of screening seasons.

Meanwhile, the multiplexes march onward. The UGC network surprised its competitors with UGC Unlimited, a ticket system whereby a monthly or annual fee gives unlimited access to the company's 56 screens across Belgium; Kinepolis, in turn, has led the way with digital cinema, installing revolutionary DLP technology in all of its Belgian outposts.

TIMINGS & TICKETS

Film programmes change over on Wednesdays, and listings can be found in most daily newspapers (keep an eye out for the supplements in *La Libre Belgique* and *Le Soir* on Wednesday) and in the pages of English-language weekly *The Bulletin*. The Belgian cinema website www.cinebel.be has the screening times for major cinemas around the country, and tickets can be booked online.

Films are screened on average four times each day, with evening showings at 7-8pm and 9-10.15pm. Features start 20 minutes after the advertised time, and average ticket prices are in the region of €9 or €11 for 3D. Outside the UGC and Kinepolis circuit, tipping attendants is expected: in return, you will find yourself being rewarded with a slim movie magazine featuring news of upcoming releases.

Belgium, rather unusually, has only two film classifications: **ENA/KNT**, meaning over-16s only, and **EA/KT**, meaning entrance is for all. Films categorised as **VO** are in their original language, invariably English, and **st. ang** are films with English subtitles. Dubbing is rare.

SPECIAL EVENTS

It's worth looking out for various mini-seasons and special events. The **Musée du Cinéma** (*see also p189*) regularly features guest directors visiting to personally present their own work – Martin Scorsese is a notable example. **Lanterne Magique** is a cinema club for youngsters at the **Palais des Beaux-Arts** (*see p65*), showing everything from *Singin' in the Rain* to spookier stuff; screenings are often preceded by a playlet introducing the themes of the films in Flemish and French. **Flagey** runs a similar season each year, *Une Séance pour Tous* (A Screening for All), in which a popular or forgotten classic is preceded by Sunday brunch.

On Fridays and Saturdays in August and September, the **Nova** cinema goes walkabout, providing free open-air screenings at sundown, showing offbeat movies in unlikely settings. The carnival atmosphere is supplemented with free concerts and finger food.

Many Brussels cinemas also offer pre-release screenings: keep an eye out for *avant-premières* (sneak previews) in magazine listings.

FESTIVALS

The **Brussels Film Festival** (*see p177*) has reinvented itself since moving to Flagey, giving attention to European filmmakers who are just starting out. Held in June, the festival guarantees fresh talent and new names; this, along with parallel screenings from better-known European names, means that it rarely disappoints. The festival bar is also good value, and usually staffed by a director or a well-known actor.

Horror flick fans can sink their teeth into the gory **Brussels International Festival of Fantastic Film**, centred at Tour et Taxis (*see p176*). The festival will be 30 years of age in 2012. It takes in a vampires' ball, a body-paint contest and late-night screenings of seriously weird cinema.

Anima (02 534 41 25, http://folioscope.awn. com), the Brussels animation festival, also has a thirtieth anniversary in 2011. It offers more than 100 films over a packed two-week period in March, and now boasts an international competition. There are fewer Belgian films at the festival than there were a decade ago, but 30,000 annual viewers still enjoy it. It's often an opportunity to get a sneak preview of upcoming US blockbusters, as well as more controversial fodder from the likes of Bill Plympton.

For many, summer means buying a season ticket for **Ecran Total** at the **Arenberg Galeries** (July-Sept), which offers a wide range of retrospectives and new cinema from around the globe.

November in St-Gilles sees the **Independent Film Festival** at the Centre Culturel Jacques Franck (*see p181*), which has eclectic programming from across the world. It runs around the same time as the **Festival of Mediterranean Film** (02 800 83 54, www.cinemamed.be).

Director's Cut

The pick of Belgium's homegrown crop.

Although its well-funded neighbour France still leads the pack in the arthouse league, Belgium should never be considered in the second division. This little country produces films that are truly at the top of their game, and some of its leading directors are finally getting much-deserved kudos from serious European actors and producers.

It helps that the French-speaking industry has a natural ally in France, and is able to use the French distribution system to widen its exposure and appeal. More international recognition, however, has come to Belgium via two Liège-based brothers, **Jean-Pierre** and **Luc Dardenne**, whose uncompromising social realism has caught the world's eye. The brothers first picked up a Palme d'Or at the Cannes Film Festival in 1999 for *Rosetta*, a film about a young woman trying to battle a desperately miserable life; then, in 2005, they lifted the prize once again for social conscience study *The Child*, which tells the story of a petty crook who sells his newborn son. Their characters are young people on the fringes of society – a fact that has led to them being compared with Lars von Trier. It's a rather tenuous link: the hand-held camerawork and long one-take shots may be similar, but the films themselves, entirely lacking in soundtracks or musical scores, are tensely individual works, set in a moody, ill-lit Belgium straight out of the songs of Jacques Brel.

Similar in cinematic style is artist-director **Bouli Lanners**, also from Liège. His first feature, 2005's *Ultranova*, was peopled with losers and loners in drab surrounds; sad, but with an irrepressible Belgian wit shining through as the film's anti-hero Dimitri tries to find himself. Not content with being on the director's side of the camera, Lanners then turned actor for Brussels-born **Stefan Liberski**'s film *Bunker Paradise*.

Flemish filmmakers tend to work on a smaller scale, but can occasionally give the francophones a run for their money. Their brightest star is **Dominique Deruddere**, who was Oscar-nominated in 2000 for his brilliant *Everybody's Famous!*, a film starring one of Belgium's finest screen and stage actors, Josse de Pauw. Deruddere's film somehow manages to encapsulate quirky Belgian humour with a wry take on what ordinary folk are prepared to do for fame (in this case, kidnap). Most recently, Felix van Groeningen's 2009 film *The Misfortunates* was nominated for an Academy Award in the Best Foreign Film category.

One film, above all others, sums up the Belgian attitude to film, life and love. **Jan Bucquoy**'s *The Sexual Life of the Belgians* continues to air at arthouse cinemas around the world; it may be getting on in years now, but it's still considered one of Belgium's finest ever cinematic exports.

ARTS & ENTERTAINMENT

Nova.

Many new Belgian and French films are also featured at the **Francophone Film Festival** (081 24 12 36, www.fiff.be) in Namur at the end of September. Flemish ones are screened at the **Flanders Film Festival** (www.filmfestival. be, 09 242 80 60), held in Ghent in October, an occasion renowned for its movie soundtrack awards. Bruges showcases world cinema at the **Nova** (050 33 54 86, www.cinemanovo.be) in March; most films have English subtitles.

CINEMAS

Actors Studio

16 petite rue des Bouchers (2nd entrance rue de la Fourche), Lower Town (02 512 16 96, information 0900 27 854, http://actorsstudio. cinenews.be). Métro/pre-métro De Brouckère. **No credit cards. Map** p315 D4.
It might take a bit of finding the first time – it's tucked into a hotel basement among the busy restaurants near the Grand'Place – but this two-screen studio is one of Brussels' little gems. If your taste leans towards Korean horror rather than the Hollywood variety, or you want to see Finnish films by the Kaurismaki brothers in VO, the Actors is for you.

Arenberg Galeries

26 galerie de la Reine, Lower Town (02 512 80 63, www.arenberg.be). Métro Gare Centrale. **No credit cards. Map** p315 D4.

Back in 1895, the magnificent Arenberg Galeries had the honour of hosting Belgium's first ever film show. Today these two arthouse screens are still Brussels' poshest cinematic address by a mile. Programming is eclectic, mixing good-looking world cinema with the French avant-garde; Ecran Total, the annual summer bash, blends recent hits with cycles devoted to well-known arthouse directors or nostalgia from yesteryear.

Aventure

57 galerie du Centre, Lower Town (02 219 17 48). Métro/pre-métro De Brouckère or pre-métro Bourse. **No credit cards. Map** p315 D4.
If you miss a big film on its first run, your best chance of catching it is to head for this rather run-down picture house, located in a shopping mall. Sound and picture quality on the two screens aren't great, but you can't fault the number of films on offer – it squeezes in more titles than anywhere else, week after week.

Flagey

Place Ste-Croix (next to place Flagey), Ixelles (02 641 10 20, www.flagey.be). Tram 81, 82 or bus 38, 60, 71. **Credit** AmEx, DC, MC, V. **Map** p322 G10.
This in-vogue cinema at the fashionable arts centre seats little more than 100 people, but the comfort is second to none. Programming is planned jointly with the Musée du Cinéma (*see right*), and blends classics such as *Cat on a Hot Tin Roof* with more adventurous international modern fare.
▶ *After the film, repair to Café Belga – open until 2am and popular with the arty crowd; see p129.*

Kinepolis

Bruparck, avenue du Centenaire, Laeken (bookings 02 474 26 00, information 0900 00 555, www.kinepolis.com). Métro Heysel. **No credit cards. Map** p326 A2.
Don't be fooled by the run-down look, or the location for that matter – Kinepolis is state of the art. With its giant screens (24 in all) and futuristic sound systems, this is total cinema, Flemish-style. Cutting-edge technology also includes one of the few servers powerful enough to download entire movies by satellite for the big screen. It also hosts the Royal National Theatre's live production screenings.

Movy Club

21 rue des Moines, Forest (02 537 69 54, http://movyclub.cinenews.be). Tram 52 or bus 49, 50. **No credit cards.**
This cavernous, out-of-the-way art deco jewel is a relic from a bygone age – and one of the city's last neighbourhood cinemas. It's a unique experience, popular with students and locals too tired to make the trek to the centre of town. Warm clothing is advisable in winter, as the heating isn't always 100 per cent reliable.

★ Musée du Cinema

Palais des Beaux-Arts, 9 rue Baron Horta, Upper Town (02 507 83 70, www.cinematheque.be). Métro Gare Centrale or Parc, tram 92, 93, 94 or bus 38, 60, 71. **No credit cards.** **Map** p317 E5.
With programming that draws on the 50,000 reels sitting in its vaults, plus live piano accompaniment to silent films every night of the year, the Film Museum is the closest you'll get to cinema heaven. Each month, three or four movie cycles focus on a director or a theme – anything from ethnographic shorts from the silent period to *Dirty Harry*-era Clint Eastwood. Tickets are cheap but the silent cinema is tiny, so book ahead.
▶ *The on-site museum displays early cinema equipment and vintage film magazines; see p64.*

★ Nova

3 rue d'Arenberg, Lower Town (02 511 24 77, www.nova-cinema.com). Métro Gare Centrale. **No credit cards.** **Map** p315 D4.
Creaky seats, trash-aesthetic decor and the most adventurous programming in the capital ensure that the Nova regularly appears on lists of the best alternative cinemas in the world. A gem that has miraculously survived on almost invisible means for more than a decade, this is also a major venue for the Brussels International Festival of Fantastic Film (see p187). The monthly Open Screens, which allow budding filmmakers to showcase their efforts, are popular, raucous affairs.

Styx

72 rue de l'Arbre Bénit, Ixelles (02 512 21 02, http://cinema-styx.wikeo.be). Métro Porte de Namur or bus 54, 71. **No credit cards.** **Map** p319 E8.
Now over 40 years old, the Styx is Brussels' most adorable fleapit. The sound quality may be less than perfect, but the programming is truly irresistible – from Truffaut retrospectives and *Amores Perros* to modern Belgian classics in the making.

UGC De Brouckère

38 place De Brouckère, Lower Town (0900 10 440, www.ugc.be). Métro/pre-métro De Brouckère. **Credit** MC, V. **Map** p315 C3.

A mid-town mecca for multiplex fans. It's not all popcorn and blockbusters, though: you can order a beer in the bar, sink back into the bucket-shaped armchairs and marvel at the gold-leaf surroundings in one of the city's biggest auditoriums. Look out for American Movie Day on 4 July, with fireworks in the streets and up to a dozen pre-release films from the US. Luckily, it's all done with style.

UGC Toison d'Or

8 avenue de la Toison d'Or, Ixelles (0900 10 440, www.ugc.be). Métro Porte de Namur. **Credit** MC, V. **Map** p319 E7.
With 15 screens (rather confusingly, at two not-quite-adjacent locations), the UGC Toison d'Or is the only serious competition to Kinepolis – and its more adventurous programming often carries the day. First-class sound and fabulous picture quality make this the best address to randomly turn up at without knowing what you want to see. On the whole, tickets aren't cheap – but the lunchtime shows are.

Vendôme

18 chaussée de Wavre, Ixelles (02 502 37 00, www.cinema-vendome.be). Métro Porte de Namur. **No credit cards.** **Map** p319 E7.
Round the corner from the Toison d'Or, this five-screen independent is a treasure, and has smartened itself up after a considerable government grant. The films are mainly European and US indie releases, but the cinema is also a regular on the local festival circuit and home to a well-loved short film festival.

UGC Toison d'Or.

ARTS & ENTERTAINMENT

Galleries

Independents and artist-run spaces set their own agenda.

Whether you're buying or just browsing, the gallery experience in Brussels lacks the stuffiness of the salons of London or Paris. Here, art is regarded as an exciting interaction between artist and public, and galleries open up in old shops, houses or disused industrial buildings with affordable, original artworks as standard.

The city is home to over 150 galleries, and new spaces appear and disappear almost overnight. Unless you're in town during Brussels Art Fair (www.artbrussels.be) in spring, exploring the wide scope of contemporary art in the capital entails some footwork. The bulk of the galleries are in the Lower Town or in the arty communes of Ixelles and St-Gilles; for more traditional and antique art, the densely packed and pricey establishments in the Sablon are the best places to unburden your wallet.

Rue de la Madeleine.

INFORMATION

To find out what's on and where, consult the English-language weekly *The Bulletin*; *Park Mail*, distributed in cinemas; and the cultural supplement *MAD* in every Wednesday edition of the French-language daily *Le Soir*. The Foundation for the Arts website (www.neca.be) also lists all current exhibitions in Brussels.

Major art museums and non-commercial galleries include the Musées Royaux des Beaux-Arts (*see p64*); the Palais des Beaux-Arts (*see p65*); the Magritte Museum (*see p64*); the Musée BELvue (*see p64*); and the Musée Communal d'Ixelles (*see p80*).

Aeroplastics Contemporary

32 rue Blanche, Ixelles (02 537 22 02, www. aeroplastics.net). Métro Louise then tram 91, 92, 93, 94. **Open** 2-6pm Wed-Sat. **Map** p319 D9.
Aeroplastics occupies a huge space in a stunning house on the Ixelles/St-Gilles border. The choice of art is somewhat incongruous with the grand setting – contemporary trends are the keynote to the high energy collection, with work by John Isaacs, John Waters, Cédric Tanguy and Terry Rodgers.

★ aliceday

1B rue des Fabriques, Ste-Catherine (02 646 31 53, www.aliceday.be). Métro Ste-Catherine. **Open** 1-7pm Tue-Sat. **Map** p316 B4.

Aeroplastics Contemporary

aliceday has an eclectic roster of superior international talents, Belgians included. Among the latter are poet/painter Walter Swennen and the ironic Jacques Lizène. Formal and cultural diversity, not to mention compelling interest, are high on the agenda, as indicated by solo shows of Kinshasa's pre-eminent popular painter Cheri Samba, furry-toy fabulist Charlemagne Palestine, Nobuyoshi Araki, Danwen Xing and Dolorès Marat.
► *In the same building, and on similarly contemporary lines, is Galerie Erna Hécey (02 502 00 24, www.ernahecey.com).*

Art en Marge
312 rue Haute, Marolles (02 511 04 11, www.artenmarge.be). Métro/pré-métro Porte de Hal or bus 20, 48. **Open** noon-6pm Wed-Fri; 11am-4pm Sat. **Map** p318 B8.
Set in the Marolles, this non-profit gallery is devoted to exhibiting 'outsider' art, also known as Art Brut: works created by artists relegated to the margins of society by mental illness and other conditions.

Atelier 340
340 drève De Rivieren, Jette (02 424 24 12, www.atelier340muzeum.be). Métro Simonis then bus 13 or tram 18, 19, 81, 94. **Open** *Exhibitions* 2-7pm Tue-Sun. **Admission** varies.
Atelier 340 provides one of the few windows on art for this northern commune and its environs. After starting up simply as a sculpture centre, this place has changed the face of the neighbourhood thanks

to its gradual physical expansion, ambitious exhibitions and their attendant publications. Run on a shoestring by a dedicated, resourceful and very small staff, it has managed not only to survive but also to preserve its autonomy for some 25 years. Admission is charged for exhibitions.

Ateliers Mommen
37 rue de la Charité, St-Josse (02 218 48 95, www.ateliersmommen.collectifs.net). Métro Madou. **Open** times vary.
If you like your art with attitude, then this is the place to go: a solid red-brick factory converted into an urban art centre with studios and exhibition spaces. The programme covers striking modern art and sculpture, installations and performance art. Wander in and out as you please, but be sure to check the website for opening times first.

Baronian_Francey
2 rue Isidore Verheyden, Ixelles (02 512 92 95, www.baronianfrancey.com). Métro Louise or tram 93, 94. **Open** noon-6pm Tue-Sat. **Map** p319 E8.
Operating from stylish quarters situated between avenue Louise and chaussée d'Ixelles, this influential gallery is Brussels' longest-running commercial showcase for modern art. Established by Albert Baronian in the 1970s, it continues to exhibit eclectic fare: from modern masters to emerging younger artists, from minimalism and Arte Povera to experimental new media.

Wiels. See p194.

Bastien

61 rue de la Madeleine, Lower Town (02 513 25 63, www.jbastien-art.be). Métro Gare Centrale.
Open 11am-6.30pm Tue-Sat; 11am-1pm Sun.
Map p315 D5.
If you're spending any length of time in town, you're bound to pass Ms Bastien's beautiful gallery, which is located a few steps down from the Gare Centrale and Albertine Library. As with most of the galleries along this stretch, Bastien is hardly revolutionary, but displays relatively modern works of a certain value. Among the artists here are Serge Vandercam, Pierre Alechinsky, Marc Chagall and Zao Wou Ki.

La Centrale Electrique

44 place Ste-Catherine (02 279 64 44). Métro Ste-Catherine. **Open** 11am-6pm Wed, Fri-Sun; 11am-8pm Thur. **Admission** €6; €2-€4.50 reductions. **Map** p315 C3.
Brussels' latest exhibition space for contemporary art is La Centrale Electrique, created in the city's first (1904) electric power plant. This sturdy industrial building is home to four major exhibitions a year.

Centre d'Art Contemporain

63 avenue des Nerviens, Etterbeek (02 735 05 31). Métro Mérode or Schuman. **Open** 9am-1pm, 2-5pm Mon-Fri. **Map** p323 K7.
You'll be hard-pressed to find many galleries in Etterbeek, the commune that has become synonymous with the bureaucracy of the EU institutions, but the French-speaking community's contemporary art outlet deserves praise for keeping a broad

view despite its cramped quarters. African and Eastern European art have figured prominently on its exhibition calendar, giving some welcome local exposure to the cultural output of these regions. Francophone Belgian artists are also showcased.

★ Espace Photographique Contretype

1 avenue de la Jonction, St-Gilles (02 538 42 20, www.contretype.org). Tram 81, 91, 92 or bus 54. **Open** 11am-6pm Wed-Fri; 1-6pm Sat, Sun.
Admission varies.
Set in the art nouveau splendour of the Hôtel Hannon (*see p39*), this non-profit photo gallery (*contretype* meaning contact print) has a lively programme of exhibitions, lectures and discussions. Shows tend to be monographic and composed of images created in Brussels – often on the gallery's own premises – by photographers invited for long-term residencies. Nominal admission charge for exhibitions.

Etablissement d'en Face Projects

161 rue Antoine Dansaert, Lower Town (02 219 44 51, www.etablissementdenfaceprojects.org). Métro Comte de Flandre or Ste-Catherine. **Open** 2-6pm Wed-Sat. **Map** p316 B3.
Among other activities, this artist-run association stages exhibitions in this unreconstituted storefront gallery. Works are by members and non-members alike. Unclassifiable and never, ever dull.

Les Filles du Calvaire

20 boulevard Barthélémy, Ste-Catherine (02 511 63 20, www.fillesducalvaire.com). Métro

ARTS & ENTERTAINMENT

Comte de Flandre. **Open** 11am-6pm Thur-Sat. **Map** p316 A3.

The Belgian outpost of the Parisian gallery of the same name, featuring predominantly young French and American artists (Steven Parrino, Barbara Gallucci, James Hyde). It occupies two floors in the Kanal 20 building (*see p59*), one of few remaining tenants in this erstwhile warren of galleries.

Jan Mot

190 rue Antoine Dansaert, Lower Town (02 514 10 10, www.janmot.com). Métro Comte de Flandre. **Open** 2-6.30pm Thur-Sat. **Map** p316 B3.

Opened in 1996 in pocket-sized premises, the gallery later moved to this well-designed (by architect Christian Kieckens) and slightly larger (although still tiny) space. Mot's stable includes Douglas Gordon, Sharon Lockhart and Pierre Bismuth.

Marijke Schreurs Gallery

475 avenue Van Volxem, Forest (02 534 18 69, www.marijkeschreurshouse.com). Tram 52 or bus 49, 50. **Open** 3-6pm Thur-Sat.

This unique gallery is situated in the home of its eponymous proprietor, who gives invited artists almost carte blanche to show or create works on all four levels of her charming 19th-century house. Themed and solo exhibitions feature site-specific installations, video, performance, photography, painting and sculpture. Hospitality is extended equally to visitors, who are welcome to attend lectures and participate in dinners and conversations organised around the art on view.

Meert Rihoux

13 rue du Canal, Ste-Catherine (02 219 14 22, www.galeriegretameert.com). Métro Ste-Catherine or Yser. **Open** 2.30-6pm Tue-Sat. **Map** p316 C2.

Meert Rihoux is a class act situated on the third floor of a converted industrial building in the heart of downtown. The featured artists include blue-chip American minimalists and conceptualists like Donald Judd, Robert Mangold, Richard Tuttle and Robert Barry; Vancouver School exponents Jeff Wall, Ian Wallace and Ken Lum; Italian abstractionists Carla Accardi and Enrico Castellani and their younger peers Liliana Moro, Grazia Toderi, Eva Marisaldi and Mario Airo; and locals Jef Geys and Sylvie Eyberg.

INSIDE TRACK
SHEER EXHIBITIONISM

At 65a rue de la Régence in Upper Town, **Sorry We're Closed** (02 538 08 18, www.sorrywereclosed.com) offers a different artistic experience. It occupies a compact white cube space, lit day and night, with a big square window facing the street. There's no entrance and no opening hours; you simply view the latest exhibition from the pavement. Artists show for two months each, and the window is never empty.

Rodolphe Janssen

35 rue de Livourne, Ixelles (02 538 08 18,
www.galerierodolphejanssen.com). Métro
Louise then tram 93, 94. **Open** 10am-noon,
2-6pm Tue-Fri; 2-6pm Sat. **Map** p319 D9.
Founded in 1991, Janssen was the first gallery in
Brussels to really commit itself to contemporary
photography. It still excels in the field, while gain-
ing notice for its shows of works in other mediums
by international artists such as Wim Delvoye, Banks
Violette and Thomas Lerooy.

Le Salon d'Art et de Coiffure

81 rue de l'Hôtel des Monnaies, St-Gilles
(02 537 65 40). Pré-métro Parvis de St-Gilles.
Open 2-6.30pm Tue-Fri; 9.30am-noon Sat.
Map p318 C9.
A unique place, consisting of a barber shop, art
gallery and antiquarian bookshop rolled into one.
Jean Marchetti began his business as a hairdresser,
then discovered art along the way. In 1976, he turned
his salon into a smart, whitewashed gallery, bringing in a daring choice of writers and artists, as well
as the likes of Jean-Pierre Maury, Stéphane
Mandelbaum and Alechinsky. Marchetti brings out
limited editions under three publishing imprints,
pairing writers with artists and producing works
that are pieces of art as well as text. As if all that
wasn't enough, there are great haircuts too.

★ Wiels

354 avenue Van Volxem, Forest (02 340 00 50,
www.wiels.org). Tram 82, 97 or bus 49, 50.
Open 12-7pm Wed-Sat; 11-6pm Sun.
Admission €6.

Housed in the industrial, modernist 'Blomme' building, Wiels is one of Brussels' most important recent
additions to the contemporary art scene. This being
Belgium, it occupies a former brewery; on entering,
you are greeted by the preserved brass tuns used by
the Wielmans brewery until it brewed its last beer
in 1988. Its opening in 2007 redrew the Brussels art
map and it is now attracting more arts projects to
the Forest area. Wiels offers six-month residencies
to Belgian artists. Entry is €6, but Wiels is included
in the Brussels Museum Card scheme. *Photo p192.*

Xavier Hufkens

6-8 rue St-Georges, Ixelles (02 639 67 30,
www.xavierhufkens.com). Métro Louise then tram
93, 94. **Open** noon-6pm Tue-Sat. **Map** p324 F12.
Occupying an elegant townhouse converted to its
present purpose, Hufkens is one of the city's most
prominent players on the international scene. The
spacious ground-floor galleries are reserved for
monographic exhibitions by the likes of Willem de
Kooning, William Eggleston and Antony Gormley;
the upper level for presentations by younger artists.

Young Gallery

75B avenue Louise, Wilchers Place, Hotel
Conrad, Ixelles (02 374 07 04, www.younggallery
photo.com). Metro Louise. **Open** 11am-6.30pm
Tue-Sat. **Map** p319 D8.
Secreted away in a courtyard behind the glitzy
Conrad Hotel, the Young is dedicated entirely to
contemporary photography, featuring the likes of
Nick Veasey, Nick Brandt, Albert Watson and Liu
Bolin. If you venture out of Brussels, it also has a
gallery by the sea in Knokke.

Young Gallery.

Gay & Lesbian

Compact, camp and cosy.

The Belgians follow a philosophy of live and let live – which means the capital is a relaxed and easy place for gays and lesbians to lead their lives. Same-sex couples have enjoyed full civil marriage rights since 2003, and the same adoption rights as heterosexual couples since 2006.

The gay quarter is concentrated in the area around the Bourse. The compact city centre and rarity of entrance fees make bar hopping an essential pastime, and there's something for everyone – although the commercial scene, as elsewhere, is dominated by clubs for the boys. Find out more at www.patroc.com.

BARS

Le Baroque
44 rue du Marché au Charbon, Lower Town (no phone). Pré-métro Bourse. **Open** 5.30pm-late Wed-Sun. **No credit cards. Map** p315 C5.
The brash and bouncy Baroque is a real party place, with funky house DJs and regular themed events – including bears' night and underwear specials.

Le Belgica
32 rue du Marché au Charbon, Lower Town (no phone, www.lebelgica.be). Pré-métro Bourse. **Open** 10pm-3am Thur-Sat; 8pm-3am Sun. **No credit cards. Map** p315 C5.
A must-visit bar, La Belgica is packed to the rafters with gay men and their friends of both sexes. But don't show up too early – it doesn't get buzzing until 11pm. And then it buzzes some. Hefty house music plays to the shoulder-to-shoulder crowd, set against a wood-panelled, shabby-chic backdrop. Looking over it all is a bust of Léopold II, who is clearly not amused. *Photo p196.*

Boy's Boudoir
25 rue du Marché au Charbon, Lower Town (02 614 58 38, www.leboysboudoir.be). Pré-métro Bourse. **Open** 6pm-5am daily. **Credit** MC, V. **Map** p315 C5.
This stalwart of the busy Charbon scene is an all-in-one, made-to-measure delight. The main bar becomes a wild dance fest as live DJs take over the music after midnight and boy, do these boys know how to party. Upstairs is a more genteel restaurant serving food until the wee hours.

Chez Maman
7 rue des Grandes Carmes, Lower Town (no phone, www.chezmaman.be). Pré-métro Bourse. **Open** midnight-dawn Thur-Sat. **No credit cards. Map** p315 C5.
A tiny bar with a big reputation, the in-your-face queer CM becomes a sweat box as the crowds pile in to see Maman strut her stuff on the bar in her size elevens. The drag is '70s in style and all mimed, but the guys and gals adore their bouffant doyenne. Outside, the doormen will make you wait if it's too busy, on a one-out-one-in basis.

Le Duquesnoy
12 rue Duquesnoy, Lower Town (02 502 38 83, www.duquesnoy.com). Métro Gare Centrale. **Open** 9pm-3am Mon-Thur; 9pm-5am Fri, Sat; 3pm-3am Sun. **No credit cards. Map** p315 D5.

INSIDE TRACK
QUEER CALENDAR

The big event on the Brussels calendar is the city's **Lesbian & Gay Pride** (www.thepride.be), which is held in May. Another annual bash with international clout is the **Gay & Lesbian Film Festival** (www.fglb.org) in January. The European gay sports tournament organised by **Brussels Gay Sports** (www.bgs.org) each September has also become an institution, with over 500 competitors taking part in 2009.

Le Belgica. *See p195.*

Probably the sleaziest doorbell in Brussels, the Duq is dark and cruisy with kinky porn on the TV and owner Gérard's favourite tracks on the sound system. Leather men, denim and wannabe skinheads all jostle for pole position, especially in the labyrinth of dark rooms in the basement and upper floors. But be warned – the stairs in this old Brussels house are not for the unfit. Occasional theme nights on Saturdays and regular Sunday afternoon parties give the place its fetish edge. And if none of this appeals, the good old Duq is also great for a beer and friendly as anything.

L'Homo Erectus

57 rue des Pierres, Lower Town (02 514 74 93, www.lhomoerectus.com). Pré-métro Bourse. **Open** 3pm-3am daily. **No credit cards. Map** p315 C4.
The name really only works in French, but you get the intended pun. Barely half a minute's walk from the Grand'Place, you can't miss this tiny bar with its Darwin-like window of apes slowly evolving into macho man. It's already a victim of its own success – you need to evolve into a snake to be able to squeeze through to the bar at peak times. But L'Homo is fun, especially when the chaps start jumping on the bar for a song. By the way, the early start can only mean one thing: afternoon tea. *Photo p198.*

La Reserve

2a petite rue au Beurre, Lower Town (02 511 66 06). Pré-metro Bourse. **Open** 11am-2am Mon, Thur, Fri; 4pm-1am Wed; 3pm-2am Sat, Sun. **No credit cards. Map** p315 C4.
Jimmy and Marcel run this bar in a scrubbed-up old house near the Grand'Place. The decor is English country pub, the atmosphere reminiscent of a gay bar in the old style, with a mixed clientele who come here to chat with the regulars. The younger boys around town smirk at its kitsch charm, but everyone goes there at some point, if only because of its user-friendly opening hours and unlikely potential as a pick-up joint. *Photo p199.*

Smouss Café

112 rue du Marché au Charbon, Lower Town (0476 28 85 40, www.smousscafe.be). Pré-metro Anneessens. **Open** 4.30pm-5am Thur, Fri; 6pm-5am Sat; 4-10pm Sun. **No credit cards. Map** p315 C5.
Smouss is one of the newest bar-cafés to open on the street of dreams, taking its position at the increasingly upscale place Fontainas end. This is a stylish place, with industrial design and stripped-back brickwork. Smart, clubby and cocktaily, it attracts a similar clientele. The Sunday tea dance has become a massive hit with all those movers and shakers who dread the peace and quiet of the day of rest.

CLUBS

Box

7 rue des Riches Claires, Lower Town (no phone, www.boxclub.be). **Open** 10pm-dawn daily. **Admission** free. **No credit cards. Map** p315 C4.
The Box has become a stalwart of the Brussels scene. At weekends, all three floors open up and resident DJs Dre and Andre1 play a mix of electro pop, techno and deep house. Special party nights at weekends add a sense of machoglam occasion – see the website for details.

La Démence

Fuse, 208 rue Blaes, Lower Town (02 511 97 89, www.lademence.com). Métro/pré-métro Porte de Hal. **Open** 10pm-noon monthly. **Admission** €20; €15 under-26s. **No credit cards.** **Map** p318 C7.

They literally bus the boys in from Lille, Paris and Amsterdam for this, Belgium's biggest gay party, with sounds – and muscles – pumping to house and techno on two floors. And when it's all too much there's a chill-out area and a room with no lights. Check website for exact dates and advance tickets. *See also below* **The International Community.**

Le You

12 rue Duquesnoy, Lower Town (02 639 14 00, www.leyou.be). Métro Gare Centrale. **Open** 11pm-5am Thur; 11.30pm-6am Fri, Sat; 9pm-3am Sun. **Admission** €9-€10. **No credit cards.** **Map** p315 D5.

You is a beacon of light on the scene, attracting a mixed party crowd of gay men and their friends of both sexes. Anything goes here, from Ibiza-style hot-pants to full drag. Thursday is You'niversity, getting the weekend going a night early. The Sunday tea dance has also become an institution, with its no-attitude music and live acts.

The International Community

Muscles from Brussels and beyond flock to La Démence.

Thierry Coppens first opened legendary gay club **La Démence** (*see above*) in Kortrijk, near the French border, in 1989. The club then found a Brussels home in 1992, at the equally legendary Fuse, where it is said techno was born. The largely French crowd moved with it, and the mega-club continues to attract around 3,000 punters from across Europe to its monthly parties – usually held the night before a bank holiday.

For those travelling from Paris, the party starts on the last Thalys train of the evening, as the hedonistas get on a fast track to Brussels. Lille? Amsterdam? London? Cologne? No problem; now that the high-speed lines are fully operational, plenty of Démencers get a late train into town then hotfoot it back the next morning. It has been estimated that there are around 30 nationalities on the Démence dancefloor, with non-Belgians making up two-thirds of the party.

La Démence has become a firm fixture on the gay calendar, pulling in men, women, transgendered, gay and straight punters alike, although the emphasis remains firmly on the 'ripple effect' – bare muscle and torsos. Different months have different themes, and 2010 saw the club branch out into occasional parties at other venues. At Easter, the boys moved across to the old Vaudeville Theatre in the Galeries St-Hubert for an atmospheric soirée of techno and progressive trance.

The Démence club night is still regarded as one of the best in Europe – not bad going, after 21 years on a notoriously fickle scene.

ARTS & ENTERTAINMENT

La Démence.

ARTS & ENTERTAINMENT

SAUNAS & GYMS

Macho II

106 rue du Marché au Charbon, Lower Town (02 513 56 67, www.machosauna.com). Pré-métro Anneessens. **Open** noon-midnight Mon-Sat; 8am-midnight Sun. **Admission** €7-€18. **No credit cards. Map** p316 C5.

The Macho is well known for its serious saunas and decently equipped fitness room. It's a big, well-kept establishment and the staff are attentive. Expect to find a youngish crowd, particularly later on in the night. A ticket allows repeat entry on the same day.

Oasis

10 rue van Orley, Upper Town (02 218 08 00, www.oasis-sauna.be). Métro Madou. **Open** noon-1am daily. *Sun brunch* noon-2.30pm. **Admission** €18; €12 reductions. **Credit** AmEx, DC, MC, V. **Map** p317 F3.

Oasis is set in a vast townhouse and the bar area is still very much a *grande salle*, with marble fireplace and corniced ceilings. Some parts are seedier, but they're meant to be. It's clean, it's popular and it has all the facilities, including a stylish whirlpool area. The stairs challenge even the most nimble-footed. On Tuesdays, it's €12 admission for all.

Spades4our

23-25 rue Bodeghem, Lower Town (02 502 07 72, www.saunaspades4.be). Pré-métro

L'Homo Erectus. *See p196.*

Anneessens. **Open** noon-midnight daily. **Admission** €12-€18; €10-€12 reductions. **Credit** AmEx, DC, MC, V. **Map** p316 B5.

Brussels' biggest and most exclusive sauna is spread over six sizeable floors. It's tastefully designed, has an excellent bar and good food, and the staff are friendly and helpful. Facilities include legitimate massage, an SM labyrinth and a cinema, as well as masses of private rooms. There is also a well-equipped fitness room and a roof terrace.

SEX SHOPS

Orly Centre

9 boulevard Jamar, Lower Town (02 522 10 50). Métro/pré-métro Gare du Midi or pré-métro Lemonnier. **Open** 10am-midnight Mon-Fri; noon-midnight Sat, Sun. **Credit** AmEx, MC, V. **Map** p318 A7.

This shop, selling mainly videos, is also a window for a three-screen cinema complex and a sauna called Club 3000. It is close to Midi station, so it is an (extremely) alternative waiting room for your train, but don't take your bags – it's dark and labyrinthine inside.

Rob Brussels @ Man to Man

11 rue des Riches Claires, Lower Town (02 514 02 96, www.rob.eu/brussels). Pré-métro Bourse. **Open** 10am-6.30pm Tue-Fri; 10am-6pm Sat. **Credit** MC, V. **Map** p315 C4.

Fetish superstore Rob adds Brussels to its international franchise, bringing with it a vast range of rubber and leather clothing and accessories, all in a stylish setting. The Man to Man moniker reminds us of a time when the emphasis was on hairdressing with the fetish as a sideline. But now things have reversed, how long will it be before the barber's chair is used as a prop rather than a seat for a crop?

WHERE TO STAY

Brussels at Heart

11 rue St-Roch, Ste-Catherine (0486 68 16 55, www.brussels-at-heart.be). Pré-métro Gare du Nord. **Rates** €99-€120 double. **Credit** MC, V.

Set in a beautiful house in a quiet street with clean grey and white interior design, Brussels at Heart is a short walk from the old centre and the gay district.

Maison Noble

10 rue Marcq, Ste-Catherine (02 219 23 39, www.maison-noble.eu). Métro Ste-Catherine. **Rates** €119-€139 double. **Credit** MC, V. **Map** p316 C2.

Brendon and Matthieu welcome guests to their stunning Brussels townhouse, in the heart of Ste-Catherine. Grand rooms with pillars and stained-glass windows and a delightful terrace make this place a home from home; note there's a €10 supplement for one-night stays.

La Reserve. *See p196.*

Music

Classical riches and cracking jazz.

Brussels may be unable to live up to the likes of London or Paris when it comes to gigs and concerts, but for a city of one million inhabitants it packs a pretty considerable musical punch. Whether you're dancing to indie hipsters at the Botanique or nodding along to avant-garde acts at the Jazz Station, there's something on offer to suit most music-lovers.

Classical music, meanwhile, is a genuinely egalitarian part of the city's cultural life, attracting a wide audience wearing everything from jeans and trainers to frocks and fox furs. The top end may be pricey, particularly when it comes to opera, but decent government subsidies mean ticket prices compare favourably to what you'll have to fork out elsewhere in Europe.

Classical & Opera

National opera house the **Théâtre de la Monnaie** holds a special place in Belgian hearts: it was an opera performance held here in 1830 that precipitated the events that led to Belgium's emergence as an independent state (*see p25*).

Heading up the National Orchestra, Austrian-born Walter Weller has introduced a series of cycles by Schubert, Beethoven and Mahler at the **Bozar**; other important venues include **Flagey**, the **Conservatoire Royal de Bruxelles** and various smaller churches and cultural centres dotted around the city.

The **Musée des Instruments de Musique** (*see p64*), housed in the superb art nouveau Old England building, is as popular for its occasional classical concerts as for its well-presented collection; sometimes, musicians play period instruments. Brussels is also a centre of excellence for early music and original instrument ensembles. Among the most notable are the pioneering La Petite Bande; Philippe Herreweghe, his orchestra Chapelle Royale and chorus Collegium Vocal; Il Fondamento; and Anima Eterna.

Contemporary classical music fans should check out the annual **Ars Musica** festival (*see p176*), where new composers are given a chance to show their pieces. Local groups specialising in new music include **Ictus Ensemble**, **Oxalys** and **Musique Nouvelle**.

INFORMATION & TICKETS

Details on all concerts can be found every Thursday in *The Bulletin*. The Philharmonic Society (02 507 82 00), based at the Bozar, organises the bulk of big-name concerts in Brussels. The group also issues a brochure of its events, which include many foreign orchestras, soloists and chamber groups. Then there's the glossy bi-monthly *Bozar Magazine*; call 02 511 34 33 for a copy, or sign up for a free electronic newsletter at www.bozar.be.

Ticket prices vary from one event to the next, even in the same venue. Philharmonic Society events are from €10 to €70, with gala concerts costing up to double the usual price. At the Théâtre de la Monnaie, expect to pay at least €10 and up to €240 for orchestra seats. Prices at other venues range from €5 to €50.

The **TIB tourist office** (*see p304*) has details of most events, and sells tickets to many concerts. You can also buy them in Brussels and Antwerp at **Fnac** (*see p156*).

VENUES

Conservatoire Royal de Bruxelles

30 rue de la Régence, Upper Town (02 511 04 27, www.conservatoire.be). Tram 92, 94. **Open** *Box office* 1hr before performance or 10 days in advance from the Palais des Beaux-Arts. **Tickets** vary. **No credit cards**. **Map** p319 D6.

The Conservatory's fine hall is a little too narrow for full-size symphonic orchestras, but perfect for chamber formations and solo recitals. Ignore the slightly off-putting peeling paint; the acoustics are excellent in a hall partially designed by French organ-builder Cavaillé-Coll. It is here that the preliminary rounds of the famous Queen Elisabeth competition (*see p206* **Inside Track**) are held – the most interesting part, according to contest connoisseurs.

★ Palais des Beaux-Arts (Bozar)

23 rue Ravenstein, Upper Town (02 507 82 00, www.bozar.be). Métro Gare Centrale. **Open** *Box office* Sept-June 11am-7pm Mon-Sat; July, Aug 11am-5pm Mon-Sat & 1hr before event. **Tickets** €10-€70; €7-€52 reductions. **Credit** AmEx, MC, V. **Map** p317 E5.
Home of the National Orchestra and seat of the renowned Philharmonic Society, the Palais is without doubt Brussels' most prestigious venue, well suited to hosting the finals of the Concours Musical International Reine Elisabeth de Belgique. Acoustics in the splendid Salle Henri LeBoeuf were greatly improved for both musicians and the public by major renovations. The smaller 400-seat chamber music hall is excellent, although concerts here are less frequent.

★ Théâtre de la Monnaie

Place de la Monnaie, 4 rue Léopold, Lower Town (070 23 39 39, www.lamonnaie.be). Métro/pré-métro De Brouckère. **Open** *Box office* (23 rue Léopold) 11am-6pm Tue-Sat & 1hr before event. **Tickets** €10-€170; €7.50-€126 under-26s. **Credit** AmEx, DC, MC, V. **Map** p315 D4.
The national opera house soaks up the lion's share of arts subsidies; hardly surprising, seeing as it's the jewel in Brussels' cultural crown. Its repertoire balances contemporary works and innovative productions of the classics, with performers not yet famous enough for prices to be out of reach.

Churches

Cathédrale des Sts Michel et Gudule

Place Ste-Gudule, Upper Town (02 217 83 45, www.cathedralestmichel.be). Métro Gare Centrale or Parc. **Open** varies. **Tickets** vary. **No credit cards. Map** p317 E4.
Brussels' most grandiose church is too large, alas, for music more complicated than Gregorian chant. Nevertheless it's the venue for quite a few major events, especially organ concerts on the excellent instrument high above the audience. The interior is just as grand as the exterior; both have undergone extensive refurbishments over the last ten years. Audiences of a thousand or so help absorb some of the ten-second echo. Sunday 12.30pm mass (10am in summer) features special concerts during much of the year; evening concerts are rarer.

▶ *The cathedral has had a long and dramatic history, and was seriously damaged by the French Revolutionary forces; see p63.*

Chapelle Royale

Eglise Protestante, 2 rue du Musée, Upper Town (02 213 49 40, www.eglisedumusee.be). Métro Gare Centrale. **Open** varies. **Tickets** vary. **No credit cards. Map** p315 D6.
A pleasure both acoustically and architecturally, for musicians and audiences alike. Too small for anything larger than a baroque chamber orchestra, the

---

THE BEST FESTIVALS

Brosella
This lovely little free jazz and folk festival, held each July in the park by the Atomium, is now over 30 years old (www.brosella.be).

Brussels Jazz Marathon
May brings a weekend of boozing and jamming, with over 400 events across the city. Special festival buses get you from one venue to another (www.brusselsjazzmarathon.be).

Couleur Café
World music takes centre stage at this amazing multicultural event, which happens in June (www.couleurcafe.org).

Festival of Flanders
Running from May to November, this classical music behemoth takes place across Flanders and Brussels. Each participating city has a different musical theme (www.festival-van-vlaanderen.be).

Festival of Wallonia
The French community's Wallonia-wide classical music festival always has a strong Brussels presence, and runs from June to October (www.festivaldewallonie.be).

Rock Werchter
Rock Werchter takes place in June and is a massive old-style rock festival, with the obligatory tents and queues for loos (www.rockwerchter.be).

Skoda Jazz Festival
This impressive countrywide jazz festival runs from October to November, drawing an international crowd (www.skodajazz.be).

ARTS & ENTERTAINMENT

Chapelle Royale. *See p201.*

venue is ideal for recitals featuring period instruments. As the maximum audience size is 150, early booking is highly advisable.

★ Eglise des Sts Jean et Etienne aux Minimes

62 rue des Minimes, Upper Town (02 511 93 84). Bus 27, 48. **Open** varies. **Tickets** vary. **No credit cards. Map** p315 D6.

This high-Baroque church, situated between the Sablon and the Marolles, has rather average acoustics but hosts a huge number of concerts. The Philharmonic Society performs some of its early music recitals here, while the imaginative Midis-Minimes summer festival (www.midis-minimes.be) attracts tourists and locals alike at lunchtimes. One Sunday morning a month during the rest of the year, the amateur/professional ensemble La Chapelle des Minimes (www.minimes.be) presents fine performances of Bach cantatas, as it has done for the last 20 years.

Occasional venues

Various unusual venues play host to sporadic concerts in and around the capital. **Château de la Hulpe** (02 653 64 04), 15 kilometres (ten miles) south-east of Brussels and the setting for the film *The Music Teacher*, hosts a summer opera calendar; elsewhere, the **Music Village** puts on a range of quality dinner concerts.

★ Flagey

Place Ste-Croix, next to place Flagey, Ixelles (02 641 10 20, www.flagey.be). Tram 81, 82 or bus 38, 60, 71. **Open** Box office 11am-10pm Tue-Sat & 1hr before event. **Tickets** vary. **Credit** AmEx, MC, V. **Map** p322 G10.

Flagey, former home of the National Radio Orchestra, folded during the 1990s, then reopened after a great deal of lengthy and very expensive renovation work. In its heyday, the main studio was acoustically one of Europe's finest, and hosted some truly memorable world premières. Now it hosts a range of contemporary and classical concerts.
▶ *Flagey is also one of the key venues for the KlaraFestival, held each September; see p178.*

Kaaitheater

20 square Sainctelette, Lower Town (02 201 59 59, www.kaaitheater.be). Métro Yser. **Open** Box office 11am-6pm Tue-Fri. **Tickets** vary; reductions under-26s. **Credit** MC, V. **Map** p316 C1.

Used mostly for staging Flemish-speaking theatre productions, this medium-sized hall also occasionally plays host to opera and contemporary music concerts; Ictus is the resident ensemble. There's also an affiliated smaller studio space at 81 rue Notre Dame du Sommeil.

Théâtre St-Michel

2 rue Père Devroye, Etterbeek (02 736 76 56, www.theatrestmichel.com). Métro Montgomery. **Open** Box office 10am-1pm Mon-Fri. **Tickets** vary. **Credit** AmEx, MC, V.

This fairly large hall, attached to one of Brussels' largest preparatory schools, has acoustics that are better suited to theatrical performances than musical recitals, but audiences and players appreciate its shape and generous volume all the same.

Rock & Pop

At the top end of the spectrum, major international artists have a range of venues to choose from. Eminem and Peter Gabriel have both played at the city's biggest (some would say too big) indoor venue, the **Forest National**, while MGMT, Goldfrapp and Iggy Pop favoured the far more intimate setting of the **Ancienne Belgique**, a renovated theatre a stroll from the Grand'Place. The other medium-sized venue, **Botanique**, is a spectacular greenhouse with three superb concert spaces.

INFORMATION, TIPS & TICKETS

For concert information, check *The Bulletin*, the French-language monthly *Kiosque* or the *MAD* supplement with *Le Soir* on Wednesdays.

For live music in small or occasional venues, look out for flyers in bars such as Au Soleil. In the city centre, the café at **Beursschouwburg** is another good source.

At many venues, including the Ancienne Belgique and Cirque Royal, queue up to pay for drinks tokens first, then use them at the bar counter; you'll have to queue twice, but it works out quicker in the long run.

ROCK VENUES

★ Ancienne Belgique

110 boulevard Anspach, Lower Town (02 548 24 24, www.abconcerts.be). Pré-métro Bourse. **Open** Box office 11am-6pm Mon-Fri. **Tickets** €10-€30. **Credit** AmEx, MC, V. **Map** p315 C4.

This place used to be old, down-at-heel and terrific (Jacques Brel put in many an electrifying performance on its stage). It's now new, shiny and – more importantly – still terrific; this place is a rare example of a renovation that transforms a venue without losing any of its spirit. Its main hall can hold 2,000, mostly standing, with an adjacent side bar poignantly decked out in posters for shows by performers no longer with us: the likes of Joe Strummer, Johnny Thunders and so on. There are lockers and pay toilets downstairs. *Photo p205.*

ARTS & ENTERTAINMENT

Beursschouwburg

20-28 rue Auguste Orts, Lower Town (02 550 03 50, www.beursschouwburg.be). Pré-métro Bourse. **Open** *Box office* 10am-6pm Mon-Fri. *Café* 8.30pm-3am Thur-Sat. **Tickets** €12; €10 reductions. **No credit cards**. **Map** p315 C4.

One of Brussels' true cultural treasures, the Beursschouwburg is funded by the Flemish Cultural Community and hosts a colourful range of events with an often eccentric vibe: concerts, club nights and jam sessions are held in either the theatre or the brilliant café, which is worth a visit even when nothing special is on. The team also organises outdoor events, concerts and street parties in July in the place de la Monnaie.

▶ *For more on the multi-talented Beursschouwburg, see p224.*

★ Botanique

236 rue Royale, St-Josse (02 226 12 11, reservations 02 218 37 32, www.botanique.be). Métro Botanique. **Open** 10am-6pm daily. **Tickets** €11-€20. **Credit** AmEx, MC, V. **Map** p317 F2.

The unmissable 'Le Bota' is managed by the French-speaking Cultural Community. The main corridor is lined with luxuriant foliage and ponds, a reminder of when the building was the centre of a vast botanical garden before the war. Audiences here revel in indie rock, with the likes of Josh Ritter, the Divine Comedy and Belgian band Balthazar appearing on stage. The best of the three separate venues in Le Botanique is the mid-sized La Rotonde (capacity 350), where the audience stands on steep steps and everyone gets a great view of the band. *See also p90* **Relics Reborn**.

▶ *Botanique hosts the Les Nuits Botanique rock festival in May, erecting an enormous marquee to accommodate the biggest acts.*

Café Central

14 rue de Borgval, Lower Town (no phone, www.lecafecentral.com). Pré-métro Bourse. **Open** varies. **Tickets** free. **Map** p315 C4.

Café Central has become one of the capital's most fashionable venues, and an epicentre of cool. There are around three concerts here each month, along with DJ nights and cult film screenings. The Central is also a participating venue in various music festivals, including the legendary Jazz Marathon (*see p176*).

Cirque Royale

81 rue de l'Enseignement, Upper Town (02 218 20 15, www.cirque-royal.org). Métro Madou. **Open** *Box office* 9am-6pm Mon-Fri; 10.30am-6pm Sat. **Tickets** vary. **Credit** MC, V. **Map** p317 F4.

This is the nearest thing Brussels has to the Royal Albert Hall. It's plush and it's spherical, with great acoustics, and it tends to draw the grand old men of rock – Johnny Hallyday is among those to have been subjected to calls for almost endless encores on its stage. There's no dancing, though – in keeping with its other role as a classical venue, you're expected to sit down and look enraptured. Even talking to your neighbour can draw disapproving glances.

Forest National

208 avenue Victor Rousseau, Forest (0900 69 500, www.forestnational.be). Tickets 077 37 38 39, www.sherpa.be). Tram 18, 52 or bus 48, 54. **Open** *Box office* 8am-10pm daily. **Tickets** vary. **Credit** MC, V.

The biggest indoor venue in Brussels, this huge concrete and metal shed can accommodate 11,000 – but you have to really like an act to want to see it here. It feels a bit like an aircraft hangar, and unless you're near the stage your idols will look smaller than they do on the telly. As long as Brussels doesn't have a regular venue between the size of Ancienne Belgique and this place, bands and their fans will have no choice but to trek to the southern edge of the city for the Forest National experience.

Grain d'Orge

142 chaussée de Wavre, Ixelles (02 511 26 47). Métro Porte de Namur. **Open** 11am-3am Fri. *Concerts* 9pm. **Tickets** free. **Credit** MC, V. **Map** p319 F7.

If you sport a flared denim suit with beer towels sewn in, you'll love this ultimate spit-and-sawdust bar. The Grain d'Orge hosts gigs every Friday night, with most of the acts tending towards American-style rock, blues or country. Everyone has a good time and, this being Belgium, a certain knowing sense of irony is all part of the fun.

Halles de Schaerbeek

22 rue Royale Ste-Marie, Schaerbeek (02 218 21 07, www.halles.be). Tickets at www.sherpa.be). Tram 92, 94 or bus 65, 66. **Open** *Box office* 2-6pm Mon-Fri. **Tickets** vary; reductions under-26s. **Credit** MC, V. **Map** p320 F1.

The Halles began life as a covered market in 1865, and is now a multi-use French cultural centre. Its mission is to promote both avant-garde and mainstream

Ancienne Belgique. *See p203.*

The old Magasin 4 was dilapidated, sweaty and graffiti-ridden. In 2010, the new M4 opened its doors just across the canal in an old industrial building. It's not so dilapidated, but it is sweaty and the graffiti makes way for neon – but it's still wonderful. Run by an association with charity status, M4 remains one of the city's wilder venues, with rock and indie bands alternated with dubstep and drum 'n' bass.

★ Recyclart
Gare de Bruxelles-Chapelle, 25 rue des Ursulines, Lower Town (02 502 57 34, www.recyclart.be). Métro Gare Centrale or bus 95. **Open** *Concerts* around 10pm Fri, Sat, last Sun of mth. **Tickets** free-€8. **No credit cards**. **Map** p315 C6.

This alternative venue, occupying several parts of a now little-used train station, is well worth a visit for the concerts, club nights and other events hosted here, from kids' puppet shows to philosophical debates. It might look as if it has been squatted by anarchists, but in fact the non-profit association that runs it has the full backing of the city and regional authorities, and the place was set up with a grant from the European Commission. It specialises in post-rock electronica, but also showcases other more traditional styles.

VK Club
76 rue de l'Ecole, Molenbeek (02 414 29 07, www.vaartkapoen.be). Métro Comte de Flandre. **Open** *Box office* 9am-6pm daily. **Tickets** vary. **No credit cards**. **Map** p316 A2.

Just as the nominally francophone Botanique has its Flemish counterpart in the Ancienne Belgique, Magasin 4 has a Flemish twin in the Vaartkapoen or VK. The place itself is great, but the area can be rough. The venue runs buses from the Gare Centrale – phone for details.

culture, running from rock and folk music to theatre and dance. Smaller concerts take place in the downstairs club, but bigger acts appear in the main hall. It looks gorgeous, and there's an awesome view from the impressive balcony, but the sound can be a little muddy. *See also p90* **Relics Reborn**.

Kultuurkaffee
Vrije Universiteit Brussel (Flemish University), boulevard de la Plaine 2, Ixelles (02 629 23 25, www.vub.ac.be/cultuur). Tram 23, 90. **Open** *Concerts* 8pm or 8.30pm Thur. **Tickets** free. **No credit cards**. **Map** p325 J14.

A good place to sample the rather hidden but often quite adventurous culture of Brussels' minority Flemish student community, akin to their British counterparts when it comes to liking late nights and a good drink. The Kultuurkaffee, with support from radio station Studio Brussel, puts on rock acts (including semi-well-known groups like Traktor), world music and the occasional Flemish oddity.

Magasin 4
51b avenue du Port, Molenbeek (02 223 34 74, www.magasin4.be). Métro Yser. **Open** 8pm on gig nights. **Tickets** €8. **No credit cards**.

JAZZ, FOLK & WORLD VENUES

Brussels has a great jazz tradition (*see p209* **All That Jazz**) and it continues to thrive here: stars to look out for include Toots Thielemans, pianist Nathalie Lorier, guitarist and composer Maxime Blésin, and sax player Steven Houben and his trumpeter son Gregory. Popular and often packed venues such as **Music Village** testify to locals' continuing enthusiasm for jazz, as do the number of jazz acts appearing at larger, more rock-oriented venues.

The **Jazz Station**, located in a disused railway station in St-Josse, was set up by the musicians' association Les Lundis d'Hortense, and is presided over by leading sax player Manuel Hermia. It provides listings and contacts at www.jazzinbelgium.org.

Brussels also stages some of the best world music around, much of it home-grown: award-winning a cappella outfit **Zap Mama** grew out

ARTS & ENTERTAINMENT

INSIDE TRACK
A RIGHT ROYAL CONCOURS

The **Concours Musical International Reine Elisabeth de Belgique** (Queen Elisabeth International Music Competition; *see p177*) is royally exclusive – not only in terms of the rarefied atmosphere and performances, but also the heeled and bejewelled crowd that is drawn to it. It was founded by the renowned Belgian violinist Eugène Ysaÿe and Queen Elisabeth of Belgium (herself a violinist); the first winner, in 1937, was David Oistrakh. Each year the focus changes between violin, piano and voice. If you can't score tickets, the concerts are shown on Belgian TV as well as online (www.cmireb.be).

of an African vocal workshop in Brussels. For visits from some of Africa's biggest stars, keep an eye out for fly posters around Matongé, the African quarter in Ixelles. For festival tips, *see p201* **The Best Festivals**.

L'Archiduc

6 rue Antoine Dansaert, Lower Town (02 512 06 52, www.archiduc.be). Pré-métro Bourse. **Open** 4pm-5am daily. **Credit** AmEx, DC, MC, V. **Map** p315 C4.

Built in the 1930s, this little art deco jewel was once an after-hours club for jazz fans. Nat King Cole used to drop by for an après-gig drink and to tinkle the ivories, and Brel was a regular. Bands at the Ancienne Belgique tend to finish the night here. Free Monday gigs (10pm) feature local musicians; Mixed and Shaken Thursdays (9pm) introduce jazz-fusion and acid jazz DJs to the mix. Ring the doorbell to enter. *See also p143*.

Candelaershuys

433 avenue Brugmann, Uccle (02 343 46 58, www.candelaershuys.be). Tram 91, 92. **Open** varies. **Tickets** €10. **No credit cards**.
Like VK (*see p205*), this is part of Brussels' local network of state-supported Flemish cultural centres. It's in a beautiful old house in a well-heeled (though not very Flemish) part of town. Just about everything goes on here, from experimental theatre group performances and poetry readings to concerts by prestigious jazz, rock and world acts. Tickets are cheap, but expect to pay up to €36 when the likes of Axelle Red turns up.

Espace Senghor

366 chaussée de Wavre, EU Quarter (02 230 31 40, www.senghor.be). Métro Maelbeek or Schuman. **Open** varies. **Tickets** €8-€12. **No credit cards**. **Map** p322 F5.

The French-speaking community restored and now runs this venue adjacent to the EU Quarter. It has an imaginative and popular programme of jazz and world music concerts, usually three or four times a month. It's not the place for a riotous night out, but the musical line-up is usually excellent.

★ Jazz Station

193-195 chaussée de Louvain, St-Josse (02 733 13 78, www.jazzstation.be). Bus 29, 63. **Open** *Bar* 11am-10pm Wed-Sat. *Concerts/rehearsals* varies. **Tickets** €6. **No credit cards**. **Map** p321 J3.

Jazz Station is set in a lovely old building, and has real artistic flair. As well as jazz concerts it offers an experimental space for new and emerging bands; during the day, jazz outfits hold open rehearsals so that serious fans can see how it's all put together. With low entry fees, a swinging bar and an exhibition space, Jazz Station is a superbly creative venue.

★ Music Village

50 rue des Pierres, Lower Town (02 513 13 45, www.themusicvillage.com). Pré-métro Bourse. **Open** 7pm-late Wed-Sat. *Concerts* 8.30pm Wed, Thur; 9pm Fri, Sat. **Tickets** €7.50-€20. **Credit** MC, V. **Map** p315 C4.

The Music Village occupies two 17th-century buildings near the Grand'Place. The club provides a home for more traditional jazz styles, as well as the occasional avant-garde act (booking advisable). Weekdays attract a lot of business visitors, but Fridays and Saturdays are reserved for performers sufficiently well known to fill the place with jazz aficionados. Dinner is optional.

New York Jazz Club

5 chaussée de Charleroi, Ixelles (02 534 85 09). Métro Louise. **Open** 10pm-1.30am Fri, Sat. **Tickets** free. **Credit** MC, V. **Map** p319 D8.

Table service pushes the drinks prices up in this smart little establishment, which also serves bistro-style food, but it's balanced out by the fact there's no entry fee. The programme is for smooth dinner-style jazz – not to everyone's taste, but popular with a well-dressed crowd keen on warming up for a late night elsewhere in the capital.

★ Sounds Jazz Club

28 rue de la Tulipe, Ixelles (02 512 92 50, www.soundsjazzclub.be). Métro Porte de Namur or bus 54, 71. **Open** 8pm-4am Mon-Sat. *Concerts* 10pm. **Tickets** free-€15. **No credit cards**. **Map** p319 F8.

Sounds continues to be a compulsory port of call for local jazz fans. Far enough out of town to discourage tourists (though only 15 minutes by bus), it attracts expats and eurocrats who like to swap their dull grey suits for glad rags. It favours modern-ish jazz, but there is also the odd big band night; Wednesdays usually bring Latino concerts. It stays open very late.

Music Village.

ARTS & ENTERTAINMENT

Tour et Taxis.

La Soupape

26 rue Alphonse de Witte, Ixelles (02 649 58 88, www.lasoupape.be). Tram 81, 82 or bus 38, 60, 71. **Open** 8.30pm-midnight concert days only. **Tickets** €8; €7 reductions. **No credit cards.** **Map** p325 G10.

Set in a side street in the ever more lively area near place Flagey and the Ixelles lakes, this intimate, fun venue specialises in *chanson française* – it holds heats for a national competition. La Soupape is a great place for discovering new talent, with many acts destined to be seen later by far more than the 50 people squeezed around its rickety tables.

La Tentation

28 rue de Laeken, Lower Town (02 223 22 75, www.latentation.org). Métro/pré-métro De Brouckère. **Open** 7pm-1am Fri, Sat, event nights. **Tickets** €5-€10. **Credit** AmEx, DC, MC, V. **Map** p316 C3.

This fine building, with its Horta staircase, was saved by the Centro Gallego, which is run by Brussels' Galician community. It has a commendably eclectic approach in its world music concerts, held twice monthly. As well as traditional Galician music, it puts on flamenco, salsa and even Flemish folk (flamenco, the Spanish for 'Flemish', was originally a perjorative catch-all for undesirables, not least Gypsies and Flemish representatives at the Spanish court). The centre also runs courses in belly dancing and the Galician bagpipes.

► *This place is also a splendid spot for a peaceful drink and a nibble on some tapas; see p142.*

Théâtre Marni

23-25 rue de Vergnies, Ixelles (02 639 09 80, www.theatremarni.com). Tram 81, 82 or bus 71. **Open** 8pm-2am Tue-Sat. *Concerts* 8.30pm. **Tickets** €5-€15. **No credit cards.** **Map** p322 G9.

This renovated theatre, a former bowling alley near place Flagey, has a wonderfully varied programme of quality jazz and world music from Belgium and beyond. Gigs take place in the large and comfortable main theatre or in the entrance hall. The organisers of the late and much-lamented Travers jazz club continue to host innovative new performers here, mainly during two seasons in May and September. Like many venues, the Marni also has a splendid bar attached, so there's no need to rush off home once the gig has finished.

Tour et Taxis

3 rue Picard, Molenbeek (02 420 60 69, www.tourtaxis.be). Métro Ribaucourt or Belgica or bus 14. **Open** varies. *Festival* last weekend in June. **Tickets** *Festival* €21/day; €50/3 days. **No credit cards.**

With parts of the site still under renovation, this vast former customs warehouse continues to provide four stages for one of the biggest world music festivals in Europe, Couleur Café (*see p201* **The Best Festivals**). There's space for a crafts village, workshops and 50 food stalls. The festival has been searching for a permanent home, but nowhere matches the lofty acreage here, turning T&T into an impromptu venue in its own right.

All That Jazz

Two major festivals make Brussels a mecca for jazz buffs.

Jazz is an international genre that works well for an international city, and bridges the local language divide – which may help to explain why it's so big here. The city has a proud jazz tradition; after all, a Belgian invented the saxophone. Django Reinhardt, Bobby Jaspar and Toots (Midnight Cowboy) Thielemans were among the local musicians who became globally famous after the war; Reinhardt and Jaspar died young, but Thielemans is very much alive, still tootling on his harmonica as he approaches 90. He is sometimes partnered on stage by the Belgian jazz guitarist Philip Catherine, who recorded with Chet Baker in the 1980s and accompanied Charles Mingus.

Jazz musicians loom large on line-ups at venues across town, and Brussels also hosts two of Europe's most notable festivals, drawing crowds from across Belgium and well beyond its borders. The **Brussels Jazz Marathon** (www.brussels jazzmarathon.be; *see also p176*) started life in 1995 as a way of kick-starting the summer festival season. For three days over the last weekend of May, the whole city gives itself over to Marathon magic. Classic jazz venues are at the core of the programme, but tiny bars also strive to find a corner for a guitarist, and hotels roll in the lobby piano for some after-dinner boogy woogy. Meanwhile, the main squares erect sound stages and beer tents to accommodate the music-hungry and booze-thirsty crowds.

In 2010, there were 125 concerts involving more than 400 Belgian and international musicians in 65 indoor and outdoor spaces. For the most part, concerts are free (though the main jazz venues may charge their usual admission prices); there's even the free Movin' Jazz bus to take audiences to outlying venues. On-board musicians keep passengers entertained, providing a jazzy interlude on wheels.

While the Marathon includes all of Brussels, autumn's **Skoda Jazz Festival** (www.skodajazz.be) does its best to get the whole country involved. The festival, which celebrated its 25th birthday in 2010, has a programme that takes in venues across Antwerp, Brussels, Ghent, Leuven, Liège and Turnhout. There are around 70 concerts in all, ranging from contemporary jazz to world, electronica and Latin – particularly Bossa Nova. It also attracts big names: Maceo Parker, Jan Garbarek, Philip Catherine and Buena Vista Social Club have all headlined.

Bruges has its own biennial festival at the end of September, **Jazz Brugge** (www.jazzbrugge.be). As the new swinger on the block, it started in 2002 when Bruges was European City of Culture. Its emphasis is on new European jazz, in a scene dominated by the USA, and it has two stellar main performance spaces: the sparkling Concertgebouw and Memling in Sint-Jan, one of the oldest hospital buildings in Europe.

ARTS & ENTERTAINMENT

Brussels Jazz Marathon.

Nightlife

The birthplace of techno parties on.

Belgium takes its clubbing very seriously, arguing that it was the birthplace of European techno thanks to the work of just one man, the legendary DJ Pierre, who placed Brussels' most enduring club, Fuse, firmly on the dance map.

Considering how compact Brussels is, the club scene is surprisingly varied and can be both heady and very hedonistic. Some reliably solid venues have been around for years; others open and close with alarming regularity. For those wanting to find a deeper head space, various full-on one-nighters pad out the regular club calendar, but be warned: their structure is loose and unpredictable, often following an impulsive instinct. Blink and you might miss something decent, but keep your eyes glued to the web and you'll be surprised at how much is going on.

ARTS & ENTERTAINMENT

INFORMATION & TICKETS

The best place to start looking for information is www.noctis.com, Belgium's best party website (*see also right* **Brussels Beats**). More and more clubs have an online presence, and many have MySpace and Facebook pages. Once in Brussels, flyers are ubiquitous in the entrances of bars and clubs.

Admission prices to clubs are reasonable, often with reductions for early entry; drinks bills are bearable, but note that credit cards are rarely accepted. One last practical point: be sure of the dress code for your party. Venues that attract professional thirtysomethings may not be overly enamoured with trainers, while the underground mob will sneer if you turn up in a pair of Gucci loafers.

INSIDE TRACK
HEAD FOR LES HALLES

It's worth keeping your eye on the **Halles St-Géry** (*see p56*). At weekends there are free entry nights at the Café des Halles, setting up at the other end of the regular café in this grand old market building. The underground vaults also open up occasionally for one-off party nights – ask at the bar for details or follow Café des Halles on Facebook.

CLUBS

★ Bazaar
63 rue des Capucins, Lower Town (02 511 26 00, www.bazaarresto.be). Bus 27. **Open** *Restaurant* 7.30pm-midnight Tue-Thur. *Restaurant & club* 7.30pm-4am Fri, Sat. **Admission** free. **Credit** MC, V. **Map** p318 C7.
A clubby, ethnic-inspired bar and restaurant above a small but regularly heaving party space – set in the cellar of the old Capucin monastery – packed with beautiful people and boasting some glorious one-off specials such as Catclub (*see p214*).

★ Beursschouwburg Café
20-28 rue Auguste Orts, Lower Town (02 550 03 50, www.beursschouwburg.be). Pré-métro Bourse. **Open** 7.30pm-late Thur-Sat (DJs from 10pm). **Admission** free. **No credit cards.** **Map** p315 C4.
A cavernous space, raw brick and red, where young, trendy Flemings dance to hard house and new-wave electronica. The joy of the Beurs is that you can come and go as you please; as the evening deepens, so does the atmosphere. As part of a new policy, right-on club nights are planned, including Fotones 5.0, an electronic experiments night.

Le Coaster
28 rue des Riches Claires, Lower Town (02 512 08 47). Pré-métro Bourse. **Open** 8pm-5am Mon-Thur; 8pm-7am Fri, Sat. **Admission** free. **No credit cards.** **Map** p315 B4.

Not a club per se, the Coaster is a wild blip in the regularised St-Géry bar scene. Two rooms crammed into a 17th-century house fill up with young guys and gals out for a night of danceable music without the rigmarole of a nightclub. There's even table football. Reasonable drinks prices, an easygoing crowd and dancing on the tables when there's no more space make Le Coaster soar like a rocket.

Dali's Bar

35 petite rue des Bouchers, Lower Town (no phone, www.myspace.com/dalisbar). Métro/pré-métro De Brouckère or métro Gare Centrale. **Open** 10pm-5am Thur-Sat. **Admission** free. **No credit cards. Map** p315 D4.
This petite club – it holds around 120 – has become a byword for partying on a human scale. Trip hop, house, chill and even didgeridoo competitions give the place an edge. Well-known DJs such as Cosy Mozzy and Svenus are happy to play here, and the 1970s disco nights on occasional Thursdays are exactly what you'd expect. But retro it ain't: Dali's keeps smack up to date with nu-jazz and electronic house events.

Factory

12 rue Fossé aux Loups, Lower Town (no phone). Métro/pré-métro De Brouckère. **Open** 10pm-6am Sat. **Admission** €10. **No credit cards. Map** p315 D3.
It may only hold around 400 people but Factory rocks on Saturday nights, pumped up to the nines by progressive house tunes and heavy one-off parties. Factory is one of the few even hardcore clubs in downtown Brussels, so getting there and crawling home is easy. Keep one eye on www.noctis.com for details of forthcoming events.

★ Fuse

208 rue Blaes, Lower Town (02 511 97 89, www.fuse.be). Métro/pré-métro Porte de Hal or bus 27, 48. **Open** 10pm-5am Thur; 11pm-7am Fri, Sat. **Admission** *before midnight* €5; *after midnight* €10. **Credit** MC, V. **Map** p318 C7.
Fuse is the only club in Brussels with a truly international reputation, and the current residents – Pierre, Deg and Seba Lecompte – draw crowds from all over Benelux, France and Germany. It also attracts international stars, with the likes of Sven

Brussels Beats

Belgian DJs may be international stars, but they remain forever local.

Among the seemingly limitless supply of beautiful people buzzing around Brussels' clubs are a few characters whose names are synonymous with creating and developing the city's eventful nightlife.

DJ Nicolas Deckmyn is one man with all the right connections. Deckmyn has been writing about the underground scene in Belgium for more than 15 years, so it's no surprise to learn that he comes from a family dedicated to entertaining – his father Jo was the founder of Schaerbeek's legendary Theatre 140 (*see p226*). Deckmyn is one half of the team responsible for creating Noctis (www.noctis.com). With its insider, word-of-mouth vibe, Noctis helps those new in town feel instantly at home while spreading the news about various underground parties that wouldn't otherwise get advertised. 'Sometimes there are more than 15 parties listed for the same night,' says Deckmyn. 'Not just house and techno, but also reggae, funk, jazz and new wave.'

Olivier Gosserie (www.myspace.com/oliviergosseries) is one of Belgium's best-loved house DJs, alongside luminaries like Cosy Mozzy (www.myspace.com/cosymozzy) and DJ Pierre from Fuse (*see above*). Gosserie continues to be lauded wherever he appears, especially at the

ultra-cool Le You (*see p214*). His new house brand, Noisy Boys, travels the world with him, whether it's in Ibiza or at his regular spot at Club Five in Washington DC. Gosserie is one of Belgum's brightest exports but remains a domestic God; you can hear him on Saturday nights (10pm-midnight) on www.funradio.be.

If these stalwarts serve as the backbone of Brussels' nightlife, then it's the feisty young pups that provide the flesh. Names to look out for include **Charles VBV** (www.charlesvbv.be), also resident at Le You for the French Kiss parties on Saturdays. Charles creates his own fat-beat tracks, intriguingly mixed with dirty house – search for his podcasts on iTunes.

Also connected to Le You is **DJ Man**, head honcho of MP Family, Belgium's biggest DJ group (www.mpfam.com), which represents the new wave of young Belgian stars. Man leads the way in VJing, playing to packed houses of up to 6,000 people at the bigger Euro parties. Other names to look out for are **Fred Hush**, a brilliant DJ/businessman who has released an album and 14 singles on his own WFC record label, and **Marco Bailey**, the techno legend who works with the likes of Sven Väth, Chris Liebing and Jeff Mills.

ARTS & ENTERTAINMENT

Recyclart.

Väth making a regular guest appearance. Fuse also hosts La Démence, the biggest and brightest gay night in Belgium (*see p197* **The International Community**). Don't come expecting a sleek super-club: Fuse is more like a disused Spanish hacienda with two floors of 2,000 people cranked to the max. It can open midweek or on Sundays; check the web.

Havana

4 rue de l'Epée, Lower Town (02 502 12 24, www.havana-brussels.com). Tram 92, 94. **Open** 7pm-2am Thur; 7pm-5am Fri; 7pm-7am Sat. **Admission** free. **Credit** MC, V. **Map** p315 C7.
In the shadow of the Palais de Justice, Havana is a classy joint carved out of an old Marollien house, attracting an international, professional crowd. You can eat, drink (three bars) or dance to Latin-based live acts, degenerating into a popular free-for-all as the evening moves into the wee hours.

Louise Gallery

Level -1, Galerie Louise, avenue Louise, Ixelles (mobile 0478 79 79 79, www.louisegallery.com). Métro Louise. **Open** 11pm-7am Fri-Sun. **Admission** varies. **No credit cards.** **Map** p315 D5.
This glam nightspot is like an underground Greek temple where stylish, high-powered worshippers lose their inhibitions between the columns and mirrors. A powerful lighting set and thumping sound system give it a hefty but highly enjoyable edge. Phone to book a table if you'd like to reserve a refuge. On Sunday, the predominantly gay Strong Cabaret takes over.

Marquee

20-22 rue Ste-Anne, Sablon (no phone, www.the marquee.be). Bus 95. **Open** 10pm-late Thur; 11pm-late Fri, Sat; 9pm-late Sun. **Admission** free. **No credit cards.** **Map** p315 D6.
This stylish club just off the posh Grand Sablon attracts a fashionable crowd. Regular club nights Ottati's on Thursdays and Borderline Corp on Sundays give way to one-off specials on Friday and Saturday nights. If you want to hang with the beautiful people, this is the place to be.

**INSIDE TRACK
GOING UNDERGROUND**

Belgium is a great place to be for one-off underground parties. Look in the foyers of bars and Le Soixante (*see right*) for flyers. If the underground scene is your thing, Facebook seems to be the online venue of choice for information and invitations; many of the clubs listed here have Facebook profiles and are a good starting point to gain entry to the unknown.

Montecristo

25 rue Henri Maus, Lower Town (02 510 05 52). Pré-métro Bourse. **Open** midnight-8am Fri, Sat. **Admission** free-€12. **Credit** AmEx, DC, MC, V. **Map** p315 C4.
It couldn't be more different from its neighbour, the art nouveau café Falstaff (*see p117*), but the Monte has made its mark on downtown Brussels in just the same way. The ground floor is a steamy Latin club with salsa at its core. At weekends, the place turns into a party palace for around 800 people. Web presence is low, so check www.noctis.com for details.

MP3 Disco Bar

17-19 rue du Pont de la Carpe, Lower Town (no phone, www.mp3bar.be). Pré-métro Bourse. **Open** 6pm-late Mon-Sat. **Admission** free. **No credit cards.** **Map** p315 C4.
MP3 is a busy late-night DJ bar in the heart of St-Géry, with a stylish interior featuring a curving bar, a row of brown stools and a bar-length mirror. Facing this is a stretch of banquettes leading to a modest raised dancefloor, two semicircles of seats and a disco ball. All of this is mere decoration – a hindrance, even – to the buzz of activity by the decks at the far end of the bar counter, and the confined but vibrant dancing post-midnight.

★ Recyclart

Gare de Bruxelles-Chapelle, 25 rue des Ursulines, Lower Town (02 502 57 34, www.recyclart.be). Métro Gare Centrale/pré-métro Anneessens or bus 27, 48. **Open** times vary. **Admission** free-€7. **No credit cards.** **Map** p315 C6.
Part of an urban regeneration project under the old Chapelle railway station, Recyclart is a hotbed of discovery. An agenda of electro sounds gives the young crowd something to funk about, as new talent gets a chance to showcase its spin-doctoring. Varied, inventive and always throbbing. Occasional exhibitions are also held.

Le Soixante

60 rue du Marché au Charbon, Lower Town (mobile 0477 70 41 56, www.myspace.com/ barsoixante). Pré-métro Bourse. **Open** 9pm-late Fri, Sat, 1st Sun of mth. **Admission** free. **No credit cards.** **Map** p315 C5.
The Soixante took over where defunct stalwart the Pablo Discobar left off. Inside it's the same crowd: twenty- and thirtysomethings knocking back cocktails and flirting to a mix of retro house and electronica. It's an unpredictable place – sometimes safe and sound, sometimes frenetic. *Photo p214.*

Wax Club

66 boulevard Anspach, Lower Town (02 503 22 32, www.thewaxclub.com). Métro/pré-métro De Brouckère or pré-métro Bourse. **Open** 9pm-late Wed-Sat. **Admission** free. **No credit cards.** **Map** p315 C4.

ARTS & ENTERTAINMENT

Le Soixante. *See p213.*

A little bit of late-night Manhattan in downtown Brussels. Well, let's not get too carried away – Wax is only on the first floor of a boxy corner building, but its wraparound floor-to-ceiling windows and outward-facing bar stools offer punters a smashing view of the urban shenanigans below. The use of so much glass and the carefully placed mirrors make the place look bigger than it really is – Wax only holds around 100 people – but it's just perfect for an hour or two.

★ Le You

18 rue Duquesnoy, Lower Town (02 639 14 00, www.leyou.be). Métro Gare Centrale. **Open** 11.30pm-5am Thur; 11.30pm-6am Fri, Sat. **Admission** €10. **No credit cards.** **Map** p315 C3.

You has made its name as a right-on gay spot (*see p197*), but this is a place where anything goes and everyone is welcome. Progressive house, breaks and trance anthems are the order of the day, with a good-looking, well-dressed crowd – although any attempt at sophistication fades once lasers start hitting mirror balls.

ONE-NIGHTERS

@Seven

Mirano Continental, 38 chaussée de Louvain, St-Josse (02 227 39 56, www.atseven.eu). Métro Madou. **Open** 7pm-1am Thur. **Admission** €7. **Credit** *bar only* MC, V. **Map** p320 G4.

Started up by German Patrick Strum, this club is a meet-and-greet concept borrowed from New York.

Deliberately international and multilingual, it reaches deep into those expat parts that other clubs can't reach. Dressy in a casual way, the after-work crowd comes here to dance and network – there are even conversation tables to help break the ice. It's a members' club (see website for details), but arrive early and you're likely to get in.

Catclub

Various venues (no phone, www.catclub.be). When Brussels-based Lady Jane decided to invite a few friends to a one-off party in 2002 she couldn't have known that Catclub would become such a highly regarded monthly night, pulling in top international DJs like Felix Da Housecat and Jeremy Caulfield. Events take place in venues on an ever-changing Brussels circuit; see website for details and also www.myspace.com/catclub_brussels.

Libertine/Supersport

1 avenue du Port, Molenbeek (no phone, http://libertinesupersport.be). Métro Yser. **Open** 11pm-6am Sat. **Admission** €5 before midnight; €10 after midnight. **No credit cards.** This is the place for some serious partying. The hedonistic crowd is a workable mix of preppy types and total alternatives, all melded together in one glorious party night. Belgian and international DJs play guest spots, starting with housey funk and moving on to thumping progressive sounds. No entry after 4am.

FURTHER AFIELD

La Bush

180 chaussée de Tournai, Esquelmes (06 955 61 17, www.labush.com). **Open** 11pm-8am Fri, Sat, nights before public hols. **Admission** free. **No credit cards.**

One of the biggest and most popular trance/deep house clubs in Belgium, with a capacity of 2,100. Friday is Clubb'in Spirit night, while Saturday's Magic Fountain is just the treatment for diehards.

★ Cherry Moon

144 Gentsesteenweg, Lokeren (09 349 01 38, www.cherrymoon.com). **Open** 10pm-7am Fri, Sat, nights before public hols. **Admission** €7-€15. **No credit cards.**

One of Belgium's biggest (room for 2,000 people) and longest-serving nightclubs, Cherry Moon has been playing hard trance and techno since 1991.

La Rocca

384 Antwerpsesteenweg, Lier (03 489 17 67, www.larocca.be). **Open** 11.30pm-7.30am Fri-Sun. **Admission** €10. **No credit cards.**

Located between Antwerp and Mechelen, La Rocca enjoys a venerated entry in Belgium's clubbing history, all-hallowed and treated with the greatest respect. No trackies or trainers.

ARTS & ENTERTAINMENT

Mirano Continental.

Sport & Fitness

Have-a-go heroes with a passion for participation.

The Belgians have always been obsessed by sport. Football, cycling, tennis and pigeon-racing all loom large in the national consciousness, and locals relish obscure participation sports such as vertical archery, which is practised in the Parc Josephat in Schaerbeek.

Eddy Merckx, five-time winner of the Tour de France, ensured that cycling is a part of Belgian life across the linguistic divide, while Walloon tennis star Justine Henin and her Fleming rival Kim Clijsters (*see right* **Comeback Queens**) epitomise the divided fan base, but have also brought the country together in their quest for sporting success.

ALL-PURPOSE STADIUMS

★ Stade Roi Baudouin
Avenue du Marathon, Laeken (02 474 39 40).
Métro Heysel or Roi Baudouin. **Map** p326 A2.
Formerly the Heysel, Belgium's national stadium was a crumbling ruin when it closed after the tragedy of 1985, when 39 fans died at a European Cup Final. Ten years later it reopened as the Roi Baudouin, a 50,000-capacity all-seater with its own métro stop. It hosts athletics events, cycling races, football matches and rugby games. *Photo p219.*

SPECTATOR SPORTS

News on all sports can be found at www.sport.be.

Athletics

The prestigious **Ivo Van Damme Memorial** (www.sport.be/memorialvandamme), held at Roi Baudouin in September, draws top stars.

Cycling

The main event on the pro circuit is the **Tour of Flanders** (www.rvv.be) on the first Sunday in April, a day race on the hills of the Ardennes. The **Grand Prix Eddy Merckx** is the main speed trial, at the Roi Baudouin in August.

Football

Belgium began an eternal rivalry with France and the Netherlands in the early 1900s. The team qualified for the World Cup six consecutive times from 1982 to 2002, making the semi-finals in 1986. In 2006 and 2010, though, they failed to qualify.

A league of four divisions is dominated by **Anderlecht**, Brussels' major club and the most recognisable name in Belgian football. To watch a First Division match you need to buy a Fan Card for €12.50, obtained from any club's ticket office. For Anderlecht, arrange one before match day. The Belgian FA runs an extensive website at www.footbel.be, while the daily sports supplement in French-language *La Dernière Heure* has comprehensive coverage of the local scene.

RSC Anderlecht
Stade Constant Vanden Stock, 2 avenue Théo Verbeeck, Anderlecht (02 522 15 39, tickets 02 529 40 67, www.rsca.be). Métro St-Guidon. **Admission** €15-€35.
No credit cards.
Anderlecht are still by far the biggest football club in the land, with the team's regular appearances in the Champions League harking back to European triumphs decades ago. On match days the football-oriented bars stretching all the way along avenue Théo Verbeeck, by the impressive stadium, are packed out with fans. The atmosphere is usually friendly, but bear in mind that the home end, stand four, is raucous, and heavy if Bruges are in town.

FC Brussels
Stade Edmond Machtens, 61 rue Charles Malis, Molenbeek (02 411 69 86, www.fc-brussels.be).

Métro Gare de l'Ouest then tram 82, 83.
Admission €15-€60. **No credit cards**.
FC Brussels was created in 2003 with the fusion of RWD Molenbeek and KFC Strombeek. After a strong start, it was relegated to the second division in 2008. FCB have a small following of fans and a lively brass band.

Royale Union St-Gilloise
Stade Joseph Mariën, 223 chaussée de Bruxelles, St-Gilles (02 544 03 16, www.rusg.be). Tram 18, 52 or bus 48, 54. **Admission** €7.50-€15.
No credit cards.
Champions before the war, and Brussels' flagship team before the arrival of Anderlecht, Royale Union St-Gilloise exist on past glories nowadays. Their pitch hewn out of the Duden forest, Union are a football romantic's dream.

Motor sport

The **Spa-Francorchamps** track, two and a half hours from Brussels, is a tricky course built into dense Ardennes forest. It hosts motorbike races, a 24-hour event and the Belgian Grand Prix between August and September (087 27 51 38, www.spa-francorchamps.be). Buses 4 and 4A run from Spa station to the track. Some prefer the motorcross equivalent, the Namur Grand Prix (www.gpnamur.com), each summer.

Tennis

For ten days in February, top players compete for a thousand diamond-studded tennis racket in the **Proximus Diamond Games** (www.sport.be/proximusdiamondgames), held at Antwerp's Sportpaleis. Any player who wins three years in a row gets to keep the prize.

PARTICIPATION SPORTS

With its large expat contingent, Brussels is full of sports clubs in almost every discipline. Most gyms, courts and clubs listed do not need long-term contracts or memberships. For youngsters, the **Brussels Sports Association** (02 354 11 14, www.bsasports.org) serves expat and local

Comeback Queens

Belgium's two first ladies of tennis continue to dominate the courts.

When it comes to tennis, Belgium can rightly claim a top spot. Two stars from separate halves of the linguistic divide have led the international women's game for most of the last decade. French-speaking Justine Henin, ranked world number one in early 2007, has won seven Grand Slam titles, three against her compatriot, Kim Clijsters; the Fleming, for her part, won the US Open as a wild card in 2009.

The girls' own stories couldn't be more different. The more popular Clijsters, or 'Kim Kong', was born in the Flemish town of Bilzen in 1983 and blessed with sporting pedigree: her footballer father Leo was an erstwhile World Cup star for Belgium; her mother Els a national junior gymnastics champion. Romantically linked with Australian tennis icon Lleyton Hewitt, Clijsters later announced her engagement to American basketball player Brian Lynch and married him in 2007.

Henin is painted as the more calculating and taciturn of the two, her career path defined by adversity and seen by many as a battle of gutsy 'Juju' against the world. Born in Liège in 1982, the elfin blonde's destiny was defined in 1992 when, taken to the Roland Garros tournament in Paris, the young Henin vowed to her mother that she would one day see her daughter play the final there. Three years later her mother died from cancer, the promise unfulfilled. Henin was forced to grow up fast, taking charge of the household and her siblings. She turned to family friend Jean-Denis Lejeune as a surrogate father; Henin's real father, José, stopped speaking to her when she became involved with tennis coach Pierre-Yves Hardenne, whom she married in 2002 and divorced five years later.

Both stars retired from the game, only to make sensational comebacks. Clijsters retired in May 2007 (her daughter was born nine months later) but came back in March 2009, winning her second US Open title and being awarded the Laureus World Comeback of the Year and WTA Comeback Player of the Year. Henin similarly retired in May 2008, but returned in 2010 at the Brisbane International as a wild card. She made it to the final, but was defeated by her great rival Clijsters in a ferociously fought match. Kim Kong and Juju remain at the top of their game, ranked world Nos.10 and 18 respectively in 2010. They also remain at the top of the Belgian sports pages for both their personal and professional lives, with the media regarding them as a match truly made in heaven.

ARTS & ENTERTAINMENT

communities, and the **British School** (www.britishschool.be) runs a Summer Sports Academy in July.

Each language community has its own sports organisation: **ADEPS** (02 344 06 03, www.adeps.be) for French speakers, and the Flemish **BLOSO** (02 209 45 11, www.bloso.be).

More information on the various sports federations can be found at www.sport.be.

Badminton

The **Brussels International Badminton Club** (www.brusselsbadminton.com) has courts in Wezembeek Oppem, Woluwe-St-Lambert and Waterloo up to four times a week for matches, coaching and casual play for its members.

The **Irish International Badminton Club** plays on Tuesday nights from September to June at the British School (*see above*). Many fitness centres (*see p220*) hire out courts, and **Move Zone** (12 rue Général Thys, Ixelles, 02 644 55 44, www.movezone.be) has five courts to rent at €15 per hour. The sports centre at **VUB university** (*see p220*) hires to non-members.

Billiards, snooker & pool

Cercle Royal de Billard Léopold

Palais du Midi, 3 rue Roger Van der Weyden, Lower Town (02 511 10 08). Pré-métro Anneessens. **Open** 2-11pm Mon-Fri; 2-6pm Sat. **No credit cards. Map** p318 B6.

Members can enjoy the baize for €4 per hour on the third floor of this sports complex. Membership is available for €30-€60 per year.

Sharkey's

32 rue Marché aux Poulets, Lower Town (02 219 49 01). Métro/pré-métro De Brouckère or pré-métro Bourse. **Open** 11am-2am Mon-Thur, Sun; 11am-4am Fri, Sat. **Admission** €10/hr. **No credit cards. Map** p315 C4.

A big and smoky games den, with rows of pool and snooker tables around a central bar.

Bowling

Brussels has a handful of bowling alleys; two of the biggest are listed below. For details of other

---

INSIDE TRACK EASY RIDER

To do some cycling out of town, use the cheap and easy bike hire scheme run by Belgian railways (02 528 28 28, www. b-rail.be) from April to September. Buy a B-Excursions Train + Vélo ticket to one of 17 stations, and pedal off on an excursion.

---

alleys and bowling clubs, refer to the **Belgian Bowling Federation** (www.bowling.be).

★ Crosly Super Bowling

36 boulevard de l'Empereur, Lower Town (02 512 08 74, www.crosly.be). Métro Gare Centrale. **Open** 2pm-1am Mon-Thur; 2pm-2am Fri, Sat; 10am-midnight Sun. **Admission** from €2.80/ game. **Credit** MC, V. **Map** p315 D5.

Twenty bowling lanes and a late bar, plus trigger-happy Q-Zar laser games for €5.

Other locations 43 quai au Foin, Lower Town (02 217 28 01).

Climbing

The **Belgian Climbing Network** (www. belclimb.net) organises expeditions for amateurs and professionals, and its website contains a decent database of routes. The Rochers de Freyr, near Dinant in the Ardennes, is the main climbing area in Belgium, with seven main crags and over 600 vertiginous lead routes to choose from.

New Rock

136 chaussée de Watermael, Auderghem (02 675 17 60, www.newtorock.com). Métro Demey or bus 72, 96. **Open** noon-midnight Mon-Fri; 1-8pm Sat; 10am-9pm Sun. **Admission** €8.50. **No credit cards.**

A seven-metre climbing wall, plus an 18-metre wall with 21 ropes for diehards. Harnesses and shoes can be hired for €2.50. *Photo p220.*

Cricket

The **Royal Brussels Cricket Club** (www.rbcc.be) is the oldest club in Belgium and today plays at a top-notch ground in Ohain. The **12 Stars Club** is an international group playing at the **British School** (*see above*) and running a Junior Cricket programme. See www.cricket-belgium.com for more details.

Cycling

Cycle tracks can be found at the Bois de la Cambre and the Forêt de Soignes. Look out for the **Dring Dring Bike Festival** in May, organised by **Pro Vélo**. For mountain biking, check out the English-speaking cycling club at www.bigm.be.

See www.visitbelgium.com for cycling tours organised by the tourist office and www.gambar.net/cyclebel for cycling routes along Belgium's waterways.

★ Pro Vélo

15 rue de Londres, Ixelles (02 502 73 55, www.provelo.org). Métro Trône. **Open** Oct-Mar

Stade Roi Baudouin. *See p216*.

ARTS & ENTERTAINMENT

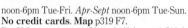

New Rock. *See p218.*

noon-6pm Tue-Fri. *Apr-Sept* noon-6pm Tue-Sun. **No credit cards. Map** p319 F7.
Pro Vélo runs tours at €9 per half day and €13 for a whole day, with bike hire available at €8 and €10. During the summer, it rents out from the Bois de la Cambre, Parc Roi Baudoin in Jette and the Woluwe Park in Woluwe-St-Pierre.

Fitness centres

ADEPS (*see p218*) runs a number of multi-functional centres; the two in the Brussels area are located in the Forêt de Soignes (02 672 22 60, www.csfds.be) and in Woluwe-St-Lambert (02 762 85 22, www.centresportifdelawoluwe.be). Elsewhere, **Sportcity Woluwe-St-Pierre** (02 773 18 20, www.sportcity-woluwe.be) has a very similar set-up.

Aspria

71b avenue Louise, Ixelles (02 542 46 66, www.aspria.be). Métro Louise. **Open** 6.30am-10pm Mon-Fri; 8am-8pm Sat, Sun. **Admission** €105-€300/day. **Credit** AmEx, DC, MC, V. **Map** p319 D8.
For the ultimate in luxury fitness and spa facilities, Aspria in the Conrad has a pool, sauna, spa treatments and superior pampering. *Photo p222.*
Other locations View Building, 26-38 rue de l'Industrie, EU Quarter (02 508 08 00); 56 rue Sombre (02 609 19 02).

Golden Club

33 place du Châtelain, Ixelles (02 538 19 06, www.goldenclub.be). Métro Louise then tram 94. **Open** 7am-10pm Mon-Fri; 10am-6pm Sat, Sun. **Admission** €15/session. **Credit** AmEx, DC, MC, V. **Map** p324 E11.
Jean-Claude van Damme started building his famously fit physique here and his former coach is still the manager – not surprisingly, the Golden Club is big on pumping iron and martial arts.

VUB Sportdienst

2 boulevard de la Plaine, Ixelles (02 629 23 11, www.vub.ac.be/sport). Métro Delta or tram 23, 90 or bus 34, 71. **Open** *Swimming pool* noon-2pm, 5-9pm Mon-Fri. *Sports centre* 9am-9pm Mon-Fri; 9am-5pm Sat; 9am-2pm Sun. **Admission** *Swimming pool* €2.90. *Sports centre* from €3.90/hr. **Credit** MC, V. **Map** p325 J14.
The excellent sports complex at the university boasts gym facilities as well as a swimming pool, sauna, squash, tennis and badminton courts, plus a climbing wall.

Winner's

13 rue Bonneels, EU Quarter (02 280 02 70, www.winnersclub.be). Métro Madou. **Open** 8am-10pm Mon-Fri; 8am-7pm Sat, Sun. **Admission** €12/day. **Credit** DC, MC, V. **Map** p320 H4.
A popular and functional multi-sports centre with climbing facilities, squash courts, gym and saunas.

Football

The three biggest expat teams in Brussels are **British United** (www.bufc.org), **FC Irlande** (www.fcirlande.be) and **Royal Brussels British** (www.rbbfc.org). British United are based in Tervuren; FC Irlande – with five full teams including veterans – train in Woluwe-St-Etienne. Royal Brussels British have six sides, also based in Tervuren.

Go-karting

City Kart
5A square Emile des Grées du Loû, Forest (02 332 36 96, www.citykart.com). Train Forest or tram 18, 52 or bus 50, 54. **Open** 5-11pm Mon-Thur; 3-11pm Fri; 2-11pm Sat, Sun. **Admission** €16/15mins. **Credit** MC, V.
A decent kilometre of indoor karting track located near to Forest railway station offering late-evening, high-octane, juvenile fun. Children are admitted from 9.30am to 2pm, weekends only.

Golf

The leafy outskirts of the city are littered with courses; for full details, consult www.golf.be. The **Royal Golf Club of Belgium** (02 767 58 01, www.ravenstein.be) in Tervuren is the top spot, while the **Brabantse Golf Club** (02 751 82 05, http://brabantsegolf.be), the first Flemish golf club in Brussels, is cheap and pleasant.

Elsewhere, the **Brussels Golf Club Academy and Training Centre** (02 672 22 22, www.brusselsgolfclub.com) offers a public course in parkland by the Forêt de Soignes, best for beginners but open to all standards. For a multi-pass package with hotels, contact 02 352 18 19, www.passbw.com.

Horse riding

The Forêt de Soignes and the Bois de la Cambre are the best options. The **Belgian Equestrian Federation** (02 478 50 56, www.equibel.be) has details of competitions and riding clubs.

Royal Etrier Belge
19 champ du Vert Chasseur, Uccle (02 374 38 70, www.royaletrierbelge.be). Bus 41. **Open** 8am-9pm daily. **Admission** varies. **No credit cards.**
Lessons are given on a long-term basis, but one-time treks can be arranged around the Bois de la Cambre.

Ice skating

An open-air rink is set up at Ste-Catherine in December (www.plaisirsdhiver.be); tickets cost €6, including skate hire.

Patinoire de Forest
36 avenue du Globe, Forest (02 345 16 11). Tram 18, 52 or bus 48, 54. **Open** early Sept-Apr 8.30am-5pm Mon-Fri; 10am-6pm, 8-11pm Sat; 10am-6pm Sun. **Admission** €5; €2.50 skate hire. **No credit cards.**
Home to the Brussels Ice Hockey Club, the Patinoire de Forest offers private lessons, ice-hockey coaching and a skating school.

Patinoire Poséidon
4 avenue des Vaillants, Woluwe-St-Lambert (02 762 16 33, www.patinoireposeidon.be). Métro Tomberg. **Open** Sept-Apr noon-10pm Mon; 10am-10pm Tue, Wed, Sat; 10am-10pm Thur; 10am-6pm Sun. **Admission** €4.50; €3.50 reductions; €3.50 skate hire. **No credit cards.**
A semi-covered, Olympic-sized rink in a sports centre that also houses a gym and swimming pool.

Rugby

The **Brussels Barbarians** is the biggest expat club (www.brusselsbarbarians.com), with two men's and one ladies' team training at the **British School** (*see p218*) on Tuesdays and Thursdays. More details at www.rugby.be.

Skateboarding & in-line skating

On Fridays in summer, 30,000 skaters wend their way through the Bois de la Cambre and the city centre; they meet at 8pm at the Attelages crossroads in the Bois de la Cambre (www.belgiumrollers.com). The Bois de la Cambre also has an outdoor skating rink at 1 Chemin du Gymnase (02 649 70 02).

A small skateboard park has been created on a square outside the old Chapelle train station.

Skiing & snowboarding

In winter, downhill and cross-country skiers flock to the Ardennes and its 70 small ski stations. Contact **Ardennes Tourism** (084 41 19 81, www.catpw.be) for details. In town, try:

Yeti Ski & Snowboarding
Drève Olympique 11, Anderlecht (02 520 77 57, www.yetiski.be). Métro Eddy Merckx. **Open** Sept-May 1-11pm Mon, Wed, Fri; 6-11pm Tue, Thur; 10am-8pm Sat, Sun. **Admission** €7.50-€10/hr. **No credit cards.**
This slope in the Parc de Neerpede sports complex is covered with a plastic carpet for the feel of snow. Equipment hire available.

Squash

Some fitness centres (*see left*) and tennis clubs (*see p222*) also have squash courts.

ARTS & ENTERTAINMENT

Belgica Squash Centre
120 avenue Jean Dubrucq, Molenbeek (02 425 30 42, www.proximedia.com/web/belgica.html). Métro Belgica. **Admission** €15/hr. **Open** 10am-1am Mon-Sat. **Credit** MC, V.
Eight squash courts and occasional tournaments.

Liberty's Squash Club
1068 chaussée de Wavre, Auderghem (02 734 64 93, www.stadium.be). Métro Hankar. **Open** 9am-midnight Mon-Fri; 9am-10pm Sat, Sun. **Admission** €9/30mins. **Credit** MC, V.
A large squash centre with 16 courts. Membership needed for phone bookings.
Other locations Stadium, 1 avenue du Sippelberg, Molenbeek (02 414 40 41).

Swimming

Proper trunks and swimming hats are required at Belgian pools.

Sportcity Woluwe-St-Pierre
2 avenue Salomé, Woluwe-St-Pierre (02 773 18 20, www.sportcity-woluwe.be). Tram 39 or bus 36. **Open** 8am-7pm Mon-Thur, Sat, Sun; 8am-8pm Fri. **Admission** €3.50. **No credit cards.**
Sportcity Woluwe-St-Pierre is a huge leisure centre with an Olympic-sized swimming pool, warm tubs and waterslide, plus tennis, squash, basketball, a solarium and steam baths.

Aspria. *See p220.*

★ Victor Boin
38 rue de la Perche, St-Gilles (02 539 06 15). Pré-métro Horta or tram 18, 81. **Open** 8am-7.30pm Mon-Fri; 9am-7.30pm Sat. **Admission** *Pool* €2. **No credit cards.** **Map** p318 A10.
A beautiful art deco pool with hydrotherapy sessions and a Turkish bath; reserved for women on Tuesdays and Fridays, men the rest of the week.

Tennis

The **Tennis Federation** (02 513 29 20, www.aftnet.be) has details of all clubs and courts; many fitness centres (*see p220*) rent courts to non-members by the hour.

★ Tennis Club de Belgique
26 rue du Beau Site, Ixelles (02 648 80 35, www.tennisclubdebelgique.be). Métro Louise then tram 93, 94 or bus 54. **Open** *To non-members* mid Apr-mid July 7am-10pm Mon-Fri. **Admission** €15-€20/hr. **No credit cards.** **Map** p319 E9.
A well-heeled club with three indoor courts, hired out to non-members on summer weekdays.

Uccle Sport
18 chaussée de Ruisbroeck, Uccle (02 376 37 79, www.ucclesport.be). Tram 18, 52 or bus 50. **Open** 8am-11pm daily. **Admission** €14-€20/hr. **No credit cards.**
Open to non-members, although paying a €25 membership fee saves €5 on rental. There are 12 clay courts and a tennis school.

Walking & running

Weekend runs for expats are organised by the **Brussels Hash House Harriers** (http://users.skynet.be/bruh3) on Saturday afternoons, and the **Brussels Manneke Piss Hash House Harriers** (www.bmph3.com). The **Irish Club** (www.irishclub.be) organises walks on Sundays. The biggest event is the **Brussels 20km** (02 511 90 00, www.20km.be) in May, when 20,000 runners head from the Bois de la Cambre to the Parc du Cinquantenaire. Meanwhile, the hilly **Brussels Marathon** (www.sport.be) is run every August.

Yoga

Contact the **Belgian Association of Yoga Teachers & Practitioners** (02 633 53 99, www.yoga-abepy.be) for your nearest centre.

Ashtanga Yoga Institutes
610 chaussée d'Alsemberg, Uccle (02 340 67 81, www.yoga-ashtanga.net). Tram 55. **Admission** €20/lesson. €20 membership. **No credit cards.**
English classes are available on request.

Theatre & Dance

Modern dance escapes the language rift that splits the theatre scene.

The performing arts in Belgium are seen as an essential part of the nation's cultural life. As such, performances are heavily subsidised to allow everyone to afford them, whether it's strictly classical fare or fluffy revue.

Brussels' official bilingual status means that spoken word theatre is organised along strict language lines – particularly in the bigger subsidised production houses, which rely on money from their regional governments.

Being free of the spoken word and therefore politics, the city's contemporary dance scene is among the best in the world, with choreographers such as Anne Teresa de Keersmaeker and Sidi Larbi Cherkaoui emerging as international names.

THEATRE

Two of Belgium's largest arts subsidies go to the **Royal Flemish Theatre** (KVS) and the **Théâtre National**. Both are resolutely representative of their language communities, and there is little crossover between the two.

For the more adventurous theatregoer, smaller venues like **Théâtre 140** lead the pack, while political posturing takes place at the tiny **Théâtre de Poche**. In summer festivals take over the city (*see pp176-181*), offering wide-ranging programmes of theatre and dance. The one truly international festival is **Kunstenfestivaldesarts**, which dives deep into the unknown (*see p229* **What's in a Name?**).

There are numerous English-language theatre groups in Brussels, organised along national lines. These include the American Theatre Company, the English Comedy Club, the Brussels Light Opera Company, the Brussels Shakespeare Society and the Irish Theatre Group. There's also Green Parrot Productions, an amateur theatre company for children and adults that specialises in popular musicals. Three of the theatre groups clubbed together to buy their own premises and are based at the **Warehouse Studio** (73 rue Waelhem, Schaerbeek, no phone), which has a small 60-seater studio space. Details of all the groups can be found at the English Language Theatre in Brussels portal, http://theatreinbrussels.com.

INFORMATION & TICKETS

The best listings can be found in *The Bulletin* on Thursdays and in *Le Soir* on Wednesdays. The season runs from September to June and venues are mostly closed in summer, which is when the performing arts festivals take over.

Ticket prices are cheap and most venues offer concessions to students, the unemployed, over-60s and groups. It's usually best to call in advance, although there is a culture of turning up on the night. Central reservations and online bookings are becoming more and more popular, but you'll pay booking fees. Smaller theatres may also charge commission for credit card bookings. Check for tickets on www.fnac.be and www.ticketclic.be – although the agencies are limited by whether the venues choose to place tickets with them.

Most theatres offload unsold tickets with **Arsène 50**, which sells them at half price plus a €1 booking fee. All the available performances are updated on the website daily. If you go to the office in person, you'll receive a voucher to exchange at the theatre 30 minutes before curtain-up, or you can book online from 2pm.

Arsène 50

Flagey, place Ste-Croix, Ixelles (no phone, www.arsene50.be). Tram 81, 82 or bus 38, 60, 71. **Open** *Ticket booth* 12.30-5.30pm Tue-Sat. *Online* 2-5.30pm Tue-Sat. **Credit** AmEx, MC, V. **Map** p315 D4.

Venues

Beursschouwburg

20-28 rue Auguste Orts, Lower Town (02 550 03 50, www.beursschouwburg.be). Pré-métro Bourse. **Open** *Box office* 11am-6pm Tue-Fri. **Tickets** €12; €10 reductions. **No credit cards**. **Map** p315 C4.

The Beurs is a centre of excellence for modern cross-form art and performance. Its overall aesthetic is industrial and minimalist, providing an understated backdrop to its innovative and highly international programme. The bar – more like a nightclub, truth be told – opens at weekends for the arty party crowd, and is pulsing until late into the night. The roof terrace bar is also packed in the summer.

★ Kaaitheater

20 square Sainctelette, Lower Town (02 201 59 59, www.kaaitheater.be). Métro Yser. **Open** *Box office* 11am-6pm Mon-Fri; 1hr before curtain-up on performance days. **Tickets** €16; €12 reductions. **Credit** MC, V. **Map** p316 C1.

The art deco Kaai is one of Brussels' most invigorating performance spaces, and stands at the forefront of the avant-garde. It has a solid stable of visiting theatre and dance companies, including Forced Entertainment (UK), the Wooster Group (USA) and Toneelgroep (NL).

▶ *Forced Entertainment are also regulars at the Kunstenfestivaldesarts in May; see p229.*

★ Koninklijke Vlaamse Schouwburg

146 rue de Laeken, Lower Town (02 210 11 12, www.kvs.be). Métro Yser. **Open** *Box office* noon-6pm Tue-Sat; 1hr before curtain-up on performance days. **Tickets** €16; €10 reductions. **Credit** AmEx, DC, MC, V. **Map** p316 C2.

Known as the KVS, the Royal Flemish Theatre is one of the big subsidised houses providing serious theatre in Dutch. Productions range from

Beursschouwburg.

weirdly modern to firmly classical, with a sprinkling of guest productions from Belgium and Europe. There is a more experimental black box studio next door, the KVS Box.

Théâtre des Martyrs
22 place des Martyrs, Lower Town (02 223 32 08, www.theatredesmartyrs.be). Metro/pré-métro De Brouckère or Rogier. **Open** *Box office* 11am-6pm Tue-Fri; 2-6pm Sat. **Tickets** €14.50-€16.50; €9-€12.50 reductions. **Credit** DC, MC, V. **Map** p315 D3.
The fresh, modern interior in a classic townhouse is representative of the Martyrs, one of the city's most

exciting theatre spaces by a long chalk, and home to three resident companies. The production style is modern and resolutely French, with an emphasis on new takes on classic playwrights: Shakespeare, Chekhov, Molière and Duras. The studio space receives smaller visiting companies.

★ Théâtre National
111-115 boulevard Emile Jacqmain, Lower Town (02 203 53 03, www.theatrenational.be). Métro/pré-métro De Brouckère. **Open** *Box office* 11am-6pm Tue-Sat. **Tickets** €19; €9-€15 reductions. Some performances vary. **Credit** MC, V. **Map** p317 D2.

Meet the Locals The Visionary Director
The irrepressible Jo Dekmine shows no signs of slowing down.

Although he claims he's not a big fan of theatre, preferring the spectacle of a good old-fashioned show, Jo Dekmine embodies the spirit of theatricality. With a shock of grey hair, mischievous black eyes and a long scarf dangling dramatically around his neck, Dekmine oozes thespia.

Now in his 80th year, Dekmine has no intention of retiring from his position as director of the groundbreaking **Théâtre 140** (*see p226*), named after its address on avenue Plasky. He's been bringing colour, innovation, style and verve to this grey community hall-style building since 1963, and he still displays an intense curiosity and a lot more energy than most men half his age.

If anyone could have turned this uninspiring space into a hotbed of raw creativity it was Dekmine, aided by his long-term business partner Renée Paduwat. In 1963, Dekmine was asked if he had any ideas about how to best utilise a 500-seater meeting place. He began with a series of shows that developed into an eclectic repertoire of dance, music, theatre, spectacle and stand-up comedy – physical and innovative performances from home and abroad. Dekmine gave Pink Floyd a leg-up in the 1960s ('they always mixed rock music and a spectacular show'), while Yes, the Soft Machine, Ian Dury, Queen, Blondie, the Yardbirds and Frank Zappa have all played on Le 140's voluminous stage. Evergreen Dekmine was even close friends with the likes of Serge Gainsbourg and Jacques Brel.

Despite such an illustrious history, Dekmine refuses to live in the past, always looking forward and embracing innovation

and new ideas. Now a grandfather of four, he performed in literary cabaret in the early years, although these days he prefers to stay behind the scenes, pulling the strings. 'It's more exciting now than in the 1960s,' he says. 'We have 20 times more shows than when we began. Le 140 must be a living theatre and a part of life.'

ARTS & ENTERTAINMENT

Théâtre National. See p225.

The little Pocket Theatre was founded by Roger Domani in 1951, and originally opened its doors on the chaussée d'Ixelles until being demolished to make way for a shopping gallery. Since then it has sat in a small building in the Bois de la Cambre, which has been the making of it. The work is demanding and hard-hitting and always pushes limits, taking world politics as its starting point.

Théâtre du Rideau de Bruxelles

Palais des Beaux-Arts, 23 rue Ravenstein, Upper Town (02 507 83 61, www.rideaudebruxelles.be). Métro Gare Centrale or Parc. **Open** *Box office* 11am-7pm Mon-Sat. *Phone bookings* 9am-7pm Mon-Sat. **Tickets** €20; €10-€15 reductions. **Credit** AmEx, DC, MC, V. **Map** p317 E5.

The Rideau has been resident at the Palais since 1943, and is an integral part of the French-language theatre scene. It appeals to the middle-class, middle-brow set, with modern classics and safe costume dramas, but every now and then surprises with an eyebrow-lifting modern piece.

Théâtre Royal des Galeries

32 galerie de la Roi, Lower Town (02 512 04 07, www.theatredesgaleries.be). Métro Gare Centrale. **Open** *Box office* 11am-6pm Tue-Sat. **Tickets** €10-€27; €9-€21 reductions. **Credit** AmEx, DC, MC, V. **Map** p315 D4.

A theatre was first built here in 1847 as part of the glass-covered Galeries St-Hubert, but was pulled down (in true Brussels style) and rebuilt in the 1950s. This gem's claim to fame is that Magritte painted a fresco on the ceiling, though the powers-that-be couldn't cope with his strange spherical bells flying through the clouds, so they placed a vast glass-balled chandelier there instead. Today the theatre is perhaps best known for its New Year revue.

Théâtre Royal du Parc

3 rue de la Loi, Upper Town (02 505 30 30, www.theatreduparc.be). Métro Arts-Loi or Parc. **Open** *Box office* 11am-6pm daily. Closed weekends when theatre is dark. **Tickets** €5-€30; €2.50-€12.50 reductions. **Credit** MC, V. **Map** p317 F5.

This stunner was built as a playhouse for the rich in 1782, and has managed to hang on to its genteel audience ever since. Most of what is performed here is described as *comédie*, but this doesn't mean funny; even Eugene O'Neill's darkly compelling *Long Day's Journey Into Night* is described here as a *'comédie dramatique'*. Expect a healthy mix of classic and contemporary playwrights.

Théâtre de la Toison d'Or

396 galeries de la Toison d'Or, Ixelles (02 510 05 10, www.theatredelatoisondor.be). Métro Porte de Namur. **Open** *Box office* 10am-4pm Mon; 10am-6pm Tue-Fri; 2-6pm Sat. **Tickets** €21; €10-€19 reductions. **Credit** AmEx, MC, V. **Map** p319 E7.

It's important to remember that this isn't truly a national theatre as such, being that it serves only the French-speaking community. Nonetheless, this is one of Belgium's most important producing houses, and one of its most heavily subsidised. The National has found great success with a mix of classical, modern, satirical and youth theatre – all played out in the most beautiful performance spaces.

★ Théâtre 140

140 avenue Plasky, Schaerbeek (02 733 97 08, www.theatre140.be). Pré-métro Diamant or bus 29, 63. **Open** *Box office* noon-6pm Mon-Fri; performances Sat. **Tickets** €14; €8 reductions. **Credit** MC, V. **Map** p321 L3.

Jo Dekmine and Renée Paduwat run the 140, as they have done for decades; the 2010 season was the theatre's 47th. Forever seeking out the new and exciting, the programme includes physical and innovative theatre from home and abroad. The after-show bar is worth a visit in itself; all in all, a marvellous place. *See p225* **Meet the Locals**.

Théâtre de Poche

1a chemin de Gymnase, Ixelles (02 649 17 27, www.poche.be). Tram 23, 90, 93, 94. **Open** *Box office* 10am-5.30pm Mon-Sat. **Tickets** €15; €10-€12 reductions. **No credit cards. Map** p324 G14.

Wolubilis.

A magnet for camp, madcap comedy and revue – Offbeat takes on Eurovision, piss-takes of the sci-fi genre, irreverent stand-up comedy and café-theatre.

Théâtre du Toone

21 petite rue des Bouchers, Lower Town (02 511 71 37, www.toone.be). Métro/pré-métro De Brouckère. **Open** *Box office* noon-midnight Tue-Sun. **Tickets** €10; €7 reductions (Tue-Thur & matinées). **No credit cards. Map** p315 D4.
This tiny place has been going for generations. It is a world-famous, world-class marionette theatre with productions in Bruxellois dialect. The atmosphere balances out incomprehension, though you may be lucky enough to catch *Hamlet* in Brussels English.

Théâtre Varia

78 rue du Sceptre, Ixelles (02 640 82 58, www.varia.be). Bus 38, 60, 95, 96. **Open** *Box office* 1-7pm Tue-Fri. *Performances* 2.30-7pm Sat of performance. **Tickets** €17-€20; €10-€15 reductions. **Credit** MC, V. **Map** p322 H8.
Firmly French in nature, the Varia mixes up a programme of new writing (Belgian and Moroccan) with modern takes on Shakespeare in translation as well as a varied dance programme. It's a space that makes an effort to welcome everyone, and even has a babysitting service.

★ Wolubilis

251 avenue Paul Hymans, Woluwe-St-Lambert (02 761 60 30, www.wolubilis.be). Métro Roodebeek or bus 29, 45. **Open** *Box office* 10am-5pm Mon-Fri; from 7.30pm on performance nights. **Tickets** €14-€45; €8-€40 reductions. **Credit** MC, V.
It took Mayor George Désir more than 20 years to realise his dream for an arts centre in the heart of Woluwe-St-Lambert, a historically creative community long lacking a worthy venue for its performing artists. In March 2006, that dream finally took the monochromatic form of the white and wildly asymmetrical Wolubilis arts centre, featuring a 486-seat theatre with a convertible stage – well suited to its broad remit of drama, music, dance, film and rock concerts. Designed by A.2R.C, the agency responsible for the extension to the Théâtre de la Monnaie, the centre also hosts the Ateliers du Temps Libre creative workshops for adults and children. There's a chance to read and refuel at the unique Cook and Book foyer on the ground floor, and it's also possible to buy a combined ticket for a buffet and show.

DANCE

The only truly classical company is the **Royal Ballet of Flanders** (www.koninklijkballet vanvlaanderen.be), which produces ballet and musical theatre of outstanding quality. Look out, too, for a wealth of visiting ballet companies, both national and international.

For such a small country Belgium has produced an astonishing array of modern dance talents, who have triumphed on the global stage. The undisputed dancing queen is **Anne Teresa de Keersmaeker**, director of the **Rosas** (www.rosas.be) company, while **Sidi Larbi Cherakou** (*see below* **Inside Track**) is an extraordinary man.

Wim Vandekeybus and his company **Ultima Vez** (www.ultimavez.com) are renowned for harsh, startling imagery with no room for compromise, while **Alain Platel's**

INSIDE TRACK
LORD OF THE DANCE

Sidi Larbi Cherakou, an astonishingly inventive young Belgian choreographer of Moroccan descent, is a force to be reckoned with in modern dance. He made his name with C de la B (*see p228*), but has since gone on to conquer the world, collaborating with everyone from Akram Khan to a group of Shaolin monks. His new company, Eastman, is currently in residence at the Toneelhuis theatre (www.toneelhuis.be) in Antwerp.

ARTS & ENTERTAINMENT

Chapelle des Brigittines.

ARTS & ENTERTAINMENT

celebrated collective **Les Ballets C de la B** (www.lesballetscdelab.be) has made a splash on the global scene with its often surreal, boldly physical performances. Another influential company is **Charleroi Danses/ Plan K** (www.charleroi-danses.be), led by a quartet of artistic directors.

Venues

★ Chapelle des Brigittines

1 petite rue des Brigittines, Lower Town (02 506 43 00, www.brigittines.be). Bus 27, 48. **Open** *Box office* 10am-6pm Mon-Fri. **Tickets** €9; €6 reductions. **No credit cards. Map** p315 C6.
The Chapelle des Brigittines, by the abandoned railway station of Bruxelles-Chapelle, is an extraordinary multimedia space: a decommissioned church taken back to its bare arches and pillars with a modern glass extension. Known primarily as a dance venue and as the centre of a summer dance festival, it is also used for theatre and art installations.

Cirque Royal

81 rue de l'Enseignement, Upper Town (02 218 37 32, www.cirque-royal.org). Métro Madou. **Open** *Box office* 10.30am-6pm Mon-Sat. **Tickets** vary. **Credit** MC, V. **Map** p317 F4.
A vast theatre space, hosting the big international tours. Come here if you want to see the St Petersburg Ballet or the Chippendales. It is one of the few venues to offer a large stage and auditorium, making it a popular place on the rock music circuit.

★ Halles de Schaerbeek

22B rue Royale Ste-Marie, Schaerbeek (02 218 21 07, www.halles.be). Tram 25, 92, 94. **Open** *Box office* 2-6pm Mon-Fri. **Tickets** vary. **Credit** MC, V. **Map** p320 F1.
This magnificent ex-agricultural hall has become a key venue for art forms across the board. Visiting dance companies love it for the ease with which they can erect giant video screens and multiple stages, and experiment with the artist-audience relationship. An important cultural centre for the local community, it's also a major venue for rock concerts.
▶ *For more on the Halles, see p90.*

Kaaitheaterstudio's

81 rue du Notre-Dame du Sommeil, Lower Town (02 201 59 59, www.kaaitheater.be). Métro Ste-Catherine. **Open** *Box office* 11am-6pm Mon-Fri; 1hr before curtain-up on performance days. **Tickets** €16; €12 reductions. **Credit** MC, V. **Map** p316 A3.
The renowned studio complex of its bigger sister, the Kaaitheater (*see p224*), Kaaitheaterstudio's stages smaller theatre productions, as well as the more esoteric dance companies, in an intimate setting. Two Belgian companies are based here: Meg Stuart's Damaged Goods and Thomas Hauert's Cie Zoo, both with an international reputation.

Théâtre les Tanneurs

75 rue des Tanneurs, Lower Town (02 512 17 84, www.lestanneurs.be). Métro/pré-métro Porte de Hal or Gare du Midi or bus 20, 48. **Open** *Box office* 10am-1pm, 2-6pm Mon-Fri; 2-6pm Sat; 1hr before performance. **Tickets** €10; €7.50 reductions. **No credit cards. Map** p318 B7.
Situated in the heart of the Marolles, Les Tanneurs has won the support of a loyal local crowd, thanks to its radical approach to theatre and dance, and its community-focused workshops and projects.

CLASSES & INSTITUTES

Maison du Spectacle – La Bellone

46 rue de Flandre, Lower Town (02 513 33 33, www.bellone.be). Métro Ste-Catherine. **Open** 10am-6pm Mon-Fri. **Map** p315 B3.
This essential reference point for theatre and dance enthusiasts includes an archive and library, and accommodates a number of government-supported arts organisations.

Vlaams Theater Instituut

19 place Sainctelette, Lower Town (02 201 09 06, www.vti.be). Métro Yser. **Open** 10am-6pm Mon-Fri. **Map** p316 C1.
The Flemish Theatre Institute is the resource centre for Flemish drama in Belgium. An archive, a library, study centre and a centre of research, the institute is regarded as the pulse of the Flemish theatre arts, including dance. It also publishes books and articles.

What's in a Name?

The festival that brings Flemish and French together.

The wackily named **Kunstenfestivaldesarts** (www.kfda.be) has method in its madness. Known simply as the KFDA, it started up in 1992 when festival director Frie Leysen decided to launch a performing arts festival to cross the language divide in Brussels. Thus the name, *Kunsten Festival* in Dutch and *Festival des Arts* in French – all melded together in a melting pot of a moniker.

Leysen succeeded: to this day, the KFDA remains the only major arts festival in Belgium where the two language communities truly work together. Now under the leadership of Christophe Slagmuylder, the KFDA co-produces around 30 international projects each year, including theatre, dance and visual art. For three weeks each May the city is taken over by the festival, which is regarded as one of the most innovative and progressive in Europe – and arts companies are knocking hard on the door to gain admittance and be part of its creative process.

Urbanism is at the heart of the KFDA experience, which offers a cosmopolitan take on how we see the world and the stories we tell to better understand our place in it. Two British companies have been festival favourites over the years: Sheffield's brilliantly experimental, boundary-breaking Forced Entertainment, and Brighton-based Lone Twin, who in 2010 presented their internationally successful *Catastrophe Trilogy* here.

As an audience member, you'll have a ball. On average, tickets are priced at around €15, and a festival pass (€130) will afford you entry to the entire programme. And the fun doesn't end when the curtain comes down, with guest DJs playing in the festival hub at the Beursschouwburg (*see p224*) until the early hours.

ARTS & ENTERTAINMENT

Time Out

timeout.com/travel
Get the local experience

Spectacular interior in the Hotel Diagonal lobby, **Barcelona**

Escapes & Excursions

Rozenhoedkaai, Bruges. *See p259.*

Antwerp

A sparkling mix of hot nightlife, hip design and huge diamonds.

Antwerp is an enigmatic place that effortlessly fuses history with red-hot fashion, cutting-edge culture and irrepressible style. This is not just a European hotspot, but rather a world heritage city of global influence and significance. At the same time Antwerp's old town is compact and manageable, defying the fact that this is Flanders' largest metropolis.

The town developed as a significant trading port in the 12th century. As the rival port of Bruges slowly silted up and the Flemish textile industry flourished, so Antwerp boomed. By the mid 16th century, it was the leading trading centre in Europe, with a population of 100,000 and a large diamond industry – set up by Jews escaping Portugal – bringing along magnificent wealth. It was a time of great cultural prestige, with new architecture reflecting the city's new status, and a raft of artists made it their home, Peter Paul Rubens (*see p239* **Rubenesque Antwerp**) and Anthony van Dyck among them.

see p239

This era of prosperity came to a savage end with the Reformation and subsequent religious riots and repression. By 1589, the population had shrunk to 42,000; the death blow was dealt by the Treaty of Munster in 1648, closing off the River Scheldt to shipping. The Industrial Revolution saw Antwerp again prosper, to the extent that it ranked as the world's third largest port at the end of the 19th century. The hosting of the World Fairs in 1885, 1894 and 1930, as well as the Olympic Games in 1920, confirmed the city's global status. Although Antwerp suffered badly during the two world wars and the interim slump, it recovered in the 1990s.

ANTWERP TODAY

Today sees Antwerp's second golden age as it positions itself as a world-class city. There's still a huge diamond business; Antwerp is the world's hub for the uncut diamond industry. And, needless to say, its rich artistic and cultural heritage is evident in the historic centre and numerous museums. The southern side, 't Zuid, around the **Fine Arts** and **Contemporary Art Museums**, is scattered with galleries and new nightclubs, restaurants and bars. To the north, the older Bonaparte dock area has an urban, bohemian air to it, as

bars vie for space with lofts, especially in the ever-ongoing renovation of the 't Eilandje quarter. The dock – built between 1853 and 1860 – is well worth exploring on foot; look out for the noted Kattendijksluis, the old sluice gate linking the dock to the river. Here you'll also find the Theater 't Eilandje, home of the **Royal Ballet of Flanders** (Westkaai 16, www.koninklijkballetvanvlaanderen.be).

Elsewhere, civil projects that ripped up the city for years are complete. The major ring roads have been rebuilt and the law courts (**Justitiepaleis**), designed by Richard Rogers, are fully functioning. In the grand old station, a new underground track now allows Antwerp

INSIDE TRACK
WHAT'S IN A NAME?

Popular legend says that Antwerp's name came from a giant called Antigoon who lived near the River Scheldt. But scholars have come up with a more likely origin – the Latin word *antiverpia*, meaning something to do with stopping sedimentation. Alas, not quite as interesting as the giant.

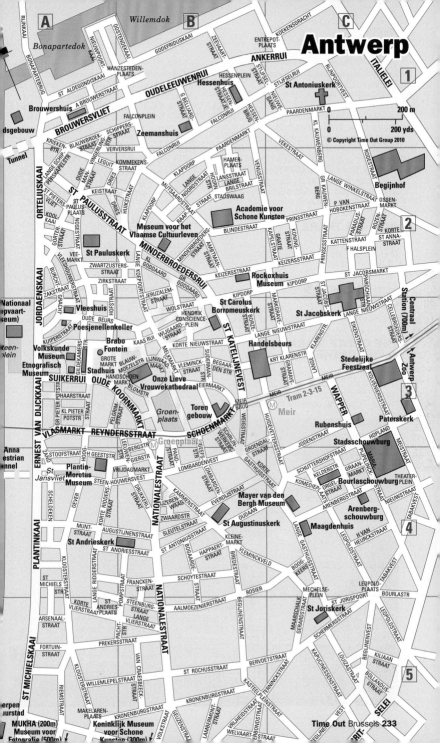

to link to Amsterdam, Brussels, Cologne and
Paris – there's even talk of trains running to
London in the future.

Then there's Antwerp's timelessness. This
is a city made for walking – no hills, streetloads
of pedestrianised areas and the air ringing with
bicycle bells. The **tourist office** (*see p243*)
sells maps for themed walks: architecture,
Rubens and fashion. Antwerp's nightlife is
among the best in northern Europe and attracts
clubbers from afar (*see p249* **Hedonistic
Antwerp**); more come for the summer arts
festival, **Zomer van Antwerpen** (June-Aug,
www.zva.be), with music, theatre and circus.

GETTING THERE

Three to four trains an hour shuttle between
Brussels and Antwerp, a 40-minute journey.

Sightseeing

Note that all museums are closed on Mondays,
and many have free admission on Fridays.

THE GROTE MARKT
& THE CATHEDRAL

Antwerp's historical centre clusters around the
lovely **Grote Markt**, with its charmingly
ornate guildhouses and 16th-century **Stadhuis**
(Town Hall). In the centre of the market square

is a 19th-century statue of Brabo, symbol of the
city. According to legend, a giant called Druon
Antigon cut off the hand of any sailor who was
unable to pay the toll for sailing on the River
Scheldt. The giant was eventually defeated by a
Roman, Silvius Brabo, who then became Duke
of Brabant. The legend curiously fits the name
of the city: with only slight alteration, Antwerp
translates as 'hand throwing' in Dutch.

The stunning 14th-century **Onze Lieve
Vrouwekathedraal** (Our Lady's Cathedral),
the largest Gothic church in Belgium, is just off
the square. The cathedral was planned to be one
of the largest in Europe, but fires, iconoclastic
fury and damage at the time of the French
Revolution resulted in the destruction of many
of its original features. A 25-year renovation
restored much of the original splendour, and
the white, light-filled interior now gleams.

The cathedral is home to a collection of
paintings and sculpture, the most celebrated of
which are by Rubens (*see p239* **Rubenesque
Antwerp**). Here you'll find four of his works:
The Raising of the Cross; *The Descent from the
Cross*; *The Resurrection*; and *The Assumption*.
The latter is set directly over the altar and may
only be viewed at a distance. Its dynamism and
dazzling colours are self-evident, but it is very
difficult to appreciate the fine details. The
other paintings are somewhat more dramatic.
The Raising of the Cross is a rich, emotional
work, although *The Descent from the Cross*
is considered the real masterpiece among them.

Grote Markt.

Designer Antwerp

The joy of Six.

The Antwerp Six designers who took the 1987 London Fashion Week by storm all still live or work in the city. They remain at the cutting edge of Belgian fashion – which in turn leads the way in Europe.

Ann Demeulemeester lives in Antwerp with photographer husband Patrick Robyn and runs a shop near the Fine Arts Museum in which her romantic, unashamedly sensuous designs speak for themselves (*see p251*). Elsewhere, bald and bearded **Walter van Beirendonck** now looks more like an ageing member of ZZ Top than an enfant terrible of the Six, designing clothes inspired by nature and technology and teaching at the Royal Academy. To showcase his own creations and those of selected friends, he runs **Walter** (*see p252*), an old garage transformed into something resembling a gallery installation. **Dries van Noten** sells his designs at **Het Modepaleis** (*see p252*).

The Six are well documented in the city's fashion museum **MoMu** (*see p242*), which showcases textile and costume collections dating from the 16th century to the present day. But while these skilled hands still lead the way, a second wave has appeared in recent years and seems to be bringing up the rear with gusto.

Martin Margiela graduated a year after the others and could almost be thought of as Antwerp's number seven. The media-shy but always daring designer now works in Paris at his own Maison Martin Margiela. Fellow student **Lieve van Gorp**, meanwhile, started her own label in the 1990s with a leather accessories collection consisting of belts and bags, while **Veronique Branquinho** and Brussels' **Olivier Theyskens** took over on the global circuit as part of the city's new generation. Branquinho opened her Antwerp flagship store in 2003 and is now teaching fashion studies in Vienna. Theyskens, for his part, is the glamorous dark prince of Belgian goth fashion; he recently dressed Madonna for the red carpet and spruced up the middle-aged **Rochas** fashion house in Paris. **Bruno Pieters** was one of Antwerp's star graduates and went straight to work as an assistant for the likes of Martin Margiela, Josephus Thimister and Christian Lacroix Haute Couture. Pieters has set out on his own with shoes, handbags, jewellery and a menswear collection.

And so it's to the future we must now look. Names that are making the pundits sit up are **Six Lee** who wowed with a conceptual menswear range in 2009; **Alexandra Verschueren** who models exquisitely detailed outfits as if made by origami; and **Léa Dickely**, a recent graduate from the Royal Academy for Fine Arts, who has made an impact with soft silhouettes and sheer, draped fabrics in greys and smokes. One thing's for sure, Antwerp is still turning out the catwalk stars of the future.

MoMu.

SEE MORE. BE MORE.

This is NEW YORK CITY

Book Now. Get More.

Glimpses of an earlier 13th-century church can be seen beneath the choir. Outside, the single spire rises 123 metres (404 feet) and would have been flanked by a twin had the money not dried up.

★ Onze Lieve Vrouwekathedraal

Handschoenmarkt (03 213 99 51, www. dekathedraal.be). **Open** 10am-5pm Mon-Fri; 10am-3pm Sat; 1-4pm Sun. **Admission** €5; free under-12s. **No credit cards. Map** p233 B3.

WEST OF THE GROTE MARKT

To the north-west of the Grote Markt, a walk along Vleeshouwersstraat, is the **Vleeshuis** (Butcher's Hall), built as a guildhouse and meat market by the Butchers' Guild in 1503. It's a puzzling construction, in late Gothic style with little turrets and walls that alternate red brick with white stone. Today the hall is used as a museum of musical instruments, representing 600 years of Antwerp's musical history. It also holds early music concerts. Much of the area in the immediate vicinity has been renovated, but the style of these new houses is insipid. The intention must have been to build in a manner that would not be at odds with the medieval and Renaissance architecture nearby; the policy is sound, but the end result makes you wish the authorities had gone for something more daring. South of here, behind the Stadhuis, is the **Volkskunde Museum** (Folk Museum).

A minute's walk west brings you around to the Scheldt and the **Steen**. This bulky castle once guarded the river and now houses the **Nationaal Scheepvaartmuseum** (National Maritime Museum). The Steen is almost as old as Antwerp itself and has thus become a noted symbol of the city. Built in 1200, it was part of the fortifications; later it served as a prison where inmates had to pay the guards for their stay – this meant that the wealthier prisoners lived in better conditions than the poorer ones, regardless of their crimes. For a while it also served as a sawmill before being turned into a museum. Today you'll find an endearingly old-fashioned collection of maps, maritime objects and countless model ships. Of more general interest are the old photos of Antwerp dock life with labelling in English. Real ships, meanwhile, can be found in the outdoor section. Spacious terraces by the castle allow for a quiet drink and a pleasant stroll by the Scheldt.

Steen (Nationaal Scheepvaartmuseum)

1 Steenplein (03 201 93 40). **Open** 10am-5pm Tue-Sun. **Admission** €4; €3 reductions; free under-19s. **No credit cards. Map** p233 A3.

Onze Lieve Vrouwekathedraal.

Vleeshuis

38-40 Vleeshouwersstraat (03 233 64 04, http://museum.antwerpen.be/vleeshuis). **Open** 10am-5pm Tue-Sun. **Admission** €5; €3 reductions; free under-19s & last Wed of mth. **No credit cards. Map** p233 A3.

Volkskunde Museum

2-6 Gildekamerstraat (03 220 86 66, http://museum.antwerpen.be/volkskunde). **Open** 10am-5pm Tue-Sun. **Admission** €3; €2 reductions; free under-19s. **No credit cards. Map** p233 A3.

NORTH OF THE GROTE MARKT

Between the Vleeshuis and the Napoleon Docks, near Verversrui, is what remains of the red-light district. Perhaps because it is so close to the historic centre, many prostitutes have been persuaded to move elsewhere. This seems a little harsh, especially seeing as many women working in the red-light district helped save rare paintings when fire broke out in 1968 in **St Paulskerk** (03 232 32 67, open May-Sept 2-5pm daily, admission free). St Paulus's 16th-century exterior is in flamboyant Gothic style and is crowned with a late 17th-century Baroque belltower. The Baroque interior contains Flemish masters (Rubens, Jacob Jordaens and Van Dyck) and carved wood panelling; there's also a treasure room. The church stands on a lively square – not as neat, perhaps, as others in the centre, but somehow more integrated into city life.

North are the docks, built under Napoleon in the early 1800s and now an upmarket area with inner-city loft living. You can get a fair picture of what the port must have been like then or take a boat around it, further north. The **Hessenhuis**, a 16th-century storehouse, is a complex devoted to social history, design and architecture. In typical Antwerp style, it also has a gay café and nightclub (*see p248*).

Hessenhuis

53 Falconrui (03 206 03 50, http://museum. antwerpen.be/Hessenhuis). **Open** *Exhibitions* 10am-5pm Tue-Sun. **Admission** varies. **No credit cards**. **Map** p233 B1.

EAST OF THE GROTE MARKT

The narrow and tortuous streets behind the cathedral emerge at the Baroque church of **St Carolus Borromeuskerk** (03 231 37 51; see schedule by door for opening times) on Hendrik Conscienceplein. On one side of this square – one of the prettiest in the city – stands the church itself; opposite is the old city library. Built for the Jesuits in the early 17th century, St Carolus is an exuberant, frothy monument to baroque excess. The façade is elaborate and ornate, with many columns and statues. Rubens produced 39 widely praised ceiling paintings and three altarpieces for the church, only for the lot to go up in smoke during a fire in 1718. Close by is the lovely **Rockoxhuis Museum**. Mayor Nicolaas Rockox was a friend of Rubens and his 17th-century townhouse is filled with period furnishings. It's more a gallery than a re-created home, though, and the main attraction is the small but perfectly formed art collection, which includes works by Matsys, Van Dyck and local boys Joachim Beuckelaer and Frans Snyders (who lived right next door). Further north is the classical **Koninklijke Academie voor Schone Kunsten** (Royal Academy of Fine Arts). It was the fashion department here that formed the driving force behind the original Antwerp Six, who famously took London Fashion Week by storm in 1987 (*see p235* **Designer Antwerp**). While it's very much a place of learning, the building and its extensive library are well worth a visit.

East of here on Lange Nieuwstraat is the fine **St Jacobskerk**. From a distance, this church looks impressive, but the closer you get the more it seems to diminish. Little houses completely surround it, only just making space for the main and side entrances. The interior is decorated in a heavy Baroque style, reflecting the fact that this was a wealthy district of

Antwerp, and the parishioners made sure the church reflected their status. It is as Rubens' burial place that St Jacob's is most well known. The artist painted the work that hangs over his tomb, *Our Lady Surrounded by Saints*, specifically for this purpose. St George is believed to be a self-portrait and the Virgin a portrait of Isabella Brant, Rubens' first wife. Mary Magdalene, meanwhile, is a portrait of Hélène Fourment, his second wife.

Not far south of the church is one of the city's major tourist draws, the **Rubenshuis**, home to the artist for most of his life. He bought it in 1611, following his return from Italy, and soon after being appointed city painter by Archduke Albrecht and Isabella. It's wise to come early to avoid the large tour parties; speed through the ugly modern ticket office outside the house itself and plunge into the wonderful interior. This is one of the most notable Baroque buildings in Antwerp, which in Rubens' time, much to his regret, was mainly Gothic. The house passed through several owners before the city of Antwerp bought it; it has since been completely renovated and the garden entirely reconstructed. Much of the furniture dates from the 17th century but was not originally in the house. Highlights include the semicircular gallery (based on the Pantheon in Rome) where Rubens displayed his vast collection of classical sculpture, and his spacious studio, overlooked by a mezzanine, where his own work could be admired by potential buyers.

Rubens was an exceptionally prolific painter (producing around 2,500 works), mainly because he didn't do all the painting himself. Canvases were mass-produced by diligent staff in his workshop; Rubens would then be on hand to direct proceedings and add the necessary key brushstrokes. With pupils such as Jordaens and Van Dyck, Rubens could clearly afford to limit the extent of his contribution to mere attentive supervision. The only real disappointment in the house is that there aren't more of Rubens' paintings out on display. Do look out, though, for an endearing self-portrait (c1630) and a later, more anxious-looking one of him in the studio.

Koninklijke Academie voor Schone Kunsten

31 Mutsaardstraat (03 213 71 00, www.artesis. be/academie). **Open** *Library* 10am-5pm Mon-Wed, Fri; 10am-6pm Thur. **Admission** free. **No credit cards**. **Map** p233 B2.

Rockoxhuis Museum

12 Keizerstraat (03 201 92 50, www.rockoxhuis. be). **Open** 10am-5pm Tue-Sun. **Admission** €2.50; €1.25 reductions; free under-19s & last Wed of mth. **No credit cards**. **Map** p233 B2.

★ Rubenshuis
9-11 Wapper (03 201 15 55, www.rubenshuis.be).
Open 10am-5pm Tue-Sun. **Admission** €6; €4
reductions; free under-19s & last Wed of mth.
No credit cards. **Map** p233 C3.

St Jacobskerk
*73 Lange Nieuwstraat (03 232 10 32,
www.topa.be/sint-jacobskerk).* **Open** *Apr-
Oct* 2-5pm Mon, Wed-Sun. *Nov-Mar* 9am-
noon Mon-Sat. **Admission** €2; €1.50
reductions; free under-12s. **No credit
cards**. **Map** p233 C2/3.

SOUTH OF THE GROTE MARKT

The south side of Antwerp is both home to the
city's older residential districts and contains
many of its best museums. A few minutes' walk
south of the Grote Markt is the Vrijdagmarkt;
each Friday bailiffs come here to auction off
debtors' seized goods. That aside, the square
is lined with idiosyncratic cafés as well as the
Museum Plantin-Moretus, home of printing
pioneer Christophe Plantin. Legend has it that
French-born bookbinder Plantin was injured in
a brawl in 1555 and, with the hush money he

Rubenesque Antwerp

Discover the city's most famous son.

As Da Vinci is to Florence and Warhol is
to New York, so Rubens is to Antwerp.
The Baroque master not only made the city
his home, he also made it his studio and
gallery, creating his major works here and
then hanging them in various churches and
private houses. He was a true celebrity
of his time; an artist, writer and diplomat
commissioned by royals and 17th-century
fat cats. The relationship between city and
man was symbiotic, an interdependence
that continues to this day.

Rubens is visible throughout Antwerp.
You can see 21 of his major oils and
sketches in the **Koninklijk Museum voor
Schone Kunsten** (*see p241*), including *The
Adoration of the Magi*, but it's also possible
to admire his paintings in the very churches
for which they were commissioned, their

scale and subject matter made to measure
for the space. The **Rubenshuis** (*see above;
pictured*), is a living memorial to the man
and his life, while his private tomb in
St Jacobskerk (*see above*) is overlooked
by his own *Mary Surrounded by Saints*.

You can follow in Rubens' footsteps and
discover the extent to which he influenced
the city and helped it flourish at the height
of its powers. A walking guide, **Rediscover
Rubens in Antwerp**, is available from the
tourist office and leads you around the
streets, alleyways and churches where the
great artist lived and worked – seeing the
paintings in situ is truly inspiring. While
Rubens has become an international
commodity, Antwerp can rest assured that
the city's most cherished son will never
truly leave home.

ESCAPES & EXCURSIONS

MoMu.

was paid, bought a printing press. The business he was to build in this immense 16th-century house became the single largest printing and publishing concern in the Low Countries (with 22 presses), as well as a magnet for intellectuals. Plantin printed many of the greatest works of his day, including an eight-volume polyglot Bible. Here you can discover all the intricacies of printing, with tours of the huge presses, a beautiful proofreading room and a foundry. There are also maps by Mercator (the famous cartographer, a contemporary of Plantin's, was born in nearby Rupelmonde), Plantin's Biblia Regia, one of the rare Gutenberg Bibles and other invaluable manuscripts. When Plantin died in 1579 the business was taken over by his son-in-law Jan Moretus and run by his family until 1865, when the city authorities bought it. In 1877, they converted it into a museum.

Equally enjoyable is the idiosyncratic **Mayer van den Bergh Museum**. A worthwhile five minutes' walk south-east from the centre, this thoroughly engaging display of the private art collection of Fritz Mayer van den Bergh is housed in a re-created 16th-century townhouse. Purpose-built in 1904 by Mayer van den Bergh's mother after the early death of her son aged 33, this immensely charming place boasts as its most prized exhibit Pieter Bruegel the Elder's astonishing *Dulle Griet* ('Mad Meg'), a Bosch-like allegory of a world turned upside down. Look out also for a hugely powerful crucifixion triptych by Quentin Matsys, works by Bouts, Van Orley, Cranach and Mostaert, plus some beautiful 15th-century carved wooden angels.

Further along, the **Maagdenhuis** is an old foundling hospital containing modest displays of art and medieval porridge bowls.

The city's major museums are a short walk further south (or tram No.8 from Groenplaats). It's a journey that art-lovers should make, especially to the **Koninklijk Museum voor Schone Kunsten** (Royal Museum of Fine Arts), the focal point of southern Antwerp. This outstanding museum, featuring Flemish painting from 1350 to the present day, is best known for its collection of Flemish Primitives and works from Antwerp's Golden Age. The Primitives include Rogier van der Weyden, Hans Memling and Jan van Eyck, whose improvements to oil painting techniques can be seen with his own unfinished picture of St Barbara. The most stunning section is the one devoted to the 17th century, with paintings by Rubens, Jordaens and Van Dyck. The Rubens works are mostly religious, with *Venus Frigida* the only notable exception; Jordaens' compositions are far less dramatic but his range of subjects more varied, such as his famous

As the Old Sang, the Young Play Pipes; Van Dyck's work is less flamboyant than either, as seen with *Portrait of the Painter Marten Pepyn*. The museum also has a large collection of paintings by James Ensor, the surrealists and the CoBrA artists.

Antwerp has a brash, optimistic attitude towards encouraging new artistic talent. The high-profile contemporary art museum **MUHKA** (Museum voor Hedendaagse Kunst van Antwerpen) displays works from the 1970s onwards. The focus is firmly on temporary exhibitions, and the strength of the museum lies in the way in which space is used in the light-flooded, mostly white-painted rooms. The result is a relaxed atmosphere, ideal for contemplating works that are not always otherwise accessible.

Meanwhile, fashion followers will adore **MoMu**, the design museum, located in the beautiful late 19th-century ModeNatie complex (www.modenatie.com). The building is home to the Flanders Fashion Institute and the fashion department of the Royal Academy of Fine Arts, as well as a trendy café-restaurant, library and workshops – but the big attraction for most visitors is MoMu. Contemporary fashion and a historic costume and lace collection are the highlights, while the overall aim is to make the museum a living space, where processes are as important as the finished product, and where fashion and design are put into a social context. The collection is being photographed and catalogued, making it available as a public archive in the museum library.

Photography buffs, meanwhile, should head to the **Museum voor Fotografie**. The latest addition, a wing designed by architect Georges Baines, contains large exhibition halls and houses the Antwerp Film Museum. The museum's photography collection is one of Europe's most important, taking an interactive approach with workshops, temporary exhibitions, film performances and lectures – plus there's a great café.

★ Koninklijk Museum voor Schone Kunsten

1-9 Leopold de Waelplaats (03 238 78 09, www.kmska.be). **Open** 10am-5pm Tue-Sat; 10am-6pm Sun. **Admission** €6; €4 reductions; free under-19s & last Wed of mth. **No credit cards**.

Maagdenhuis

33 Lange Gasthuisstraat (03 223 53 20). **Open** 10am-5pm Mon, Wed-Fri; 1-5pm Sat, Sun. **Admission** €3; free under-19s. **No credit cards. Map** p233 C4.

Mayer van den Bergh Museum

19 Lange Gasthuisstraat (03 232 42 37, http://museum.antwerpen.be/mayervandenbergh).

ESCAPES & EXCURSIONS

Diamond district.

ESCAPES & EXCURSIONS

Open 10am-5pm Tue-Sun. **Admission** €4; €2 reductions; free under-19s. **Credit** MC, V. **Map** p233 C4.

★ MoMu

28 Nationalestraat (03 470 27 70, www.momu. be). **Open** 10am-6pm Tue-Sun. **Admission** €6; €1-€4 reductions; free under-12s. **No credit cards**. **Map** p233 B4.

MUHKA

16-30 Leuvenstraat (03 260 99 99, www.muhka.be). **Open** 11am-6pm Tue, Wed, Fri-Sun; 11am-9pm Thur. **Admission** €5; €4 reductions; free under-13s. **Credit** V.

Museum voor Fotografie

47 Waalsekaai (03 242 93 00, www.foto museum.be). **Open** 10am-5pm Tue-Sun. **Admission** free. **No credit cards**.

Museum Plantin-Moretus

22 Vrijdagmarkt (03 221 14 50, http:// museum.antwerpen.be/plantin_moretus). **Open** 10am-5pm Tue-Sun. **Admission** €6; €1-€4 reductions; free under-18s. **No credit cards**. **Map** p233 A4.

THE LEFT BANK

South of the Steen, in St Jansvliet, you'll find the entrance to the 600-metre (1,969-foot) **St Anna pedestrian tunnel**, which connects the right and left banks. Wooden escalators take you underground from the art deco bulkhead, then it's a ten-minute walk to the other side of the river and a great view of the Antwerp skyline. Antwerp was built mainly on the right bank of the Scheldt and consequently the left bank isn't too lively. Architect Le Corbusier had a plan to move the administrative buildings to the left bank, thinking that this was the only way in which it might have a real chance to develop, but the project was turned down. Nevertheless, the left bank can claim the only beach in Antwerp, the **St Anna Strand**. Despite the reappearance of fish in the river, it is still considered unsafe to swim in the Scheldt. The beach is a good 15 minutes' walk north once you reach the west bank.

CENTRAAL STATION, THE DIAMOND DISTRICT & THE MEIR

Antwerp's striking **Centraal Station** is east of the centre. Built in 1905 by Louis Delacenserie in iron and glass, and featuring an impressive dome, majestic stairs and lashings of lavish gold decoration, it's a surprising and splendidly ostentatious construction. Inside it is a monument to classic and contemporary design. Next to the station is Antwerp's extensive **Zoo**, the biggest in Belgium and one of Europe's oldest (opened in 1843). The original architecture, needless to say, is more impressive than the animals' cramped living quarters.

West of Centraal Station is the **diamond district**, a predominantly Jewish area. The Diamantsbeurs in Pelikaanstraat is heavily guarded. The **Provinciaal Diamantmuseum**, on a square facing Centraal Station, has three floors of treasures. Visitors are taken on an interactive tour showing how rough diamonds become polished and end up as jewellery. The locality shines less than the stones in which it trades; there is a visible police presence.

The **Meir**, Antwerp's main shopping street, takes you from the station to the historic centre. Don't let the elaborate window displays cause you to miss some remarkable 19th-century buildings, such as the art deco **Boerentoren**, the first skyscraper in Europe. Just off the Meir, the **Handelsbeurs** (Stock Exchange) is on the site of one of the oldest stock exchanges in all of Europe. The original building was replaced in the 16th century; the current structure dates from 1872.

Further afield, it's well worth getting out to the truly splendid **Openlucht Museum voor Beeldhouwkunst Middelheim**. This open-air sculpture museum has works from Rodin to the present day, including Belgian artists Panamarenko and Vermeiren. It's about five kilometres from the city centre: city trams No.7 and No.15 stop a 15-minute walk short of it; buses No.18 and No.32 go closer, or it may be easier to take a taxi. The biennial summer exhibition of international sculpture here should not be missed.

Antwerp Zoo

26 Koningin Astridplein (03 202 45 40, www.zooantwerpen.be). **Open** *Jan, Feb, Nov, Dec* 10am-4.45pm daily. *Mar, Apr, Oct* 10am-5.30pm daily. *May, June, Sept* 10am-6pm daily. *July, Aug* 10am-7pm daily. **Admission** €19.50; €14.50 reductions; free under-3s. **Credit** AmEx, DC, MC, V.

Openlucht Museum voor Beeldhouwkunst Middelheim

61 Middelheimlaan (03 828 13 50, www.middelheimmuseum.be). **Open** *Oct-Mar* 10am-5pm Tue-Sun. *Apr, Sept* 10am-7pm Tue-Sun. *May, Aug* 10am-8pm Tue-Sun. *June, July* 10am-9pm Tue-Sun. **Admission** free. **No credit cards**.

Provinciaal Diamantmuseum

19-23 Koningin Astridplein (03 202 48 90, www.diamantmuseum.be). **Open** 10am-5.30pm daily. Closed Wed. **Admission** €6; €4 reductions; free under-12s. **Credit** MC, V.

TOURIST INFORMATION

For details of local churches, see www.topa.be.

Toerisme Antwerpen

13 Grote Markt (03 232 01 03, www.visit antwerpen.be). **Open** 9am-5.45pm Mon-Sat; 9am-4.45pm Sun. **Map** p233 A3.
Another branch of the tourist office can be found at Centraal Station.

ESCAPES & EXCURSIONS

Centraal Station.

HOTELS

Hotels are plentiful, but you need to book in summer. Rack rates for a standard double room are shown here; research or contact the tourist office for cheaper prices. Breakfast is included unless otherwise indicated.

Diamond Princess

2 St Laureiskaai (Bonapartedok), 2000 Antwerp (03 227 08 15, www.diamondprincess.be). **Rates** €87. **Credit** AmEx, DC, MC, V. **Map** p233 A1.
This five-deck 'boatel' has 57 luxuriously furnished en suite rooms. There's a restaurant, 'beach deck' (terrace), bar, library and disco.

★ Greta Stevens – Miller's Dream

35 Molenstraat, 2018 Antwerp (03 259 15 90/ http://users.pandora.be/molenaarsdroom). **Rates** €70-€110. **No credit cards**.
This beautiful colonial-style house is near the park, south of Britselei. Three stunning, spacious en suite B&B rooms are decorated with modern art.

Hilton

Groenplaats, 2000 Antwerp (03 204 12 12, www.hilton.com). **Rates** €350. Breakfast €25. **Credit** AmEx, DC, MC, V. **Map** p233 B3.
The Hilton offers the usual facilities and a range of extras, but in a stylish building with more charm than you might expect.

Hotel Prinse

63 Keizerstraat, 2000 Antwerp (03 226 40 50, www.hotelprinse.be). **Rates** €135. **Credit** V. **Map** p233 C2.
A 16th-century private house with a striking modern interior, lovely courtyard and 35 en suite rooms.

Hotel Villa Mozart

3 Handschoenmarkt, 2000 Antwerp (03 231 30 31). **Rates** €150. **Credit** AmEx, DC, MC, V. **Map** p233 A/B3.
The 25 luxury rooms and suites here, in the centre of the old town, are decorated in Laura Ashley style. Hotel services include a sauna and babysitting.

New International Youth Hostel

256 Provinciestraat, 2018 Antwerp (03 230 05 22, www.niyh.be). **Rates** €61. **Credit** (online bookings only) AmEx, MC, V.
A ten-minute walk south of the station, this hostel has only 30 rooms so booking is essential. Rooms are for one, two, four or eight people; six of the rooms have an en suite bathroom.

Radisson Blu Astrid

7 Koningin Astridplein, 2018 Antwerp (03 203 12 34, www.parkplaza.com). **Rates** €300. **Credit** AmEx, DC, MC, V.
It may appear to be made from Lego, but the Astrid's interior is much easier on the eye. Facilities include a pool, sauna and gym.

'T Sandt

17 Zand, 2000 Antwerp (03 232 93 90, www.hotel-sandt.be). **Rates** €180. **Credit** MC, V. **Map** p233 A4.
All rooms in this 19th-century building by the Scheldt are suites and very spacious; each is decorated in a different style. An Italianate garden and rooftop terrace bar are further attractions.

Vandepitte B&B

49 Britselei, 2000 Antwerp (03 288 66 95). **Rates** €70. **No credit cards**. **Map** p233 C5.
Its south Antwerp location is somewhat uninspiring and two of the three rooms are small (although one does have a bathroom to die for), but Vandepitte makes up for it with its show-stealing penthouse: black stone floors, views over Antwerp, a flash stereo, ethnic art and bags of space. The breakfast is equally impressive.

★ De Witte Lelie

16-18 Keizerstraat, 2000 Antwerp (03 226 19 66, www.dewittelelie.be). **Rates** €250. **Credit** AmEx, DC, MC, V. **Map** p233 C2.
The building may be 17th-century, but the interior is utterly contemporary. You can expect good-sized rooms, lashings of low-key luxury and a generous breakfast. Ten suites too.

Gay accommodation

b+b2000 Guesthouse

8 Van Boendalestraat, 2000 Antwerp (03 234 12 10, www.bb2000.be). **Rates** €59 double. **No credit cards**.
Friendly B&B in a period terraced house with good-sized, comfortable rooms and shared lounge areas.

G8 Gay Guesthouse

8 Geulincxstraat, 2060 Antwerp (mobile 0477 62 62 81, www.g8.be). **Rates** €60. **No credit cards**.
A no-nonsense bed-and-breakfast place catering more for the fetish-type crowd.

EATING & DRINKING

Restaurants

Amadeus

20 Sint-Paulusstraat (03 232 25 87, www.amadeusspareribrestaurant.be). **Open** 6.30-11pm Mon-Thur; 6-11pm Fri-Sun. **Main courses** €18. **Credit** AmEx, DC, MC, V. **Map** p233 A2.
This spare-rib restaurant, accommodated in an old art nouveau glass factory, has a USP. A litre of house red sits unceremoniously on the table at arrival – drink as much or as little as you like, you're

De Kleine Zavel. See p246.

charged only for the amount you quaff. Then there are the ribs, as many as you can eat with the accompaniment of your choice. No cutlery necessary.

De Broers van Julienne

45-47 Kasteelpleinstraat (03 232 02 03, www. debroersvanjulienne.be). **Open** noon-10pm Mon-Sat; 5.30-9pm Sun. **Main courses** €13. **Credit** MC, V. **Map** p233 C5.

There's a certain hush about this charming meat-free restaurant. It's all to do with the decor and reading-room atmosphere created in a calm colonial style, with a pretty garden under shady trees in summer. The food is prepared using natural and organic ingredients. A shop and bakery at the front are equally classy.

Ciro's

6 Amerikalei (03 238 11 47, www.ciros.be). **Open** 11am-11pm daily. **Main courses** €20. **Credit** MC, V.

Ciro's was last decorated in 1962 and as such seems to have gone full circle in its own retro way. The crowds come for the steak and chips, regarded as the best in Antwerp. New ownership has changed nothing, which is what everyone wants.

★ Désiré de Lille

14-18 Schrijnwerkerstraat (03 232 62 26, www. desiredelille.be). **Open** 9am-10pm daily. **Main courses** €13. **No credit cards**. **Map** p233 B3.

Désiré started off as a funfair stand, selling freshly made waffles, fruit-filled doughnuts and *laquemants*, a kind of baked pancake. It trades in a genteel 1930s restaurant, with big windows opening up to the street, its interior filled with banquettes and railway carriage lights. A glass pergola at the back gives a conservatory feel and leads to a magnificent garden.

Het Nieuwe Palinghuis

14 Sint-Jansvliet (03 231 74 45, www. hetnieuwepalinghuis.be). **Open** noon-3pm, 6-10pm Wed-Sun. **Main courses** €30. **Credit** MC, V. **Map** p233 A4.

Boating collectibles set the tone, the walls hung with prints of 19th-century Antwerpenaars fishing their cotton smocks off – even the loo seats have shells embedded in them. Fish is the order of the day – eel, scallops with truffles and naughty pot mussels in cream with garlic. Pricey but worth every penny.

Hippodroom

10 Leopold de Waelplaats (03 248 52 52, www.hippodroom.be). **Open** noon-2.30pm, 6-11pm Mon-Fri; 6-11pm Sat. **Main courses** €25. **Credit** AmEx, MC, V.

Hippodroom's long, slender dining room – complete with massive works of art and minimally set tables – contrasts perfectly with its turn-of-the-century exterior. Its confident aesthetic style extends to the menu: Iranian caviar, sushi, French-inspired fillet of lamb with truffle risotto, and vegetarian options.

Izumi

14 Beeldhouwersstraat (03 216 13 79, http://www2.resto.be/izumi). **Open** noon-2pm, 6.30-10.30pm Tue-Sat. **Main courses** €18. **Credit** AmEx, DC, MC, V.

Izumi has been nestling in its old Antwerp townhouse since 1978, and now has an unassailable reputation as the best Japanese restaurant in the city. Dutch chef-owner Ed Balke spent four years mastering the art of Japanese food preparation, and in 1999 teamed up with Takeati Kato, a sushi chef from Hiroshima. The result is pure Japanese culinary art, prepared in the time-honoured fashion and heavy on the fish and seafood: belly of tuna, fried eel with cucumber, squid, octopus, urchin, marinated seaweed, and full spreads of sushi, sashimi and teriyaki. If you find it difficult to choose from the carte, the range of set menus should make life easier.

★ De Kleine Zavel

2 Stoofstraat (03 231 96 91, www.kleinezavel.be). **Open** noon-2.30pm, 6-10.30pm Mon-Thur; noon-2pm, 6.30-11pm Fri; 6.30-11.30pm Sat; noon-2pm, 6-10.30pm Sun. **Main courses** €28. **Credit** AmEx, DC, MC, V. **Map** p233 A4.
Set in a long room among beer and wine crates, the KZ is one of Antwerp's dining hotspots, with chef-owner Carlo Didden serving up imaginative French- and Med-inspired food to a discerning yet unpretentious crowd. Rare meats, foie gras and wild mushrooms all find a place with style. *Photo p245.*

Lucy Chang

16-17 Marnixplaats (03 248 95 60, www.lucychang.be). **Open** noon-midnight daily. **Main courses** €13. **No credit cards**.
The first thing you see in here is an oriental market stall, to the right of which is a long, low bar. This is designed for those who want to pop in and just take a small plate of dim sum or a bowl of noodle soup. The food is from Laos, Vietnam, Thailand, Malaysia and China, and is designed as one-dish meals, where everything comes at once and can be shared.

Maritime

4 Suikerrui (03 233 07 58, www.maritime.be). **Open** noon-2.30pm, 6-9.30pm Mon, Tue, Fri-Sun. **Main courses** €28. **Credit** AmEx, DC, MC, V. **Map** p233 A3.
Maritime looks classically Belgian with its wooden beams, chi-chi chairs and red tablecloths. The food is equally classic, with a heavy leaning to eels and mussels – and not just eels in green sauce – try them in cream or fried in butter, or have a go at mussels in a Madras curry sauce. Lobster is popular too. All in all, the perfect spot for a fishy treat.

Het Pomphuis

Droogdok, 7 Siberiastraat (03 770 86 25, www.hetpomphuis.be). **Open** 11am-2.30pm; 6-11pm Mon-Fri; 11am-11pm Sat, Sun. **Main courses** €28. **Credit** AmEx, DC, MC, V.
This magnificent old building, the pumphouse for the dry dock, was converted back in 2003 into an equally magnificent restaurant. Massive arched windows and lofty ceilings surround crisply laid

tables. The menu is unusual for Antwerp, with dishes such as goats' cheese salad with dates, apples and beetroot syrup.

Sombat Thai Cuisine

1 Vleeshuisstraat (03 226 21 90, www.sombat.be). **Open** noon-2.30pm, 6-10.30pm Tue-Fri; 6-11pm Sat, Sun. **Main courses** €25. **Credit** AmEx, DC, MC, V. **Map** p233 A3.
Owner Sombat opened Les Larmes du Tigre in Brussels before setting up this expansive restaurant in the shadow of the Gothic Butcher's Hall. Mixed dishes are popular here, so spring rolls turn up with minced pork in a banana leaf, crispy noodles and dipping sauces. Regarded as Antwerp's finest Thai.

Zuiderterras

37 Ernest van Dijckkaai (03 234 12 75). **Open** 9am-midnight Mon-Thur; 9am-1am Fri-Sun & June-Aug. **Main courses** €28. **Credit** AmEx, MC, V. **Map** p233 A3.
It's worth walking along the quay just to get a look at this sleek, shiny building. The Bob van Reeth creation has a circular bar and a terrace looking over the river. The modern European menu (bouillabaisse with grilled focaccia) may be on the expensive side but it's a wonderful place to be at sunset.

Bars

The local beer is De Koninck (www.dekoninck.be) and is ubiquitous. Rather than asking for it

Het Pomphuis.

INSIDE TRACK ELIXIR OF LOVE

Locally made Elixir d'Anvers is a traditional digestif in Antwerp. First produced in 1863, it is distilled using pure alcohol and 32 different herbs. It may not be to everyone's taste, but it takes Antwerpenaars back to when they were young; grandma would often give a wee dram on a sugar cube.

by name, the locals simply request a *bolleke* (a ball-shaped glass) or a *fluitje*, a tall flute glass. Local gin, genever, comes in many flavours.

Bar Tabac

43 Waalsekaai (03 238 19 37, bartabac.be). **Open** 9pm-late Wed-Sun. **No credit cards**.
BT doesn't really start to shake its tail feather until gone midnight, when a superb soundtrack (from Madonna to Serge Gainsbourg via most points in between) complements an atmosphere rarely more than a couple of notches from cool. If you've had an evening of indistinct drinking in designer bars and were wondering exactly why Antwerp is hyped to the nines, breeze into the Bar Tabac, particularly on a Sunday night, and all will become clear.

Berlin

2 Kleine Markt (03 227 11 01). **Open** 8am-late Mon-Fri; 10am-late Sat, Sun. **Credit** AmEx, MC, V. **Map** p233 B4.
Dark and broody but with the utmost taste, Berlin has become something of an institution with singles, couples and families – a big play area at the back with tables for mum and dad to knock back the tequilas has made sure of that. Food is served throughout the day but watch out, evenings and weekend afternoons can be a bit of a scrum.

Café Beveren

2 Vlasmarkt (03 231 22 25). **Open** noon-late Mon, Thur-Sun. **No credit cards**. **Map** p233 A3.
This is your actual dockside Antwerp, the kind of spot you might find in Rotterdam or Hamburg, where age-mellowed regulars fumble with their reading glasses before another round of cards. The red-lined banquettes encase the café in a lost era – note also the fully working De Cap fairground organ and old Rowe Ami jukebox, and watch out for spontaneous outbreaks of old-time dancing.

Den Engel

5 Grote Markt (03 233 12 52, www.cafeden engel.be). **Open** 9am-late daily. **No credit cards**. **Map** p233 A3.
Antwerp's bar of all bars. It isn't fab or fashionable, and whatever edges it once cut blunted long ago; it is simply an institution, ramshackle relief from the

official goings-on next door at the Town Hall. Councillors clink glasses with nervous fiancés, journalists accept drinks and gossip from politicians, while locals of all ages provide a cheery backdrop. Next door's Den Bengel (the Miscreant) copes with the overflow from Den Engel (the Angel).

Entrepôt du Congo

42 Vlaamsekaai (03 257 16 48). **Open** 8am-3am Mon-Fri; 8am-4am Sat, Sun. **No credit cards**.
This pioneering enterprise began the regeneration of the southern quaysides into the trendy quarter of galleries and designer bars it is today. A century ago, Congo boats would dock here, unloading crates of colonial plunder into this grand corner edifice. Now a classy, bare wood-and-tile interior displays only one deference to decoration: a framed portrait of King Baudouin in postage-stamp humour over the bar. The place is still justifiably popular, despite a plethora of competition a mere anchor's toss away – perhaps it's the excellent bar food.

'T Oerwoud

2 Suikerrui (03 233 14 12). **Open** noon-late daily. **Credit** AmEx, MC, V. **Map** p233 A3.
A step back from the quayside, two steps from the brazen tourism of the town centre and opposite the medieval fortress of the Steen, 'T Oerwoud (the Jungle) is a relaxing lunch spot – salads, soups and pastas, many served until late – but also operates as a busy pre-club livener. Spotlights blaze over the curved bar, speakers boom with popular dance sounds, and the nachos machine and upholstered leather seating of the chill-and-chat back area soon become buried in a fug of Bastos.

De Pelikaan

14 Melkmarkt (03 227 23 51). **Open** 9am-late daily. **No credit cards**. **Map** p233 B3.
The downtown and ever downbeat Pelican has been dragging writers, designers and musicians through its doors and keeping them glued to its bar counter for longer than most care to remember. Set in the shadow of the cathedral, it makes no effort to appeal to curious passers-by, leaving the dressing up to tackier venues nearby. It isn't even dressed down: it's just got out of bed and put on whatever it could find on the bedroom floor, invariably the same as what it found there yesterday. Enter, drink, swap stories, get drunk, go home. Perfect. *Photo p248*.

De Vagant

25 Reyndersstraat (03 233 15 38, www. devagant.be). **Open** 11am-late Mon-Sat; noon-late Sun. **No credit cards**. **Map** p233 A/B3.
Genever was to Antwerp what gin was to London, the opiate of historic port cities drowned in a sea of cheap alcohol. Prohibition arrived in 1919 and wasn't repealed until 1984. This bar opened a year later, with 200 types of once-forbidden genever in

myriad strengths and flavours, accompanied by small chunks of cheese and deft slices of meat. Sipped and not slammed, genever boasts a proud history detailed on the drinks menu and celebrated in an exquisite interior of old flagons and pre-prohibition posters. Upstairs, a restaurant serves dishes concocted from the stuff.

Het Zand

9 Sint-Jansvliet (03 232 56 67). **Open** 11am-late daily. **No credit cards. Map** p233 A2.
Located by the grand entrance of the St Anna foot tunnel, Het Zand displays the calculating hand of the Celtic fraternity. Yet, despite the fading promise of a peeling Guinness gift shop sign, this is essentially a boozy hostelry in the classic Antwerp tradition. Het Zand is as close as you're ever likely to get to sitting in a pre-war Antwerp living room – with a bar attached. Wooden tables heave under heavy lunches, old geezers prop up the tall brick bar, while the unusual local tradition of displaying death masks of former regulars is upheld overhead.

Gay & lesbian bars & clubs

Antwerp is a gay mecca, with a few hotspots that even the Dutch cross the border for. See www.gay-antwerp.com for information. Unless stated, the venues below have no entry fee.
See also right **Hedonistic Antwerp**.

Atthis

27 Geuzenstraat (03 216 37 37, www.atthis.be). **Open** 8.30pm-2am Fri, Sat. **No credit cards. Map** p233 B5.

A women-only private club that's a little more refined than most in Belgium. There's a video library and a lesbian centre under the same name.

Boots

22 Van Aerdstraat (03 233 21 36, www.the-boots.com). **Open** 10.30pm-4am Fri; 10.30pm-5am Sat; 5-10pm Sun. **Admission** €7. **No credit cards.**
The great-grandaddy of Belgium's cruisy bars and probably the sleaziest to boot. Stairs lead up and up through a dark bar area into an even darker play area where anything that can happen is likely to happen. There is a strict dress code, but you can change on the premises. You'll also need ID to secure a temporary membership.

Hessenhuis

53 Falconrui (03 231 13 56, www.hessenhuis. com). **Open** 10.30am-late daily. **No credit cards. Map** p233 B1.
By day, Hessenhuis acts as a museum and art gallery (*see p238*), but at night it transforms itself into a popular pre-club destination, attracting townie gays and their female friends. The interior is a combination of modern and rustic, though the clientele is full-on chic, ready to party and enjoy the live entertainment or theme nights. Breakfast is served on Sundays.

Kinky's

10 Lange Beeldekensstraat (03 295 06 40, www.kinkys.be). **Open** 7pm-4am Mon; 2pm-3am Tue, Thur; 8pm-5am Fri; 6pm-5am Sat. **Admission** €7.50-€10.50. **No credit cards.**

De Pelikaan. *See p247.*

Hedonistic Antwerp

Stay fashionable after dark.

The reputation of Antwerp's nightlife comes from its status as a fashion capital, a gay centre and a city at ease with itself. Locals sashay from one spot to another in a bid to decide what's hot and what's not. Us mere mortals can try and keep up by checking **www.noctis.com** or dropping into urban shops like **Fish & Chips** (*see p251*) to pick up flyers.

A quick word about what to wear: only the more underground clubs will welcome skate shoes and baggy jeans; in the mainstream, it's always best to dress to impress. One exception is **Petrol** (21 d'Herbouvillekaai, 03 226 49 63, www.petrolclub.be), a laid-back place where funky house alternates with electronica, drum 'n' bass and reggae, and where people can be whatever they want.

A good nightlife starting point is the legendary **Café d'Anvers** (15 Verversrui, 03 226 38 70, www.cafe-d-anvers.com; *pictured*), which was a church and cinema before its transformation into a kicking club

in 1991. Expect progressive house from Thursday to Saturday, with resident DJs including local luminaries like DJs Isabel, Prinz and Bartholomeo.

Industria (10 Indiestraat, 03 234 09 92, www.clubindustria.be) is one of Antwerp's more sparkling sin bins. It's set in a beautiful old factory space with progressive house and funky soul, but be aware it closes in the summer. For one-off parties, it's a good idea to click on to **www.5voor12.com**, a production company that stages major club events throughout the country as well as irregular nights at **De Cinema** (12 Lang Brilstraat, 03 226 49 63, www.decinema.be). This particular venue accommodates **Couleur d'Anvers**, a night of African and black music.

As a fully fledged international hotspot, Antwerp is now also included on the tour circuit of various travelling superclubs, including **Sensation** (www.sensation-white.com), which calls into town every spring for a major party.

ESCAPES & EXCURSIONS

Located near the train station, Kinky's caters for a fetish crowd. Special themed parties mean special dress codes, so check the agenda before you go.

Oink Club
3 Van Schoonbekeplein (03 485 54 40, www.oink oinkbar.be). **Open** 9pm-3am Sun-Thur; 9pm-6am Fri, Sat. **No credit cards**.
The name says it all: in Oink's own words this is Antwerp's piggest fetish bar. It's also one of the biggest, with two floors of dark and mysterious spaces above the industrial-style bar.

Popi
12 Plantinkaai (03 238 15 30, www.popi.be). **Open** 2pm-late Mon-Fri; 11am-late Sat, Sun. **No credit cards**.

Brash, cheeky (its name refers to the Russian for backside) and impossibly pink, Popi doesn't take itself in the least bit seriously. Abba, Eurotrash and drag sum up the free-fall entertainment. Popi is almost ten years old, but it still doesn't know – or care – what it wants to be when it grows up.

★ Red & Blue
11-13 Lange Schipperskapelstraat (03 213 05 55, www.redandblue.be). **Open** 11pm-7am Sat & special nights. **Admission** €10 plus €2 membership. **Credit** AmEx, MC, V. **Map** p233 A2.
The name comes from the club's location in the old red-light district. The girls may have moved on, but the boys have arrived and plan to stay. Saturday's men-only night is regarded, along with Brussels' La Démence (*see p197*), as Belgium's best, with Dutch

dance divas pouring across the border (Fridays are mixed). More than a disco, R&B is an event – Grace Jones once drove through the sweaty dancers in a stretched limo. Serious party time.

GALLERIES

Antwerp's thriving contemporary art scene is conveniently centralised near the Waalsekaai, between the **Royal Museum of Fine Arts** and the **MUHKA**.

Micheline Szwajcer

14 Verlatstraat (03 237 11 27, www.gms.be). **Open** 10am-6pm Tue-Fri; noon-6pm Sat. Szwajcer represents some of Belgium's finest artists, from Guy Mees and Marthe Wery to the younger Ann Daems and David Claerbout.

Stella Lohaus

47 Vlaamsekaai (03 248 08 71, www.stella lohausgallery.com). **Open** 2-6pm Wed-Sat & by appt.

Offbeat Antwerp

Get off the main drag for some consumer chic.

For shoppers arriving by train, the walk into town from the station naturally draws you into the pedestrianised Meir, full of samey chain shops and cheap thrills. However, there's another way of getting around Antwerp that involves a bit of free spirit and dog-legging, but which also allows you to find shopping gems you may otherwise miss.

Just before you enter the Meir, turn left and you'll come to Hopland, a long street that runs parallel to the main drag. You can't miss No.47, a renovated old school building now home to **Donum** (*see p253*), an excruciatingly trendy interiors shop. On the other side of the road are some seriously classy little fashion stores, among them **Bruno Atognini**, **Le Chapeau** and **Bâton Rouge**. At the end of this block at No.2 is the incongruous glass box that is the **Grand Café Horta**, filled with original ironwork from Victor Horta's Maison du Peuple in Brussels. Left of this is Vogelenmarkt, with a fancy little food market (until 5pm Sat) and general market (until 1pm Sun).

If you then wind your way along the side of the Bourla theatre you'll pass the museum-like **Vrouyr**, a stunning shop selling antique and modern rugs (4 Kommedieplaats, www.vrouyr.com), before eventually coming to Korte Gasthuisstraat, a small, car-free street that is part of an area known as the *Wilde Zee* (*see also right*). This is where more discerning Antwerpenaars come for their food specialities. **Burie Confiserie** (No.41) has been around since 1920 and is truly a sweetshop of childhood dreams, while **Burie**'s chocolate shop at No.3 is another box of delights. **Goossens** (*see p252*) is reputed to be the best baker in Antwerp; if you want to buy a loaf or cake you'll have to

join the nattering queue on the street – just like the good old days. At No.11 is another Antwerp legend, **Philip's Biscuits** (*see p252*), selling snappy biccies by weight or in nifty packets. At the end of the street on the little square you'll see **Van Bladel** at No.25, a fresh fish merchant with a deli counter offering the likes of paella or dressed crab for a luxury takeaway lunch.

For bearings, remember that you're roughly following the route of the Meir and heading towards the river. Lombardenvest is a street dotted with one-off shops, the most endearing of them all being **Huis A. Boon** at No.4 (*see p252*), selling leather gloves (including made-to- measure) in an old shop lined with tiny drawers and mirrors from another age. Crossing Nationalestraat into Steenhouwersvest you'll hit another enclave of designer one-offs, including **Diane Von Furstenberg** at No.44.

At the other end of the scale but equally satisfying is **Episode** (No.24A), a sprawling warehouse of second-hand clothing perfect for a rummage. Right over the road at No.27 is **De Cognatheek**, a temple to fine brandy, selling that and nothing else and reeking of exclusivity as a direct result. By contrast, **Bazar Bizar** (No.18, www.bazar bizar.be) is a charming ethnic home furnishings shop smelling of incense. At No.24 is **Francis**, selling original furniture from the 1930s to the '50s – worth a look.

From here you have a choice. Either left into Kloosterstraat for random junk, **Nadine Wijnants**' jewellery shop (*see p252*) or **Chelsea** (No.10) for a dive into its second-hand vinyl (also pop along to **Cru**, 19 St Michaelstraat, for cheap and cheerful '60s gifts). Alternatively, turn right for the Grote Markt or Groenplaats and a well-deserved drink. Without realising it, you've walked miles.

ESCAPES & EXCURSIONS

For over a decade, this gallery has stood by countless top concept artists including Joelle Tuerlinckx, Sven't Jolle, Angel Vergar and Job Koelewijn.

Zeno X
16 Leopold de Waelplaats (03 216 16 26, www.zeno-x.com). **Open** 2-6pm Wed-Sat.
Zeno X puts on exhibitions from Belgium's Raoul De Keyser and Luc Tuymans, along with other equally acclaimed artists. The gallery has another site at 37 Appelstraat in Borghout.

SHOPPING

Antwerp's role as one of the world's most celebrated fashion hubs (*see p235* **Designer Antwerp**) has made it a clothes shopper's paradise. The main shopping drag with all the international chains is the **Meir**, the traffic-free stretch between the station and the city centre. **Huidevetterstraat** to the south is more upbeat with some one-off boutiques, and things start to get really interesting around **Schutterhofstraat**, home to chic bathroom shops, contemporary jewellers and various understated designer clothing stores. The avant-garde core is the warren of streets known as the *Wilde Zee* (Wild Sea). Here **Kammenstraat** is the place to go for upbeat streetwear and retro shops; **St Antoniusstraat** is where Walter van Beirendonck hangs out; and **Nationalestraat** is home to Dries van Noten's temple of fashion.

Antwerp also has a well-deserved reputation for its fine antiques and endlessly charming bric-a-brac shops, most of which can be found in the district of St Andries: head for **Lombardenvest**, **Steenhouwersvest** and **Kloosterstraat** (*see also left* **Offbeat Antwerp**).

Fashion & accessories

Ann Demeulemeester
Leopold de Waelplaats (03 216 01 33, www.ann demeulemeester.be). **Open** 11am-7pm Mon-Sat.
Credit AmEx, DC, MC, V.
Demeulemeester, the star member of the Antwerp Six, designs clothes that are slick yet sensual, soft with big attitude and all seemingly right for the times. Her minimalist shop is in a different part of Antwerp from any of her contemporaries, but fittingly located opposite the Fine Arts Museum.

Christa Reniers
22 Drukkerijstraat (03 233 26 02, www. christareniers.com). **Open** 11am-1pm, 2-6pm Thur-Sat. **Credit** AmEx, MC, V. **Map** p233 B4.
Brussels-based Reniers is considered Belgium's top jewellery designer, creating rings, chokers and bracelets in silver and gold.

XSO. See p252.

Closing Date
15 Korte Gasthuisstraat (03 232 87 22). **Open** 11am-6.30pm Mon-Sat. **Credit** AmEx, DC, MC, V. **Map** p233 B4.
Clubbers with cash and eccentrics with panache gather here to pore over racks of clothes by the likes of Owen Gaster, Dsquared2 and Amaya Arzuaga.

Coccodrillo
9a/b Schuttershofstraat (03 233 20 93, www.coccodrillo.be). **Open** 10am-6pm Mon-Sat. **Credit** AmEx, DC, MC, V. **Map** p233 C4.
Prada, Patrick Cox, Jil Sander, Ann Demeulemeester, Dries van Noten and Helmut Lang are among those represented at this full-on fashion footwear mecca.

Erotische Verbeelding
165 Kloosterstraat (03 226 89 50, www.erotischeverbeelding.com). **Open** 11am-6pm Mon-Sat. **Credit** AmEx, MC, V. **Map** p233 A5.
This women-only store stocks sex aids, tasteful-looking dildos, a smattering of S&M and slinky lingerie in a safe and sophisticated environment.

★ Fish & Chips
36-38 Kammenstraat (03 227 08 24, www. fishandchips.be). **Open** 10am-6.30pm Mon-Sat. **Credit** AmEx, MC, V. **Map** p233 B4.
Antwerp's chaotic temple to cool. On Saturdays, DJs spin in a booth overhanging the ground floor, which boasts skater gear and raver labels.

ESCAPES & EXCURSIONS

Huis A. Boon

4 Lombardenvest (03 232 33 87,
www.glovesboon.be). **Open** 10am-6pm Mon-Sat.
Credit AmEx, DC, MC, V. **Map** p233 B4.
Huis A. Boon is a wonderfully evocative time
capsule of a glove shop, with hundreds of different
pairs for men and women displayed on dark shelves
and in little drawers.

Louis

2 Lombardenstraat (03 232 98 72). **Open**
10am-6pm Mon-Sat. **Credit** AmEx, MC, V.
Map p233 B4.
Louis was one of the first boutiques to champion
Belgian fashion, and is now a shrine for fashion-
conscious men and women. Martin Margiela,
Veronique Branquinho, Rick Owens and Raf Simons
are staple labels.

Het Modepaleis

16 Nationalestraat (03 470 25 10, www.dries
vannoten.be). **Open** 10am-6.30pm Mon-Sat.
Credit AmEx, DC, MC, V. **Map** p233 B4.
Dries van Noten sells his own collections in this
landmark building dating from 1881. Both the men's
and women's floors offer top-level flair.

Nadine Wijnants

26 Kloosterstraat (mobile 0484 643 303,
www.nadinewijnants.be). **Open** 11am-6pm
Fri, Sat or by appt. **Credit** MC, V.
Map p233 B3.
One of the top jewellery designers in Belgium,
Wijnants creates charming, affordable pieces with
semi-precious stones, silver, bronze and gold plate.

SN3

46-48 Frankrijklei (03 231 08 20, www.sn3.be).
Open noon-6.30pm Mon; 10am-6.30pm Tue-Sat.
Credit AmEx, DC, MC, V.
Housed in a former cinema, this slightly snobby
designer boutique carries principal collections by the
likes of DKNY, Gaultier, Dior, Galliano and Prada.

★ Verso

11 Lange Gasthuisstraat (03 226 92 92,
www.verso.be). **Open** 11am-7pm Mon-Thur;
11am-9pm Fri, Sat. **Credit** AmEx, DC, MC, V.
Map p233 C4.

Set in an old bank, Verso is a temple to cutting-edge
design. Fashionistas glide around fingering style
from the likes of Helmut Lang, Miu Miu, YSL,
Armani and Versace. So exclusive it hurts.

Walter

12 St Antoniusstraat (03 213 26 44, www.walt.de).
Open 1-6pm Mon; 11am-6.30pm Tue-Sat. **Credit**
AmEx, DC, MC, V. **Map** p233 B4.
This creation by Walter van Beirendonck and Dirk
van Saene feels more like a gallery, but designer
labels include Van B's own collections.

XSO

13-15 Eiermarkt (03 231 87 49). **Open** 10am-
6pm Mon-Fri; 10am-6pm Sat. **Credit** AmEx, DC,
MC, V. **Map** p233 B3.
Set in a quiet courtyard in the centre of town, this
shop mixes Japanese purity (white walls, slate
floors) with Italian flair. Labels include Issey
Miyake, Kenzo and Giorgio Armani. *Photo p251.*

Food & confectionery

Chocolatier Goossens

6 Isabellalei (03 239 13 10). **Open** 9am-6pm
Mon-Sat. **No credit cards**. **Map** p233 B4.
Probably the finest chocolatiers in Antwerp. Teddy
bears, chocolate lips and even Kama Sutra reliefs
made from 100% cocoa butter make perfect gifts.

★ Goossens

31 Korte Gasthuisstraat (03 226 07 91).
Open 7am-7pm Tue-Sat. **No credit cards**.
Map p233 B4.
Founded in 1884, this small and popular traditional
bakery offers a good choice of pastries and cakes,
all displayed on metal racks.

Philip's Biscuits

11 Korte Gasthuisstraat (03 231 26 60).
Open 10am-6pm Mon-Sat. **No credit cards**.
Map p233 B4.
The place for macaroons, *speculoos* (ginger biscuits)
and hand-shaped butter biscuits.

Vervloet Kaashandel

28 Wiegstraat (03 233 37 29). **Open** 8am-6pm
Mon-Sat. **No credit cards**. **Map** p233 B3.
Luc Wouters specialises in cheeses from Belgium,
including his own hard goat's cheese variety.

Gay & lesbian

Toys 4 Boys

6 Nosestraat (03 232 08 27, www.toys4boys
leather.com). **Open** 11am-8pm Thur-Sat; 2-5pm
Sun. **Credit** AmEx, MC, V. **Map** p233 A2.
An atmospheric shop selling a range of fetish gear,
including bespoke leather and rubber clothes. Dutch
couple Marcel and Cor also offer a piercing service.

Wakko.

'T Verschil
33 Minderbroedersrui (03 226 08 04,
www.verschil.be). **Open** 11am-6pm Wed-Sat;
1-6pm Sun. **Credit** MC, V. **Map** p233 B2.
Books, DVDs and videos for gays and lesbians.
In the cellar is an old café to help with the browsing.

Health & beauty

Soap
13 Plantinkaai (03 232 73 72). **Open** 9am-
6.30pm Mon-Thur; 9am-8pm Fri; 9am-6pm Sat.
Credit MC, V. **Map** p233 A4.
The salon where Belgium's ultra-stylish get their
hair dyed, fried or laid to the side.
Other location 2 Korte Schipperskapelstraat
(03 213 10 13).

Wakko
3 St Rochusstraat (03 233 46 04, www.wakko.be).
Open 10am-6pm Tue, Wed, Fri, Sat; 10am-8pm
Thur. **Map** p233 B5.
Wakko is one of the wackiest hairdressers around,
a kitsch temple to hair, colour and extensions.

Home furnishings

Avant-Scène
33 Leopoldstraat (03 231 88 26). **Open** 11am-
6pm Tue-Sat. **Credit** MC, V. **Map** p233 C3.
Pieces from Belgium's foremost furniture designers,
including the Van Severen brothers and Xavier Lust.

Donum
47 Hopland (03 231 39 18, www.donum.be).
Open 10am-6pm Mon-Fri; 10am-6.30pm Sat.
Credit AmEx, DC, MC, V. **Map** p233 C3.
This interior design shop is seriously cool. Set in
an old school, Italian design is the order of the day.
There is also an interior design service.

Scapa World
*26-30 Hopland Complex, Hopland (03 226
79 93).* **Open** 10am-6.30pm Mon-Sat. **Credit**
AmEx, DC, MC, V. **Map** p233 C3.
Ralph Lauren springs to mind as you enter this
gleaming homestore. Turkish, Irish and Austrian
cultures influence the clothes and home furnishings
on display. Great household linen too.

'T Koetshuis (Chelsea)
*10 Kloosterstraat (03 248 33 42, www.antiek-
koetshuis.be).* **Open** noon-6pm Tue-Sat; 1-6pm
Sun. **No credit cards**. **Map** p233 A4.
Its official name is Chelsea, but 'T Koetshuis (coach-
house) is what you'll find written over the door. The
art deco and art nouveau furnishings are chosen and
displayed with care, so don't expect any bargains.

Music & books

Bilbo
Oude Korenmarkt 12 (03 226 8480). **Open**
10am-6pm Mon-Fri; 10am-6.30pm Sat. **Credit**
AmEx, DC, MC, V. **Map** p233 A3.
Packed with new and used vinyl and CDs offering
rock, indie, techno, house – anything, really.

Mekanik Strip
*73 St Jacobsmarkt (03 234 23 47, www.mekanik-
strip.be).* **Open** 10am-6.30pm Mon-Fri; 10am-6pm
Sat. **Credit** AmEx, DC, MC, V. **Map** p233 C2.
A huge selection of English, French and Dutch
comics, plus magazines, books, videos, posters,
Tintin collectibles and its own gallery.

THEATRE & DANCE

★ deSingel
25 Desguinlei (03 248 28 28, www.desingel.be).
Open Box office 10am-7pm Mon-Fri; 4-7pm Sat.
Tickets €10-€40. **Credit** MC, V.
Antwerp's modern equivalent to Brussels' Bozar,
with cutting-edge dance and theatre in a massive
concrete setting, and an intelligent agenda of events.

Vlaamse Opera
*8 Van Ertbornstraat (03 202 10 11, www.vlaamse
opera.be).* Box office: *3 Frankrijklei (070 22 02 02).*
Open Box office 11am-5.45pm Tue-Sat. **Tickets**
€4-€70. **Credit** AmEx, DC, MC, V.
The Flemish Opera productions are divided between
the opera house in Ghent and the old but acoustically splendid Antwerp Hall.

Bruges

People, people everywhere, but plenty of space to think.

Bruges, with its modest population of 116,000, is mobbed by about three million tourists every year, many of them from Britain, making it the most popular destination in Belgium for foreign visitors.

Despite large crowds, it is a romantic, atmospheric and historical city that invites gentle wandering and an exploration of its squares, alleyways and quays. The city gained new credibility as a supporting character in the 2008 film *In Bruges*, which showed the old centre at its most subtle and mysterious. By far the easiest and most enjoyable way to visit Bruges is on foot. It's compact, largely traffic-free and always easy to get around – and anything has to be better than one of those horse-drawn carriages.

ESCAPES & EXCURSIONS

HISTORY

The British people have always been seduced by Bruges. One of the earliest English settlers was Gunhilde, the sister of King Harold, who settled here after the Battle of Hastings in 1066. By the Middle Ages, the city was teeming with English wool merchants, including one William Caxton, who picked up the art of printing in Flanders. Charles II spent several years in exile in Bruges and English Catholic nuns founded a convent within the city walls.

The city enjoyed its own golden age in the 15th century when it was a flourishing port and trading city. Merchants came here from all over Europe to trade in wool, lace and diamonds, constructing impressive Gothic brick houses and banks along the canals and narrow lanes in the northern quarter. This glorious period is also reflected in the rich collections of art in the museums and churches.

It all came to an end when the Zwin estuary began to silt up, cutting the city off from the sea. Trade moved to Antwerp and Bruges went into hibernation for 300 years, missing out on the Industrial Revolution and the prosperity of the rest of the country. In the early part of the 19th century, British tourists passed through the town on their way from the battlefield at Waterloo. Many were seduced by its sleepy charm and crumbling monuments untouched by industry. They urged the city fathers to preserve its character by constructing new buildings in a retro Bruges Gothic style. By the mid 19th century, 1,000 British had settled here, opening shops, hotels and tearooms.

BRUGES TODAY

Bruges acquired a nickname, the Venice of the North, and was soon swamped by tourists. By the 1980s, it was all getting far too much for local residents, who put up posters in their front windows bearing the slogan 'SOS Brugge'. The city council was soon goaded into action. The city used its year as European City of Culture in 2002 to embark on major projects designed to change its image. Bruges finally abandoned its love affair with Gothic (real and fake) and the planning department approved the construction of the brutally modern, controversial red hulk of the **Concertgebouw** (34 't Zand, 070 22 33 02, www.concertgebouw.be, *photo p256*), a new concert hall seating 1,200 people.

Two new bridges were built in the south of the city, including Jürg Conzett's sleek one spanning the Coupure canal, and a daring

---

INSIDE TRACK
SEE IT, BUY IT, TAKE IT HOME

There is a central museum shop in Bruges at 16 Dijver (no phone, open 10am-6pm Tue-Sun), located in a former coach house and attached to the Brangwyn Museum-Arentshuis (*see p260*).

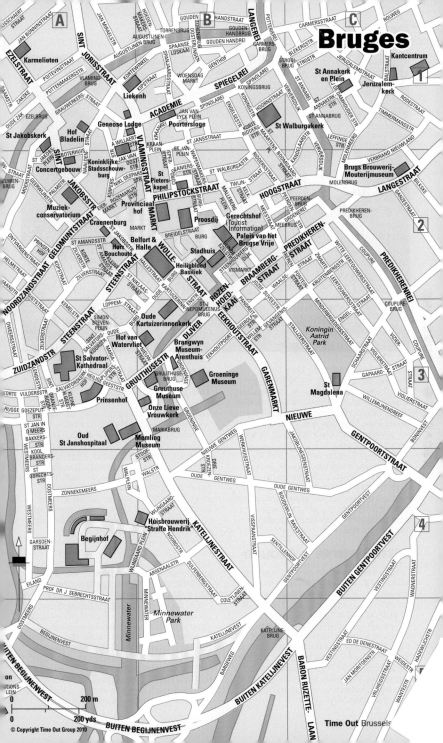

Concertgebouw. *See p254.*

pavilion was added on the Burg by the Japanese architect Toyo Ito. Museums were also given a radical makeover: the **Memling Museum** was redesigned and a spectacular Gothic loft opened to the public, while the **Groeninge Museum** was given a new look that downgrades the world-famous Van Eycks from their star position.

Bruges still has far too many touristy chocolate shops and lace emporia, its boat trips are a let-down, and there are too few modern art galleries and new-style cafés. It is best approached *à deux* on a winter break. Wander by the canals, take in a couple of sights, enjoy a Flemish beer – and maybe then the city will begin to work its spell.

GETTING THERE & AROUND

From Brussels, there are two trains an hour (50 minutes). It's a 15-minute walk to the centre, or you can take a taxi or bus from outside the station. To call a cab, Taxi Snel (050 36 36 49, www.taxisnel.be) is as good as any.

Several shops rent out bicycles by the hour, the day or the week; hire is €5-€10 a day. Try 't Koffieboontje, 4 Hallestraat (050 33 80 27, www.hotel-koffieboontje.be) or Eric Popelier, 14 Hallestraat (050 34 32 62, www.fietsen popelier.be). For details of various guided bike tours contact Quasimundo (050 33 07 75, www.quasimundo.com).

SIGHTSEEING
The Markt & the Burg

The traditional starting point for any visit is the main square, the **Markt**. Its most striking monuments are the **Halle** (Cloth Hall) and the **Belfort** (Belfry). Both the belfry and market square are symbols of the civic pride and great mercantile power of medieval Bruges; the view from the top of the 80-metre (263-foot) belfry makes the climb – all 366 steps – worth the effort. The city's carilloneur climbs up every Sunday to play at 2.15pm, also giving ringings on the stroke of 9pm on Mondays, Wednesdays and Saturdays in the summer.

Most buildings on the square are modern reconstructions, including **Craenenburg**, built on the site of the same house where Emperor Maximilian was held prisoner by local citizens. The building contains a popular Bruges café with a typical Old Flemish interior (*see p266*).

The statues at the centre of the square are of Jan Breydel and Pieter de Coninck, who both inspired locals to slaughter several thousand French citizens at the start of the 14th century, an early example of ethnic cleansing known as the *Brugse Metten*. The statues were unveiled by King Léopold II, who is said to have spoken Dutch for the first time during the ceremony.

From here it's a very short walk to the **Burg**. This beautiful square was the site chosen by

Baldwin I to build a castle in the ninth century. The site is these days occupied by the **Stadhuis** (Town Hall), built in splendid Gothic style in the 14th century. The lavish Gothic Hall on the first floor boasts a spectacular ceiling, while the walls are painted with scenes relating the history of the city, often with more verve than accuracy. The paintings date from the early 20th century.

On one corner of the Burg stands the Old Recorders' House, the **Paleis van het Brugse Vrije**, originally built in the 16th century and renovated in the 18th. The façade overlooking the canal is all that remains of the original structure; the rest is neo-classical in style. Inside the palace there's only one room that can be visited, with an impressive chimney piece (1528) of black marble and oak by Lanceloot Blondeel, running almost the whole length of one wall.

The oldest building on the Burg, tucked away in a corner next to the Stadhuis, is the easily missed **Heiligbloed Basiliek** (Basilica of the Holy Blood). The bizarre interior is well worth a look. The Lower Chapel was built in the 12th century in honour of St Basil and is in a pure Romanesque style. Its refined sobriety is in surprising contrast to the generous interior of the Upper Chapel, which was built in the 12th century in Romanesque style, then rebuilt in Gothic style and finally heavily altered in the 19th century. The decorated wooden ceiling, many of the colourful frescoes, the marvellous stained-glass windows and globe-shaped pulpit all date from the last reconstruction.

It is in this Upper Chapel that the crystal phial containing two drops of holy blood, stored in a silver tabernacle, is exhibited every Friday.

This is one of the holiest relics of medieval Europe. The phial is supposed to have been given to Thierry d'Alsace by the Patri of Jerusalem during the second Crusade. Legend has it that the blood contained within the phial liquefied every Friday, but the miracle is said to have stopped working in the 15th century.

The relic is carried through the streets every year on Ascension Day. The Procession of the Holy Blood, a major traditional event in Bruges, dates back to the early Middle Ages and still involves thousands of participants dressed in rich costumes, plus musicians and even animals.

★ Belfort

Markt. **Open** 9.30am-5pm daily. Last entry 4.15pm. **Admission** €8; €6 reductions; free under-6s. **No credit cards**. **Map** p255 B2.

Heiligbloed Basiliek

13 Burg. **Open** *Apr-Sept* 9.30am-noon, 2-6pm Tue-Sun. *Oct-Mar* 10am-noon, 2-4pm Tue, Thur-Sun; 10am-noon Wed. **Admission** *Chapel* free. *Treasury* €1.50. **No credit cards**. **Map** p255 B2.

Paleis van het Brugse Vrije

11a Burg (050 44 82 60). **Open** 9.30am-12.30pm, 1.30-5pm daily. **Admission** Combined ticket with Stadhuis €2; €1 reductions; free under-6s. **No credit cards**. **Map** p255 B2.

Stadhuis

12 Burg (050 44 81 13). **Open** 9.30am-5pm daily. **Admission** Combined ticket with Paleis van het Brugse Vrije €2; €1 reductions; free under-6s. **No credit cards**. **Map** p255 B2.

ESCAPES & EXCURSIONS

Markt.

Grand Day Out

A walk around Bruges' cultural hotspots.

Bruges is certainly well endowed in the art department; visiting everything in one day is impossible, but you can pick from the best to plan your own mini grand tour.

A good starting point is the Burg, just east of the Markt. The **Stadhuis** (*see p257*) dates from 1376 and features some magnificent 19th-century murals illustrating scenes from the city's past. From the Burg it's a short walk to the **Groeninge Museum** (*see p260*), located by the Dijver canal and home to an impressive collection of Belgian art from Hieronymus Bosch (including *The Last Judgement*) and Jan van Eyck.

Next door, the **Forum+ [Concertgebouw]** serves as a unique platform for modern art (exhibitions are staged every three months). Even further along the Dijver, the **Brangwyn Museum-Arentshuis** (*see p260*) is an elegant 18th-century mansion containing many works by Bruges-born British painter Frank Brangwyn (1867-1956), famous for his scenes from the hard lives of local dock and factory workers. The **Gruuthuse Museum** (*see p261*) is also

well worth a visit, with a truly bizarre collection of busts, ceramics and sculpture, taking in everything from the kitchen sink to the guillotine. Then on to the simply stunning **Onze Lieve Vrouwkerk** (*see p261*), a short walk around the corner on Mariastraat; the church's 122-metre (400-foot) steeple dominates the Bruges skyline, but once inside it's Michelangelo's beguiling sculpture of the *Madonna and Child* that will take your breath away.

If you're squeamish, it might be worth avoiding the **St Janshospitaal** (*see right*), also on Mariastraat, with its gruesome depictions of medieval hospitals. Its chapel, however, is a more sedate monument to the genius of 15th-century artist Hans Memling, who created many of his best works for the hospital, including a shrine to St Ursula. There are more medical curiosities in **Onze Lieve Vrouw ter Potterie Museum** (*see p262*), an historic hospital set inside a 13th-century church; it's also a calm spot in which to unwind after such an intense culture overdose.

Stadhuis.

Museums along the Dijver

From the Burg, head south to the **Vismarkt**
(Fish Market), taking the narrow Blinde
Ezelstraat (Blind Donkey Street). The fish
market still takes place every morning from
Tuesday to Saturday. The walk east from here
follows the **Groenerei** canal, one of the most
attractive waterways in Bruges. The water,
trees and gabled houses – especially the Pelican
House at No.8 – make it a favourite romantic
spot. It can be noisy during the day, so come
back after dark, when most tourists have gone,
to look at the beautiful floodlit bridges.

Just west of Vismarkt is Huidevettersplaats
(Tanners' Square), which in turn leads to the
Rozenhoedkaai. The grand view of the canal,
bordered by ancient buildings and trees, has
captivated photographers since the mid 19th
century, but it can get a bit too crowded. The
quay leads to another picturesque canal, the
Dijver. The main attractions here are the
Groeninge Museum, famous for its collection
of Flemish art, and the nearby **Brangwyn
Museum-Arentshuis**. Set in the intimate
Arentspark, this small museum is named after
the Bruges-born British painter and engraver
Frank Brangwyn, whose own works are on
display inside. Next to the Brangwyn Museum,
the **Gruuthuse Museum** is set inside an
extensive 15th-century mansion originally
belonging to the powerful Gruuthuse family,
who had a monopoly on *gruut*, a mixture of
dried flowers and plants used in the brewing
process before hops became more fashionable.
Lodewijk van Gruuthuse was also a diplomat,
patron of the arts, friend of Edward IV of
England and Knight of the Golden Fleece; he
also invented a rather nastier version of the
cannonball. His motto, '*Plus est en vous*', is
reproduced around the palace, which was
bought by the city and opened as a museum.

The furniture in the reception hall dates from
the 16th, 17th and 18th centuries, as do all the
silverware and ceramics. The bust of Charles V,
showing a young and candid emperor, is one
of the most important pieces in the collection.
Many other exhibits are objects from daily life,
including the ancient musical instruments in
the music cabinet and a large collection of lace.
Lace-making is a Bruges tradition that dates
back to the Middle Ages, when lace was made
with imported linen, always by women and
often in convents and *béguinages* (houses for
lay sisters). In the 17th century, Bruges, Ghent,
Brussels and Mechelen were unrivalled in the
art. *See p267* **Needle Works**.

A small stone bridge leads from Arentspark
to the **Onze Lieve Vrouwkerk**, the Church of
Our Lady. The bridge is constantly blocked as
tourists take photographs, but few realise the

View from the **Rozenhoedkaai**.

bridge was built as recently as 1910. A cobbled
lane leads to the church, an imposing brick
structure with a massive tower, best seen from
the garden. The church is famed for its works of
art, which include Michelangelo's *Madonna and
Child*. The modest sculpture was ordered by the
Piccolomini family for Siena Cathedral, but a
Bruges merchant later purchased it when the
family failed to pay their debts. The sculpture is
an early work by the artist and one of the few to
have left Italy during his lifetime. In the choir
are the burial tombs of Charles the Bold and his
daughter, Mary of Burgundy. In stark contrast
to her husband, Maximilian of Austria, Mary
was loved by locals, having died young after
falling from her horse. Their joint mausoleum
(overlooked by a giant altar painting of the
crucifixion by Bernard van Orley) is both
lavish and solemn. A graceful brass sculpture
of the princess lies over the adorned base;
the monument for Charles the Bold, made
at a later date, is very similar in style.

Directly opposite the church is the medieval
St Janshospitaal, which was still in use as a
hospital in the early 20th century. The street
outside was raised in the 19th century, so that
the entrance to it, like that of the Onze Lieve
Vrouwkerk, now lies below ground level. The
former hospital wards – with their vast oak
ceilings – are now occupied by an interesting
museum of local history and medicine. The
exhibits include old photographs, paintings and

Groeninge Museum.

a rather grim collection of surgical instruments. Within the hospital's ancient chapel is the renovated **Memling Museum**, dedicated to the 15th-century painter Hans Memling. This is a small, remarkable collection of the Frankfurt-born artist, who lived and studied in Bruges. Memling undertook many commissions for the English aristocrat John Donne and the Italian banker Portinari. His talent as a portrait artist and his hunger for detail are quite astonishing. Like all of the Flemish Primitives, Memling believed that the material world was a product of divine creation, and that it was necessary to reproduce God's work as faithfully as possible. His use of colours is brilliant and the scenes always carefully composed. He ended his days as a patient of the hospital and carried out several commissions for the institution.

The Mystical Marriage of St Catherine is one of several similar works by Memling (another is in New York's Metropolitan Museum). In the central panel, Jesus, sitting on Mary's lap, is sliding a ring on St Catherine's finger. Although Memling's paintings are often said to be rather devoid of feeling, here the colours are vivid and passionate. The *Sibylla Sambetha* is believed to be a portrait of Marie Moreel, whose father commissioned many works from Memling. Also on display is a shrine made by Memling in 1489, which contains the relic of St Ursula. The story of the pagan martyr St Ursula and the 11,000 virgins was a highly popular legend; the shrine is shaped like a Gothic cathedral and decorated with scenes of the saint's life.

Over the canal from the Memling, the **Groeninge** is the most prestigious museum in Bruges, covering 600 years of Belgian painting. Pride of place goes to its outstanding collection of Flemish primitives, in particular works by Jan van Eyck. No master illustrates the concept of 15th-century painting better than Van Eyck, who created the illusion of texture and detail by inventing a technique of applying oil and varnish in painstaking layers. The colours are not only longer lasting, but the malleability of the paints enabled him to achieve a subtlety of clarity and hue. His virtuosity and strict attention to detail were such that many artists travelled to Flanders to learn his secrets. His most striking work is the *Madonna with Canon George van der Paele*. Chief curator Manfred Sellink commissioned an unconventional, stark white redesign of the museum in 2002 – Van Eyck's *Madonna* dominates room 2. Also keep an eye out for pieces by the likes of Memling, Rogier van der Weyden, Hieronymus Bosch and Gerard David. There are some good examples of Belgian surrealism – Ensor, Magritte, Delvaux – in the later rooms.

Brangwyn Museum-Arentshuis
16 Dijver (050 44 87 63). **Open** 9.30am-5pm Tue-Sun. **Admission** €2; €1 reductions; free under-6s. **Credit** AmEx, MC, V. **Map** p255 B3.

★ Groeninge Museum
12 Dijver (050 44 87 43). **Open** 9.30am-5pm Tue-Sun. **Admission** €8; €6 reductions; free under-6s. **Credit** AmEx, MC, V. **Map** p255 B3.

ESCAPES & EXCURSIONS

Gruuthuse Museum
17 Dijver (050 44 87 62). **Open** 9.30am-5pm
Tue-Sun. **Admission** €6; €5 reductions; free
under-6s. Ticket includes entry to Church of
Our Lady. **Credit** AmEx, MC, V. **Map** p255 B3.

★ Memling Museum
38 Mariastraat (050 44 87 70). **Open** 9.30am-
5pm Tue-Sun. **Admission** €8; €6 reductions;
free under-6s. **Credit** AmEx, MC, V.
Map p255 A3.

★ Onze Lieve Vrouwkerk
Mariastraat. **Open** 9.30am-5pm Tue-Fri; 9.30am-
4.45pm Sat; 1.30-5pm Sun. **Admission** *Church*
free. *Choir* €2; €1 reductions; free under-6s.
No credit cards. **Map** p255 B3.

Begijnhof & Minnewater Park

Coming out of St Janshospitaal, turn right on
Katelijnestraat and you find the **Begijnhof**,
one of Bruges' most charming locations by far.
Founded by Margaret of Constantinople in
1245, it features rows of modest whitewashed
houses around an inner lawn, covered with
daffodils in spring. The atmosphere is calm and
serene, far removed from the crowded streets
around. There are no longer any *béguines* (lay
sisters) in Bruges; the last ones died in the
1930s. The women you see walking around the
Begijnhof today are Benedictine nuns. It is
possible to visit the church, and one of the
houses is also open to visitors.

At the Begijnhof's southern entrance is the
picturesque **Minnewater Park**, with swans,
lawns and small houses. Before the Zwin silted
up, barges and ships would penetrate this far
into the city. The 16th-century lock-keeper's
house is still standing on the north side of the
lake, next to a 1398 guard tower. The lake is
named after a woman called Minna who, legend
has it, fell in love with a man of whom her
father disapproved. She fled his house and hid
in the woods by the lake. Unfortunately, her
beloved was a little slow in finding her and
Minna died in his arms. The heartbroken man
still found enough strength in him to change
the course of the water, bury Minna's body and
let the waters flow over the grave again.

Walking back towards the Markt, you see the
huge **St Salvator-kathedraal**, surrounded by
old trees. Work on the cathedral first began in
the tenth century, but after four fires and the
Iconoclastic Riots nothing of that period has
survived except the base of the tower. This
troubled history is also largely responsible for
the varied and eclectic style of the interior. The
choir dates from the 14th century, although part
of an even older 13th-century construction still
survives. The painted columns, similar to those

in the Upper Chapel of the Heiligbloed Basiliek,
are a relatively recent addition, as are the
stained-glass windows. There are several
paintings by Bernard van Orley in the right
transept, but the lighting is bad and they are
difficult to see. However, the treasury has been
restored and relit, allowing visitors to admire a
spectacular painting by Dirk Bouts known as
the *Hippolytus Altarpiece*.

St Salvator-kathedraal
St Salvatorskerkhof (www.sintsalvator.be).
Open 2-6pm Mon; 8.30am-noon, 2-6pm Tue-Fri;
8.30am-noon, 2-3.30pm Sat; 9-10.15am, 2-5pm
Sun. **Admission** *Church* free. *Treasury* €3.
Map p255 A3.

St Anna quarter

The area of St Anna, north-east of the Burg,
is a poorer and more populated area, and less
visited by tourists. There are fewer shops and
the bars are mostly frequented by locals, yet it's
packed with charm. Follow Hoogstraat east of
the Burg and turn left on Verversdijk canal,
which is lined with impressive 18th-century
houses. Down the little lane on the left, the
Jesuit church of **St Walburga**, built between
1619 and 1641, is decorated with tall, solid, grey
Tuscan-style columns. The style is Baroque and
the dominant colours gold and white, yet the
interior is more harmonious than overbearing.

Back on the Verversdijk, cross the diminutive
bridge to reach the 17th-century **St Annakerk**,
a rather austere building from the outside, but
with a luxurious interior.

Immediately behind St Anna, on the corner
of Peperstraat and Jeruzalemstraat, the
Jeruzalemkerk was built by a wealthy family
of Italian merchants, the church still belonging
to its descendants. It's a curious, three-level
building, supposedly constructed according to
the model of the Holy Sepulchre in Jerusalem.
Highlights within include a crucifix decorated
with bones and skulls over the altar, a copy of
the tomb of Christ in the crypt and some fine
stained glass. Next door, the **Kantcentrum**, or
Lace Museum, has women who are still able to

> ### INSIDE TRACK
> ### TWO WHEELS GOOD
>
> Bruges, being flat, is perfect for cycling,
> and it is also the traditional start of the
> famous Tour of Flanders road cycling race.
> The Ronde van Vlaanderen (www.rvv.be) is
> one of Belgium's biggest sporting events
> and always takes place on the 14th
> Sunday of the year (in April).

ESCAPES & EXCURSIONS

demonstrate the intricate skills of lace-making (*see p267* **Needle Works**). Walking north on Balstraat brings you to the **Engels Klooster**, an English convent and church located on Carmersstraat. Ring the bell and a nun will appear to show you inside the church.

The houses in this part of town are a long way from the flamboyant style of the historic centre. This is no longer an open-air museum, but a living community where many elderly people live in tiny 19th-century houses. The numerous *godshuizen* (almshouses) are evidence of the rampant poverty that overtook the city after the 15th century. As the city's fortunes declined, people abandoned the city, leaving behind vast empty spaces. Richer citizens took it upon themselves to build almshouses to shelter the poor and elderly. There are about 30 of these *godshuizen* in Bruges, some still fulfilling their original role. The entrance is usually marked by a small statue of the Virgin Mary. Once inside, you will often find a little courtyard surrounded by small almshouses, each with its own highly individual character. The lawns are carefully tended and the gardens planted with flowers.

A ten-minute walk down the Potterierei brings you to the almost forgotten **Onze Lieve Vrouw ter Potterie Museum**, a former hospital dating back to the 13th century. You can wander through evocative rooms filled with Baroque paintings, sculpture and furniture.

Jeruzalemkerk

3a Peperstraat (050 33 00 72, www.kant centrum.com). **Open** 10am-5pm Mon-Sat. **Admission** Combined ticket with Kantcentrum €2.50; €1.50 reductions. **No credit cards.** Map p255 C1.

Kantcentrum

3a Peperstraat (050 33 00 72, www.kant centrum.com). **Open** 10am-5pm Mon-Sat. **Admission** Combined ticket with Jeruzalemkerk €2.50; €1.50 reductions. **No credit cards.** Map p255 C1.

Onze Lieve Vrouw ter Potterie Museum

79 Potterierei. **Open** 9.30am-12.30pm, 1.30-5pm Tue-Sun. **Admission** €2; €1 reductions.

St Annakerk en Plein

J De Damhouderstraat. **Open** *Apr-Sept* 10am-noon, 2-4pm Mon-Fri; 10am-noon Sat. **Admission** free. Map p255 C1.

St Walburgakerk

Koningstraat & Hoornstraat. **Open** *Apr-Sept* 10am-noon, 2-5pm, 8-10pm Mon-Sat; 2-5pm Sun. **Admission** free. Map p255 B1.

Tourist information

Toerisme Brugge

Bruges railway station (050 44 46 46, www.brugge.be). **Open** 10am-5pm Mon-Fri; 10am-2pm Sat, Sun.
Concertgebouw, 34 't Zand (050 44 46 46, www.brugge.be). **Open** 10am-6pm daily.

WHERE TO STAY

Bruges has more than 100 hotels. The hotel sector is seriously challenged by an ever growing number of small B&Bs (*gastenkamers*), often located in lovingly restored houses in the old quarters. Many hotels close in January and early February. For details, check www.hotels-brugge.org. The tourist information office (*see above*) manages a free accommodation booking service. Prices listed here are for a double room and include breakfast unless otherwise stated.

Hotels

Golden Tulip Hotel de' Medici

15 Potterierei, 8000 Bruges (050 33 98 33, www.hoteldemedici.com). **Rates** €219. **Credit** AmEx, DC, MC, V. Map p255 B1.
A modern hotel in a good canalside location near the historic centre. The interior is clinically efficient, but rooms are spacious and comfortable. The hotel has a recreation centre with sauna, steam bath and gym.

Hotel Acacia

3A Korte Zilverstraat, 8000 Bruges (050 34 44 11, www.hotel-acacia.com). **Rates** €128. **Credit** AmEx, DC, MC, V. Map p255 A2.

Hotel Die Swaene.

There has been a hotel on this site since the 1430s. The original building was demolished in the 1960s; the current hotel is now part of the Best Western chain. Centrally located, it has 48 rooms (all en suite), plus an indoor swimming pool, sauna and jacuzzi.

Hotel Adornes

26 St Annarei, 8000 Bruges (050 34 13 36, www.adornes.be). **Rates** €140. **Credit** AmEx, MC, V. **Map** p255 C1.
This friendly family hotel in a canalside location near St Annakerk is ideal for exploring the historic centre and the quiet Guido Gezelle quarter to the east. Rooms are comfortable and stylish.
▶ *The hotel also offers free parking spaces and free bicycles.*

Hotel Aragon

22 Naaldenstraat, 8000 Bruges (050 33 35 33, www.aragon.be). **Rates** €158. **Credit** AmEx, DC, MC, V. **Map** p255 A2.
An appealing hotel right in the heart of the historic merchant quarter, opposite a palace once owned by a Medici banker. The 42 rooms are done out in a comfortable English style and the location is quiet.

★ Hotel De Orangerie

10 Kartuizerinnenstraat, 8000 Bruges (050 34 16 49, www.hotelorangerie.com). **Rates** €179; €20 breakfast. **Credit** AmEx, DC, MC, V. **Map** p255 B2/3.
This central 15th-century convent, by a canal, has 20 rooms, all individually decorated by Antwerp interior designer Pieter Porters. He is also responsible for decor in De Tuilerieën (7 Dijver, 8000 Bruges, 050 34 36 91, www.hoteltuilerieen.com), a mansion from the same era under the same hotel ownership.

★ Hotel Die Swaene

1 Steenhouwersdijk, 8000 Bruges (050 34 27 984, www.dieswaene-hotel.com). **Rates** €195; €20 breakfast. **Credit** AmEx, DC, MC, V. **Map** p255 B2.
Right in the centre of the city, this 15th-century mansion next to a canal is wonderfully romantic: real Venice of the North stuff. All 22 rooms are individually decorated; some have four-poster beds. There's a candlelit restaurant, pool and sauna too.

Hotel Ter Reien

1 Langestraat, 8000 Bruges (050 34 91 00, www.hotelterreien.be). **Rates** €125. Closed early Jan-early Feb. **Credit** AmEx, MC, V. **Map** p255 C2.
A pleasant canalside hotel with a seductive inner courtyard, close to the centre. Rooms are bright and comfortable. The house was the birthplace of Fernand Khnopff, the symbolist artist who painted views of deserted Bruges quays.

Relais Oud-Huis Amsterdam

4a Genthof, 8000 Bruges (050 34 18 10, www.martins-hotels.com). **Rates** €149; €20 breakfast. **Credit** AmEx, DC, MC, V. **Map** p255 B1.
A splendid hotel set in a beautifully renovated 17th-century house, overlooking one of the canals. With its carved wooden staircase, chandeliers, antique furniture and bare wooden beams, the opulent interior is staggering. There's also an extremely pretty interior courtyard.

Romantik Pandhotel

16 Pandreitje, 8000 Bruges (050 34 06 66, www.pandhotel.com). **Rates** €200; €20 breakfast. **Credit** AmEx, DC, MC, V. **Map** p255 B3.

This charming 23-room hotel in a leafy corner of Bruges occupies an 18th-century carriage house. Expect a friendly welcome.

B&Bs

Absoluut Verhulst

1 Verbrand Nieuwland, 8000 Bruges (050 33 45 15, www.b-bverhulst.com). **Rates** €95. **No credit cards. Map** p255 C2.

The Verhulsts run this B&B in a 17th-century house with creaking floorboards. There are three light, stylish rooms, including a duplex and a loft sleeping up to five people. Bikes can be rented for the day.

★ Baert Gastenkamer

28 Westmeers, 8000 Bruges (050 33 05 30, www.baert-gastenkamer.be). **Rates** €85. **No credit cards. Map** p255 A3.

Huub Baert and Jeannine Robberecht run a stylish B&B in a restored stable building that belonged to a convent. They offer two bright rooms, both with private canalside terraces that catch the sun. Born and bred in Bruges, Huub is an expert on local history. He offers a Bruges beer to guests on arrival and sends them on their way with a box of chocolates.

★ Dieltiens

40 Waalsestraat, 8000 Bruges (050 33 42 94, http://users.skynet.be/dieltiens). **Rates** €80. **No credit cards. Map** p255 B2.

A very stylish B&B run by Koen and Annemie Dieltiens in a beautiful 18th-century mansion in the heart of Bruges. There are only three rooms, so book in advance. There is also a studio apartment to rent in a small, renovated 17th-century house nearby.

Gheeraert

9 Ridderstraat, 8000 Bruges (050 33 56 27, http://users.skynet.be/brugge-gheeraert). **Rates** €70. **No credit cards. Map** p255 B2.

This exquisitely decorated townhouse, just a couple of minutes from the Burg, has three second-floor guest rooms. All are decorated in a classy, pared-down style and hung with prints by Flemish Masters. The breakfast is notable. The Gheeraerts also rent out self-catering holiday flats in the area.

Kwalito

44 Ezelstraat, 8000 Bruges (050 34 23 26, www.bedandbreakfast-kwalito.com). **Rates** €90. **Credit** MC, V. **Map** p255 A1.

The Depoorter-Clement family runs this lovely little guesthouse next door to their grocery of the same name, so you're guaranteed fresh bread for breakfast. Every room has a kitchen corner, with a microwave. The centre is a short walk away.

Van Nevel

13 Carmersstraat, 8000 Bruges (050 34 68 60, www.bbeurope.net/Belgium/van_nevel.htm). **Rates** €60. **Credit** MC, V. **Map** p255 C1.

Craenenburg. *See p266.*

Near the church of St Anna, ten minutes from the centre in a quiet area, the Van Nevels rent out two well-equipped rooms in a 16th-century house.

Youth hostels

Bauhaus

135-137 Langestraat, 8000 Bruges (050 34 10 93, www.bauhaus.be). **Open** 24hrs daily. **Rates** from €20 per person. **Credit** AmEx, MC, V. **Map** p255 C2.

This is one of Bruges' largest youth hostels, with 80 rooms sleeping two, three, four or eight. The decor is a mix of colonial and religious. There's bike rental, an internet café and bar. It's also possible to rent a flat for up to 12 people.

Snuffel

47-49 Ezelstraat, 8000 Bruges (050 33 31 33, www.snuffel.be). **Rates** from €15 per person. **Credit** AmEx, MC, V. **Map** p255 A1.

For bargain hunters, the Snuffel offers hostel-like accommodation in rooms sleeping groups of four, six, eight or 12 people.

EATING & DRINKING

It's not difficult to eat well in Bruges if you avoid the tourist traps on the Markt and by the Begijnhof. Places range from more traditional Flemish taverns offering honest fare for around €15 to the sublime three-starred **De Karmeliet**.

Restaurants

Bistro De Schaar

2 Hooistraat (050 33 59 79, www.bistro deschaar.be). **Open** noon-2.30pm, 6-11pm Mon-Wed, Fri-Sun. **Main courses** €20. **Credit** MC, V.

Located out of the tourist centre, just off Predikherenrei, this cracking little bistro offers a modern take on cosy rusticity. Grills are popular, as are less traditional dishes such as prawns in garlic or cheese-filled ravioli.

★ Bistro Refter

2 Molenmeers (050 44 99 00). **Open** noon-2pm, 7-10pm Tue-Sat. **Menus** €35. **Credit** AmEx, DC, MC, V. **Map** p255 C1.

A new bistro opening from Geert van Heck of De Karmeliet (*see right*). It's called Refter because it's in the refectory of the old Carmelite building it occupies, though the decor is now ultra sleek and modern. This place is much more affordable than its three-star sister; it's a set menu-only bistro, which makes everything that little bit easier.

Eetcafé de Vuyst

15 Simon Stevinplein (050 34 22 31, www. eetcafedevuyst.be). **Open** 10am-6pm Mon,

Wed-Fri; 10am-9.30pm Sat, Sun. **Main courses** €18. **Credit** DC, MC, V. **Map** p255 A3.

A fun café-bar with newspapers on the walls and glass-topped tables containing original paintings. There are various *moules* options, as well as salads, crêpes and a good-value three-course lunch.

★ In Den Wittekop

14 St Jacobstraat (050 33 20 59, www.inden wittenkop.be). **Open** noon-2pm, 6-10pm Tue-Sat. **Main courses** €23. **Credit** AmEx, MC, V. **Map** p255 A2.

Despite being close to the tourist centre, this ageing café offers an authentic Bruges experience, along with classic *steak frites* and eels cooked in a variety of ways.

★ De Karmeliet

19 Langestraat (050 33 82 59, www. dekarmeliet.be). **Open** noon-2pm, 7-10pm Tue-Sat. **Main courses** €70. **Credit** AmEx, DC, MC, V. **Map** p255 C2.

At the three Michelin-starred De Karmeliet, chef Geert van Hecke's staples include rabbit, local breeds of chicken, truffles and scallops. Special menus cover such themes as 'the flat country'. The decor is airy and modern, and you can see Geert at work at the back of the dining room. This is a cathedral to high dining but expect to pay for it.

Parkrestaurant

1 Minderbroedersstraat (050 34 64 42, www.parkrestaurant.be). **Open** 11.30am-10pm Tue-Sun. **Main courses** €25. **Credit** AmEx, MC, V. **Map** p255 C2.

An elegant and friendly restaurant located in a patrician mansion facing the city's main park. The chefs produce some truly wonderful dishes using Ardennes beef, fresh salmon, Ostend sole and Sisteron lamb. The garden is an idyllic spot for a summer meal.

De Stove

4 Kleine St Amandstraat (050 33 78 35, www.restaurantdestove.be). **Open** 7-10pm Mon,

ESCAPES & EXCURSIONS

Tue, Fri; noon-2pm, 7-10pm Sat, Sun.
Main courses €25. **Credit** AmEx, MC, V.
Map p255 A2.
A beguiling little restaurant, just off one of the main shopping streets, serving a variety of hearty meat and fish dishes. The interior is traditional Flemish with an ancient iron stove and chimney.

Tanuki
1 Oude Gentweg (050 34 75 12, www.tanuki.be).
Open noon-2pm, 6.30-9.30pm Wed-Sun.
Main courses €22. **Credit** AmEx, MC, V.
Map p255 B4.
Tanuki's oriental minimalism offers a truly striking contrast to the mostly Flemish restaurants in the neighbourhood. Sushi and sashimi are a speciality, always fresh and reliably tasty.

Cafés & bars

B-Café
25 Wollestraat (050 33 42 29, www.b-online.be).
Open noon-6.30pm Mon, Tue, Thur-Sat; 3-6pm Sun. **Credit** AmEx, MC, V. **Map** p255 B2.
Stylish café above the design store B (*see right*), whose decked terrace offers unexpected views of the city spires. Excellent pasta, bruschetta and coffee.

Bean Around the World
5 Genthof (050 70 35 32). **Open** 10am-7pm Mon, Thur-Sat; 11.30am-7pm Wed. **Credit** MC, V. **Map** p255 B1.
A relaxing American coffee shop run by Californian Oline Aucoin offering free local and international newspapers, an internet terminal and free Wi-Fi. A perfect place for tourists and locals to come and tap on their iPads over a great cuppa.

★ Brugs Beertje
5 Kemelstraat (050 33 96 16, www.brugs beertje.be). **Open** 4pm-1am Mon, Thur, Sun; 4pm-2am Fri, Sat. **Map** p255 A3.
Drinkers rave about this dark brown pub that sells no less than 300 different beers. Set up by 'beer professor' Jan De Bruyne, it's now mainly run by his wife Daisy, who takes a more lenient run line when asked for 'a lager'.

Craenenburg
16 Markt (050 33 34 02, www.craenenburg.be).
Open 7am-midnight daily. **No credit cards.**
Map p255 A/B2.
Set on the site of the house where Maximilian of Austria was held captive, this is a typical Bruges tavern with yellowed walls, wooden tables and elaborate stained glass. *Photo p264.*

Het Dagelijks Brood
21 Philipstockstraat (050 33 60 50). **Open** 8am-6pm Mon, Wed-Sun. **No credit cards.**
Map p255 B2.

The Bruges branch of popular bakery chain Le Pain Quotidien. Decorated with effortlessly rustic flair, it's an excellent place to stop for snacks, salads and thick-cut sandwiches made with its traditional sourdough bread.

'T Estaminet
5 Park (050 33 09 16). **Open** 11.30am-3am Mon-Wed, Sun; 4pm-3am Thur; 11.30am-6am, Fri, Sat. **Credit** MC, V. **Map** p255 C2.
An old Bruges tavern facing Astrid Park in a quarter seldom reached by tourists. The owner has built up what is undoubtedly one of the best jazz collections in Bruges, attracting writers, politicians and women with dogs.

Est Wijnbar
7 Braambergstraat (050 33 38 39, www.wijn barest.be). **Open** 4pm-late daily. **No credit cards. Map** p255 B2.
A beautiful wine bar where you can sample 90 different wines, in a classy setting. Hosts intimate jazz concerts every Sunday from 8pm; entry is free.

De Garre
1 De Garre (050 34 10 29). **Open** noon-midnight Mon-Thur; noon-1am Fri; 11am-1am Sat; 11am-midnight Sun. **No credit cards. Map** p255 B2.
At the end of the shortest blind alley in Bruges (off Breidelstraat), this bar sells 130 different beers. It's set in a 16th-century house with wooden beams, brick walls and authentic Bruges atmosphere.

Joey's Café
16a Zuidzandstraat (050 34 12 64). **Open** 11.30am-late Mon-Sat. **No credit cards.**
Map p255 A3.
Located in the Zilversteeg shopping centre, Joey's is a dark candlelit café run by a local musician. The relaxed mood and good sounds draw a lively crowd, with a summer terrace and live music once a month.

Prestige
12-14 Vlamingstraat (050 34 31 67). **Open** 7.45am-6pm Tue-Sun. **No credit cards.**
Map p255 B2.
An elegant tearoom near the Markt, perfect for breakfast or a lunchtime bowl of own-made soup. Anyone looking for an afternoon sugar rush should try the coffee served with four miniature cakes.

De Proeverij
6 Katelijnestraat (050 33 08 87, www. deproeverie.be). **Open** 9.30am-6.30pm daily. **No credit cards. Map** p255 B4.
De Proeverij is a stylish café with pale green walls in a busy street. Coffee comes with a saucer of whipped cream and chocolates from Sukerbuyc (*see p268*) opposite. The hot chocolate is served as a dish of pure melted chocolate, which you add to a mug of steaming milk.

De Republiek
*36 St Jacobsstraat (050 34 02 29, www.
derepubliek.be/index2.html).* **Open** 11am-late
daily. **No credit cards. Map** p255 A2.
This candlelit café attached to an arts complex is a
good place to pick up word-of-mouth tips on jazz,
films and dance events.
▶ *Here you'll also find the late-night Cactus Club
(www.cactusmusic.be), the main place in town for
both DJs and live music.*

The Top
*5 St Salvatorskerkhof (050 33 03 51, www.cafe
thetop.be).* **Open** 6pm-2am daily. **No credit
cards. Map** p255 A3.
This lively bar lurks in the shadow of St Salvator
Cathedral, attracting a mixed crowd ranging from
young locals looking for a wild night out to tourists
hunting for decent dance sounds in the early hours.

De Versteende Nacht
11 Langestraat (050 34 32 93). **Open** 5pm-late
Mon-Sat. **Entry** *Concerts* free-€3. **Credit** MC, V.
Map p255 C2.
The manager of this jazz café is a huge fan of comic
strips and his bar is appropriately filled with comic
books, its walls covered with cartoons. Weekly live
jazz sessions draw the crowds on Wednesday nights.

SHOPPING
Dig a bit deeper, and you can find a lot more
than twee boutiques peddling chocolate and
lace. The main shopping street is **Steenstraat**,
which runs from the Markt to 't Zand and has
the usual international chains. **Geldmunt** and
Noordzandstraat have the fashion boutiques.
Wollestraat has its share of lace shops, plus
some smaller specialised stores too.

Design

★ B
25 Wollestraat (050 49 09 32, www.b-online.be).
Open 10am-1pm, 2-6pm Mon-Sat. **Credit** AmEx,
DC, MC, V. **Map** p255 B2.
A stunning contemporary design shop founded by
Katrien van Hulle, offering what she calls 'Belgian
products with an A label'.

Callebert
25 Wollestraat (050 33 50 61, www.callebert.be).
Open 3-6pm Mon, Sun; 10am-noon, 2-6pm Tue-
Sat. **Credit** AmEx, DC, MC, V. **Map** p255 B2.
International contemporary furniture and design in
a stylish shop next door to B. Check out ceramics by
Pieter Stockman and itect Bob van Reeth, or furni-
ture by the Van Severens brothers.

Fashion

L'Héroine
*32 Noordzandstraat (050 33 56 57,
http://users.skynet.be/fb143674).* **Open**
10am-6.30pm Mon-Sat. **Credit** AmEx, DC,
MC, V. **Map** p255 A2.
The upper floor of this lovely boutique has dresses
by Belgian designers Mieke Cosyn, Kaat Tilley and

Needle Works
Belgium is considered the cradle of lace.

The discovery of various bobbin-shaped
bone instruments has led some experts
to assert that lace-making actually dates
back to ancient Rome. There's no doubt,
though, that by the 15th century this
popular pastime had become an art in the
Low Countries, with Charles V ordering its
tuition in schools and convents.

There are four separate kinds of lace and
two main techniques still practised in the
Flemish regions. Although tourists should
be wary of machine-made lace imported
from Taiwan, they can still find the genuine
article at many specialist outlets. In the
region of Aalst, artisans create Ribbon lace,
also known as Renaissance or Brussels
lace, as it is mostly sold in the capital.
Bobbin lace, sometimes called Duchess,
is a speciality of Bruges, featuring delicate
flower patterns that are both costly and

highly time-consuming to produce, involving
up to 400 bobbins at any given time.

The oldest type of lace is Needlepoint;
it's no longer made commercially, but you
can still find examples in Bruges' rococo
Lace Emporium (9 Wollestraat, 050 34
04 72), which hosts lace-making
demonstrations. Techniques have changed
dramatically: a veil made for Queen
Elizabeth I famously required 12 million
stitches and some 12,000 hours of labour;
today Princess lace, as it is known, is only
half handcrafted, the netting done by
machine. Flowers, stalks and leaves are
later added by hand. You can spot machine-
made material: the netting will always be
very regular, an impossible feat for even
the most nimble-fingered lace maker. You
can see all these techniques at the lace
museum at the **Kantcentrum** (*see p262*).

Ann Huybens. Downstairs is menswear by Dries van Noten, womenswear by Martin Margiela and jewellery by Antwerp duo Wouters & Hendrix.

Joaquim Jofre

7 Vlaamingstraat (050 33 39 60). **Open** 9.30am-6.30pm Mon-Sat. **Credit** AmEx, DC, MC, V. **Map** p255 B2.

Worth checking out just to marvel at the art deco interior fittings imported from the owner's home country of Spain. The women's clothes are classic, well cut and beautifully finished, and there is also a good line-up of accessories, including hats.

Olivier Strelli

3 Eiermarkt (050 34 38 37, www.strelli.be). **Open** 10am-6.30pm Mon-Sat. **Credit** AmEx, MC, V. **Map** p255 A2.

This Brussels designer has established a loyal following in West Flanders with his sober fashions for men and women.

Other location 19 Geldmuntstraat (050 33 26 77).

Rex Spirou

18 Geldmuntstraat (050 34 66 50, www.rex-spirou.com). **Open** 9.30am-6.30pm Mon-Sat. **Credit** AmEx, DC, MC, V. **Map** p255 A2.

This wild store decorated by young graffiti artists sells streetware by name brands. The shop has managed to evade a local law banning neon signs – you may need sunglasses to look at the website.

Gifts

'T Apostelientje

11 Balstraat (050 33 78 60, www. apostelientje.be). **Open** 1-5pm Tue; 9.30am-12.15pm, 1.15-5pm Wed-Sat; 9.30am-1pm Sun. **Credit** AmEx, DC, MC, V. **Map** p255 C1.

A lot of lace around town is passed off as authentic Bruges handiwork even when it's machine-made and imported from abroad. The genuine article is sold here by a mother (in the business for 20 years) and her daughter, who has written several books on the subject. *See also p267* **Needle Works**.

Bottle Shop

13 Wollestraat (050 34 99 80). **Open** *Summer* 9am-11pm daily. *Winter* 9am-7pm daily. **Credit** MC, V. **Map** p255 B2.

Stockist of 850 types of local drinks: Trappist brews, hard-to-find Gueuze beers and genevers. Standard varieties will be cheaper in the supermarkets.

★ Diksmuids Boterhuis

23 Geldmuntstraat (050 33 32 43). **Open** 9am-12.30pm, 1.30-6.30pm Mon-Sat. **No credit cards**. **Map** p255 A2.

A rustic, friendly shop selling butter, cheese and smoked ham fresh from the Flemish polders. Popular with locals and tourists alike.

Dumon

6 Eiermarkt (050 34 62 82, www.chocolatier dumon.be). **Open** 10am-6pm Mon, Tue, Thur-Sat; 10am-5pm Sun. **Credit** AmEx, DC, MC, V. **Map** p255 A2.

A tiny basement chocolate shop that may well prove difficult to pass by. Friendly staff and a huge range of chocolates – equal parts divine and devilish.

De Patience

2 Spinolarei (050 34 21 89, www.bnart.be). **Open** 2-6pm Thur-Sat. **No credit cards**. **Map** p255 B1.

A gallery and shop run by US calligrapher Brody Neuenschwander, who worked on Greenaway's *Prospero's Books* and *The Pillow Book*. His postcards make rather eccentric souvenirs.

Soap Story

47 Noordzandstraat (050 34 44 01, www.the soapstory.com). **Open** 10am-6pm daily. **Credit** AmEx, DC, MC, V. **Map** p255 A2.

The Soap Story sells blocks of soap by weight in weird and wonderful scents and colours. Under the same ownership as the Bottle Shop (*see left*).

Sukerbuyc

5 Katelijnestraat (050 33 08 87, www. sukerbuyc.be). **Open** 8.30am-6.30pm daily. **No credit cards**. **Map** p255 A3.

A family-run chocolate shop that sells rich dark chocolates made with 100% cocoa butter and sugar-coated sweets for Catholic christenings. The name means sugarbelly in English.

Tintin Shop

3 Steenstraat (050 33 42 92, www.tintinshop brugge.be). **Open** 9.30am-6pm Mon-Sat; 11am-6pm Sun. **Credit** AmEx, MC, V. **Map** p255 A2.

Cartoon books, T-shirts and toys featuring the famous Belgian boy reporter.

Music & books

De Reyghere

12-13 Markt (050 33 34 03, www.dereyghere.be). **Open** 8.30am-6.15pm Mon-Sat. **Credit** AmEx, DC, MC, V. **Map** p255 B2.

Established in 1888, De Reyghere specialises in international newspapers, books on Bruges and fiction, including a small section of English novels. Guidebooks are sold next door.

Rombaux

13 Mallebergplaats (050 33 25 75, www. rombaux.be). **Open** 9am-12.30pm, 2-6.30pm Mon-Fri; 9am-6pm Sat. **Credit** MC, V. **Map** p255 B2.

One of the most comprehensive classical music shops in Belgium, Rombaux has been run by the same family for three generations. The shelves are filled with every imaginable CD recording.

Ghent

A thoroughly modern time warp.

Architecturally, Ghent is stuck in a medieval time warp with its compact, traffic-free centre cut through with canals and little trip-trap bridges. It has more listed buildings than the rest of Belgium put together, an ancient castle and a cathedral holding some of the world's most important works of art. But as crucial as Ghent's history is to its identity, it doesn't allow the past to hinder its present. Ghent is a thriving port, university city and the nerve centre of Belgium's digital industries.

Apart from an annual ten days of madness in July (*see p278* **Ghent Goes Wild**), the city remains quietly unassuming and tends not to scream its riches from the rooftops. The locals seem to prefer it that way, perhaps aware they could have another Bruges on their hands if they don't watch out. Ghent wants to share its lovely old town and is proud to show it off, but seemingly wants visitors to go there of their own accord – to take time to understand its ways rather than piling off a bus in a scrum of flying lace and bad holiday snaps. Ghent has the pedigree of a wealthy city state and it's not interested in cross-breeding.

HISTORY

Ghent's history is rich and erratic, combining periods of great glory and wealth with suffering and persecution. In the Middle Ages, when it was the centre of the cloth and wool trade, it was the largest town in western Europe and the university was considered one of the most scholarly. This wealthy, well-educated city later provided rich pickings for Martin Luther and his followers, which led Ghent into a nightmare scenario of heretic bonfires and the infamous iconoclastic fury of 1566, when no church, monastery or convent remained undamaged. In 1540, Ghent-born Emperor Charles V returned to the city in a rage after its citizens refused to pay higher taxes. He ordered the rebellion's ringleaders executed and then forced 50 of the city's elders, dressed only in white shirts and with nooses tied around their necks, to beg for mercy. Local residents became known as *stropdragers*, or noose-wearers.

GHENT TODAY

Known as Gent to the Flemings and Gand to the Walloons, the capital of East Flanders and Belgium's second port – it's on the banks of two rivers, the Leie and the Ketel – is 56 kilometres (35 miles) north-west of Brussels. Yet it could be another world. There's a flavour of wealth in the air, a sense of studied pride and, above all, organisation. Transport is a good case in point; escalators from the train station platform lead you directly down to the tram, which in turn delivers you deftly into the centre of town. The good thing about Ghent is that it works. The streets are calm and uncluttered, yet the cafés and bars around the Korenmarkt are packed and energetic, giving Ghent a sophisticated atmosphere all of its own, a place where both young and old have a feeling of belonging, and where visitors are welcomed – but left largely to their own devices.

GETTING THERE & AROUND

Ghent is just half an hour by train from the centre of Brussels. Four fast trains an hour shuttle between the two cities. From Gent St Pieters station take the No.1 tram into town (pay at the platform machines). If you arrive by car, follow the signs reading 'P-route'; this will take you through streets where you are allowed to park and, eventually, to a multi-storey car park.

INSIDE TRACK
JUST TO BE CLEAR

Ghent is served up in three different ways:
Gent = Dutch/Flemish
Gand = French
Ghent = English

SIGHTSEEING

The must-see attractions are the towers of **St Niklaaskerk**, the **Belfort** and **St Baafskathedraal** (and the view of the three together); Van Eyck's truly stunning *The Adoration of the Mystic Lamb* in St Baafskathedraal (*see p273* **A Lamb's Tale**); and **Gravensteen castle**. The first half of August is quiet as Ghent recovers from its raucous July festival.

St Michielsbrug to St Baafskathedraal

St Michielsbrug is a good place to start any tour of the city. One of the single best views of the cathedral is from this bridge over the Leie, which overlooks the **Graslei** (Herb Quay; *photo p274*) and **Korenlei** (Corn Quay). Both are lined with beautiful houses, most built during the Flemish Renaissance but some dating back as far as 1000. Just south of the bridge, on the west side of the river, is **St Michielskerk**, standing alongside the former Dominican

monastery Het Pand, part of the University of Ghent – the public are free to wander around. On the other side of the bridge stands **St Niklaaskerk**, an outstanding piece of Scheldt Gothic architecture built in the 13th century. Its interior is dominated by an over-the-top Baroque altarpiece.

Next door stands the **Stadhuis** (Town Hall), designed to be the largest town hall in Europe. Building began in 1518 but had to be halted because of religious strife and diminishing funds (the bickering contributed to that tantrum of Charles V's). Work resumed at the end of the 16th century, and the result of this staggered construction process is clearly visible. One part, decorated with countless statues, is in an ornate Gothic style, while the more sober section of the façade reflects post-Reformation taste. Check with the **tourist office** (*see p274*) for details of official guided tours.

Across the Botermarkt from the Stadhuis soars the lofty **Belfort** (Belfry), first built in the 14th century and later heavily restored. Its interior – containing both a carillon and a bell museum – is worth the entrance fee for the view over the city and the neighbouring cathedral.

Ghent's first cathedral was founded (as St Peter's) by the Brabant-born St Bavo in the seventh century. Built over six centuries, the current **St Baafskathedraal** (also known as St Bavo's) is remarkable as much for its high and late Gothic style as for the noted works of art it contains. Laurent Delvaux's elaborate rococo pulpit, in oak and marble, is the first thing you see on entering, and Peter Paul

St Michielsbrug.

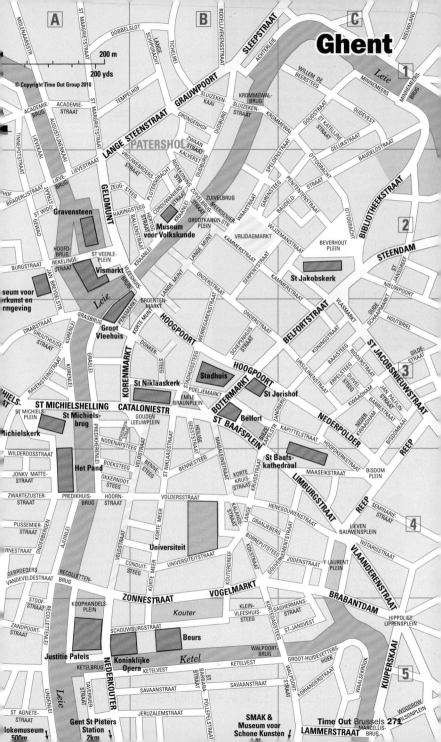

Ghent

St Baafskathedraal.

Nov-Mar 10.30am-4pm Mon-Sat; 1-4pm Sun.
Apr-Oct 9.30am-5pm Mon-Sat; 1-5pm Sun.
Admission €4; €1.50-€3 reductions; free
under-7s. **No credit cards**. Map p271 C4.

Gravensteen castle & around

Surrounded by water on the north-west edge
of the centre is **Gravensteen castle**. Built
in 1180 by Philippe of Alsace, Count of
Flanders, on the site of the first count's original
stronghold, this is the only medieval fortress in
Flanders. The arrestingly grim structure lost
its military function centuries ago – it was
subsequently used as a mint, a court of justice
and even a cotton mill. It has a small collection
of torture instruments.

Next door to the castle, on St Veerleplein, a
bas-relief Neptune towers over the entrance to
the **Vismarkt** (Fish Market), while across the
water stands the **Museum voor Sierkunst
en Vormgeving** (Museum of Decorative Arts
and Design). Located in an 18th-century house,
this superb collection includes beautiful royal
portraits alongside crystal chandeliers, silk wall
coverings and ornate tapestries. The furniture,
most of it French, includes baroque, rococo and
Louis XVI pieces. A more modern extension
houses temporary exhibitions. There is also a
stunning collection of modern design, including
art nouveau pieces by Victor Horta, Paul
Hankar and Henri van de Velde.

Just east of the castle on the Kraanlei is the
quirky **Museum voor Volkskunde** (Folklore
Museum, also called Het Huis van Alijn). Set
inside 18 almshouses, with a garden and chapel,
this museum is aimed primarily at children, but
parents will also enjoy it. It aims to show life in
Ghent in the 19th century, and has candlestick-
makers, cloth-makers, reconstructed sweet
shops, pubs and a chemist.

Patershol, the atmospheric tangle of streets
north of here, is packed with fine restaurants
and bars, patronised by young professionals.
Over the Leie, **Vrijdagmarkt** is a vast square
that used to be the focal point of political life
and quarrels in the Middle Ages, and is still a
marketplace; restaurants and bars line its sides.
There are market stalls on many squares and
markets most days of the week, plus a decent
fruit and vegetable market in **Groentenmarkt**
every morning. You'll come across several
excellent traditional bakeries and cheese shops
in the area, and plenty of cafés and tearooms.

Outside the historical centre, the Leie along
Lievekaai and **St Antoniuskaai**, north of
the castle, provides a charming walk.

★ Gravensteen
St Veerleplein (09 225 93 06). **Open** *Oct-Mar*
9am-5pm daily. *Apr-Sept* 9am-6pm daily.

Rubens' *Entry of St Bavo into the Monastery* is
displayed in the north transept. Its undisputed
masterpiece is *The Adoration of the Mystic
Lamb* by Hubert and Jan van Eyck (*see right*
A Lamb's Tale). The painting is on display
in the De Villa Chapel, crowded in high season
but worth the wait. The picture depicts a scene
from the Apocalypse according to St John,
the colours so bright and glistening that the
painting lights up the whole chapel.

The 12th-century crypt is the oldest part of
the cathedral. Although it contains tombs and
the usual religious paraphernalia, it's actually
most notable for its frescoes and for Justus van
Gent's painting *The Calvary Scene*.

South and west of the cathedral are Ghent's
shopping streets, such as crowded **Veldstraat**,
south from St Niklaaskerk, and the more
attractive **Magaleinstraat** and **Koestraat**,
south of the Belfort.

Belfort
St Baafsplein (09 375 31 61 07 72). **Open** 10am-
6pm daily. **Admission** €5; €3.75 reductions; free
under-19s. **No credit cards**. Map p271 B3.

★ St Baafskathedraal
*St Baafsplein (09 225 49 85, http://users.
skynet.be/sintbaafskathedraal-gent)*. **Open** *Nov-
Mar* 8.30am-5pm Mon-Sat; 1-5pm Sun. *Apr-Oct*
8.30am-6pm Mon-Sat; 1-6pm Sun. **Admission**
free. *The Adoration of the Mystic Lamb* **Open**

Admission €8; €6 reductions; free under-19s.
No credit cards. Map p271 A2.

Museum voor Sierkunst en Vormgeving

*5 Jan Breydelstraat (09 267 99 99, http://
design.museum.gent.be)*. **Open** 11am-6pm Tue-
Sat; 10am-5pm Sun. **Admission** €5; €3.75
reductions; free under-19s. **Map** p271 A2.

Museum voor Volkskunde

*65 Kraanlei (09 269 23 50, www.huis
vanalijn.be)*. **Open** 11am-5pm Tue-Sun.
Admission €2.50; €1.75 reductions; free
under-6s. **No credit cards**. Map p271 B2.

South of St Pieters station

The area between St Pieters station and the city
centre is home to three intriguing museums.
Along the west side of the River Leie is the
former Abdij (Abbey) van de Bijloke. The red-
brick abbey was founded in the early 13th
century and maintained its religious function
until it was promptly closed down by the
invading French revolutionaries in 1797. Up
to 2009 it housed the old Bijlokemuseum, but
from October 2010, **STAM**, the Museum of
the City of Ghent, takes pride of place.

South of here, across the river (a five-minute
walk from the train station; 25 minutes from the
centre) is **Citadelpark**, laid out in the 1870s
on the site of a Habsburg castle. Here is where
you'll find the outstanding **SMAK** (Stedelijk
Museum voor Actuele Kunst – Museum of
Contemporary Art). Generally thought to be
Flanders' finest collection of modern art, it
boasts first-rate works by Francis Bacon,
Joseph Beuys and David Hockney. There's also
a good spread of minimal and conceptual art,
the 1960s well represented with pieces by
Christo, Warhol and Broodthaers.

A Lamb's Tale

Van Eyck's striking altarpiece is an artistic enigma.

St Baafskathedraal (*see left*) is crammed
with works of art, including a Rubens,
but attentions most usually focus on a
complex altarpiece completed in 1432.
The Adoration of the Mystic Lamb, made
up of 12 panels in two rows, is attributed
to Jan van Eyck, although a Latin inscription
on its border – not to mention a rather
mysterious fingerprint – suggests that
his brother Hubert may have at least
started the painting.

The altarpiece was originally designed for
a private chapel belonging to the wealthy
cloth merchant Joost Vijd and his equally
influential wife Elisabeth Borluut; the
couple unfolded the panels (eight of them
painted on both sides) on Sundays and
high days for public viewing. Throughout the
centuries, ordinary folk piled in to see the
painting, endowing it with an almost cult
following. In 1934, the unthinkable finally
happened and the lower left panel, *The
Just Judges*, was stolen; it was never
recovered and has thus become one of
Belgium's greatest unsolved mysteries,
with many claiming that it was destroyed
long ago. A copy was made by Jef
Vanderkeven in 1945, and it is his
replacement panel that we see today.

Because of the highly sensitive nature of
the painting itself and the ever increasing
number of visitors, *The Adoration of the
Mystic Lamb* now sits securely in a
separate area of its own. Entry costs €4
and also includes the loan of a recorded
commentary. Because the painting is
so rich in detail, this comes highly
recommended, taking you as it does
through the complexity of the painting
panel by panel until an overall picture
of its fascinating story emerges.

The top central panels hold a mystery
of their own. Here you'll see Mary and
John the Baptist flanking a figure in the
middle; certain elements suggest the figure
is Jesus, but others give it a God-like
appearance. The truth is that no one knows
for sure, though Van Eyck may even have
been trying to combine characteristics
of both – something extremely rare in
medieval painting. On each side of the
central panel are some highly animated
depictions of Adam and Eve; Adam looks
as though he's walking right out of the
painting, while Eve appears to be having
a bad hair day. As if Original Sin wasn't
enough, the couple also offended 19th-
century moralists by being so blatantly
naked – a more modest clothed copy was
made for each of them, and can still be
seen displayed outside the Vijd chapel.

Het Lam Gods, as locals know it, is one
of the most influential paintings of the
Flemish School, and gives an insight into
the lives and beliefs of another age while
remaining a genuine enigma to the last.

ESCAPES & EXCURSIONS

Graslei. *See p270.*

Facing SMAK is **Museum voor Schone Kunsten** (Museum of Fine Arts). A major refurbishment has spruced the whole thing up.

Museum voor Schone Kunsten

1 Fernand Scribedreef, Citadelpark (09 240 07 00, www.mskgent.be). **Open** 10am-6pm Tue-Sun. **Admission** €5; €3.80 reductions; free under-12s, all 10am-1pm Sun. **No credit cards**.

★ SMAK (Stedelijk Museum voor Actuele Kunst)

Citadelpark (09 240 76 01, www.smak.be). **Open** 10am-6pm Tue-Sun. **Admission** €6; €4 reductions; free under-18s. **No credit cards**.

STAM (Museum of the City of Ghent)

2 Godshuizenlaan (09 269 87 90, www.stamgent.be). **Open** 10am-6pm Tue-Sun. **Admission** €6; €4.50 reductions; free under-19s. **No credit cards**.

Tourist information

City of Ghent Tourist Office

Belfort, 17A Botermarkt (09 266 56 60, www.visitgent.be). **Open** *Nov-Mar* 9.30am-4.30pm daily. *Apr-Oct* 9.30am-6.30pm daily. **Map** p271 B3.

WHERE TO STAY

At Christmas, Easter and especially during the Gentse Feesten in mid July (*see p278* **Ghent Goes Wild**) you should book at least a month

in advance of your visit. To do this, you can contact the tourist office (*see left*). Staff will check availability within your price range, then reserve free of charge when you call them back 30 minutes later. Alternatively, visit www.gent-hotels.eu.

The **Guild of Guesthouses in Ghent** (www.bedandbreakfast-gent.be) has 66 families who offer B&B accommodation, from a room in a cosy private home to a self-contained suite in a 17th-century cloister. Check the website for a list with descriptions; the tourist office also has an album of snapshots. Prices listed here are for a double room and include breakfast unless otherwise stated.

Adoma

19 St Denijslaan, 9000 Ghent (09 222 65 50, www.hotel-adoma.be). **Rates** €67. Breakfast €6. **Credit** AmEx, DC, MC, V.

A bargain – and it has the advantage of being a stone's throw from the station (a tram ride from the centre). The rooms are comfy and all have phones and TVs. There's also a car park and Wi-Fi.

Boatel

44 Voorhoutkaai, 9000 Ghent (09 267 10 30, www.theboatel.com). **Rates** €140. **Credit** AmEx, DC, MC, V.

This former transport boat moored near Dampoort train station, ten minutes' walk from the centre of town, has been converted into a seven-room hotel, complete with original woodwork and portholes. Known for serving a good breakfast.

Brooderie

8 Jan Breydelstraat, 9000 Ghent (09 225 06 23, www.brooderie.be). **Rates** €70. **No credit cards**. **Map** p271 A2.

Charming three-room B&B in a gabled house overlooking the canal in the centre. The light-filled rooms are clean and fresh; toilets and shower are shared.
► *Brooderie is also a bakery with a health-food café (open 8am-6pm Tue-Sun).*

Cour St Georges

2 Botermarkt, 9000 Ghent (09 224 24 24, www.courstgeorges.be). **Rates** €105. **Credit** AmEx, DC, MC, V. **Map** p271 B3.

Facing the Stadhuis and by the Belfort, the Cour dates back to 1228 – Charles V and Napoleon were guests. The smallish rooms aren't as characterful as they might be but have all the mod cons.

De Draecke Youth Hostel

11 St Widostraat, 9000 Ghent (09 233 70 50, www.vjh.be). **Rates** from €17.80 per person. **Credit** MC, V. **Map** p271 A2.

Set in a pretty part of the centre, De Draecke is ideal if you're on a tight budget. There are 106 beds in rooms sleeping two to six people, all en suite.

Erasmus

25 Poel, 9000 Ghent (09 224 21 95, www.erasmushotel.be). **Rates** €120. **Credit** AmEx, MC, V. **Map** p271 A3.

A cosy hotel five minutes' walk from the centre. The owners have preserved the authentic character of the 16th-century building while providing the 11 well-furnished rooms with every desirable modern comfort in mind.

★ Gravensteen

35 Jan Breydelstraat, 9000 Ghent (09 225 11 50, www.gravensteen.be). **Rates** €165. **Credit** AmEx, DC, MC, V. **Map** p271 A2.

A beautiful hotel in a 19th-century *hôtel particulier*. The Second Empire style is imposing and impeccable; the 49 elegant rooms are all equipped with modern facilities. The hotel has a bar and car park.

La Maison de Claudine

20 Pussemierstraat, 9000 Ghent (09 225 75 08, www.bedandbreakfast-gent.be). **Rates** €80. **No credit cards**. **Map** p271 A4.

For a classy B&B with a whiff of the bohemian about it, La Maison is hard to beat. Two luxury suites and one room (all non-smoking) are available. The largest suite is an enormous penthouse in the eaves, with fine views over the towers of Ghent. The other suite is a self-contained former coach house, which looks out on to the walled garden.

PoortAckere Monasterium

56 Oude Houtlei, 9000 Ghent (09 269 22 10, www.poortackere.com). **Rates** €115. Breakfast €15. **Credit** AmEx, DC, MC, V.

Not far from the centre, this renovated convent dates from 1278 and now houses a hotel, restaurant and concert venue, all arrayed around two lovely walled gardens. Some bedrooms are rather spartan, others are more luxurious, but all are fresh and clean.

EATING & DRINKING

Your impression of Ghent nightlife will depend on which area of town you visit and the evening you happen to choose. The southern part of the

Medieval Ghent.

city is certainly livelier and has the trendiest bars, largely because this is the student area and attracts a younger crowd. Most students, however, go home for the weekend and their big night out is usually Thursday. On Saturday the crowd is older and somewhat smarter. If it's quiet, don't worry – most locals don't think about going out for a drink until after ten.

Patershol, north of the historic centre, also has plenty of bars. With its canals and medieval streets free of traffic, it can be magical in the evening. Bars and restaurants here tend to be more elegant than in the student area.

Restaurants

Avalon
32 Geldmunt (09 224 37 24, www.restaurant avalon.be). **Open** 11.30am-2.30pm Mon-Thur; 11.30am-2.30pm Mon-Sat. **Main courses** €11. **Credit** MC, V. **Map** p271 A2.
Avalon is an unpretentious little lunchtime place with a rustic interior and a quiet walled garden terrace. More café than restaurant, it serves mostly vegetarian food; satisfying soups, own-made quiches and bountiful salads are the order of the day.

Le Baan Thai
57 Corduwanierstraat (09 233 21 41). **Open** 6.30-10pm Tue-Sat; noon-2pm, 6.30-10pm Sun. **Main courses** €15. **Credit** AmEx, DC, MC, V. **Map** p271 B2.

This pretty restaurant, set back from the street and overlooking a courtyard, serves excellent Thai food to eat in or take away. Booking essential.

Belga Queen
10 Graslei (09 280 01 00, www.belgaqueen.be). **Open** noon-2.30pm, 7-11pm Mon-Wed; noon-2.30pm, 7pm-midnight Thur-Sat; noon-2.30pm, 6.30-11pm Sun. Main courses €28. **Credit** AmEx, DC, MC, V. **Map** p271 A3.
This fancy, expensive restaurant-cum-cocktail lounge, set on the town's most beautiful quayside, attracts hordes of nouveaux riches from the suburbs. The food is haute Belgian with excellent seafood. All this under the 13th-century beams of an imposing old grain store.

★ De Blauwe Zalm
2 Vrouwebroersstraat (09 224 08 52, www. deblauwezalm.be). **Open** 7-9.30pm Mon, Sat; noon-1.30pm, 7-9.30pm Tue-Fri. **Main courses** €30. **Credit** AmEx, DC, MC, V. **Map** p271 B2.
The most talked-about restaurant in town, thanks to the expertise of chef Danny de Cleyn and interior designer Hans Wyers – one responsible for the exquisite fish dishes, the other for the striking piscine decor. Sure, it's as pricey as it gets in Ghent, but you're getting a standard of cooking, presentation and service that would put many restaurants in Antwerp to shame. Recommended.

Brasserie Keizershof
47 Vrijdagmarkt (09 223 44 46, www.keizershof. net). **Open** noon-2.30pm, 6-10.30pm Tue-Sat. **Main courses** €17. **Credit** AmEx, MC, V. **Map** p271 B2.
A high-ceilinged, beautifully renovated restaurant in the centre of town. The wide-ranging menu has plenty of traditional Ghent dishes on offer, and also features fish, pasta, steaks and French standards. Prices are reasonable.

C-Jean
3 Cataloniëstraat (09 223 30 40, www.c-jean.com). **Open** noon-2pm, 7-9pm Tue-Sat. **Main courses** €28. **Credit** AmEx, MC, V. **Map** p271 B3.
C-Jean enjoys an excellent local reputation, and deservedly so. The food is first-rate and reasonably

ESCAPES & EXCURSIONS

Georges.

priced. Ghent specialities feature heavily, as do a variety of fish and shellfish dishes.

★ Faim de Toi
10 Belfortstraat (09 223 63 93, www.faimde toi.be). **Open** noon-2pm, 6-10pm Tue-Fri; 6-10pm Sat. **Main courses** €25. **Credit** AmEx, DC, MC, V. **Map** p271 C3.
Classy and utterly contemporary, Faim is an embodiment of what cool Ghent is all about. The menu here is a modern take on local classics, giving the old green eels a lighter lift and presenting fillet of bream with chorizo oil. There are also fab salads and pastas. There's a funky lounge bar to chill in alongside Ghent's modish media types.

Georges
23-27 Donkersteeg (09 225 19 18, www.georges seafood.be). **Open** noon-2.15pm, 6.30-9.30pm Wed-Sun. **Main courses** €25. **Credit** AmEx, DC, MC, V. **Map** p271 B3.
A father-and-son fish restaurant that has been in the same family since 1924. The prices are a tad steep, but the fish is ultra-fresh and expertly cooked. The scrupulously clean fishmonger's next door, with its tanks of lobsters, is under the same ownership and a good advert for the restaurant.

De Hel
81 Kraanlei (09 224 32 40). **Open** noon-2pm, 6-10pm Mon, Fri, Sun; 6-10pm Thur, Sat. **Main courses** €22. **Credit** AmEx, MC, V. **Map** p271 B2.
In years past De Hel had devilish decor to match its name. Now the design of this cosy, wood-beamed restaurant changes regularly – with the exception of an old Chinese room that can be booked for dinner. Flemish and French cuisine is served – specialities include *waterzooi* and eel dishes – although you might also find the likes of goat curry.

'T Klokhuys
65 Corduwaniersstraat (09 223 42 41, www. klokhuys.com). **Open** 6-11pm Mon; noon-2.15pm, 6-11pm Tue-Sun. **Main courses** €18. **Credit** AmEx, MC, V. **Map** p271 B2.
Green banquettes line the walls and dried hops snake along the ceiling at rustic 't Klokhuys. Expect a selection of local regional dishes – such as chicken casserole or stewed eels in chervil sauce – with an emphasis on seasonal produce.

La Malcontenta
7-9 Haringsteeg (09 224 18 01, www. lamalcontenta.be). **Open** 6-11pm Wed-Sat. **Main courses** €12. **Credit** AmEx, MC, V. **Map** p271 A2.
Don't be misled by the name of this restaurant: the interior and staff may be a touch casual, but the kitchen's keenly priced specialities from the Canary Isles are a treat – try the seafood pancake or the squid in spicy tomato sauce. Tapas available too.

Pakhuis
41 Schuurkenstraat (09 223 55 55, www. pakhuis.be). **Open** noon-11pm Mon-Thur; noon-midnight Fri, Sat. **Main courses** €25. **Credit** AmEx, DC, MC, V. **Map** p271 A3.
This large renovated storage depot is worth visiting as much for its architecture as its French-Italian

ESCAPES & EXCURSIONS

food: the cast-iron pillars, wrought-iron balustrades, parquet floor and impressive oak bar are the main features of a classic interior. You can gawp with just a drink if you don't fancy eating.

Vier Tafels

6 Plotersgracht (09 225 05 25, www.viertafels.be). **Open** 6-10.30pm Mon; noon-2pm, 6-10.30pm Tue-Sun. **Main courses** €20. **Credit** AmEx, DC, MC, V. **Map** p271 B2.

One of the most popular restaurants in Patershol. It's not as expensive as other places nearby, but the food is every bit as good with top-notch global favourites and Ghent specialities. It also features a bar, Virus, for a pre-meal tipple.

Wok Away

11 Korenmarkt (09 233 90 00, www.wokaway.be). **Open** 11.30am-8pm daily. **Main courses** €4. **No credit cards**. **Map** p271 A3.

Ghent Goes Wild

Don't miss Belgium's biggest party.

The start of August is a slow time in Ghent. Restaurants and bars pull their shutters down and locals slope around wearing shades and looking sheepish. This is the aftermath of Belgium's wildest party, the mother of all street festivals that takes place each July.

De Gentse Feesten (09 210 10 10, www.gentsefeesten.be) is a home-grown bash with centuries of history, aimed firmly at locals but attracting more visitors every year as news of its good-natured vibe spreads. Indeed, so rapid is its rise that the city fathers commissioned a study on the impact of the 1.5 million visitors crammed into the old town centre over the ten-day period. It certainly transforms the city: the normally quiet cobbled streets resound with rock music, jazz bands and street theatre; the clean, ordered life of Ghent billows with excitement and an increase in discarded fast-food cartons.

Urban dross, some may think, but the truth is that the Gentse Feesten is the happiest, most relaxed street party that you could hope to see. Sure, it's one big piss-up, with folk of all ages staggering their way through the countless knees-ups keeping bars going till dawn, but there is never any trouble. Let's just say that again: there is *never* any trouble; not a punch, not a brawl, nothing trashed – except the good people of Ghent, who know how to behave even when beer-soaked.

The festival got under way in its current form in 1970, when the local folk singer Walter De Buck decided to get people on to the streets for a bit of popular culture while giving artists from all over the country an opportunity to promote themselves to a wider audience. He organised a ten-day programme of entertainment on the little square by St Jacob's church, and once the city council sat up and got involved, it all

started to snowball. The festival is these days based around three sub-festivals: **International Street Theatre** (www.istf.be), **International Puppet Buskers** (www.eftc.be) and the highly infectious **10 Days Off** techno festival (www.10daysoff.be). Yes, even the clubbing goes on for ten days – free shuttle buses get you out to the Vooruit centre where the vast party thumps ever on.

Leading up to the Feesten in early July is the Gent Jazz Festival (ww.gentjazz.com), a sort of taster of things to come. Top headline acts appear here along the lines of Norah Jones and Toots Thielemans – even Madness have made an appearance.

All these provide the frame on which hangs the rest: dance lessons at **Baudelo Park**; the alternative music acts at the **Trefpunt** (www.trefpuntvzw.be); free entrance to all the city's museums. On top of that, each of Ghent's squares is musically themed to help the ten days swing by: the **Korenmarkt** is for pop acts, **Groentenmarkt** is country and western music, **Beverout Plein** offers rock 'n' roll, and the free-for-all **Vlasmarkt** next door just goes for whatever takes its fancy. Nor is it all simply music, madness and a sea of booze; the cultural life of the city also thrives (there are around 700 theatre performances each year). There's stuff for kids too: ask at the tourist office for the *Kinderfestivalpocket*, a guide to children's activities during the festival.

Local tradition marches on too; there is still the Stroppenommegang (Procession of the Noose-Wearers) and the famous Kouter Ball, which has been going strong in these parts since 1843 and gives citizens an opportunity to turn out in their best. The Gentse Feesten is mad, wild, good-natured and friendly; it's a time when the folk of Ghent can celebrate in their own batty, rather bohemian way. It's a true class act.

ESCAPES & EXCURSIONS

This Asian fast-food restaurant is deservedly popular with the young Ghent crowd, with speedy service and great flavours. The restaurant turns into a loungey cocktail bar in the evening.

Cafés & bars

★ Café Charlatan
6 Vlasmarkt (09 224 24 57, www.charlatan.be). **Open** 7pm-late daily. **No credit cards.** **Map** p271 C3.
Describing it as a music café doesn't begin to tell the story – although there is live music most evenings at 10pm, with a live radio link-up. The back room opens at weekends from 1am for urban house, disco and other danceable tunes. All sorts of performances take place, but Charlatan is simply a damn good hangout for musicians, night owls and locals who refuse to go home. It's undoubtedly at its brilliant best during the awesome Gentse Feesten (*see left* **Ghent Goes Wild**), when this is simply *the* place to be at eight in the morning.

Damberd Jazz Café
19 Korenmarkt (09 329 53 37, www. damberd.be). **Open** 11am-late daily. **No credit cards. Map** p271 A3.
An art nouveau jazz venue on two floors. The ambience is friendly and the crowd all ages. There's live jazz (see website for details), but the place is mainly used as a comfortable and convenient meeting place slap in the centre of town.

De Dulle Griet
50 Vrijdagsmarkt (09 224 24 55, www. dullegriet.be). **Open** 4.30pm-1am Mon; noon-1am Tue-Sat; noon-7.30pm Sun. **No credit cards. Map** p271 B2.
De Dulle Griet was the first pub in Belgium to specialise in local Flanders beers, so it's not surprising that its dimly lit and curious interior has welcomed many a tourist. It's still a lot of fun, though, mainly because locals love it as well – some indulge in the bizarre house custom of exchanging their shoe for a beer, and have the waiter then winch it up in a basket. Go figure – it's Ghent, after all.

'T Galgenhuisje
5 Groentenmarkt (09 233 42 51). **Open** 11am-late daily. **No credit cards.** **Map** p271 B3.
A working and highly popular pub since the late 17th century, 't Galgenhuisje means 'the gallows' – a reference to its rather grisly medieval function.
▶ *Downstairs, in the 14th-century cellar, a restaurant serves fish and grilled meats.*

★ Hotsy Totsy
1 Hoogstraat (09 224 20 12, www.hotsytotsy.be). **Open** 6pm-late Mon-Thur; 8pm-late Fri-Sun. **No credit cards.**

Limonada.

The Hotsy Totsy jazz bar is a veritable Ghent institution. The venue pulls in a varied crowd who come to enjoy the strong drinks, jazz and eclectic stand-up comedy performances – check website for details. Despite the heavy wooden door and curtains, it's open to all, a ten-minute walk from the centre.

Limonada
7 Heilige Geeststraat (09 224 40 95, www.limonada.be). **Open** 8pm-late Mon-Sat. **No credit cards. Map** p271 B3.
A laid-back bar with an atmosphere more akin to Antwerp than alternative Ghent.

Mosquito Coast Travel & Adventure Café
28 Hoogport (09 224 37 20, www.mosquito coast.be). **Open** 11am-late Tue-Sat; 3pm-late Sun. **No credit cards. Map** p271 B3.
An ideal place to meet like-minded adventurers. The cosy bar is littered with second-hand guidebooks, plus decent wines, snacks, cocktails and tapas. It moved from its original venue lock stock and barrel in 2005, but you'd never know it.

Pink Flamingo's Lounge
55 Onderstraat (09 233 47 18). **Open** noon-midnight Mon-Wed; noon-3am Thur, Fri; 2pm-3am Sat; 2pm-midnight Sun. **No credit cards. Map** p271 B2.
This pub is well known for its collection of kitsch, which changes every three months. The place is

Café de Video.

packed with dolls, records, cartoon books, religious figurines and tat of every description.

Rococo
57 Corduwaniersstraat (09 224 30 35).
Open 9pm-late Tue-Sun. **No credit cards**.
Map p271 B2.
Located in Patershol, Rococo is one of Ghent's moodier bars. Artists gather around candlelit tables and a piano sits in one corner, sometimes too tempting for the would-be *chanteur* who's had a few too many. There's also an outdoor café at the back.

★ Den Turk
3 Botermarkt (09 233 01 97, http:// cafedenturk.be). **Open** 11am-late daily.
No credit cards. **Map** p271 B3.
Dating all the way back to 1340, Den Turk is the oldest pub in Ghent, although you wouldn't know it from its distinctly ordinary decor. It plays host to regular jazz (plus a dash of blues and flamenco) and you can munch on a sizeable choice of snacks.

'T Velootje
2-4 Kalversteeg (09 223 28 34). **Open** times vary; phone for details. **No credit cards**.
Map p271 B2.
One of the oldest brick houses in Ghent, partly built on the ruins of a Roman fortress, 't Velootje is crammed with religious objects and antique bicycles. Look for the blue-and-white 'Pater Lieven' sign on the apricot-painted house, or you'll miss it.

★ Het Waterhuis aan de Bierkant
9 Groentenmarkt (09 225 06 80, www.waterhuis aandebierkant.be). **Open** 11am-late daily.
Credit MC, V. **Map** p271 B3.
A good stop for beer-lovers, with an excellent range of brews (including 14 on draught and all six Trappists), all described on the menu. Its riverside location makes it extremely popular.

CLUBS & DANCE FESTIVALS

Cool and sophisticated Ghent goes for a subtle inner-city nightlife, with student bars, jazz cafés and all-hours lounge bars to keep night owls alert. Clubs are generally advertised as 'parties', so keep your eye out for flyers. Start at **Oude Beestenmarkt**, where folk happily bar hop in, out and back again; **Café de Video** (No.7, www.cafevideo.be) is a hotspot right now, with **Suite 16** (No.5, www.suite16.be) keeping the punters awake with a full agenda of live music and DJs. For more serious clubbing, Ghent's reputation rests on one venue: **Culture Club** (174 Afrikalaan, 09 267 64 42, www.cultureclub.be). Its classy design and heavy duty light shows make it a must for those into house, R&B and hip hop, with special electro and techno parties adding the necessary layers. Beyond the ring, and a five-kilometre taxi ride away, the **Mega-Temple** (5 Solariumdreeft, Destelbergen, www.mega-temple.be) is a national legend, and still keeps a happy 1,500-strong crowd moving to usually commercial, uplifting sounds.

The main dance party is the **10 Days Off** festival (www.10daysoff.be), part of the **Gentse Feesten** (*see p278* **Ghent Goes Wild**), with ten nights of quality electro-dance featuring a range of top-class international DJs. **I Love Techno** (www.ilovetechno.be), one of Europe's biggest festivals, takes place in the cavernous Flanders Expo centre on Ghent's Maaltekouter.

FILM

At the beginning of October, Ghent hosts the annual **Flanders International Film Festival** (www.filmfestival.be). Prizes are awarded and the odd celebrity pops by. Among the local cinemas hosting the event, and used throughout the year, are **Kinepolis** (12 Ter Platen, 09 265 06 00, www.kinepolis.be), **Sphinx** (3 St Michielshelling, 09 225 60 86, www.cinebel.com) and **Studio Skoop** (63 St Annaplein, 09 225 08 45, www.cinebel.be).

SHOPPING

Ghent's central shopping district is highly compact, completely pedestrianised and generally free of overwhelming crowds.

Veldstraat is the main drag, with the usual international chain stores and department giant Inno. **Bennesteeg** has Ghent's most upscale fashion boutiques, and streets **Volder**, **St Niklaas** and **Magelein** feature more quirky addresses. All the shops listed below are closed on Sundays.

Fashion & accessories

Ann Huybens
4 Trommelstraat, bottom of Kalversteeg (09 224 36 16, www.annhuybens.com). **Open** 2-6pm Wed, Fri, Sat or by appt. **Credit** V. **Map** p271 B2.
Ann Huybens' ready-to-wear wild wedding dresses are sold in all the hippest bridal shops, but this is her own boutique. Get fitted out for a bespoke gown or choose from a limited selection on the shelves.

Ill'mus
18 Jan Breydelstraat (09 233 40 90). **Open** 10am-1pm, 1.30-6pm Tue-Sat. **Credit** AmEx, MC, V. **Map** p271 A2.
Upscale fashion labels include Ghost, DKNY Jeans and Georges Rech for women, plus Paul Smith and Kenzo for men.

Lena Lena at M
19 Bennesteeg (09 233 79 47). **Open** 2-6pm Mon; 11am-6pm Wed-Sat. **Credit** AmEx, DC, MC, V. **Map** p271 B4.

INSIDE TRACK MUSEUM PASS

You can buy a **Museum Pass** (€20) from the tourist office (*see p274*) that gives entry to all the city's museums for three days. In addition, you can use all the inner-city buses and trams for free.

Miet Crabbé is the designer behind this label for fashion-conscious voluptuous women. One half of the shop has decorative homeware by other Belgian designers, including Christophe Coppens.

Movies
5 St Pietersnieuwstraat (09 223 59 12, www. movies.be). **Open** 10.30am-6.30pm Mon-Fri; 10am-7pm Sat. **Credit** AmEx, DC, MC, V.
Since 1984, Movies has offered a range of high-quality designer fashion in a pleasant environment. Streetwear labels include the likes of Adidas, Fornari, G-Star and Schott.

Het Oorcussen
7 Vrijdagmarkt (09 233 07 65, www.oorcussen.be). **Open** 1.30-6pm Mon; 10.30am-6pm Tue-Sat. **Credit** AmEx, MC, V. **Map** p271 B2.
This stylish boutique in a 16th-century house offers exclusively Belgian designers: Dries van Noten, Dirk Bikkembergs, Ann Demeulemeester, AF Vandevorst and Martin Margiela. There's also

Pink Flamingo's Lounge. *See p279.*

ESCAPES & EXCURSIONS

a small collection of jewellery and accessories by Wouters and Hendrix.

Orsacchino
7b Gouvernementstraat (09 223 08 47).
Open 10.30am-6.30pm Mon, Wed-Sat.
Credit MC, V. **Map** p271 B/C4.
Sophisticated, daring lingerie and bathing costumes for men and women. Men are restricted to D&G, but women can also pick from Joop, André Sardá and Pain de Sucre.

Food & confectionery

★ Het Groot Vleeshuis
7 Groentenmarkt (09 223 23 24, www.groot vleeshuis.be). **Open** 10am-6pm Tue-Sun.
Credit MC, V. **Map** p271 B3.
The great butcher's hall is a cavernous medieval space dedicated to the regional products of East Flanders. Here you can find sausages, hams, regional beers and *cuberdons*, red syrupy triangles of sugary confection.

Temmerman
79 Kraanlei (09 224 00 41). **Open** 11am-6pm Tue-Sat. **No credit cards. Map** p271 B2.
Temmerman is a confectioner of great charm, with an absolutely fabulous assortment of chocolates, biscuits, sweets, edible sugared flowers, honey and teas. Every type of sweet has a history attached and the staff are happy to tell you all about it.

★ Tierenteyn-Verlent
3 Groentenmarkt (09 225 83 36, www.tierenteyn-verlent.be). **Open** 8.30am-6pm Mon-Fri; 8.30am-12.30pm, 1-6pm Sat. **No credit cards.**
Map p271 B3.
This shop, with the same original fittings as when it first opened in 1858, specialises in mustard. A huge vat prepared according to a family recipe of 1790 stands in one corner, and can be bought by the gram and taken home in containers sold in the shop. Other spices are stocked, along with every type of mustard seed imaginable.

Vishandel de Vis
48 Voldersstraat (09 224 32 28, www.devis.be).
Open 10am-6.30pm Mon; 9am-6.30pm Tue-Sat.
Credit MC, V. **Map** p271 B4.
A first-class and fiercely popular food shop specialising in fresh fish and all kinds of seafood: the fresh variety on slabs, ready-to-eat winkles and live oysters; freezer cabinets stuffed with bags of shellfish and fish suppers; and a *traiteur* with a wonderful selection of various take-home-and-heat recipes for that home-made look.

Music, books & comics

De Kaft
44 Kortrijksepoortstraat (09 329 64 38, www.dekaft.be). **Open** 10am-6pm Mon-Sat.
No credit cards.
This quirky second-hand shop sells an eclectic range of books, comics, vinyl, CDs, posters, videos and computer software. It's neat and tidy – not always the case with nearly new shops – so you should find what you're looking for.

Music Mania
197 Bagattenstraat (09 225 68 15, www.music maniarecords.com). **Open** 11am-7pm Mon-Sat.
Credit MC, V.
Three floors covering every type of music you can imagine, although drum 'n' bass, jazz and reggae are specialities. The shop used to be known for its heavy metal selection, which is still good. Although no second-hand CDs are sold, you should find some bargains on the third floor. Check out the vinyl as well.

Souvenirs

★ The Fallen Angels
29-31 Jan Breydelstraat (09 223 94 15, www. the-fallen-angels.com). **Open** 1-6pm Mon, Wed-Sat. **Credit** MC, V. **Map** p271 A2.
A wonderful place to browse for an original souvenir from the many boxes of vintage postcards of Ghent. The shop also stocks a selection of antique toys.

Het Oorcussen. *See p281.*

Day Trips

Gothic cities and seaside escapes.

Nowhere's far in Belgium. The excellent train network can speed you back and forth to all parts of the country in the same day; the sandy coast, the forested Ardennes and the major Gothic cities are all within striking distance of the capital.

Remember that Brussels is a bilingual island, surrounded by Flemish territory – so the moment you leave the capital, signposts and place names change to Flemish (Bruges becomes Brugge, for example). The bulk of Flanders lies to the north, east and west of Brussels, while the boundary of the French-speaking region of Wallonia is to the south of the city.

Ostend & the North Sea Coast

The Belgians are justly proud of their 67 kilometres (42 miles) of coastline. Not only does it provide a punctuation mark to their territory, but its sands are some of the finest in northern Europe. At low tide the soft beaches can stretch for several hundred metres, providing a safe play area and a paddler's paradise. And despite the cold, grey North Sea, which can whip up a fair wind all year round, the stalwart Belgians arrive in droves; in summer it's shoulder-to-shoulder solid, while in winter it's full of retired folk and city types with second homes.

This tourist invasion of the dunes has its downside; massive building projects along the coastline have left it overdeveloped in a mish-mash of styles, a sort of Benidorm *à la belge*, where apartment blocks, villas and commercial enterprises vie for the perfect sea view. But all is not lost: the coast is redeemed by its broad promenades, which separate sand from cement and provide a safe passage for hired bikes, tandems and pedal cars, as well as plenty of long, lazy strolling.

Another charming feature uneclipsed by the building work is the humble beach hut. They remain in rows all along the Belgian coast as a testament to the 19th century, when they were drawn by horse to the water's edge for modest mixed-sex bathing. ('Horror!' cried the English,

but that didn't stop the young Victoria popping over for a dip.) Today the huts are painted up a treat in ice-cream colours and can be hired or bought, although families tend to pass them down from generation to generation.

OSTEND

Thanks to its royal connections, Ostend is considered the queen of the Belgian seaside resorts. Léopold I built a house here, but it was Léopold II, master builder of Belgium, who commissioned several villas and gave Ostend its royal character.

Despite criticism that he was neglecting the capital, Léopold II spent much of his time here – partly because it provided the perfect hideaway for his numerous affairs. His association with the town meant it became a highly fashionable resort in the late 19th and early 20th centuries; so fashionable, in fact, that it rivalled Monte Carlo for wealth, casinos and racecourses. World War II finally put paid to all that, and serious aerial bombardment destroyed much of the old fabric, including the original casino, resulting in the curious blend of imperialistic grandeur and 1960s and '70s blocks that you'll see today.

The atmosphere in Ostend is pretty typical seaside stuff, with the long, wide promenade and soft, flat sands giving it a calm air. The *Mercator*, an old Belgian navy training ship from the '30s, still stands in the yacht harbour, while the **Souikom** harbour is now used mainly for water sports.

Ostend.

A plethora of events takes place throughout the summer, from sporting get-togethers (sailing, cycling, windsurfing) to artistic shindigs (a major theatre festival takes place in July and August; www.theateraanzee.be). One of the oddest events by far is September's shrimp-peeling competition in the **Visserskai**, the fishermen's harbour, which provides the wonderful sight of the daily catch coming in.

The wind can be biting in winter, but hardy Belgians use their holiday flats year round, so Ostend is never really empty. Over the Christmas and New Year period there is a skating rink and an atmospheric Christmas market, along with fireworks on the beach on 31 December, and the strange but spectacular communal ritual of burning Christmas trees on the beach after Twelfth Night.

A smattering of architectural gems from old Ostend remain. **Fort Napoleon**, built in 1812, is the only intact Napoleonic fortress in Europe, while over at the western end of the promenade Léopold II's **Galeries Royales** (*photo p287*) comprise a stately colonnade crowned with a belle époque pavilion. Léopold's own former villa is now a luxurious hotel, the **Thermae Palace** (*see right*). In the church of **St Peter and St Paul** is a darker relic; the marble mausoleum housing the first Léopold's beloved

wife, Louise-Marie, who died in Ostend in 1850. The twin-towered church also houses stained-glass depictions of the Belgian kings.

The crowning glory of the post-war period is **Ostend Casino**, built in 1953 and the fourth to stand on the spot. The walls of the gaming room are decorated with frescoes by Paul Delvaux, although you have to take a place at the tables to see them. The casino is also used as a multi-purpose arts complex in summer.

Ostend's artistic reputation stems from its link to the expressionist painter James Ensor, who lived, worked and died here. A trail of 15 panels reproducing his often macabre works are dotted around town, while his home and studio, the **Ensorhuis**, is open to the public. So small was its upstairs workshop that Ensor could never fully unfurl his ultimate masterpiece, *Christ's Entry into Brussels*. The house used to belong to his aunt, who sold seashells and other souvenirs, and the shop continues this tradition.

The Provincial Museum for Modern Art joined forces with the old Museum of Fine Arts in 2009, and is now known as the **Art Museum aan Zee**. It exhibits local modern art from the expressionists to the present day and includes video art and installations by Panamarenko, the man with the flying machines.

Art Museum aan Zee
11 Romestraat (059 50 81 18, www.pmmk.be).
Open 10am-6pm Tue-Sun. **Admission** €5.
No credit cards.

Ensorhuis
27 Vlaanderenstraat (059 50 81 18).
Open 10am-noon, 2-5pm Mon, Wed-Sun.
Admission €2. **No credit cards**.

Where to eat & stay

It's no surprise to learn that fish is the order of the day in Ostend. For a quick bite go to the Visserskai, where small stands sell fishy finger food – prepared crab, mussels and fresh young herring (*maatjesharing*) – and, yes, you do eat them raw. You shouldn't go wrong in any one restaurant in Ostend, but among the pick of the bunch are **'T Vistrapje** (37 Visserskaai, 059 80 23 82, www.vistrapje.be, menus €34-€60) or, over at No.30, the **Thermidor** (059 70 24 27, main courses €25) – guess what's on the menu there.

For something ritzy, try **Savarin** (75 Albert I Promenade, 059 51 31 71, www.savarin.be, main courses €30); prices are lower at lunch. The **Art Café** (3 Romestraat, 059 80 56 86, main courses €10) is buzzier. Nightlife and drinking haunts are around Langestraat and Van Iseghemlaan. Irish pubs abound, but one bizarre place is the **Cosy Corner Inn** (76a Langestraat, 059 70 92 61), full of atmosphere and bonhomie.

Hotels tend to be smarter than those at most seaside resorts. At the top end, Léopold's old villa, the **Thermae Palace Hotel**, is one of Ostend's finest (7 Koningin Astridlaan, 059 80 66 44, www.thermaepalace.be, €170-€195 double; *photo p288*). The modern **Hotel Europe** is only 50 metres from the promenade, and is reasonably priced and comfortable (52 Kapucijnenstraat, 059 70 10 12, www.europe hotel.be, €80-€105 double). A decent place near the railway station is the art deco-style **Hotel Louisa** (8B Louisastraat, 059 50 96 77, www.hotellouisa.be, €90 double). For a budget option try **Hotel Orbit** (46 Torhoutsesteenweg, 059 50 14 42, €60 double). For more options, see www.hotels-belgium.com/oostende/hotels.htm. You can book via the tourist office (*see below*).

Getting there

The motorways to the coast can be a nightmare, particularly at weekends and in the summer, and parking comes with its own problems. By far the best way to get to Ostend is by taking the inter-city train from Brussels; the journey time is just over an hour.

Tourist information

Toerisme Oostende
2 Monacoplein, 8400 Oostende (059 70 11 99, www.toerisme-oostende.be). **Open** 10am-6pm Mon-Sat; 10am-5pm Sun.

ALONG THE COAST

A good way to pop into other resorts is to take the coastal tram (*see below* **Beside the Seaside**). **De Haan** (www.dehaan.be) has a

---

Beside the Seaside

All aboard Belgium's splendid coastal tram.

One of the glories of the Belgian coast is the Kusttram, the quaint coastal tram that runs along its length from De Panne to Knokke. It's not just a major civil engineering success story; it also makes life easier for locals, allowing them to travel the coast in style, while at the same time providing tourists with a unique sightseeing opportunity.

The tram – run by Flemish public transport company De Lijn (059 56 52 11, www.delijn.be/dekusttram) – makes 69 stops along its route, including all 16 coastal towns. It also ties in neatly with most major railway stations, making that final leg of the trip more bearable. Knokke station to Blankenberge seafront? No problem at all.

In summer, one tram goes by every ten minutes (20 minutes in low season), and a €5 daily pass allows you to hop on and off when and where you like. Hardier travellers hoping to do the whole journey in one go need to set aside around two hours and 20 minutes, and should consider bringing along a cushion to ease the bumpy ride.

The real benefit of the tram is the flexibility it offers tourists: if you've had enough of sunbathing crowds, hit the tram and head for some quiet dune walking; if the kids are screaming, pile aboard and go to a water park or funfair. Alternatively, if you'd rather laze on the beach sipping Belgian beer all day, forget the car and take the tram to the sands. What more could you ask for?

delightfully unspoilt, sandy, seven mile-long beach, and is particularly geared up for kids' activities. It's also proud of its pine-wooded dunes, which hug the seashore and are laid out with ramblers' walkways. This is one of the few spots where belle époque architecture, harmonious pastel façades and winding lanes have not given way to high-rise blocks.

Blankenberge (www.blankenberge.be) also boasts sandy dunes, a 1930s pier, a harbour and a lengthy promenade, with steep ladder-type steps down to the bathing huts and beach. The town is stuffed with attractions, including the **Sea Life Centre** and the **Serpentarium** reptile park.

Even **Zeebrugge**, known mostly as a ferry port, is worth a look around. It is now Belgium's main fishing port, and the new fish market is a sight in itself. The old one has been converted into a major maritime theme park, **Seafront Zeebrugge**, where, among other things, you can clamber around a real Russian submarine and a lightship.

For those that prefer their coastline rugged and unspoilt, it's well worth heading to the area around **Zwin**, where the dunes are rigorously protected in order to provide a sanctuary for indigenous birds and wildlife at **Het Zwin Nature Reserve** (see p290 **Where the Wild Things Are**). Zwin is at the northernmost end of the coastal zone, furthest from Ostend and close to the Dutch border.

Close by Zwin is the posh resort of **Knokke-Heist**, with its designer shops, swanky restaurants and exclusive beach clubs, not to mention the very select **Royal Tennis Club du Zoute** (7 Astridlaan, 050 60 28 60), and **Royal Zoute Golf Club** (050 60 12 27, www.zoute.be). More downmarket but still a place to see and be seen is **Surfers Paradise** (13 Acacialaan, 050 61 59 60, www.surfers paradise.be), a semi-exclusive beach area where you can hire boards and play it cool. The **Casino Knokke** (509 Zeedijk, 050 63 05 00, www.casinoknokke.be) is so much more than a gaming house. Set in a beautiful 1920s building, it has two nightclubs and a function room that draws international stars. It is also an art gallery of sorts, with frescoes by Keith Haring and Paul Delvaux alongside works by the likes of Spilliaert. But it is the *Enchanted Fields* murals in the dining room that attract most attention, as they are the work of Belgium's René Magritte. Naturally you need to be an appropriately dressed paying punter to partake, but once inside the atmosphere is relaxed and fun (you'll need your passport).

★ Het Zwin

8 Graaf Léon Lippensdreef, Knokke-Heist (050 60 70 86, www.zwin.be). **Open** *Easter-Sept*

9am-7pm daily. *Oct-Easter* 9am-5pm daily. Closed Wed Nov-Mar. **Admission** €5; free-€4.20 reductions. *With Butterfly Park* €8.40; €2.70-€4.20 reductions. **Credit** phone for details.

Sea Life Centre

116 Albert I Laan, Blankenberge (050 42 43 00, www.sealife.be). **Open** from 10am daily; check website for closing times. **Admission** €16.50; €13-€15 reductions. **Credit** MC, V.

Seafront Zeebrugge

Vismijnstraat 7, Zeebrugge (050 55 14 15, www.seafront.be). **Open** 10am-6pm daily; closed early-late Jan. **Admission** €10.50; €8.50 reductions. **No credit cards**.

Serpentarium

146 Zeedijk, Blankenberge (050 42 31 62, www.serpentarium.be). **Open** times vary. **Admission** €8.50; €6-€7.50 reductions. **No credit cards**.

Where to eat & stay

In Knokke-Heist, smart dinners, smart discos and the smartest of casinos are likely to inflict some serious damage on your wallet. If seafood's your thing, you could try **Aquilon** (6 Elizabethlaan, 050 60 12 74), famed for its lobster and lavish use of truffles. **Ter Dijcken** (137 Kalvekeetdijk, 050 60 80 23) is a classic French/Belgian establishment. Main courses at both are around €40. For a simpler lunch of *moules-frites*, you really can't go wrong at **'T Kantientje** (103 Lippenslaan, 050 60 54 11, main courses €20).

If you want to stay the night, **La Réserve** (160 Elizabethlaan, 050 61 06 06, www.la-reserve.be, €250-€550 double) is reopening in 2011 in the full-on five star style. The cheaper **Parkhotel** (204 Elizabethlaan, 050 62 36 08, www.parkhotelknokke.be, €95-€145 double) is a decent alternative, close to the beach and decorated in modern style.

Leuven

The picturesque yet ever lively city of Leuven (Louvain in French), just east of Brussels, is Belgium's equivalent to Cambridge or Oxford. It is home to one of the world's oldest Catholic universities (founded in 1425) and survived two bouts of bombing during the World Wars. It was also the scene of sustained linguistic battles in the mid-1960s. After four years of fighting, the university was split; the Flemings stayed and a new campus was built for francophones in Louvain-la-Neuve. Today it seems tranquil enough; bicycles dominate the quiet city centre, with many streets closed to cars. There's a fine network of cycle paths, and bike hire shops are scattered around town.

Leuven considers itself the beer capital of Belgium, and it's no idle boast. The huge Interbrew conglomerate has its brewery here, while Domus (Tiensestraat 8, www.domus leuven.be) is a smaller operation. You can sample its amber-hued Nostra Domus beer and unfiltered, malty lager, Con Domus, on a brewery tour, or at one of the terraces on the bar-starred central **Oude Markt**. In August, Oude Markt becomes the stage for the outdoor rock festival **Marktrock** (www.marktrock.com).

The town centre (a ten-minute walk from the train station, along Bondgenotenlaan) is focused on **Grote Markt**, where you'll find the city's architectural highlights. The impressive and elaborate **Stadhuis** (Town Hall), built between 1439 and 1469, is a masterpiece of Brabant late Gothic architecture. Its delicate pinnacles, towers and intricate detailing have a fairy-tale harmony, and bear testament to the city's prosperous past: Leuven grew rich from the cloth trade, and was the capital of Brabant. The original plan for statues in each of the 282 niches proved too ambitious, however; the money ran out, and it wasn't

Galeries Royales, Ostend. *See p284.*

ESCAPES & EXCURSIONS

until the mid 19th century that the majority of niches were eventually filled with non-medieval figures such as Napoleon and members of Belgian royalty.

The Town Hall faces Leuven's other major Gothic building, **St Pieterskerk** (016 22 69 06, closed Mon) – a church with an unhappy past. Begun in the 1420s, on the site of a Romanesque basilica, it was intended to have three spires, the central one soaring to 170 metres (558 feet) high. Sadly, the marshy subsoil proved unable to support such a structure; work lasted 70 years, and the prematurely capped towers mark the builders' insurmountable problem. The exterior was then badly battered during both World Wars. Inside, though, Gothic harmony is re-established in the vertiginous nave. The ambulatory contains a small but worthwhile museum, the **Treasury of St Peter**, with a copy of Roger van der Weyden's *Descent from the Cross* and two rare surviving triptychs from his apprentice Dirk Bouts, the city painter of Leuven.

In September 2009, the brand new Museum Leuven, known simply as **M**, opened up, taking in the collection from the old Vander Kelen museum as well as recreating the old rooms of the original building. The permanent collection is based around two important periods; late Gothic and the 19th century

Stroll south from St Pieterskerk along Naamsestraat to the Baroque mid 17th-century **St Michielskerk**, then continue on down to **Groot Begijnhof**, just off the street to the right. Founded around 1230, this gorgeous and extensive complex (with its 62 houses, ten convents, church and squares) once played home to lay sisterhoods (*béguines*), but is now mostly student accommodation.

If you want a change from culture, hot shops include **Profiel** (37 Mechelsestraat, 016 23 72 62, www.profiel-leuven.be), which stocks cutting-edge womenswear by Ann Demeulemeester, Dries van Noten and Kaat Tilley, together with lesser-known and much cheaper labels. Men have **Jonas** opposite (No.34, 016 23 41 04, www.jonasmen.be) for casual fashion from Antwerp Sixer Dirk Bikkembergs and Paul Smith. For comic strip annuals, call by **Het Besloten Land** (16 Parijsstraat, 016 22 58 40, www.hbl.be) – the shop is piled high with titles in French, Dutch and English.

On Saturday mornings there's a food market on **Brusselsestraat**, where local farmers come to sell their produce. **Elsen** (36 Mechelsestraat, 016 22 13 10, www.elsenkaasambacht.be) is run by a professional cheese ripener who picks up his specials from the food market outside Paris. If you ask him nicely he'll show you the special ripening chambers.

Thermae Palace Hotel. *See p285.*

★ M – Museum Leuven

Leopold Vanderkelenstraat 28 (016 27 29 29,
www.mleuven.be). **Open** 11am-6pm Tue,
Wed; 11am-10pm Thur; 11am-6pm Fri-Sun.
Admission €9; €5-€7 reductions; free under-13s.
Credit AmEx, MC, V.

Where to eat & stay

Make a beeline for the Oude Markt area, just
south of the Grote Markt, and pick one of
the many bars or cafés that line the square.
If you fancy making a real night of it, **Silo** (39
Vaartkom, 0496 23 72 52, www.silo.be) is one of
Belgium's best clubs, set in an old warehouse.

For dinner head to Parijsstraat, which runs
parallel with the Oude Markt on the west side.
There are restaurants to suit most tastes and
budgets. Top choices include the global fusion
Kapsiki at No.34 (016 20 45 87), which has
vegetarian mains at €18, and upmarket
restaurant-traiteur **Il Pastaio** at No.33 (016
23 09 02, www.ilpastaio.be, closed Sun, main
courses €14). The pasta is made in-house; try
the scampi, tomatoes, basil and olive oil sauce.

For quieter dining, consider **Ombre ou
Soleil** (20 Muntstraat, 016 22 51 87, main
courses €30), where the menu is Med simplicity
and the ambience is relaxed. On the same
street, **Oesterbar** (No.23, 016 29 06 00,
www.oesterbar.be, main courses €30)
specialises in fish and oysters and boasts an
open log fire in winter. Or there's the trendy,
five floor **De Blauwe Zon** (28 Tiensestraat,
016 22 68 80, main courses €20), whose kitchen
serves up modern fusion cuisine and wicked
steaks. For a true gourmet experience go for
smart **Belle Epoque** (94 Bondgenotenlaan, 016
22 33 89); in fair weather you can sit outside in
the pretty courtyard. Expect to pay from €60
per person, and book ahead at the weekend.

To extend your stay, try the peaceful
Daniels B&B at 14 Cardenberch (016 23 87 80,
www.jeffsguesthouse.be, €90 double), which
has just one calm, tastefully muted suite.
Martin's Klooster (22 Predikherenstraat, 016
213 141, www.martins-hotels.com, from €235
double) is a more opulent option, with 40 sleek,
modern rooms in a 16th-century country house.

Getting there

There are five trains an hour from Brussels
to Leuven. The journey takes 30 minutes.

Tourist information

Leuven Tourist Office

1 Naamsestraat, 3000 Leuven (016 20 30 29,
www.leuven.be). **Open** *Mar-Oct* 10am-5pm daily.
Nov-Feb 10am-5pm Mon-Sat.

INSIDE TRACK BIKE ON BOARD

All trains in Belgium have space for bikes;
you can buy a single bicycle ticket for €5
or a day pass for €8 valid on any train.
If you're loading up the bike in Brussels,
it's best to go from Gare du Midi or Gare
du Nord, as stops at Gare Centrale are
too short. You can also hire bikes for
a full day or half day from stations in
Blankenberge, Bruges, Ghent, Knokke
and Ostend. Call 02 528 28 28 or visit
www.b-rail.be for details.

Liège

Liège is the third largest city in Belgium after
Brussels and Antwerp. Despite being just 16
kilometres (ten miles) from the Dutch border, its
French-speaking residents are considered to be
the most dedicated Francophiles in the country.
Liège is also known as Outremeuse, meaning
'beyond the River Meuse'; one part of the city
is named exactly that, and is renowned for its
rebellious nature. It also holds its own cultural
festival every 15 August to celebrate local
folklore and tradition.

The city is the de facto capital of the
Ardennes and of its own province. For centuries
it was an independent power, governed by a
succession of powerful prince-bishops between
the tenth century and 1794, when French
Revolutionary armies ousted the last of the
ruling priests and destroyed the cathedral.
The city got back on its feet in the 1800s and
enjoyed prosperity as a coal and steel centre;
it is still home to a sizeable Italian population,
after immigrants came here to work in the
mines following World War II. In more recent
times the local heavy industry declined, which
accounts for the down-at-heel feel of some of
the less prosperous neighbourhoods.

Today, Liège is probably most famous as
the birthplace of Georges Simenon, the prolific,
pipe-smoking author who wrote over 500
novels and, so the legend goes, slept with more
than 10,000 women. He was born in 1903 at
24 rue Léopold, a stone's throw from the
Outremeuse district where he grew up: the
building is now a discount junk shop. (Opposite
is a nightlife must-try, the Maison du Pequet,
pequet being a local variety of gin with freshly
squeezed fruit juices.)

Simenon started his writing career as a cub
reporter on the *Gazette de Liège*, wrote his first
novel at the age of 17 and set many of his
stories in Liège; he later admitted that almost
all of his settings – even those in the US –
were based on his home town.

ESCAPES & EXCURSIONS

Where the Wild Things Are

Get back to nature at one of Belgium's biggest protected reserves.

You might think that there's little more to the Belgian coastline than dunes, dunes and yet more dunes, but you'd be wrong. Endless sandscapes abound, of course, but the dunes along this coast enjoy a surprising amount of diversity. Some are covered with hardy, spiky marram grass; others with deciduous trees or unique salt-water plants, attracting rich birdlife.

Knokke-Heist, created by the building of dykes to protect the area around the *zwin* or sea-arm, is the most northerly of Belgium's many resorts, separated from Zeeland in the Netherlands by the stunning nature reserve **Het Zwin** (*see p286*). This wild area was formerly the estuary of the river of the same name, which silted up over the ages, causing serious damage to the commercial port potential of both Bruges and Damme.

While most of the land behind the coast has been reclaimed for cultivation, an area of 150 hectares (370 acres) near the sea has been designated a protected habitat of mudflats, marshes and dunes, creating a plant and bird sanctuary. The reserve needs constant maintenance, and only a third of the total area is accessible to the public. Nevertheless, the park makes a wonderful hiking destination, complete with lagoons, salt marshes and low pine tree plantations, while the man-made dyke allows visitors to walk across the marshes from park to sea, observing many beautiful birds and plants.

Some 100 species of bird nest in Het Zwin, including visitors such as avocets, egrets and harriers, which come to lay their eggs, spend the winter or search for food. At the entrance to the nature reserve, various species are kept in ponds and aviaries so that visitors can see them close up without disturbing those in the wild. Budding botanists can also study the unusual plants that flourish in the wetland conditions, including sea lavender, glasswort, samphire and saltbush.

Besides Het Zwin, the region also has 12 kilometres of sandy beaches, a handful of seaside resorts, a butterfly garden with over 400 exotic varieties and over 3,500 hectares (8,648 acres) of polders (tracts of land reclaimed from the sea) with signposted walking and cycling routes.

Amateur detectives can pick up a few leads of their own on the two-hour 'Sur les traces de Simenon' audio tour of the city (€6), starting at the **Maison du Tourisme** (*see p292*). The war memorial outside the Town Hall lists one Arnold Maigret, who furnished the writer with a surname for his famous detective, the star of no less than 75 novels. The church of St-Pholien, in Outremeuse, is a grislier landmark: a young cocaine addict was found hanged from its door handle in 1922, inspiring Simenon's 1931 thriller *Le Pendu de St-Pholien*.

The main railway station in Liège is two kilometres south of the centre on place Guillemins, and is home to a small information office (04 252 4419, closed Sun). It's a 25-minute walk to the heart of the city, the charmless place St-Lambert. Here you'll find the **Palais des Princes-Evêques**, the grand former home of the prince-bishops, dating from the 16th century but much altered over the centuries. The Palais now serves as the court for Liège Province, and only the outer courtyard is generally accessible to the public.

The older part of the city lies east of here, in the shadow of the steep Montagne de Bueren, atop which stand the remains of the ramparts of the **Citadelle**. It's a stiff climb, but rewarded with a fabulous panorama of the city. Parallel to the bottom of the hill runs Féronstrée, the backbone of this part of Liège.

Many of Liège's museums are either on or just off Féronstrée. The **Musée de l'Art Wallon** boasts over 3,000 paintings and sculptures, giving a sample of the best of Brussels and Wallonia; naturally, both René Magritte and Paul Delvaux are represented here. A little further along Féronstrée are the delightfully presented 18th-century furniture and furnishings of the **Musée d'Ansembourg** – including its famous six-faced clock.

The **Grand Curtius** is an ambitious expansion of the Musée Curtius which reopened in 2009, resulting in a new four-in-one museum complex. The 17th-century Renaissance palace now houses the immense collection of arms and armour of the Musée d'Armes, the glass artefacts of the Musée du Verre (some dating back to ancient Egypt), and the many decorative and historic pieces of the Musée d'Archéologie and Musée d'Arts Décoratifs (some with religious significance, and made with precious metals and stones).

The area south and west of place St-Lambert is an appealing place to wander, with its pedestrianised streets and multitude of bars, restaurants and shops; it's also liberally sprinkled with churches. On place Cathédrale, the **Cathédrale St-Paul** was begun in the 14th century but not finished until the 19th; its exterior may be unremarkable, but inside are some vibrant 16th-century ceiling paintings and vivid stained glass.

South of the cathedral, by avenue Maurice Destenay, is the church of **St-Jacques**, founded in the 11th century. Only the western wing of the original church survives, with Gothic and Renaissance styles mingling in the rest of the church. The most notable feature of **St-Denis**, set between the cathedral and place Lambert, is its immense, 16th-century retable. West of here, on place Xavier Neujean, stands **St-Jean** (closed Oct-May; call 04 223 4566 for reservations). Dating from the tenth century, it was originally modelled on Charlemagne's church at Aachen, although only the tower remains of the original structure. Note that most churches have restricted visiting hours on Sunday, and also close at lunchtime.

A key figure in Liègeois lore is Tchantchès, a character with a huge nose and a passion for fighting and drinking. He's most often found today in puppet form, and is celebrated in the **Musée Tchantchès** at 56 rue Surlet (04 342 7575, www.tchantches.be). From October to Easter, you can catch a puppet show on Wednesdays at 2.30pm and Sundays at 10.30am. The other main attraction on this side of the river Meuse is further south, by the tree-lined Parc de la Boverie: the **Musée d'Art Moderne**, which houses works by Chagall, Gauguin, Monet and Picasso, among others (*see right* **Inside Track**).

★ Cathédrale St-Paul

Place Cathédrale (www.cathedraledeliege.be). **Open** 8am-noon, 2-5pm daily. **Admission** €4. **No credit cards**.

Grand Curtius

13 quai de Maestricht (04 221 9404, www.grandcurtiusliege.be). **Open** 10am-6pm Mon, Wed-Sun. **Admission** €9; €5 reductions; free under-12s. **No credit cards**.

Musée d'Ansembourg

114 Féronstrée (04 221 9402). **Open** 1-6pm Tue-Sun. **Admission** €5. **No credit cards**.

Musée d'Art Moderne (MAMAC)

3 parc de Boverie (04 343 0403, www.mamac. be). **Open** 1-6pm Tue-Sat; 11am-4.30pm Sun. **Admission** €5; €3 reductions; free under-12s. **No credit cards**.

★ Musée de l'Art Wallon

86 Féronstrée (04 221 9231, www.museeart wallon.be). **Open** 1-6pm Tue-Sat, 11am-4.30pm Sun. **Admission** €5; €3 reductions; free under-12s. **No credit cards**.

Where to eat & stay

It's easy to eat well in Liège. Diagonally opposite the end of the rue du Pot d'Or is **Le Bruit Qui Court** (142 boulevard de la Sauvenière, 04 232 1818, www.bruitquicourt.be, main courses €14), a late-opening brasserie in a former bank that serves pasta, salads and grilled fish.

As Ouhès (19-21 place du Marché, 04 223 3225, www.as-ouhes.be, main courses €17) serves local specialities such as *boulets* (Liège's own traditional meatballs) and mashed potato mixed with black pudding. Nearby is the diminutive **L'Eurèye** (9 place du Marché, 04 223 2813, main courses €15), which also serves classic Liègois dishes and is generally packed. Just up the road, **Le Bistrot d'en Face** (8-10 rue de la Goffe, 04 223 1584, www.lebistrotdenface.be, main courses €17), attracts the more adventurous gourmets with a menu that includes pig's ears, herrings in oil and other hearty local fare.

Rue Tête de Boeuf is probably the best starting point for bars, although they are sprinkled around the city. If you've had a long night, you could have coffee and breakfast at **Café Lequet** (17 quai sur Meuse, 04 222 2134), an old haunt of the Simenon family, which opens its doors at 6am on Sundays and serves a famous meatball and chips. It's the perfect spot to greet a new day in passionate, mysterious, hard-living Liège.

The **Hotel Hors-Château** (62 rue Hors-Château, 04 250 6068, www.hors-chateau.be, €95 double) is a smart contemporary place to stay, set in a renovated 18th-century house in the old town.

ESCAPES & EXCURSIONS

Getting there

From Brussels, there are four trains an hour to Liège. The journey takes 65 minutes.

Tourist information

City of Liège Tourist Office
92 Féronstrée, 4000 Liège (04 221 9221, www.liege.be). **Open** 9am-5pm Mon-Fri; 10am-4.30pm Sat; 10am-2.30pm Sun.

Maison du Tourisme
35 place St Lambert, 4000 Liège (04 237 9292, www.liege.be). **Open** 9am-5pm Mon-Fri; 10am-4.30pm Sat; 10am-2.30pm Sun.

Namur

Some 60 kilometres (37 miles) south-east of Brussels is Namur, the capital of French-speaking Wallonia. It's a pretty, cobbled little city located at the confluence of the rivers Sambre and Meuse. Once of strategic military importance – hence its hilltop citadel – the town's attraction now lies in its cosy old squares and pedestrianised streets, lined with grand houses, chic shops, busy cafés and some excellent restaurants.

Namur was subjected to numerous invading forces, each struggling for control of the mighty **Citadelle de Namur**, one of the largest forts in Europe. Although it has been fortified for 2,000 years, the citadel's current structure dates mainly from the period of Dutch rule between 1815 and 1830. It sprawls over some 200 acres; there are five self-guided walking tours year round and, from April to November, a tourist train and tour guides to take visitors through the underground passages where soldiers could live for up to a month without venturing above ground. You'll also find some exhibitions, an open-air theatre and children's amusements.

Also on the site is **Parfums Guy Delforge** (60 route Merveilleuse, 081 22 12 19, www.delforge.com, admission €3.50), Belgium's only perfume manufacturer. At 3.30pm on Saturdays, and Tuesday to Saturday in the school holidays, guided tours demonstrate the different stages of perfume making, from the raw materials kept cool deep inside the citadel to the end product.

Down in the town itself there are a number of museums worth investigating. The **Trésor du Prieuré d'Oignies** is a modest but worthwhile collection of 13th-century gold and silver work by Brother Hugo d'Oignies – treasures that were hidden away from French revolutionaries and Nazi soldiers during two of the more recent invasions of Namur. Just

around the corner is the **Musée Archéologique**, where you'll find a relief model of Namur. Before air reconnaissance and satellite imaging, monarchs had scale models made of towns so that they could plan their line of attack (or defence) should war break out. The model of Namur, a copy of the original made in the 18th century for Louis XV, is an immaculate representation of how Namur would have looked; model-maker Larcher d'Aubancourt walked around the town measuring every inch of ground.

Walk through the pedestrianised old town and you'll find the **Musée Félicien Rops**, located in an 18th-century manor house. Namur-born artist Rops was notorious during his lifetime for his epicurean appetites, his fascination with the occult and the erotic nature of his drawings. The museum has more than 1,000 works, plus an important collection of 2,000 engravings. In another magnificent 18th-century mansion, the **Musée de Groesbeeck de Croix** re-creates an aristocratic abode from the Enlightenment. Highlights include the kitchen and the French garden – an oasis in the heart of the city.

Compared with the abundance of exquisite medieval gold and 19th-century symbolist pornography it offers, Namur's ecclesiastical sights are disappointing. The best is the Baroque **Eglise St-Loup** on rue du Collège, with a lovely interior built for the Jesuits in the early 17th century. It was here that Baudelaire collapsed and died from a stroke in 1866. East of St-Loup, 16th-century **Eglise St-Jean Baptiste** overlooks place du Marché-aux-Légumes; west of St-Loup, past the former Jesuit college of the Palais Provincial, the **Cathédrale St-Aubain** stands on the square of the same name. A grand neo-classical pile, it was built in the mid 18th century on the site of two old churches. Its treasures are now in the **Musée Diocésian** (www.musee-diocesain-namur.be; admission €3), which has amassed pieces from churches across the region, including a golden crown reliquary from the 13th century that is said to include two thorns from Jesus's crown.

The best shopping can be found along the traffic-free streets between the cathedral and rue de l'Ange. Wine shop **Grafé Lecocq** (3 rue du Collège, www.grafe.be) has extensive cellars, covering much of the subterranean level of the cathedral. For jewellery, head for **Maya** (15 rue de la Halle, www.mayajewellery.be), with tempting pieces from the likes of Christa Reniers and Annick Tapernoux.

★ Citadelle de Namur
64 route Merveilleuse (081 65 45 00, www.citadelle.namur.be). **Open** *Apr-Sept*

11am-6pm daily (last admission 5pm).
Admission €9; €6 reductions. **Credit** MC, V.

Musée Archéologique

Rue du Pont (081 23 16 31). **Open** 10am-5pm
Tue-Fri; 10.40am-5pm Sat, Sun. **Admission** €3;
€1.50 reductions. **No credit cards.**

★ Musée Félicien Rops

*12 rue Fumal (081 22 01 10, www.musee
rops.be).* **Open** *Sept-June* 10am-6pm Tue-
Sun. *July, Aug* 10am-6pm daily. **Admission**

€3; €1.50 reductions; free under-12s.
No credit cards.

Musée de Groesbeeck de Croix

3 rue Saintraint (081 24 87 20). **Open** 10am-
noon, 1.30-5pm Tue-Sat. **Admission** €3;
€1 reductions. **No credit cards.**

Trésor du Prieuré d'Oignies

17 rue Julie Billiart (081 25 43 00). **Open** 10am-
noon, 2-5pm Tue-Sat; 2-5pm Sun. **Admission** €2.
No credit cards.

Dancing in the Streets

The weird but wonderful Binche Carnival.

For most of the year, Binche is a quiet town
in Belgium's industrial rustbelt, not far from
Charleroi. There's little for tourists to do,
aside from surveying the palace ruins and
strolling along a stretch of the old city
walls. Arrive on Shrove Tuesday (Mardi
Gras), though, and you'll find yourself
plunged into one of the most spectacular
carnivals in Europe (064 33 67 27 or visit
www.carnavaldebinche.be).

Don't get the wrong idea; it's not like
carnival in Cologne, and you won't get
kissed by a transvestite in an extravagant
wig. Carnival here is a serious business,
involving months of preparation. Strict
rules and rituals cover every aspect of
the festival, from the mysterious symbols
stitched on to the costumes to the timing
of the parades. The participants, known
as Gilles, have to be male, Belgian and
born in the town; the women's role is to
make the costumes.

Records of the festivities date back to
the 14th century, but the turning point
came in 1549 when Mary of Hungary,
governor of the Low Countries, put on an
extravagant procession in honour of her
brother, Charles V. At the same time, in
another corner of his empire, explorers
were discovering the civilisations of South
America, so the nobles in Binche decided
to dress up as Incas.

Carnival season starts in early January
with a calendar of balls, processions and
rehearsals. Eight days before Shrove
Tuesday, thousands take to the streets
wearing masks in a ceremony known as
Trouilles de Nouilles. But the main events
are packed into three strenuous days,
starting on the Sunday before Shrove
Tuesday. From 3pm, the Gilles parade
through town in their spectacular

costumes, accompanied by brass bands,
drummers and revellers in fancy dress.

Shrove Monday is more relaxed, with
a children's parade, barrel organ music
and dancing in the streets. The next
morning, the Gilles are roused before dawn,
helped into their costumes and given a
glass of champagne. The streets are soon
filled with groups of Gilles dancing to a
hypnotic drum beat. They eventually arrive
at the cobbled square by the town hall,
where they put on wax masks decorated
with a moustache and glasses, then begin
a slow, stamping clog dance.

It goes quiet around lunchtime, when
the Gilles retire to quaff oysters and
champagne while everyone else tries to
squeeze into a café. The revellers regroup
at about 3.30pm for the main parade,
when the Gilles don huge headdresses
decorated with ostrich feathers. They set
off on a slow dance, accompanied by boys
laden with baskets of blood oranges. Now
the rowdy part begins, as the boys start
hurling the oranges at the crowd; they
are meant as gifts, and you must never
throw one back.

The people of Binche were enormously
proud when an international committee
voted in 2003 to include Binche Carnival
on the UNESCO World Heritage list. One of
the delegates happened to suggest to the
organisers that it might be a good idea to
allow women a greater role; she was lucky
that no one had any oranges to hurl.

The Musée International du Carnaval
et du Masque (10 Rue Saint Moustier,
064 33 57 41, www.museedumasque.be)
has a fascinating collection of masks and
costumes from around the world. Note
that, like most things in Binche, it is closed
during carnival time.

Where to eat & stay

For refreshment, the area west of central place d'Armes is your best bet. The tiled **Tea Time Café** (35 rue Saint-Jean, 0496 52 44 22) is an ideal snack stop between sightseeing. For something more substantial, **Brasserie Henry** (3 place St-Aubain, 081 22 02 04, www.brasseriehenry.net, main courses €17) serves up local specialities and international favourites in very generous portions. At the family-run **La Bonne Fourchette** (112-116 rue Notre Dame, 081 23 15 36, main courses €20), located between the citadel and the Meuse, you'll find classic Wallonian cuisine.

Gourmet fare can be sampled at **La Petite Fugue** (5 place Chanoine Descamps, 081 23 13 20, www.lapetitefugue.be, main courses €25), where mains might include lobster with fennel and ratatouille or a delicious sole meunière.

If you're after a quiet drink, go straight to **Le Chapitre** at 4 rue du Séminaire, with its extensive beer list; for something a little more lively, try **Le Monde à l'Envers** at 28 rue Lelièvre. There are a handful of cafés lining place du Marché aux Légumes, including the **Piano Bar** (No.10, 081 23 06 33), which hosts jazz and rock concerts most weekends.

The pick of the limited accommodation is **Hotel Les Tanneurs** (13 rue des Tanneries, 081 24 00 24, www.tanneurs.com, €40-€215 double). Thirty rooms have been created in an old tannery, each priced according to their size and facilities (some have their own jacuzzi and hammam). It has a charming rustic restaurant, and also offers half-board accommodation. The run-of-the-mill but affordable **Hotel Ibis** (10 rue du Premier Lanciers, 081 25 75 40, €63-€95 double) is also centrally located.

Getting there

From Brussels, up to five fast trains an hour make the 60-minute journey to Namur.

Tourist information

Maison du Tourisme de Namur
Square Léopold, 5000 Namur (081 24 64 49, www.namurtourisme.be). **Open** 9.30am-6pm daily.

Office du Tourisme
Hôtel-de-Ville, 5000 Namur (081 24 64 44, www.namurtourisme.be). **Open** 8am-4.30pm Mon-Fri.

Waterloo

The Battle of Waterloo (*see p21*) evidently wasn't fought with the tourists of today in mind; the battlefield lies close to a motorway, a long way from the centre of Waterloo itself. The scattering of tourist attractions include the quarters used by Napoleon and Wellington and the impressive Butte du Lion, a huge monument built by the Dutch on the spot where the Prince of Orange was wounded. From the top of this 226-step vantage point, the battleground seems remarkably small.

A notable historic relic in its own right is the **Panorama**, a circular building showcasing a panoramic painting made in 1912 by Louis Dumoulin to mark the centenary of the battle. The sites have recently undergone extensive renovations, and at the heart of it all is the **Lion Mound Hamlet Visitors Centre** (315 Route du Lion, 02 385 1912, www.waterloo 1815.be), selling various passes to the sights. There is also a Discovery Tour (€12; €9 reductions), which enables visitors to survey the battlefield from the back of a specially modified truck.

In April, there are demonstrations of artillery fire on the field with cavalry and infantry in authentic period uniform. There is also a partial reconstruction in June to mark the anniversary of the battle itself (18 June), and every five years the battle is re-enacted in its entirety – the next one is due in 2015 (*see p178*).

Getting there

The easiest way to get to Waterloo from Brussels is by car; take the ring road west to junction 25. Otherwise, there are five trains an hour to Waterloo station and the journey takes around 20 minutes. It's a one-kilometre walk from the station, although there are taxis.

Tourist information

Office de Tourisme de Waterloo
218 chaussée de Bruxelles, 1410 Waterloo (02 352 09 10, www.waterloo-tourisme.be). **Open** *Apr-Sept* 9.30am-6.30pm daily. *Oct-Mar* 10.30am-5pm daily.

Directory

Getting Around

DIRECTORY

ARRIVING & LEAVING

By air

Brussels Airport
0900 700 00,
www.brusselsairport.be.
Brussels' main airport is at Zaventem, 14 kilometres (nine miles) north-east of the capital, and has good road and rail connections into the city centre. You'll find the information desk (open 7am-10pm daily) in the check-in area. Hotel information and a phone link for reservations are in the arrivals section. Hotel shuttle buses run from level 0.

A train service, **Airport City Express** (02 528 28 28, www. b-rail.be), runs to Gare du Midi, Gare Centrale and Gare du Nord. Tickets cost €5.10, first-class €6.70. There are four trains an hour from 6am to midnight; journey is 20mins. Women travelling alone at night are safest to alight at Gare Centrale.

The **Airport Line** bus No.12 (070 23 2000, www.stib.be) leaves the airport three times an hour between 6am and 7pm Mon-Fri, making five stops on its way to the EU Quarter; it costs €3 (or €5 from the driver). Outside of these times you need to take the No.21, which makes most in 20 stops. **De Lijn bus 471** (070 220 200, www.delijn.be) also travels between Brussels Gare du Nord and the airport; a single ticket costs €2 (or €3 from the driver). A **Brussels Airlines Express** bus (052 33 40 00) runs hourly to Antwerp from 5am (7am Sun) to midnight and costs €10 for a single ticket.

Taxis wait by the arrivals building and should display a yellow and blue licence. The fare to central Brussels is around €40 – many accept credit cards but check first. Wheelchair users can book a taxi from **Taxi Hendriks** (02 752 98 00, www.hendriks.be).

Car rental desks in the arrivals hall are open from 6.30am to 11pm daily. *See p298* **Car hire**.

Ryanair (www.ryanair.com) serves what it calls 'Brussels South', situated 55 kilometres (34 miles) away in **Charleroi** (07 125 12 11, www.charleroi-airport.com). Bus A connects with arrivals and runs the 20-minute journey to Charleroi train station, where a half-hourly train takes 50 minutes to reach Brussels (combined ticket with city transport €11.30).

Brussels City Shuttle (no phone, www.voyages-lelan.be) runs a bus (€13 one-way) from Charleroi airport to Brussels Gare du Midi. Journey time is about an hour. Taxis from Charleroi to central Brussels cost about €95.

By rail

There are up to ten Eurostar trains a day between Brussels and London, with a journey time of one hour 50 minutes. Check in at least 30 minutes before departure.

Eurostar St Pancras
08432 186186, www.eurostar.com.

Eurostar Gare du Midi
02 528 28 28, www.eurostar.com.
Open 8am-8pm Mon-Fri; 9.30am-5.30pm Sat, Sun. **Credit** AmEx, MC, V. **Map** p318 A7.

By car

To drive to Brussels from the UK, Eurotunnel can transport you and your vehicle from the M20 near Folkestone to Coquelles near Calais in 35 minutes. There are motorway connections to Brussels from there. It's a 24-hour service with up to three trains an hour 7am-midnight and one every two hours during the night. There are facilities for the disabled. Tickets can be bought from a travel agent, Eurotunnel's website or call centre, or, more expensively, on arrival at the tolls. Hertz and Eurotunnel have a Le Swap rental system for a left-hand and right-hand drive rental car in France and the UK.

Eurotunnel
UK 08443 353535, www.eurotunnel. com. **Open** 8am-7pm Mon-Fri; 8am-5.30pm Sat & hols; 9am-5.30pm Sun. **Credit** AmEx, DC, MC, V.
Ticket prices depend on time and length of travel, with cheaper fares available for advance booking. Fares start at £53 single. Discounts for online booking and frequent travellers.

By coach

Eurolines (UK)
08717 818 818, www.eurolines.co.uk. **Open** 8am-8pm daily. **Credit** AmEx, DC, MC, V.
A return fare from London to Brussels starts at around £55 with advance booking discounts and cheaper rates for children and senior passengers.

Eurolines (Brussels)
80 rue du Progrès, Schaerbeek (02 274 13 50, www.eurolines.be). *Métro/pré-métro Gare du Nord.* **Open** 8.30am-8.30pm daily. **Credit** AmEx, DC, MC, V. **Map** p317 D2.
Eurolines buses depart from CCN Gare du Nord (80 rue du Progrès) and offer services to 500 destinations in 34

countries. A return ticket to London Victoria costs from €31 with the journey taking around seven hours.

PUBLIC TRANSPORT

Brussels' cheap, integrated public transport system is made up of métro, rail, buses and trams, with tickets allowing for any changes en route up to an hour. A map is invaluable, as stations are not well signposted.

Métro, trams & buses

The public transport network in the capital is run by **STIB/MIVB** (Société des Transports Intercommunaux de Bruxelles). Maps and timetables are available from info centres at Gare du Midi, Porte de Namur and Rogier. **De Lijn** runs suburban buses from its main Gare du Midi terminal. Public transport operates from around 5.30am to midnight, depending on location.

De Lijn
070 220 200, www.delijn.be. **Open** *phone calls only* 7am-7pm Mon-Fri; 10am-6pm Sat, Sun. Flemish buses operating from Brussels and around Flanders. Fares are based on zones and the cost of a ticket is €1.20 for one or two zones (€2 if bought from the driver) and €2 for three or more zones (€3 if bought from the driver).

STIB/MIVB
14 galerie de la Toison d'Or, Ixelles (0900 10 310, www.stib.be). Métro Porte de Namur. **Open** 10am-6pm Mon-Sat. **Map** p318 D7.

Tickets, lines & passes

Tickets are sold at métro and rail stations, on buses and trams, at STIB info centres and at newsagents. Points of sale for monthly passes are métro Porte de Namur, Gare du Midi, Rogier and Merode, SNCB stations and online. Tickets must be validated, by using the machines at métro stations and on trams and buses at the start of the journey. They are then valid for one hour on all forms of transport and with unlimited changes but revalidate each time.

A new electronic system of ticketing is being gradually introduced across the STIB network so there are currently two types of ticket; **Jump** is a card system offering single, five or ten journeys as well as one or three day passes –

validate these in the orange machines. **MOBIB** is the new electronic system – touch the card on the red reader to validate the fare. A MOBIB card requires a €5 refundable deposit and a passport photograph. Fares for MOBIB are slightly cheaper than Jump.

The **Brussels Card** for tourists offers unlimited public transport for one, two or three days, plus admission to 30 museums, for €24, €34 or €40 respectively. Children under six travel free if accompanied by an adult with a valid ticket.

A **night bus** service, NOCTIS, was introduced in 2007. The 11 routes run on Friday and Saturday only and end at 3am. A single journey is: Jump €1.70, MOBIB €1.60 or €2 from the driver.

Métro stations are indicated by a white letter 'M' on a blue background, while red and white signs mark tram and bus stops. Brussels is served by four métro lines (1, 2, 5, 6) and two pré-métro underground tram lines (3, 4) running north–south through town, linking Gare du Nord and Midi.

Fares

One journey
Jump €1.70, MOBIB €1.60.
Ten journeys
Jump €12.40, MOBIB €11.30.
One day
Jump €4.50, MOBIB €4.20.
Three days
Jump €9.50, MOBIB €9.20.

Belgian railways

SNCB (02 528 28 28, www.b-rail.be) runs an efficient, cheap national rail system. Most tourist spots are an hour or so from Brussels. Tickets can be bought online and printed at home or at the station, but leave plenty of time for queues.

Brussels has three linked mainline stations: **Gare Centrale** (1km from the Grand'Place), **Gare du Midi** (South Station) and **Gare du Nord** (North Station). All have baggage facilities. Midi's left luggage office is by the Eurostar terminal. *See p301* **Lost Property**.

Disabled travel

For those travelling outside Brussels by train or on certain bus services, the disabled passenger pays and any accompanying person travels free. Contact the train station in advance for travel with a wheelchair, which is carried free.

There are al[...]
blind (call S[...]

TAXIS

Ranks are [...]
stations ar[...]
Porte de Namur, place d Espag...,
the Bourse and De Brouckère. Taxis can take up to four people and the tip is included in the meter fare. If you have a complaint to make against a driver, or you've lost an item in a taxi, record the registration number of the vehicle and contact the taxi service of the Ministry of Brussels Capital Region on 0800 147 95 or www.brusselstaxi.be. The clock starts at €2.40 (€4.40 after 10pm) and is then charged at €1.23 per kilometre if the journey is inside the 19 communes – double if not.

Autolux
02 411 41 42, www.autolux.be.
Taxis Bleus
02 268 00 00, www.taxisbleus.be.
Taxis Verts
02 349 49 49, www.taxisverts.be.

DRIVING

It's not easy driving around Brussels. You're better off taking public transport or walking. Dents on the right side of many cars show the damage caused by the '*priorité à droite*' rule, the reason for so many accidents. Cars must give way to any vehicle from the right, even on a major road, unless marked otherwise. A white sign with a yellow diamond on your road means cars from the right must stop for you.

A comprehensive tunnel system links major points in the city, making it possible to traverse Brussels without seeing the light of day. The inner ring is a pentagon of boulevards (marked with signs showing a blue ring on which the yellow dot is your current location). The outer ring is a pear shape, divided into an east and west motorway ring.

The speed limit on motorways is 120kph (75mph), on main roads 90kph (56mph), and in built-up areas 50kph (31mph). There are no tolls on Belgian roads. The wearing of seat belts is compulsory in the front and rear of the car. The legal maximum blood alcohol level is 0.5g/l (approx one glass of wine). A driving licence from your home country is acceptable if you are staying less than 90 days in Belgium. If your car is towed, go

DIRECTORY

DIRECTORY

earest police station to get a
ment releasing it. Police may
e you the document free of
narge or demand a nominal fee,
depending on the area of town.
They will then give the address
of the garage holding your car.
Present the police letter there and
pay another fee – the sum can vary
– to get your car back. On-the-spot
fines are common for speeding.

It takes 40 minutes to reach
Antwerp, 50 minutes to reach
Ghent, and 90 minutes for Liège
and Bruges. Calais and Amsterdam
are two-and-a-half hours away,
Paris three hours. Names are
signposted in two languages
(except in Flanders); Antwerp
is given as Anvers/Antwerpen,
Ghent is Gand/Gent, and Bruges
is Bruges/Brugge.

For information on importing
a car, registering a vehicle or
getting a licence in Belgium,
see www.mobilit.fgov.be.

Breakdown services

In the event of a breakdown, there
are two organisations you can call:

**Tourist Club Belgique
(TCB)**
*24hr emergency service 070 344 777,
enquiries (9am-5pm Mon-Fri) 02 233
23 27, www.touring.be.*

**Royal Automobile Club
de Belgique**
*24hr emergency service 02 287 09 00,
enquiries (8.30am-5pm Mon-Fri) 02
287 09 11, www.racb.com.*

Car hire

To hire a car, you must have a full
current driving licence (normally
with a minimum of one year's
driving experience) and carry a
passport or identity card, as well
as a credit card in your name. The
major car hire companies can be
found in the arrivals hall of
Zaventem airport and at Gare du
Midi. Hire rates at the airport can
be steeper than those you'll be
quoted in town.

Avis
070 223 001, www.avis.be.

Budget
02 721 50 97, www.budget.be.

Europcar
02 348 92 12, www.europcar.be.

Hertz
02 717 3201, www.hertz.be.

Repairs & services

Carrosserie Européenne
*933 chaussée d'Haecht, Evere (02 231
00 69, www.carrosserie-europeenne.be).*
Also check 'Auto-carrosseries –
reparations/Carrossierie
herstellingen' in the *Yellow Pages.*

CYCLING

Cycling on the main roads in central
Brussels can be a daunting
prospect. However, cycling the back
streets and out of town is generally
safe. Lanes are shown by two
broken white lines and are less
secure than the cycle tracks, which
are separated from the traffic. Some
city lanes go against the flow of
traffic. A map of local lanes and
tracks can be found at **Pro-Vélo**.
In Brussels city, the rent-a-bike
scheme **Villo!** allows you to rent a
bike from any of 180 bike stations.

Pro-Vélo
*15 rue de Londres, Ixelles (02 502 73
55, www.provelo.org).*
Organises guided tours at 2pm
(Dutch), 2.30pm (French) on Sundays
from April to October. Tours cost €9
half-day, €13 whole day. Bike hire
costs €8 half-day, €10 whole day.

Villo!
078 05 11 10, www.villo.be.
Villo! is an urban cycling scheme that
allows you to hire a city bike for any
period. For visitors there is an option
of a one or seven-day basic registration
(€1.50 or €7) bought from any of the
stations using your bank debit card.
You are then able to use the bikes
when you like using a pin number.
The first 30 minutes are free, then start
from 5c for the next 30 minutes and
€1 for the next hour. Bikes can be
picked up and dropped off at any of
the stations – maps are on the stations
or there are apps available for WAP
and iPhones. See website for details.

WALKING

The centre of town, although
uneven, is easy to navigate, with
many traffic-free streets around the
Grand'Place. The only real slog is
the walk up to the Upper Town. The
Institut Geographique National
(02 629 82 82, www.ngi.be) has
maps of trails outside the centre.

GUIDED TOURS
Bus tours

There are two main hop-on-hop-
off bus tour companies, both

offering 24hr tickets. They also
both run day trips to Antwerp,
Bruges and Ghent.

For pre-booked groups,
Brukselbinnenstebuiten (02 218
38 78, http://brukselbinnenstebuiten.
vgc.be) is a non-profit association
running small bus tours with local
guides. Prices start at €170 for a
half-day. They also organise
walking tours. **ARAU** (*see below*)
runs an art nouveau bus tour with
an English-speaking guide.

Brussels City Tours
*02 513 77 44, www.brussels-city-
tours.com.* **Tickets** €8; €10
reductions; free under-4s. **Credit**
AmEx, DC, MC, V.
Buses run every 30 minutes 10am-4pm
Sun-Fri, 10am-5pm Sat. The best place
to join this tour is at the Bourse.

Visit Brussels Line
www.city-discovery.com. **Tickets**
€17.99; €9.99 reductions. **Credit**
AmEx, DC, MC, V.
Buses run every hour 10am-4pm daily.
Join at Gare Centrale.

Walking tours

Be.guided (mobile 02 495 538 163,
http://www.beguided.be) is a new
walking tour service starting in
October 2010. All guides are
recognised by Tourism Flanders.

Brussels Walks, or **Klare
Lijn** (0493 50 40 60 mobile,
www.brusselswalks.be), organises
walks (€10) starting at the BIP
tourist centre (*see p304*) at 2pm
on Saturdays during the summer –
see website for dates.

ARAU (02 219 33 45,
www.arau.org) organises themed
walks with an English-speaking
guide – see website for details.
Walking tours cost €10.

Boat tours

Between May and September
there are canal and river cruises
in and around Brussels
(www.brusselsbywater.be).
These include a trip on the
Brussels sea canal. Boarding is
at 6 avenue du Port (métro Yser).

River Tours
*84 boulevard d'Ypres, 1000
Brussels (02 218 54 10,
www.rivertours.be).* **Brussels
canal tour** *45min tour* 2pm,
3pm, 4pm, 5pm Tue-Sun. **Tickets**
€4; €1.25-€3 reductions. *90min
tour* noon Tue-Sun. **Tickets**
€6; €1.25-€5 reductions.
No credit cards.

Resources A-Z

AGE RESTRICTIONS

In Belgium, you have to be 18 to vote or marry, and 16 to smoke, drink and/or have sex. For driving, the minimum age is 18 though car hire firms won't rent to under-21s.

BUSINESS

Chambers of commerce

American Chamber of Commerce (AmCham)
41 rue du Commerce, 1000 Brussels (02 513 67 70, www.amcham.be).
British Chamber of Commerce
11 blvd Bischoffheim, 1000 Brussels (02 540 90 30, www.britcham.be).

Conferences

Brussels International
02 513 89 40, www.brussels international.be.
This non-profit bureau is supported by the City of Brussels and its services are free of charge.
Management Centre Europe
118 rue de l'Aqueduc, Ixelles (02 543 21 00, www.mce.be).
International business and training organisation, hosting a variety of large seminars and conferences.

Couriers

DHL *02 715 50 50, www.dhl.be.*
FedEx *02 742 02 02, http://fedex.com/be.*
UPS *078 250 877, www.ups.com.*

Office services

Papeterie du Parc Léopold
177 rue Belliard, 1040 Brussels (02 230 69 12, www.parcleopold.com).
Top quality stationers in EU Quarter.
Regus *02 234 77 11, www.regus.com.*
International company that rents out fully equipped offices; six locations in Brussels, including the airport.

Secretarial services

Manpower *0800 243 43, www.manpower.be.*
Tempo Team *02 555 16 11, www.tempo-team.be.*

Translators & interpreters

Aplin *02 808 07 65, www.aplin.be.*

CONSUMER

To complain about shops that sell faulty merchandise or for general consumer protection issues, contact Economie (02 277 54 85, www.mineco.fgov.be).

If you are dissatisfied with the hygiene standards in a restaurant, café, food store or supermarket, contact the Federal Agency for the Safety of the Food Chain (02 211 82 11, www.afsca.be).

To complain about a taxi driver, call the taxi service of the Ministry of Brussels Capital Region on 0800 147 95. Operators can take your call in English; have the number of the taxi to lodge a complaint.

CUSTOMS

The following customs allowances apply to those bringing duty-free goods into Belgium from outside the European Union:

● 200 cigarettes or 100 cigarillos or 50 cigars or 250g (8.82oz) smoking tobacco.
● Two litres of still table wine and either one litre of spirits/strong liqueurs (over 22% alcohol) or two litres of fortified wine (under 22% alcohol)/sparkling wine/ other liqueurs.
● 500g coffee or 200g coffee extracts/essences.
● 50g perfume.
● 250ml toilet water.
● 100g tea or 40g tea extracts/essences.
● Other goods for non-commercial use up to a maximum value of €300 for land or sea arrivals, €430 for air arrivals.

If you are travelling from an EU member state, you are allowed to bring in as large a quantity of duty-paid goods as you can carry. But if you bring more than 110 litres of beer, 90 litres of wine, ten litres of spirits and 800 cigarettes you could be asked to pay an additional tax. There's no limit to the amount of foreign currency that can be brought in or out of Belgium.

DISABLED

New buildings in Brussels are required by law to be fully accessible to people who are not fully mobile and most of the big

hotels are wheelchair-friendly. That said, the cobbled pavements are very uneven and there are steep hills. Tactile pavement slabs are installed at all road crossing points. The many older buildings are often not equipped to handle disabled visitors. Public transport is becoming more adapted for disabled passengers, with all trams and buses having low-level platform for access and new buses having retractable ramps. Many métro stations are equipped for wheelchairs. A STIB minibus (02 515 23 65, www.stib.be), with vehicles equipped for wheelchairs, is available to transport disabled travellers door-to-door 6.30am-11pm for the same price as a métro ticket (book in advance). STIB has also installed braille information panels and floor-level tactile guides in all métro stations.

ELECTRICITY

The current used in Belgium is 220V AC. It works fine with British appliances (which run on 240V), but you'll need an adaptor. American appliances run on 110V and you'll need to buy a converter. Good hotels will supply adaptors and converters.

EMBASSIES

It's advisable to telephone to check the opening hours of the embassies listed below. You may also need to make an appointment to see someone. Be aware that different departments within the embassies often keep different, and usually shorter, hours. In emergencies it's worth ringing after hours; there may be staff on hand to deal with crises. For embassies not listed, check the *Yellow Pages* or www.brussels.info/embassies.
American Embassy
27 boulevard du Régent, 1000 Brussels (02 811 40 00, www.usembassy.be).
Australian Embassy
6-8 rue Guimard, 1040 Brussels (02 286 05 00, www.belgium. embassy.gov.au).
British Embassy
10 avenue d'Auderghem, 1040 Brussels (02 287 62 11, http:// ukinbelgium.fco.gov.uk).

Canadian Embassy
2 avenue de Tervuren,
1040 Brussels (02 741 06 11,
www.ambassade-canada.be).
Irish Embassy
180 chaussée d'Etterbeek,
1040 Brussels (02 282 34 00,
www.embassyofireland.be).
New Zealand Embassy
Level 7, 9-31 avenue des Nerviens,
1040 Brussels (02 512 10 40,
www.nzembassy.com/belgium).

EMERGENCIES

The general standardised
emergency number to call
throughout Europe is **112**.
If you need to telephone the
fire brigade or an ambulance, call
100. For the police, the number is
101. The Belgian Red Cross also
offers a 24-hour ambulance service
that can be reached at **105**.
For the Belgian Poison
Control Centre: 070 245 245,
www.poisoncentre.be.

GAY & LESBIAN

**English-speaking Gay Group
in Brussels** *www.eggbrussels.be.*
Hosts informal parties every month
for people of all nationalities.
**International Lesbian & Gay
Association** *02 609 54 10,*
www.ilga-europe.org.
Network of international bodies that
campaigns against discrimination
against gays and lesbians.
Rainbowhouse *02 503 59 90,*
www.rainbowhouse.be.
A meeting and information point.
Tel Quels *Helpline 02 502 00 70,
bar 02 275 06 03, www.telsquels.be.*
This collective organises events and
activities for parents, students and
singles among others.

HEALTH

Belgium has an excellent healthcare
system, with a ratio of one doctor
for every 278 people, and well-run,
modern hospitals. You'll also find
that many doctors speak English.

Accident & emergency

The following hospitals can provide
24-hour emergency assistance. Call
105 for a 24hr ambulance service.
Cliniques Universitaires St-Luc
*10 avenue Hippocrate, Woluwe-
St-Lambert (02 764 11 11,
www.saintluc.be). Métro Alma.*
Hôpital Brugmann
*4 place van Gehuchten, Laeken (02
477 21 11, www.chu-brugmann.be).
Métro Houba-Brugmann.*

Hôpital Erasme
*808 route de Lennik, Anderlecht (02
555 31 11, www.erasme.ulb.ac.be).
Métro Erasme.*
Hôpital St-Pierre
*322 rue Haute, Lower Town (02 535
31 11, www.stpierre-bru.be). Métro/
pré-métro Porte de Hal/bus 27, 48.*
Map p318 C8.
**Hôpital Universitaire des
Enfants Reine Fabiola**
*Paediatric emergency room, 15 avenue
Jean-Jacques Crocq, Laeken (02 477
21 11, www.huderf.be). Métro
Houba-Brugmann.*

Complementary &
alternative medicine

Acupuncture, homeopathy,
osteopathy and chiropractic
medicine are recognised, but
alternative medicine in Belgium is
still behind many other European
countries. See www.homeopathy.be
for doctors and dentists who
subscribe to homeopathic
principles. There are homeopathy
sections in many pharmacies.

Contraception & abortion

Condoms are widely available
and are sold at most chemists
and supermarkets (although
condom vending machines are not
widespread). Birth-control pills can
be bought at pharmacies with
a doctor's prescription.
Abortion is legal up to the 12th
week of pregnancy. After that, in
cases of foetal abnormality or
health risks to the mother, the
agreement of two independent
doctors is required.

Dentists

Dental care in Belgium is of a high
standard. The Health Unit at the
American Embassy (02 508 22 25)
can provide a list of English-
speaking dental practitioners, as
can the Community Help Service
helpline (02 648 40 14). Call 02 426
10 26 for a current list of dentists on
duty in evenings and at weekends.

Doctors

Call 02 479 18 18 to find doctors, or
click on www.mgbru.be. You are
free to choose any doctor no matter
where you live and without a
referral. You can often walk in
without an appointment during
weekday office hours. If you are too
sick to go in to the surgery, some
doctors will make house calls. After
hours, you can often reach your

physician (or one on call) through
an answering service. Even if
you're insured, expect to pay for
your visit on the spot in cash. Keep
receipts to claim reimbursement
from your insurance company.

Hospitals

Outpatient clinics at private or
university hospitals have a good
reputation for their state-of-the-art
technology, but often suffer from
bureaucracy and crowded waiting
rooms. Despite the drawbacks, they
have a concentration of specialists
in one place, as well as laboratory
and X-ray facilities. For details of
emergency hospitals, *see left*. A full
list is available at www.hospitals.be.

Opticians

There are many opticians around
Brussels (*see p172*). The American
Embassy (02 508 22 25) can provide
a list of English-speaking ones.

Pharmacies

Pharmacies (*pharmacies/apotheeks*)
in Belgium are clearly marked with
a green cross. Most are open 9am-
6pm Mon-Fri. Most also open on
Saturday mornings or afternoons.
Phone 0900 105 00 for the nearest on
weekend or night duty, or enter your
postcode at www.pharmacie.be to
find the nearest one open.

STDs, HIV & AIDS

Aide Info SIDA
*02 514 29 65, www.aideinfosida.be
(see also below* **Helplines***).*
Le Centre Elisa
*11 rue des Alexiens, 1000 Brussels
(02 535 30 03, www.stpierre-
bru.be/fr/service/autres/elisa.html).*
Anonymous HIV and STD tests.

HELPLINES

Brussels' large foreign community
has established an extensive
network of support groups. Unless
indicated in the listings, the groups
below are for English speakers.
Aide Info Sida *0800 20 120.*
Open 6-8pm Mon-Fri.
Alcoholics Anonymous *02 216 09
08, www.aa-europe.net/countries/
belgium.htm.* Open 24hrs daily.
Community Help Service (CHS)
02 648 40 14, www.chsbelgium.org.
Open 24hrs daily.
Drugs information *02 227 52 52.*
Open 24hrs daily.
Rape Crisis *02 534 36 36.*
Open 9.30am-5.30pm Mon-Fri.

DIRECTORY

Suicide Prevention *0800 32 123.*
Open 24hrs daily.
Victim Support *02 537 66 10.*
Open 9am-5pm daily.

ID

Belgium has an identity card system; citizens are expected to be able to show their card and thus prove their identity at any time. As a visitor, you are also expected to carry some sort of photographic ID, such as your passport, with you at all times.

INSURANCE

As members of the European Union, both the UK and Ireland have reciprocal health agreements with Belgium. You'll need to apply for the necessary European Health Insurance Card (EHIC) at home first. British citizens can obtain this by telephone, 0845 605 0707 or online, www.ehic.org.uk. Try to get the EHIC at least two weeks before you travel.

For long-term visitors, after six months of residence you are eligible for cover under Belgium's basic health insurance system, the *mutuelle*. You are allowed to choose whichever *mutuelle* best meets your needs. For phone numbers consult the local *Yellow Pages* under '*Mutualités/Ziekenfondsen*'.

INTERNET

Central Brussels has few cybercafés, though some small telephone cabin shops offer internet. Many bars and cafés are now offering Wi-Fi connections, as are hotels. Retailer Fnac has a cybercafé (*see p156*).

LEFT LUGGAGE

Main train stations have left-luggage offices, open 6am-midnight. Smaller stations have coin-operated lockers.

LIBRARIES

Bibliothèque Royale de Belgique
4 boulevard de l'Empereur, Upper Town (02 519 53 11, www.kbr.be). This is the state library, holding everything published in Belgium, as well as foreign publications. Details of the library's vast catalogue are accessible on the website.

ULB (Université Libre de Bruxelles)
50 avenue Franklin Roosevelt, Ixelles (02 650 47 00, www.bib.ulb.ac.be).

Although the ULB library is intended for students at the university, it's also open to non-students. It has a large collection of materials in English in various media, accessible on the website.

LOST PROPERTY

Report lost belongings to the nearest police station or police HQ at 30 rue du Marché au Charbon, Lower Town (02 279 79 79); bear in mind you may have trouble finding an English speaker. You must ask for a certificate of loss for insurance purposes. If you happen to lose your passport, contact your embassy or consulate (*see p299* **Embassies**). Below are details for items lost on public transport.

Air

Aviapartner
02 723 07 07, www.aviapartner.aero. **Open** *Phone enquiries* 6am-10pm daily.
Belgian Ground Services (BGS)
02 723 60 11, www.flightcare.be. **Open** *Phone enquiries* 7am-11pm daily.

Airport

Brussels Airport
02 753 68 20, www.brusselsairport.be. **Open** 8am-4.15pm Mon-Fri.

Métro, buses & trams

STIB/MIVB
Porte de Namur, Ixelles (02 515 23 94). **Open** 8.30am-4pm Mon-Fri. Lost property office located at Porte de Namur métro.

Rail

For articles left on a train, enquire at the nearest station or check with the main rail lost property office at Gare du Midi (02 224 88 62). The website (www.b-rail.be) has an online form to register any loss.

Taxis

If you have the number of the taxi where you left your item, or want to report an item found in a taxi, call the taxi service of the Ministry of Brussels Capital Region on 0800 147 95. There is an online form to register loss at www.brusselstaxi.be.

MEDIA

Most newsagents and kiosks in Brussels stock the leading papers and magazines from Britain, France, Germany, the Netherlands and elsewhere (including the US). But the local press is still surprisingly broad, and runs the gamut from the conservative (*De Standaard*) to the more outrageous (*Humo*, *Ché*). Belgians are even more spoilt for choice when it comes to television. Cable TV has been available since the 1960s, and 95 per cent of households receive around 40 television channels, many of them from overseas.

Newspapers

La Dernière Heure
www.dhnet.be
Popular right-leaning French-speaking tabloid.
L'Echo
www.lecho.be
Pre-eminent French-speaking business paper in Belgium.
European Voice
www.european-voice.com
This weekly English-language paper specialises in the workings of the EU.
Het Laaste Nieuws
www.hln.be
Once renowned as the traditionally liberal Flemish daily, HLN also takes an interest in the seamier side of life.
La Libre Belgique
www.lalibre.be
Catholic French-language daily with a serious tone and look.
Metro
www.metrotime.be
This free newspaper is available at most metro stations in French (green) and Dutch (blue).
De Morgen
www.demorgen.be
Once the staple of socialist workers, De Morgen has evolved into a more general left-wing Flemish daily.
Le Soir
www.lesoir.be
The most widely read francophone daily, an independent-minded, quality broadsheet. Wednesday's issue contains *MAD*, an indispensable supplement with the week's listings.
De Standaard
www.standaard.be
The biggest Dutch-speaking daily takes few risks, opting for a conservative Catholic angle on most issues.
Vlan
www.vlan.be
Thousands of ads from property to cars to jobs to junk appear in this paper every Sunday.

Magazines

The Bulletin
www.ackroyd.be
Brussels' only English-language weekly every Thursday. It comes with

DIRECTORY

arts and entertainment listings including TV schedules.

Dag Allemaal
www.dagallemaal.be
Dutch-language TV and radio listings magazine.

Kiosque
www.kiosque.be
Pocket-sized, French-language monthly listings mag with small English section.

La Libre Match
Joint venture between *Paris Match* and *La Libre Belgique*.

The Ticket
www.theticket.be
Pocket-sized arts and entertainment listings magazine in French and Dutch.

Le Vif-Express/Knack
www.levif.be
These sister publications in French and Dutch are the country's only news magazines.

Radio

To keep anglophone US and UK pop/rock music at bay, radio stations receiving subsidies must make at least 60 per cent of their music broadcasts in the language of the region from which the station is funded. Commercial stations are free to play as they choose. Frequencies for the same station differ in other parts of the country. French-speaking radio includes Bruxelles-Capitale (99.3 MHz), the Brussels-only news station; La Première (92.5 MHz), state-owned and solid; Radio Contact (102.2 MHz) and Radio 21 (93.2 MHz), both popular and poppy. Musique 3 (91.2 MHz) is classical. Flemish radio stations include VRT1 (91.7 MHz), classical and talk; VRT2 (93.7 MHz), Top 40 and oldies; VRT3 (89.5 MHz), high culture. Studio Brussel (100.6 MHz) plays alternative rock and indie.

Television

Cable TV gives Belgians easy access to BBC1 and BBC2, CNN and MTV, as well as channels from France, the Netherlands, Germany, Spain, Portugal and Italy. The main Belgian television channels include: Kanaal 2, showing anglophone series and films in original language, and the state-run RTBF1 & 2. The Flemish version is VRT.

MONEY

There are euro banknotes for €5, €10, €20, €50, €100, €200 and €500, and coins worth €1 and €2 plus 1, 2, 5, 10, 20 and 50 cents.

ATMs

ATMs are somewhat difficult to find in the city centre. Gare du Midi has ATMs at the bottom of the Eurostar escalator. As well as using a debit card to withdraw euros, you can also obtain a cash advance on most major credit cards from ATMs. Just keep in mind that cash advance fees can be steep.

Banks

Most banks open from 9am to 3.30-5pm, Monday to Friday. A few have half-days on Saturdays. Some also close for lunch. There will usually be staff members who speak English.

Bureaux de change

Banks are the best places to exchange currency. After banking hours you can change money and travellers' cheques at bureaux de change around the centre of town (the money exchange at 88 rue Marché aux Herbes, just off the Grand'Place, is open 10am-7pm Mon-Sat and 11am-6pm Sun) or at offices in the Gare du Midi (7am-11pm daily) and Gare Centrale (8am-9pm daily). Several banks at the airport give cash advances on credit cards, and convert currency. Most open early and close at 10pm.

Credit/debit cards

Most large shops, hotels and restaurants accept credit cards, including Visa, Mastercard and American Express. Debit cards from other European countries are accepted in most places.

Report thefts immediately to the police and to the 24-hour services listed below.

American Express
02 676 21 21,
www.americanexpress.com.

Diners Club
02 626 50 24, www.dinersclub.be.

Mastercard
toll free 0800 150 96,
www.mastercard.com/be.

Visa International
toll free 0800 183 97,
www.visaeurope.com.

Tax

Belgian VAT is 21 per cent, but if you're a non-EU resident, want to make a purchase of more than €145 and plan to take the purchase out of the country within three months, you can buy tax-free. Look for the 'Tax-Free Shopping' logo on shop

windows. Bring your non-EU passport to make a purchase and you will be given a Tax-Free shopping cheque that can be stamped by customs officials in the airport and then cashed at the Europe Tax-Free shopping desk. (Allow plenty of time in the airport for extra queues.) Shopping tax-free in shops without the Tax-Free logo is more complicated, but usually still possible. You need to request an itemised invoice at the shop and have it stamped by a customs agent when you leave Belgium. Then mail the invoice to the shop, which will send you the refund. This works best if you happen to be flying out of Zaventem – customs officials at Charleroi airport are notoriously impossible to locate.

OPENING HOURS

Many offices close for lunch or close early on Friday, although this is not official. Most shops open from 9am to 6pm, though certain groceries and supermarkets stay open till 9pm. Department stores open until 9pm on one day a week, usually Friday. For late-opening shops, look for a 'Night Shop' sign.

Most museums are open 9am to 5pm Tuesday to Saturday, and sometimes on Sunday. Nearly all are closed on Mondays. Several only open from Easter Sunday to September. Thus, all in all, it's wise to call the museum, particularly if it's a smaller one, before visiting. For banking hours, *see left* **Money***; for post office hours, see below* **Postal services***.*

POLICE STATIONS

For the police, call 101. The central police station in Brussels is at 30 rue du Marché au Charbon (02 279 79 79, www.polbru.be). For other emergency numbers, *see p300* **Emergencies***.*

POSTAL SERVICES

Post offices are generally open 9am to 5pm Monday to Friday, but times can vary. The central office at **place de la Monnaie** is open until 7pm. Queues in post offices can be long and slow, though a ticketing system is now in place.

Letters mailed to the UK and other European countries usually take two days; the US takes about five days. A letter weighing up to 50g costs 90c to any country in Europe. A letter up to 50g to any country in the rest of the world costs €1.05. Price is determined by the size of the envelope. Stick to using local Belgian envelopes, as non-standard sizes – even if different by only a fraction of an inch – can send the cost of postage soaring. Staff will measure to ensure the correct dimensions. Sending a postcard is the same price as a letter.

For postal information and to find the nearest post office to you, refer to the website www.post.be.

Central Post Office
1 boulevard Anspach, Lower Town (02 226 21 11). Métro/pré-métro De Brouckère. **Open** 8am-7pm Mon-Fri; 10.30am-4.30pm Sat.

Packages

Packages weighing more than 2kg (4.4lbs) are taken care of by Kilopost or Taxipost, managed by La Poste (www.post.be). Just take any package weighing up to 30kg (66lbs) to the nearest post office. *See also p299* **Couriers**.

RELIGION

Many churches and synagogues hold services in English. For places away from the centre, it is advisable to call for directions. See the 'Religious Services' section at www.xpats.com for a list.

Holy Trinity Church *29 rue Capitaine Crespel, Ixelles (02 511 71 83, www.htbrussels.com). Métro Louise.* **Map** p319 D8. Holy Communion in English is on Sundays at 9am, 10.30am and evening praise is at 7pm. An African-style afternoon praise session is at 2pm.
Beth Hillel Reform Synagogue of Brussels *80 rue des Primeurs, Forest (02 332 25 28, www.beth-hillel.org). Tram 52 or bus 54.* **Services** 8pm Fri; 10.30am Sat.
Grande Mosquée de Bruxelles & Centre Islamique *14 Parc du Cinquantenaire, EU Quarter (02 735 21 73, www.centreislamique.be). Métro Schuman.* **Map** p323 K5.
International Protestant Church *International School of Brussels, 19 Kattenberg, Watermael-Boitsfort (02 673 05 81, www.ipcbrussels.org). Tram 94 or bus 95.* **English service** 10am Sun.
Quaker House *50 square Ambiorix, EU Quarter (02 230 49 35, www.quaker.org/be-lux). Métro Schuman.* **Map** p321 J4. **Meetings** 11am Sun, 12.30pm Wed.
St-Nicolas *1 rue au Beurre, Lower Town (02 267 51 64). Métro/*

pré Métro Bourse. **Map** p319 E6.
Mass in English 10am Sun.
Our Lady of Mercy Parish *Place de la Ste-Alliance, Uccle (02 354 53 43, www.olm.be). Bus 43.* **Mass in English** 5pm Sat; 10am Sun.

SAFETY & SECURITY

While generally safe, Brussels is starting to gain some of the less desirable attributes of a big city. Pickpockets and bicycle thieves have become part of the city's landscape, especially in crowded tourist areas during the day, and after dark in the grey streets downtown between the Grand'Place and the Gare du Midi. Gangs of pickpockets work the major railway stations, the pré-métro tram serving Midi and incoming international trains. Take the sort of precautions you would in any big city. (*See also p300* **Emergencies**.)

SMOKING

Smoking in confined public places is banned by law. This amounts to no smoking in train stations (except on open-air platforms) and public buildings such as town halls and theatres. In 2007, a law came in that banned smoking in restaurants if the establishment cannot provide a separate smoking area.

STUDY

Brussels is a major European study centre. There are universities that teach in French and Dutch, and many that offer courses in English.

Language schools

Classified ads on www.xpats.com and www.expatica.com are full of people willing to exchange conversation or teach one-to-one. There are numerous language schools throughout Brussels. The Alliance Française (02 788 21 60, www.alliancefr.be) is the leading French-language school, while the big international schools include Amira (02 640 68 50, www.amira.be), Berlitz (02 649 61 75, www.berlitz.be) and Language Studies International (02 217 23 73, www.lsi-be.net). Fondation 9 (02 627 52 52, www.fondation9.be) offers lessons in all EU languages.

Universities

The two main Brussels universities are split according to language but have large numbers of foreign

students. The French-speaking Université Libre de Bruxelles or ULB (50 avenue Franklin Roosevelt, Ixelles 02 650 21 11, www.ulb.ac.be) is the largest with 18,000 students, of whom a third are foreign. The Dutch-speaking Vrije Universiteit Brussel or VUB (2 boulevard de la Plaine, Ixelles 02 629 21 11, www.vub.ac.be) has 9,000 students and two campuses. Although most courses are taught in Dutch, there are a number of English-language postgraduate degrees. Vesalius College (2 boulevard de la Plaine, Ixelles 02 629 28 21, www.vesalius.edu) is part of the VUB and linked with Boston University Brussels (174 boulevard du Triomphe, Ixelles 02 640 74 74, www.bu.edu/brussels). There are also excellent centres of art and design. The most famous is the Ecole Nationale Supérieure des Arts Visuels de la Cambre (21 Abbaye de la Cambre, Ixelles 02 626 17 80, www.lacambre.be). It offers courses in architecture, graphic design and fashion. The Académie Royale des Beaux-Arts de Bruxelles (144 rue du Midi, Lower Town (02 506 10 10, www.arba-esa.be) is best known for painting and sculpture.

TELEPHONES

Belgacom is the major operator. For a longer stay here, sign up for one of its special packages for free or cheaper calls to a country of your choice (see www.belgacom.be or call 0800 401 00 for English customer service). Telenet (0800 666 11, www.telenet.be) is Belgacom's main rival and also offers a range of services with competitive deals. For a short-term stay, you can use one of the many telephone cards available in newsagents, post offices and supermarkets.

Dialling & codes

To make an international call from Belgium, dial 00, then the country code (Australia 61, Canada 1, France 33, Germany 49, Ireland 353, New Zealand 64, Netherlands 31, UK 44, USA 1), then the number. When in Belgium, dial the city code and number (Antwerp 03, Bruges 050, Brussels 02, Ghent 09, Liège 04), even when in the city itself. To call Belgium from abroad, first dial the international access code, then 32, then drop the 0 of each city code. 0800 numbers are free inland. See www.goldenpages.be or http://whitepages.truvo.be for telephone listings.

DIRECTORY

Public phones

Public telephone booths are a rarity since the mobile phone revolution, but look in stations, post offices and other usual locations. There are several close to the Grand'Place, around place de Brouckère and the Bourse. Many public phones accept only prepaid telephone cards – coin phones are rare. You can buy phone cards at newsstands, post offices, train stations and supermarkets.

Operator services

Operator assistance
1324 all languages.
Directory enquiries
1405 (English enquiries for numbers).

Mobile phones

Belgium is part of the GSM mobile network. You can rent GSM phones at the airport or from some car hire agencies. The rental fee is usually low but the cost per call is high. Network providers include Proximus (02 205 40 00, www.proximus.be), Mobistar (0495 95 95 00, www.mobi star.be) and Base (0486 19 19 99, www.base.be).

TIME

Belgium is on Central European Time, one hour ahead of GMT, six hours ahead of US Eastern Standard Time and nine hours ahead of US Pacific Standard Time. Clocks go back an hour in the autumn and forward an hour in the spring.

TIPPING & VAT

Service and VAT are included in hotel and restaurant prices, though people often throw in a few extra euros if the service has been exceptional. Tips are also included in metered taxi fares, although taxi drivers expect extra tips from foreigners. At cinemas and theatres, tipping the attendant 20c to 50c for a programme is expected.

TOURIST INFORMATION

For visitors from the UK, the site for Brussels and Wallonia is www.belgiumtheplaceto.be as well as www.visitflanders.co.uk. For tourist information tailored to the North American market, see www.visitbelgium.com.

Brussels Info Point (BIP)
2-4 rue Royale, Upper Town (02 513 89 40, www.biponline.be).
Open 9am-6pm daily.
There is also a small tourist office in the Hôtel de Ville on Grand'Place, same details as above.

VISAS & IMMIGRATION

EU nationals and citizens of Iceland, Monaco, Norway, Liechtenstein and Switzerland can enter Belgium without a visa or a time limit. EU nationals only need to show a valid national ID card to enter. Citizens of Australia, Canada, New Zealand, Japan and the United States, among other countries, are permitted to enter Belgium for three months with a valid passport. No visa is needed. For longer stays, they must apply for a Schengen type D visa from the Belgian consulate in their own country before entering Belgium. *See right* **Working in Brussels** for more information on long stays.

WHEN TO GO

Winters are cold and damp, sometimes with considerable snowfall. Summers are warm. Rain can fall all year round. The biggest drawback to winter in Brussels is the shortness of the days. The sky is dark until 8.30am and after 4pm in the shortest months.

Public holidays

Belgian public holidays are: New Year's Day (1 Jan); Easter Sunday; Easter Monday; Labour Day (1 May); Ascension Day (6th Thur after Easter); Pentecost Whit Monday (7th Mon after Easter); Belgian National Day (21 July); Assumption (15 Aug); All Saints' Day (1 Nov); Armistice Day (11 Nov); and Christmas Day (25 Dec). If a holiday falls on a Tuesday or Thursday, most offices, by tradition, will 'make the bridge' *(faire le pont/de brug maken)* and observe a four-day weekend. The French and Flemish communities celebrate separate regional holidays – 11 July for the Flemish-speaking community and 27 September for the French-speaking.

WOMEN

Downtown Brussels in the daytime is open and female-friendly; women can enjoy a drink alone in a café with very little or no hassle. After dark, unaccompanied women should avoid the gloomier areas towards the Gare du Midi and Gare du Nord. *See p303* **Safety & security**.

WORKING IN BRUSSELS

EU nationals and citizens of Iceland, Norway and Liechtenstein do not need a work permit. However, you are required to register and get a residence permit. To register you must go to the town hall of the commune in which you are living. For a list of communes and links to their respective sights see www.bruxelles.irisnet.be. If you live or work in Belgium, you must carry your Belgian identity card *(carte d'identité/identiteitskaart)* with you at all times. If you don't have one, carry your passport.

Non-EU citizens do need a work permit, which is usually granted to the employer. For information about the types of work permit see the official Brussels Region website www.bruxelles.irisnet.be or the federal Office des Etrangers https://dofi.ibz.be. For Brussels commune see www.brussels.be. Working illegally is not recommended. For employment laws see www.meta.fgov.be.

THE LOCAL CLIMATE

Average temperatures and monthly rainfall

	High (°C/°F)	Low (°C/°F)	Rainfall (mm/in)
Jan	7/45	2/36	53/2.1
Feb	10/50	2/36	43/1.7
Mar	13/55	4/39	49/1.9
Apr	17/63	6/43	53/2.1
May	20/68	9/48	65/2.6
June	23/73	12/54	54/2.1
July	25/77	15/59	62/2.4
Aug	26/79	16/61	42/1.6
Sept	23/73	12/54	54/2.1
Oct	20/68	8/46	60/2.4
Nov	14/57	4/39	51/2.0
Dec	7/44	3/37	59/2.3

Vocabulary

Although officially bilingual, Brussels is a largely French-speaking city. For this reason, we have usually referred to Brussels' streets, buildings and so on by their French name. In town, all street signs are given in both languages (as they are on our street maps, starting on p315).

French is also the language of Wallonia (the south), while Flemish, a dialect of Dutch, is the language of Flanders (the north). The French frown upon the easier Belgian numerical use of *septante*, *huitante* instead of the complicated French *soixante-dix* and *quatre-vingt*; the Flemings think that the Dutch spoken in Holland sounds like English. There is also a small German-speaking enclave in the east of the country. In the **Trips Out of Town** chapter (*see pp232-294*) we use Dutch for place names in Flanders.

English is widely spoken in Brussels and Flanders, but attempts to speak French in Flanders will fall on deaf ears at best. Simply put, the Flemings won't speak French and the French can't speak Dutch – but the issue is far more politically vexed than that. If you can't speak Dutch, use English if the following modest vocabulary doesn't stretch.

Words and phrases are listed below in **English**, then French, then *Dutch* – with pronunciation for Dutch given in brackets.

USEFUL EXPRESSIONS

Good morning, hello bonjour *hallo* ('hullo'), *dag* ('daarg')
Good evening bonsoir *goedenavond* ('hoo-dun-aav-ond')
Good night bonne nuit *goedenacht* ('khoo-dun-acht')
Goodbye au revoir *tot ziens* ('tot zeens'), *dag* ('daarg')
How are you? comment allez-vous? *hoe maakt u het?* ('hoo markt oo hut')
How's it going? ça va? *hoe gaat het?* ('hoo hart hut')
OK d'accord *okay, in orde, goed* ('okay', 'in order', 'hoot')
Yes oui *ja* ('yah')
No non *nee* ('nay')
Please s'il vous plaît *alstublieft* ('als-too-bleeft')

Thank you/thanks merci *dank u* ('dank oo'), *bedankt* ('bur-dankt')
Leave me alone laissez moi tranquille *laat me met rust* ('laat mu mat rust')
How much?/how many? combien? *hoeveel, wat kosthet?* ('hoofail' 'vot cost hut')
I would like... je voudrais... *ik wil graag...* ('ick will hraak')
My name is... je m'appelle... *mijn naam is...* ('mine narm iss')
Left/right gauche/droite *links/rechts* ('links'/'reckts')
Open/closed ouvert/fermé *open/gesloten* ('open'/'he-slo-tun')
Good/bad bon ou bonne/mauvais or mauvaise *goed/slecht* ('hoot'/'sleckt')
Well/badly bien/mal *goed/slecht*
Stamp timbre *postzegel*
Toilet WC *toilet* ('twalet')
Do you know the way to... est-ce que vous savez où se trouve...*weet u de weg naar...* ('vait oo de veg nar...')

LANGUAGE EXPRESSIONS

Do you speak English? parlez-vous anglais? *spreekt u Engels?* ('spraykt oo engels?')
I don't speak French/Dutch je ne parle français *ik spreek geen Nederlands* ('ick sprayk hain nay- der-lants')
Speak more slowly, please parlez plus lentement, s'il vous plaît *kunt u wat trager spreken, alstublieft?* ('kunt oo waht tra-her spray-cun, als-too-bleeft')
I don't understand je ne comprends pas *ik begrijp het niet* ('ick be-gripe hut neet')

EATING & DRINKING

I would like to reserve a table... je voudrais réserver un table... *ik zou graag een tafel reserveren...* ('ick zoo hraak an ta-full ray-sir-va-run')
...for two people/at eight o'clock ...pour deux personnes/ a vingt heures ...*voor twee personen/ om acht uur* ('for tway per-sone-an/om acht oor')
Can I have the bill, please? l'addition, s'il vous plaît *mag ik de rekening, alstublieft?* ('mach ick de ray-cun-ing, als-too-bleeft')

Two beers, please, deux bières, s'il vous plaît *twee bieren/pilsjes/pintjes, alstublieft* ('tway beer-an/pils-yes/pint-yes, als-too-bleeft')

ACCOMMODATION

Do you have a room... avez-vous une chambre... *heeft u een kamer...* ('hay-ft oo an kam-er')
...for this evening/for two people? pour ce soir/pour deux personnes? *voor vanavond/voor twee personen?* ('vor vanarfond/ vor tway per-sone-an')
Double bed un grand lit *een tweepersoonsbed* ('an tway per-sones-bed')
With bathroom/shower avec salle de bain/douche *met badkamer/douche* ('mat bat camer/doosh')
Expensive/cheap cher/pas cher *duur/goedkoop* ('doer/hoot-cope')

NUMBERS

zero zéro *nul;* **1** un/une *een;* **2** deux *twee;* **3** trois *drie;* **4** quatre *vier;* **5** cinq *vijf;* **6** six *zes;* **7** sept *zeven;* **8** huit *acht;* **9** neuf *negen;* **10** dix *tien;* **11** onze *elf;* **12** douze *twaalf;* **13** treize *dertien;* **14** quatorze *veertien;* **15** quinze *vijftien;* **16** seize *zestien;* **17** dix-sept *zeventien;* **18** dix-huit *achtien;* **19** dix-neuf *negentien;* **20** vingt *twintig;* **30** trente *dertig;* **40** quarante *veertig;* **50** cinquante *vijftig;* **60** soixante *zestig;* **70** septante *seventig;* **80** huitante *tachtig;* **90** nonante *negentig;* **100** cent *honderd;* **thousand** mille *duizend;* **million** million *miljoen.*

DAYS & MONTHS

Monday lundi *maandag;*
Tuesday mardi *dinsdag;*
Wednesday mercredi *woensdag;*
Thursday jeudi *donderdag;*
Friday vendredi *vrijdag;*
Saturday samedi *zaterdag;*
Sunday dimanche *zondag.*
January janvier *januari;*
February février, *februari;*
March mars *maart;* **April** april, *april;* **May** mai *mei;* **June** juin *juni;* **July** juillet *juli;* **August** août *augustus;* **September** septembre *september;* **October** octobre *oktober;* **November** novembre *november;* **December** décembre *december.*

Further Reference

BOOKS

Art & architecture

Meuris, Jacques
René Magritte
The world of the surrealist painter, in words and pictures.
Rombout, Marc
Paul Delvaux
Excellent selection of colour plates, plus biographical text.
Shinomura, Junichi
Art Nouveau Architecture, Residential Masterpieces 1892-1911
The selection of photographs of the Musée Horta would be a fine addition to anyone's coffee table.
White, Christopher
Pieter Paul Rubens: Man and Artist
A lavishly illustrated look at the Antwerp-born artist.

Fiction, drama & poetry

Baudelaire, Charles
Amoenitates Belgicae
A scathing look at the Belgians and their culture.
Brontë, Charlotte
The Professor
Charlotte Brontë's first novel was set in Brussels, and she struggled to find a publisher for it, even after the huge success of her later works.
Villette
Brussels was the model for the town of Villette in her final novel, based on her experiences there.
Claus, Hugo
The Sorrow of Belgium
Milestone novel, set during the Nazi occupation, by a major Flemish-language novelist.
Conrad, Joseph
Heart of Darkness
Conrad's masterpiece features early scenes in a corrupt, cheerless Brussels, unnamed but still clearly identifiable.
Hergé
The *Tintin* books
Belgium's most famous author needs only one name, where others require two, and no introduction.
Hollinghurst, Alan
The Folding Star
Fictional art history and sexual obsession in a dreary city in northern Belgium.

Martin, Stephen (ed)
Poetry of the First World War
An anthology, with poems about the battlegrounds of Flanders.
Maeterlinck, Maurice, et al
An Anthology of Modern Belgian Theatre
Works by Maeterlinck, Crommelynck and de Ghelderode.
Meades, Jonathan
Pompey
Portrait of Belgium's imperial escapades in the Congo.
Royle, Nicholas
Saxophone Dreams
A magical-realist adventure set in the landscapes of Belgian surrealist Paul Delvaux, including a role for Delvaux himself.
Sante, Luc
The Factory of Facts
Autobiographical account of growing up in Belgium in the '50s.
Simenon, Georges
Maigret's Revolver
Simenon was prolific but maintained the quality of his writing. Any title by the Liège-born master of the crime/detective fiction genre is worth a read.
Thackeray, William Makepeace
Vanity Fair
The middle section describes the social scene in Brussels on the eve of the Battle of Waterloo.
Yourcenar, Marguerite
Zeno of Bruges
The wanderings of an alchemist in late medieval Europe.

Food & drink

Hellon, John
Brussels Fare
Recipes from Belgian restaurants.
Webb, Tim
Good Beer Guide to Belgium & Holland
Excellent guide for beer lovers from the Campaign for Real Ale.
Wynants, Pierre
Creative Belgian Cuisine
Anyone who has eaten at the wonderful Comme Chez Soi (*see p115*) will need no further encouragement.

History & politics

Since Belgium did not exist until 1830, few books deal specifically with its history. Instead, the

determined reader should search for books about Spain, Austria, the Netherlands, etc.
Glover, Michael
A New Guide to the Battlefields of Northern France and the Low Countries
Covers Waterloo as well as the World War I battlefields.
Kossman, EH
The Low Countries
Dull but informative history of Belgium 1780-1940.
Parker, Geoffrey
The Dutch Revolt
Excellent history of the decline of the Spanish empire in the 16th century.

Travel

Bryson, Bill
Neither Here Nor There
Belgium and Brussels fill two amusing, if predictable, chapters of Bryson's European travels.
Pearson, Harry
A Tall Man in a Low Land
Entertaining and affectionate travelogue.

WEBSITES

www.agenda.be
Comprehensive listings.
http://belgianbeer board.com
Readable Belgian beer site.
www.alltravelbelgium.com
Handy hotel website, with availability search and option to book online.
www.brusselstourism. eu.com
Comprehensive tourism site.
www.belgianstyle.com/ mmguide
Fun but fact-filled guide to the beers of Belgium.
www.ebrusselshotels.com
Descriptions, reviews, prices and photos of the capital's hotels.
www.belgiumtheplaceto.be
Everything covered, from health to transport.
www.expatica.com
Expat website.
www.resto.be
Excellent site with detailed search engine and customer reviews of restaurants around Belgium.
www.trabel.com
Travel in Belgium.

Content Index

INDEX

Venue Index

INDEX

INDEX

INDEX

Maps

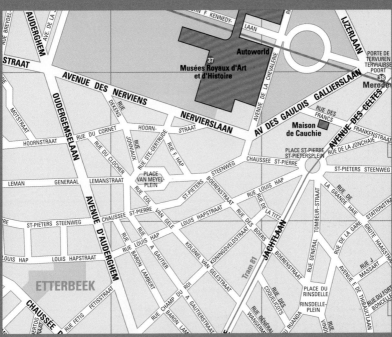

Place of interest and/or entertainment . . . . . .

Railway or bus station . . . .

Park . . . .

Hospital/university . . . .

Area . . . . **IXELLES**

Tram route . . . . ——

Métro/pré-métro route . . . . ——

Pedestrianised zone . . . . ▭

Métro/pré-métro station . . . . Ⓜ

Post office . . . . ✉

Hotel . . . . ⓲

Restaurant/café . . . . ㊎

Pub/bar . . . . ㉍

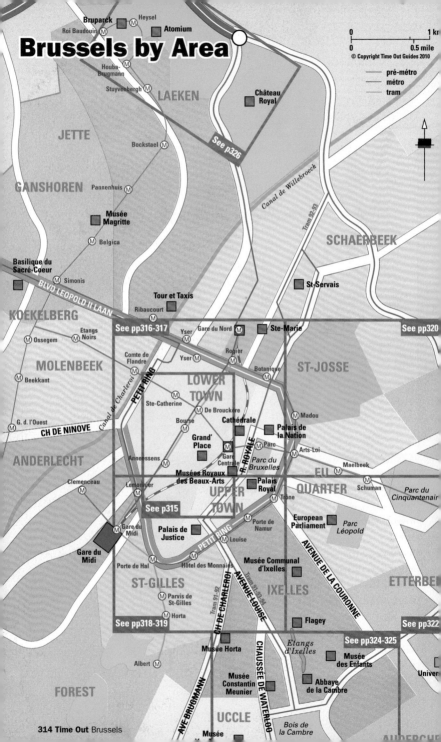

Brussels by Area

	0	1 km
	0	0.5 mile

© Copyright Time Out Guides 2010

— pré-métro
— métro
— tram

Bruparck

Heysel

Roi Baudouin

Atomium

Houba-
Brugmann

LAEKEN

See p326

Château
Royal

Stuyvenbergh

JETTE

Bockstael

GANSHOREN

Pannenhuis

Musée
Magritte

Belgica

SCHAERBEEK

Basilique du
Sacré-Coeur

Simonis

St-Servais

BLVD LEOPOLD II LAAN

KOEKELBERG

Etangs
Noirs

Tour et Taxis

Ossegem

Ribaucourt

See pp316-317

Yser

Gare du Nord

Ste-Marie

See pp320

MOLENBEEK

Beekkant

Comte de
Flandre

Yser

Rogier

ST-JOSSE

Botanique

LOWER
TOWN

G. d. l'Ouest

Ste-Catherine

De Brouckère

Madou

CH DE NINOVE

Bourse

Cathédrale

Palais de
la Nation

Arts-Loi

ANDERLECHT

Anneessens

Grand'
Place

Gare
Centrale

Parc du
Bruxelles

Maelbeek

Clemenceau

Lemonnier

Musées Royaux
des Beaux-Arts

Palais
Royal

EU
QUARTER

See p315

UPPER
TOWN

Trône

Schuman

Parc du
Cinquantenair

Gare du
Midi

Palais de
Justice

Porte de
Namur

European
Parliament

Parc
Léopold

Gare du
Midi

Porte de Hal

Louise

Hôtel des Monnaies

Musée Communal
d'Ixelles

AVENUE DE LA COURONNE

ETTERBEE

ST-GILLES

Parvis de
St-Gilles

IXELLES

See pp322

Horta

Flagey

See pp318-319

Albert

Etangs
d'Ixelles

See pp324-325

FOREST

Musée Horta

Univer

Musée
Constantin
Meunier

Musée
des Enfants

Abbaye
de la Cambre

UCCLE

Bois de
la Cambre

AUDERGH

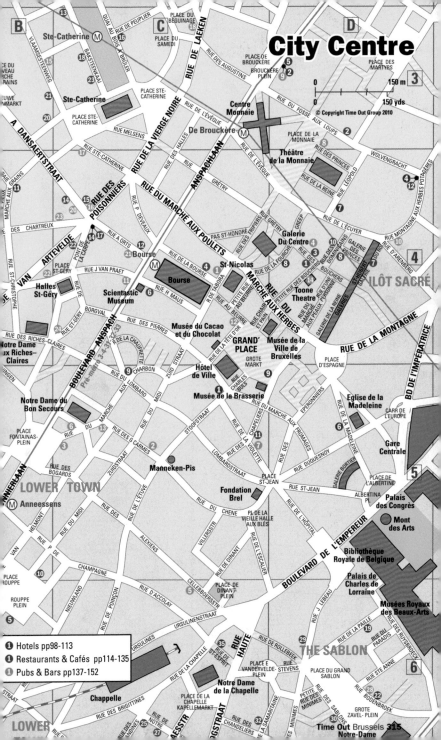

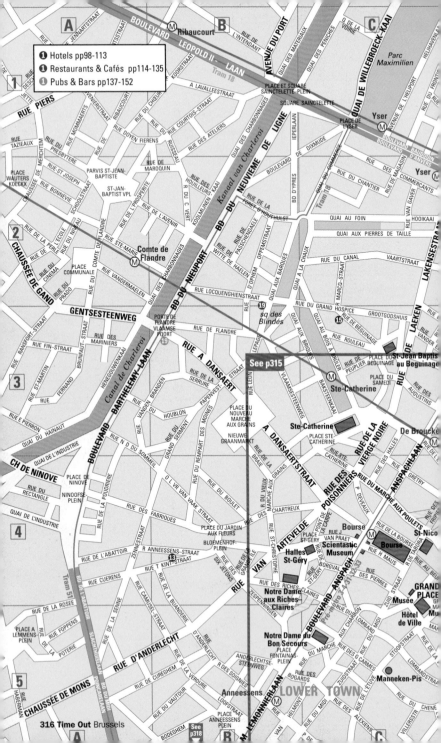

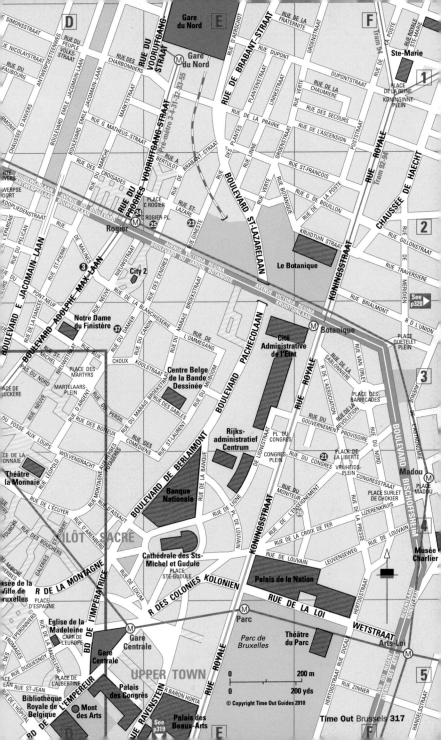

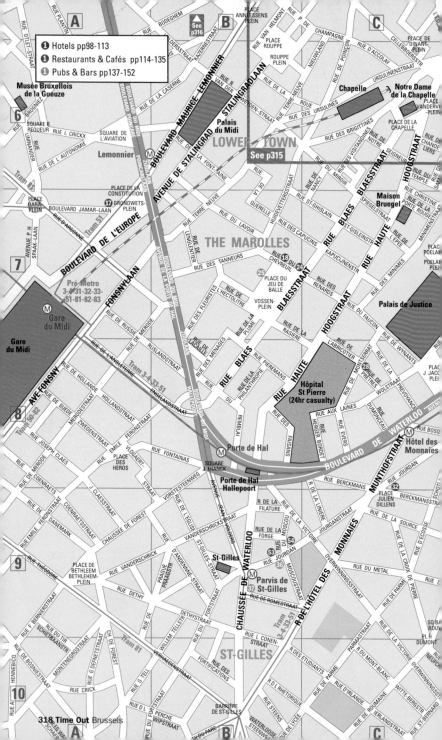

Legend:
1. Hotels pp98-113
2. Restaurants & Cafés pp114-135
3. Pubs & Bars pp137-152

Musée Bruxellois de la Gueuze

Chapelle

Notre Dame de la Chapelle

Palais du Midi

LOWER TOWN
See p315

Lemmonier

PLACE DE LA CONSTITUTION

GRONDWETS-PLEIN

THE MAROLLES

Maison Bruegel

Pré-Métro
3-4-31-32-33-51-81-82-83

PLACE DU JEU DE BALLE

Gare du Midi

Palais de Justice

Gare du Midi

Hôpital St Pierre (24hr casualty)

Porte de Hal

Hôtel des Monnaies

Porte de Hal Halleport

St-Gilles

Parvis de St-Gilles

ST-GILLES

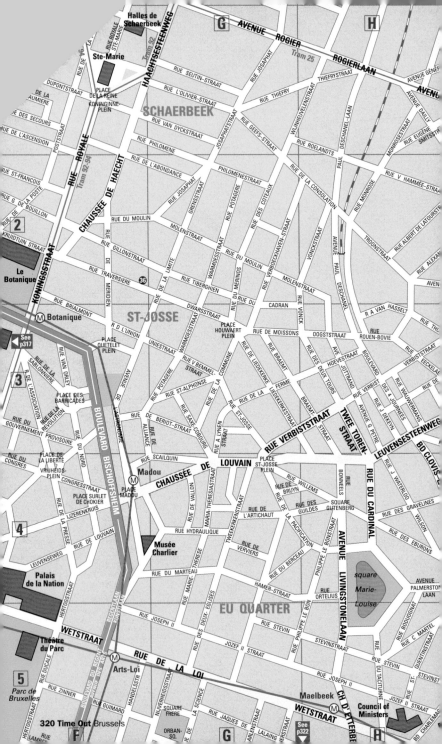

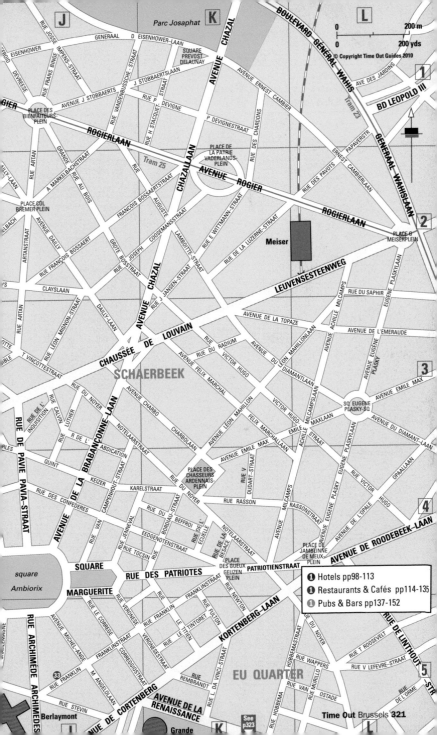

❶ Hotels pp98-113
❶ Restaurants & Cafés pp114-135
❶ Pubs & Bars pp137-152

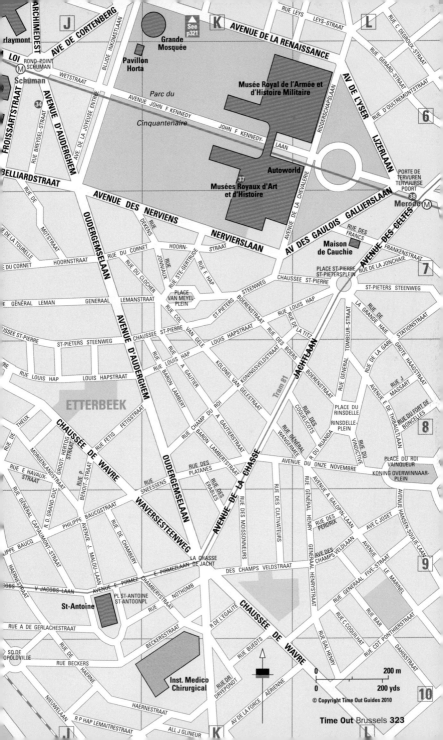

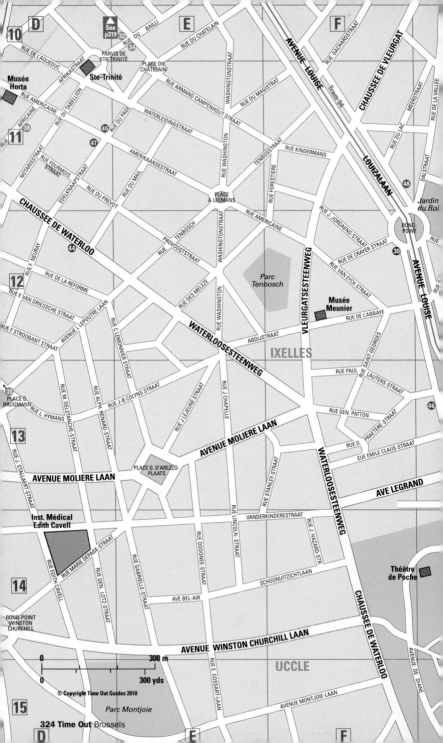

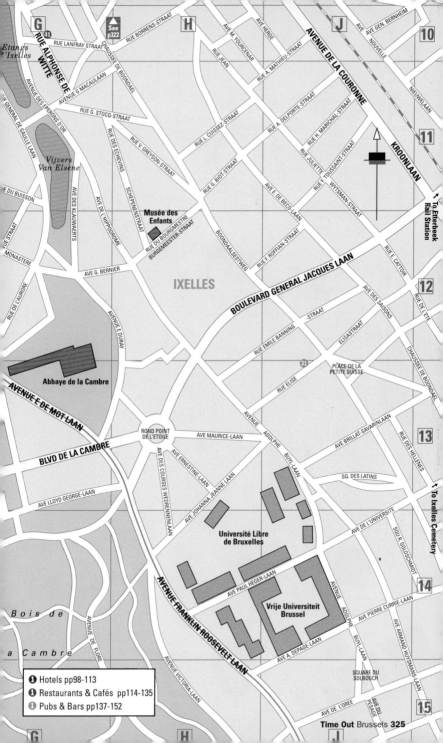

Étangs
d'Ixelles

RUE ALPHONSE DE WITTE

RUE LANFRAY STRAAT

See p.322

RUE BORRENS-STRAAT

CHAUSSÉE DE BOONDAEL

AVENUE M. YOURCENAR

AVE HERGÉ

RUE JEAN

RUE A. MATHIEU STRAAT

AVENUE DE LA COURONNE

AVE NOUVELLE

AVE GEN. BERNHEIM

NIEUWELAAN

AVENUE G. MACAULAIN

RUE DES ÉPERONS D'OR

AVENUE DES ÉPERONS D'OR

AVENUE GÉNÉRAL DE GAULLE LAAN

RUE G. STOCQ-STRAAT

RUE DES ÉCHEVINS

RUE V. GREYSON-STRAAT

SCHEPENENSTRAAT

RUE L. CUISSEZ-STRAAT

RUE A. DE PORTE-STRAAT

RUE H. MARICHAL-STRAAT

RUE JULIETTE

RUE F. TOUSSAINT-STRAAT

WYTSMAN STRAAT

KROONLAAN

11

To Etterbeek
Rail Station

Vijvers
Van Elsene

AVE DES KLAUWAERTS

AVE DE L'HIPPODROME

RUE G. BIOT-STRAAT

AVE E. DE BECO-LAAN

Musée des
Enfants

RUE DU BOURGMESTRE
BURGEMEESTER-STRAAT

BOONDAALSESTEG

RUE F. ROFFIAAN-STRAAT

RUE E CATTOR

RUE DU BUISSON

RUE STRAAT

RUE MONASTÈRE

AVE DES KLAUWAERTS

AVE G. BERNIER

IXELLES

BOULEVARD GENERAL JACQUES LAAN

AVE DES SASSONS

RUE DE L'ÉTÉ

12

RUE DE LAUROIRE

AVENUE E DURAY

RUE EMILE BANNING

-STRAAT

ELISASTRAAT

CHAUSSÉE DE BOONDAEL

Abbaye de la Cambre

AVENUE E DE MOT LAAN

ROND POINT
DE L'ÉTOILE

AVE MAURICE-LAAN

RUE ÉLISE

31

PLACE DE LA
PETITE SUISSE

AVENUE ADOLPHE

BUYL-LAAN

AVE BRILLAT-SAVARIN LAAN

RUE DES HÉLÈNES

13

To Ixelles Cemetery

BLVD DE LA CAMBRE

AVE DES COURSES WEDRENNENLAAN

AVE ERNESTINE-LAAN

AVE LLOYD GEORGE-LAAN

AVE JOHANNA JEANNE LAAN

SQ. DES LATINS

AVE DE L'UNIVERSITÉ

SQU R. GOLDSCHMIDT

Université Libre
de Bruxelles

AVENUE FRANKLIN ROOSEVELT LAAN

AVE PAUL HEGER-LAAN

Vrije Universiteit
Brussel

AVENUE ADOLPHE

BUYL-LAAN

AVE PIERRE CURRIE-LAAN

14

AVE ARMAND HUYSMANS-LAAN

Bois de

AVENUE DE FLORE

AVE A. DEPAGE-LAAN

AVENUE VICTORIA-LAAN

SQUARE DU
SOLBOSCH

AVE DU
PESAGE

a Cambre

AVE DE L'ORÉE

15

❶ Hotels pp98-113
❶ Restaurants & Cafés pp114-135
❶ Pubs & Bars pp137-152

Time Out Brussels **325**

Laeken

Domaine Royal de Laeken

Château Royal

© Copyright Time Out Group 2010

400 m
400 yds

Street Index

STREET INDEX

Street Index

STREET INDEX

Street Index

STREET INDEX

Advertisers' Index

Please refer to the relevant pages for contact details.

INDEX

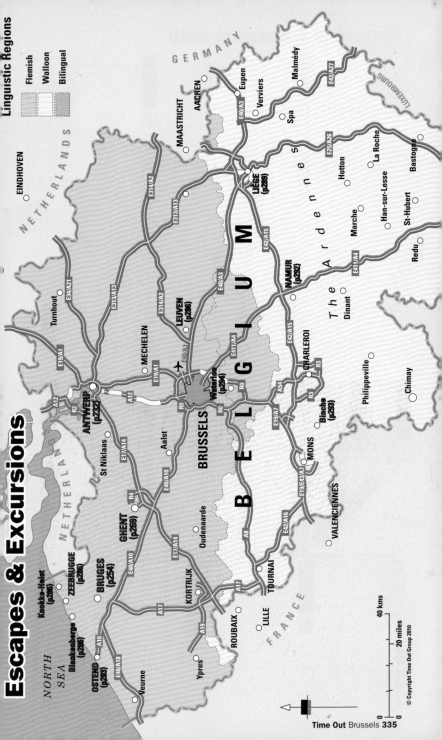

Escapes & Excursions

Linguistic Regions

- Flemish
- Walloon
- Bilingual

NORTH SEA

NETHERLANDS

GERMANY

LUXEMBOURG

FRANCE

BELGIUM

BRUSSELS

Knokke-Heist (p206)
Zeebrugge (p206)
Blankenberge (p206)
Ostend (p203)
Veurne
Ypres
Bruges (p254)
Ghent (p269)
Kortrijk
Oudenaarde
Aalst
St Niklaas
Antwerp (p232)
Turnhout
Mechelen
Leuven (p206)
Waterloo (p294)
Mons
Binche (p253)
Tournai
Valenciennes
Roubaix
Lille
Charleroi
Philippeville
Chimay
Namur (p292)
Dinant
Liège (p209)
Eupen
Verviers
Spa
Malmédy
The Ardennes
Marche
Hotton
La Roche
Han-sur-Lesse
St-Hubert
Redu
Bastogne
Eindhoven
Maastricht
Aachen

40 kms
20 miles

© Copyright Time Out Group 2010

Time Out Brussels **335**

Brussels transport map

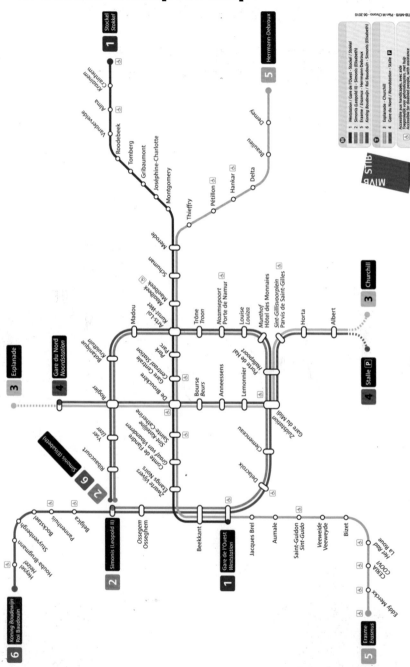